Children Moving

A Teacher's Guide to Developing a Successful Physical Education Program

SECOND EDITION

George Graham
Virginia Tech.

Shirley Ann Holt/Hale
Linden Elementary School, Oak Ridge, Tennessee

Melissa Parker
University of South Carolina

Mayfield Publishing Company
Palo Alto, California

Library of Congress Catalog Card Number: 86-061127
International Standard Book Number: 0-87484-727-3

Manufactured in the United States of America

10 9 8 7 6 5 4 3 2 1

Mayfield Publishing Company
285 Hamilton Avenue
Palo Alto, California 94301

Sponsoring editor: James Bull
Manuscript editor: Eva Marie Strock
Managing editor: Pat Herbst
Art director: Cynthia Bassett
Designer (interior and cover): Albert Burkhardt
Illustrator: Mary Burkhardt
Production manager: Cathy Willkie
Compositor: Graphic Typesetting Service
Printer and binder: R. R. Donnelley

Text and illustration credits follow the index.

Contents

PART THREE Movement Concepts   155

PART FOUR Skill Theme Development   243

PART SIX Physical Fitness and Mainstreaming   673

PART SEVEN **The Future**   713

Preface

The preface for the first edition of *Children Moving* began with the following paragraph: "We are teachers of children first. And writers second. As teachers we have worked in suburban, small town, private, and inner-city schools. We have taught on playgrounds and fields, in classrooms, gymnasiums and hallways, and in rooms that seemed no larger than closets. We have worked with children from three to twelve, black and white, rich and poor. Some of them loved physical education. Others hated it. A few were ambivalent. We have worked for administrators who were cooperative and helpful, and for some who were indifferent. We have known hostile, apathetic, eager, and supportive parents."

Since 1980, when we wrote that paragraph, our beliefs about children and physical education have remained virtually the same. What *has* changed is our understanding and knowledge about how to share this information with others. Since the first edition was published, we have listened intently to and carefully observed our colleagues in public and private schools, our undergraduates at the beginning of their careers, university professors, and presenters at workshops and conferences. Just as important, we, ourselves have continued to teach children. Those who are familiar with the first edition will quickly realize that we have learned a great deal from our listening and watching. The result is that the second edition of *Children Moving* is a major revision, and many of the changes are the direct result of the comments, questions, and suggestions offered by our students and advocates of the earlier text.

One major change is the addition of four new chapters—Chapter 2, "Teaching by Skill Themes," Chapter 29, "Physical Fitness in Children's Physical Education," Chapter 30, "Mainstreaming Children with Handicapping Conditions in Physical Education," and Chapter 31, "Building Support for Your Program." A second important revision is our attempt to answer the question "Where do we begin?" In each of the appropriate chapters, we have included guides for assessing the children's skill development and understanding of movement concepts. In addition, each skill theme and movement concept chapter has been revised using a scripted format to acquaint beginning teachers with how an experienced teacher might phrase a task or make a suggestion about improving the quality of a skill. Another major revision is the inclusion of questions at the end of each chapter to help readers check to see how well they have understood important ideas. Finally, we have added an appendix that outlines four yearly programs of physical education for children based on skill themes and movement and fitness concepts. The four outlines, two for beginning and two for experienced classes, provide general guidelines for both two-day-a-week and five-day-a-week programs.

The new edition of *Children Moving*, like its predecessor, is designed for the teacher who truly wants children to improve their motor skills and develop positive attitudes about physical activity. It's more than simply a compilation of games and activities that will keep children "busy, happy, and good."

The book is divided into seven parts. Part One is an overview of the ideas that guide our teaching. In Chapter 1, we acquaint the reader with the major purposes of children's physical education and our philosophy, and we provide a definition and examples of reflective teaching. In Chapter 2, we answer many questions that are often posed by teachers who have not been exposed to a program based on skill themes and movement concepts. The third chapter describes the actual content of children's physical education and provides an overview of the way the skill themes are organized. A system for assessing children's physical abilities in order to provide tasks that match their skill levels is described in Chapter 4, the final chapter in Part One.

Teaching skills are the focus of Part Two. In this part, we emphasize the importance of knowing how to teach. We describe, with examples, the teaching skills that, from our own experience and also through a review of the related research, we have found to be prerequisites of successful teaching. Preactive skills (those used prior to teaching), active skills (those used while teaching children), and postactive skills (those used after the lesson has been concluded) are discussed in the chapters in Part Two.

This is a book about children and about the teaching process in the real world. It is not about homogeneous classes of children or about perfect or predictable situations—there are none. We stress teaching skills as much as content in an effort to help teachers increase their effectiveness. You may find less theory and more application than you expect. For readers who are particularly interested in the theoretical foundation for our work, we have cited sources.

The third and fourth parts of the text contain the scripted material. Part Three describes how we teach the movement concepts of space awareness, effort, and relationships and includes a new feature of the second edition— assessment guides to help you determine where you should begin with your children and also to help you to informally and quickly assess their progress.

The eleven chapters in Part Four describe the development of the skill themes. Assessment guides are also included with each of these chapters to help you determine whether tasks at the precontrol, control, utilization, or proficiency level will be most appropriate for a particular group of children. The scripted format and ideas for improving the quality of the children's movements (refinements) are designed to help you gradually adjust to this approach to teaching. With experience you will find that you rely far less on the script as you develop your own ways of presenting tasks to children and providing feedback.

Part Five discusses how the skill themes and movement concepts are combined and taught in the context of games, dance, and gymnastics. At the suggestion of many readers of the first edition, we have placed this material later in the book to emphasize the fact that typically those three contexts of physical activity are for children who are developmentally more mature.

The next part is composed of Chapters 29 and 30, which were not in the first edition. In Chapter 29, we describe the important physical fitness concepts that children need to understand if they are going to develop a healthy lifestyle. We present a number of ideas for teaching these concepts in class, and we also suggest ways for children to incorporate them into their lives before and after school and at home. In Chapter 30, we describe practical techniques for teaching children with handicapping conditions who are often mainstreamed into physical education classes.

The final part of the book begins with a chapter describing strategies for teachers to use to gain support for their programs from other teachers, parents, and administrators. Part Seven concludes with a statement of our dreams about physical education for tomorrow's children.

The ideas we share in the new edition of *Children Moving* have evolved over a period of years. Some of our ideas you will recognize as similar to the ideas of other educators. Some are unique. We believe that teaching is an ongoing developmental process that has a certain similarity to the way children develop. Our philosophy continues to evolve and develop, as do our teaching skills. We hope that by sharing with you our beliefs and our ways of teaching, we are encouraging you to think about the teaching process and so to develop your own philosophy and techniques.

We want physical education to be an enjoyable and worthwhile experience for every child. And we want the youngsters in our classes to learn movement skills that will enhance their lives—as children now and as adults in the years to come. Sometimes, in the midst of working with many children day after day, it's hard to remember how important and lasting an impact a good teacher can have on a child. We try—as we hope you will—to make a difference in the lives of the children we have the privilege to teach. We hope that by sharing our ideas and experiences you will also come to share our commitment to making the world a better place for children to grow and develop.

ACKNOWLEDGMENTS

We wish to express our appreciation to the children of the following elementary schools: Linden in Oak Ridge, Tennessee; Christ the King in Atlanta, Georgia; Codwell in Houston, Texas; Barnett Shoals and Gaines in Athens, Georgia; Heathwood Hall, B. C. Grammar School No. 1, and Herbert A. Wood in Columbia, South Carolina. These children helped us with the photographs and artwork for the book, and many of them also contributed to our understanding of reflective teaching.

To those administrators and friends who supported our efforts through their encouragement and cooperation—especially Ida Lou Stephens, Robert Smallridge, Angela McCormick, Ken Dawkins, Kim Thomas, Tom and Laraine Ratliffe, Karyn Hartinger, John Lockamy, Barbara Moody, Ken Hirth, Wendy Weathers, Clay Thurston, and the South Carolina Special Olympics—we offer special thanks.

L. David Dwinell once again worked under less than ideal circumstances to provide us with a wealth of perspective and varied photographs that truly capture the essence of *Children Moving*. For his willingness and efforts we are grateful.

We also want to thank our colleagues for their helpful suggestions and insights: Sandy Beveridge, University of Utah; John Haubenstricker, Michigan State University; Dolly Lambdin, University of Texas; Pamela Milchrist, California State University at Sacramento; James Robertson, Springfield College; and Carol Workman, University of Utah.

Finally, we want to thank countless numbers of teachers and students who have made so many positive and helpful comments since the first edition of *Children Moving* was published. Your support and encouragement for our efforts have been most appreciated—and highly valued.

George Graham

Shirley Ann Holt/Hale

Melissa Parker

RHYMES AND REASONS

John Denver

So you speak to me of sadness and the coming of the winter,
Fear that is within you now that seems to never end,
And the dreams that have escaped you
                and the hope that you've forgotten,
And you tell me that you need me now,
                and you want to be my friend.
And you wonder where we're going,
                where's the rhyme and where's the reason,
And it's you cannot accept it is here
We must begin to seek the wisdom of the children
And the graceful way of flowers in the wind.

For the children and the flowers are my sisters and my brothers,
Their laughter and their loveliness would clear a cloudy day
Like the music of the mountains and the colors of the rainbow
They're a promise of the future and a blessing for today.

Tho the cities start to crumble and the towers fall around us,
The sun is slowly fading and it's colder than the sea.
It is written from the desert to the mountains they shall lead us
By the hand and by the heart they will comfort you and me.
In their innocence and trusting they will teach us to be free.

For the children and the flowers are my sisters and my brothers,
Their laughter and their loveliness would clear a cloudy day
And the song that I am singing is a prayer to non-believers,
Come and stand beside us, we can find a better way.

PART one

Overview

In the first four chapters we describe key aspects of the approach we call reflective teaching. Chapter 1 discusses why reflective teaching is necessary, citing such factors as class size, discipline, and facilities and equipment. The chapter goes on to describe critical variables that significantly influence one's success as a teacher, including considerable practice, high success rates, and structured learning. We don't believe that a single approach succeeds for every teacher in every school; we feel teachers should try to reach every child by matching the physical education program to the environmental characteristics of a particular school.

Chapter 2, "Teaching by Skill Themes," answers many of the questions that typically arise when individuals haven't experienced, either as a student or as a teacher, a curriculum organized by skill themes. The question/answer format also addresses several of the organizational and teaching process concerns typically involved in teaching by skill themes.

Chapter 3, "Program Content," describes our alternative to the usual organization of the elementary school curriculum into games, gymnastics, and dance categories and a rationale for organizing a curriculum this way. We stress the skill themes and movement concepts approach and present ways to vary such contexts.

Because our programs aren't organized by grade level or age, Chapter 4 discusses our approach to organizing program content according to generic levels of skill proficiency. We describe the four levels of proficiency—precontrol, control, utilization, and proficiency—and show how skill levels can be used in teaching.

Each chapter ends with a summary and reading comprehension questions to test your overall grasp of key points. The references are also excellent sources for further reading.

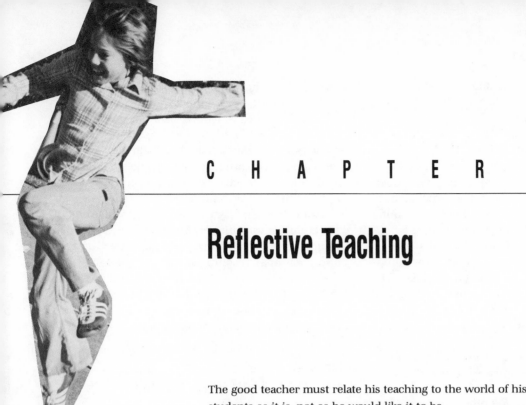

CHAPTER 1

Reflective Teaching

The good teacher must relate his teaching to the world of his students as it is, not as he would like it to be.

Herbert Foster

Physical education is more than recess, more than simply a time to play. It's a time for learning. Our first aim is to help children improve their movement skills. Girls and boys who participate in our program for a year, or for several years, should have better physical skills than children of equal ability who never participated in organized physical education classes. In addition to helping children become more skillful, we attempt to help them feel good about themselves as movers so that they'll learn to feel comfortable participating in new and different activities. We try to help children experience success in physical education so that they'll enjoy and participate in physical activity both at school and at home. If we give children a good foundation of skill development, cognitive understanding, and posi-

tive attitudes toward themselves in physical activity, they'll be well on their way to becoming adults who derive the benefits of physically active and healthy lifestyles.

In any physical education class you'll find children who are there because they must be, not because they want to be. And you'll find some who are eager to become skillful enough to participate in varsity athletics. We're determined to foster the development and enthusiasm of all the children in our classes. We want them all to experience success and pleasure and a sense of competence.

No two children are exactly alike. There are obvious physical differences and more subtle personality and individual differences. What is exciting to one child is boring to another. Some youngsters are able to accomplish a great deal on their own; other children require almost constant monitoring if they are to accomplish anything. For each child who delights in the challenge and camaraderie of a team game, another prefers the challenge and satisfaction of individual activities.

Children are different, and so are the schools they attend. Some school buildings have open designs, but others are divided into permanent classrooms. Administrators can be strict, stultifying, or supportive. Fellow teachers can be cooperative or competitive, helpful or obstructive. Gymnasiums, plentiful physical education equipment, adequate field space, and small class sizes are basic necessities in some elementary schools; other schools view such facilities as frills. Parents are concerned, meddlesome, apathetic, helpful, or unavailable.

How is a teacher to succeed amid this diversity? We have no magical answers. But we are convinced that a linear approach* to teaching is not effective, and so we coined the term *reflective teaching*. In reflective teaching, the successful teacher who achieves professional satisfaction employs a variety of teaching skills that interact effectively with the particular teaching environment.

The concept behind what we call reflective teaching is not new. Indeed, most likely reflective teaching has been practiced since the beginning of formal education. Nor are we attempting to add another term to an already cumbersome educational jargon. We're trying to convey the concept that effective[†] teaching is situational rather than generic. For example, a teacher who succeeds in suburbia may fail in the ghetto, unless he or she adapts techniques and skills to the specific educational environment. For many teachers, the results of attempting to transplant predesigned programs of education without considering the ecology of a

given school have been disastrous for both the children and the teachers.

In this book, reflective teaching doesn't refer to any particular methodology or style of teaching; it refers to the many teaching skills employed by individuals who are respected as master teachers. The reflective teacher is one who can design and implement an educational program that is congruent with the idiosyncrasies of a particular school situation. *Invariant teaching*, unlike reflective teaching, is characterized by the use of one approach in all teaching situations (see Table 1-1). We use the terms reflective teaching and invariant teaching to more clearly define and clarify *some* of the components that seem to collectively constitute "good" and "bad" teaching.

THE NEED FOR REFLECTIVE TEACHING

The casual observer who visits a number of classes or schools may not be conscious of the differences in teaching environments. However, an experienced teacher is often aware of those differences and can describe how they influence students, teachers, and teaching (Locke, 1975). Each teaching environment is composed of a variety of factors, as Figure 1-1 illustrates.

Our conversations with teachers as well as our own experiences have revealed that the same characteristics substantially influence what are generally called good or bad teaching situations. Physical education teachers most commonly mention the following five variables as illustrating the need for reflective teaching: socioeconomic status of the children, size of the classes, the teacher's education and experience, equipment and facilities, and discipline. These variables are now discussed in detail.

Socioeconomic Status of Children

The behavioral characteristics of children of low socioeconomic status (SES) and those of middle-

---

*Dwight Allen defined *linear thinking* as searching for the answer to a problem by investigating a single solution without considering feasible alternatives (Allen, 1975).
[†]We use the terms *successful teaching* and *effective teaching* to indicate that, because of the teaching process, the outcome of a given educational experience results in the sought-after physical, affective, and cognitive effects.

T A B L E 1-1 / Components of Reflective Teaching and Invariant Teaching

Variable	The reflective teachers	The invariant teachers
Planning	Adjust lesson plans to differences between classes and children	Use the same plan for each primary grade and the same plan for each intermediate grade
Progression within and between lessons	Base progression on such factors as youngster's (1) rate and extent of improvement; (2) physical skill needs; (3) interest in a particular topic or activity	Base progression on such factors as: (1) six-week units; (2) amount of material to be covered in a semester or year; (3) a predetermined formula for progression
Methodology	Vary the methodology according to such factors as: (1) kinds of children in the class; (2) purpose of the lesson; (3) ability of the children to accept responsibility	Employ the same methodology with all classes and hope that the children will eventually fulfill the teacher's expectations
Curriculum	Design curriculum for each unique class of children after examining the children to determine their abilities and needs	Use predetermined curricular content without considering such factors as children's ability, community influences, or children's interests
Equipment and facilities	Modify activities and lessons to available equipment and facilities	Teach activities and lessons that use available equipment and facilities
Discipline	Attempt to understand management problems and then seek the causes, modifying teaching procedure accordingly	Assume that the children are misbehaving and resort to punitive measures to modify individual and class behavior
Evaluation	Regularly evaluate the children and seek evaluative information about their teaching from children and colleagues	Evaluate sporadically and often base evaluation on whether children liked the lesson, how long they remained interested, and how well they behaved

high SES are different. For many years, elementary school teachers have recognized these learning style differences. Nevertheless, many teacher education institutions prepare teachers as if children from the inner city were just like children from suburbia—but they're not.

Recent research on teaching effectiveness has demonstrated certain differences. One research summary, for example, pointed out that low SES children succeed better (as evidenced by achievement scores) when a direct (teacher-dominated) style of teaching is used. Middle SES students seem to achieve more when teachers use a less direct pattern of instructional interaction (Rosenshine, 1976).

We're not aware of any studies that have demonstrated a relationship between SES and achievement in physical education. But our experiences in elementary schools are consistent with research data indicating that in middle-high SES schools, teaching styles are less direct than in low SES schools (Chapter 4). The socioeconomic status of the children within a school or class has an obvious impact on the teacher that seems to demand

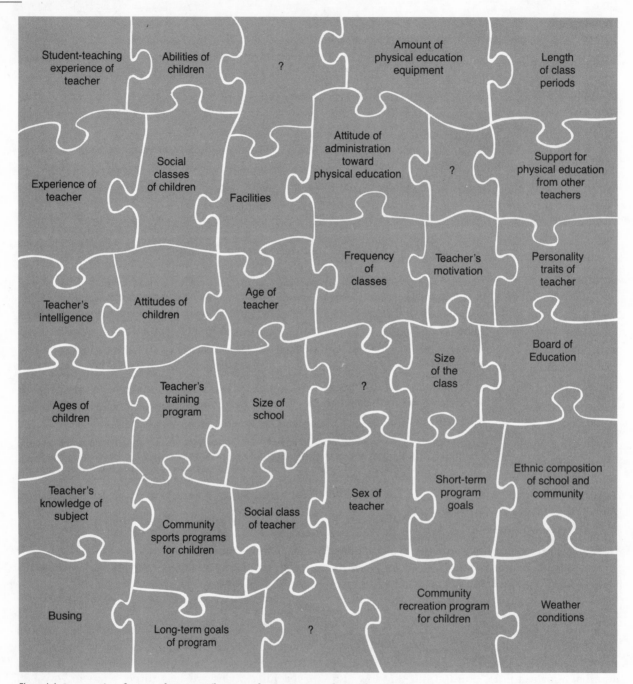

Figure 1-1 Interacting factors that contribute to the unique ecology of each school.

Some inner-city youngsters often test their teachers according to rules governing their street corner behavior rather than by their teachers' middle-class rules and expectations. This testing by street corner rules happens to teachers and administrators in inner-city schools every day. And most of the teachers and administrators neither realize nor understand what is happening. Indeed, until you actually experience this testing—when all your middle-class niceties do not count a damn and you wonder why this kid is doing that to you because you are not as prejudiced as the others and you really want to help blacks—it will be hard, if not impossible, for you to understand what I am talking about.

Herbert Foster,
Ribbin', Jivin' and Playin' the Dozens

reflective teaching. And yet socioeconomic status is but one of many variables.

Class Size

Another variable—one that is particularly important to the physical education teacher—is class size. Physical education classes are historically the largest classes in a school. A person doesn't need much teaching experience to realize that the number of students within a given class, other variables excluded, significantly dictates what a teacher can accomplish. Lessons that are possible with twenty-five children are difficult, if not impossible, with one hundred children.

For teachers to do more than provide direc-

Some teachers have a gymnasium or multipurpose room in which to teach physical education; they may have plenty of equipment.

At the heart of complexity in the gym is *numbers*. That the teacher is one and the learners are many is a fact of life which shapes every aspect of the teacher's experience. What many outsiders fail to appreciate is that an average class contains a lot of kids for one person to handle *even if there were no intent to teach anything*. This failure particularly is true of parents who often feel qualified as experts on child management because they deal more or less successfully with their own children in groups rarely exceeding three or four.

Larry Locke, "The Ecology of the Gymnasium: What the Tourist Never Sees"

tions to a mass of children, they must have opportunities to observe and analyze and to give children feedback. The logistical problems of providing individual instruction for each child in a class of fifty children who meet for half an hour are overwhelming. The educational literature supports this viewpoint: "The more successful teachers did more tutorial teaching. They spoke to the class as a whole in order to provide structure and give general direction, but most of their actual instruction was given in small groups or to individuals" (Good, Biddle, & Brophy, 1975, p. 70). Class size can determine the teaching approach that a given teacher can use to foster a successful educational experience.

Teacher's Experience

Roland Barth, in *Open Education and the American School* (1972), described his attempt to transplant a program of open education into what had been a traditional school. Barth was aided by a group of apparently enthusiastic teachers who were committed to the concept of open education but had little experience. Reflecting on the results of the unsuccessful experiment, Barth offered the following insight (pp. 143–144):

> Successful teachers in informal classrooms have often taught several years in traditional classes. They are experienced teachers who have turned to informal methods when they found the transmission-of-knowledge model inadequate. These teachers are fully capable of running a class like a Marine drill sergeant if need be. They don't want to do this, and rarely need to; but they know, parents know, and the children know that strength and confidence underlie their permissiveness and kindness. In such classrooms a child can experiment as the agent of his own learning, just as he can explore being naughty—with the confidence that a strong authority figure is there to back him up in case things go awry.

As Barth suggested, experienced teachers often possess teaching skills that permit them to function effectively in a variety of circumstances—to teach reflectively.

Facilities and Equipment

A fourth variable is the adequacy of the facilities and equipment within a particular school. Established programs of physical education often include adequate equipment supplies and a reasonable solution to the use of indoor space during inclement weather. On the other hand, fledgling programs of physical education frequently severely lack physical education equipment. In some schools, physical education classes are forced to use classrooms, cafeterias, or even hallways on rainy days.

Some teachers are masters of improvisation, but others can't function without adequate facilities and equipment. The teaching skills acquired during student teaching, when equipment and facilities were ideal, often must be adapted to less desirable conditions. You may find that there is only one ball per class, instead of one ball per pupil. You may find yourself, on a rainy afternoon

Some teachers teach most of their lessons outside because they don't have an appropriate indoor facility for physical education; they may also have limited equipment.

teaching in a classroom instead of on a playground. Different environments call for different teaching skills.

Discipline

Another variable that contributes to the need for reflective teaching is generally referred to as *discipline*—the process of dealing with children who behave in ways the teacher considers unacceptable. The ability to effectively discipline children is a major concern in education today, among parents as well as teachers.

The ability to manage a class of children effectively is also one of the few teaching skills that educators agree is a prerequisite to successful teaching. A teacher must be able to create and maintain an appropriate environment if children are to learn. Some teachers are able to maintain desirable student behavior by simply glancing occasionally at certain children within a class. Other teachers spend most of their time trying to maintain order. We believe that specific teaching skills can be effectively employed to create and sustain an appropriate environment.

Unfortunately, many textbooks—and many teachers—underplay the role of discipline. These texts and teachers assume that a "good" teacher doesn't have discipline problems (Siedentop, 1983). Our experience suggests otherwise. During a teaching career, a teacher encounters many kinds of classes. Some will test the teacher's ability to maintain appropriate behavior; others are cooperative. Successful teachers are able to work effectively with both types of classes.

RESEARCH ON SUCCESSFUL TEACHING

Although many variables interact to create the idiosyncrasies of a particular teaching situation, the five variables just discussed are the most common concerns of elementary school physical education teachers. What can a teacher do to promote learning and enhance the development of positive attitudes in these varying environments?

The answer to this frequently asked question is becoming increasingly clear, based on research completed in the last ten years (Berliner, 1984; Gage, 1984; Graham & Heimerer, 1981; Rink, 1985; Rosenshine, 1983; Siedentop, 1983). It would take a book by itself to discuss all the pertinent research; however, three major points are especially significant if we want children to become skillful movers with positive attitudes toward physical activity:

1. Children need considerable and appropriate practice.
2. Practice needs to be at high rates of success.
3. Environments need to be structured intentionally for learning.

Considerable and Appropriate Practice

Successful teachers give children plenty of opportunities to practice (Berliner, 1984; Fisher, Berliner, Filby, Marliave, Cahen, & Dishaw, 1980; Gage, 1984; Graham & Heimerer, 1981; Rink, 1985; Rosenshine, 1983; Salter & Graham, 1985; Siedentop, 1983). For example, if we want children to become skillful throwers, they'll need thousands and thousands of chances to throw. When they throw, they'll need to throw appropriately, using the correct form and technique. In addition to practicing throwing correctly, the children will need to throw a variety of objects (e.g., beanbags, small balls, large balls, Frisbees, footballs) to become adept at throwing in the different contexts they'll experience as adolescents and adults. They'll need to practice throwing to partners, at targets, for distance, and against opponents. Simply playing in a game, such as kickball, provides neither the amount nor type of throwing that is worthwhile practice for most children.

High Success Rates

There is a strong, positive relationship between high success rates and student achievement (Anderson, Evertson, & Brophy, 1979; Berliner, 1984; Brophy, 1983; Fisher et al., 1980; Rosenshine, 1983). And greater student satisfaction also results from success rather than failure (Berliner, 1984). When a child isn't very skilled, a task that is too hard can lead rapidly to feelings of despair, frustration, and boredom. Failure often leads to off-task behavior.

Rosenshine (1983) suggested that we may never be able to give specific answers as to how high success rates should be, but that 80 percent appears appropriate when working on new material. This implies that teachers

1. Teach new material in small steps, to lessen the possibility for error
2. Practice to the point of overlearning, i.e., beyond the point where children simply succeed occasionally

The skill theme chapters (15 to 25) are organized according to these two principles. The material in those chapters is presented sequentially, in small steps, and review suggestions for revisiting material taught previously are included.

Structured Learning

The third point for successful teaching focuses on the learning environment (Chapter 7). Learning a motor skill doesn't happen haphazardly. Teachers plan and teach for learning (Berliner, 1984; Fisher et al., 1980) by structuring the learning environment so that the children know what is expected of them. Successful teachers spend time discussing a lesson's goals or structures and giving directions about what to do. If you watch a lesson being taught by a successful teacher, the purpose of the lesson will be clear to you and, more importantly, to the children. The children know what they're expected to learn because the teacher tells them what they'll be practicing during that lesson.

The implementation of these three characteristics of successful teaching will vary, depending upon the contextual factors, including the five we discussed. Reflective teachers, however, adjust to their environment so that the children have much appropriate practice, at high success rates, in environments that are structured for learning.

SUMMARY

The reflective teacher assesses the ecology of the teaching environment to define the variables that will determine the most effective physical education program for a particular situation. Then the teacher plans the teaching process that will be most effective.

The teacher considers the characteristics of each class and the abilities of the individual students. A reflective teacher doesn't expect all children to respond in the same way or to achieve the same level of skill. A reflective teacher is continually observing and analyzing, a process that facilitates revision of expectations and adaptation of all the components of the program so that the effectiveness of the teaching program is constantly being improved. The reflective approach to teaching requires that teachers constantly and accurately monitor as they attempt to design and implement a physical education program for a given school.

Effective teachers typically structure their lessons so that children have numerous opportunities to practice the skill that is the major focus of a lesson. They also structure the practice activities so that children have high rates of success along with specific feedback about the best ways to perform the skill.

READING COMPREHENSION QUESTIONS

1. What is reflective teaching? What are its basic characteristics?
2. What does a linear approach to learning mean?
3. Why and how does class size affect teaching?

4. What factors, typically beyond the teacher's control, contribute to the dissimilarity of teaching situations?

5. Define the term *generic.*

6. Can a teacher learn to discipline classes, or is maintaining appropriate behavior an inborn ability? Explain your answer.

7. In your own words, explain the major implication of reflective teaching.

8. The final section of Chapter 1 discusses three characteristics of effective teaching. Using the same format as in Table 1-1, develop your own table, with the columns headed "successful teaching" and "unsuccessful teaching." Under each heading, give an example of successful and unsuccessful teaching for the categories of "practice," "success rate," and "structured learning." (Many of the examples will probably come from your own experiences in physical education.)

REFERENCES

Allen, D. (1975). The future of education—Where do we go from here? *Journal of Teacher Education, 26,* 41–45.

Anderson, L., Evertson, C., & Brophy, J. (1979). An experimental study of effective teaching in first grade reading groups. *The Elementary School Journal, 79,* 193–223.

Barth, R. (1972). *Open education and the American school.* New York: Agathon Press.

Berliner, D. (1984). The half-full glass: A review of research on teaching. In P. Hosford (Ed.), *Using what we know about teaching.* Alexandria, VA: Association for Supervision and Curriculum Development.

Brophy, J. (1983). Classroom organization and management. *The Elementary School Journal, 83,* 265–286.

Fisher, C., Berliner, D., Filby, N., Marliave, R., Cahen, S., & Dishaw, M. (1980). Teaching behaviors, academic learning time and student learning: An overview. In C. Denham & A. Lieberman (Eds.), *Time to learn.* Washington, D.C.: U.S. Department of Education, National Institute of Education.

Foster, H. L. (1974). *Ribbin', jivin' and playin' the dozens: The unrecognized dilemma of inner-city schools.* Cambridge, MA: Ballinger.

Gage, N. (1984). What do we know about teaching effectiveness? *Phi Delta Kappan, 66*(2), 87–93.

Good, T. L., Biddle, B. J., & Brophy, J. E. (1975). *Teachers make a difference.* New York: Holt, Rinehart and Winston.

Graham, G., & Heimerer, E. (1981). Research on teacher effectiveness. *Quest, 33*(1), 14–25.

Locke, L. F. (1975, Spring). The ecology of the gymnasium: What the tourist never sees. *Southern Association of Physical Education for College Women Proceedings.*

Rink, J. (1985). *Teaching physical education for learning.* St. Louis: Mosby.

Rosenshine, B. (1976). Recent research on teaching behaviors and student achievement. *Journal of Teacher Education, 27,* 61–64.

Rosenshine, B. (1983). Teaching functions in instructional programs. *Elementary School Journal, 83,* 335–351.

Salter, W., & Graham, G. (1985). The effects of three disparate instructional approaches on skill attempts and student learning in an experimental teaching unit. *Journal of Teaching in Physical Education, 4*(3), 212–218.

Siedentop, D. (1983). *Developing teaching skills in physical education* (2nd ed.). Palo Alto, CA: Mayfield.

Teaching by Skill Themes

The concept of progressions in skill development is as old as
education itself. However, in physical education we have often
been accused of adjusting our content to those who learn
most rapidly to the exclusion of those who learn slowly. In
other words, we have focused on the end product without
providing for the increments or stages in skill development
that occur between rudimentary and highly skilled
performance.

Vern Seefeldt

If you glanced at the
table of contents and read Chapter 1, you noticed
that this book is different from what you may have
been expecting. Most of us recall elementary school
physical education programs that were very different from those described here. You might be
asking, "Where's Duck, Duck, Goose? Where are
Brownies and Fairies? Red Rover, Red Rover? Why
don't they have chapters on basketball and softball? What about kickball?" Obviously, these games
aren't in *Children Moving*, for a very good reason.

Our approach is different. Our main goals are
to help children become skillful movers and develop
positive attitudes toward themselves and toward
physical activity. To accomplish these goals, our
primary focus is on skill themes and movement
concepts, as explained in this chapter's series of
questions and answers.

What Are Skill Themes?

Skill themes are fundamental motor patterns
(movements) that are used in games, gymnastics,
and dance. These patterns are combined and
modified into more specialized skills once the basic
skills become automatic to the children (Gallagher,
1984; Seefeldt, 1979). One of our major goals is to
help children cross what Seefeldt (1979) termed
the proficiency barrier between a fundamental
motor pattern and the automation of that skill so
the skill can be used in a complex environment,
often as a sports skill (Figure 2-1). Children need
help crossing that barrier; they can't do it "naturally."

The experiences in our physical education
lessons are organized according to the child's

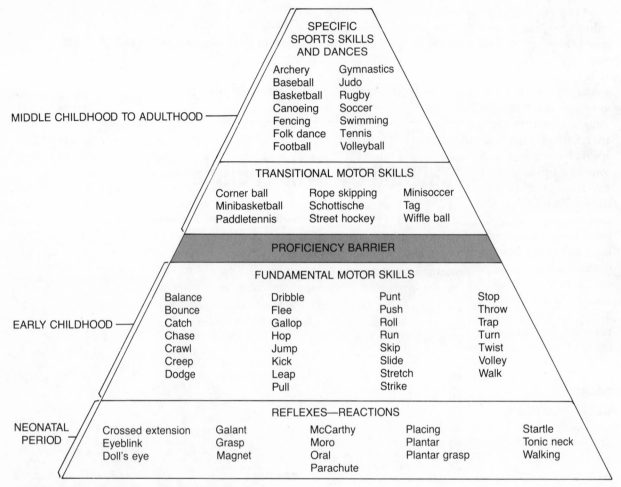

MIDDLE CHILDHOOD TO ADULTHOOD

SPECIFIC SPORTS SKILLS AND DANCES

Archery   Gymnastics
Baseball   Judo
Basketball   Rugby
Canoeing   Soccer
Fencing   Swimming
Folk dance   Tennis
Football   Volleyball

TRANSITIONAL MOTOR SKILLS

Corner ball   Rope skipping   Minisoccer
Minibasketball   Schottische   Tag
Paddletennis   Street hockey   Wiffle ball

PROFICIENCY BARRIER

FUNDAMENTAL MOTOR SKILLS

EARLY CHILDHOOD

Balance   Dribble   Punt   Stop
Bounce   Flee   Push   Throw
Catch   Gallop   Roll   Trap
Chase   Hop   Run   Turn
Crawl   Jump   Skip   Twist
Creep   Kick   Slide   Volley
Dodge   Leap   Stretch   Walk
           Pull   Strike

REFLEXES—REACTIONS

NEONATAL PERIOD

Crossed extension   Galant   McCarthy   Placing   Startle
Eyeblink   Grasp   Moro   Plantar   Tonic neck
Doll's eye   Magnet   Oral   Plantar grasp Walking
                             Parachute

Figure 2-1 Sequential progression in the achievement of motor proficiency. *Source:* Adapted from "Developmental Motor Patterns: Implications for Elementary School Physical Education" by V. Seefeldt, 1979, in C. Nadeau, W. Halliwell, K. Newell, & C. Roberts (Eds.), *Psychology of Motor Behavior and Sport—1979*, Champaign, IL: Human Kinetics.

developmental level (Thomas, 1984) by focusing on individual skills. These individual skills—skill themes—comprise the content (along with movement concepts) of our program. Each skill theme is a series of tasks designed to lead the children to higher levels of skill proficiency. For younger, less skilled children, the tasks are relatively simple. As the children improve, the task from one skill theme is combined with a task from another skill theme. For example, running, throwing, and catching are practiced together, similar to the way they might be used in a game of baseball or basketball. By focusing on separate skill themes initially, the children are able to learn to move more efficiently and effectively. The process is analogous to the way children study the meaning of a single word before using the word in a sentence or a paragraph.

Prior to teaching by skill themes, we often found that "the game" and its rules were taking precedence over learning to move well. We emphasize skill acquisition in a variety of contexts to help children make the transition from basic use of the skills (precontrol and control levels) to higher, more specialized, automatic use of the skills (utilization and proficiency levels). (Levels are defined later in the chapter.) Our theme approach implies that the skill will be revisited over a period of years, but in increasingly complex environments. Jumping, for example, might initially be studied as a two-foot takeoff and a two-foot landing. As the children learn to jump and land with increasing adeptness, jumping and landing are then practiced as part of a routine in gymnastics or dance, along with rolling, transferring weight, and balancing. The skill themes are described more completely in Chapter 3, and Table 3-1 (p. 30) lists the skill themes. Chapters 15 to 25 completely describe the skill themes and the tasks used to help children become skillful movers.

What Are Movement Concepts?

Movement concepts aren't movements themselves; they indicate how, where, with whom, or with what a movement will be performed. The concepts are used in conjunction with skill themes to enhance the quality of the children's movements by broadening both the range and the depth of the tasks that are studied as part of a skill theme. For example, running is a movement, part of the skill theme of traveling. For children to run effectively when they're playing games, they need to be able to apply the movement concepts of running in different pathways, changing speeds and directions, and running in relation to others. Correctly applying and teaching the concepts will help enable the children to perform the skills and to perform them well. Table 3-2 (p. 30) lists the movement concepts; Chapters 3 and 12 to 14 fully explain the concepts.

How Is a Skill Theme Developed in a Lesson?

Actually, a skill theme is developed over a series of lessons, typically over a number of years. In an individual lesson, only a very small part of a skill theme is taught, depending upon the youngsters' ability. As the children become more skillful, the skill theme tasks are varied to become more difficult and challenging. For example, children in kindergarten might practice striking a balloon with a lightweight racket. Fifth-graders might also be working on the same skill theme—striking with rackets—but in a game situation that involves trying to keep a tennis ball in play with a partner. Chapter 24, "Striking with Rackets and Paddles," describes the progression and tasks for this particular skill theme.

Where Are the Activities for the Skill Themes Listed in the Book? What Do You Teach?

The activities (tasks) are contained in the movement concept chapters (12 to 14) and skill theme chapters (15 to 25). These are the tasks the children practice during class. The end of Chapter 22, "Throwing and Catching," for example, includes a variety of games for children. Once children have acquired the basic skills, we encourage the youngsters to use them in games. In fact, if they don't use the skills in gamelike activities, they never become adept at playing games. This idea is expanded upon later in this chapter.

An analogy to math will help you understand the use of movement concepts and skill themes in physical education. Before youngsters are ready to solve practical problems in math, such as counting change, figuring the cost of two toys, or calculating percentage, they need to learn the basics of counting, adding, subtracting, multiplying, and dividing. Similarly, children must learn the basics in physical education. Before children can play softball effectively, they need to be able to throw, catch, run, and strike a pitched ball with a bat. There are many activities they can practice, however, that lead up to playing softball.

Then Children Don't Learn to Play Sports by Participating in Low-Organized Games Designed to Lead up to Sports?

Exactly. Just look at a group of high school youngsters playing softball in a physical education class. Many of them have played hours of lead-up games to softball as well as the actual game, and yet many are virtually unable to throw, catch, and bat successfully. This situation is comparable to being unable to add or divide simple numbers in a math class. These high school youngsters simply never learned the basic skills needed to play softball successfully.

Is Every Student Expected to Be a Good Athlete in All Sports?

No. That's simply unrealistic, given the limited amount of time allotted to physical education. It is reasonable, however, to think that children can acquire the basic skills in physical education. Our experience was that in far too many elementary schools children were enjoying physical education but weren't learning anything. We weren't satisfied with this. We wanted children to enjoy our classes, but we also wanted them to *learn* something. This is why we chose to develop the content by using skill themes and movement concepts.

Isn't This a Harder Way to Teach? How Do Experienced Teachers React to Developing the Content This Way?

Initially it is harder. Anything new is harder. Some teachers try it for a few weeks and give up. Others stick with it and find that, in the long run, it's better for the children. At times teachers find it's tempting to take the easy way. It's far less trouble, for example, to teach a game like kickball and then let the children play kickball for weeks on end. The outspoken, athletic children like it, and, once the teams have been chosen, the teacher can sit back and simply watch the children play and settle the occasional argument. The problem, once again, as our experience and an increasing body of research suggest, is that the children don't learn much of anything in programs where children simply play games all the time.

How Do Athletic Coaches Feel About Your Approach to Developing the Content?

They like it. Ask any coach, and he or she will tell you that they wish they had more time to devote to fundamentals. That's exactly what we're doing in our programs: teaching the fundamentals. In fact, the better we develop fundamental skills in our programs, the more time coaches have to devote to other aspects of the sport.

Do Junior High and High School Physical Education Teachers React the Same as the Coaches?

Yes they do. They appreciate it when children have focused on the fundamentals for several years. In addition, it's easier for teachers to teach sports and lifetime activities like tennis and golf when chil-

dren have acquired the basic skills but haven't yet been introduced to the "official" version of the sports.

Isn't It Difficult to Maintain Youngsters' Interest in a Program That Emphasizes the Fundamentals?

Ideally, children begin this program in kindergarten. When they do, this is really the only program they know, so their interest is high. When we introduce this program to children in the fourth and fifth grades, some of them initially have a difficult time adjusting, particularly the highly skilled children who enjoy playing games they dominate. In time, however, children learn to enjoy this program because they're improving. We also attempt to adjust the activities to the youngsters' skill level (Chapter 4), and this makes the lessons more interesting.

What Does "Adjusting the Activities" Mean?

In essence, this is the concept of reflective teaching. If a boy can't catch a ball, for example, then he isn't going to enjoy playing a game of softball in which the score is kept and winning is important. For this child we provide noncompetitive activities that he can succeed at. In the same class, however, a girl may have played softball on a team for several years and be very good. We try to provide her with gamelike activities related to softball in which she and a group of classmates may choose to keep score. In reading and math classes, for more effective learning the children are grouped by ability. Although it's harder to do this in physical education, we do provide different tasks based on the youngsters' ability. We group children by four skill levels: *precontrol, control, utilization,* and *proficiency.* Children at the precontrol level are unable to consciously control or replicate a particular movement. Control-level children are able to replicate particular movements that now respond

more accurately to the child's intentions. Children at the utilization level are able to move automatically and reflexively and are therefore ready to study combinations of skill themes. Children at the proficiency level are challenged by repeating movements exactly or using movements in dynamic, unpredictable situations because they've gained control of the movement. (Skill levels are explained more fully in Chapter 4.) In addition, the tasks in each skill theme chapter are arranged from simple to complex, based on these four skill levels.

What About Dance and Gymnastics?

Initially our focus is on helping children develop and learn the basic skills. As children learn these skills, the skills are placed into the contexts of dance and gymnastics (and also games). It's important to understand that the purpose of dance, gymnastics, and games extends beyond simply skill improvement. Dance is a form of expression by moving to rhythm alone or with others. Gymnastics is a series of acrobatic skills combined into smooth-flowing, repeatable sequences performed on the floor and/or apparatus to demonstrate strength, balance, and body control. Games are organized activities using manipulative skills and played for the enjoyment and satisfaction of cooperating and competing with others.

Dance, gymnastics, and games require the use of skills that are best learned initially *outside* these contexts. As explained in the next few answers, however, it's ineffective to always practice the skills outside these contexts, so the contexts of dance, gymnastics, and games are interwoven throughout the movement concept and skill theme chapters. The chapters on games, dance, and gymnastics (Chapters 26, 27, 28, respectively) illustrate this approach.

An analogy with reading also illustrates this point. We teach children to read; as adults they choose what they'll read. Our goal is to provide a solid foundation for the variety of games, gymnastics, and dance situations the children will experience later in adolescence and as adults. Right now the children might tell us they aren't interested in some skills. But twenty years from now, who knows?

Don't Some Skills Need to Be Taught Differently from Others?

Yes they do. Skills can be classified along a continuum from "open" to "closed." Closed skills such as bowling and the free throw in basketball require identical performances each time, and there is relatively little interference from the outside. Dance and gymnastics are classified as consisting primarily of closed skills. Open skills are those typically used in team sports that require not only the execution of the skill but the ability to determine the influence of a variety of other factors, such as the speed at which a teammate is traveling and the location of an opponent. Dribbling a basketball in a five vs. five game and deciding whether to pass or spike a ball in a volleyball game are examples of open skills.

As you read the skill theme chapters (15 to 25), you'll see that initially even the open skills are practiced in environments that are more or less static (precontrol and control levels). As soon as the children experience success, however, the tasks are changed so that the environment gradually becomes more dynamic and unpredictable, thereby more closely resembling the environment that the skills will be used in during actual game play (utilization and proficiency levels).

Is This the Way the Skill Theme Chapters Are Organized?

Yes. A logical sequence, based on what we know about open and closed skills, is presented in each skill theme chapter. Essentially, each skill is divided into a series of tasks, from simple to complex; the tasks progress from easy to difficult (from precontrol to proficiency level). The tasks are phrased as we'd say them, although we know that, in fact, you probably won't phrase them exactly the same way. But this is a good place for you to start. The tasks also include examples of extending, refining, and applying the skills.

What Do "Extending," "Refining," and "Application" Mean?

These terms are used to describe content development in physical education (Rink, 1985). *Extending* means modifying a task, typically to make the task more difficult. For example, if children are simply dribbling a ball with their feet in general space, a teacher can extend the task by presenting an additional challenge: asking the children to vary the speed, from slow to fast, when they hear a drumbeat.

Refining is maintaining the same task but focusing on the way it's being accomplished, the quality of the movement. If the children continue to try to vary their speed of dribbling a ball with their feet and the teacher observes that there really isn't much difference in the speed, the teacher might refine the task by stating, "When you're dribbling slowly, you'll want to keep the ball close to you by just touching the ball with your foot. When you want to speed up, however, you'll have to give the ball a soft kick to allow you to run and dribble the ball." The task stays the same—dribble and change speeds—but the teacher focuses on the quality of the movement; i.e., how the movement is being performed. The tasks in the skill theme chapters aren't intended to be completed in a few lessons or in a couple of weeks. They literally take years to develop from the precontrol through proficiency levels. Refinement is a key if children are really going to be good at a skill. A physical education teacher who doesn't refine a skill is like a math teacher who never corrects the children's math papers and just keeps progressing from subtraction to multiplication to division without ever helping children learn the procedures correctly. Refinement means working with the children to be sure that they're actually learning the skill, not simply going through a series of tasks one after another.

Suppose our teacher now says to the children, "On the signal, change from slow dribbling to fast dribbling to slow dribbling. I'll give the signal five times. See how many times out of the five you can change without losing control." This is an example of a task application. The children will be competing with an established standard. *Application* can be competition with a standard, as above; with time; with a previous record the child has achieved; or with another child (for those youngsters ready for competition). Task application heightens the youngsters' interest, requires accountability in the execution of the task, and provides several forms of competition when appropriate.

As you read the movement concept and skill theme chapters, you'll see that the tasks, as phrased in each of those chapters, are extended, refined, and applied. We explained these terms now so you'd be able to understand how the tasks are developed in Parts Three and Four. Additional explanations are in Chapter 9.

This Sounds So Complicated. Are You Sure All This Is Really Necessary to Teach Physical Education to Children?

This approach really is necessary if children are going to increase their skillfulness. When teachers don't understand and use this approach, some children may enjoy physical education, but they really don't learn much.

Don't You Teach Fitness?

Yes, we teach children to understand important fitness concepts (Chapter 29). The sad truth is, however, that most children don't have physical education often enough during the week to improve both fitness and skill levels. For this reason we advocate teaching the concepts of fitness, thereby enabling children to develop the knowledge and attitudes that are prerequisites to a lifetime of healthy living.

As a Beginning Teacher I Really Feel Overwhelmed, and This Is Only Chapter 2!

We certainly understand your feeling. It should make you feel better to know that the remainder of the book develops the idea of teaching by skill themes. Thus, by the time you've read the entire book, the ideas will be clearer and make more sense. Don't give up. There's much new information and terminology, but stick with it—the children you teach will benefit.

READING COMPREHENSION QUESTIONS

1. Why aren't games like basketball and Duck, Duck, Goose included in this book?
2. In your own words, define skill theme.
3. Why don't children learn to play sports by participating in low-organized games?
4. Explain the difference between an open skill and a closed skill.

5. In your own words, explain extending, refining, and application, with an example of each term.
6. Why does teaching physical education have to be so complicated?

REFERENCES

Gallagher, J. (1984). Making sense of motor development: Interfacing research with lesson planning. In J. Thomas (Ed.), *Motor skill development during childhood and adolescence.* Minneapolis: Burgess.

Rink, J. (1985). *Teaching physical education for learning.* St. Louis: Mosby.

Seefeldt, V. (1979). Developmental motor patterns: Implications for elementary school physical education. In C. Nadeau, W. Halliwell, K. Newell, & C. Roberts (Eds.), *Psychology of motor behavior and sport—1979.* Champaign, IL: Human Kinetics.

Thomas, J. (1984). Children's motor skill development. In J. Thomas (Ed.), *Motor skill development during childhood and adolescence.* Minneapolis: Burgess.

C H A P T E R **3**

Program Content

A physical education program for children which begins with an organized sport is analogous to a language arts program beginning with a Shakespearean sonnet.

Iris Welsh [student]

Typically, children who are learning to read are taught to recognize letters, then parts of words, then complete words, and finally sentences. Children who are studying mathematics learn to solve problems after they've grasped the basic functions of numbers and signs. Children learning to play a musical instrument study the scale before attempting a song. In physical education, however, children frequently are taught games, dances, or complex gymnastic stunts before they're able to perform the necessary skills. Too often children know the rules for a game or the formation of a dance but don't have the skills needed for successful and enjoyable participation. Our way of teaching children how to participate effectively in various activities is to focus on the development of the skills necessary. We call this approach *teaching by skill themes*.

CHARACTERISTICS OF THEMES

In music, a theme recurs in different parts of a song, sometimes in exactly the same way, at other times in a slightly different form. *The Random House Dictionary of the English Language* defines a theme as "a short melodic subject from which variations are developed." In physical education, various movements can be thought of as a theme.

By revisiting a movement—sometimes in the same context as before, sometimes in a slightly different context, and sometimes in a radically different context—we provide children with variations of a skill theme. These variations lead to proficiency as well as diversity. Jumping can be presented as jumping from an object—a box or a

23

table—and landing softly. This movement can be revisited with a slight variation: jumping from an object and landing facing in a different direction from the takeoff position. Jumping for distance or leaping in synchronization with the leap of a partner would be radically different, yet the theme would still be jumping (Gallagher, 1984).

Some movements, such as jumping, traveling, and balancing, can be focused on in games, gymnastics, and dance contexts. Other movements, such as throwing and dribbling, are primarily used in only one of those three areas. Whenever possible, we point out to students the similarities in movements used in different contexts, to enhance students' cognitive understanding of the principles that underlie successful performance of a movement. We're not certain that this influences skill performance (transfer of learning), but it doesn't seem to have any adverse effects.

The instructor who teaches by themes can focus on helping children become skillful movers. Youngsters will have plenty of opportunities as they grow older to learn games, dances, and gymnastics activities, but first they must learn the basic skills needed for successful participation.

Many adults choose to not play tennis or swim or dance. They don't enjoy these activities because they don't possess the skills needed to participate successfully. An unskilled adult, attempting to learn

Fundamental activities such as running, jumping, skipping, sliding, catching, kicking and striking are the basic components of the games, sports and dances of our society. Children who possess inadequate motor skills are often relegated to a life of exclusion from the organized and free play experiences of their peers, and subsequently, to a lifetime of inactivity because of their frustrations in early movement behavior.

Vern Seefeldt, John Haubenstricker, Sam Reuschlein

Essentially, the notion is that these elements are learned in early life through the various activities performed (such as jumping, throwing, striking, and the like), and then when a new act is to be learned in later life, the student can piece together these elements in a more efficient way to achieve the new motor goal. The assumption is that by jumping over objects of various sizes, shapes, heights, et cetera, the student will have more effective "elements" for the performance of the next jumping tasks (e.g., the running long jump in high school).

Richard Schmidt, "Schema Theory: Implications for Movement Education"

a complex set of dance steps, may be embarrassed and frustrated. So too will the adult who is trying to learn to play tennis but cannot even hit the ball into the opponent's court.

The instructor who teaches by themes and focuses on basic skills can also involve children in games, dance, and gymnastics. The primary goal, however, is to give children opportunities to use skills in appropriate contexts. The theme being studied determines the activity to be taught, *not* vice versa.

SUPPORT IN THE LITERATURE

Teaching by themes is not a novel idea; it is used in approaches described in certain elementary school physical education textbooks (Gallahue, 1982; Kirchner, Cunningham, & Warrell, 1978; Krueger & Krueger, 1982; Logsdon et al., 1984; Stanley, 1977). The research literature in two related areas—motor skill development and cognitive processing—supports the emphasis on skill themes in physical education programs for children rather than the more complex games, gymnastics, and dance.

Motor Skill Development

The emphasis in the area of motor skill development (often referred to as motor development) has been on the development of *individual* motor skills. The thrust of research in this area has been to observe children over a long period of time, to understand how different motor skills develop. Based on this research, it's obvious that a basic skill such as throwing or striking evolves through a number of distinct patterns or stages (Gallahue, 1982; Roberton & Halverson, 1984; Wickstrom, 1983).

Figure 3-1 illustrates the developmental sequence of throwing. It's important to emphasize that people don't attain the final segment, Mature Throwing Pattern, simply as a matter of growth. Many adults don't use this pattern when they throw a ball, probably because they were never taught to throw properly in physical education rather than because they didn't have practice throwing (Seefeldt, 1979).

A simple review of these sequences rapidly reveals that not all children are ready for organized games or sports, for example. The emphasis initially then is on matching the task to the child's developmental level to help the child move toward a "mature" pattern (Seefeldt, 1979).

The ages four to nine have been suggested as critical years for learning motor skills (Pangrazi, Chomokos, & Massoney, 1981). The key to helping children improve, however, is to understand their developmental readiness (Gallahue, 1982; Roberton & Halverson, 1984; Seefeldt, 1979). Four to nine are critical years, yet children vary within these ages—they're not all at the same skill level. The challenges the reflective teacher thus faces are to

1. Understand the progression and development of the basic skills (Chapters 15 to 25)
2. Learn to assess each individual child's level of skill proficiency (Chapter 4)
3. Develop the ability to observe children in a class, analyze their movement, and then prescribe an appropriate modification of a task (Chapter 9)

The research on the development of basic motor skills is enormously helpful in teaching successfully. A knowledge of this research also emphasizes the necessity of varying tasks for individual children rather than thinking, for example, that all seven-year-olds have identical skill levels.

Cognitive Processing

Research on motor skill development clearly indicates that tasks for young children need to be straightforward, not complex, because youngsters haven't yet developed the motor pattern to the stage that it's automatic and performed without major concentration.

Research on how children understand, remember, and process information about motor skills also supports the notion that initial experiences need to be less complex than those presented to more skilled children (Gallagher, 1984; Thomas, 1984). The following excerpt from Thomas (1984, p. 101) illustrates the basic premise behind understanding youngsters' cognitive process:

A young child dribbling a soccer ball down the field is concentrating on controlling the ball. Having to consider another player (defensive) when planning and controlling the ball may be more than the child can handle (attention capacity is exceeded). An older child may have learned the dribbling skill well (the skill has become less demanding on attention or more automatic) and can consider the defensive player in planning appropriate movements. However, a coach yelling, "Cut to your left and pass the ball, to Susie!" frequently results in a loss of ball control. In this case, attending to the coach results in more than the child can do while simultaneously controlling the ball and planning movements. Again, the attentional capacity of the (cognitive) system is exceeded.

Stage 1:   The throwing motion is essentially in a forward direc-
tion.The feet usually remain stationary. The force to propel the
object is produced almost exclusively by arm movement—
primarily forearm extension. There is little or no trunk rotation.

Stage 3:   The arm and leg on the same side of the body
provide the action. The object to be thrown is placed in a position above the shoulder as the leg steps forward. Little or no
rotation of the spine or hips occurs in preparation for the throw.
The follow-through phase includes flexion of the hip, and the
trunk rotates toward the opposite side.

Figure 3-1 Developmental stages of throwing. *Source:*
Adapted from "Developmental Sequence of Throwing"
by V. Seefeldt & J. Haubenstricker, 1978, Athens:
University of Georgia; and *Fundamental Motor
Patterns*, 2nd ed., by R. L. Wickstrom, 1977,
Philadelphia: Lea & Febiger.

Stage 2:   The hips, spine, and shoulders rotate as one unit. During the preparatory phase, the hand grasping the object is placed behind the head. The child may step forward with either leg, and the throwing arm is brought forward across the body. The arm is continually held in an extended position, giving the appearance of a sling motion.

(continued)

Earlier research by Schmidt (1977) also supports teaching by skill themes. In describing a concept he calls *schema theory*, Schmidt presented the results of studies that suggest that "a variety of movement experiences produces an increased capacity to move." Schema theory suggests that teaching by themes is an efficient way to enhance transfer of basic movements, or movement elements, to more complex movements used later in life.

Not all studies of schema theory substantiate the positive implications we describe. Our experience, however, suggests that teaching by themes is an effective way to help children become skillful movers. We've found that, when using skill themes, we're able to focus on providing children with appropriate movement experiences. When instructors use game, gymnastics, and dance units, children learn how to do the activity but don't necessarily improve their skills. The purpose of

<u>Stage 4:</u>   The leg opposite the throwing arm moves forward as the arm is moved above the shoulder (windup). There is little or no rotation of the hips and spine during the windup phase. The motion of the trunk and arm resembles those of stages 1 and 3. The stride forward of the leg opposite the throwing arm provides a wide base of support and greater stability during the force production phase of the throw.

<u>Mature throwing pattern:</u>   The windup phase begins with the throwing hand moving in a downward arc and then backward as the opposite leg moves forward. The hips and spine rotate into a position for forceful derotation. As the foot opposite the throwing arm strikes the floor, the hips, spine, and shoulders begin derotating in sequence. The leg opposite the throwing arm begins to extend at the knee, providing an equal and opposite reaction to the throwing arm. The arm opposite the throwing limb also moves forcibly toward the body to assist in equal and opposite reaction.

Figure 3-1 (continued)

TABLE 3-1 / Skill Themes

Locomotor skills	Nonmanipulative skills	Manipulative skills
Walking	Turning	Throwing
Running	Twisting	Catching and collecting
Hopping	Rolling	Kicking
Skipping	Balancing	Punting
Galloping	Transferring weight	Dribbling
Sliding	Jumping and landing	Volleying
Chasing, fleeing, and	Stretching	Striking with rackets
dodging	Curling	Striking with long-handled
		implements

TABLE 3-2 / Movement Concepts

Space awareness (where the body moves)		Effort (how the body moves)		Relationships
Location:	Self-space and general space	Time:	Fast/slow Sudden/sustained	Of body parts: Round (curved), narrow, wide, twisted, symmetrical/ nonsymmetrical
Directions:	Up/down Forward/backward Right/left	Force:	Strong/light	
		Flow:	Bound/free	
Levels:	Low/middle/high			With objects and/ or people: Over/ under, on/off, near/far, in front/ behind, along/ through, meeting/ parting, surround- ing, around, alongside
Pathways:	Straight/curved Zigzag			
Extensions:	Large/small Far/near			With people: Leading/following, mirroring/match- ing, unison/con- trast, alone in a mass, solo, part- ners, groups, between groups

physical education in elementary school is to help children learn to become skillful movers. The individual who is a skillful mover can play a sport far more successfully than can the individual who knows a great deal about playing the sport but lacks the necessary skills. Teaching by themes emphasizes the acquisition of appropriate skills.

SKILL THEMES AND MOVEMENT CONCEPTS

We use the terms *skill themes* and *movement concepts* to differentiate between the movements (skill themes) and the ideas (movement concepts) used to modify or enrich the range and effectiveness of skill employment. Skill themes are the major focus of our teaching (Table 3-1); movement concepts are usually subthemes (Table 3-2).*

The distinction between skill themes and movement concepts can be clarified by a comparison to grammar. Skill themes are always verbs— they're movements that can be performed. Movement concepts are always modifiers—they describe how a skill is to be performed. This distinction also clarifies how movement concepts are employed to embellish, enhance, or expand the quality of a movement. A verb by itself—strike, travel, roll—is typically less interesting than when it is modified by an adverb—strike hard, travel jerkily, roll smoothly. Skills can stand by themselves. You can roll or gallop or jump, but you can't slow or high or under. Concepts modify skills.

The curricular interaction between the skill themes and movement concepts listed in Tables 3-1 and 3-2 can be represented schematically by five concentric circles (Figure 3-2). (For easier reference, we call this figure "the wheel," a term our students coined.) The two inner circles represent the skill themes; the three outer circles represent the movement concepts.

The first inner circle is the general categories of the skill themes from Table 3-1: manipulative, nonmanipulative, and locomotor skills. The next inner circle contains the breakdown of the skills in each category, such as walking and running for locomotor skills, turning and twisting for nonmanipulative skills, and throwing and kicking for manipulative skills.

The outer circle is the three categories of the movement concepts from Table 3-2: space awareness (where the body moves), effort* (how the body moves), and relationships. The fourth circle from the center subdivides each of the three movement concept categories. For example, space awareness is subdivided and includes location and directions; the subdivision of effort includes time and force; and among the relationships subdivisions are body parts and people.

Finally, in the third circle, the movement concepts are subdivided even further. The teaching concepts that we use, primarily as subthemes to enhance skill acquisition, are listed in this circle.

In the wheel, the two inner circles representing the skill themes are stationary. The three outer circles are connected to each other but are able to rotate around the two inner circles. This rotation illustrates the idea that the same movement concept can be used to enhance the development of different skills. The concept of levels in space, for example, is useful for refining such skills as catching, striking, volleying, and balancing. The concept of fast and slow can be applied to the study of such skills as traveling, rolling, dribbling, transferring weight, and dodging. At times, some concepts serve as subthemes for other concepts. For example, fast or slow may modify pathways, and forward and backward may be used to modify over and under.

---

*The major source for this explanation of skill themes and movement concepts is *Physical Education: A Movement Orientation*, 2nd ed., by Sheila Stanley, 1977, New York: McGraw-Hill.

*Some movement analysis frameworks include the concept of space (direct and flexible) as a quality of movement. In our teaching, however, we use this concept so infrequently that we don't include it in our discussion of the qualities of movement.

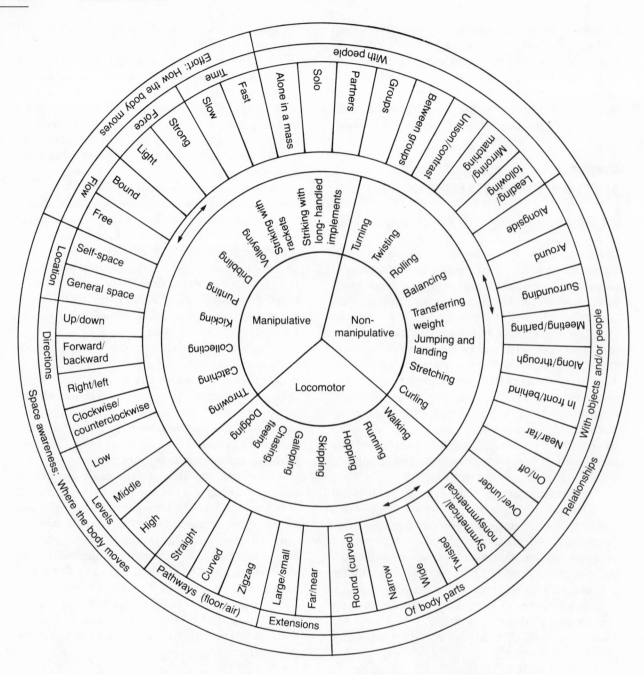

Figure 3-2 Movement analysis framework (wheel) depicting the interaction of movement concepts and skill themes.

The wheel graphically helps children understand the interaction between skill themes and movement concepts. Mount the wheel on a piece of cardboard (a manila folder works well) or on poster board. Cut the wheel between the second and third circles, and glue the outer three circles onto a second piece of cardboard. Attach the two inner circles to the second piece of cardboard by a clasp that lets the inner circles rotate.

CONTEXT VARIATION

Initially, movement concepts are taught as themes. The children study the vocabulary that is used to describe movement, and they learn to execute movements that express an understanding of each movement concept (Chapters 12 to 14). After the children have learned this movement vocabulary, the movement concepts are taught as subthemes that foster the acquisition of particular skills.

When teaching a skill, we provide experiences that progress from simple to complex. The expe-

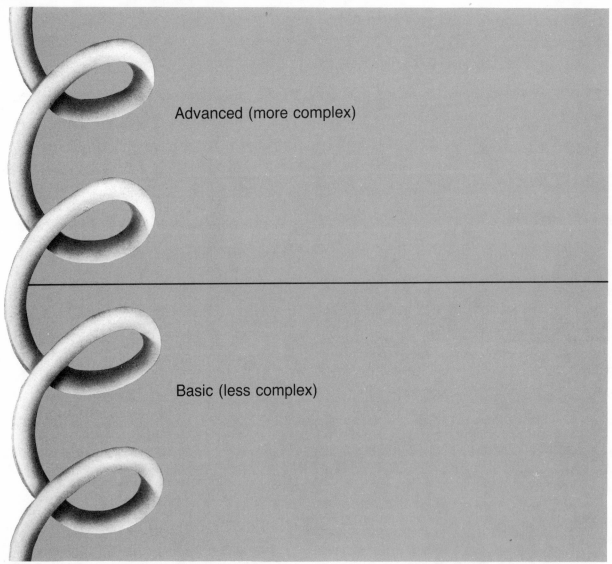

Advanced (more complex)

Basic (less complex)

Figure 3-3 Progression spiral illustrating the contextual variations in which skill themes can be studied.

riences are generally made more difficult by combining the skill with appropriate concepts. Skills are combined to increase the challenge of a task. We change the context in which the skill is practiced by focusing on different concepts or different combinations of skills.

Each skill theme (Part Four) is represented by a spiral that indicates the progression from simple to complex (Figure 3-3). This progression is facilitated by varying the contexts in which a skill is practiced to make the skill increasingly more challenging. The spiral is a graphic reminder that the same context (task) may be revisited and that, when appropriate, the context can be varied to give the learner a more difficult challenge.

The concepts of faster or slower, for example, can be used to increase the challenge of a task. But the use of the concept depends on the skill theme being studied. The context variation for the skill theme of rolling or of transferring weight can be made more difficult by challenging the children to move more slowly. But with a skill like dribbling, which is easier to perform at a slower rate, the challenge "dribble faster" increases the complexity of the task. In short, there's no standard formula that can be used as a guide for varying the contexts in which all skill themes are studied. Each skill theme is different.

The spirals aren't intended to suggest the length of time to be spent studying a particular theme. In reflective teaching, the context is varied when appropriate for a particular class or child.

Finally, the spiral represents a progression from the precontrol level up to the proficiency level (see Chapter 4). When the context of a movement is varied, many children regress to a previous level. This doesn't mean that children will drop from the utilization or proficiency level to a precontrol level each time the context of a task is varied. But the teacher can expect to observe a variation in skill performance each time the context of a task is varied.

The progressions in Part Four are based on our knowledge of the pertinent literature and on years of teaching experience. But you may find that a different ordering of the context variations is more appropriate for a particular teaching situation. Each child, each class, each teaching environment differs from all others, and the reflective teacher adapts to these differences.

SUMMARY

Teaching by themes is an alternative to teaching games, gymnastics, and dance. The focus is on the acquisition of specific skills and the use of those skills in a variety of contexts, rather than on, for example, the skills needed to play a particular game. Some skills are studied in games, dance, and gymnastics contexts, while others may be studied in only one or another of these contexts.

The research literature on motor skill development and cognitive processing in children supports teaching by skill themes. Both related areas indicate that initially the focus of a physical education program should be on helping children improve their fundamental skills in relatively uncomplex environments. Schema theory suggests that the individual who learns a variety of skills early in life has an enhanced ability to become proficient in later years. In other words, teaching by themes appears to enhance transfer of learning.

Movement concepts are used to develop the range and efficiency of skill employment. Once children have acquired a functional understanding of a concept—such as the ability to travel in different directions or to differentiate between fast and slow movements—concepts are used as subthemes to increase the range and repertoire of their movement abilities.

A teaching progression for skill themes can be represented graphically by a spiral that depicts the contextual variations in which a particular skill theme can be studied. The spiral is a visual reminder that each task is revisited to enhance skill acquisition and retention and that skills are best learned when presented in a progression from basic to advanced.

READING COMPREHENSION QUESTIONS

1. What do children need to learn in physical education before they're ready to play a game? Why?
2. What is a skill theme?
3. Briefly describe the support in the research literature for teaching by skill themes.
4. What are movement concepts? How do they modify skill themes?
5. How can you distinguish skill themes from movement concepts?
6. What does revisiting themes mean?
7. What does the spiral indicate about skill development? (Use Figure 3-2, the wheel, to explain your answer.)
8. What skill themes relate generally to game contexts? To dance contexts? To gymnastics contexts?
9. Indicate how one skill theme can be used to modify another.
10. Give an example of how the space awareness concepts are important in varsity team sports.

REFERENCES

Gallagher, J. (1984). Making sense of motor development: Interfacing research with lesson planning. In J. Thomas (Ed.), *Motor skill development during childhood and adolescence* (pp. 123–138). Minneapolis: Burgess.

Gallahue, D. (1982). *Developmental movement experiences for children.* New York: Wiley.

Kirchner, G., Cunningham, J., & Warrell, E. (1978). *Introduction to movement education* (2nd ed.). Dubuque, IA: Brown.

Krueger, H., & Krueger, J. (1982). *Movement education in physical education* (2nd ed.). Dubuque, IA: Brown.

Logsdon, B., Barrett, K., Broer, M., Ammons, M., Halverson, L., & Roberton, M. (1984). *Physical education for children: A focus on the teaching process* (2nd ed.). Philadelphia: Lea & Febiger.

Pangrazi, B., Chomokos, N., & Massoney, D. (1981). From theory to practice: A summary. In A. Morris (Ed.), *Motor development: Theory into practice* [Monograph 3 of *Motor Skills: Theory into Practice*].

Roberton, M., & Halverson, L. (1984). *Developing children—their changing movement.* Philadelphia: Lea & Febiger.

Schmidt, R. A. (1977). Schema theory: Implications for movement education. *Motor Skills: Theory Into Practice, 2,* 36–48.

Seefeldt, V. (1979). Developmental motor patterns: Implications for elementary school physical education. In C. Nadeau, W. Halliwell, K. Newell, & C. Roberts (Eds.), *Psychology of motor behavior and sport.* Champaign, IL: Human Kinetics.

Stanley, S. (1977). *Physical education: A movement orientation* (2nd ed.). New York: McGraw-Hill.

Thomas, J. (1984). Children's motor skill development. In J. Thomas (Ed.), *Motor skill development during childhood and adolescence* (pp. 91–104). Minneapolis: Burgess.

Wickstrom, R. L. (1983). *Fundamental motor patterns* (3rd ed.). Philadelphia: Lea & Febiger.

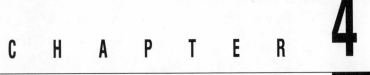

Determining Generic Levels of Skill Proficiency

Where parents have a voice in physical education programs, they usually insist that the curriculum includes the dances, games and sports skills of their culture. At the elementary level these activities are often preceded by the fundamental skills that are combined into more complex tasks as age and skill levels increase. . . . Teachers are to concentrate on the process of learning by selecting the appropriate content for whatever level of development the child demonstrates.

Vern Seefeldt

Historically, elementary school physical education textbooks have used grade levels as guidelines for determining what to teach and when to teach it. Activities thought to be appropriate for first-grade children are described in one section, second-grade activities in another section, and so forth. We found, when teaching, that organizing content by grade levels doesn't work well. One third-grade class is different from another third-grade class, in both ability and interest. And within each third-grade class there's a substantial range of differences. The convenience of organizing curriculum by grade

level can't be denied. But we wanted an approach that would better match the range of differences that are characteristic of children. Both age and sex are inadequate guidelines for curriculum construction. Six-year-old boys have a wide range of abilities and interests, as do ten-year-old girls. And so we began to examine the possibility of organizing a curriculum based on children's levels of motor skill proficiency.

The concept of levels of motor ability isn't new. It is supported by research in motor development (McClenaghan & Gallahue, 1978; Roberton & Halverson, 1984; Seefeldt, 1979; Thomas, 1984; Wickstrom, 1983); motor learning (Gentile, 1972); and curriculum theory (Jewett & Mullan, 1977). The problem was to assimilate the available research and formulate a practical model, grounded in research, that could be used effectively in actual teaching situations. Stanley (1977) proposed four levels of skill proficiency: precontrol, control, utilization, and proficiency. We've adapted these levels as a guide to organizing lesson content to match the skill abilities of children.

Note that we use the levels of skill proficiency to describe a youngster's proficiency for each skill theme, e.g., kicking, jumping and landing, hitting a ball with a bat. The skill levels do *not* pertain to the movement concepts because the concepts aren't skills; they represent cognitive understanding expressed through versatile and efficient use of the skill themes. As you read further, this point will become clearer. For now, however, just remember that the four levels of skill proficiency apply to the skill themes only.

IDENTIFYING LEVELS OF SKILL PROFICIENCY

Precontrol Level

The initial level is characterized by lack of ability to either consciously control or intentionally replicate a movement. For example, a child at the precontrol level who is bouncing a ball spends more time chasing after the ball than bouncing it—the ball seems to control the child. A child who tries to do a forward roll may complete a revolution on a mat or may get stuck, not rolling at all, or rolling half forward and half to the side and finishing flat on his or her back. A child's efforts to strike a ball with a racket are characterized by frequent misses, mishits, and an inefficient and inconsistent striking pattern. Successful skill performances are accidents. Most preschool and kindergarten children are at the precontrol level. By the time children are in the first grade, however, you'll observe many of them entering the control level.

Movements at the precontrol level are characterized by inconsistency, and successful skill performances are often accidental rather than intentional.

Control Level

The control level is characterized by less haphazard movements—the body appears to respond more accurately to the child's intentions. The child's movements often involve intense concentration because the movements are far from automatic. A movement that is repeated becomes increasingly uniform and efficient. At this level, a cartwheel a child performs is identifiable as a cartwheel; a child is able to travel in a previously identified direction while briefly taking full weight on her or his hands. When a child tries to throw a ball at a target, the ball travels in the direction of the target, usually.

Many first- and second-grade children are at the control level. You'll begin to observe that some children involved in certain youth sports pro-

Control-level movements often involve intense concentration.

At the utilization level, movements are more reflexive and require less concentration.

grams are at the next level, utilization. This is true only for their sport, however. For example, children involved in afterschool gymnastics programs may be approaching the utilization level in the skill themes of rolling or transferring weight, but they may be at the precontrol level for throwing and catching or kicking a ball.

Utilization Level

The utilization level is characterized by increasingly automatic movements. A child at this level is able to use a movement in different contexts because he or she doesn't need to think as much about how to execute the movement. Dribbling a ball in a situation similar to a game is appropriate for a child at the utilization level. When children

at the previous level (control) try to dribble a ball, they spend more time chasing the ball than dribbling because they're unable to focus on dribbling a ball while trying to travel away from an opponent. A cartwheel, as one in a sequence of three movements, is also an appropriate task for a child at the utilization level.

As children get older, the gap between the skill levels widens. Children in the fourth and fifth grades who are involved in youth sports programs are often at the utilization level in the skill themes used in their sport, but not necessarily in other skills. In the same class, however, it's not uncommon to have children who have remained at the precontrol level, primarily because of their lack of activity beyond formally organized physical education classes.

OBSERVABLE CHARACTERISTICS OF THE GENERIC LEVELS OF SKILL PROFICIENCY

Precontrol Level

1. Child is unable to repeat movements in succession; one attempt doesn't look like another attempt to perform the same movement.
2. Child uses extraneous movements that are unnecessary for efficiently performing the skill.
3. Child seems awkward and frequently doesn't even come close to correctly performing the skill.
4. Correct performances are characterized more by surprise than by expectancy.
5. When the child practices with a ball, the ball seems to control the child.

Control Level

1. The child's movements appear less haphazard and seem to conform more to the child's intentions.
2. Movements appear more consistent, and repetitions are somewhat alike.
3. The child begins to correctly perform the skill more frequently.
4. The child's attempt to combine one movement with another or perform the skill in relation to an unpredictable object or person is usually unsuccessful.
5. Because the movement isn't automatic, the child needs to concentrate intensely on what he or she is doing.

Utilization Level

1. The movement becomes more automatic and can be performed successfully, with concentration.
2. Even when the context of the task is varied (slightly at first), the child can still perform the movement successfully.
3. The child has developed control of the skill in predictable situations and is beginning to be able to move skillfully in unpredictable situations. The child can execute the skill the same way consistently.
4. The child can use the skill in combination with other skills and still perform it appropriately.

Proficiency Level

1. The skill has become almost automatic, and performances in a similar context appear almost identical.
2. The child is able to focus on extraneous variables—an opponent, an unpredictable object, the flow of travel—and still perform the skill as intended.
3. The movement often seems effortless as the child performs the skill with ease and seeming lack of attention.
4. The movement can be performed successfully in a variety of planned and unplanned situations as the child appears to modify performance to meet the demands of the situation.

Proficiency Level

The fourth level, proficiency, is characterized by somewhat automatic movements that begin to seem effortless. At this level the child gains control of a specific movement and is challenged by the opportunities to employ that skill in changing environments that may require sudden and unpredictable movements. The challenge of repeating movements exactly and with ever-increasing degrees of quality is also appropriate for children at this level. Rarely are elementary

Children at the proficiency level are challenged by dynamic, unpredictable situations.

school children at the proficiency level in a skill. We do observe them, but they're certainly in a minority. In almost every instance, their proficiency is a result of their extensive involvement in afterschool youth sports programs.

INFLUENCE OF YOUTH SPORTS

One of the strongest influences today on children is youth sports. Many children participate in a number of sports, starting as early as age four. Throughout the book we refer to these children, who may be better skilled than their counterparts who don't participate in youth sports. This doesn't imply that youth sports coaches are necessarily better "teachers." It does reinforce the importance

of practice, however. Children who play on youth sports teams have many more opportunities to practice than children who participate in physical activity only during organized physical education classes.

It's encouraging to note that the entire youth sports scene has improved drastically over the past few years. In many communities, parents and coaches have begun to understand that children aren't professional athletes and so have started to appreciate children as children rather than expecting them to perform as adults. The criticism once leveled at youth sports coaches is no longer universally justified. As in every endeavor, however, there are exceptions. Nevertheless, today there are a number of very positive, useful programs for children. As professional educators, we can help our children by observing the programs in our community and encouraging the children to participate in the worthwhile programs. We also have a responsibility to speak out when necessary to improve the programs that may be psychologically and physically damaging to children. Many youth sports coaches particularly need our assistance with organizing practice and helping children improve their skills. Just watch a few practices and you'll observe that many of the well-meaning parents simply don't have the background to design appropriate, interesting, helpful practices for children. Our experience has been that if approached properly, youth sports coaches value and appreciate our expertise.

TASK-SPECIFIC LEVELS

The levels of motor skill proficiency are task-specific and not age-related. This means that a child who is at the proficiency level in one skill (for example, at striking a ball with a racket) isn't necessarily at the proficiency level in related skills (such as striking a ball with a bat or a club). Thus, a child's level of motor skill proficiency is evaluated for specific skills.

Age is not an indicator of motor skill proficiency. If it were, all adults would be skillful at ball games, for example, and we know this isn't true. It isn't unusual to observe children in the fourth and fifth grades who are at a precontrol level when a new skill is introduced, one that they've never practiced. Generally, however, because of their physical maturation and previous experiences, they move from the precontrol level more rapidly than younger children.

USING SKILL LEVELS IN TEACHING

The levels of motor skill proficiency are a basis for the design of experiences appropriate to each level of skill ability. In most classes (third grade and above) you'll find that the children range across three levels for a particular skill: precontrol, control, and utilization. When this is true, a single game or task will be inappropriate for at least some of the children. Typically in physical education, tasks or games that seem appropriate for the middle skill level have been selected, leaving children at the extremes either bored or left behind because the activity is too easy or too hard.

There are ways of matching the requirements of the task to the skill level of children, however. Two such approaches we call *teaching by invitation* and *intratask variation*. It's important to state that these aren't ideas you'll want to try as an inexperienced teacher. But in time, when you've established a positive learning environment and are beginning to feel comfortable seeing all that is going on in your classes, you'll want to experiment with these approaches.

Teaching by Invitation

Teaching by invitation, the first approach, is actually inviting children to stay with the same task or to change to another, typically more difficult one. The *child* makes the decision to change, however; the teacher simply presents ideas. The following example from an actual lesson illustrates this approach.

A class of second-graders is asked to choose a beanbag or yarn ball and begin throwing and catching to themselves while remaining in self-space. The teacher observes that most children are catching with two hands but some are ready to practice one-handed catches. She says, "You may want to continue catching with two hands, *or* you may want to try catching with one hand." The choice is the children's!

The teacher then spends several minutes working with children individually, helping them improve their catching. She then makes the decision, again based on her observation, that *some* of the children are ready to progress to another challenge. The teacher stops the class and says, "You may want to continue catching with two hands, with one hand, *or* you may want to try catching far away from your body so that you have to stretch to make the catches."

If you were observing this lesson, you'd notice that most of the children make decisions that are congruent with their skill level. The poorest catchers, for example, would continue to work on two-handed catches, while the better catchers would eagerly accept the challenge of stretching to catch.

Of course, there will always be exceptions. Our experience suggests that the most frequent exception is when children are invited to continue to work alone *or* with a partner. Often we find that children who we feel would benefit from continuing to work alone will choose to work with a partner—simply because they enjoy socializing with

a friend. We respect this decision, however, and understand it, even though we may not always agree with it.

Does teaching by invitation guarantee meeting the catching needs of every child in a class? Hardly! We've found, however, that once an appropriate learning environment has been created, children respond very well to teaching by invitation.

Intratask Variation

Teaching by invitation allows the children to make their own choice about adjusting the difficulty of a task. Intratask variation requires that the teacher makes the adjustments for individuals as she moves from child to child. The advantage of this approach is that the teacher is able to better match the task to the skill level of the individual child rather than stating the task to the entire class. The disadvantage is that it is done individually and therefore is a slower process. The following example, using the skill theme of throwing and catching, illustrates intratask variation.

With an inexperienced class, one of our initial throwing and catching challenges is: "Find a small or large ball, a yarn ball, or beanbag that you want to practice with. Throw and catch to yourself. Try to stay in your self-space." For some of the children, this will be an appropriate, interesting challenge; for others, however, the task may be inappropriate. This is when intratask variation is used.

As we travel around the area, we observe the success rate of individual children, their throwing and catching patterns, and their levels of skill proficiency. Using this information, we can give individual children variations of the initial task—variations within the theme of throwing and catching. We might ask one child to "Make your catches at different levels." A more skilled youngster could be challenged to "Jump to catch the ball." A child who is having little success might be asked if a larger ball or a beanbag would be more interesting.

The teacher who uses intratask variation effectively needs a thorough understanding of the skill theme that is being taught. This understanding of the different skill themes comes with time and practice. Initially, however, when a teacher begins using intratask variation, we encourage the teacher to be thoroughly familiar with the entire spiral for that skill theme. Specifically, we encourage the teacher to have a minimum of five tasks for each of the four levels of skill proficiency that can be presented to children. We suggest that the teacher write these tasks on a 5 × 8 card that can be kept in a pocket for quick reference. It's easy to know the progressions at home but much different when you're trying to keep thirty children on task and participating successfully.

SUMMARY

Organizing curriculum by grade level or age is convenient. Yet, because of the range of skills found at any grade level or age, age and grade level are inadequate indicators of children's skill levels. We adapted the concept of generic levels of motor skill proficiency. Assessment of children's skills in terms of these levels is a basis for planning appropriate activities. The four levels of motor skill proficiency are: (1) precontrol, (2) control, (3) utilization, and (4) proficiency.

Children at a precontrol level are unable to consciously control or replicate a particular movement. At the control level, the child's body appears to respond more accurately to the child's intentions, and movements become increasingly similar. Movements are even more automatic and reflexive at the utilization level; children can use a movement in a variety of contexts. At the proficiency level, a child has gained control of a movement and is challenged by the goal of repeating movements exactly or using movements effectively in dynamic, unpredictable situations.

The generic levels of skill proficiency are task-related—that is, a person at the utilization level in one skill may be at the control level in another skill. Age and skill level are not necessarily related.

Two approaches that experienced teachers use to help match the children's skill level and the difficulty of a task are teaching by invitation, used with the whole class, and intratask variation, individually prescribed by the teacher.

READING COMPREHENSION QUESTIONS

1. What is the purpose of the generic levels of skill proficiency?
2. In your *own* words, explain the differences among the four levels of skill proficiency.
3. What does task specific mean?
4. Why isn't age an indicator of motor skill proficiency?
5. Explain the basic differences between teaching by invitation and intratask variation.
6. Why are teaching by invitation and intratask variation useful for teachers?
7. On the following graph, estimate your skill level for each skill theme listed. Plot each point. Which skill themes do you need the most work on? Why are you less advanced at these skills than at the others? Did you rate yourself at the proficiency level for any of the skills? If so, why do you think you attained the proficiency level in that skill?

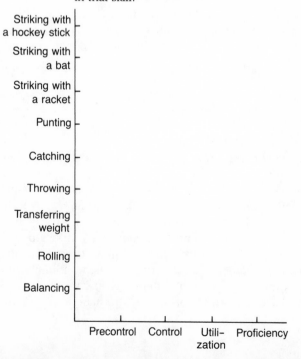

REFERENCES

Gentile, A. (1972). A working model of skill acquisition with application to teaching. *Quest, 17,* 3–23.

Jewett, A., & Mullan, M. (1977). *Curriculum design: Purposes and processes in physical education teaching-learning.* Washington, D.C.: American Alliance for Health, Physical Education, and Recreation.

McClenaghan, B., & Gallahue, D. L. (1978). *Fundamental movement: A developmental and remedial approach.* Philadelphia: Saunders.

Roberton, M., & Halverson, L. (1984). *Developing children—Their changing movement.* Philadelphia: Lea & Febiger.

Seefeldt, V. (1979). Developmental motor patterns: Implications for elementary school physical education. In C. Nadeau, W. Halliwell, K. Newell, & C. Roberts (Eds.), *Psychology of motor behavior and sport.* Champaign, IL: Human Kinetics.

Stanley, S. (1977). *Physical education: A movement orientation* (2nd ed.). New York: McGraw-Hill.

Thomas, J. (Ed.) (1984). *Motor skill development during childhood and adolescence.* Minneapolis: Burgess.

Wickstrom, R. (1983). *Fundamental motor patterns* (3rd ed.). Philadelphia: Lea & Febiger.

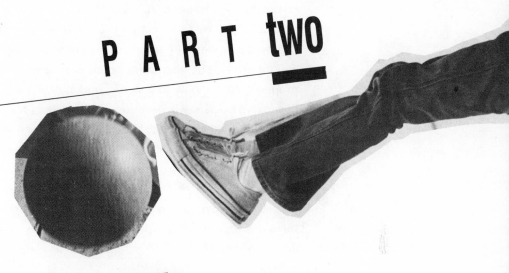

P A R T two

Teaching Skills

The successful teacher must know not only what to teach but how to teach. Part Two focuses on the teaching skills that such a teacher of physical education needs.

Chapter 5, "Planning," and Chapter 6, "Organizing for Learning," discuss lesson planning skills and ways to organize classes to maximize learning. A poorly planned or inappropriately organized lesson often will fail, regardless of a teacher's ability to interact with children. Chapter 5 describes step-by-step effective planning for the year and the day and covers such important points as how to record progress, design lessons, and actually enjoy planning. Chapter 6 details the various instructional approaches, including the inquiry and child-designed approaches; assorted formats that can be used for lessons, such as task sheets, contracts, and learning stations; and how to combine the approaches and formats.

Chapters 7 to 9—"Establishing an Environment for Learning," "Discipline: Maintaining Appropriate Behavior," and "Observation Techniques," respectively—discuss skills used in the instruction process. Most of these skills involve direct interaction with children. Chapter 7 includes ideas for differentiating between (*a*) physical education class as a learning experience and (*b*) recess. The chapter elaborates on various ways to establish the proper attitudes, how to foster a good atmosphere in the classroom, and how to set up safety procedures.

Chapter 8 has practical ideas on discipline, including approaches for working with both individual children and entire classes. Specific examples from actual teaching situations illustrate how to increase appropriate and decrease inappropriate behavior and how to maintain proper behavior. The teacher is shown how to interact positively with the children; work with them one on one; apply "punishment," such as time-outs and desists; and follow worthwhile reward systems, such as class rewards, tokens, and behavior games.

Chapter 9 focuses on the process of teaching physical education and includes a discussion of teacher feedback and how it's used in task extension, refinement, and application. Teachers are also told how to use the two observation techniques of back to the wall and scanning and how to plan for observation.

The final two chapters in this part, "Evaluating Student Progress" (Chapter 10) and "Assessing Your Teaching Performance" (Chapter 11) are devoted to postactive teaching skills. Behavior is observed and data collected during a lesson; evaluation and assessment are conducted after a lesson or at the end of a teaching day. Chapter 10 describes the three evaluation systems; how to evaluate the domain by inventories, student logs, and standardized test; and how to find time to perform evaluation. Chapter 11 details how the teacher can assess alone, via tape recording, and using written instruments; assess with the help of a student; and assess with the help of a peer. Also covered is a practical way to combine these three methods.

As with Part One, the ends of the chapters here in Part Two contain useful reading comprehension questions and references.

Planning

"Will you please tell me which way I ought to go from here?"
"That depends a good deal on where you want to get to," said the Cat.
"I don't care much where," said Alice.
"Then it doesn't matter which way you go," said the Cat.

Lewis Carroll

Planning is one of the least enjoyable aspects of teaching. And yet it's essential because failure to plan appropriately can lead to lessons that are disastrous. Disorganization and an excessive amount of time spent on management characterize the lessons of the teacher who hasn't planned effectively.

Inappropriate planning can also have long-term implications. One of the important tasks of physical education in elementary school is to provide a variety of learning experiences that give children a broad foundation of movement abilities. Children who are skillful in only a few activities, typically games, may be the products of programs characterized by inefficient planning. Instructors who don't plan are likely to teach only what they know well and the children enjoy, which often results in an unbalanced program over the years.

Because planning is typically done during the teacher's own time rather than during school time, there are strong temptations to avoid it. It can be much more pleasant to watch television, go to a ball game, or just go to bed early. But planning, even though you may consider it as onerous as homework, *is* necessary.

REFLECTIVE PLANNING

The reflective planner considers many factors when trying to devise the best lessons possible under the circumstances. Planning can't be reduced to an exact formula, but certain factors will always influence the effectiveness of a lesson. Each factor is important, and all interact to determine the teaching environment for which the reflective teacher must plan. When planning, we consider class size, frequency of class meetings, available equipment and facilities, personal characteristics of the children, and children's skill levels and interests.

Class size often determines the amount and types of information that can be presented. It's fairly safe to assume, for example, that a class of fifteen children will accomplish significantly more in a year's time than a class of sixty (Glass, Cahen, Smith, & Filby, 1979).

Frequency of class meetings is the second fac-

Teachers, not properly prepared, turned to elementary game books and exercise charts, or called upon their knowledge of athletics to design programs for children. As a result, many new local guides, even today, reflect programs of simple circle and low organized games, a few singing games, miscellaneous rhythmical activities, calisthenic programs familiar to every serviceman, watered-down secondary sports programs, and the inevitable relays with long waiting lines.

Such stereotyped programs spell the potential demise of elementary physical education. Limited programs make it appear that any aide or para-professional who has a short course or reads a book can perform the task. Parents, principals, and superintendents recall these kinds of programs as part of their childhood experiences, observe them in their own schools, and on that basis often reject the need for well-prepared teachers and for physical education in the curriculum.

Margie Hanson, "Professional Preparation of the Elementary School Physical Education Teacher"

---

tor. Classes that meet once or twice a week accomplish far less than classes that meet daily because you can't present as much material in one or two days as you can in five. And children, particularly the younger ones, tend to forget what they learned a week earlier. The teacher who meets a class once a week must plan on spending part of each lesson reviewing last week's lesson. This review time reduces the time that can be spent presenting new information.

To learn and understand a concept or skill, a child needs a multitude of experiences with a particular task or challenge. When the amount of *available equipment and facilities* is limited, all the children must wait and each child has fewer opportunities to use the equipment. One result is that children learn more slowly than they would with adequate equipment that would increase learning opportunities.

Equipment also dictates which experiences can be presented. In gymnastics, for example, children who have progressed beyond the initial stages of skill development need apparatus—tables, beams, and vaulting apparatus—that allows them to work off the floor because only with such equipment will they continue to be challenged. Similarly, nylon hose rackets are appropriate for children who are just beginning to learn to strike with implements. But wooden paddles or rackets are essential if the children are to remain interested in and challenged by the skill theme of striking with implements.

Facilities also influence planning. Kicking can be studied briefly in a limited indoor space. But children can learn much more about kicking when they can practice it outdoors in a larger area that has a smooth surface. Thus, lack of adequate outdoor facilities may prevent you from devoting as much time as you'd like to a particular skill theme.

Similarly, the kind of available indoor space influences planning. Most teachers, for example, prefer to teach dance indoors. Hallways, classrooms with furniture pushed aside, school foyers—all these indoor areas can be used for teaching. But these aren't ideal settings for teaching many movement themes. It's extremely difficult, for example, to teach locomotor activities in a crowded classroom. However, you can effectively teach the concepts of symmetrical and nonsymmetrical shapes in a crowded, indoor area.

How responsible are the students? Children's ability to function in a variety of environments also influences planning (see Chapters 6 and 7). During the first few meetings of a class you can gather observations about *children's characteristics;* this information is useful when you plan lessons for a particular class. Some classes and some individual children can cooperate with others and work well in less than optimum circumstances. The teacher of such a class can provide experiences that wouldn't succeed with less responsible children. To illustrate, some children in a class are able to work effectively without constant supervision—perhaps in a hall outside the classroom. The teacher of this class can send some children into the hall to work on a particular topic, decreasing the number of children working in the classroom and thus increasing the space available to all the children. Children can study a skill theme more effectively, and for longer, if the class can be split up. The enthusiasm and cooperativeness of a class also influence the way different themes and concepts can be studied.

The four factors just mentioned are easier to assess than *children's skill levels and interests.* The teacher must have this information to decide what material is appropriate and how to present that material. A teacher wants to challenge the students but not overwhelm them, so that they will continue to be interested and will want to learn.

If you decide that your class needs to be introduced to the concept of levels (Chapter 12), many factors, including the children's ages and skill levels, will determine your plan for this lesson. Young, unskilled children often enjoy the challenge of taking different body parts into different levels—for example, "Can you move your elbow into low level?" "Can you move an ankle into high level?" Children in intermediate grades might be bored by that task and so would probably learn more

One way of discovering what age youngster to begin working with is to visit a lot of schools. Try to find teachers you like and respect, and spend a few days working alongside them. Don't visit for an hour or two. It is important to stay all day (or if you have time, all week) to get a sense of the flow of time and energy working with that age person involves. Of course, your rhythm as a teacher might be different, but it is important to have a sense of what it is like to be with young people all day before becoming a teacher.

> Herbert Kohl,
> *On Teaching*

effectively if challenged to catch or strike a ball at different levels.

When teaching children in the upper grades, it's important to consider the types of movement experiences to which they've already been exposed. You'll want to take advantage of skills learned in earlier experiences, and you'll also want to avoid repetition of material with which students are already familiar. For example, if the children are proficient in the skills used in softball, you may decide to minimize the amount of time spent on the skill theme of striking with bats.

The movement concept chapters (12 to 14) and the skill theme chapters (15 to 25) contain an Assessment Guide that tells you how to obtain a broad, general estimate about the skill level of a particular class. The Assessment Guide is a quick way of answering the question, "Where should I start with this class?"

EFFECTIVE PLANNING

The experienced teacher is often able to plan more effectively than the neophyte. A beginning teacher

T A B L E 5-1 / School Year Overview Form—Activities for an Inexperienced Class

Content	Percentage of class meetings (%)	Approximate number of days
Establishing a learning environment	5	9
Movement concepts:		
Location	5	9
Directions, levels, pathways, extensions	10	18
Relationships with objects and people	10	18
Effort	10	18
Skill themes:		
Traveling	10	18
Throwing, catching, kicking, punting	15	27
Dribbling, volleying, striking	5	9
Shapes, turning, twisting, stretching, curling	10	18
Balancing, transferring weight, rolling	10	18
Jumping and landing	5	9
Fitness concepts	5	9
	100	180

Note: This overview is for a class that meets every day. It will vary depending upon the ecology of the teaching situation, as described in Chapter 1.

may work hard to plan appropriately, but because of the factors just discussed, the lessons may be unsatisfactory. In contrast, a more experienced teacher can often predict accurately whether a lesson will succeed or fail with a particular class. Many experienced teachers have also developed the ability to modify a plan during the lesson, to make it more successful. The inexperienced teacher must observe carefully and consider the many factors that influence a class. Gradually, with accumulating experience and hard work, you'll find that you're increasingly effective at creating reflective lesson plans.

Effective planning is best explained by dividing the process into three steps. Step 1 is determining the skill themes and movement concepts that will be taught during a year as well as the emphasis each theme or concept will receive. This emphasis is expressed in percentage figures. In

step 2, these percentages are translated into days, organized into a progression, and placed on a daily calendar. Step 3 is planning for each day's lessons.

Step 1: Planning the Year

You need to establish a rough estimate of how much time you want to devote to various skill themes and movement concepts. For example, how many days will you spend teaching pathways? Levels? Throwing and catching? Weight transfer? Your first estimates won't be permanent, but they're necessary if you're going to avoid a lopsided curriculum that emphasizes a few skills and concepts but neglects others.

We've found the easiest way to estimate is to use percentages. To make these decisions, review the movement concepts and skill themes in Chapter 3, jotting down the themes and concepts and

T A B L E 5-2 / School Year Overview Form—Activities for an Experienced Class

Content	Percentage of class meetings (%)	Approximate number of days
Establishing a learning environment	5	9
Movement concepts:		
Space awareness	5	9
Effort	10	18
Relationships	10	18
Skill themes:		
Traveling	5	9
Throwing, catching, kicking, punting	20	36
Dribbling, volleying, striking	15	27
Balancing, transferring weight, rolling	15	27
Jumping and landing	5	9
Fitness concepts	10	18
	100	180

Note: This overview is for a class that meets every day. It will vary depending upon the ecology of the teaching situation, as described in Chapter 1.

some idea of the percentage of time you'll need to spend on each area. For example, if your children need to spend much time practicing kicking, you may want to allocate 10 to 15 percent of that year's lessons to kicking. On the other hand, if they're skilled at kicking, you may want to do nothing more than review kicking, so you'll allocate 5 percent or even less to kicking.

Tables 5-1 and 5-2 are overview forms for the school year; they'll give you an idea of what such an outline might look like for an inexperienced class (Table 5-1) and an experienced class (Table 5-2). As you can see, the overview for the inexperienced class allocates more time to studying the movement concepts than does the overview for the experienced class, which focuses more on the skill themes.

Once you've determined the percentages (and are sure they total 100 percent for the school year),

translate them into school days. For example, if your children have physical education every day, then your academic year is approximately 180 days. However, if your children have physical education only twice a week, then your overview will have only seventy-two days. When you know the number of days you meet the children for the year, you can translate your percentages into the actual number of class meetings. Teachers who teach their children every day, for example, can devote eighteen days to teaching effort concepts if they decide to devote 10 percent of their classes to teaching time, force, and flow. Teachers whose children have physical education only twice a week, however, have about only seven days to devote to teaching effort (10 percent of seventy-two is about seven).

As you begin to develop your own school year overview, the Assessment Guides in the chapters

PLANNING THE SCHOOL YEAR

The chapters in Parts Three and Four are arranged in a developmentally logical sequence. The first three chapters (Chapters 12 to 14) focus on the movement concepts of space awareness, effort, and relationships, respectively. These concepts are initially taught as movement vocabulary words. Once the concepts are understood, they're used to enhance and embellish the study of individual skill themes (refer to Chapter 3 for a more thorough explanation). The remaining chapters (15 to 25) offer ideas for developing eleven skill themes.

When planning the school year, it's necessary to focus on the movement concepts *before* the skill themes. Children need to be taught (or to review) the movement vocabulary before it can be used successfully in the study of different skill themes. For example, pathways is a movement concept that is a subtheme for skill themes such as throwing and catching, traveling, dribbling and chasing, fleeing and dodging (Chapter 12 explains pathways). Rather than breaking the continuity of several lessons on the skill theme of traveling to explain a con-

cept such as pathways, we find it more satisfactory to teach pathways and other movement concepts first. Then when we want children to travel in different pathways, there's no need to stop and explain pathways. The children already know this movement concept, and the emphasis can remain on traveling.

We'd like to provide an exact, step-by-step progression for the school year, including a day-to-day outline that teachers could follow with every class they teach. This is unrealistic, however, because teaching situations are too different and varied. The planning guide examples in this chapter are intended only as aids to understanding the process of effective planning. Once an individual obtains a teaching position, it is that person's responsibility to develop yearly and daily plans that reflect the uniqueness of the particular teaching environment. Four sample daily calendars have been developed to help get you started (see Appendix A), but you'll find that you need to change them once you get to know your children's needs and interests.

in Parts Three and Four will give you a good idea of the areas in which your children need the most practice. (Ways to use these Assessment Guides are explained later in this chapter.)

Step 2: Day-by-Day Outline

The next step is to outline the sequence of lessons for each skill theme or movement concept. For example, let's assume you've decided to devote approximately 10 percent of the lessons for a particular class to the skill theme of jumping and landing. The day-by-day outline for this skill theme (Table 5-3) would show an appropriate progres-

sion for that particular theme. In devising that progression, you'd take into consideration the five factors, discussed earlier, that influence the teaching environment, and you'd use the information in Chapter 17, "Jumping and Landing." The outline would list an activity for each day devoted to the skill theme.

In Chapter 17, as in all the other skill theme chapters, we present "activities leading to skill theme development" at the precontrol, control, utilization, and proficiency levels. (In Chapters 12 through 14, we present "activities leading to movement concept understanding.") The names of the activities at the precontrol and control levels in

In most classrooms, ... there is no time to reflect or hold at a particular point and drift for a while. There is little time to celebrate communal achievement or discuss and respect boredom and weariness. Yet it seems to me that it is crucial that the rhythm of the school year be adjusted to the organic rhythms of individual classes. Learning cannot be parceled out evenly over all the days of the year, and every day cannot be expected to contain the same amount of material to be covered. There must be peaks and valleys, variations in the quality and quantity of work done at different times.

Herbert Kohl,
On Teaching

TABLE 5-3 / Sample Sequence of Jumping and Landing Skill Theme: Eighteen-Day Sequence for an Inexperienced Class (10 Percent of a Year's Lessons)

Day	Lesson focus
1	Jumping and landing: basic patterns
2	Jumping for distance
3	Jumping for height
4	Landing on one foot
5	Jumping over a swinging rope
6	Jumping over low obstacles: hoops
7	Jumping over low obstacles: hurdles
8	Jumping to form a body shape during flight
9	Traveling, jumping, and body shapes
10	Performing jumping sequences and making body shapes
11	Jumping rhythmically
12	Jumping in rhythmical sequences
13	Jumping a turned rope
14	Jumping a self-turned rope
15	Jumping using buoyant and yielding landings
16	Jumping over equipment using buoyant landings
17	Jumping on and off equipment using buoyant and yielding landings
18	Jumping and landing task sheet

Note: These sequence ideas from Chapter 17 are only a starting point, but they can be varied to suit the needs of classes, groups, and individuals. Some classes, for example, might need to spend several days on jumping for height. Other individuals, those who are adept at jumping and landing, could be individually challenged to make shapes in the air while others in the class are still attempting to take off and land on two feet without falling down (intratask variation). Once a teacher understands a sequence, it's easier for him or her to logically rearrange the sequence to suit the needs of various individuals and groups.

Chapter 17 are the items listed under "lesson focus" in Table 5-3. Each activity in the movement concept and skill theme chapters can be the focus for a day's lesson.

Obviously a lesson sequence will vary with the skill level of the class, the amount of time available, and other factors. In Table 5-3, the teacher decided that with an inexperienced class of first-graders he would begin with a lesson focused on two-foot takeoffs and two-foot landings. If his class had been more experienced (for example, a fourth grade that he had worked with for the past three years), he might have decided to quickly review two-foot takeoffs and landings in the first lesson and then proceed to jumping over obstacles or jumping rhythmically—activities that would not be taught until days 6 and 7 or 11 with an inexperienced class.

The beginning teacher will have to experiment with devising the sequence. This process of sequencing lessons to enhance learning movement concepts or skill themes is a valuable one. With practice, each teacher learns to predict, with increasing accuracy, the appropriate emphasis that a theme or concept should receive in a given class.

And experience helps the teacher adjust the sequence of the lessons to account for individual differences within a class and among classes. Once the teacher has outlined a sequence, he or she can rearrange that sequence without losing sight of the intended direction or progression of the skill theme or movement concept.

Once the theme or concept has been outlined and arranged into a progression, the next step is to insert the progression into a daily calendar (Fig-

Grade Level _____

Week 1	Week 2	Week 3	Week 4	Week 5	Week 6
M T W T F	M T W T F	M T W T F	M T W T F	M T W T F	M T W T F
Week 7	Week 8	Week 9	Week 10	Week 11	Week 12
M T W T F	M T W T F	M T W T F	M T W T F	M T W T F	M T W T F
Week 13	Week 14	Week 15	Week 16	Week 17	Week 18
M T W T F	M T W T F	M T W T F	M T W T F	M T W T F	M T W T F
Week 19	Week 20	Week 21	Week 22	Week 23	Week 24
M T W T F	M T W T F	M T W T F	M T W T F	M T W T F	M T W T F
Week 25	Week 26	Week 27	Week 28	Week 29	Week 30
M T W T F	M T W T F	M T W T F	M T W T F	M T W T F	M T W T F
Week 31	Week 32	Week 33	Week 34	Week 35	Week 36
M T W T F	M T W T F	M T W T F	M T W T F	M T W T F	M T W T F

Figure 5-1 Daily calendar.

ure 5-1). Decisions on the number of days in a row to focus on a theme or concept are based on the teacher's knowledge of all the factors that make up the learning environment.

Here are helpful guidelines for developing your day-to-day outlines:

1. The first time you introduce a concept or theme, the children will need several lessons in a row to grasp the major ideas. Later in the year, they'll need less time. Mass the practice in the beginning of the year; distribute it later.

During weeks 4 and 6, for example, four lessons may be devoted to jumping and landing. The remainder of the year, jumping and landing are the major focus of the lesson for only two days in a row. This same principle applies to any skill theme or movement concept: massed practice during initial learning, distributed practice later.

2. The older the children, the longer they're able to remain on the same skill theme. For example, children designing games or dances typically need several days in a row for this task.

As the children become more skilled, you'll notice that it becomes easier to remain on a skill theme than it was initially.

3. It isn't very effective to focus on a skill once a year and then never revisit it. Three weeks of practice on the skill theme of rolling in February, for example, probably won't lead to the long-term learning that three weeks of practice, one week each in October, February, and April, will cause.

4. To get you started, a major task is generally appropriate for the focus of a day's lesson. If you think the children will find a single task too strenuous or uninteresting, you may want to combine a major task from two different chapters. For example, you may want to combine the ideas under the heading Jumping a Turned Rope (p. 316) with the major task Traveling in Pathways (p. 434) from Chapter 21. This will give the children variety. Although most of our lessons focus on one major movement concept or skill theme, there's certainly no valid reason to not focus on two themes or concepts in a single lesson.

Our experience has been that it's often difficult for beginning teachers to develop a daily calendar. In an attempt to make this process easier (and better), four sample daily calendars are included in Appendix A. Two calendars are for classes that have physical education five times a week (180 days a year); two are for classes that meet twice a week (72 days a year). Two of the calendars are for grades K–2, and two are for grades three through six.

You'll find that you'll want to change these calendars as you plan your year, but they're a helpful start. To the right of each activity is a page number, which indicates the corresponding page in the text you can refer to for a thorough explanation of each task and how it can be presented to children.

Once an outline has been written, it is used only as a guide and changed as often and as much as a particular situation requires. You should write your outlines in pencil, leaving much space for changes.

Learning is not totally predictable. If the study of a particular topic is going especially well, we don't change simply because the daily outline tells us to change. If several lessons on a particular topic have proven ineffective, it's possible to change to a different focus even though the daily outline calls for teaching three more lessons on that topic.

The children's needs and interests are the guide for the lessons to be presented. No outline, however theoretically sound it may be, can unfailingly reflect the progress and the interests of all the children being taught.

Step 3: Planning Daily Lessons

Short-term planning is typically done after school and in the evenings. This is the step in which the specific variations among individuals and classes are taken into account. Long-term planning is typically done before the school year begins, before teachers know the individual children they'll be teaching. Thus, it is in daily lesson planning that individual variations can be accommodated.

Lesson ideas are generated from a number of sources, including notes from classes, your own and others' observations, books, workshops, conferences, articles, and discussions. Planning for lessons involves sifting through sources and then designing lessons to match the needs and characteristics of a particular class. We've found few, if any, predesigned lessons that worked for us the way they supposedly worked for their authors. And so, instead of including specific lesson plans, this book contains tasks for development to encourage you to develop your own plans.

To plan effectively, you need to consider the vital information in the sample guide for lesson planning (Figure 5-2). We've found this form useful for planning lessons and for improving our teaching. It is presented here only as a guide; you may want to change it or adapt it to your particular style of lesson planning.

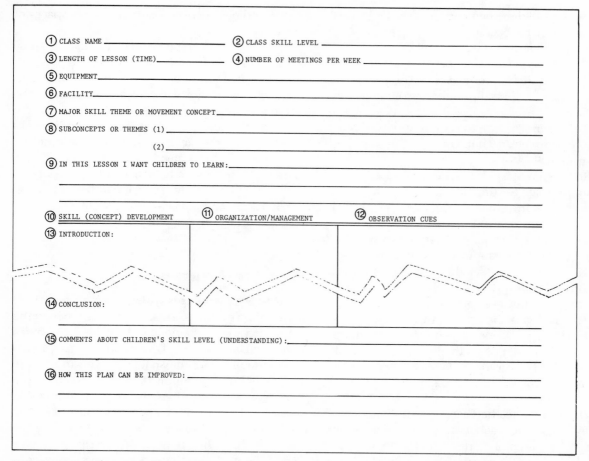

① CLASS NAME _____   ② CLASS SKILL LEVEL _____
③ LENGTH OF LESSON (TIME)_____ ④ NUMBER OF MEETINGS PER WEEK _____
⑤ EQUIPMENT_____
⑥ FACILITY_____
⑦ MAJOR SKILL THEME OR MOVEMENT CONCEPT_____
⑧ SUBCONCEPTS OR THEMES (1) _____
                        (2) _____
⑨ IN THIS LESSON I WANT CHILDREN TO LEARN:_____

⑩ SKILL (CONCEPT) DEVELOPMENT   ⑪ ORGANIZATION/MANAGEMENT   ⑫ OBSERVATION CUES
⑬ INTRODUCTION:

⑭ CONCLUSION:

⑮ COMMENTS ABOUT CHILDREN'S SKILL LEVEL (UNDERSTANDING):_____

⑯ HOW THIS PLAN CAN BE IMPROVED: _____

Figure 5-2 Sample lesson planning form.

The lesson planning form has sixteen different parts. Each part, along with suggested modifications, is discussed in the order in which a plan is typically completed. (Figure 5-3 shows a completed plan.)

1. Class Name. This part isn't necessary for a classroom teacher. Physical education specialists may want to make a plan for each of their classes or, when their teaching load is particularly heavy, list the grade level as a general guide, e.g., 2nd/3rd grade. Another alternative is to just list the skill level of the class. Teachers with heavy loads, e.g.,

thirty different classes in a week, use the same basic plan for each grade level and then make individual notes about different classes as suggested at the end of this form (part 15).

2. Skill Level. This gives the teacher a general idea of the skill level of the class. The information is based on observations and assessments (explained later in this chapter).

3. Length of Lesson (Time). This refers to the length of a class, e.g., 10:00 to 10:30, or twenty-five minutes.

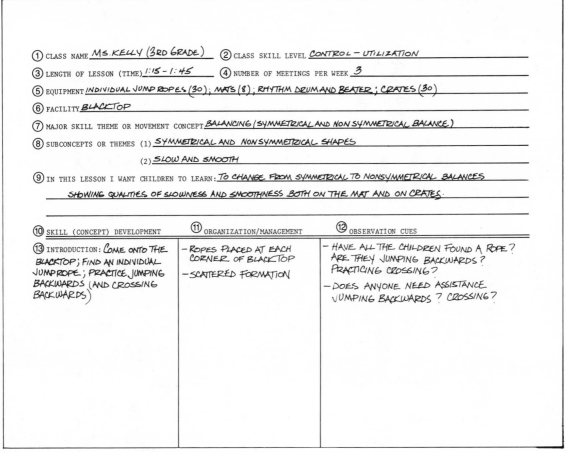

① CLASS NAME *Ms. Kelly (3rd Grade)*   ② CLASS SKILL LEVEL *CONTROL – UTILIZATION*

③ LENGTH OF LESSON (TIME) *1:15 – 1:45*   ④ NUMBER OF MEETINGS PER WEEK *3*

⑤ EQUIPMENT *INDIVIDUAL JUMP ROPES (30); MATS (8); RHYTHM DRUM AND BEATER; CRATES (30)*

⑥ FACILITY *BLACKTOP*

⑦ MAJOR SKILL THEME OR MOVEMENT CONCEPT *BALANCING / SYMMETRICAL AND NON SYMMETRICAL BALANCE)*

⑧ SUBCONCEPTS OR THEMES (1) *SYMMETRICAL AND NONSYMMETRICAL SHAPES*

　　　　　　　　　　　(2) *SLOW AND SMOOTH*

⑨ IN THIS LESSON I WANT CHILDREN TO LEARN: *TO CHANGE FROM SYMMETRICAL TO NONSYMMETRICAL BALANCES SHOWING QUALITIES OF SLOWNESS AND SMOOTHNESS BOTH ON THE MAT AND ON CRATES.*

⑩ SKILL (CONCEPT) DEVELOPMENT	⑪ ORGANIZATION/MANAGEMENT	⑫ OBSERVATION CUES
⑬ INTRODUCTION: *Come onto the blacktop; find an individual jump rope; practice jumping backwards (and crossing backwards)*	– *ROPES PLACED AT EACH CORNER OF BLACKTOP* – *SCATTERED FORMATION*	– *HAVE ALL THE CHILDREN FOUND A ROPE? ARE THEY JUMPING BACKWARDS? PRACTICING CROSSING?* – *DOES ANYONE NEED ASSISTANCE JUMPING BACKWARDS? CROSSING?*

Figure 5-3 Sample lesson planning form filled out. This plan is based on the tasks suggested in Chapter 19 in the section titled "Balancing Symmetrically and Nonsymmetrically." As suggested in this chapter, the plan has been changed somewhat from the actual tasks.

(continued)

4. Number of Meetings per Week. This information is especially helpful for specialists who meet certain classes a different number of times per week from others.

5. Equipment. A list of the equipment that will be needed is a handy way to check before the lesson to make sure everything is ready. It's easy to forget, so this list is necessary.

6. Facility. Some teachers have to change facilities during the day, such as from a cafeteria to a classroom. This is a handy reminder, and for those who have limited indoor space, it's a helpful reference when they must teach indoors.

7. Major Skill Theme or Skill Concept. This section is taken from the day-to-day outline (Table 5-3) and typically will be a major task from one of the move-

—ROPES BACK WHERE YOU GOT THEM. GROUPS OF FOUR. EACH GROUP CARRY A MAT TO A SELF-SPACE (ONE PERSON AT EACH CORNER OF THE MAT). SIT ON YOUR MAT WHEN YOU ARE READY.	— MATS IN FOUR LOCATIONS ON BLACKTOP (2 PER LOCATION) CRATES (BOXES) 8 ROPES STACK OF 2 MATS	—ARE ROPES PLACED BACK WHERE THEY BELONG? — ARE ALL FOUR CHILDREN CARRYING THE MATS ACCORDING TO INSTRUCTIONS? —ARE CHILDREN SITTING ON MATS WHEN THEIR MAT IS IN A SELF-SPACE?
— EACH TAKE A CORNER OF THE MAT. BALANCE ON YOUR BACK WITH YOUR ARMS AND LEGS EXTENDED — WIDE.	—FOUR STUDENTS TO A MAT; MATS SPREAD OUT OVER BLACK TOP	— ARE STUDENTS BALANCED ON THEIR BACKS? — ARE THE ARMS AND LEGS EXTENDED WIDE?
—MAKE THE SHAPE (ARMS) AND LEGS EXACTLY THE SAME ON BOTH SIDES. WHAT DO WE CALL THIS TYPE OF SHAPE?	— SAME	—ARE THE ARMS AND LEGS PLACED SO THAT THE SHAPES ARE SYMMETRICAL?
— CHANGE THE SHAPE (STILL ON YOUR BACK) SO THAT IT IS STILL SYMMETRICAL.	— SAME	—ARE THE SHAPES DIFFERENT, BUT STILL SYMMETRICAL?

Figure 5-3 (continued)

ment concept or skill theme chapters. (The daily calendars in Appendix A are good guidelines for planning these topics.)

8. Subconcepts or Subthemes. Although not always necessary, this section is a reminder of the points that will be emphasized along with the major task. Jumping, for example, might be a subtheme of a lesson on catching; speed might be a subconcept of a lesson on pathways. It's important to note that any concept or skill can be a major focus of a lesson or a minor focus or subtheme.

9. In This Lesson I Want Children to Learn. This section is really the statement of objectives. Most education and physical education teachers have plenty of practice writing objectives, so this point isn't emphasized here. What is important is that the teacher be able to clearly state what she or he expects to see at the end of the lesson. Others should be able to see it also. Failure to write this statement means that often the teacher is simply "doing stuff" rather than actually teaching to help children improve.

In this section, a statement such as "to throw

— STAY BALANCED ON YOUR BACK BUT CHANGE TO A NONSYMMETRICAL BASE.	— SAME	— ARE THE SHAPES NON SYMMETRICAL? STILL ON THEIR BACKS?
— BALANCE ON YOUR SHOULDERS, BACK OF HEAD AND ARMS. CREATE A SYMMETRICAL SHAPE WITH YOUR LEGS. ON THE FIRST DRUMBEAT, CHANGE TO A NONSYMMETRICAL SHAPE; ON THE NEXT DRUMBEAT, BACK TO A SYMMETRICAL SHAPE.	— SAME	— ARE THE CHANGES MADE ON THE DRUMBEAT? ARE THE SHAPES CORRECT? SYMMETRICAL — NONSYMMETRICAL — SYMMETRICAL?
— USE THE SAME THREE SHAPES BUT CHANGE SLOWLY AND SMOOTHLY FROM ONE SHAPE TO THE OTHER. START AND STOP ON YOUR OWN.	— SAME	— LOCATE SEVERAL CHILDREN WHO ARE PERFORMING THE TASK AS SLOWLY AND SMOOTHLY AS REQUIRED.
— WATCH (____, ____). NOTICE HOW SLOWLY AND SMOOTHLY THEIR SHAPES CHANGE	— SAME	— ARE THE CHILDREN WATCHING THE DEMONSTRATORS?
— PRACTICE AGAIN, TRYING TO MAKE YOUR SHAPE CHANGES SLOW AND SMOOTH.	— SAME	— ARE THE SHAPES SLOW AND SMOOTH?

(continued)

better" is so vague as to be useless, as is the statement "to practice throwing." In contrast, the statement "to use opposition when they throw a ball overhand to a partner" is more helpful because it describes an action that is observable. It's clear what this teacher has in mind—and an observer would be able to tell whether the teacher had accomplished the objective at the end of the lesson.

10. Skill (Concept) Development. This part of the lesson contains the actual content; the content is from Chapters 12 to 25, as well as other sources. In the beginning, teachers often find it helpful to be very thorough. In fact, some teachers in the first few lessons actually write down exact statements from the book. Before long, however, this isn't necessary; it's enough to simply write down the "big ideas." Statements such as "Throw and catch with a partner—emphasizing opposition" or "Run, stop, and balance on one foot" are sufficient reminders when a teacher has some experience.

11. Organization/Management. This section is often overlooked in lesson planning, but it's very important.

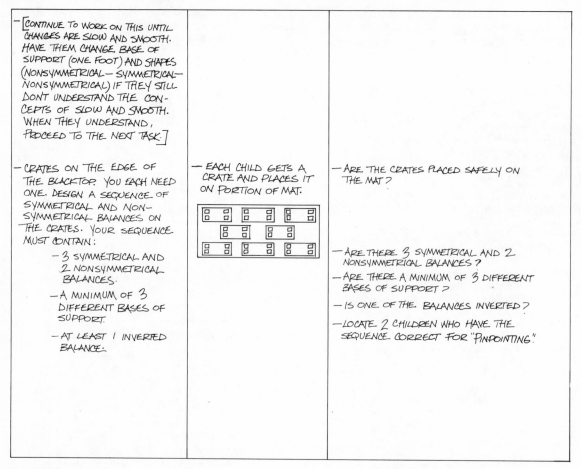

— [CONTINUE TO WORK ON THIS UNTIL CHANGES ARE SLOW AND SMOOTH. HAVE THEM CHANGE BASE OF SUPPORT (ONE FOOT) AND SHAPES (NONSYMMETRICAL — SYMMETRICAL — NONSYMMETRICAL) IF THEY STILL DON'T UNDERSTAND THE CONCEPTS OF SLOW AND SMOOTH. WHEN THEY UNDERSTAND, PROCEED TO THE NEXT TASK.]		

— CRATES ON THE EDGE OF THE BLACKTOP. YOU EACH NEED ONE. DESIGN A SEQUENCE OF SYMMETRICAL AND NON-SYMMETRICAL BALANCES ON THE CRATES. YOUR SEQUENCE MUST CONTAIN:
  — 3 SYMMETRICAL AND 2 NONSYMMETRICAL BALANCES.
  — A MINIMUM OF 3 DIFFERENT BASES OF SUPPORT.
  — AT LEAST 1 INVERTED BALANCE.
	— EACH CHILD GETS A CRATE AND PLACES IT ON PORTION OF MAT.	— ARE THE CRATES PLACED SAFELY ON THE MAT?
		
		— ARE THERE 3 SYMMETRICAL AND 2 NONSYMMETRICAL BALANCES?
		— ARE THERE A MINIMUM OF 3 DIFFERENT BASES OF SUPPORT?
		— IS ONE OF THE BALANCES INVERTED?
		— LOCATE 2 CHILDREN WHO HAVE THE SEQUENCE CORRECT FOR "PINPOINTING."

Figure 5-3 (continued)

Carefully thinking through this section before a lesson may mean virtually no wasted waiting time for the children.

In this section we jot down our organizational patterns. For example, every child has a ball in self-space; four children to a mat; a diagram of where each of the six stations will be located in the room. Decisions about how to get a partner (someone with the same color shirt) or how to put children into groups (by birthdays) are other organizational tips to include in this section. Completing this section forces the teacher to plan ahead. Typically the organization necessary to complete each task is included on the same line as the task statement (Figure 5-3).

12. Observation Cues. The observation cues remind you of what to look for in the lesson. In the beginning, you may want to write down a statement; later, an abbreviated reminder will be sufficient. You'll find that some of the cues will be unnecessary as you observe that the children are already meeting the criteria called for in the cue.

For example, a cue we use frequently is, "Are

[PINPOINT TWO CHILDREN WHO HAVE SEQUENCE CORRECT. DIRECT THE CHILDREN TO WATCH FOR THE DIFFERENT SHAPES, INVERTED BALANCE.]	—TWO CHILDREN DEMONSTRATE.	—ARE THE CHILDREN PAYING ATTENTION AND OBSERVING?
—ONCE YOU HAVE MEMORIZED YOUR SEQUENCE, FOCUS ON DOING IT SMOOTHLY AND SLOWLY. THE SPEED SHOULD BE EVEN THROUGHOUT—NO JERKINESS.	—ALL WORKING ON CRATE— INDIVIDUALLY.	—ARE THE SEQUENCES SMOOTH AND SLOW-FLOWING? —ARE THEY DOING THE SHAPES CORRECTLY—SYMMETRICAL (3); NONSYMMETRICAL (2); 1 INVERTED; 3 DIFFERENT BASES OF SUPPORT?
—WHEN YOU THINK YOU HAVE YOUR SEQUENCE "PERFECTED," LET ME KNOW AND I WILL COME BY AND LOOK AT IT. WHEN I HAVE LOOKED AT IT (AND APPROVED IT), YOU MAY WANT TO CREATE A DIFFERENT SEQUENCE OR YOU MAY WANT TO WORK WITH A PARTNER (WHO HAS HAD A SEQUENCE APPROVED) TO CREATE A MATCHING SEQUENCE.	—ALL WORKING ON CRATE— INDIVIDUALLY.	—WHEN I WATCH INDIVIDUALS, I NEED TO BE SURE THAT: ① SEQUENCE IS CORRECT ② IT FLOWS SMOOTHLY FROM ONE BALANCE TO ANOTHER

(continued)

the children using all the general space?" If the children are using the space appropriately, this cue wouldn't necessarily be stated to the children as a reminder. In contrast, if the cue was "bending knees upon landing from a jump" and we observed that the children weren't bending their knees upon landing, the cue would be used as a task refinement (Chapter 9).

13. Introduction. Typically, we begin our lessons with activity as soon as possible. In fact, when the children are ready, we prefer to have them enter the gym and begin practicing with no instruction from us. Sometimes we challenge them to remember from the previous lesson: "Next time when you enter the gym, find a rope and begin jumping." Sometimes we use a chalkboard or bulletin board:

1. Enter the gym quietly.
2. Take off your shoes and socks and place them neatly against the wall.
3. Find a ball and begin dribbling in general space.

This section on the form reminds us to be sure to plan an introduction to the lesson.

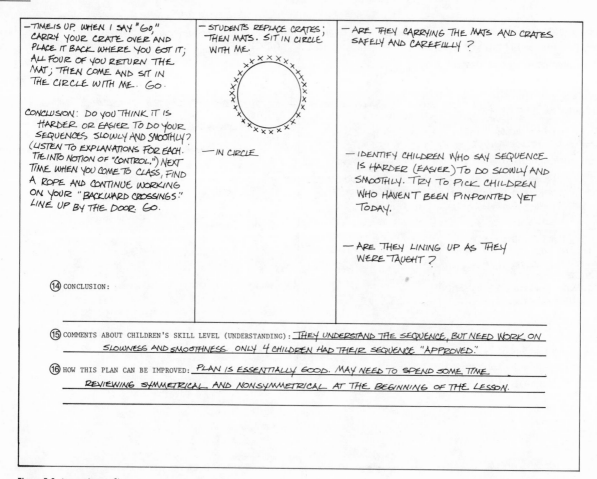

—TIME IS UP. WHEN I SAY "GO," CARRY YOUR CRATE OVER AND PLACE IT BACK WHERE YOU GOT IT; ALL FOUR OF YOU RETURN THE MAT; THEN COME AND SIT IN THE CIRCLE WITH ME. GO.

CONCLUSION: DO YOU THINK IT IS HARDER OR EASIER TO DO YOUR SEQUENCES SLOWLY AND SMOOTHLY? (LISTEN TO EXPLANATIONS FOR EACH. TIE INTO NOTION OF "CONTROL.") NEXT TIME WHEN YOU COME TO CLASS, FIND A ROPE AND CONTINUE WORKING ON YOUR "BACKWARD CROSSINGS." LINE UP BY THE DOOR. GO.

⑭ CONCLUSION:

—STUDENTS REPLACE CRATES; THEN MATS. SIT IN CIRCLE WITH ME.

—IN CIRCLE

—ARE THEY CARRYING THE MATS AND CRATES SAFELY AND CAREFULLY?

—IDENTIFY CHILDREN WHO SAY SEQUENCE IS HARDER (EASIER) TO DO SLOWLY AND SMOOTHLY. TRY TO PICK CHILDREN WHO HAVEN'T BEEN PINPOINTED YET TODAY.

—ARE THEY LINING UP AS THEY WERE TAUGHT?

⑮ COMMENTS ABOUT CHILDREN'S SKILL LEVEL (UNDERSTANDING): THEY UNDERSTAND THE SEQUENCE, BUT NEED WORK ON SLOWNESS AND SMOOTHNESS. ONLY 4 CHILDREN HAD THEIR SEQUENCE "APPROVED."

⑯ HOW THIS PLAN CAN BE IMPROVED: PLAN IS ESSENTIALLY GOOD. MAY NEED TO SPEND SOME TIME REVIEWING SYMMETRICAL AND NONSYMMETRICAL AT THE BEGINNING OF THE LESSON.

Figure 5-3 (continued)

Once the children have had a few minutes (typically no more than five), we call them in and explain the purpose of the day's lesson. During this time we attempt to create an interest in the lesson by using *set induction* (Graham, 1975); this term means that you create a reason for the lesson by creating a cognitive interest in what is about to be practiced. Examples of set induction include reasons for practicing, challenges to find different ways to solve a problem, questions to see if children can improve from past performances, comparisons with other sports or athletes. Typically, this takes no more than two to three minutes, and then the children begin actually practicing on the major focus of the lesson.

14. Conclusion. The conclusion, at the end of the lesson, also typically takes no more than two or three minutes. This is a time to comment on the children's behavior and their skill improvement; remind them of the important cues, e.g., bent knees when landing; encourage them to practice with parents and friends; and/or remind them about beginning the next class if they come into the gym and begin activity on their own.

15. Comments About Children's Skill Level (Understanding). This section is completed after the lesson. Typical comments might be that the children need more practice because they didn't accomplish the objective of the lesson or that they seem to be ready to move to a harder task. This also is the place to record comments about individual children in the class, an especially important step when you revisit this skill or concept in a few weeks. As suggested in the beginning of this section, teachers with many classes a week use essentially the same plan for each grade level, recording the differences in a separate notebook or on 5 × 8 cards, for example, by listing the classroom teacher's name.

16. How This Plan Can Be Improved. Many teachers refer to last year's plans as they plan for the next year. This section of the plan is especially helpful as you review lessons from a previous year.

As you've already concluded, a well-done plan is somewhat lengthy. For this reason many teachers find it helpful to write a brief outline of the plan on a 5 × 8 card that they carry with them during the lesson as an uncumbersome reminder.

As you review these sixteen steps for the lesson plan, you may find that certain steps are unnecessary for your situation. That is to be expected—we suggest that you adapt this form to meet your needs and then mimeograph plenty of copies for the year.

USING THE SKILL ASSESSMENT GUIDES

Each movement concept and skill theme chapter (Chapters 12 to 25) contains one or more Assessment Guides, which are actually skill tests. These guides give a teacher a formative evaluation of the children's status for that particular theme or concept. The Assessment Guides are designed to help answer questions such as "At what skill level are the children?" or "Where do I begin?" The two examples in Figures 5-4 and 5-5 are from Chapter

Figure 5-4 Movement concept Assessment Guide from Chapter 12, "Space Awareness."

ASSESSMENT GUIDE / Levels

TASK   Skip around the space, and on the signal freeze in a body shape that is, as much as possible, at the level called out.

GUIDE   You'll know the children understand the concept of levels when you observe that:

1. Their body shapes are, as much as possible, at the level indicated.
2. They don't hesitate between the traveling and freezing action; they automatically freeze at the level indicated.

You'll know the children still don't understand the concept of levels when you observe that:

1. Only part of their body shapes are at the level indicated.
2. They have to stop and think before they freeze; they don't automatically freeze at the level indicated.

ASSESSMENT GUIDE / Volleying

Note to Teachers. Mark a line on the wall approximately three feet above the floor. Mark the second line seven feet from the floor so it's directly above the three-foot line. A dotted line of plastic colored tape works well; a continuous line of tape isn't necessary.

TASK   Stand eight to ten feet from the wall (you can mark a line on the floor). Drop the playground ball so it bounces one time; then strike the ball with your open palm so the ball travels to the wall and hits between the tape marks. After the ball bounces one time on the floor, strike it again to the wall. The pattern will be: strike ball with palm, ball hits wall, ball bounces on floor, strike ball again, ball hits wall . . . Try to keep the pattern going at least five times. You may choose to hit with either hand or with both hands.

GUIDE   The children are ready for precontrol- or control-level tasks when you observe that:

1. They're unable to strike the ball between the tape marks.
2. They catch the ball each time rather than continuously hitting.
3. They're unable to hit the ball five times in a row.

The children are ready for utilization- and proficiency-level tasks when you observe that they're capable of striking the ball between the tape marks five times without breaking the pattern.

Figure 5-5 Skill theme Assessment Guide from Chapter 23, "Volleying and Dribbling."

12, "Space Awareness," and Chapter 23, "Volleying and Dribbling."

Notice that the Assessment Guide for Chapter 12 doesn't include references to skill levels because, as explained earlier, the generic levels of skill proficiency apply to the skill themes (Chapters 15 to 25), not to the movement concepts. The Assessment Guide for Chapter 23 includes general references as to the appropriate task level, based on the children's performance. Because of the nature of the assessment, the guide must be general, so the teacher will have to judge the exact place to begin.

Another important point is that the Assessment Guides aren't intended to be used with every

child twice a year, for example. We suggest that they be used when needed to obtain an estimate of either the skill level or the improvement of a class. There are several ways to use the Assessment Guides without having children wait in line; following are four suggestions:

1. Organize the class into stations (Chapter 6). You can be at one of the stations administering one assessment as the children rotate to your station. If you're new to a school, you may want to administer several different assessments to obtain a general estimate of the children's abilities.

2. Set up several group games, e.g., modified vol-

leyball (p. 522) or minisoccer (p. 442). Rotate one side out of the games at a time and administer an assessment to that group. For example, in a class of thirty, if there were two games of minisoccer with six per side, you could work with a group of six to conduct an assessment. Although you wouldn't want to do this often, it is another way to ascertain the children's progress.

3. Select a group of six to eight children that represents the range of ability for a given grade level. Arrange to work with this group during one of your planning periods so you can administer several assessments.

4. In some schools, parents, aides, or high school students can learn to use the different Assessment Guides to determine the needs of the children in particular grade levels. This is also helpful for measuring children's progress from year to year.

CHANGING ACTIVITIES

Deciding when to continue focusing on a concept or theme and when to change can be a difficult decision. Probably the least efficient guide is time. That is, it isn't usually productive to plan to spend five minutes on one idea and ten minutes on another, or a week on a theme. We've found that observation, using the techniques suggested in Chapter 9, can provide cues about the skill levels of the children in a class. Some cues are more valuable with some activities than with others.

We use five criteria when reflecting on a particular activity and making appropriate decisions:

1. What success rate is being achieved, by individual children and by the class as a whole?

2. Are children able to perform this movement effectively, using correct motor patterns?

3. How many children are on-task and how many are off-task?

4. Are the children interested in the activity?

5. How much time has been allocated to this activity in the long-term plan for the year?

Because we want the children to succeed more than fail, we prefer that the children experience success 70 to 80 percent of the time. You can assess the success rate for an entire class by using the scanning technique (Chapter 9) to determine how well the children are able to accomplish a task. For example, if the children have been challenged to "Dribble a ball with one hand as you travel through general space" and we observe that most of the children are chasing after the ball rather than dribbling under control, we'd refocus the lesson. In contrast, if the task appeared too easy for the class, we'd also refocus the lesson.

Verbal and nonverbal indicators can also be cues about how appropriate a task is. Relatively quiet involvement in an activity, for example, often indicates the appropriateness of a challenge. Unusual loudness, in contrast, may indicate a general lack of interest. Obviously this too depends on the class and on the individuals in the class. Some children seem to complain about everything and consequently are inaccurate barometers.

The final criteria, the long-term plan for the year, is probably the least important of the five, but it does influence decisions about whether to continue with an activity. Even though the children may be infatuated with a particular theme, if a disproportionate amount of time is devoted to one theme or concept, other topics will receive less attention. We do adjust our long-term plans regularly, but we also try to give children the variety of experiences that is so important to overall development.

The successful teacher is able to use cues to make informed decisions about the appropriateness of a particular activity. A decision to refocus within a lesson or between lessons is, for an effective teacher, a conscious decision based on data.

RECORDING PROGRESS

A reflective teacher must record the progress that a particular class, group, or individual makes during a lesson. An elementary school physical education specialist may teach eight to twelve classes a day. Each group and each student will progress to a different degree and in a different way. A reflective teacher, whose approach takes these differences into consideration, will need notes on which to base the next day's (or week's) lessons.

You can write brief comments in a standard planning book or on index cards. Notes summarizing what was accomplished during a lesson are helpful when planning the next day's lessons. Whenever possible, the day's schedule should include five or ten minutes between classes; you can use this time for recording observations and, if necessary, arranging equipment for the next class. When a schedule doesn't include time for writing notes, particularly when teaching a class as individuals (see Chapter 6), a cassette tape recorder is helpful. Just a few words on tape can help you remember the details of an important observation you made during the first lesson of the day. What seemed so clear at 9:00 A.M. is often opaque by 4:00 P.M.

LESSON DESIGN

If children are to develop into skillful movers, they must do more than play games. Children need opportunities to practice skills in meaningful contexts. A successful teacher is able to create practice situations that are enjoyable, appropriately de-

signed, and allow for maximum participation. The teacher who can design interesting and exciting practice situations will rarely hear the question— asked so often by highly skilled unchallenged children—"When do we get to play a game?"

Interesting Lessons

Many children, particularly younger ones, don't understand the need to practice in order to become more skillful. Nor do they care. Many children are interested only in the present and have little concern about the future, which seems remote. Young children more easily accept and enjoy lessons with immediate meaning. For example, we wouldn't teach second-graders how to turn on one foot by having them perform a mass drill because such an exercise would make little sense to them. We might have them jog around the gym and instruct them to "Spin around on one foot when you hear the drum and then continue jogging." On the next drumbeat we might ask them to "Pivot on the other foot" or to "Spin in the opposite direction." Later, when the children are able to travel dribbling a ball, we might ask them to "Spin on the drumbeat while continuing to dribble a ball." We don't teach skills as if all children really want to learn the skill because they intend to play on a varsity team in high school—they don't.

Variety in a lesson also makes the lesson more enjoyable. We try to give children a number of related practice opportunities in a single lesson, rather than having them practice the same skill the same way the entire lesson.

Appropriate Lessons

Children want to be challenged and successful at the same time. The ideal task is difficult enough so that the child can't do it as intended every time yet easy enough so that the child is successful much of the time. If a small child tries to make a basketball go through a ten-foot-high basket, his success rate may be so low that he'll quickly lose interest. If the same child is given options—for example, shooting at a basket seven feet high or shooting through a hoop suspended from a pole—his interest will remain higher for longer, and so his skills will improve.

Maximum Participation

One of the clearest differences between more effective and less effective teachers is that the students of more effective teachers actually spend more time practicing than do the children of less effective teachers (Gage, 1978; McDonald, 1976; Rink, 1985; Rosenshine, 1983; Siedentop, 1983). The value of practice may seem obvious, yet frequently practice is neglected, particularly in teaching games. When a class of thirty children is practicing a skill such as throwing or catching and uses only three or four balls, the children's skills will improve less than the skills of children whose teacher designs the same lesson so that there is a ball for every two children in the class.

Remember, though, that not all children have learned to practice on their own. Making more equipment available doesn't guarantee increased practice time. In fact, we've observed instances where the children in a class actually practiced more when there were only three or four balls available because most of the students in the class hadn't yet learned to work on their own.

MAKING PLANNING ENJOYABLE

Planning is hard work. It takes time and energy to plan effective lessons that are exciting and interesting to children. Teachers who fail to plan well tend to return to old standbys—kickball, dodgeball, and four square—that contribute minimally to children's physical education.

You'll always be able to find something to do that is more interesting than planning lessons. So it's a good idea to devise ways to make planning easier and more fun. We've found the following ideas helpful:

If this project doesn't interest you, *leave it alone*, don't imagine that you can make exciting for children what to you is only a bore. Find instead something to do that you can throw yourself into. Let the students see *you* genuinely interested. Let them see *your* intelligence, imagination, and energy at work.

John Holt,
Freedom and Beyond

A bride served baked ham, and her husband asked why she always cut the ends off. "Well, that's the way my mother always did it," she replied. The next time his mother-in-law stopped by, he asked her why she cut the ends off the ham. "That's the way my mother did it," she replied. And when grandma visited, she too was asked why she sliced the ends off. She said, "That's the only way I could get it into the pan."

Muriel James and Dorothy Jongeward,
Born to Win

1. Set aside some time each day specifically for planning. Then you won't be constantly trying to find time to plan. Some people find that planning at school before they leave for home is effective; others prefer to arrive at school early to plan the day.
2. Try to become excited about your plans. When you're excited about trying to present an idea in a new and interesting way, planning is fun and your enthusiasm is communicated to your students.

3. Don't hesitate to experiment. The worst that can happen is that a lesson won't work as planned. When this happens, we tell the children we were trying a new idea and it didn't work. Children understand and sometimes make worthwhile suggestions about how the idea might be improved.

When you set aside appropriate amounts of time, try new ideas, and attempt to make lessons exciting, planning becomes more enjoyable. And your attitude toward teaching will be affected. Most of us experience uncertainty when beginning a lesson (or anything else) for which we're unprepared. When you've planned a lesson thoroughly, the assurance and enthusiasm you feel can be contagious.

SUMMARY

Planning is a crucial, although not necessarily enjoyable, facet of teaching. Successful teachers plan effectively, not only from day to day but for the entire year. Plans should be used as helpful but not immutable guides. As the teacher learns about the individual children and the ecology of the particular teaching situation, plans can and should be adapted.

Long-term plans provide an outline of the general topics to be covered throughout a year. When this outline is done as a school year overview (Tables 5-1 and 5-2), the percentages can be reflected in a daily calendar (Figure 5-1), which gives the teacher a guide for determining what will be taught on a particular day. When daily lesson planning is based on the long-term plans, the teacher can make certain that appropriate topics are adequately studied.

A format for planning daily lessons (Figure 5-2) should include space for: recording information about a lesson's major focus, writing the progression of the activities, important organization and management information, teaching cues, and introducing and concluding the lessons. Teachers should keep track of individual student progress and write helpful objectives as well as criteria for determining when to change to a different theme or concept. Guidelines for designing successful physical education lessons for children include ideas for making lessons enjoyable and appropriate and for maximizing the children's desire to participate in physical education lessons.

READING COMPREHENSION QUESTIONS

1. Why is it important to do both short- and long-range planning? What can happen when a teacher doesn't plan the entire year ahead of time?
2. What does the term *reflective planning* mean?
3. Using Tables 5-1 and 5-2 as examples, develop a school year overview for a program in which you meet with the children a total of seventy-two days per year. Be certain

that the percentages add up to 100. Change at least three of the "content" categories from the way they're included in the tables.

4. Use Table 5-3 as an example to develop an eighteen-day sequence for another skill theme.

5. Use the guide for planning lessons (Figure 5-2) to write your own plan. (Do *not* use the same skill theme.) Describe the teaching situation for which you're creating the plan. The completed plan (Figure 5-3) will help you in this task.

6. Describe how the Assessment Guides are used by referring to an example from one of the movement concept chapters and one from the skill theme chapters. Do *not* use the ones shown in this chapter.

7. Explain the purpose of the sample daily outlines in Appendix A. Which of these four outlines do you think you'd find most helpful? Why?

REFERENCES

Gage, N. L. (1978). *The scientific basis of the art of teaching*. New York: Teachers College Press.

Glass, G. V., Cahen, L., Smith, M., & Filby, N. (1979, April–May). Class size and learning. *Today's Education*, 42–44.

Graham, G. (1975, March). A bridge between what is and what could be. *The Physical Educator*, 14–16.

Hanson, M. (1972, June). Professional preparation of the elementary school physical education teacher. *Quest*, 98–106.

Holt, J. (1972). *Freedom and beyond*. New York: Dutton.

James, M., & Jongeward, D. (1973). *Born to win*. Reading, MA: Addison-Wesley.

Kohl, H. (1976). *On teaching*. New York: Schocken.

Mager, R. F. (1973). *Measuring instructional intent, or got a match?* Belmont, CA: Fearon.

McDonald, F. (1976, Spring). Report on Phase II of the beginning teacher evaluation study: Overview of the ethnographic study. *Journal of Teacher Education*, 39–42.

Rink, J. (1985). *Teaching physical education for learning*. St. Louis: Mosby.

Rosenshine, B. (1983). Teaching functions in instructional programs. *Elementary School Journal*, *83*, 335–351.

Siedentop, D. (1983). *Developing teaching skills in physical education*. (2nd ed.). Palo Alto, CA: Mayfield.

CHAPTER 6

Organizing for Learning

The key to success in such trial runs (individualizing), I've found, is to go at it quietly, carefully and watchfully. Don't try to change the whole world, even the small world of your own gymnasium, on the first try.

Dolly Lambdin

What is the best way to organize a class for learning? Some teachers rarely vary the organization of their classes; others often do. When deciding how to organize a particular class, the reflective teacher considers such factors as the goals of the lesson, how much responsibility the class is ready for, how many decisions the children are capable of sharing in, and whether the lesson will fail if the students are allowed to choose among several activities. The factors discussed in Chapter 1 and the teacher's experience with different organizational patterns will influence this decision. This chapter is an introduction to the variety of organizational patterns that teachers might use in their classes.

In our teaching we typically use three instructional approaches:

1. Direct
2. Inquiry, either convergent or divergent
3. Child-designed

We also use a variety of lesson formats; the four we use most often are

1. Whole class
2. Learning center or station
3. Task sheet
4. Contract

The following two main sections describe each of the three approaches and four formats, with examples of when and how to use them in teaching. It's important to stress that one particular approach or format isn't inherently better than

> Individualizing is not so much a method of instruction as it is a distinct way of thinking about learning and the respective roles of teacher and student.
>
> Larry Locke and Dolly Lambdin,
> "Teacher Behavior"

another. Rather, one is better for a specific purpose, as will become clear as you read the chapter's explanations.*

INSTRUCTIONAL APPROACHES

An analysis of our teaching would reveal that the direct and the inquiry approaches are used more often than the child-designed approach. Although we don't use the third approach as often, asking children to design their own games, dances, or gymnastic sequences does enhance the children's creativity and imagination.

Direct Approach

With the *direct approach*, the teacher tells the children exactly what to practice, shows them how to practice, and guides their practice. Thus the children make few decisions themselves. This approach has proven highly effective when a teacher's goal is to have the children learn a specific skill and perform that skill correctly in a specified manner. For example, if your goal is to teach the overhand throw, you want the children to step with the foot

*For a more thorough understanding of techniques for organizing, see the text *Teaching Physical Education*, 2nd ed., by Muska Mosston, 1981, Columbus, OH: Merrill. There is a brief introduction to the entire spectrum of teaching styles in Michael Goldberger's October 1984 article, "Effective Learning Through a Spectrum of Teaching Styles" in the *Journal of Physical Education, Recreation, and Dance*, pp. 17–21.

> Teachers have to learn how to provide transitions for their pupils. It is not possible for most young people to make choices after five or six years of being told what to do every minute they are in school. It is equally hard for them to share resources, help other students, or decide what they want to learn after years of being expected to hoard, compete, and conform. Transitional situations often have to be provided. Some students need workbooks for a while; others want to memorize times tables or have weekly spelling tests. Young people are no different from adults. When faced with new possibilities they want something old and predictable to hold onto while risking new freedom. Inexperienced teachers often make the mistake of tearing down the traditional attitudes their students have been conditioned to depend upon before the students have time to develop alternative ways of learning and dealing with school. In their impatience they become cruel to students who do not change fast enough or who resist change altogether. One just cannot legislate compassion or freedom. Teaching as a craft involves understanding how people learn; as an art it involves a sensitive balance between presenting and advocating things you believe and stepping away and encouraging your students to make their own sense of your passion and commitment.
>
> Herbert Kohl,
> *On Teaching*

opposite their throwing hand, sequentially rotate their hips and shoulders, extend their arm almost fully, and follow through (Chapter 22). Some children may learn this correct way of throwing without assistance from the teacher, but many won't.

Recent research (Graham & Heimerer, 1981;

Rink, 1985; Rosenshine, 1983) identified five aspects of direct instruction that are particularly important when a teacher's goal is teaching a specific skill:

1. Initially the teacher gives the student a clear idea of what is to be learned. The teacher or a student *correctly* demonstrates the skill, along with the important cues. For example, if the teacher is focusing on landing from a jump, she or he emphasizes in the demonstration that to attain a soft, quiet landing, the ankles and knees must be flexed prior to landing.

2. Next, the teacher gives specific feedback. In our example, the children now practice flexing their knees and ankles prior to landing; the teacher specifically tells them how well they're flexing their knees and ankles. The teacher tells the children *exactly* what they are (or are not) doing correctly so that they can improve. Once the children have the "big" idea—soft, quiet landings—the teacher helps them land softly and quietly by structuring appropriate tasks and giving them information about how well they're performing the task. The teacher proceeds in small steps, but at a brisk pace.

3. In the third aspect, the teacher gives explanations and instructions clearly and repeats the cues often. At the end of a lesson, we often ask the children to repeat the cues so that we know if we've been effective. The question "What are the important things to remember when you're trying to land softly and quietly from a jump?" will tell you whether or not the children have really remembered your teaching cues related to soft, quiet landings.

4. One of the most important and obvious factors in the direct approach is often overlooked. Children need *considerable* opportunities for practice if they're going to actually *learn* to land softly and quietly. For this reason we always try to structure the learning situation so that the children have plenty of practice. Most of the time we're able to arrange the environment so that children rarely, if ever, have to wait. We try to have all the children active a minimum of 60 percent of the lesson, more when possible (Chapter 11).

5. High success rates are also important for learning, especially the basic skills. We try to provide tasks that allow children to be successful about 80 percent of the time. This motivates the children and also allows them to grasp one skill before moving onto the next level. If children can't land softly and quietly when they jump from the floor, for example, then obviously they won't be able to land effectively when they jump from a bench or a wooden box. (Teaching by invitation and intratask variation are helpful techniques for adjusting tasks to match the differing skill levels of children in the same class, as explained in Chapter 4.)

As Mosston (1981) pointed out in his description of the command style of teaching, this type of instruction has a right response the teacher is looking for, one she or he helps the children to accomplish. Just any response is not acceptable. For example, if a teacher's goal for a lesson is to teach the children to use opposition when they throw overhand, she'll need to give the children plenty of practice opportunities and feedback to be certain that they step with the opposite foot before moving on to another aspect of the overhand throw. If the teacher doesn't require the children to practice stepping with the opposite foot until the movement is overlearned, the children will quickly forget the concept of opposition once the task changes. The teacher will find herself continually reminding children to "Step with the opposite foot when you throw." The proof of this statement can be found in any high school softball class: Watch the students play a game and see how many are inefficient throwers who've never learned the concept of opposition when they throw. They were taught the concept, but never to the point of learning it.

Inquiry Approach

In the elementary school, we use the direct approach for teaching specific skills to children who are developmentally ready to learn mature versions of the skill. We don't use the direct approach exclusively, however. We've found the *inquiry approach* valuable in certain circumstances.

The inquiry approach encourages children to think and solve problems rather than to simply copy a teacher's or student's correct performance of a skill. In this approach, the teacher typically asks questions. We've found this approach especially helpful for encouraging children to think on their own, to discover new and different approaches to performing skills, and to solve questions related especially to teamwork and strategy. Inquiry is also an important approach for those children who aren't developmentally ready to learn a mature version of a skill but who simply need opportunities to explore movement. Typically these children are preschoolers through grade two, although there are always exceptions. We actually use two versions of inquiry, depending upon the purpose of our lesson: convergent or divergent inquiry.

Convergent Inquiry. Convergent inquiry encourages children to discover the same answer(s) to a series of questions the teacher asks. The teacher guides the children toward one or more correct answers. Mosston (1981) suggested that children can discover ideas, similarities, dissimilarities, principles (governing rules), order or system, a particular physical activity or movement, how, why, limits (the dimension of "how much," "how fast," etc.), and other elements. When we want the children to learn one of these elements, we often use the discovery approach to better involve the children in their learning.

It's important that the teacher formulate in advance the questions to be asked so he or she has some idea of the sequence of questions that will lead the children to the solution. The teacher must ask questions in relevant small steps, rather than spanning too wide a gap. Equally important, the teacher needs to wait for the answer rather than becoming impatient and telling the answer.

The following sequence illustrating Mosston's classic slanty rope technique is a very good example of convergent inquiry encouraging children to find ways of avoiding eliminating others from activity. This excerpt is from page 166 of his work.

Step 1: Ask two children to hold a rope for high jumping. Invariably they will hold the rope horizontally at a given height (for example, at hip level).

Step 2: Ask the group to jump over. Before they do so, you might want to ask the rope holders to decrease the height so that everybody can be successful.

Step 3: After everyone has cleared the height, you ask, "What shall we do now?" "Raise it!" "Raise it!" is the answer—always! (The success of the first jump motivates all to continue.)

Step 4: Ask the rope holders to raise the rope just a bit. The jumping is resumed.

Step 5: "Now what?" "Raise it!" the children will respond.

Step 6: Raising the rope two or three more times will create a new situation, a new reality. Some children will *not* be able to clear the height. In traditional situations these children will be *eliminated* from the jumping, and only some will continue; there will be a constantly diminishing number of active participants. The realization of individual differences becomes real; the *design* for opportunity for all has not yet come about.

Step 7: Stop the jumping and ask the group, "What can we do with the rope so that nobody will be eliminated?" Usually one or two of the following solutions are proposed by the children: *(a)* Hold the rope higher at the two ends and let the rope dip in the center. *(b)* Slant the rope! Hold the rope high at one end and low at the other.

Divergent Inquiry. In divergent inquiry, the teacher outlines a problem and then challenges the children to find many answers. This technique encourages children to find movement alternatives. A typical divergent question is, "Find at least three different ways to travel under the hoop (supported on cones) and at least three different ways to travel over the hoop."

In the divergent inquiry approach, the teacher must be careful to not impose personal values on the children's responses. The emphasis is on obtaining a *variety* of responses, not a single answer. For this reason, Mosston (1981) warned of two verbal behavior patterns that we try to avoid when using divergent inquiry. "You can do better than that" in response to a child's movement indicates that the teacher doesn't really value the response or that the teacher has a particular response in mind. Another counterproductive verbal behavior is a statement such as "Stop. Everyone watch Penny." After Penny finishes her movement, the teacher says, "Terrific Penny." This behavior by the teacher, while perhaps innocent in nature, suggests to students that there's a right answer and therefore encourages the children to attempt to find a correct answer (convergent) rather than searching for a variety of alternatives, the goal of divergent inquiry.

Child-Designed Approach

The *child-designed approach* urges children to design their own activities. This approach encourages creativity in the children and also lets them invent and develop activities that match their skill level, or the skill level of the group in which they're working. We ask the children to design their own games, dances, and gymnastics routines.

Moderation is the key to success. If you simply say to children, "Make up your own game. It has to include throwing and catching," the result may be a disaster. We know from experience. Try to give children more specific suggestions for designing activities:

"Design beginning and ending movements for the balance, roll, balance sequence you've been practicing."

"You've been practicing five movements: leaping, spinning, sinking, exploding, and freezing. Use them in a repeatable sequence that flows together smoothly."

In time, the situation can be structured so that the children contribute more and more. By initially restricting the children's input, you limit the amount of time the children spend making decisions. These decisions are important to children, and so some children take a substantial amount of time to design an activity. You want the children to contribute to their own learning, but you also want them to be active in physical education class. At times this can be a dilemma!

An environment in which children are designing their own activities is a complex one in which to teach. Should you assist or stay away, encourage or simply observe, offer an idea for restructuring an activity or let the children work it out? And these decisions are even more complicated when a variety of projects is going on simultaneously. Child-designed activities are challenging for the children and for the teacher.

SELECTING AN APPROACH

A question frequently asked is, "Which approach should I use?" The answer, obviously, is a question: "What is your goal?"

If the children are developmentally ready, and you want them to learn a specific skill that has correct and incorrect ways of being performed, the direct approach will best serve the purpose. If you want to enhance cognitive understanding while provoking curiosity, the inquiry approach is best. When you have the time and want to emphasize the children's involvement in decision making while also fostering their creativity, use the child-designed approach.

Another frequently asked question relates to

which approach to use in a lesson. The answer is that, in fact, there are some lessons in which we use all three approaches. For example, upon entering the gym, the teacher says, "Select a rope and find at least six different ways to jump" (divergent inquiry approach). After three minutes, the children put away their ropes, and the teacher explains and demonstrates the overhand throw and focuses specifically on opposition (stepping with the foot opposite the throwing hand) and extension (extending the elbow as the ball is released). Thus teacher explanation, demonstration, and specific practice tasks comprise this part of the lesson (direct approach). In the final part of the lesson, the teacher tells the children to make up their own throwing game. The groups may be no larger than three, and the game has to include everyone using the overhand throw (child-designed approach).

As we indicated at the beginning of the chapter, no approach is better than another. Some approaches are better for accomplishing different purposes than others. The reflective teacher uses all three approaches to best meet the needs of the children and personal teaching goals.

LESSON FORMATS

The lesson format is the way the class is organized for learning a lesson. The four lesson formats we most frequently use are:

1. Whole class
2. Learning centers or stations
3. Task sheets
4. Contracts

As with the three approaches, our decision as to the best format depends upon many factors, but our most important consideration is always our goal for the lesson.

Whole Class Lesson Format

The lesson format we use most often is working with the entire class on the same task at the same time. All the children practice the same skill or concept, work on discovering a solution, or invent a gymnastics sequence. This format works best when a teacher is new to teaching and hasn't worked with the children for long. Once the teacher has established a learning environment, teaching by invitation and intratask variation are helpful for changing the tasks to better match the children's interests and abilities (Chapter 4). The whole class format requires less time for organization than the other three formats, an important consideration for teachers who meet with their children only once or twice a week.

Learning Center or Station Format

One alternative to teaching the class as a whole is to organize the children so that they can work in groups. The children won't all be involved in the same activity simultaneously, and so they (and the teacher) should be ready to have more than one activity happening at the same time. Planning, observation, and sometimes management may be more difficult for the instructor, but the teacher will be able to better match the lesson to the students' varying abilities.

When learning centers (stations) are used, the teacher sets up several activity areas in the teaching space. The class is then divided into groups, one for each learning center. It's wise to start with just a few learning centers—perhaps three. The number of centers can be increased gradually as the children learn to work responsibly at their centers. Stopping when asked, rotating systematically, and not interfering with others are skills that need to be practiced before learning centers can be used effectively.

One advantage of learning centers is that practice situations can be set up that, if the entire class were involved, would involve waiting in lines for turns (see Figure 6-1). When the children are able to function in the environment of learning centers, they can be allowed to choose the learning centers at which they'd like to work. Eventually they can rotate from one learning center to another

*Teaching a class as a whole is an effective method of
organizing instruction.*

*Directions written on poster boards increase time
spent in activity.*

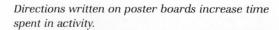

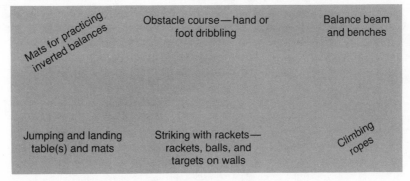

Figure 6-1 Arrangement of learning centers in the teaching space.

at their own discretion. You may want to write task descriptions on poster boards and place one at each learning center. This technique decreases substantially the time spent instructing the class as a whole.

The three instructional approaches can be used with learning centers or stations. For example, as the following list explains, it's possible to use all three approaches in the learning center shown in Figure 6-1:

- *Inverted balance*—Practice the handstand and headstand as taught in class and diagrammed on the poster (direct approach).
- *Jumping and landing*—Find four different ways to jump from the table to the mat. Be sure to land on your feet each time (divergent inquiry approach).
- *Striking with rackets at targets*—With your partner, make up a game. You both must use the racket to strike the ball to the target at the wall. You'll need to decide (1) the distance you want to be from the wall, (2) the boundaries (being considerate of other's space), (3) if you want to keep score or not and how you want to score if you decide to keep score (child-designed approach).

Task Sheets

Another format for individualizing instruction is to give each child a series of challenges that she

can practice at her own pace (Mueller, 1976). Each child is given task sheets (see Figure 6-2). Each task sheet contains a progression of activities and includes spaces for child-designed activities. When a task has been successfully accomplished, the student records it on the task sheet, with that day's date, and asks the teacher, a parent, or an older child or partner to observe the accomplishment and sign the task sheet.

Initially an entire class works on the same task sheet. As the children learn to use the task sheets, we let them pick from sheets on several different skill themes. Writing and refining group task sheets is time consuming, but the sheets can be valuable when you begin to individualize instruction.

Depending upon how the task sheet is phrased, the sheet can use either a direct or inquiry approach. In the example in Figure 6-2, the stem "I am able to . . ." suggests a more direct approach. On the other hand, the stem "Find . . . different ways to . . ." encourages discovery by the children, suggesting the divergent inquiry approach.

Contracts

As children become accustomed to working on their own, the teacher can use independent contracting to make instruction more personal (Gotts, 1976; Locke & Lambdin, 1976). A teacher who uses independent contracting is saying to the students,

Name _____ Teacher _____

BALANCE TASK SHEET

Date Accomplished	Verification	Challenge
		I am able to walk forward the entire length without falling off.
		I am able to walk leading with my right side the entire length without falling off.
		I am able to walk leading with my left side the entire length without falling off.
		I am able to walk backward the entire length without falling off.
		I am able to walk forward (with my hands folded on my head) the entire length without falling off.
		I am able to walk forward the entire length with an eraser balanced on my head.
		I am able to walk backward the entire length with an eraser balanced on my head.
		I am able to walk along the beam, pick up a beanbag, and walk to the other end without falling off.
		I am able to walk along the beam, balance on one knee, and walk to the other end without falling off.
		I am able to walk the entire length of the balance beam without falling off, keeping my eyes closed all the way.
		I am able to bounce a ball across the beam without a miss.
		I am able to roll a ball along a beam without either the ball or myself touching the ground.
		I am able to walk along the beam, do a complete turn on one foot only, and walk to the end without falling off.
		I am able to walk along the beam twirling a hoop on one arm, without falling off.
		I am able to walk along the beam balancing a wand in one hand without falling off.
		I am able to hop along the beam on one foot without falling off.
		I am able to throw a ball back and forth to a partner ___ times without a miss, while standing on the end of a beam.
		I am able to jump rope on a balance beam ___ times without a miss.
		I am able to do a forward roll on the beam.
		I am able to jump onto the beam from a spring board without losing my balance.
		I am able to . . . .
		I am able to . . . .
		I am able to . . . .

Figure 6-2 Task sheet.

"I trust you to make intelligent and responsible decisions about what you need to practice."

We've used the written contract illustrated in Figure 6-3. Each child writes down the skill or activity she or he will be practicing or playing, the goal to be achieved, the time to be spent practicing each activity, and (when appropriate) the name of a practice partner. Recognizing the dynamic nature of a physical education class, we let the children change their contracts during class, as long as they write down all changes. We encourage the children to save time by coming to physical education

Name_____

Contract for_____, 198_____
            (date)

Time	Activity	Goal	Partner

COMMENTS:

1) Did you accomplish your goal?

2) What do you need to work on during the next class?

3) Do you want to tell me about the class?

Figure 6-3 Individual contract.

class with their contracts already completed for that day. In the final few minutes of a class, we ask the children to evaluate their accomplishments for that day.

When you first use independent contracting, it's wise to restrict each child to a single skill theme.

We attempt to work with children as individuals.

As the children become accustomed to the system, you can gradually increase the number of choices.

SELECTING A LESSON FORMAT

How do you determine which lesson format is best with a given class? An assessment of the eagerness and achievement level of a class can provide guidance. The model we use theorizes that classes can be neatly subdivided into high and low eagerness and achievement levels (Figure 6-4).

We assume that children who are eager to participate in physical education require less teacher direction, as do children who have high ability levels. Children who don't enjoy physical education and don't have well-developed skills seem to require more direct teacher attention. When this is true, the model in Figure 6-4 is a useful, generalized guide for determining the best organizational pattern for a class.

Children who are high achievers and highly eager are assumed to function well in a personalized instructional setting. Highly eager, low-achieving students seem to do well in an individualized instructional setting if the teacher is efficient at skills such as prompting, cueing, and reinforcing to keep the children focused on the task at hand. Students who are low in eagerness and high in achievement often seem to function well in groups, particularly if the teacher is enthusiastic and an efficient motivator. Low achievers who are also low in eagerness often require teachers who are direct with them initially, until the children discover success and the personal satisfaction that can be derived from involvement in physical activity.

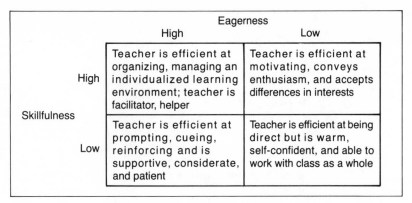

		Eagerness	
		High	Low
Skillfulness	High	Teacher is efficient at organizing, managing an individualized learning environment; teacher is facilitator, helper	Teacher is efficient at motivating, conveys enthusiasm, and accepts differences in interests
	Low	Teacher is efficient at prompting, cueing, reinforcing and is supportive, considerate, and patient	Teacher is efficient at being direct but is warm, self-confident, and able to work with class as a whole

Figure 6-4 Model for determining class organization pattern based on the children's skillfulness and eagerness.

In respect to my own growth, whether in tennis or any other aspect of development, I have found it helpful to look at myself as the seed of a tree, with my entire potential already within me, as opposed to a building, which must have stories added to it to achieve a greater height. This makes it easier for me to see that it doesn't help me to try to be what I'm not at any given moment, or to form concepts of what I should be, or to compare myself to other trees around me. I can understand that I need only use all the rain and sunshine that come my way, and cooperate fully with the seed's impulse to develop and manifest what it already uniquely is.

Timothy Gallwey,
The Inner Game of Tennis

Obviously this model is an oversimplification and should not be used as a concrete, universally applicable guideline. It does, however, provide a perspective that can help you to decide which organizational pattern to use with a particular class at various times during their physical education experience.

COMBINING THE APPROACH AND FORMAT

A teacher who understands the three instructional approaches and the four lesson formats can begin to use them in lessons when the children are ready. We've found that not all approaches can be used equally well with all the lesson formats; certain approaches work better with certain lesson formats than others. Figure 6-5 illustrates the approaches we've found most effective with each format.

Both the direct and the inquiry approaches work best when the class is taught as a whole, with learning centers, and with task sheets. We use contracts only with the direct approach because the children are expected to be practicing specific skills rather than creating routines or discovering alternative ways of moving. We've used task sheets with both the direct and inquiry approaches but not with the child-designed approach, although there may be times when that approach would be appropriate and effective.

LESSON FORMAT

	Whole Class	Learning Center/Station	Task Sheet	Contract
Direct	X	X	X	X
Inquiry	X	X	X	
Child-Designed	X	X		

INSTRUCTIONAL APPROACH

Figure 6-5 Matching instructional approaches with lesson formats.

It takes experience, including defeat, failure, and frustration to develop skills as a teacher. It takes years to become established in a new community and then more time to develop an organization strong enough to fight oppressive schools effectively. With the best will in the world, it also takes years to learn to build the right tone in a class and equip the room sensibly, to develop an eye for children in trouble, to know how to support students and how to make demands on them without oppressing them, to know when to add something new or step back and leave the children alone. Teaching is no simple matter. It is hard work, part craft, part art, part technique, part politics, and it takes time to develop ease within such a complex role. However, for many of us the effort makes sense, for one gets the opportunity to see young people grow while one has a positive and caring role in their lives.

Herbert Kohl,
On Teaching

SUMMARY

One of the myriad questions that a teacher must answer is, "What is the best way to organize the class for learning?" The answer depends upon a number of factors, the primary one being the teacher's goal for a particular lesson or series of lessons. Classes can then be organized based on three different instructional approaches and four lesson formats.

The three instructional approaches are direct, inquiry, and child-designed. Use the direct approach when the students are to learn a specific skill technique. Use the inquiry approach to stimulate thinking and enhance students' involvement on a cognitive level. In convergent inquiry, the students discover the answer to a problem based on a series of questions the teacher asks. Divergent inquiry encourages the children to find many answers, rather than one, to the teacher's question or statement. The child-designed approach encourages creativity and inventiveness; the children are involved in actually creating their own games, dances, and sequences.

The four lesson formats are whole class, learning center or station, task sheets, and contracts. Each of the three instructional approaches can be used with both whole class and learning center or station formats. Task sheets are used primarily with a direct approach, although they can also be used with an inquiry approach. Contracts are typically used only with a direct approach; i.e., the students are expected to practice a specific skill or movement.

Which approach and format the teacher selects depends upon that teacher's goals. Ideally, over a period of weeks, both the teacher and the children learn to work effectively when any of the formats or approaches are used in a class. But because this doesn't happen easily or quickly, an assessment of the achievement and eagerness levels of the children in a class can be useful when a teacher is making decisions about the organizational pattern that will work best.

READING COMPREHENSION QUESTIONS

1. Explain the differences among the three instructional approaches described in this chapter. Include a reason for using each approach.
2. What criteria might a teacher use for selecting an approach to use in a lesson?
3. Give two examples of convergent inquiry and two examples of divergent inquiry, written in the actual form that they would be stated.
4. This chapter provides an example that indicates how all three approaches might be used in a single lesson. Use different content (skill themes) and write three parallel but different examples. Use the example in the book as a model.
5. Explain the four different lesson formats described in this chapter.
6. Select a skill from one of the skill theme chapters (15 to 25) and develop a task sheet similar to the one in this chapter. Include at least six different tasks, ranging from precontrol through utilization levels.
7. Why do the authors suggest that a direct approach may not be best for preschoolers up through grade two? In your answer, explain the term *developmentally ready*.

REFERENCES

Gallwey, T. (1974). *The inner game of tennis.* New York: Random House.

Goldberger, M. (1984, October). Effective learning through a spectrum of teaching styles. *Journal of Physical Education, Recreation, and Dance,* 17–21.

Gotts, S. L. (1976). Student-teacher contracts. In D. Hellison (Ed.), *Personalized learning in physical education.* Washington, D.C.: American Alliance for Health, Physical Education, Recreation, and Dance.

Graham, G., & Heimerer, E. (1981). Research on teacher effectiveness. *Quest, 33*(1), 14–25.

Kohl, H. (1976). *On teaching*. New York: Schocken.

Lambdin, D. (1976). Quiet individualizing: What one teacher did. In D. Hellison (Ed.), *Personalized learning in physical education*. Washington, D.C.: American Alliance for Health, Physical Education, Recreation, and Dance.

Locke, L. F., & Lambdin, D. (1976). Teacher behavior. In D. Hellison (Ed.), *Personalized learning in physical education*. Washington, D.C.: American Alliance for Health, Physical Education, Recreation, and Dance.

Mosston, M. (1981). *Teaching physical education* (2nd ed.). Columbus, OH: Merrill.

Mueller, R. (1976). Task cards. In D. Hellison (Ed.), *Personalized learning in physical education*. Washington, D.C.: American Alliance for Health, Physical Education, Recreation, and Dance.

Rink, J. (1985). *Teaching physical education for learning*. St. Louis: Mosby.

Rosenshine, B. (1983). Teaching functions in instructional programs. *Elementary School Journal, 83*, 335–351.

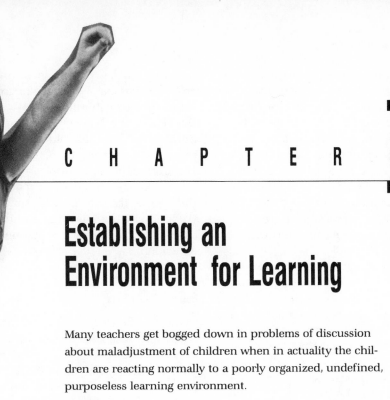

C H A P T E R **7**

Establishing an Environment for Learning

Many teachers get bogged down in problems of discussion about maladjustment of children when in actuality the children are reacting normally to a poorly organized, undefined, purposeless learning environment.

James DiViglio

To teach effectively, it's necessary to build an environment in which learning is allowed to occur because such an atmosphere is a necessary, although not sufficient, condition for learning. Establishing a learning environment involves using those procedures necessary to place students in contact with, and to keep them in contact with, the subject matter for as long as necessary.

One of the most important factors in establishing a learning environment is also one of the least tangible: teacher attitude. The teacher's self-image and feelings about teaching, about physical education, and about children all influence attitude. The teacher who is enthusiastic conveys this attitude to the children, and as a result their enthusiasm for physical education is heightened. The teacher who views physical education as a

time for learning and work communicates this feeling to the children by the way he or she demands that all the children adhere to certain criteria for behavior.

The clearest evidence of the influence of teacher attitude on the atmosphere of a learning environment can be obtained by observing one class of children with several different teachers. The same children may be businesslike and involved with one teacher and apathetic or frivolous with another teacher only thirty minutes later. Clearly teacher attitude has a significant influence on the learning environment.

History, science, even music and art classes are all thought of as a time for learning. But it's not uncommon for children, parents, and even some teachers to think of physical education as free time, a break from the work of the academic subjects taught in classrooms. In fact, many teachers refer to physical education class as recess.

Children definitely need a break from routine. Recess is free time and provides that needed break. Physical education, however, is an educational experience designed to enhance motor skill learning and to foster the development of positive attitudes toward physical activity. The difference between physical education and recess must be clear to children, parents, and teachers if students are to benefit appropriately from the time devoted to physical education.

A physical education teacher's first goal is to establish an environment in which learning will occur. From the first day, the pupils must understand that physical education is not a break, but a time for learning motor skills and fitness concepts. Once children understand this, the teacher's task is much easier. Remember, though, that a learning environment isn't established in a single lesson; with some classes, the process may take several weeks.

Some educators use the terms "developing a learning environment" and "discipline" as if they were synonymous, but we don't. Discipline is required when a child's behavior is disruptive and the teacher needs to prevent the disruption from occurring again (see Chapter 8). When a learning environment is being established, the focus is on fostering acceptable behavior and creating an atmosphere appropriate for a physical education class. Some discipline may be required in a physical education class, as in any class. An established, consistent, positive environment in the gymnasium, where the students know exactly what is expected of them, will reduce the need for discipline and stimulate enthusiasm for learning.

FOSTERING APPROPRIATE ATTITUDES

When they begin school, most children have few preconceptions about how a physical education learning environment will be structured. In a short time they learn to behave according to their teachers' expectations. If youngsters are allowed to develop unacceptable behavior in physical education class, the teacher will find it increasingly difficult to alter the children's behaviors. For this reason it's crucial that teachers establish an appropriate learning environment during their very first lessons with the students. How well they do this will set the tone for the remainder of the year. We've found the following techniques helpful in establishing a learning environment in physical education.

Getting Off to a Good Start

Typically, the first day a class meets, the teacher goes over those logistical and organizational rules and procedures she or he feels are essential for effective class functioning. Many times we've seen this done only in the first lesson via a lecture; the rules and procedures are never taught and never reviewed again, unless something goes wrong. In recent years, it has become increasingly obvious how really important the first few days of school are (Brooks, 1984): The environment for the entire year is established. The students learn what is appropriate behavior in the gymnasium, and they learn what will be expected of them in physical education. It is then that they learn the class rules, both stated and nonstated. When a situation arises and is consistently treated the same way, the students know the teacher means what has been said. Now is when behavior is established that will typify a class for the remainder of the year. We've found the following suggestions helpful for getting off to a good start. Figure 7-1 provides a checklist of items to ensure that you're ready for the beginning of the school year.

1. Before you ever meet your students, decide what is appropriate behavior for your physical education class.
2. Set out that appropriate behavior in clear, simple rules.
3. Anticipate problems in the content or gym-

CHECKLIST FOR THE BEGINNING OF SCHOOL

Item	Check When Done	Notes
1. Are your teaching areas and equipment ready?		
2. Have you decided your class rules, procedures, and consequences?		
3. Are you familiar with the parts of the school that you may use (halls, cafeteria, playgrounds, multipurpose room) and any procedures associated with their use?		
4. Do you have complete class rosters for each class you teach?		
5. Do you have file information on your students, including any comments from previous teachers and information on health problems?		
6. Do you know if any of your students have handicapping conditions?		
7. Do you have an adequate amount of equipment for all students?		
8. Have you established the procedure for the arrival and departure of the students from the physical education area?		
9. Are the children's name tags ready? Do you have some blank ones for unexpected students?		
10. Do you have your first day's plan of activities ready?		
11. Do you have rainy day activities planned?		
12. Do you have a letter ready to send home to the parents with information about the school year and what materials or clothing the child will need to bring to school?		
13. Do you know how to obtain assistance from school staff members (e.g., school nurse, office personnel, resource teachers, and the custodians)?		

Figure 7-1 Checklist for the beginning of school. *Source: Adapted from Classroom Management for Elementary Teachers* by C. Evertson, E. Emmer, B. Clements, J. Sanford, & M. Worsham, 1984, Englewood Cliffs, NJ: Prentice-Hall.

nasium routine and develop ways to prevent or reduce those problems.

4. Plan very specific activities for the first few sessions of the school year. Teach the rules of behavior as well as classroom procedures (e.g., what to do when arriving in class; how to take out, set up, and take down equipment; what to do in a fire drill). You can most easily do this by planning what these procedures will be, designing situations that will allow students to practice the procedures, and teaching those procedures via direct instruction (see Chapter 6).

   After you initially teach these routines, practice them for several sessions so that you're sure the students understand and know them. If you ask those teachers whose gymnasiums are known for much on-task behavior and a productive learning environment what they taught the first few weeks of school, they'll almost always answer with some variation of "How to behave in physical education." Time spent teaching behavior in the beginning of the year allows much more time to be spent learning and much less time repeating what should have already been habit during the remainder of the year.

5. Instruct the group as a whole for the first few weeks of school. Whole class instruction (see Chapter 6) is best because it gives the teacher an opportunity to see who follows directions and allows the teacher a chance to reinforce appropriate behavior. Don't begin individual or small group work until you're certain students understand what is expected of them.

6. In the early days, routinely check individually with students to determine how they're settling in and to gain other information that may be relevant to the physical education and school setting.

Establishing Rules of Behavior

If children understand the behavioral boundaries within which they're expected to function, they're less likely to test your flexibility and more likely to cooperate. A few rules, stated clearly and adhered to consistently by the teacher, can be helpful to everyone:

1. When the teacher gives a signal (with words, a drumbeat, or a whistle), the children are expected to stop and listen.
2. Children are expected to work without interfering with other children or preventing others from working.
3. Children are expected to treat equipment carefully, as if it were their own.
4. Children are expected to stay within assigned boundaries.

These rules are necessary to group survival. Figure 7-2 is an example of gymnasium rules that we've found successful for eliciting the sought-after learning environment. You may wish to establish different rules; if so, the following general guidelines are helpful for establishing the rules of behavior:

1. State rules positively. Whenever possible, avoid using the words "don't," "not," and "no."
2. Keep the number of rules to the minimum necessary. A good guide is to state no more than seven rules.
3. Post rules so they can be easily seen and read.
4. Explain why the rules are necessary. Children are far more cooperative with rules that make sense to them than with seemingly arbitrary regulations.
5. Make sure the children understand the rules. You can most easily accomplish this by actually teaching and practicing the rules. To teach rules most efficiently, first describe and demonstrate the desired behavior, have the children actually rehearse the correct behavior (this usually takes more than one rehearsal), and then finally provide feedback, especially the first time children are actually asked to use a routine.
6. Design, teach, post, and practice the consequences established for breaking the rules.

P.E. CLASS RULES

1. TEACHER SPEAKS, STOP, EQUIPMENT DOWN, LISTEN.
2. THE EQUIPMENT IS FOR YOU, TREAT IT THAT WAY.
3. ALL ACTIVITY STARTS AND STOPS ON THE TEACHER'S SIGNAL.

4. BE POLITE, COURTEOUS AND HELPFUL TO OTHERS.
5. ALWAYS MOVE UNDER CONTROL AND WATCH FOR OTHER STUDENTS.

Figure 7-2 Example of gymnasium rules.

7. Especially in the beginning, prompt students toward appropriate behavior and reinforce appropriate behavior. Let students know when they've done something correctly.

One of the obvious questions, although students don't always ask it, is "What happens when one of the rules is broken?" No matter how well we teach, some of the children will break some of the rules, so we find it helps at the outset of the

year to describe the consequences for breaking a rule. These consequences are for relatively minor offenses; major offenses are discussed in Chapter 8, "Discipline: Maintaining Appropriate Behavior."

The teacher needs to develop consequences appropriate to the particular teaching situation. Many teachers use a series of consequences similar to the following:

1. The first time a child violates a rule—e.g., the

AVOIDING BEHAVIOR PROBLEMS WHEN CHOOSING PARTNERS OR GROUPS

Many activities for children involve working with a partner. In some classes, the act of finding a partner creates many behavior problems. Children argue over who is going to be whose partner, other children will be left out, the time used in deciding partners takes longer than the task itself, and then children want to change partners. The same problems occur, even more so, when dividing children into groups and/or teams. For avoiding such problems as much as possible, we've found the following techniques helpful:

Getting Partners

1. Put a time limit on how long children can take to choose partners, e.g., "by the time I count to 5."
2. Put restrictions on who may be partners, e.g., "someone you've never worked with before," "the person sitting next to you," "the person who sits next to you in class," or "someone you know you can work with in a productive manner."
3. Decide ahead of class who'll be partners.
4. Hand out color codes (pieces of paper, stickers, or marking pen marks on the hand) at the beginning of class; the children who match up are partners.

Dividing into Groups and/or Teams

1. Have children choose partners; then put one partner on one team and one on another. This works well for making teams equal.

2. Assign each student a color or number (the number of colors or numbers equals the number of groups you desire) at the beginning of the year or month. When groups are to be formed, the teacher simply says, "Reds here," "Blues here," "Purples here," and "Greens here." (This is also an efficient way to take roll in your class.)
3. Divide teams by certain generic characteristics, e.g., eye color, month of birth, number of siblings, or first letter of names.
4. Divide groups ahead of time.

Whatever you do, don't take more than sixty seconds, and most importantly, don't alienate anyone. Under no circumstances should selecting partners or dividing children into groups be a popularity contest.

child fails to stop and listen—give the child a *verbal* warning.

2. The second time a child violates a rule in that class, have the child "sit out" (also called time-out) until the child comes to you and tells you why he or she was told to sit out.

3. If the child violates a rule a third time, have the child sit out the remainder of the class.

Although sitting out the remainder of the class may seem a bit harsh, as teachers we need to be able to teach. A child who is continually disruptive receives a substantial amount of our attention—attention that other children in the class deserve just as much.

As much as possible, the consequences should be noninterruptive. We try to deliver a consequence with a word or two and avoid interfering with the learning experiences of the rest of the class. One final comment about time-out: It is effective when the children find the lesson interesting. If the lesson is uninteresting, dull, or inappropriate for a child, then time-out becomes a reward rather than a consequence for off-task behavior.

Setting Performance Standards

Set high but reasonable expectations for students and communicate them to the children. These expectations apply to both managerial and instructional aspects of the class. We've found that an easy way to do this is to teach with a *critical demandingness* (Brophy & Evertson, 1976), which means that we set standards and consistently adhere to them so that the children know exactly what is expected. For example, we've established performance standards for many of the daily management tasks, such as putting away equipment or lining up to go back to the classroom.

Performance standards are really a way for teachers to communicate exactly what they expect. When these expectations are clear, the children understand what the teachers desire. For example, children know that they're to put away the ball if the teacher has clearly stated this expectation. When the expectation isn't clear, however, several children may throw their ball from halfway across the gym, hoping that somehow the ball will land in the appropriate container or location. But the expectation is that children will *place*, not throw, the ball into the appropriate box (or hoop). Unfortunately, with some classes it takes several practice episodes until the children learn that the teacher means business. The children need to learn that the expectation that they put the ball away rather than throwing it isn't something the teacher hopes for—it's something the teacher *insists* upon, to

avoid the chaos and disruption that can occur when standards for performance aren't set and adhered to.

STOPPING AND LISTENING

One of the seemingly hardest things to teach children in physical education is to stop activity quickly and listen to the teacher. When a teacher must spend time quieting the children so that the entire class can hear an explanation or comment, the amount of time left for activities is decreased. Physical activity, by its nature, is noisier than classroom activity, and children tend to be even louder on a playground than in a gymnasium. Thus it's imperative that children learn to respond quickly and appropriately to the teacher's signal for quiet. Listening games can be used to teach children to listen as they move and to respond quickly to the teacher's signals.

You might initially assign a criterion of five seconds as a reasonable amount of time for the children to stop and be listening after they hear the stop signal. If the entire class is stopped and listening in five seconds or less, we praise them. If they aren't stopped and listening, explain that taking more than five seconds is too slow and they'd better practice again because it's a waste of time to take that long. Gradually, raise the standards as the children become more proficient. The children often view these races against the clock as fun games and delight in praise from the teacher when they perform well. They also enjoy trying to beat their own records. This approach provides far more time for activity and instruction. As the children learn the value of spending less time on management tasks, you can eliminate these races against the clock.

Teachers must be clear, concise, and to the point. As a general rule, once a class has begun, we try to keep our verbal explanations to less than sixty seconds. Although this isn't always possible (or even appropriate), it does help to increase the children's willingness to stop and listen to us.

LISTENING GAMES

In a successful learning environment, noise rarely exceeds a reasonable level that can be thought of as "busy noise." Hollering, shrieking, and yelling are appropriate at recess. In physical education class, the children shouldn't be expected to be silent, but they should be able to hear a teacher speaking in a reasonable tone, considerably below a shout. You can use the games described below to establish an appropriate noise level; the objective of these games is to teach the children to listen for the teacher as they move.

Purpose of Listening Games

These listening games are designed to help the children learn to stop as quickly as possible when responding appropriately to the teacher's verbal challenge. Try not to single out children who are slow, and don't use penalties as a form of discipline. Embarrassment and punishment are both counterproductive; you want children to enjoy exercise, not to think of it as unpleasant.

Stop and Go

Children travel in general space in a scattered formation. Once the children are able to (1) walk without touching others and (2) stay far away from others as they walk, you can begin to play Stop and Go. When you say "stop," the children should stop and freeze instantly. When you say "go," they should begin to travel again. Don't shout the signals—*speak* them, so that the children become accustomed to listening for your voice at a reasonable level.

Body Parts

This game focuses on the different body parts. Once the children have adjusted to Stop and Go, they enjoy the challenge of touching the floor with different body parts—elbow, seat, knee, wrist, waist, left hand, or right foot—as quickly as they can when you say "stop."

Traveling

When children have learned to travel using different locomotor patterns, variations in these patterns are appropriate. Call out different ways of traveling—skipping, hopping, crab-walking, galloping—and challenge the children to change from one to another as rapidly as possible. The challenge of this game is increased when you combine traveling and the concept of direction—for example, gallop backward or hop to the right.

Circles

This game can be played on a painted playground surface or in a gymnasium. Before class, draw circles, triangles, squares, and so on on the ground. The object is for the children to move as quickly as possible to the shape you name; for example, if you call out "circle," the children stand on a circle as quickly as possible. You can use colors instead of or in combination with shapes if the surface you're using is painted various colors. The terms you use will be determined by your pupils' knowledge of colors and shapes.

Numbers

In one version of this game, the children stop with the appropriate number of body parts touching the ground. For example, if you call out "three," the children should stop with three body parts touching the ground.

In a second version, the children stop in groups. The number the teacher calls determines the size of the group. This game is helpful when you want the children to form into groups of three, four, or five in a hurry.

Combinations

As children learn each variation, they find it challenging and fun to play several games at once. For example, you might call out a body part or a color or a locomotor pattern or a number. Children thrive on increasingly difficult games.

Switch and Rotate

This game is primarily to teach listening, but it's more appropriate for older children. The object of the game is to stay so close to a partner that, when the teacher says "stop" and the players freeze, the follower can still touch the leader. When the teacher says "switch," the partners change roles and the follower becomes the leader.

You can make this game more difficult by increasing the size of the group, from two to three, then four, then five. The object of the game remains the same: Each child should be able to touch the person in front as soon as you say "stop." When you add the challenge "rotate," the leader goes to the end of the line and becomes a follower. Children find the challenge of listening and responding instantly while trying to remain close to the children in front of them fascinating. You can make this game more challenging by varying the locomotor patterns, e.g., from walking to skipping to hopping to galloping to running.

ESTABLISHING CLASSROOM ATMOSPHERE

When establishing a classroom atmosphere, it's very important that teachers be consistent in what they expect from one day to the next, to avoid *slippage* (letting the children become lax as the year progresses). A good way to maintain consistency is to effectively use the management techniques suggested by Kounin (1970).

Consistency

Students learn best when the gymnasium is a predictable place to be. Rules and procedures must be followed in a routine fashion. For example, if one day children are allowed to take out equipment mats by dragging them across the floor but the next day four people are required to carry each mat, what Doyle (1979) calls ambiguity exists: The students really don't know what is expected of them. These misleading practices must be eliminated, and the function of the gymnasium must follow a set routine so that procedural aspects of the class occur the same way each time.

Monitoring and Teacher Reaction

The following techniques are effective for monitoring and subsequently handling student behavior during class:

1. The teacher's movement patterns are unpredictable. The teacher varies the way she or he moves through the class during activity and stands in various places to instruct the class.
2. The teacher scans the class frequently to "catch students being good." To scan, quickly look across the class in a predetermined direction, usually left to right, at regular intervals.
3. The teacher provides clear and precise directions and repeats them at least once for clarity; the teacher then asks questions to check for understanding.
4. The teacher possesses "withitness": He or she appears to have eyes in the back of his or her head (Kounin, 1970).
5. The teacher can *overlap* (attend to two issues simultaneously) (Kounin, 1970).
6. The teacher avoids *dangles* (issues left in midair) (Kounin, 1970).
7. The teacher avoids *flipflopping* (terminating

one activity, starting another, and returning to the first activity) (Kounin, 1970).

8. The teacher uses *targeting* (directs interactions toward the appropriate student (Siedentop, 1983).

9. The teacher displays the skill of *timing* (the lag time between student action and teacher behavior). As a general rule, the shorter the lag time, the better (Siedentop, 1983).

Figure 7-3 Checklist for a productive learning environment.

	CHECKLIST FOR A PRODUCTIVE LEARNING ENVIRONMENT	
Item	Check When Done	Notes
1. Were rules reviewed?		
2. Were rules followed?		
3. Was positive feedback given when students practiced a procedure correctly?		
4. Were directions and demonstrations given so all children could see and hear?		
5. Was inappropriate behavior stopped immediately?		
6. Were rules and procedures posted so all could see and read them?		
7. Was equipment gotten safely and efficiently?		
8. Did all children know the stop signal?		
9. Were any new students spoken to individually at least once?		
10. Did class begin immediately when students entered the area?		
11. Was student's appropriate behavior rewarded in some way?		
12. Were the designed consequences administered to all students who displayed inappropriate behavior?		

Use of these skills enables a teacher to avoid what Kounin (1970) called the *ripple effect*, which occurs when one class member involves several others in a rapidly spreading circle of off-task behavior. The classic example of the ripple effect resulting from ineffective targeting and timing is attempting to identify who started a fight:

TEACHER: All right, who started the fight?

TED: Ray pushed me first.

RAY: Well, Ted threw a rock at me.

TED: But I was aiming for Bobby because he called me a dumbbell.

If a teacher practices these techniques consistently and regularly, the functioning of the gymnasium is more likely to progress in a manner that enhances learning. Furthermore, discipline problems, although they won't vanish, will be curtailed.

TEACHING SAFETY PROCEDURES

As with other aspects of the learning environment, safety needs to be taught. We can't expect children to learn and practice safety simply by listening once or twice to explanations of safety procedures.

General safety procedures can easily be taught at the beginning of the school year by incorporating them with and encompassing them by other gymnasium rules and procedures. These safety procedures must be explained and then taught as well as practiced.

We've found that special safety procedures, ones that deal with specialized equipment or unique situations, are most effectively taught at the time that situation occurs. Again, the procedures shouldn't be glossed over; students should thoroughly understand them before the teacher proceeds.

It's beneficial to explain why selected behaviors are inappropriate and safety procedures necessary. Explaining the possible harmful consequences of such actions helps children understand the need for stated practices. As with all ongoing gymnasium rules, consequences for breaking safety rules must be stated; they might easily be included in the general rules for behavior. The children need to understand that safety is *their* responsibility as well as the teacher's.

A TIME FOR REFLECTION

Quite often it's very easy to forget what actually happened in a class—how much you accomplished, what you didn't accomplish, what was understood and misunderstood. Figure 7-3 is a checklist of the critical aspects presented in this chapter; during the beginning of the year, it helps to refer to it often. As the year progresses, you may want to use the checklist once a day or even once a week. If you consistently find items that aren't checked, you may want to begin to modify some of your teaching behaviors.

SUMMARY

A teacher must distinguish between physical education and recess. Once children truly understand the difference between "purposeful practice" (physical education class) and "doing your own thing" (recess), they're far more willing to participate in the development of a learning environment.

A new teacher needs to begin to develop a learning environment immediately, as does the teacher working with a new class. Designing lessons that involve the children in activity most of the time is one positive approach to establishing a learning environment. Excessive management time and waiting time, often the result of poor organization, tend to hinder the creation of an appropriate atmosphere.

When children have acquired suitable listening skills and safety practices, when they accept the responsibility for their own actions and cooperate with others, the alternatives for class organization are increased significantly. The teacher who clearly states and consistently adheres to rules of behavior and standards for performance will have productive lessons and enthusiastic students.

READING COMPREHENSION QUESTIONS

1. What is physical education? What is recess?
2. What is discipline? How does discipline differ from establishing a learning environment?
3. What three activities can you use to teach children to listen in a physical education environment?
4. List five guidelines for establishing rules of behavior in the gymnasium.
5. In your words, what does critical demandingness mean?
6. Why are the first lessons of the year so important? List five suggestions for those lessons.
7. Why are effective monitoring skills important? Name three monitoring skills a teacher should employ.

REFERENCES

Brooks, D. (1984, April). *Communicating competence: Junior high teacher behavioral expression during the first day of school.* Paper presented at the annual meeting of the American Educational Research Association, New Orleans.

Brophy, J. E., & Evertson, C. M. (1976). *Learning from teaching: A developmental perspective.* Boston: Allyn and Bacon.

DiViglio, J. (1972). Guidelines for effective interdisciplinary teams. *The Clearing House, 47,* 209–211.

Doyle, W. (1979). Making managerial decisions in classrooms. In D. L. Duke (Ed.), *Classroom management.* Seventy-eighth Yearbook of the National Society for the Study of Education, part 2. Chicago: University of Chicago Press.

Evertson, C., Emmer, E., Clements, B., Sanford, J., & Worsham, M. (1984). *Classroom management for elementary teachers.* Englewood Cliffs, NJ: Prentice-Hall.

Kounin, J. (1970). *Discipline and group management in classrooms.* New York: Holt.

Rosenshine, B., & Berliner, D. (1978). Academic engaged time. *British Journal of Teacher Education, 4*(1), 3–15.

Siedentop, D. (1983). *Developing teaching skills in physical education* (2nd ed.). Palo Alto, CA: Mayfield.

Discipline: Maintaining Appropriate Behavior

Many teacher-trainees are quite simply afraid that they will not be able to control their students, let alone teach them anything. They should be afraid. They have had precious little in their undergraduate curriculum which would provide the kinds of experiences necessary to understand the problems and gain the skills necessary to feel confident about their abilities as educators.

Daryl Siedentop (1972)

Disciplining children is one of the least enjoyable tasks of teaching, but it is something that *all* teachers must do. The notion that only poor teachers have to discipline children is simply not accurate.

From our viewpoint, discipline is the presence and maintenance of behavior supportive of learning. We follow a positive approach to dealing with inappropriate behavior, an approach that lets a teacher both create a positive atmosphere and teach students appropriate behavior for the gymnasium. In this situation, the teacher's primary task with regard to discipline is to first employ techniques that create appropriate behavior and second, use techniques that reduce inappropriate behavior.

It's normal for teachers to be concerned about discipline. Fuller (1969) and Fuller, Parsons, and Watkins (1974) found that preservice teachers' primary concerns about teaching can be stated as follows: "Will I be able to control the children?" "Will the children like me?" Our experiences with beginning teachers as well as our own teaching experiences suggest that most preservice teachers ask these questions. The difference between so-called good teachers and poor teachers is not their concern about discipline—all teachers encounter deviant behavior and must find ways of dealing with it. Rather, the more successful teachers are able to minimize the amount of time they devote to discipline. Even the teacher who establishes and explains rules of behavior, teaches with a critical demandingness, and sets and adheres to performance standards can't be sure that a class will perform as expected. In many classes there will be some children who find it difficult to function in a school environment, not only in physical education but in other classes as well. Occasionally an entire class has difficulty adhering to the behavioral boundaries the teacher has established.

Whether an individual, several children, or most of the children refuse to abide by the rules, your first response might well be to examine your performance as a teacher. When children react in unexpected ways, you may, upon reflection, find that their reactions are justified. Children are incredibly honest. A teacher may not want to know or believe that a lesson is a dud, but the children will let the teacher know. Occasionally it's the teacher's behavior, rather than the children's, that needs to be changed.

If you determine that the lesson is appropriate and your performance as a teacher is satisfactory, you can then look for other causes of disruptive behavior. Try not to view disruptive behavior as a personal affront. Instead, deal with it in two phases: short-term, reacting appropriately; long-term, seeking to understand the cause.

Comparing a referee or umpire's job with the teacher's need to discipline children places a teacher's job in perspective. Those referees respected by players and coaches share the following characteristics: They're fair, consistent, accurate, and unemotionally involved. As teachers, we should keep these good characteristics in mind as we reflect on how we help children work within our guidelines.

Although a referee's job is less enjoyable than a player's or coach's, at least to us, it's an important aspect of organized sport. Similarly, enforcing discipline is an important role for a teacher. In physical education, as in sports, there will be violations and infractions.

If you observed an effective teacher near the end of a school year, you'd see few, if any, discipline problems because the teacher handled them effectively at the beginning of the year. That teacher no longer needs the short-term techniques we describe in this chapter.

Our goal is to help children become intrinsically motivated so they can benefit from and enjoy physical activity. In some situations, this motivation will occur naturally, so few of the techniques described will be necessary. In other teaching situations, however, many of the techniques will be needed. In either situation, we want to use less and less of these techniques so that the children participate in physical education because they like it and feel it is valuable rather than because of an external reward or motivator. Our explanation of effective techniques for helping children work within our guidelines (Chapter 1) is divided into three steps: increasing appropriate, decreasing inappropriate, and maintaining whole-class appropriate behavior.

INCREASING APPROPRIATE BEHAVIOR

For behavior that doesn't conform to the expectations established for the specific setting, the teacher must first attempt to increase appropriate behavior. Five techniques teachers have found useful for increasing appropriate behavior are positive interaction, ignoring inappropriate behavior, nonverbal teacher interactions, eliminating differential treatment, and person-to-person dialogue.

Positive Interaction

Bane and Jencks concluded that "the primary basis for evaluating a school should be whether the teachers and students found it a satisfying place to be" (1972, p. 41). One of the most powerful methods of creating this environment is to interact with students in a positive way when they behave in an appropriate manner. In essence, this is emphasizing the positive rather than the negative. Many children who are known throughout the school as discipline problems have become accustomed to hearing nothing but negative comments about their behavior. Catching them in the act of doing something right and praising them for it can dramatically change their behavior (Siedentop, 1983).

But note that praise shouldn't be contrived and meaningless, offered with no genuine feeling, as is often the case. Give praise frequently but not

---

The class proceeded through its parody of education, following a formula validated in a thousand classrooms I have visited and countless thousands I have not. First step in the formula is an assumption, an untested hypothesis which becomes valid merely because (and as soon as) it is assumed: Children who do not easily take the imprint of their teacher's own education and values, who are not ductile enough to be drawn wire-thin so that they may slip through traditional holes in the fabric of society—these are not "promising children" and the best that can be hoped for from them is good behavior (silence) and early withdrawal (dropout). Since silence is their most positive attribute, they should be left unmolested during the class hour so long as they practice that virtue.

Perhaps worst of all the many dreadful aspects of this assumption is that *the children know it*. They know—and will tell you, as they told me, if they are asked—that a few of them are regarded as "good material" and the rest are nothing: "ever' time I go to her class, she make me feel like I was nothin'." Snapper, Rubbergut's half brother, said it. He said it for all the children who drown in the well of silence.

Daniel Fader,
The Naked Children

Every person needs recognition. It is expressed cogently by the lad who says, "Mother, let's play darts. I'll throw the darts and you say 'Wonderful.' "

Dale Baughman

---

so profusely that it seems trivial. And give it only when a child actually displays appropriate behavior. All children are capable of receiving some type of praise—catch them being good!

This sounds like common sense, but research (Hamilton, 1974; Hughly, 1973; Rife, 1973) has shown that this isn't the prevalent mode of operation in the gymnasium. The following list includes examples of verbal positive interactions in the left column, nonverbal ones in the right column. A simple tally by a student or from an videotape will give you an idea of how you're doing.

Verbal positive statements	Nonverbal positive interactions
Good	High five
Terrific	Smiling
Right	Clapping
Nice job	Thumbs up
Way to go	Winking
That's it	Pat on the back
Thank you	Shaking hands
Great	Arm around a
You did it this time	student
Beautiful	Giving an OK sign
Excellent	
Nicely done	
OK	
All right	

Ignoring Inappropriate Behavior

The opposite of emphasizing appropriate behavior with positive interactions is ignoring inappropriate behavior. Many of us teachers find that praising appropriate behavior is hard, but ignoring inappropriate behavior is even more difficult. Evertson, Emmer, Clements, Sanford, and Worsham (1984, p. 102) suggested that inappropriate behavior should be ignored when it meets the following three criteria:

1. It is of short duration and not likely to spread or persist.
2. It is a minor deviation.
3. Reacting to it would interrupt a lesson or call attention to the behavior.

Student behaviors that could be ignored in a physical education setting include occasional calling out during discussions, brief whispering, short periods of inattentiveness or nonpractice, and occasional continuation of activity after the stop signal. Thus, unless a behavior is harmful to other students, causes a safety problem, or seriously disrupts other students, reacting to it would consume too much of your energy, interrupt your lessons constantly, and detract from your classroom climate (Evertson et al., 1984).

To be completely effective, a teacher must both ignore minor inappropriate behavior while simultaneously praising appropriate behavior. Yet, when we've become accustomed to saying, "Sh-h," "Hurry up!"; "I'm waiting for you to get quiet."; or "Tommy!!!", it's not easy to change to phrases such as, "Jody was quiet when she heard the stop signal"; "Terrific, you were ready to go in 10 seconds today"; "Tommy, you showed thoughtfulness when you helped Jay up after he fell down." Such interactions, which can create appropriate behaviors in children, imply, for many of us, that the teacher is letting Tommy or the students who aren't yet quiet get away with inappropriate behavior. For many of us this is a risky action because the perceived implication is that our control is in jeopardy. In reality, the teacher who ignores simple inappropriate behavior while praising appropriate behavior is teaching children what desired behavior is while simultaneously creating an atmosphere that is warm and conducive to learning.

There's a subtle innuendo with the praising appropriate behavior/ignoring inappropriate be-

In the inner city, teachers and students do not respect the same rules. Many of the youngsters want their teachers to play the game of teaching and learning by the rules and regulations they know and understand, and that are important to them—not by the rules that are important to their teachers. They want their teachers to be humanly and emotionally tough enough to make them control their behavior, since they in fact gain strength to behave from the emotional strength of their teachers. They want teachers who will "make me work and not let me get away with anything" (told to me and my university students by innumerable so-called inner city school "discipline problems").

Herbert Foster,
Ribbin', Jivin' and Playin' the Dozens

havior scenario. For example, if a teacher used *both* sets of examples described in the previous paragraph, what message would the students receive? The answer is confusion. Students would assume they could receive reinforcement and adult attention for either appropriate or inappropriate behavior.

Ignoring inappropriate behavior is for many of us a very uncomfortable and awkward act. A good way to assess your skill in praising the good and ignoring the inappropriate is to tape-record your lessons and count how often you say something positive and the number of times you say something negative. Remember that even little things such as "Hurry up!" and "Sh-h" count as negative interactions. Don't be surprised at what you first discover about your behavior; look at it as a challenge to improve.

Nonverbal Teacher Interactions

A number of simple nonverbal techniques are often sufficient to prompt appropriate student behavior.

Sometimes just the physical proximity of the teacher will solicit the desirable behavior from some students. For example, when giving directions or speaking to the class as a whole, the teacher merely stands near the student displaying inappropriate behavior. Another technique for increasing appropriate behavior is to borrow the equipment the student is using for purposes of demonstration. Finally, often even less obvious actions work. For example, simple eye contact or a signal, such as nodding the head, will redirect the student.

Eliminating Differential Treatment

Often a stranger can walk into a classroom and after a few minutes pick out the "discipline problems" in a group of children he or she has never seen before. Frequently these are the children whose names the teacher is constantly calling out—"Cecil, are you listening? Daphne, sit down, please." It's not uncommon to see the same children singled out frequently. And typically these children are masters of brinkmanship; they know just how far they can go without actually being disciplined.

Because they covet adult attention, they persist in their deviant behavior, so avoid singling out these children, if possible.

One way to spot differential treatment of students in your classes is to tape-record a few lessons. Place a tape recorder in the gymnasium or attach it to a belt around your waist. (This observation and assessment technique is discussed further in Chapter 11.) After you've taped several lessons, listen to the tapes and record the number of times you call each child's name and the number of reprimands or desists that you issue to individual children.

A simple way to record your tally is to use a copy of the class roster that has two columns to the right of the names (see Figure 8-1). The first column is a tally for each time you call a child's name; the second column is a tally for each time you give a reprimand to or there is a negative interaction with a specific child. If, after you complete your tallies, you find that you repeatedly single out the same few children and/or interact negatively with those children, you know you need to take steps to change your teaching behavior (see Chapter 11).

Figure 8-1 Chart for helping a teacher identify differential treatment.

	Name Called	Reprimand
Mike	|||		
Sue		
Rich	||		
Bill		
Don	~~||||~~ ||||	||||
Billie			

I have tried to respond to what children say rather than to what I expect or want them to say. Responding to children in this way is not a natural act; I have often been chagrined or embarrassed to discover myself listening to myself (rather than to the child) and answering a question both unasked and unintended. Or, worst of all, I have an answer that was not only unwanted but unmanageable by the child. In this, as in so much else, adult responses are inferior to children's, for children are usually too wise to burden adults with information they cannot handle.

Daniel Fader,
The Naked Children

Person-to person dialogue can be an effective strategy for reaching alienated students.

Person-to-Person Dialogue

Another successful technique is the person-to-person dialogue. Arrange a time to meet with a child away from the class (not immediately before or after). You might say to the child, "Willie, you don't seem to be enjoying our physical education class. I'd like you to come to my office after school today so that we can talk about it." The purpose of this meeting is to try to determine the reasons for the child's behavior in your class. This is *not* a time for a lecture; instead, teacher and pupil should have a dialogue. We've found that a statement such as the following enables many children to begin a discussion of their concerns: "Willie, I'd like to talk to you about physical education class. Is there something I do that bothers you?"

This statement takes the focus from the child and places it on the teacher. Many children are quite candid about what's bothering them. Remember, this is a dialogue, not a lecture. Explaining to the child something of how and why you teach is constructive and often productive. Lecturing to the child about his behavior or threatening him with future punishments is counterproductive. This dialogue is not teacher-to-child but person-to-person. Often the temptation to lecture, accuse, or blame a child is strong, but succumbing to this temptation is the quickest way to destroy any rapport between student and teacher. If a child trusts you enough to talk candidly about his concerns and you threaten or lecture him, communication ceases. Many children—especially those who need individual attention the most—have been betrayed before, and so they're likely to be sensitive and wary. Use of teacher power in this situation reinforces a child's belief that he cannot trust teachers and that being honest only gets him into more trouble.

Some children never want to participate in physical education class. A person-to-person dialogue is often helpful here, as is a conference with the child's other teachers. Some children are simply being obstinate or are genuinely lazy. Others may be afraid of participating in physical activity because they've already had unsatisfactory experiences at home or on the playground. If a child has a legitimate reason, we respect the child and attempt to create a satisfactory alternative. Transferring the child to another physical education class or arranging a one-to-one teaching situation often leads, in time, to participation with the regular class. Forcing a child to participate in physical education classes without first understanding the reason for the reluctance may not be in the child's best interests. Once a teacher understands why a child is reluctant to participate, the teacher can make an informed decision about the most appropriate course of action.

DECREASING INAPPROPRIATE BEHAVIOR

Although our first strategy in dealing with inappropriate behavior is to attempt to increase appropriate behavior, we all know this doesn't always work. At times a teacher must decrease inappropriate behavior. When this is necessary, the teacher should have a repertoire of strategies available. Teachers in physical education have found the following techniques useful: desists, time-out, behavior contracts, letters to parents, and involving the principal. Note that all the techniques fit the psychological definition of the term *punishment*—they decrease the likelihood of an inappropriate behavior recurring. These techniques should *not* be emotionally laden, associated with acts of anger, or said in a raised voice. Also, any action the teacher takes to decrease inappropriate behavior should be accompanied by actions to build appropriate behavior.

Desists

Sometimes it's impossible to ignore inappropriate behavior, so it must be reprimanded. Kounin (1970) called this technique a desist. Using verbal desists effectively is a skill, and a desist can result in behavior change. Kounin established several con-

ditions that must be present for a desist to be effective:

1. A desist must be clear. "Ellen, stop doing that" isn't enough. The desist must contain exact information about what the student is doing wrong. For example, "Ellen, stop hitting the basketball with the tennis racket; it'll ruin the tennis racket" is clear and specific. The student knows exactly what she is doing wrong.
2. A desist must be firm. Firmness is the degree to which the teacher follows through on the desist, so that the student is aware the teacher means what was said. Brooks (1984) found that teachers who giggled or laughed after they delivered desists weren't taken seriously. Ways of implying firmness when delivering a desist include moving a bit closer to the student, looking the student momentarily in the eyes, and keeping a straight face when delivering the desist.
3. A desist must be well timed; a behavior must be desisted immediately, before it's allowed to spread to other students.
4. A desist must be appropriately targeted; it must be directed at the original offender, not a second or third party.
5. A desist mustn't be harsh. Kounin found that rough desists simply upset children and weren't effective. Firmness doesn't mean harshness or punitiveness; it is simply meaning what you're saying.

Time-Out

Time-out is like the penalty box in ice hockey. During a time-out, a child is told to withdraw from class for a specific amount of time or until the child is ready to function according to the rules. When ready to return to class, the child simply rejoins the activity or reports to the teacher for instructions. The time-out procedure should be taught with all other procedures at the beginning of the year, so that subsequently the teacher can give a time-out with no explanation and without interrupting the rest of the class.

BEHAVIOR CONTRACT

Kim Thomas and Mr. Diller agree that the following plan will be in effect for the next two weeks.

Starting date _____   Ending date_____

Kim will

1. Not interrupt other students' work by trying to knock their equipment away

2. Not disturb class by talking while the teacher is talking

3. Participate in all activities and try hard to improve her skills in throwing

Mr. Diller will

1. Give Kim individual help on throwing

2. Count one point for each day that Kim meets the three points stated above

3. Let Kim help with the physical education equipment for one week if she earns five points during the two weeks of the contract

Signed _____

_____

_____

Figure 8-2 A typical behavior contract. *Source:* Adapted from *Developing Teaching Skills in Physical Education,* 2nd ed., by D. Siedentop, 1983, Palo Alto, CA: Mayfield.

For a time-out situation to be effective, the following conditions must be present.

1. The student must find physical education enjoyable; if not, the time-out itself may be a reward instead of a punishment.
2. The time-out area should be a clearly designated place where social contact with classmates isn't possible.
3. The length of the time-out can be at the discretion of the child (as suggested in Chapter 7). Some teachers prefer to specify the length of the time-out, e.g., three minutes. If the time-out is going to be timed, an egg timer or clock helps children determine when the specified amount of time has passed.

Behavior Contracts

A behavior contract is a formal agreement between a student and the teacher regarding behavior in the physical education setting. The contract includes a statement of the desired behavior, the contingencies (how much, for how long), and the rewards that will be earned if the behavior and the contingencies are met (Siedentop, 1983). When using a behavior contract, remember that students must have a role in defining all three aspects of the contract: behavior, contingencies, and rewards. After all has been agreed upon, it is very important that both parties (sometimes a third party as a witness) sign the agreement. The student should be made aware of the importance of the agreement and, just as the teacher does, view it as a formal agreement, not to be taken lightly. Figure 8-2 is an example of a behavior contract with one student.

Letters to Parents

Desists, time-out, and behavior contracts work with some children, not with others. When a child continues to misbehave and present problems, a letter to a parent can be effective in obtaining that child's cooperation. But this technique should be used only after other approaches have proven unsuccessful.

The letter to the parents lists specific violations. The child is to have the letter signed by a parent and then return it to the teacher. Such a letter is usually followed by improvements in behavior. When that occurs, you can send home a letter, as soon as possible, that reports the improvements as clearly as the earlier letter reported violations. This second letter congratulates the child on improved behavior and, like the first one, requires a parent's signature. Some parents may have never before received a positive comment about their child from a school. Figures 8-3 and 8-4 are two suggested report forms.

Involving the Principal

Sending a disruptive child to the principal may or may not be successful. When you send a child to the principal, you're acknowledging—to yourself and to the child—your inability to cope with the situation. You're also placing the child in a situation you can't control.

Some principals are positive and helpful in working with disruptive children. Others use threats or corporal punishment, techniques likely to temporarily improve the child's behavior but permanently damage the child's enthusiasm and trust.

Only when you've tried every other possible technique to deal with behavior detrimental to the child and classmates should you send a child to a principal. If you must do this, we hope yours is a principal who can help you and the child to better understand each other's needs and situations, so that you can work together more successfully.

```
                        ELEMENTARY SCHOOL

                PHYSICAL EDUCATION BEHAVIOR REPORT

     NAME _____  DATE _____

          Educational research has consistently shown that
     when a teacher spends class time managing discipline
     problems, less "teaching" and student "learning" occur.
     Disruptive behavior, therefore, is a primary reason for
     poor student achievement.

          We regret to inform you that your child exhibited
     the following misbehavior during physical education
     class today:


Fought with others      _____      Refused to participate    _____

Argued with others      _____      Lazy; no hustle or energy  _____

Mistreated equipment    _____      Late to class              _____

Disrupted the work                 Disruptive in hallway      _____
  of others             _____

Discourteous to others  _____      Continually off-task; not
                                     following teacher's
Frequently clowned                   directions               _____
  acting foolish
  and silly             _____      Spoke using foul language  _____

Talked while teacher               Did not listen to
  was talking           _____        teacher                  _____

    Teacher's Comments:_____

    _____

    _____

    _____


     Please discuss today's incident with your youngster.  We are
concerned about the harm your child's behavior is causing himself and
his classmates.  We will keep you informed of his behavioral progress
during the coming weeks.

     Thank you for your cooperation.

                        TEACHER_____


                   PARENT'S SIGNATURE_____
```

Figure 8-3 Report for parents.

MAINTAINING APPROPRIATE BEHAVIOR IN ENTIRE CLASSES

Some classes have a more difficult time than others learning to abide by the class rules. When the race-against-the-clock games and performance standards don't result in the desired outcome, it's necessary to use more sophisticated techniques. Four approaches that have proven successful are Hellison's system, class rewards, token systems, and behavior games.

```
                          ELEMENTARY SCHOOL

                   PHYSICAL EDUCATION BEHAVIOR REPORT

    Name_____ Date_____

         Educational research has shown that when a teacher spends
    class time managing discipline problems, less teaching and less
    learning occur.  Therefore, when disruptive behavior is non-
    existent in a class situation, greater student achievement is
    likely to result.

         We are glad to inform you that your youngster's behavior in
    physical education class has improved._____
    consistently exhibits the following exemplary behaviors:

    _____ Listens to the teacher   _____ Is courteous to others

              Is on-task, following   _____ Treats equipment with care
    _____     directions

    _____ Is eager to participate  _____ Plays safely

         Your child is doing a wonderful-terrific-dynamite job in
    physical education and we are proud of him/her.  You are to be
    commended for preparing your youngster to function so well in school.
    We are more effective teachers because of your efforts.

         Thank you for your cooperation.

                                TEACHER: _____
```

Figure 8-4 Report for parents.

Hellison's System for Developing Self-Responsibility

During his work with high-risk, alienated youth, Don Hellison developed a system for leading youngsters to become responsible initially for their own behavior and then, in time, to work success- fully with other students. It's important to point out that this isn't a quick-fix approach to class discipline but a program designed to be imple- mented throughout the year. From irresponsibil- ity, the youngster progresses through four levels of awareness: self-control, involvement, self-responsibility, and caring. (The following information is insufficient for enabling a teacher to implement the program. If you're interested in implementing this approach, a complete description is in Hellison's 1985 text, *Goals and Strategies for Teaching Physical Education.*)

Level 0: Irresponsibility. Students at this level are not motivated to participate in physical activity. They often make excuses and blame others for their behavior. Their behavior includes discrediting or making fun of other students' involvement and interrupting, intimidating, and verbally or physically abusing other students.

Level 1: Self-Control. At level 1, children are helped to shift responsibility for their behavior from an external force, usually the teacher, to themselves. At this point they're able to control their behavior enough so they don't interfere with other children. They do this without very much prompting from the teacher and without constant supervision.

Level 2: Involvement. Children at level 2 not only show self-control but are involved in the lessons. They willingly, even enthusiastically, play, accept challenges, and practice motor skills under the teacher's supervision.

Level 3: Self-Responsibility. The goal at this level is for children to both work without direct supervision and to eventually take responsibility for their interests and actions. This implies that they begin to identify their own needs and interests and plan and develop their own programs. This goal assumes that children are able to independently reflect, plan, work, and play if given proper guidance and appropriate guidelines within which to work.

Level 4: Caring. The goal of level 4 is to encourage children to reach out beyond themselves to others—to genuinely care for others. Children at this level extend their sense of responsibility by cooperating, giving support, showing concern, and helping others.

Class Rewards

A class as a whole earns class rewards for abiding by the class rules. The first step is to establish a reward that will have meaning to a particular age of students—posters, banners, and free time have been used successfully. When an entire class does well for a day (week, month), it receives the reward. For example, if a class consistently does better than the performance standards established for management tasks over a given period of time, it receives a poster or banner to display in its room. Some teachers provide a reward for a class-of-the-week. We prefer, however, to reward *every* class for doing well, not just one.

Token Systems

Time-out penalizes disruptive behavior; a token system rewards desirable behavior. A token system is a program with academic, organizational, or managerial outcomes accompanied by a system in which students can earn "tokens" that can be exchanged for various rewards (Siedentop, 1983). The intent is to reward appropriate behavior and so encourage all children to behave appropriately.

The teacher initially explains to the class that a particular rule or procedure is being violated or not being accomplished as efficiently as possible. In doing this, the teacher must define very clearly the behaviors that are to be improved. After the behaviors have been defined, rewards must be developed. This is best done with the students' input, by having them rank available awards (as presented by the teacher) according to their desirability. The higher the ranking, the more the students will be motivated by the reward; the lower the ranking, the greater the probability it won't do much to encourage children to change their behavior. After the behaviors and rewards have been established, the rate of exchange must be agreed upon: how many tokens it will take to acquire the different rewards.

For example, the teacher explains to the class that some students aren't stopping and listening as soon as they hear the stop signal. The teacher explains that, beginning today, as soon as he gives the stop signal, he'll check off on a class list the names of the children who stop and listen within five seconds after the signal is given. Students who earn five checks during the class will be given a reward.

Successful rewards in physical education include a student-of-the-day or -week award, whereby the student is given a badge to wear until the next physical education class and the student's name is displayed on a bulletin board in a prominent place; extra physical education time; special privileges, such as helping the teacher with other classes or after school; and free-choice times. With free-choice times, children who've earned three tokens, for example, may choose an activity for the last five minutes of class while the remainder of the class continues with the ongoing activity. Jumping rope, shooting baskets, or climbing on the playground apparatus are typical free-choice token system rewards.

No matter what the reward, it's most effective if the children themselves have had a part in deciding what it will be. Gradually the length of time in which a reward is earned can be lengthened from a day to a week to a month. Once children have learned to abide by the rules that are vital for the successful functioning of a large group, token systems become unnecessary.

Behavior Games

A more sophisticated and persuasive approach to class discipline is described in Siedentop's *Developing Teaching Skills in Physical Education* (1983). Siedentop suggested the use of a behavior game the class plays, in which appropriate behavior is learned via the game. Certain standards for performance are established, and all the students in a class have the opportunity to earn the reward. This format can be modified. The standards can be raised gradually, the number of signals can be decreased, and the time period over which the game is played can be extended, from one week to two weeks to a month. Siedentop emphasized that the purpose of this game is to elicit the desired behavior, so that the behavior game eventually can be eliminated. Behavior games aren't intended to be a permanent feature of a program; they can be effectively employed when the behavior of a class as a group is exceptionally deviant. As with the class rewards, the key to success is a reward that the class as a whole finds desirable. Remember, what appeals to one class may not appeal to another.

FORMAT FOR A BEHAVIOR GAME

1. The class is divided into four groups. Groups are allowed to choose a name for their team.
2. It is emphasized that each team can win and that teams are competing against a behavior criterion rather than against each other.
3. Four to six behavior rules are explained thoroughly.
4. Rewards are discussed and decided on by the group.
5. The game is explained. Points will be awarded each time a signal goes off (the students won't know when the signal will occur). The teacher will check each group when the signal occurs. If all team members are behaving according to the rules, the team gets one point. If any team member is breaking any of the rules, the team gets no point.
6. A cassette audiotape is preprogrammed with a loud noise to occur periodically (a bell or a buzzer works well). Eight signals are programmed. The intervals between

the signals vary. Several tapes are prepro-grammed. When class begins, the teacher simply turns on the tape recorder with the volume up (often he or she doesn't know when the signals will occur).

7. When the signal occurs, the teacher quickly glances at each team and makes a judg-ment on their behavior. Teams that win a point are praised and told about their point. Teams that do not win a point are told why. (After doing this for a few days, the teacher can usually manage this kind of behavior game easily, not taking more than 15 or 30 seconds at each signal to record and announce points.)

8. At the end of the period, the teacher totals the points and posts the scores for the day.

9. At the end of a specified period (ranging from one day to as long as 8 weeks), the rewards are earned by each team that has met the criterion.

10. If one player on a team loses more than two points for his or her team two days in a row, the team meets and decides whether this player should sit out from gym class for a day (this "doomsday" con-tingency very seldom needs to be used).

11. With each consecutive game played, it is possible to reduce the number of signals per class and increase the length of the game. As good behavior becomes the norm for the class, the game can gradually be phased out.

Daryl Siedentop, *Developing Teaching Skills in Physical Education*

CORPORAL PUNISHMENT

We're unalterably opposed to corporal punish-ment. For some teachers a spanking or a paddling seems to be—inappropriately—a cathartic that may help the teacher but is more likely to harm the child. There are times when the temptation to paddle or strike a continually misbehaving child is almost overwhelming. And yet, according to our observations, it is the same few children who receive the vast majority of the paddlings. Obviously, this shows that for many children paddling doesn't achieve the desired result. And simultaneously, it proves to these children that physically striking another person is a legitimate alternative when no other course of action appears effective. Interest-ingly, many of the children who are continually the recipients of corporal punishment are being punished for fighting or hitting others. Occasion-ally a first paddling achieves the desired result. One cannot help but wonder, however, about the long-term impact of such an experience on a child. Use of corporal punishment is inhumane, ineffec-tive, and an admission of failure.

SUMMARY

Discipline is the presence of appropriate behavior that supports the educa-tional goals of the specific situation. During the time needed to establish a learning environment, behavior inappropriate for the setting may occur. When it does, the teacher should first make certain that the lesson plans are pedagogically sound. If they are, then it is appropriate to focus on the students' behavior. It's important to understand that problems with inappropriate behavior are normal; *all* teachers will encounter some children who are off-task.

There are two phases to managing inappropriate behavior: the immediate response (short-term) to the situation and the long-term strategy. The long-term strategy involves recognizing the need to prevent the recurrence of the behavior by finding out what triggered it and developing ways of helping students learn more constructive means for dealing with inappropriate behavior. Short-term techniques give a teacher practical skills to use instantly when undesirable behavior occurs. This discussion dealt almost exclusively with short-term techniques under the assumption that it is only after the teacher has acquired and consistently used these techniques with positive results is she or he comfortable with addressing the long-term aspects of inappropriate behavior. The techniques presented are simply a way of dealing with the immediate inappropriate behavior; as a learning environment is developed and students accept the responsibility for their own behavior, such techniques should no longer be needed and can gradually be faded out.

When inappropriate behavior first occurs, the teacher should use the techniques that have been found effective for increasing appropriate behavior: positive interaction, ignoring inappropriate behavior, nonverbal teacher interactions, reminding interactions, eliminating differential treatment, and person-to-person dialogue. For those times when teachers find it necessary to decrease inappropriate behavior, successful techniques include desists, time-out, behavior contracts, letters to parents, and involving the principal. Remember that strategies to reduce inappropriate behavior should *always* be accompanied by techniques to increase appropriate behavior. Techniques for refocusing an entire class that is off-task include Hellison's system for developing self-responsibility, class rewards, token systems, and behavior games.

READING COMPREHENSION QUESTIONS

1. What should your first step be when you find most of the students in your class misbehaving? Why?
2. What is discipline as we defined it? How does it differ from the traditional approach to discipline?
3. What are the two phases in dealing with inappropriate behavior in the gymnasium?
4. What is the first strategy for maintaining an effective learning environment in the gymnasium? What techniques can be used to accomplish this goal?
5. Why are positive interactions with students so important, especially in the beginning of the year?
6. When should you ignore inappropriate behavior?
7. What does differential treatment of children mean? How can you determine if you are doing this?
8. What is the major point to remember in a person-to-person dialogue with a student?

9. What is the second strategy for handling inappropriate behavior in the gymnasium? What techniques can be used to accomplish this goal?
10. What are the characteristics of an effective desist?
11. What is a time-out? What points should you remember when using a time-out? When is a time-out not effective?
12. When is a a letter to parents useful? What should you include in the letter?
13. What is a token system? Describe how one works.
14. What is a behavior game? How is it played?
15. Why should many of the techniques discussed in this chapter *not* be necessary as the school year progresses?

REFERENCES

Bane, M. J., & Jencks, C. (1972, Sept.). The schools and equal opportunity. *Saturday Review of Education*, 37–42.

Evertson, C., Emmer, E., Clements, B., Sanford, J., & Worsham, S. (1984). *Classroom management for elementary teachers*. Englewood Cliffs, NJ: Prentice-Hall.

Fader, D. (1971). *The naked children*. New York: Macmillan.

Foster, H. L. (1974). *Ribbin', jivin' and playin' the dozens*. Cambridge, MA: Ballinger.

Fuller, F. (1969, March). Concerns of teachers: A developmental conceptualization. *American Educational Research Journal*, 207–226.

Fuller, F., Parsons, J., & Watkins, J. (1974, April). *Concerns of teachers: Research and reconceptualization*. Austin: University of Texas.

Hamilton, K. (1974). *The effects of a competency-based format on the behavior of student teachers and high school pupils*. Unpublished doctoral dissertation, The Ohio State University, Columbus.

Hellison, D. (1985). *Goals and strategies for teaching physical education*. Champaign, IL: Human Kinetics.

Hughly, C. (1973). *Modification of teacher behaviors in physical education*. Unpublished doctoral dissertation, The Ohio State University, Columbus.

Kounin, J. (1970). *Discipline and group management in classrooms*. New York: Holt.

Rife, F. (1973). *Modification of student-teacher behavior and its effect upon pupil behavior*. Unpublished doctoral dissertation, The Ohio State University, Columbus.

Siedentop, D. (1972, June). Tilting at windmills while Rome burns. *Quest*, 94–97.

Siedentop, D. (1983). *Developing teaching skills in physical education* (2nd ed.). Palo Alto, CA: Mayfield.

C H A P T E R **9**

Observation Techniques

It is vital for a teacher to observe children, whatever the subject or situation. It is through observation that the successful teacher assesses the moods, attributes, needs, and potential of individuals and groups.

E. Mauldon and J. Layson

The ability to observe—to see with understanding—is crucial for a reflective teacher. The instructor who designs and implements a successful physical education program for an individual school or class must be able to observe perceptively, accurately, and continuously and then translate the data gained from the observation into usable information.

Hoffman (1977), for example, reported a study that compared physical education teachers' observational-analysis ability with that of a group of softball players and coaches who had no professional training in physical education. The study revealed that the softball players scored significantly higher than the teachers who had degrees in physical education. Hoffman also provided evidence that the skill of observational analysis can

be learned. "Data from the only training study conducted to date have indicated that thirty-five minutes of well-organized discrimination training can bring about significant gain in the ability to detect errors in a fundamental skill" (p. 45). Neither study was conducted in a field-based setting.

Accurate observational analysis is difficult in a nonteaching environment. The complexity is increased considerably, however, when the teacher attempts to observe the movement and behavioral characteristics of individual children while simultaneously monitoring the work of an entire class during a physical education lesson (Barrett, 1977, 1979, 1983).

The following vignette from Larry Locke's "The Ecology of the Gymnasium: What the Tourist Never Sees" is an extremely accurate insight into the complexity of the process of teaching. Locke describes a two-minute observation of a class of thirty-four fourth-grade children during a gymnastics unit:

> Teacher is working one-on-one with a student who has an obvious neurological deficit. She wants him to sit on a beam and lift his feet from the floor. Her verbal behaviors fall into categories of reinforcement, instruction, feedback, and encouragement. She gives hands-on manual assistance. Nearby two boys perched on the uneven bars are keeping a group of girls off. Teacher visually monitors the situation but continues work on the beam. At the far end of the gym a large mat propped up so that students can roll down it from a table top, is slowly slipping nearer to the edge. Teacher visually monitors this but continues work on the beam. Teacher answers three individual inquiries addressed by passing students but continues as before. She glances at a group now playing follow-the-leader over the horse (this is off-task behavior) but as she does a student enters and indicates he left his milk money the previous period. Teacher nods him to the nearby office to retrieve the money and leaves the beam to stand near the uneven bars. The boys climb down at once. Teacher calls to a student to secure the slipping mat. Notes that the intruder, milk money now in hand, has paused to interact with two girls in the class and, monitoring him, moves quickly to the horse to begin a series of provocative questions designed to reestablish task focus.

As Locke so aptly reminded us after painting this accurate picture of the complexity of teaching:

> That was only 120 seconds out of the 17,000 the teacher spent that day in active instruction. A great deal of detail was unobserved or unrecorded over those two minutes, and nothing in the record reflected the invisible train of thought in the teacher's mind.

PLANNING FOR OBSERVATION

When teaching physical education, a person is constantly bombarded by seemingly hundreds of ideas in just a few seconds, so here we've provided a procedure for observing that we've found valuable as we attempt to see and understand all that is going on in our classes. Because teaching is so complex, it's important that a teacher knows what to look for in a particular lesson prior to conducting the lesson itself. This requires some advance planning (Chapter 5). When we don't plan beforehand, we often find it difficult to decide what to observe during a lesson, so our lessons lack focus or direction. It's almost as if we were just "doing things" with children rather than actually teaching. For this reason, when we plan we develop observation cues (Chapter 5) that remind us what to look for. Our observation cues fall into four categories: safety, on-task behavior, class movement patterns, and individual movement patterns.

Safety

The teacher's initial and constant attention must always be directed toward the children's safety. Whenever the teacher observes an unsafe situation, the teacher should remember that safety must take priority over everything else going on in the lesson. If the teacher has stated a task so that the children are responding unsafely, the class must be stopped and the task restated. If equipment is unsafe or being used unwisely, the class must be stopped to make the use of the equipment safe. Safety is the initial focus of any lesson and must be the uppermost consideration as teachers work with children.

We teach the children about safety as well so that they're able to understand some of the hazards they may encounter if they aren't careful. Initially, we explain the reasons for our safety procedures, to enable children to better understand

Although we don't like to even think about it, legal liability is an increasing concern of teachers, particularly those of physical education. We strongly encourage you to be certain to teach safety rules similar to those just described and to include the rules in the written lesson plan so that they're part of a permanent record in the unfortunate event you have to document safety precautions. Most of these safety rules should be taught in the first few weeks of school (Chapter 7) and then reinforced throughout the year. Again, as you observe, make sure safety is constantly the forefront of your focus.

and make intelligent decisions about their own safety. That's not enough, however. We need to constantly be aware of unsafe conditions. Following are several of the safety precautions we constantly keep in mind as we observe the classes. Certain of these precautions are also described in Chapter 7, "Establishing an Environment for Learning."

1. The children are required to work independently without pushing, shoving, tripping, or otherwise interfering with other children.
2. The children are required to work in a space reasonably distant from others (the concept of self-space). When the youngsters get too close, for example, when striking with rackets, we stop the lesson and make them adjust their space.
3. Depending on the surface, our children work in tennis shoes or barefoot. We don't allow stocking feet, especially on hardwood or linoleum floors because they're so slippery. The children enjoy sliding, but this is a definite hazard.
4. In lessons on skill themes, such as rolling, transferring weight, and balance (gymnastics context), we don't allow I Dare You and Follow the Leader games.
5. Unless otherwise indicated, in lessons in which gymnastics apparatus is being used, we allow only one child on the equipment at a time. This condition changes once the learning environment has been effectively established.

On-Task Behavior

Once you've observed that the environment is safe, your next focus is to determine if children are on-task. Are they actually doing what you asked them to do? For example, if you asked your class to throw and catch with a partner, are they indeed doing so? Or are they kicking the ball; running around chasing one another; not working with a partner but in groups of four or five? If so, these are off-task behaviors and need to be attended to immediately. Stop the lesson!

There are three reasons why children may be off-task:

1. The children are trying, but the task was stated unclearly. You must restate the task.
2. The task is too hard or too easy (success rate will help you here). Many of the children are either bored or frustrated. In either event, restate or change the task.
3. The children haven't yet learned to be on-task. If so, you'll have to once again practice the appropriate behavior in physical education class (Chapter 7). Although this isn't particularly enjoyable for either the children or the teacher, it's necessary because constant off-task behavior simply can't be tolerated; it's not fair to either the teacher or the children, especially those children who are working so hard to be on-task and do what the teacher asks.

The reality of teaching, unfortunately, is that every class always has one or two children who tend to be off-task more than others. What do you do with them? After all, it's not fair to punish the entire class because of the behavior of one or two children. Refer to Chapter 8 for ideas about appropriate behavior.

Class Movement Patterns

When you've determined that the class is working safely and on-task, begin observing the entire class to see how they're accomplishing the task. Constantly be on the alert, however, for unsafe and off-task situations.

As you scan the entire class to see how they're moving, you'll make one of three decisions, based on what you observe the majority of the children doing. The three decisions are whether to (1) extend the task, (2) refine the task, or (3) apply the task (Rink, 1985).

Extending the Task. You may decide that even though the children are on-task (doing what you asked), the task isn't appropriate for them. If, for example, you observe that most of the children can do the task easily (100 percent success rate), you'll want to make the task more difficult; if the task is too hard (50 percent success rate), you'll want to make the task easier. In the movement concept chapters (12 to 14) and the skill theme chapters (15 to 25), a solid box (■) signifies the extension of a task (see Figure 9-1).

Refining the Task. If the children seem to find the difficulty of the task challenging yet manageable (about an 80 percent success rate), you'll want to refine the task, which involves focusing on how the movement is being done, the quality of the movement. This is one of the most valuable functions a teacher can perform to help children improve their skills as movers. In the movement concept and

Figure 9-1 This task from Chapter 21 illustrates the format of the activities in Parts Three and Four. The solid box indicates the extension of the task; the open boxes indicate refinements to the task.

Kicking a Stationary Ball from a Stationary Position

Place the balls for kicking approximately ten feet from the wall around the gymnasium.

Stand behind a "kicking" ball. Use your instep (shoelaces) to kick the ball to the wall. Kick it hard!

- □ Contact the ball below the center so it travels forward at a low level.
- □ Kick hard so the ball hits the wall with enough force to rebound back to you.
- □ Place your nonkicking leg alongside (not behind) the ball.
- □ Center your weight over your nonkicking leg for good balance.

Place a series of two-inch colored tape markers on the walls of the gym, approximately three feet above the floor.

- ■ Kick the ball so it contacts the wall below the tape line. (*Teacher or child demonstrates.*)
- □ Practice kicking with both your right and your left foot until you can kick three times in a row with each foot.

Figure 9-2 Illustration from Key Observation Points: Kicking in the Air (Chapter 21). "Is the child's kicking foot extended for contact on the shoelaces, not on the toes?"

skill theme chapters, an open box (□) identifies task refinements (see Figure 9-1).

Task refinements focus your attention on the quality of the children's movement. Each open box (as shown in Figure 9-1, which is an activity in Chapter 21, "Kicking and Punting") is a cue for observation. Record this cue on your lesson planning form (Figure 5-2, p. 58) in the "observation cues" column, and be sure to watch for the designated action as you proceed through the task.

Chapters 15, 17, 18, 21, 22, 24, and 25 have Key Observation Points that will help you become a better observer. Before you teach a lesson from one of those chapters, you'll want to refer to the Key Observation Points drawings to help determine what you'll be looking for. Figure 9-2 is a portion of one of the Key Observation Points sequences in Chapter 21.

An example of how the illustrations of correct and incorrect performances in the Key Observation Points are used for task refinement is helpful here. We'll use an illustration from Chapter 22, "Throwing and Catching."

Let's say that for this lesson you've decided that your second-graders need practice throwing overhand. You select a series of tasks from Chapter 22 that will help them become better throwers. You also decide that your major focus for the lesson will be the use of opposition, i.e., the children step with the foot opposite their throwing hand. Figure 9-3 (taken from one of the Key Observation Points in Chapter 22) is a guide so that you know specifically what to look for. Once you've defined the task ("Throw the ball as hard as you can against the wall. Remember to step with the foot on the other side of your body from your throwing arm."), observe to see which children are using opposition and which ones aren't. If you observe that

Figure 9-3 Illustration from Key Observation Points: Throwing (Chapter 22). "Does the child take a forward step on the foot opposite the throwing arm?"

It's easy to confuse success at a task with the way the task is being performed (the quality of the movement). Refinement (improving the quality of the movement) is constantly necessary, even for children at the proficiency level. If you watch a professional team at practice, you see a great deal of refinement even for these excellent players. Success is there, but the quality of the performance (the way the skill is performed) needs constant and consistent refinement. If this is true for the best athletes in the world, it is certainly true for our children.

most of the children aren't using opposition, stop the class and remind them to use opposition (or remind children individually). You may also demonstrate the correct performance yourself, or pick several children who are using opposition as models. Then the children can return to their practice.

Refinement continues until the children are using opposition. The decision as to whether to

Recently I observed a teacher attempting to teach a child how to run and kick a stationary ball. The child was unable to adjust her run to enable her to arrive at the ball in a proper kicking position. After each unsuccessful attempt (the ball was barely moving as the child appeared almost to step on the ball rather than kick it), the teacher would say to the child, "No, that's not it!" The child knew she had failed as she watched the ball erratically dribble away from her foot, and yet the teacher offered no prescription for improvement. Rather than giving a student a statement of results they can readily observe, the successful instructor offers a prescription for practice, i.e., refinement.

refine or extend, however, can be made only through effective observation, which is why we recommend focusing on just one aspect of a movement at a time, rather than trying to focus on all the Key Observation Points that are pictured.

Applying the Task. The third decision, applying a task, is based on the teacher's observation, for example, that the children are now beginning to use opposition but they need more practice with it. Application means that the children are asked to compete against a set standard or time, a prior performance, or another child. Using the throwing example in Figure 9-3, it's clear that second-graders who are just learning to use opposition aren't ready to play a competitive game requiring the overhand throw. Therefore the teacher selects the following application task: "Continue throwing hard against the wall. Every time the ball reaches the wall on a fly, take one step backward. See how far from the wall you can get. When the ball doesn't reach the wall on a fly, take one step forward."

Application also involves using the movement in a more complex environment. This is challenging to the children and worthwhile practice as well. Children at the utilization level in throwing, for example, need and want to throw against an opponent to a partner who is running. When the teacher turns a task like this into a game, the task application decision has been made. Again, this is based on the teacher's observation, to determine when children are ready for these kinds of tasks.

Individual Movement Patterns

Teaching children individually is something we try to do as teachers. Obviously, however, it's not an easy job. Chapter 4 described two approaches to working with individuals: teaching by invitation and intratask variation. Use of these approaches involves the ability to observe individuals and yet maintain the focus on the entire class. This may sound easy; it isn't.

We encourage teachers to focus initially on the entire class using a technique called scanning

The first time I taught the whole class [twenty-six children] I had a great deal of trouble seeing individuals in the class. All I saw, no matter how hard I tried, was a mass of individuals. I couldn't see individual performances.

Fran McGillan [as a junior in college, the first time he taught an entire class of twenty-six children]

(described in a later section). By working with individuals too early (intratask variation), the teacher may lose focus on the entire class. We've seen this happen frequently with beginning teachers. The teacher becomes so involved helping an individual child that she loses focus on the entire class; suddenly she looks up and finds a number of children are off-task or that an unsafe condition has developed. This is *not* to suggest that teachers don't work with children individually—we certainly do. But teachers must make sure that they don't become so involved with one child that they forget to concentrate on the whole class. As Locke's vignette suggests, this is a real challenge.

When we work with individuals, essentially we use the same process as for the entire class. We extend, refine, or apply the task (intratask var-

iation); we vary the task for different children. If you ever have an opportunity to watch a master teacher, you'll see that she's constantly using intratask variation as she travels from child to child, extending the task for some, refining the task for others, while simultaneously remaining conscious of the entire class, their safety, and their on-task behavior. Now you can better understand why it's so important to spend time establishing a learning environment at the beginning of the year.

COMBINING OBSERVATION ASPECTS

Our description of the four aspects of the lesson—safety, on-task behavior, class movement patterns, and individual movement patterns—was rather easy to follow. When teaching, however, a teacher is rarely able to focus on any one aspect at a time. As suggested in Locke's vignette, the teacher must virtually concentrate simultaneously on the four aspects. Figure 9-4 is a schematic overview of the four major questions that we ask ourselves when we teach. Note that the arrows between the questions go both ways, indicating that the observational focus isn't linear but that there's a constant interplay between the questions.

Figure 9-4 Questions used to guide observation for reflective teaching.

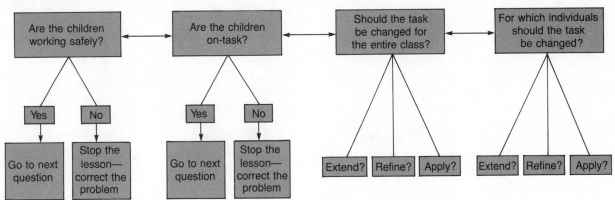

OBSERVATION TECHNIQUES

In addition to knowing the right questions to ask, other tips will also help you learn to be a better observer. The two observation techniques we've found helpful seem simple, but it has been our experience that many teachers are unaware of them. The techniques are *back to the wall* and *scanning*.

Back to the Wall

To determine whether the class is functioning appropriately, a teacher must be in a position to observe the entire class. This position is called back to the wall. The teacher is on the outside of the area in which the children are working, so that

Be gentle with yourself. Don't be disappointed initially if, in the relative tranquility after you've finished teaching, you find that you made some apparently obvious errors. Observation appears easy to the spectator, but the complexity of teaching and observing movement can be fully appreciated only when one assumes the role of the teacher. In time and with practice, you'll become increasingly satisfied with your ability to observe and analyze movement.

she or he can see the entire class. When a teacher enters the middle of an instructional area, he or she is unable to see part of the class (Figure 9-5).

Figure 9-5 Teacher's ineffective position for observation.

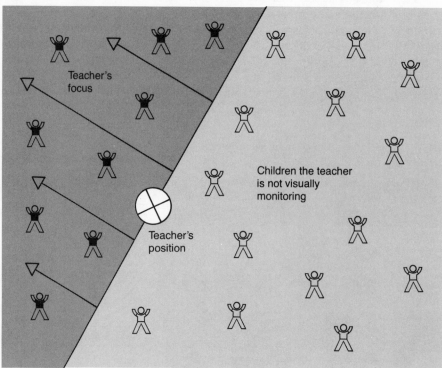

The back-to-the-wall technique allows the teacher to view all children simultaneously.

The ability to observe all that is going on, particularly with classes that are difficult to manage, is important for both effective classroom management and comprehensive observation. When a teacher is sure that a class is capable of working without constant monitoring, he or she can ignore the back to the wall technique, except when using it to observe the whole class.

Remember, though, that the teacher who is in a position to observe an entire class isn't necessarily observing effectively. It's not unusual for a teacher to become so focused on the movement or behavior of a particular individual or group that she or he becomes oblivious to other children within the class.

Scanning

The teacher who wants to observe the class as a whole can maintain an appropriate focus by scanning (Siedentop, 1983). Using a left-to-right sweep, the teacher can glance at an entire class in just a few seconds and accurately assess how all the children are working. For example, if you want to determine the number of children who are actively practicing a given movement, you could quickly observe the class from left to right, counting as you scan. By comparing the number practicing a particular movement with the total number of children in the class, you can rapidly (in no more than fifteen seconds) assess the way the class is working. This observation technique can be used for obtaining information about the appropriateness of the movement, the behavior of an entire class, or the behavior of individuals within the class.

When using both techniques, the focus should be on the four observation aspects described. The teacher is constantly asking the four questions illustrated in Figure 9-4. When we're standing with our back to the wall, scanning the class, a fifth question is also helpful: "How would this lesson appear to someone who just walked over to observe?" For example, we think of the principal, a parent, one of our college professors. Sometimes our answer to this question is surprising. Some lessons look better than we feel they are going; others look worse when viewed from an outsider's perspective. True, we're not teaching to please others, but considering how others would view the lesson helps provide some insights.

SUMMARY

Observing—the ability to see with understanding—is a crucial skill the reflective teacher should learn. One critical aspect of accurate and successful observation is planning ahead of time. By planning ahead, a teacher knows what he or she will be looking for in regards to the lesson's objectives. The key points for observation, called observation cues, are: safety, on-task behavior, class movement patterns, and individual movement patterns; the four cues are interrelated.

Task extension, task refinement, and task application are also part of the observation process. Also part of the process of observing effectively is analysis of success rate, to determine whether or not to change the task the children are working on. Successful observers use the two techniques of remaining on the periphery of the class (back to the wall) and scanning (periodically checking to see what the entire class is doing).

READING COMPREHENSION QUESTIONS

1. In reflective teaching, what is the purpose of observation?
2. Why is observation in physical education so difficult?
3. In your own words, explain the key observation points that a reflective teacher watches for regarding safety.
4. What does off-task behavior look like? Give three examples.
5. Distinguish among extending, refining, and applying a task. Explain how the solid boxes (■) and open boxes (□) are used in Chapters 12 to 25.
6. Using a chapter other than 21 or 22, locate a page with Key Observation Points. Explain how you would use the illustrations in the Points to refine a task. You'll need to state the task and then how you'd refine it, based on the illustrations.
7. Why was Figure 9-4 included in this chapter?
8. Describe how you would use the scanning and back-to-the-wall techniques in your teaching.

REFERENCES

Barrett, K. R. (1977). We see so much but perceive so little: Why? *Proceedings: 1977 National Conference of the National College for Physical Education for Men and the*

National Association for Physical Education of College Women. Chicago: Office of Publications Services, University of Illinois.

Barrett, K. R. (1979, January). Observation for teaching and coaching. *Journal of Physical Education and Recreation,* 23–25.

Barrett, K. R. (1983). A hypothetical model of observing as a teaching skill. *Journal of Teaching in Physical Education, 3*(1), 22–31.

Hoffman, S. J. (1977). Toward a pedagogical kinesiology [Monograph 28]. *Quest,* 38–48.

Locke, L. F. (1975, Spring). The ecology of the gymnasium: What the tourist never sees. *Southern Association of Physical Education for College Women Proceedings.*

Mauldon, E., & Layson, J. (1965). *Teaching gymnastics.* London: MacDonald & Evans.

Rink, J. (1985). *Teaching physical education for learning.* St. Louis: Mosby.

Siedentop, D. (1983). *Developing teaching skills in physical education* (2nd ed.). Palo Alto, CA: Mayfield.

Evaluating Student Progress

In light of the influence of self-concept on academic achievement, it would seem like a good idea for teachers to follow the precept I saw printed on an automobile dragstrip racing program: Every effort is made to insure that each entry has a reasonable chance of victory.

William Purkey

It's naive to assume that children who attend physical education class regularly are learning to move efficiently and effectively. They may be. But the only way to be certain is to use an evaluation instrument designed to assess improvement in children's movement abilities.

Evaluation is also a direct way for teachers to assess their effectiveness. If the children are learning what the teacher intends them to learn, then the instructor has some assurance that he or she has been successful. But if the children show little or no improvement, then the teacher has reason to question his or her effectiveness.

As physical educators, we're concerned with not only the children's physical development but also their attitudes about physical education and themselves as movers. Evaluation provides information about our success in both the affective and motor domains.

SUMMATIVE AND FORMATIVE EVALUATION

Evaluation can be divided into two types: summative and formative. *Summative evaluation* (McGee, 1977; Safrit, 1973) is generally performed as a culminating activity after a unit or series of lessons to indicate a student's ability when she or he has completed the study of a particular skill. In comparison, *formative evaluation* is frequent, even daily, assessment of a child's abilities, knowledge, or attitudes. The teacher incorporates this information into lessons that give the child appropriate experiences. McGee (1977) illustrated the differences between formative and summative evaluation with the following questions:

Summative	*Formative*
How far can Terry jump?	How many times can Terry jump?
	Does Terry have enough body control to jump long and short distances?
	What can Terry do to improve his body control?
What is Terry's fitness percentile?	Does Terry have enough strength and endurance to keep moving in the lesson?
	What can Terry do to improve his stamina?
Did Terry learn to jump?	How can Terry use his body in a lot of jumping patterns?
	What can Terry do to get more arm movement into the jump?

Summative evaluation is analogous to taking a trip and finding out, after arriving at what you think is your intended destination, that you took a wrong turn and really aren't where you intended to be. Formative evaluation is a road map, providing information during the trip through physical education so that changes and corrections can be made along the way. And this is an important aspect of evaluation: Evaluation is used to determine not only how much or how well students have learned, but also what areas should be emphasized in the curriculum.

The current philosophy of elementary physical education programs stresses the concepts of alternatives, choices, flexibility, variety, versatility, and other such words that refute the concept of only-one-acceptable-way to do a task. While earlier a teacher may have been primarily interested in how far a child could jump, now that teacher is interested in the variety of ways the child can jump with good body control. This change in philosophic position, which has changed the methodology and content emphases of physical education in the elementary schools, has likewise changed the role of evaluation. Both product and process evaluation continue to be needed, but the emphasis has changed from a product to a process orientation. The teacher-centered program was generally product oriented using summative evaluation. The current student-centered program is process oriented stressing formative evaluation. Consequently, the growth process in developing movement patterns is more essential than the final product measure.

Rosemary McGee,
Evaluation of Processes and Products

EVALUATION SYSTEMS

Many physical education teachers have developed their own evaluation system. Such a system also serves as a report to parents. This practice saves the teacher considerable time and provides a guide for evaluating both the children's progress and the success of the physical education program itself. Some teachers also keep tape recorders nearby when they're teaching. By making brief comments into the tape recorder, at the end of a class for example, the teacher can remember progress an

A tape recorder is a quick, convenient way to record observations.

individual child made and record it on the appropriate form later in the day.

The three evaluation systems discussed in this chapter were developed by Karyn Hartinger, an elementary school physical education specialist in Portland, Oregon; Angela McCormick, a teacher at Heathwood Hall Episcopal School in Columbia, South Carolina; and Tom Ratliffe, an assistant professor at the University of Massachusetts. Each teacher adapted the system to suit individual needs; all three persons used the concept of reflective teaching to develop their evaluation system. In each

system, evaluation is designed to be formative and ongoing, serving as a guide for the teacher rather than being something done once a year in the last few weeks of school.

Hartinger System

Karyn Hartinger developed her system as a practical and realistic way of following or tracking the progress of several hundred children over a period of several years. She used the movement concept and skill theme chapters to outline the important areas she wanted her children to learn throughout elementary school (Figure 10-1). She then arranged with her school district to print these forms on carbon-backed paper so that there are five copies.

The first year, Hartinger writes the name of each child on an individual form. That year she assesses the progress of each child, checks the appropriate lines, then tears off the top page for the parents. She keeps the five copies (carbons), which give her an automatic record. The second year, when she gets ready to assess the child's progress, she simply writes in the date for that year on the carbon copies, checks the new lines on which the child has made satisfactory progress, and sends the top carbon to the parent. For years three through five, the parents receive the top carbon. A child who attends Atkinson School, where Karyn teaches, thus receives a report during each of their five years at the school.

Another advantage of the Hartinger system is that it gives the teacher a practical approach to evaluating the curriculum. Each year the teacher will have to focus on the skills and concepts included on the progress report if the child is expected to make progress. This has a subtle advantage of keeping a teacher on-task regarding a curriculum's scope and sequence.

McCormick System

The system Angela McCormick developed also includes a report to parents. McCormick, however,

Physical Education Skill Sheet

1 - 5th Grades

Name _____   Dates _____

The skills listed below should be accomplished by the time your child has completed the fifth grade. (A check ✓ in front of the skill shows the student is proficient in that task.) This sheet will be following your child through grades 1 - 5.

MOVEMENT CONCEPTS

____ Quick starts/stops on signal
____ Understands **general space**
____ Understands **self-space**
____ Moving in different **directions**
____ Knows **right/left**
____ Change direction quickly
____ Moving at 3 different **levels**
____ Travel different **pathways**
____ Repeat specific **pathways**
____ Moving at different **rates**

TRAVELING

____ Crawling
____ Walking
____ Running
____ Skipping
____ Sliding
____ Galloping

JUMPING

____ Two feet to two feet
____ Hop
____ Leap
____ One foot to two feet
____ Run and jump
____ Distance
____ Height
____ Rhythmic jumping
____ long rope
____ short rope
____ Over obstacles
____ Jump and turn
____ Control / soft landing

ROLLING

____ Log roll
____ Forward roll
____ Backward roll
____ Shoulder roll

____ Variation roll
____ Jump off, land, & roll
____ Jump over, land, & roll
____ Dive roll

BALANCING

____ One leg
____ Different body shapes
____ Tripod
____ Bridge
____ Walk on low beam
____ Walk on high beam
____ Variety of stunts on beam
____ Small base of support
____ Pushing
____ Pulling
____ Lifting
____ Climbing rope (1/3 up)
____ Climbing rope (2/3 up)
____ (Option) (top)
____ Cartwheel
____ Roundoff

KICKING

____ Stationary ball on the run
____ Ball rolled by someone
____ Distance
____ Dribbling the ball
____ Dribbling around obstacles
____ Kicking at a target
____ Passing to a partner
____ Use variety parts of the foot
____ Accuracy
____ Moving target
____ Accuracy while traveling
____ One-to-one situation
____ Volleying to self
____ Kick to a target against a defense
____ Gamelike situation

THROWING

____ Body mechanics
____ To self
____ To wall
____ Stepping w/opposite foot
____ Using more body parts to increase
     the force
____ Follow through
____ To stationary target
____ To partner
____ Accuracy while traveling
____ Accuracy to a traveling partner
____ Hit a moving target
____ Dynamic situation
____ Against an opponent
____ Without being intercepted
____ Accuracy w/consistency
____ Gamelike situation

CATCHING

____ Body mechanics
____ To self at various heights
____ Thrown by a skilled thrower
____ Bounce to self & catch
____ Catch at different levels
____ Catch in different directions
____ Catch with an implement
____ Catch wall rebound
____ Stationary partner
____ Moving with partner
____ In the air
____ Outmaneuvering defender
____ Intercept
____ Off-balance catching
____ Gamelike situation

VOLLEYING

____ Striking balloon with hand
____ Striking balloon w/other parts
____ Striking ball with hands
____ Striking ball w/other parts
____ Striking balloon w/partner
____ Striking ball w/partner
____ Striking ball to target (over)

DRIBBLING

____ Bounce ball - stationary
____ Bounce ball - moving
____ Bounce ball (eyes up)
____ Using either hand
____ Changing directions
____ Around stationary obstacles
____ Traveling - changing hands
____ Change speed of dribbling
____ Keep ball away from opponent
____ Gamelike situation

STRIKING WITH RACKETS
AND PADDLES

____ Striking a balloon (repeatedly)
____ Self-tossed ball
____ Striking a ball up/down (repeat)
____ Against the wall (repeat)
____ Over the net (repeat)
____ With a partner
____ Performing offensive/defensive
     moves
____ Gamelike situation

LONG HANDLED IMPLEMENTS

____ Striking stationary object/floor
____ Striking off a batting tee
____ Traveling - object on floor
____ Striking suspended object
____ Striking to stationary partner
____ Striking to stationary target
____ Striking a pitch ball
____ Strike self-toss ball
____ Traveling - dodging stationary
     objects
____ Traveling - dodging moving objects
____ Pass to moving partner
____ Pass & receive while moving
____ Striking for distance
____ Direct speed, distance, & pathway
     of object
____ Gamelike situation (hockey)
____ Gamelike situation (bat)

PUNTING

____ Drop ball, then punt (alternate)
____ Distance
____ Accuracy
____ Catch pass, then punt
____ Gamelike situation

MUSIC

____ Claps to a beat
____ Moves to a beat
____ Follows a specific pattern/dance
         "   (moderate difficulty)
____ Creative movement

Figure 10-1 Example of a carbon-back form used for tracking students' progress. *Source:* Developed by Karyn Hartinger, Portland, Oregon.

Heathwood Hall Episcopal School

19 **84** -19 **85**

Name: _Mary Johnson_   Grade: _3_

Homeroom Teacher: _Walker_

Subject _Physical Education_   Teacher: _McCormick_

Term	First Quarter	Second Quarter	Third Quarter	Fourth Quarter
Grade		*S+*		
Parent's Initial				

O = Outstanding   N = Needs Improvement
S = Satisfactory   U = Unsatisfactory

EXEMPLARY BEHAVIORS

	Seldom				Usually
Listens					✓
Is on-task					✓
Is eager to participate					✓
Works well with others					✓
Treats equipment with care					✓
Works safely					✓

FOUR LEVELS OF MOTOR SKILL PROFICIENCY

Precontrol — Unable to consciously control or replicate a particular movement.

Control — Responds more accurately to intentions; and particular movements can be replicated.

Utilization — Moves automatically and reflexively; can use movement in a variety of ways.

Proficiency — Has gained control of a movement and is challenged by repeating movements exactly or using movements effectively in dynamic, unpredictable situations.

(OVER)

Figure 10-2 Example of a report form that is sent to parents. *Source:* Developed by Angela McCormick, Heathwood Hall Episcopal School, Columbia, South Carolina.

MOTOR SKILL DEVELOPMENT

	Precontrol	Control	Utilization	Proficiency
running			✓	
taking weight on hands				✓
tossing and catching			✓	
throwing			✓	
kicking				✓

COMMENTS

First Quarter: _____

_____

Second Quarter _Mary works hard in class. I'd like_
to encourage Mary to practice running so that
she can increase her speed.

I will encourage her, too. Thanks - B. J.

Third Quarter _____

_____

Fourth Quarter _____

_____

Please initial and return this card in the report folder.

Figure 10-2 (continued)

includes each child's skill level for the skill themes she worked on during that reporting period (Figure 10-2). The front page of the report includes the child's name, teacher's name, and a checklist of exemplary behaviors that are important to the establishment of a positive learning environment. The front page also includes a brief description of each of the four skill levels. On the back side of the report, McCormick writes in the skill themes that have been practiced during that quarter and checks the child's appropriate skill level. That page also has a place for writing comments to the parents. At Heathwood Hall, each teacher is required to send a progress report for each child to the parents four times a year.

Ratliffe System

In contrast to the Hartinger and McCormick systems, Tom Ratliffe's system was designed for the teacher, not the parents, as a more objective way of assessing the children's progress in skill development. The names of the children in the class are listed in the left-hand column. The following rows of columns record each child's skill level on the particular tasks that are the primary focus for a particular period (Figure 10-3). The teacher observes and then records each child's progress on the checklist with the appropriate letter: PC for precontrol, C for control, U for utilization, and P for proficiency.

The Ratliffe system is also different because it includes a series of tests Ratliffe devised to determine how a child is progressing (Ratliffe, 1984). The Assessment Guides in each of the skill theme chapters can be used to measure children's progress over a period of months and years. The obvious advantage of using the same assessment task over several years is that it is a relatively objective measure of a child's progress.

As Ratliffe noted in his article, it takes time for the teacher to learn the four generic levels so that quick classifications can be made, but these are skills that a teacher can learn through practice. (This is also true for the McCormick system.) The

Class: Horton

Names	Punting 10/16/82	Punting 11/8/82	Throwing	Catching		
Joe	PC	C				
Susie	PC	C				
Tom	C	U				
Pat	C	C				
Nick	U	U				

Figure 10-3 Sample check sheet physical education teacher uses. *Source:* Developed by Tom Ratliffe, University of Massachusetts.

important point is to select a system that will suit your needs and then adapt it to make it succeed for you.

EVALUATING THE AFFECTIVE DOMAIN

There are two evaluation techniques we've found helpful for assessing children's attitude about physical activity. One is a paper and pencil test, a self-efficacy inventory. With the other technique, over a period of several days or weeks the children write in a student log their feelings about physical education.

Self-Efficacy Inventory

Self-efficacy, a term derived from Bandura's work (1977), is defined as one's perceived competence in performing a given task. Bandura maintained that a person's perception of personal competence greatly influences motivation. Information on self-efficacy is very helpful to us as we deter-

> To begin with, I've found that there is no else like me, anywhere, like snow flakes. No one else feels completely the way I do. No one else sees things in the same scope as I do. So my first discovery about myself is that I'm me.
>
> From a High School Composition

mine the focus and emphasis of our programs. One of our goals is to help children develop positive feelings of self-efficacy related to a broad range of skills and activities.

Self-efficacy is also thought to be influenced by previous mastery experiences. Lockamy (1984) developed a system to measure children's self-efficacy in relation to their motor ability. His system can be modified to provide an occasional assessment of how children are feeling about their ability to perform certain skills and tasks in a physical education program.

Lockamy asked the children ten questions related to his physical education program (Figure 10-4). Each question starts with the stem, "How do you feel about your ability to...." (You'll want to change the questions to match the activities you've been focusing on in your program.) By placing an X over one of the three faces, the child is able to tell you how she feels about her ability to do a backward roll or punt a ball, for example. It shouldn't take the children any longer than fifteen minutes to complete such a form.

Student Logs

The use of student logs (Norris, 1976) for evaluating children's feelings about physical education is a much more open-ended technique. The children are simply asked to record their feeling periodically about physical education class. As you might expect, these logs often yield fascinating insights into how children perceive physical education class (Figure 10-5). You probably won't want to use this technique with more than two classes at a time, and then only for a few weeks. The purpose is simply to gain an understanding of how individual children are feeling about physical education. We collect the logs periodically and write comments in them when appropriate.

One of the best ways to encourage the children to keep a log is to give them a college blue book. Whenever possible, encourage children to keep their logs in the classroom and to bring the logs to physical education classes periodically. Usually the students have time to write in their logs sometime during the school day. Many classroom teachers encourage the children to keep up with their logs because they believe this is good writing practice. One of the quickest ways to discourage children from writing in their logs is to correct for grammar, punctuation, and spelling.

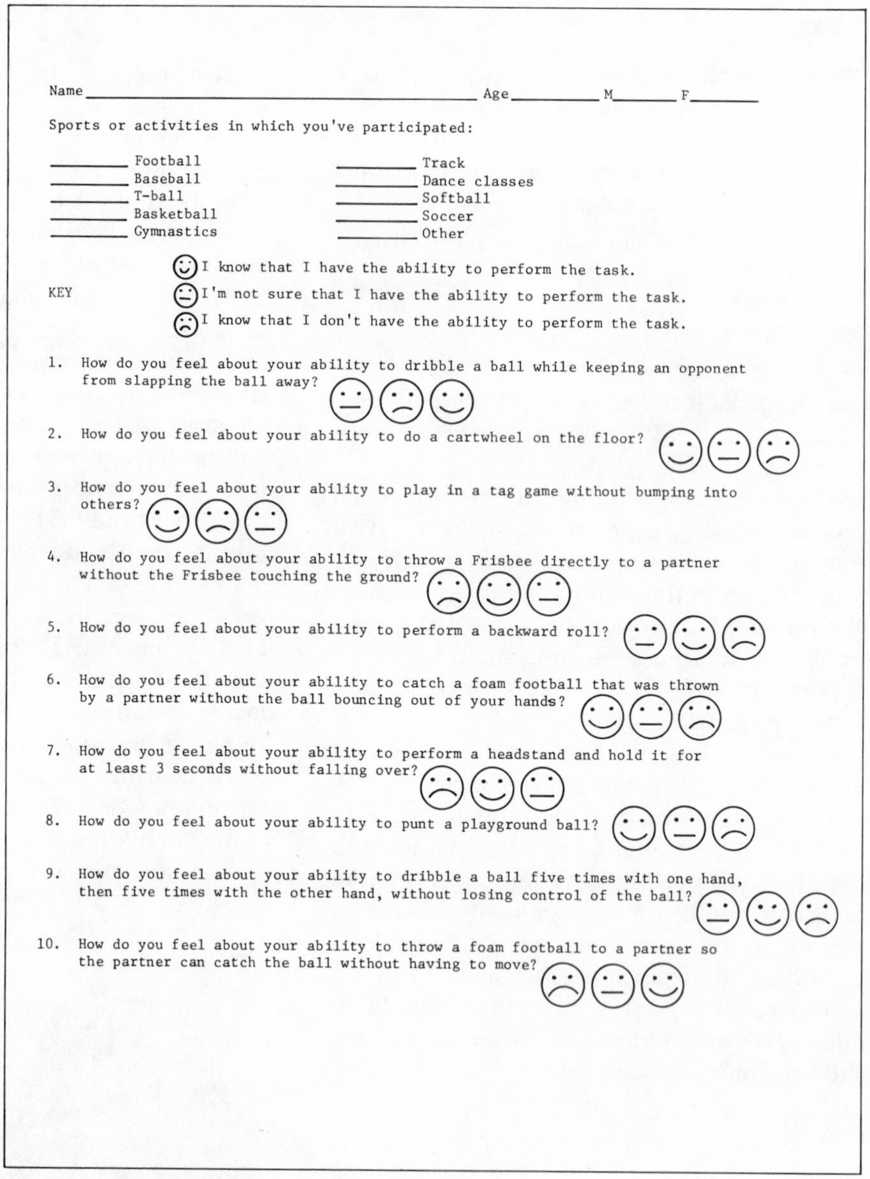

Name _____ Age _____ M _____ F _____

Sports or activities in which you've participated:

_____ Football   _____ Track
_____ Baseball   _____ Dance classes
_____ T-ball   _____ Softball
_____ Basketball   _____ Soccer
_____ Gymnastics   _____ Other

KEY   ☺ I know that I have the ability to perform the task.
       ☹ I'm not sure that I have the ability to perform the task.
       ☹ I know that I don't have the ability to perform the task.

1. How do you feel about your ability to dribble a ball while keeping an opponent from slapping the ball away?

2. How do you feel about your ability to do a cartwheel on the floor?

3. How do you feel about your ability to play in a tag game without bumping into others?

4. How do you feel about your ability to throw a Frisbee directly to a partner without the Frisbee touching the ground?

5. How do you feel about your ability to perform a backward roll?

6. How do you feel about your ability to catch a foam football that was thrown by a partner without the ball bouncing out of your hands?

7. How do you feel about your ability to perform a headstand and hold it for at least 3 seconds without falling over?

8. How do you feel about your ability to punt a playground ball?

9. How do you feel about your ability to dribble a ball five times with one hand, then five times with the other hand, without losing control of the ball?

10. How do you feel about your ability to throw a foam football to a partner so the partner can catch the ball without having to move?

Figure 10-4 Self-efficacy inventory. *Source:* From "The Relationship of Self-Efficacy to Motor Skill Level, Gender, Age and Previous Experience" by J. Lockamy, 1984, unpublished master's project, Athens: University of Georgia.

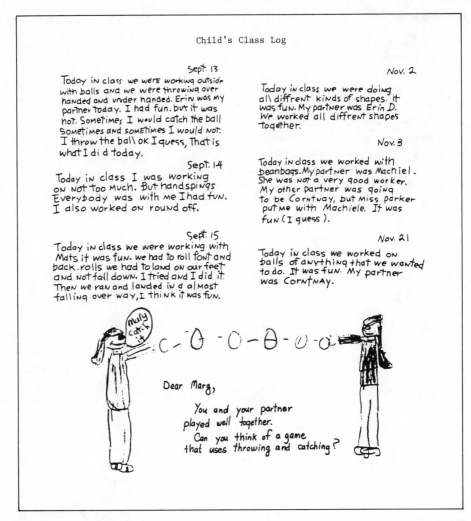

Figure 10-5 Child's class log.

This is *not* the purpose of the logs. Again, the logs are only intended to help teachers learn about children's perceptions of physical education class.

STANDARDIZED TESTS

Although we don't base grades on performances on standardized tests, we believe such tests do have a place in the physical education program.

For example, children enjoy and are challenged by comparing their current performances with their past performances on the American Alliance for Health, Physical Education, Recreation and Dance (AAHPERD) Health-Related Fitness Test (Chapter 29).

When you administer a standardized test, it's a good idea to keep the results private, rather than reading them out to each class or posting the scores on a bulletin board. If children choose to share their scores—and many do—that's up to them.

Whenever a value is set forth which can only be attained by a few, the conditions are ripe for widespread feelings of personal inadequacy. An outstanding example in American society is the fierce competitiveness of the school system. No educational system in the world has so many examinations, or so emphasizes grades, as the American school system. Children are constantly being ranked and evaluated. The superior achievement of one child tends to debase the achievement of another.

Morris Rosenberg,
Society and the Adolescent Self-Image

Our purpose, however, is not to have children compare themselves with others but to determine whether or not their efforts have resulted in improvement.

Many other instruments can be utilized to assess student progress. For those interested in obtaining additional information and practical examples of tools for evaluation, see McGee's excellent reference, "Evaluation of Processes and Products" (1984).

FINDING TIME TO CONDUCT EVALUATIONS

No instructor who teaches several hundred children each week—as many physical education instructors do—has the time needed to use all the evaluation techniques described in this chapter. But a reflective teacher is aware of these techniques and uses them with different classes for different purposes. Perhaps you'll have one class at a time keeping logs. And you may be able to send only one written report a year to parents.

Select from the various evaluative techniques those that are most appropriate; each technique provides a different type of information. For example, logs provide fascinating insights into how children are progressing in designing their own games or dances, but a checklist would be far less appropriate for that purpose. In contrast, a checklist is useful for assessing children's individual abilities in a new situation, for example, a class of kindergarten children or during a teacher's first year in a new school.

Even when you narrow down the evaluation system(s) to be used with your classes, time can still be a problem. For example, it's counterproductive to evaluate one child while the others stand in a line waiting their turn. The same is true for administering the Assessment Guides in Chapters 12 to 25. There are at least four ways to minimize the waiting time for children during evaluation.

1. Set up stations or learning centers (Chapter 6). Stay at one of the stations and conduct the evaluation for the children at that station. If you plan to do this, be certain that the children are familiar with the other stations so you can devote most of your time to conducting the assessments rather than explaining procedures at the other stations.
2. Ask the classroom teacher (or another teacher, aid, parent, high school student) to assist with the class. They can either give the evaluation while you work with the other children, or supervise most of the class while you work with a few children at a time. If the adult helping you is relatively inexperienced in physical education, you'll probably want to set up a game situation that will simply require monitoring rather than expecting the adult to actually teach.
3. Videotape the children so that you can make your judgments about skill levels and progress during your planning time or after school.
4. Use a tape recorder as you teach, and use the class list as a guide for observing each child; then make comments about the child's ability level and improvement.

SUMMARY

Evaluation is a necessary process for determining whether children are actually learning in physical education. Evaluation of student progress is also a direct way of assessing one's effectiveness as a teacher. Summative evaluation is generally performed at the end of a unit or topic of study. Formative evaluation is an ongoing process that provides guidance for future lessons while tending to minimize comparisons between children.

Instruments for evaluating a student's progress include checklists, individual records, student logs, and standardized tests. Evaluation can be used as a basis for grades, as a basis for progress reports to parents, and for discovering children's individual needs and interests. Progress reports to parents, as an alternative to a single grade, are the preferred mode of reporting student progress whenever feasible.

READING COMPREHENSION QUESTIONS

1. What is summative evaluation? Give an example.
2. What is a formative evaluation? Give an example.
3. What do the authors propose that a child be graded on? Why?
4. How can a class be organized to minimize waiting time during evaluation?
5. What is the purpose of having children keep a log? How does the log work?
6. Explain the difference between grading and evaluation.
7. Select one of the three evaluation systems (Hartinger, McCormick, or Ratliffe) and provide an argument for using that system as opposed to the other two. Imagine that you're actually teaching as you write your answer.
8. Explain why evaluation is necessary in children's physical education.

REFERENCES

Bandura, A. (1977). Self-efficacy: Toward a unifying theory of behavioral change. *Psychological Review, 84*(2), 191–215.

Lockamy, J. (1984). *The relationship of self-efficacy to motor skill level, gender, age and previous experience.* Unpublished master's project, University of Georgia, Athens.

McGee, R. (1984). Evaluation of processes and products. In B. J. Logsdon et al., *Physical education for children: A focus on the teaching process.* Philadelphia: Lea & Febiger.

Norris, G. (1976). *Perceptions of an elementary school physical education learning environment reflective of humanistic tenets as seen by participants and selected observers.* Unpublished research paper, University of North Carolina at Greensboro.

Purkey, W. (1970). *Self-concept and school achievement.* Englewood Cliffs, NJ: Prentice-Hall.

Ratliffe, T. (1984). Evaluation of students' skill using generic levels of skill proficiency. *The New Physical Educator, 41*(2), 64–68.

Rosenberg, M. (1965). *Society and the adolescent self-image.* Princeton, NJ: Princeton University Press.

Safrit, M. J. (1973). *Evaluation in physical education.* Englewood Cliffs, NJ: Prentice-Hall.

Assessing Your Teaching Performance

While it is true that a few individuals have used systematic observation for many years to analyze skill performance, most have ignored the objective route. Far too much guess work has been used. Student teachers have been angered by the high degree of subjectivity shown by supervisors; practicing teachers have complained about the prejudicial nature of their promotion evaluations; students have been frustrated in their endeavors to seek helpful means by which they can work for self-change. In general, the act of teaching has lacked scientific inquiry.

John Cheffers

To become a truly effective teacher, you must accurately and relevantly assess your teaching performance. Historically, a number of informal (and in many instances inaccurate) approaches to obtaining information about teaching have been used. For example, an assessment based on how much the students like a teacher doesn't provide much useful information about that teacher's performance, nor does a principal's evaluation based on a five-minute, once-a-year visit to the gymnasium. Some student teachers receive feedback from their supervisors that is both helpful and accurate. Few teachers, however, continue to receive throughout their teaching careers the amount and type of feedback vital to improving teaching performance. And this is unfortunate.

The notion that anyone who receives a teaching certificate is a qualified teacher is quickly becoming discredited, and it's about time. No airline would hire a novice pilot to fly an airplane with 200 passengers. No doctor would be permitted to perform a major operation alone the day after graduating from medical school. Pilots and doctors must complete extensive internships before they're assigned major responsibilities. This hasn't been true for teachers.

In most states, when a teacher is certificated (usually with only brief student teaching experience), the teacher is given complete responsibility for a class of children. The assumption is that anyone who is certificated knows how and what to teach and requires little, if any, assistance. But in teaching, as in all human activities, experience enhances proficiency. Beginning teachers can benefit from professional guidance. With appropriate assistance, they'll become better teachers sooner.

Some school districts, recognizing inexperienced teachers' need for professional guidance, employ educators who use clinical supervisory techniques (Krajewski, 1976) to work with beginning instructors. In other school districts, however, inexperienced teachers must discover for themselves how to teach and what to teach. Individuals who are trying to improve their teaching effectiveness without assistance from school district or university personnel can use self-evaluation techniques. We've divided these techniques into three categories: (1) those that can be utilized without assistance; (2) those that require student assistance; and (3) those that use peer assistance.

Regardless of who is performing the assessment, the first step in assessing your teaching performance is deciding what is important to look at and what to look at first. We stated in Chapter 7 that establishing a learning environment was a necessary but not sufficient condition for learning. Therefore, decide if a learning environment has indeed been set up. If it has, you can begin to assess some aspects of effective teaching (see Chapter 1) while occasionally rechecking how well the learning environment is being maintained. The box below is a checklist to help you decide what to look for, based on your questions about your teaching.

DETERMINING WHAT TO OBSERVE

If you're having problems with inappropriate behavior, select one or more of the following to do:

1. Look at your plans for potential breakdowns.
2. Transcribe all your instructions to the class and check for clarity. Did you know what was supposed to happen?
3. Tape your lesson for analysis of general time usage. Was there an extreme amount of management time? Waiting time?
4. Record your feedback. Was inappropriate behavior handled promptly and consistently, or did you nag often?

To check the atmosphere of your class, do one or more of the following:

1. Tally your feedback.
2. Check for differential treatment of students.
3. Check student interaction patterns.

To assess the instructional environment, select from the following:

1. Check your task development.
2. Assess each student's practice opportunities.
3. Check the general use of class time.
4. Tally feedback with specific attention to skill feedback.

UNASSISTED ASSESSMENT

You can learn much about your teaching without relying on others for observation, interpretation, or analysis. You can learn, for example, the amount of time you spend actually talking to the entire class or to individuals within a class. You can discover which children receive most of your attention and whether you spend more time discussing their movement or their behavior. How do children react to your teaching performance? How, and how often, do you use positive or negative comments? How much time do the children spend getting out or putting away equipment? You can answer these and other key questions with self-assessment techniques.

Tape-Recorded Self-Analysis

One of the simplest techniques for analyzing teaching performance is to tape-record verbal interactions and instruction. If you strap a portable cassette tape recorder around your waist, you'll be able to record both interactions with individual children and instructions to the entire class. The children quickly become accustomed to seeing the tape recorder, and before long they forget about it. By taping different classes, you can obtain answers to such important questions as:

What percentage of a lesson did I spend talking to the entire class? To groups? To individuals?

Are my verbal comments clear? Do I repeat myself frequently?

What percentage of my comments to the children are positive? Negative? Neutral? Do I nag children?

Do I interact with many children in a class? Or do I focus on just a few, constantly calling their names?

How do I develop content?

These and many other questions can be answered by making tape recordings. Finding the answers involves defining what you want to assess, listening to the tape, tallying the number of times each behavior occurs or recording the length of time something occurs, and then determining percentages.

For example, you easily determine the percentage of positive, negative, general, or nagging comments you made to children by using a feedback checklist (Figure 11-1), which records two broad categories of feedback: skill and behavior. Skill feedback relates to the movement aspect of the class; behavior feedback relates to the conduct of the students in the class.

Skill feedback is subdivided into positive or corrective aspects. An example of positive feedback is, "Susie, that was a good serve"; an example of corrective is, "Susie, next time try to throw the ball a little higher." Corrective feedback always contains a statement about how to improve a skill.

Behavior feedback is subdivided into positive and negative categories. Positive behavior feedback refers to affirmative comments made regarding someone's behavior, such as, "Tom, I like the way you stopped and listened so quickly." Negative behavior feedback includes disapproving comments about behavior. "Sarah, you know better than that" is negative behavior feedback.

As you listen to your tape, tally each feedback statement you hear into one of the categories in Figure 11-1. After you've tallied all your feedback comments, total the number of comments in each column.

Another useful type of information from tape-recorded analysis is how to develop content when you teach. As described in Chapters 2 and 9, the three categories of task or content development are extension, refinement, and application. Extension tasks involve changing the complexity of a task by making it more complex or less complex. Examples are being asked to bounce a ball in self-space or being asked to bounce a ball while traveling in general space.

Refinement tasks deal with the qualitative

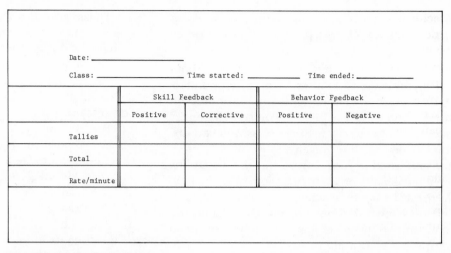

Figure 11-1 Feedback checklist.

aspects of a skill, such as asking the students to bounce a ball without looking at it or to bounce the ball using their fingertips. A refinement task always seeks to improve the quality of student performance. Application tasks take the student focus

Figure 11-2 Graph for determining content development.

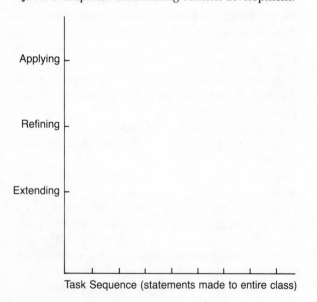

off of how to do the movement and shift it to how to use the movement. This is most often seen in either self-testing or competitive experiences.

Figure 11-2 is a graph for determining how content is developed in a lesson. Before using this chart, listen to your tape and write down, in order, every task presented during the class session. Then categorize each task as extending, refining, or application. (For this project, record only tasks given to the entire class, not feedback suggestions given to individual students.)

After you've labeled the tasks, plot them on your graph in the order in which they occurred. Once you've finished, you'll have a picture of how you developed content in your lesson. In most instances you'll be working toward extension tasks followed by several refining tasks, although this pattern will vary, depending upon the purpose of the lesson, student ability, etc. Application typically follows refinement, although this will vary as well.

Feedback and content are only two examples of data you can collect from a tape recording of your teaching. For most of the questions you want to ask about your teaching, you can develop similar, uncomplicated systems that will give you the specific information you want to know. The secret to developing such systems is to define the behavior (what you want to observe or listen to) very precisely so that you can tell when it does and doesn't happen. It doesn't help very much to say, "I want to find out if I was clear or not when I talked to students"; you need to define what "clear" means to you. It could mean that students didn't have to ask you questions about how to do a task after you gave the task; it could mean that you didn't mumble and slur your words when you gave a task; or it could mean that you didn't have to turn the tape recorder up to 9 to be able to hear yourself. Whatever it is, define it and then try to assess it by listening to your tape.

Once you've obtained baseline data about your teaching performance, you can measure improvement over a period of weeks or months. You may find it challenging to set teaching goals for yourself: "During this class I want to interact at least once with every child in the class," or "During this class I want to make at least 80 percent of my comments positive." When you listen to a tape after a class, you'll learn whether you've achieved your goal.

Written Instruments

A written instrument, completed by the children, can provide information about your teaching. The children can circle appropriate faces (Figure 11-3) to indicate their responses (Cheffers, Mancini, & Zaichowsky, 1976; McGee, 1984). You can hand out answer sheets and then read the questions to the whole class. When you read the questions to the entire class, you minimize reliance on children's ability to read.

Be careful in interpreting the results of such an instrument, and remember that it is only one of many techniques that can be used to obtain information about your teaching performance. Judiciously employed, however, such an instrument can provide valuable insights about the children's reaction to your teaching.

STUDENT-ASSISTED ASSESSMENT

Mature, responsible students can help you assess your teaching performance by using techniques that they can learn in just a few minutes. Such instruments will provide information that cannot be obtained by the unassisted techniques.

Teacher Pathway

Give the student a sketch of the teaching area— the gym or playground. Have the student trace the pathway that you make during the lesson. This is especially helpful when you're learning to increase your effectiveness as an observer (Chapter 9). You can also teach the student to make a mark on the pathway each time you interact individually with a child.

Interaction Patterns

It's important to interact, verbally or nonverbally, with each child during each lesson. An interaction checklist (Figure 11-4) can be used to obtain infor-

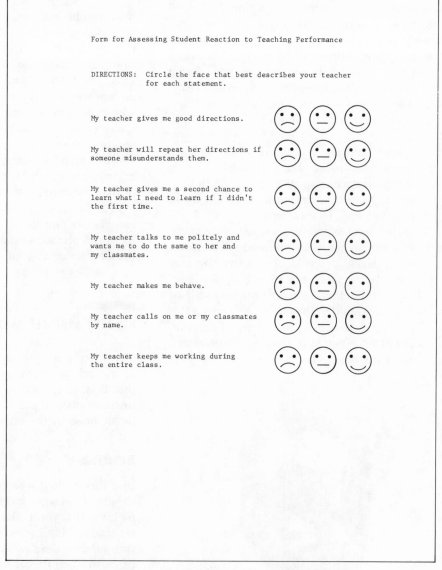

Form for Assessing Student Reaction to Teaching Performance

DIRECTIONS: Circle the face that best describes your teacher
             for each statement.

My teacher gives me good directions.

My teacher will repeat her directions if
someone misunderstands them.

My teacher gives me a second chance to
learn what I need to learn if I didn't
the first time.

My teacher talks to me politely and
wants me to do the same to her and
my classmates.

My teacher makes me behave.

My teacher calls on me or my classmates
by name.

My teacher keeps me working during
the entire class.

Figure 11-3 Form for assessing student reaction to
teaching performance.

mation about your patterns of interaction with an entire class.

Select a student who knows the names of all the children in the class. Give that student a checklist form on which you've listed the names of the entire class. Ask the student to make a tally, in the appropriate column, across from the name of each child you talk to, touch, or smile at during one class period. At the conclusion of the lesson, you can use the completed checklist to analyze your teaching pattern.

You may also find interesting information in

Interaction Checklist Form

CHILDREN'S NAMES	TYPES OF INTERACTION		
	TALKED TO	SMILED AT	TOUCHED
NICK	II		I
TOM	III	I	
ANNA	III	I	
KEN	I	I	I
MELINDA			
LAURA		I	
HAL	II		I
MEGAN		I	
KELLY	I		
PATRICK	I		I
JEANNETTE	I	II	
JOSH			
BENJIE		I	

Figure 11-4 Interaction checklist form.

an analysis of the gender and race of the children you interact with. If you're unintentionally favoring one group over another, you should be aware of that.

Another type of analysis enables the teacher to determine whether there's a disparity in his or her interactions with different children. Is the teacher interacting more with the most skilled children than with the least skilled ones? Or do the interaction patterns indicate some other distribution of attention? Again, the teacher uses the information on an interaction checklist that a stu-

DATE _____

Teacher _____   Observer _____

Theme of Lesson _____

OBSERVATIONAL DATA

Names of Children	Practice Opportunities			
	ROLL	CATCH	KICK	THROW

Figure 11-5 Practice opportunity checklist.

dent has filled in. The teacher selects the students who've been observed to be the most skilled and the least skilled—each group should include about 25 percent of the class. From an analysis of the interactions with each group and a comparison of these two interaction patterns, the teacher can determine the group to which he or she is devoting more time.

Practice Opportunities

Effective teachers give children plenty of practice opportunities. One way to indirectly assess the

Students can be trained to collect data on teaching performance.

number of practice opportunities students are getting in a class is to teach a student helper to observe and record the number of practices for selected students (Figure 11-5). You may want to select the children to be observed, or the student helper, if qualified, can select two or more children to observe. This technique works best when the lesson focuses on easily observed movements, such as rolls, catches, or kicks, that can be written on the form before the lesson.

DATE _FEBRUARY 12_

Teacher _LINDA KOBEL_   Observer _JUDY MITCHELL_

Theme of Lesson _KICKING AND CATCHING_

OBSERVATIONAL DATA

Names of Children	Practice Opportunities KICKS	CATCHES	Teacher Feedback MOVEMENT POSITIVE	NEGATIVE	BEHAVIOR POSITIVE	NEGATIVE
MARK	THL THL IIII	THL IIII	II	I	II	
VIRGINIA	THL II	III	IIII		II	
TODD	THL THL THL THL	THL THL THL III	III		I	I
JEFF	I THL THL	THL THL		THL	I	III
SUSIE	THL THL THL III	THL THL II	III	I	II	I

Figure 11-6 Practice opportunities and teacher feedback checklist.

PEER-ASSISTED ASSESSMENT

Some children could learn to use the data-gathering systems described below, but it's more realistic to seek the help of a colleague who's willing to help you assess your teaching performance. Such an arrangement can be mutually beneficial since the systems described in this section can be easily adapted for use in a classroom setting. Thus, if there's only one physical education specialist in the school, a classroom teacher could work as peer assistant, with the specialist.

Feedback and Practice Opportunity Checklist

This system goes a bit further than the practice opportunity checklist and the feedback checklist described in the previous sections. Using the form shown in Figure 11-6, a colleague selects several children, without your knowledge, and records their practice opportunities. She also codes feedback statements you make to the students being observed. Each statement is coded as related to the child's movement or behavior, and each statement is coded as positive or negative when possible—that is, if the statement is clearly positive or negative. Neutral statements are not recorded under the behavior heading.

The statement "Nice catch, Virginia" would be coded on the checklist as Movement, Positive. The statement "Jeff, you never listen!" would be coded as Behavior, Negative. This observation system is relatively simple to learn and can be used reliably after just a few minutes of practice.

Duration Recording System

Duration recording, which is a bit more difficult to use than the teacher feedback checklist, indirectly assesses teacher performance by measuring what the students are doing (Siedentop, 1983). This system includes four categories of student behavior: (1) instruction time, (2) management time, (3) activity time, and (4) waiting time. The total amount of time, in minutes and seconds, is determined for each of the four categories. These minutes and seconds can then be converted into percentages that permit comparisons with previously coded lessons.

The duration recording system form (see Figure 11-7) contains three time bars, each bar representing ten minutes and organized by ten-second segments. The form lists the code the peer assistant should use to report what is happening:

I for instruction; M for management; A for activity; and W for waiting time.

The peer assistant records the exact time the lesson begins—the time at which the teacher gives a starting signal or the children begin to practice one or more activities. From that moment until the end of the lesson, the peer assistant, using a watch with a second hand, marks the time bars to reflect what is happening in the class. The assistant draws a line through the bar when there is a change in student behavior and indicates the change by writing the appropriate letter over the next space in the bar. At the end of the lesson, the time is recorded. The peer assistant uses the definitions and examples in Table 11-1 as guides to accurate coding.

After the lesson, the teacher uses the information on the duration recording system form to figure out what percentage of class time was spent in each category. The following procedure should be used: Add up the time for each of the four categories. Divide each category total by the total lesson time, and then multiply each by 100. The calculations at the bottom of Figure 11-7 illustrate how the percentages for that sample lesson were determined.

In the beginning, the peer assistant may be uncertain about how to code a particular event. This is not uncommon when one is learning to use any type of analysis system. The assistant should make a decision and then code other such events the same way. That will enable you to compare a succession of lessons to determine what progress you're making.

COMBINING ASSESSMENT TECHNIQUES

Many observation systems have been developed to analyze the teaching performance of physical education teachers (Darst, Mancini, & Zakrajsek, 1983; Rink, 1983; Siedentop, 1983). As you become accustomed to using different systems, you can begin to code additional teacher or student behav-

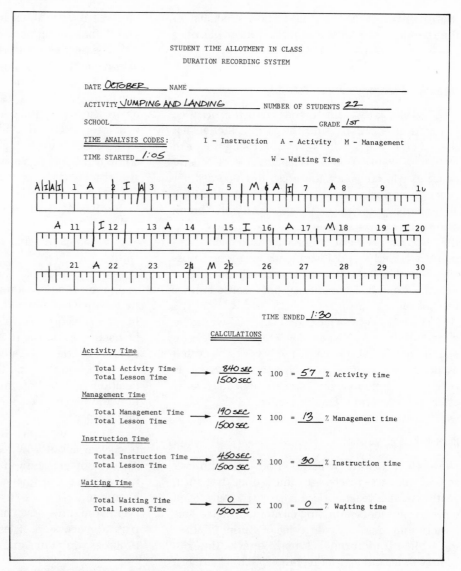

Figure 11-7 Student time allotment in class duration recording system. *Source*: Adapted from an instrument developed by the Physical Education Department, Ohio State University.

ior simultaneously—for example, how many students are off-task at a particular moment or how many positive and negative feedback statements the teacher makes. Remember that what is measured or how it is measured is less important than the continuing effort to systematically assess and improve your teaching performance. Relying on your subjective judgment ("I think I'm getting better") or that of a colleague ("That lesson looked good") is not nearly as effective as collecting and

TABLE 11-1 / Duration Recording System Coding Guide

Category	Definition	Examples
Instruction	Time when students have an opportunity to learn. They may be receiving verbal or nonverbal information. Most students (51 percent or more) are *not* engaged in physical activity.	Listening to a lecture, watching the teacher or another student demonstrate a skill, participating in a class discussion, answering teacher's questions
Management	Time when the opportunity to learn is *not* present. Most students (51 percent or more) are involved in activities only indirectly related to class learning activity. There is no instruction, demonstration, or practice.	Changing activities, numbering off for an activity, listening for roll call, getting out or putting away equipment, getting into line
Activity	Time when most students (51 percent or more) are involved in physical movement consistent with the specific goals of the particular lesson.	Performing exercises; designing a game, dance, or gymnastic sequence; participating in a group or individual game; providing assistance for a partner; waiting in line for a turn
Waiting	Time not defined by the other three categories.	Waiting for class to begin, or waiting for instruction to resume when it has been interrupted by another teacher, student messenger, parent, principal, or public address system

Source: Adapted from an instrument developed by the Physical Education Department, Ohio State University, Columbus, Ohio.

Instructional time is recorded when the opportunity to learn is present but the students aren't active.

Waiting time can be the time when students are waiting for class to begin.

Activity time is recorded when the children are involved in movement that is consistent with the teacher's goals.

analyzing relatively objective data that you can refer back to in a few days, months, or even years.

BEING OBSERVED

Because many of us are reluctant to be observed while we teach, it may be less threatening to begin your assessment process with the unassisted or student-assisted instruments. When you've progressed to the point where you want more complex data and can no longer use students to help

obtain data, be thoughtful about whom you ask to observe you. We've found it easier and more comfortable to use a colleague who is a friend and nonjudgmental, someone you're willing to expose both your good points and weaknesses too. For most of us, it takes a while to build up to this point—take it slowly.

Always remember that you're obtaining this information to help improve your teaching. The information is yours to do with as you wish; no one else needs to see it unless you want them to. When viewed this way, assessing your teaching performance can be interesting and challenging, not threatening.

A SUPPORT GROUP

The techniques described for analyzing one's teaching are effective approaches to improving performance. But successful teaching is more than using specific teaching behaviors in predetermined ways. Teaching can never be totally reduced to specific formulas of behavior that guarantee success for all teachers with all classes. However, systematic observation can help answer some questions and provide information that can influence a teacher's success. There are other questions that require careful thought and analysis, questions that cannot be answered solely by systematic observation. Sometimes we need to sit down with colleagues who'll listen carefully and help us understand (analyze) a particular situation. This is what a support group does. Teachers form support groups to build helping relationships between two or more individuals who've learned to trust one another. These individuals share their concerns, questions, dreams, and hopes about themselves as teachers.

If you're not careful, teaching can be a lonely and difficult profession. As the poster depicting an exhausted teacher at the end of an obviously difficult day reminds us: "No one ever said teaching was going to be easy." When your teaching isn't going well, or when you've had a spectacular day, a support group can provide comfort and encouragement. It's reassuring to have a stable group of colleagues who'll listen carefully, verbally applaud your successes, and help you analyze your concerns.

Most teachers occasionally gripe about teach-

Elementary school physical education teachers have been observed who clocked as little as three and a half minutes of significant face-to-face contact with other adults between the hours of 7:30 A.M. and 4:30 P.M. The teacher can be psychologically alone in a densely populated world. The physical (architectural) isolation of the gym located away from the political heartland of the school and the social isolation of the physical educator role which may make the teacher peripheral to the real business of the school, both seem to sustain and intensify the feeling of isolation. Teaching physical education in some schools is a lonely job, awash in an endless sea of children.

Larry Locke,
"The Ecology of the Gymnasium:
What the Tourist Never Sees"

ing conditions, parents, administrators, or fellow teachers. We all have our down days. Within a support group, however, complaining is inappropriate because it's often toxic and tends to contaminate the thinking of others. A support group is designed to make people feel better about their teaching, not worse.

Teaching will never be an exact, predictable science. There will always be some art to teaching effectively. Systematic observation techniques and support groups are two approaches to improving both teaching performance and one's personal satisfaction and enthusiasm for teaching.

SUMMARY

Teaching is a developmental process. Because effective teaching involves learning, it takes time and experience to become a successful teacher. Unfortunately, many school districts don't seem to recognize this fact, so many inexperienced teachers find themselves on their own before they're actually ready to face teaching alone. The teacher who wants to become more effective can use various observation techniques to obtain data that *are* helpful. These techniques are classified into three categories: (1) unassisted, (2) student-assisted, and (3) peer-assisted.

When no one is available to help, a teacher can use written instruments and tape-recorded self-analysis to obtain information about teaching performance. A teacher's pathways, interaction patterns, and the number of practice opportunities given to children can be assessed with student assistance. A peer can provide even more technical information by using a feedback and practice opportunity checklist or a duration recording system.

A very different but equally valuable aid is the support group. Such a group, made up of fellow teachers, can provide comfort and encouragement for all participants. When a group of peers actively listens to each other's questions and helps clarify each other's thoughts, the teaching attitude of all the members is improved.

READING COMPREHENSION QUESTIONS

1. Identify two self-evaluation techniques you can use by yourself. What information can you obtain from each technique?
2. When would you want to use written instruments?
3. What is the use of knowing the pathway you traveled during class?
4. What kind of analysis can you make from student-teacher interactions?
5. How does the combined feedback and practice checklist work?
6. What is duration recording? What categories does it contain? How is each category defined?
7. How does a duration recording system work?
8. What are support groups? What is their value?

REFERENCES

Cheffers, J. (1977). Observing teaching systematically. *Quest, 28,* 17–28.

Cheffers, J., Mancini, V., & Zaichowsky, L. (1976). The development of an elementary physical education attitude scale. *The Physical Educator, 32,* 30–33.

Darst, P., Mancini, V., & Zakrajsek, D. (Eds.). (1983). *Systematic observation instrumentation for physical education.* West Point, NY: Leisure Press.

Krajewski, R. J. (Ed.). (1976, Winter). Clinical supervision. *Journal of Research and Development in Education,* 58–66.

Locke, L. F. (1975, Spring). The ecology of the gymnasium: What the tourist never sees. *Southern Association of Physical Education for College Women Proceedings.*

McGee, R. (1984). Evaluation of processes and products. In B. Logsdon et al., *Physical education for children: A focus on the teaching process.* Philadelphia: Lea & Febiger.

Rink, J. (1985). *Teaching physical education for learning.* St. Louis: Mosby.

Siedentop, D. (1983). *Developing teaching skills in physical education* (2nd ed.). Palo Alto, CA: Mayfield.

P A R T three

Movement Concepts

The three chapters in this section explain the concepts of space awareness (Chapter 12), effort (Chapter 13), and relationships (Chapter 14) and present ideas for teaching them to children. Because these are concepts rather than actual skills, levels of skill proficiency are not discussed. As children study space awareness, effort, and relationships, they learn to demonstrate, through movement, their understanding of the meaning of each concept. Once children have acquired this functional understanding, the concepts are used primarily as subthemes to enhance the range and quality of skill development that result from the study of the various skill themes (Chapters 15 to 25).

12

Space Awareness

All movement takes place in space. Because children who develop a keen space sense will be better able to move safely as they travel through physical education environments, it's beneficial to focus on the concept of space awareness at the beginning of the physical education program.

Children can be made aware of the different aspects of space and then challenged to think about spatial considerations as they engage in game, gymnastics, and dance experiences. As children move their bodies in differing ways through varying spatial conditions, they begin to feel and understand space in new ways. As relationships between the body and space become clear, adeptness at controlling movements in functional or expressive physical education activities is enhanced. For example, children learn to maneuver across a large span of climbing equipment, traveling around, over, and under other youngsters without bumping any of them or losing control of their own movements.

Recall from earlier chapters that the movement analysis framework consists of both movement concepts and skill themes. Space awareness—where the body moves—is one of the three categories of movement concepts. The space awareness categories are in the shaded portion of the wheel (Figure

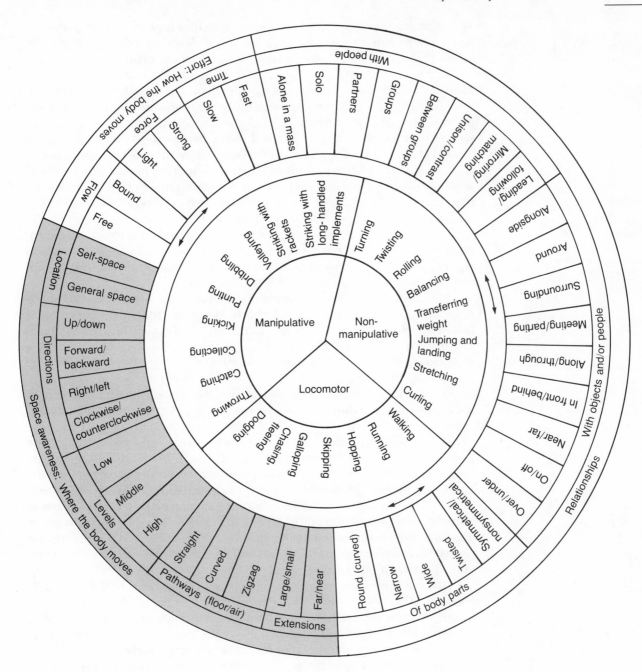

Figure 12-1 Movement analysis framework: Space awareness concepts.

12-1). The position of space awareness on the wheel indicates that it is a movement modifier or concept. In other words, it describes *how* a skill is to be performed as opposed to stating *what* skill is to be performed.

The space awareness section is subdivided into five categories that delineate various aspects of space: location, directions, levels, pathways, and extensions. In turn, each of these categories is further subdivided into specific components that are the working or teachable aspects of space awareness. For example, the location category is subdivided into general space and self-space. Study Figure 12-1 to determine all the subdivisions for each of the separate aspects of space. It helps to think of the three outermost portions of the wheel as three levels of the same idea. The first level or outside ring describes the idea, the second ring gives the categories that make up the idea, and the third ring defines what is found in each category.

Activities in this section are planned as beginning tasks to not only introduce but to teach children the five categories of space indicated in the second ring of the wheel. Children *must* understand these concepts before they attempt to apply them in conjunction with skill themes.

We usually begin by acquainting children with the two basic orientations of location: self-space and general space. These two ideas are crucial to all future learning; they're the foundation upon which everything else is built. *Self-space* is all the space that the body or its parts can reach without traveling away from a starting location. *General space* is all the space, within a room or a boundary, that the body can penetrate by means of locomotion.

The remaining four categories describe the relationships of the body to the space aspects of directions, levels, pathways, and extensions. *Directions* in space are the dimensional possibilities into which the body or its parts move or aim to move—up and down, forward and backward, right and left, clockwise and counterclockwise. *Levels* in space are divided into low, middle, and high. Low level is the space below the knees. Medium level is the space between the knees and the shoulders when the child is in a standing position. High level is the space above the shoulders. *Pathways* in space are the floor patterns (straight, curved, and zigzag) the body can create by traveling through space. The term *pathways* also denotes the possible floor or air patterns of a thrown or struck object—for example, the arched flight of a basketball set shot or the curved path of a pitcher's curveball.

The category *extensions* includes the size of movements of the body or its parts in space (for example, small arm circles or large arm circles) and the distances from the center of the body that the parts reach to carry out a movement. The tennis serve a skilled player performs is a far extension, while a tennis serve a beginner executes is often close to the body.

To help determine if children understand a specific aspect of the concept, use the Assessment Guides that accompany the discussion of each concept. If your students are able to carry out the tasks described in the Assessment Guides, they may begin to combine the concept with skill themes. This doesn't mean that you should disregard the activities we've provided. To ensure understanding, you'd be wise to use the tasks intermittently or for warm-up.

The ideas for developing each space concept are stated in direct terms. Remember, though, that the method used to study each concept can be varied according to your purposes and the characteristics of the children in your class (see Chapter 6).

DEVELOPING THE CONCEPT OF SELF-SPACE

We've found that the best way to teach the concept of *locations* is to focus on the two components—self-space and general space—separately. We first teach self-space and then proceed to general space. You should repeat all the activities involved in teaching self-space and general space until it's clear that the students understand the distinction between the two concepts as well as the need to use space effectively.

If children understand the concept of self-space, their awareness of movement possibilities in the space immediately surrounding their bodies increases. Without a keen sense of the relationship of self-space to surrounding space,

When appropriately challenged, young children become enthralled with the process of exploring space.

children's range of potential movements is restricted. When young children are introduced to a wide repertoire of movement skills in self-space, they begin to build a foundation of nonlocomotor skills (such as twisting and turning) that can be used to enhance the development of concepts and of other skills.

Each individual is surrounded by a self-space as he or she travels—the possible movements into space immediately surrounding the body will be the same regardless of location. But children will understand this concept most easily if they learn it while remaining stationary. Staying in one location will clarify for the children the difference between the movements possible in the space immediately surrounding the body and the movements possible when the body travels through a general space.

ASSESSMENT GUIDE / Self-Space

TASK   Jump on two feet in self-space.

GUIDE   You'll know the children understand the concept of self-space when you observe that they can jump in self-space without moving out of their self-space.

You'll know the children don't understand the concept of self-space when you observe that:

1. They travel around the entire available space when jumping.
2. They briefly travel outside their self-space and then return to it when jumping.

TEACHING THE CONCEPT OF SELF-SPACE

We give the children activities they can accomplish in one location, without traveling. In addition to building their movement vocabularies, the absence of locomotion enhances kinesthetic awareness of stretching, curling, twisting, and swinging (nonlocomotor) movements.

Activities Leading to Movement Concept Understanding

Exploring Self-Space

While standing in a place all by yourself, not traveling anywhere else, move your arms in as many places as possible around your body. Pretend that everything around you is poison and you're on an island in the middle of that poison, with all your friends on islands of their own. You can't reach your friends on their islands, and they can't reach you. You're stranded.

Youngsters discover that a variety of nonmanipulative movements are possible in self-space.

■ This time, still staying in a place by yourself, try to move your legs all around you. Try places that you think are hard to get, like behind you or way out to the side; come very close to falling off your island.

■ Once you think that you're very good with moving your arms and legs without leaving the space you're in, try to pick other parts you can move without leaving your space. Use parts you think would be really hard to move around in your space without moving your whole body from your island. Explore your whole island.

□ The area that you've just explored is called *self-space;* it's like your own island or armor that travels with you wherever you go. Your self-space belongs to you, and no one else is allowed in it unless you let them. Remember too that you're not allowed in anyone else's self-space unless they invite you.

Even with the best analogies in the world, sometimes it's still difficult for children, both young and old, to understand the concept of self-space. When this happens, we've used hula hoops, carpet squares, ropes shaped into circles,

and X's marked on the floor to help children differentiate and remember what their self-space really looks like. As soon as children understand what self-space is and are able to consistently remain in self-space, you can remove these prompts.

Curling, Stretching, and Twisting in Self-Space

While staying in self-space, where you can't touch anyone else, curl your body up very tightly so that you look like a little ball. Now that you're curled up, begin to stretch, ever so slowly, until you're stretched as tall and wide as possible. As you stretch, remember that you can't leave your own space. You're in your own birdcage.

■ Now that you know you can move in your space or birdcage, practice these stretching and curling actions. First pretend that you're trying to reach the cookie jar that is on a shelf at the very top of your cage. Stretch as tall as you can to get it. Now, just as you have two cookies in your hand, your mother walks in. Sink very quickly back to the floor and make yourself very small to try and hide from her.

■ This time, a big spider is on the floor of the cage, near your feet. Stretch tall; you're trying to reach the top rungs of your cage to pull yourself up out of the spider's way. Now the spider climbs to the top; shrink very small and try to get away from the spider.

■ Now that you've practiced your stretching and curling actions, you're going to add twisting actions to them. You want to twist your *whole* body, not just one part. To start, make believe the cookie jar is on the very back of the shelf, behind two boxes; as you stretch, twist your body so you can get to the cookie jar.

■ Stretch toward the top of the birdcage (as you did to get away from the spider). Now pretend that suddenly you have an itch in the middle of your back. Hold on to the top of the cage with one hand and try to scratch your back with your other hand.

Moving the Whole Body in Self-Space

So far, all you've done in self-space are curl, stretch, and twist; you really haven't moved your whole body using any kind of specific movement. This time, let's practice walking in place in self-space. Remember that you can't go anywhere off your island or out of your birdcage—that's all the area you have.

Other actions to practice in self-space: skipping, hopping, jumping.

*Teaching children to travel safely through a general
space is one of our first objectives.*

DEVELOPING THE CONCEPT OF GENERAL SPACE

General space is all the space, within a room or boundary, into which an individual can move by traveling away from the original starting location (self-space).

We help the children learn different ways of traveling safely through general space by providing appropriate movement tasks. Once the children are able to travel safely (without bumping and under control) in general space, they're ready to experience more complex tasks that include several concepts in combination, such as speed, pathways, and directions. Manipulating balls as one travels through general space is an even more difficult challenge.

ASSESSMENT GUIDE / General Space

TASK   Travel on your feet through the general space you have to move in.

GUIDE   You'll know the children understand the concept of general space when you observe that:

1. They're able to travel around the whole space without bumping into each other.
2. They travel around the entire space, using the corners and empty spaces in the room, not just the middle.

You'll know the children don't understand the concept of general space when you observe that:

1. They constantly run into each other as they travel.
2. They travel in a large circle in the middle of the area.

TEACHING THE CONCEPT OF GENERAL SPACE

Activities in this section are designed to help children learn to travel safely and efficiently through general space. You can increase the complexity of the activities by focusing on the concepts of speed, pathways, and directions and on the manipulation of objects through general space. Traveling in general space is an excellent warm-up or limbering activity that you can use each day.

Activities Leading to Movement Concept Understanding

Exploring General Space

Find a space by yourself and stand there. I'll know you're ready when I see you standing very still in a space where you can't touch anyone else. When I say "Go," begin to walk around the room, trying not to come near anyone else and at the same time not leaving any empty spaces in the room. When I say "Freeze," stop very quickly right where you are. When you stop, you shouldn't be able to touch anyone else.

■ This area that you just moved in is called *general space;* it's all the space available for you to move in. As you move in general space, your self-space goes with you, like a bubble that surrounds you, so that you're protected. Let's try the same activity again, only this time move a little faster through general space. Remember that as you move and when you stop, you shouldn't be able to touch anyone else.

Increase the speed only when you observe that the children are able to travel without bumping into one another; for some classes this will take several days. Always start slowly.

■ This time, instead of walking through general space, you're going to jog *(or skip, leap, hop, gallop, etc.)* through general space. Remember to always stay as far away from other people as you can. Think about visiting different places in the area, such as the corners and the middle of the area.

After you give the stop signal, you can further concept development by giving the children feedback, e.g.,

1. *Praise youngsters who stop in isolated areas.*
2. *Praise youngsters who stop quickly and safely.*
3. *Point out congested or vacant spaces.*
4. *Praise youngsters who've avoided collisions by traveling defensively.*

Reducing the Size of the General Space

Spread out and find a space by yourself. On the signal, begin to travel on your feet in general space, not touching anyone else. The hard part this time will be that I'm going to keep making your space smaller as you move. For me to do that, you must always stay in front of me; I'll keep moving forward until your general space is very small.

To do this activity, you should face the children while standing at the edge of the general space. All the children should be moving within the boundaries. When you want the space to become smaller, take a step or two toward the center of the general space (the idea is a whole wall moving forward at one time).

Dodging in General Space

Divide the class in half. Have half the children line up on one side of the area, half on the other side.

We're going to play a game now. The object of the game is for both groups to get to the other side of the area without touching anyone else. The hard part is that both groups will be moving at the same time. Remember, all of you in both groups are trying to switch sides without touching anyone else. I'll watch very carefully to see if I can find anyone touching.

Other locomotor patterns can be used: slow jogging, hopping, skipping, leaping, galloping. Youngsters can travel at fast speeds, such as running, only after they've had much practice.

Traveling Over, Under, and Around Obstacles in General Space

For this activity you'll need small obstacles, such as hoops and ropes on the floor, milk crates, and low benches, all spread out in various places around the area.

Travel around the space without touching any piece of equipment or any other person. You may go over, under, or around any of the obstacles, but don't touch anyone or anything. Remember, if someone else is at a piece of equipment, go on to another one; don't wait in line.

DEVELOPING THE CONCEPT OF DIRECTIONS

Directions in space are the dimensional possibilities into which the body or its parts move or aim to move—up and down, right and left, forward and backward, clockwise and counterclockwise. There is no universally correct direction; direction is a function of the body's orientation in space. Forward and backward, for example, depend on the way a person is facing rather than a location in a room. Left and right refer to the respective sides of the body, not a certain wall or location in a gymnasium. Because the concepts of right and left (sideways) and clockwise and counterclockwise require cognitive as well as physical maturation for correct execution, it's not uncommon to find that children learn the directions forward and backward and up and down before they learn the directions of right and left and clockwise and counterclockwise.

ASSESSMENT GUIDE / Directions

TASK   Walk quickly in general space. When I call out a direction, change the direction you're traveling in to a new direction, as quickly and smoothly as possible.

GUIDE   You'll know the children understand the concept of directions when you observe that:

1. They change direction within two steps after hearing the command.
2. They travel in the correct directions.
3. They change direction without hesitation.

You'll know the children don't understand the concept of directions when you observe that:

1. They take several steps to change direction.
2. They travel in incorrect directions.
3. They have to stop and think before they're able to change direction.

TEACHING THE CONCEPT OF DIRECTIONS

These activities provide ideas for helping children understand the concepts of forward and backward, up and down, sideways, clockwise and counterclockwise, and right and left. As the children become more capable, the complexity of the tasks is increased—the children are challenged to combine two or more direction concepts and to move in different directions in relation to objects or people.

Activities Leading to Movement Concept Understanding

Traveling in Different Directions

On the signal, walk as you'd usually walk, with the front of your body going first. This direction is called *forward.*

■ This time, walk with your back going first. This direction is called *backward.* Sometimes going backward is hard because you have to look over your shoulder to see where you're going.

■ Now walk with one side of your body going first. This direction is called *sideways.* You can move to either your right or left side. Let's practice both ways. First move with your right side going first. When you hear the beat of the drum, (*if you don't have a drum, use a tin can, a baby rattle, or a New Year's noisemaker*), change so that your left side goes first.

Moving Clockwise and Counterclockwise

Rotation *describes movement in clockwise or counterclockwise directions. When we want children to turn, spin, or pivot, using the terms right and left is inaccurate. The terms clockwise and counterclockwise, however, indicate the appropriate direction in which the movement is to be made.*

Look down at the floor. Imagine that there's a clock on the floor in front of you. Slowly turn around, turning in the direction the hands on the clock move. This direction is called *clockwise.* Now turn in the other direction. This direction is called *counterclockwise.*

■ Now practice the different directions some more. See if you can spin clockwise on one foot. Now change and spin counterclockwise on the same foot. Swing your arms in the direction you want to spin and see if you can spin all the way around before you stop. Is it easier to spin in a clockwise or a counterclockwise direction? Why do you think so?

■ This time try jumping. Stay in your self-space, and jump and see if you can turn all the way around so that you land facing the same direction you were when you started. Be careful to not fall down; if you do, it doesn't count.

Try turning clockwise and counterclockwise when you jump. Can you turn farther in one direction than the other?

■ Find a partner. One of you spin or jump and turn while the other watches. See if your partner can tell you whether you were spinning (turning) in a clockwise or counterclockwise direction. Take turns.

■ Now you're going to try something different. Travel in general space. When you hear one drumbeat, spin in a clockwise direction and keep traveling. When you hear two drumbeats, spin in a counterclockwise direction and keep traveling. If you hear three drumbeats, change the way you're traveling, for example, from a skip to a slide. Do you think you can remember all this? Let's see!

You can also teach and reinforce the concepts of clockwise and counterclockwise when working with several of the skill themes, such as dribbling in a clockwise or counterclockwise direction and pushing a ball with a field hockey stick in both directions.

Exploring Directions

In your self-space, point with the body part named in the direction that I call out. *(You can continue the list with any body part.)*

With your foot, point forward.

With your elbow, point backward.

With your hip, point to the left.

With your left foot, point forward.

□ As you point, make sure the direction you're pointing to is very clear—so I could always tell which way to go if you were trying to point out a direction.

Changing Directions on Signal

Now that you know which directions are which, move a little faster when you practice them and mix them all up. On the signal, begin to travel in general space in a forward direction. After that, each time you hear the signal, change the direction you're moving in. For example, if you start out moving in a forward direction, the first time you hear the signal you change to a sideways direction; the next time you hear the signal, you change to a backward direction; and the next time, you change back to a sideways direction. Remember to make your directions very clear.

While the children are waiting for the signal, have them think about how they're going to change direction.

■ This time the changes of direction are going to be a bit harder. They'll be in code. One beat of the drum means forward. Two beats of the drum means sideways. Three beats of the drum means backward. Spread out in general space in a space by yourself. When you hear the beat of the drum, begin to travel in the direction indicated by the code. When you hear the next beat of the drum, change and travel in the direction that it indicates. Listen very carefully to the drumbeats because I might try to trick you.

Turning While Moving in Different Directions

Spread out around the outside of the room and face the wall. When you hear the drumbeat, begin to travel around the space by using a sliding pattern. As the drum beats again, turn, without stopping, to face the inside of the room— keep sliding. Each time the drum beats, change the way you're facing and continue moving sideways. When you do this, I'm looking for turns that are smooth and slides that don't stop as you turn.

DEVELOPING THE CONCEPT OF LEVELS

Levels are the horizontal layers in space where the body or its parts are positioned or can move. Low level is the space below the knees, close to the floor. A stamp or twist of the foot is an action at a lower level. Crawling, creeping, or rolling are locomotor actions performed at a low level.

Medium level is the space between low level and high level—the area between the knees and shoulders. Catching a thrown ball, for example, typically occurs in middle level.

High level is space above the shoulders, toward the ceiling. Although one can't move the whole body into high level, actions such as stretching the arms up high or standing on the balls of the feet bring body parts into a high level. A jump can take much of the upper body into a high level, while part of the body remains at a medium or low level because of the pull of gravity.

ASSESSMENT GUIDE / Levels

TASK   Skip around the space, and on the signal freeze in a body shape that is, as much as possible, at the level called out.

GUIDE   You'll know the children understand the concept of levels when you observe that:

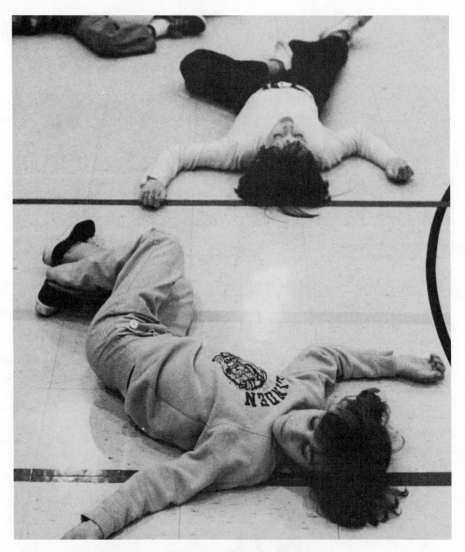

Children explore low level, as close to the floor as possible.

1. Their body shapes are, as much as possible, at the level indicated.
2. They don't hesitate between the traveling and freezing action; they automatically freeze at the level indicated.

You'll know the children still don't understand the concept of levels when you observe that:

1. Only part of their body shapes are at the level indicated.
2. They have to stop and think before they freeze; they don't automatically freeze at the level indicated.

TEACHING THE CONCEPT OF LEVELS

The activities in this section give children movement challenges that help them learn to move the body, body parts, and objects into different levels in space.

Activities Leading to Movement Concept Understanding

Traveling and Freezing at Different Levels

Spread out and find a space by yourself. On the signal, begin to travel in general space. When you hear the drumbeat, freeze where you are, with your whole body at a low level.

■ This time, travel and on the signal freeze with your body at a low level and a body part at a high level. Make it very clear which part is at a high level.
■ This time, when you stop, freeze with your body at a medium level. Remember that a low level means below your knees, a medium level is from about your knees to your shoulders, and a high level is above your shoulders. Make your levels very clear.

Traveling with Body Parts at Different Levels

Travel around general space with as many of your body parts as possible at a low level. Remember that your body parts should always be at a low level when you're traveling, not just when you freeze.

■ As you travel this time, try to have as many body parts as possible at a medium level. Remember that it isn't possible to have all body parts at a medium level as you travel because your feet always have to be on the floor, but have as many parts as possible at a medium level and none at a high level.
■ This time as you travel, have as many parts as possible at a high level. This activity is harder than the other two, so be very careful that all possible body parts are at a high level.

Rising and Sinking to Create Different Levels

Find a space by yourself and get into a low position that you like. I'm going to beat the drum very slowly eight times. As I beat the drum, rise very slowly to

Teachers often ask, "How do I accommodate different skill levels in one class?" More specifically, "How do I do this with little equipment?" We've found that the best way is to vary the major task for individual children according to their needs (see Chapter 6). Often you can reduce or increase the complexity of the task without substantially changing the equipment used. Consider the task of throwing a ball to a partner so that the partner is fully extended to catch. You can reduce the complexity of this task by changing the equipment from a ball to a beanbag or by having the partner use an outstretched arm as the target. Then, by changing the task so that the throw forces the partner to take a step to catch the ball, you increase the complexity of the same task.

The teacher should make such changes by moving from group to group, observing, and modifying accordingly. In this way the entire class is then practicing variations of the same task.

the eight beats until you attain a position of stillness with as many body parts as possible at a high level. Remember to rise slowly. But also remember that you have only eight beats in which to get to a high level, so judge your movement so you get there in time. After you've reached your high position, on the next eight beats slowly sink back to your low position. The sequence then goes like this: a low position, eight beats to get to a high still position, eight beats to return to your low position. Let's try it.

Traveling While Rising and Sinking

As you travel around the space this time, I'll give you drumbeats to guide your actions. The drumbeats will be in counts of four, with the accent on the first beat. Start by traveling at a low level. On the accented first beat, quickly jump and stretch into a high level and then immediately return to a low level of travel until the next accented beat. Your movement should look like this: travel low, jump high, travel low, jump high, travel low, etc.

□ Make your jump very clear and as high as possible and your travel at a low level very clear. I should be able to easily tell the difference between the two levels.

DEVELOPING THE CONCEPT OF PATHWAYS

A pathway is an imaginary design that the body or its parts when moving through space create along the floor or through the air. A pathway is also the trail of an object (a ball or hockey puck) as it travels from one player to another or toward a goal.

At first, young children may have difficulty understanding the concept of pathways in space. However, a class of young children can become enthralled with the process of discovering and experimenting with the many pathways the body can travel. A teacher can plan experiences that enable youngsters to recognize pathways and to effectively use knowledge of pathways to improve control of travel. For instance, even very young children can come to understand that a curved or angular pathway is effective for avoiding collisions when traveling through a crowd.

ASSESSMENT GUIDE / Pathways

TASK   Travel around the general space. Each time you hear the drumbeat, I'll call out a pathway to travel. As soon as you hear the pathway, quickly change to the new pathway.

GUIDE   You'll know the children understand the concept of pathways when you observe that:

1. They travel the correct pathways.
2. They change pathways without hesitation.
3. The speed of their travel doesn't change as they change pathways.

You'll know the children don't understand the concept of pathways when you observe that:

1. They travel incorrect pathways.
2. They have to stop and think before they change pathways.
3. The speed of their travel changes as they change pathways.

TEACHING THE CONCEPT OF PATHWAYS

Children learn to travel in straight, angular, and curved pathways, and in combinations of these pathways, by experiencing the activities in this section. More difficult activities involve manipulating various objects in pathways and traveling in relation to others along various pathways.

Activities Leading to Movement Concept Understanding

Exploring Pathways

Place tape markings on the floor, similar to those shown in Figure 12-2.

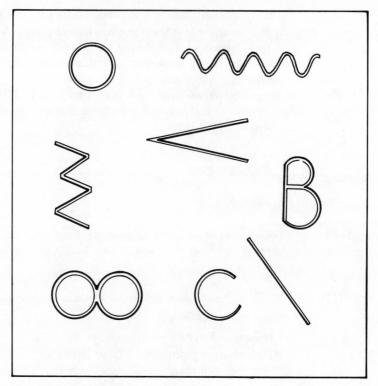

Figure 12-2 Pathways taped on the floor.

Today you're going to learn about pathways. A line that doesn't turn or twist and is always straight is called a *straight pathway*. A line that circles around is called a *curved pathway*. A semicircle is a curved pathway. A line that looks like a lot of Z's put together is a *zigzag pathway*. Now find a space on one of the pathways marked on the floor. Travel along that pathway on your feet; be able to tell me what kind of pathway it is when I ask you.

■ This time as you travel, change your directions, sometimes going forward along your pathway, sometimes sideways, and sometimes backward. Try out all directions on your pathway.

■ Now change the way that you travel along your pathway. Sometimes you may want to hop, sometimes leap, sometimes run. Find at least four different ways that you can travel along your pathway.

During the activity, have the children regularly change places so that they're on a different pathway.

MR. JENNING'S KINDERGARTEN CLASS DISCOVERS PATHWAYS

Teacher: Hey gang! How did we get to the physical education space today?

Children: We walked!

Teacher: Yes! And what parts of our bodies did we use?

Children: Our feet . . . our legs.

Teacher: You got it! Tell me, did we leave a trail behind us? Any footprints on the floor?

Children: No! (Loud and laughing)

Teacher: I don't see any either. But what if our shoes were muddy. Would we have left a trail?

Children: Yeah! But Mrs. Farmer (the principal) sure would be mad!

Teacher: I think she would be, too! But if we did leave muddy footprints from your classroom all the way to the physical education space, what would our path look like?

Children: Long . . . Messy . . . We go by the library.

Teacher: I think you're all right. I have an idea . . . Let's look at the chalkboard. Here's your room way over here and this is where the physical education space is. Look at our pathway. Although we didn't leave any real footprints, we did follow a path. We follow this same pathway each time we come to the physical education space. Tell me, is our path just one straight line or did we make any turns?

Children: We turned when we came out of the room. At the library.

Teacher: You people are sharp today. Hey! Can you think of any other pathways you follow each day?

Children: We go to lunch . . . Walk to school . . . Down to the playground.

Teacher: We follow a lot of pathways each day. Let's see if we can have some fun with pathways today. Pick a spot somewhere on the outside of the room (for example, a brick, a picture) and when I say "Go," you stand up and walk in a straight line to your spot and freeze. Here we go!

Using Pathway Maps

For each child in the class, draw a card, similar to one shown in Figure 12-3.

Figure 12-3 Pathway cards.

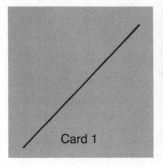
Card 1

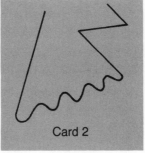
Card 2

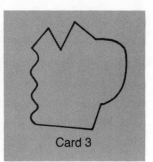
Card 3

Take a card and find a space by yourself. Travel on your feet and follow the pathway indicated on your card. Pretend that your card is a map showing the route to take to get to a new place. Keep practicing your pathway until you're very sure it's just like the one on the card and you can do it the best you can. Be able to tell me the name of the pathway you're following whenever I ask you.

■ Now trade cards with someone else and practice that pathway until you think it's perfect.

Designing Pathways

Pick a spot on the wall across the room from you. Remember where your spot is, and in your mind plan a pathway that will take you from where you are now to that spot. Think about it a long time so you can remember it when you start to move. When I give the signal, travel along your made-up pathway until you get to the spot you've picked out. Stop still when you get there. On the next signal, travel back to the place you started from, following the same pathway you took coming over. This is similar to following a path through the woods: You can't go off the path or you'll get lost.

■ Now I am *not* going to give you the signal any more. Practice your pathway on your own until you have it memorized and can repeat it exactly every time.

Creating Follow the Leader Pathways

Find a partner and stand in a space by yourselves. I'll know that you're ready when I see each of you standing quietly in your own space. Decide which of you is going to be the leader. On the signal, the leader travels a pathway to somewhere else in the room. On the second signal, the leader freezes and the follower moves along the same pathway the leader took until the follower catches up with the leader. After doing this three times, the leader and follower switch places. The secret is for the follower to watch the leader very closely. In the beginning, the leader should not make up hard pathways. Followers, remember to copy the leaders' pathway exactly.

Traveling Pathways and Obstacles

Divide the class in half. One-half of the class assumes still positions at various places in the general space; the other half spreads out around the perimeter of the space.

Now you're going to travel in pathways that go around, over, and under obstacles in your way. Always remember that your classmates are the obstacles, so you have to be very careful of them. You can't touch anyone else. People who are obstacles must remember to stay very still so as to not interfere with anyone who's moving. Obstacles, go find a position in a space by yourself that you can hold still. It can be any position that you like—a bridge, a statue, or a balance. Those of you on the side of the space, pick a point on the other side of the room and plan a pathway to get there. Remember that your pathway can go over, under, or around any of the obstacles. Think about it and really make it different from anything you've done before. *(Give the children a few seconds to plan their pathway and the obstacles time to select their position.)* On the signal, follow your pathway to the point you picked on the other side of the room. Freeze when you get to the point you picked. On the next signal, try to retrace your pathway until you get back to your starting position.

- Now, on your own, practice your pathway four times. Remember to avoid running into other travelers as you cross the space.
  □ Always have a clear beginning and end to your pathway. After four times, have a seat at the place where you end up. Remember, no touching.

When all have completed their pathways, have the students switch places and perform the activity. You can enhance activities such as these by asking children who're doing the activities correctly to demonstrate for the rest of the class.

Following the Dots Pathways

Each student will need a pencil and a card with dots randomly plotted on it. Spread carpet squares on the floor in a pattern similar to that of the dots on the card.

Connect the dots on your card to form any design you like. After you've finished connecting the dots, follow the path that you drew from one carpet square to the other. Make sure you know the type of pathway you've designed because I might ask you.

- Now trade maps with someone else. Follow that person's map. Figure out if that pathway is different from yours.

Combining Pathways, Levels, and Directions

For each child, you'll need a task sheet similar to that in Figure 12-4.

This activity lets you combine pathways, levels, and directions. It's also a good way to test yourself. Once you think you're able to perform a challenge, have a friend watch you and sign the line on the Task Sheet beside the challenge. When you're finished, I'll come and check you out. You may use a friend to help you if you want extra help. *(Younger children can use a smile face instead of having someone else initial the sheet.)*

Name —————————— Teacher ————————————		
Pathways, Levels, and Directions Task Sheet		
Date	Who Watched	Challenge
		I can walk forward in a straight pathway.
		I can walk backward in a straight pathway.
		I can walk sideways in a straight pathway.
		I can walk forward in a curved pathway.
		I can walk backward in a curved pathway.
		I can walk forward, low, and curved.
		I can walk backward, high, and zigzag.
		I can run sideways, medium, and curved.
		I can slide backward, medium, and zigzag.
		I can
		I can
		I can
		(Make up three things you can do on your own using pathways, levels, and directions.)

Figure 12-4 Task sheet for levels, pathways, and directions.

DEVELOPING THE CONCEPT OF EXTENSIONS IN SPACE

Extensions in space are best understood as two separate possibilities. First, extensions are spatial relationships of body parts to the entire body. Body extremities can be held in close to the body, as in a curl, or they can be opened up, as in a stretch. Extensions are also the size of movements in space. Movements with extremities held close to the body are small movements, such as putting a golf ball; those with the extremities extended or opened up are large movements, such as driving a golf ball.

ASSESSMENT GUIDE / Extensions

TASK   Travel around general space. On the signal, freeze in a position that shows a near or close extension. On the next signal, change your extension to a far extension.

GUIDE   You'll know the children understand the concept of extensions when you observe that:

1. They don't hesitate when performing the extensions.
2. Their close extensions have all body parts close to the center of the body and their far extensions have as many body parts as possible far away from the centers of their body.

You'll know the children still don't understand the concept of extensions when you observe that:

1. They perform incorrect extensions.
2. They have to stop and think before they perform the task or change from one extension to the next.
3. They have to look at other children to see what extension is being called for.
4. They perform the extensions with only a few body parts and some parts are, in fact, at the wrong extension.

TEACHING THE CONCEPT OF EXTENSIONS IN SPACE

The concept of extensions is taught through learning experiences that give children an operational understanding of the differences between large and small and near and far extensions (movements).

Activities Leading to Movement Concept Understanding

Exploring Extensions

Find a space by yourself. With your hands, explore all the space close to your body. Remember to not reach very far from your body; this is an extension near your body.

■ Now, without leaving your self-space, explore all the space that is far away from your body. Try to reach as far as you can without leaving your space. Remember to explore above and behind as well as in front of you. This is called an extension that is far away from your body. We call these *near* and *far* extensions.

Traveling and Extensions

Travel around the room. When you hear the beat of the drum, freeze in a position where your body reaches as far into space as possible. Be very sure that all possible body parts are as far away from the center of your body as you can get them.

■ This time as you travel, when you hear the drumbeat, freeze with all body parts as close to your body as possible. Remember to keep all your body parts as close to yourself as you can.

■ Now the traveling will change. When you hear the sound of the drum, jump high into the air, extending your arms and legs as far away from your body as possible. When you land, hold a position very still, with all body parts very close to the center of your body.

□ Really try to make a clear difference between the faraway and near extensions.

Changing from One Extension to Another

Find a space by yourself and get into a tight position you like. I'll beat the drum six times, in slow beats. On the first six beats, gradually extend all body parts far away from your body. On the next six beats, slowly move to your tight curled position. The movement then goes like this: first a tight, curled position; on six beats, slowly move to a spread-out position; on the next six counts, slowly move back to a near extension.

□ Try to make the extensions you use very clear. We'll practice this activity a number of times so you can work on doing your best possible.

Using Extensions and Imagery

As you travel around general space, pretend you're carrying an object you don't want anyone to see or that you're trying to hide or protect something, such as a baby bird, a $1 million jewel, or a lot of money. As you walk, think very carefully about how you'd actually really carry the object you've chosen.

■ Now, instead of having an object you want to hide, you have one you're proud of and want to show off—maybe a trophy that you just won. How would you carry it? Go!

□ In which activity did you use a near or small extension? In which activity did you use a large or far extension?

The child responding to the challenge of catching at a low level must have a functional understanding of the concept of space.

APPLYING THE CONCEPT OF SPACE AWARENESS

Self-space and general space are often appropriate beginning concepts for children who have had little experience in formal physical education classes. One of the important skills that children need to develop early is the ability to occupy an area or to travel in an area while maintaining awareness of others. Self-space and general space are helpful concepts to use when teaching these skills.

The concepts of directions, levels, and pathways are usually introduced after children have developed the ability to differentiate between self-space and general space. Until the children actually acquire a functional understanding of directions, levels, and pathways (high, medium, low levels; forward, sideways, backward directions; straight, zigzag, and curved pathways), the observational focus is primarily on the concept rather than on correct performance of a skill. For example, if you ask the children to throw so the ball starts off at a high level, you're less interested in the actual mechanics of throwing than in the child's ability to release the ball at a high level. Once you're confident that the children are able to apply the concepts, you can focus more on appropriate skill technique.

Most children take a longer time to grasp the concepts of right and left, air pathways, and extensions. Thus it's wise to introduce the other concepts to children before focusing on these three ideas.

The ability to understand the concept of right and left is related to cognitive maturation. Some children will need more time and more practice opportunities than others to master left and right. Many children easily acquire cognitive understanding of the concepts of extensions and air pathways for objects, but most require a certain degree of skill before they can express these ideas in movements. Children with immature throwing and kicking patterns, for example, have difficulty propelling objects so that they travel in different (but intended) air pathways. Children with immature striking or catching patterns are unable to consistently catch or strike an object far from or near to the body.

If you wait until children have developed the skills that are related to these concepts, you'll find that the pupils grasp the concepts more easily than if you try to teach the concepts and then the skills. There's no universally successful sequence for the introduction of these concepts. The reflective teacher uses all available information and makes judgments about the most appropriate time, sequence, and duration for introducing and studying the concepts of space awareness and the application of the concepts to specific skill-practice situations.

READING COMPREHENSION QUESTIONS

1. What is the primary reason for focusing on the concept of space at the beginning of a physical education program?
2. What does the term *space awareness* mean? What are the characteristics of someone who is "aware of space"?
3. What directions in space are studied in this program? Why do children find some directions harder than others to understand?
4. Distinguish the three levels of space from each other.
5. List the three types of pathways an individual might travel. Explain the difference between a floor pathway and an air pathway.
6. Give two examples of a far extension and two examples of a near extension.
7. Why have children study self-space while they are stationary rather than traveling?
8. What does it look like when children are able to travel safely in general space?
9. What does *travel defensively* mean? Does the term relate to the speed of travel in general space? How?

13

Effort Concepts

Too often no conscious, planned attempt is made to help children understand the effort concepts of time, force, and flow and the application of these concepts to specific skills.* Many teachers don't feel comfortable teaching these concepts, which are vague and abstract. It is not like teaching a child to strike a ball with a paddle, where the objective of striking is obvious and the result easily perceived. Despite the hesitancy of many teachers to undertake the teaching of effort concepts, there is agreement that an applied understanding of these concepts is essential in skill development, from beginning through advanced levels.

The concept of effort defines how the body moves. The concept is divided into three components: time, force, and flow, which are defined by observable characteristics that can be taught to children. Figure 13-1 conceptualizes this idea and puts it into perspective with the other movement concepts and skill

*Some movement analysis frameworks include the concept of space (direct and flexible) as a quality of movement. In our teaching, however, we use this concept so infrequently that we've chosen not to include it in the discussion of the qualities of movement.

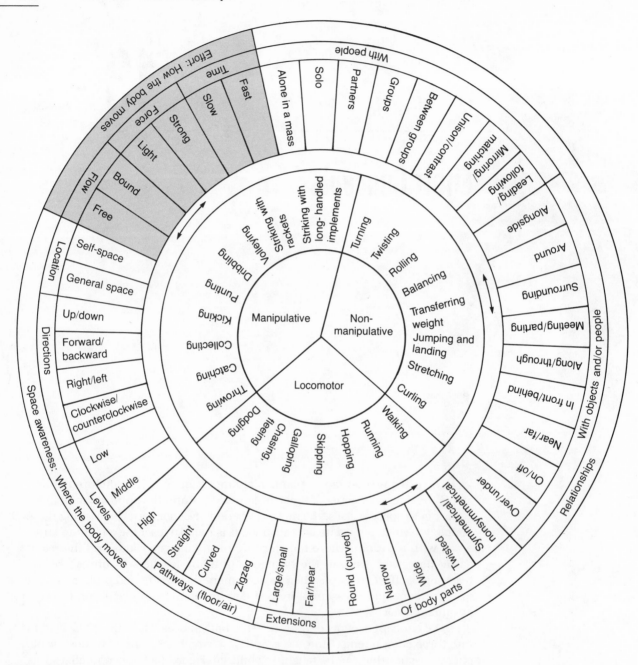

Figure 13-1 Movement analysis framework: Effort concepts.

themes. The effort category is in the shaded portion of the framework. The outside ring defines the concept; the second ring states the components of the concept; and the third ring defines the three components.

Highly skilled (proficiency level) movers have developed an internalized, almost reflexive knowledge of the proper amount and degree of time, force, and flow. They're able to adjust the quality of movements in relation to the demands of a situation—harder or softer, faster or slower, bound or free.

We begin to teach effort concepts to children by providing experiences to help them understand the contrasts of fast-slow, strong-light, and bound-free. Once the children have grasped the differences between the extremes, we focus on the concepts as they apply to specific skills (such as throwing, striking, and transferring weight) and in different situations (for example, to assist in the expression of an idea or to accomplish a particular strategy). As children become more skillful, we focus on the gradations among the extremes. To illustrate, initially we might ask children to travel rapidly and to travel slowly. As children develop the ability to differentiate between the extremes, we focus more on the movement possibilities that occur between the extremes—faster, slower, accelerating, decelerating, sudden changes of speed.

Many of the activities in this chapter use imagery to help children distinguish among different effort concepts. It's important to keep in mind that the focus is on the movement qualities of the various images rather than on the images. For example, when we say "Move like a hippo," we're not asking the children to pretend to be hippos; we're using this task to help the children envision a slow, lumbering movement. Chapter 27 contains additional information about the appropriate use of imagery in teaching movement.

DEVELOPING THE CONCEPT OF TIME

Time to a young child is the ticktock of a watch, the cuckoo on a clock, or the numbers racing by on a digital timepiece. When spoken of in relation to movement, time is fast—being able to run like the wind; being the fastest in the class; zip, dash, zoom.

In an activity in which speed is often the measure of success, children often have difficulty comprehending slowness and seeing the importance of this rate of movement. Yet the performer executing a walkover on the balance beam grasps the concept of slowness, as does the leaping dancer who seems to remain suspended in the air while the hands and arms express a certain feeling or emotion.

Changes in the time of a movement usually occur without forethought as children adapt to different situations—speeding up or slowing down, to maintain possession, to avoid being tagged, to get in open space and receive a pass. Many movements and specific skills dictate the rate of movement. A handspring is done quickly, but a back walkover is performed slowly. In some activ-

Young children enjoy the sensation of a fast run.

Slowness is necessary in executing an inverted balance.

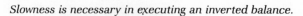

ities, the child is free to assess a situation and then perform a skill at the best rate. For example, a movement executed quickly in dance or gymnastics elicits feelings of power and speed; the same movement executed slowly expresses the ultimate in control.

We begin teaching the concept of time to young children by contrasting the extremes. Gradually we advance to work that focuses on degrees of speed along a continuum—the ability to execute movements at varying speeds for the purpose of adapting, changing, or creating a situation.

ASSESSMENT GUIDE / Time

TASK Travel slowly in general space. On the beat of the drum, change your speed to fast; on the next beat of the drum, go back to slow; on the next beat, go back to fast. Remember to only go as fast as you can and still be able to control your movement.

Note to Teachers. Don't try this task with children until you're reasonably confident that they can travel safely in general space.

GUIDE You'll know the children understand the concept of time when you observe that:

1. They change speed smoothly and without hesitation.
2. The difference between their fast and slow movements is clear.

You'll know the children don't yet understand the concept of time when you observe that:

1. They fall down when asked to stop when moving at a fast speed.
2. They have to stop and think about the change in speed.
3. There's no discernible difference between their fast and slow movements.

TEACHING THE CONCEPT OF TIME

These activities are designed to help children develop a functional understanding of time by giving them experiences that contrast fast and slow actions of the total body and body parts, experiences that focus on acceleration-deceleration. When children are traveling fast, try to keep the activity period short, to avoid undue fatigue.

Activities Leading to Movement Concept Understanding

Exploring Time

Find a space by yourself. Without leaving your space, try to keep up with the beat of the drum. The beat will be very loud and quick to begin with, so you'll want your movements to be very sharp and quick. The trick to having very quick actions is to make them very short; something that's really quick can't go on for very long. This action is called a *sudden* movement.

■ This time the beat of the drum will be slower and longer. Try to move your whole body as slowly as the drumbeats, much like a balloon floating through the air or a feather being dropped from a high building.

□ Think about moving every part of your body slowly, not just your arms but your head, shoulders, back, stomach, legs, everything. This action is called a *sustained* movement.

Using Different Speeds in Self-Space

In a space by yourself, bring your hands together very slowly, as if to catch an insect that might try to fly away. At the very last moment before your hands are going to touch, quickly separate them as if you're surprised to find out that the insect is a bee. Remember when you do your slow movements to make them very slow but to always keep your hands moving; make your quick so quick that it's like a flash of lightning.

□ Let's try those movements five more times. You can bring your hands together any way you want as long as you do so slowly, and then quickly take them away any way you want. Remember to make your slow and quick movements as clear as they can be. Five times. Go.

■ Now on your own find other body parts that you can bring together slowly and then quickly pull apart. Try to find at least three combinations. Practice each movement so that the difference between fast and slow is very clear.

This activity is more difficult than it sounds because it is asking for extremes of a movement. You can have children practice this activity over and over; always ask for faster and slower actions than the children previously exhibited.

Moving at Different Speeds

On the signal, move as fast as you can, but remain in self-space; on the next signal, freeze in a balanced position that you can hold very still. Remember to try to go as fast as you can, but you must be able to stop on the signal without falling over.

■ Now, on the start signal, move as slowly as you can. Try to move very slowly, but always keep moving. On the stop signal, freeze in a balanced position. Remember to stay in your self-space.

■ Your first movement was at a fast speed, your second at a slow speed. Could you tell the difference? Again you're going to practice both fast and slow speeds. Try to make the movements very clear so I can really tell the difference between them. As you move, I'll call out fast or slow, and you change your speed accordingly. So if I call out slow, move very slowly, and if I call out fast, move fast. Listen very carefully because I might try to trick you. Make your fast really fast and your slow really slow.

Once the children demonstrate an understanding of speed in self-space, you can transfer these same tasks to traveling in general space.

Traveling and Freezing by Using Changes in Time

This time, begin your traveling with a quick explosion of speed and keep going at a fast speed; then freeze very quickly in a balanced position. The movement should be like this: Begin really fast as if you've been shot out of a cannon, then move fast as if you're running from someone, then freeze quickly as if someone has surprised you and you can't move. Make each segment of your traveling very clear so that I can tell when you change from one part to the other. I'll give you the start signal; then you're on your own.

A young boy's attempt at a strong shape.

■ Now that you've practiced sudden starts, traveling fast, and then freezing, you're going to make up a sequence using those speeds. Choose one sudden start, fast travel, and freeze position that you really like and practice it until you can do it smoothly and with control. Each of the three parts should be very clear and very different from each other. After you think the sequence is really good, practice it three more times. Remember to start and end in the same place each time. Your three movements should look the same every time, as if they'd been videotaped.

■ Now begin very slowly, as a car does on a cold morning. As you warm up, gradually increase your speed until you're moving fast. Then, freeze suddenly. The sequence should look like this: a slow start, a gradual increase to fast speed, then a freeze. This is different from your last traveling action, so make that difference very clear.

■ Now, by yourself make up a sequence that includes a slow start that gradually increases to a fast speed and suddenly freezes. Practice the sequence until you're ready to show someone else, who, after seeing it, should be able to tell you what the three parts were.

Children often equate slowness with heavy, jerky, stiff actions rather than with graceful movement. Examples of slow-moving animals can be useful here.

Combining Imagery and Time

This time you're going to practice traveling the way different things that move fast or slow do. Remember that you aren't really trying to act like the things you're pretending to be; you're just trying to move at the speed they move. Let's practice one movement. On the signal, move as a turtle would move. Think carefully about it—a turtle moves very slowly. Now try moving as fast as a rabbit. Go really quickly.

■ How does a new race car move? Let's try to go as fast as a race car can. There's only one thing different about this race car: It goes so fast that it can't make any noise. So go as fast as a silent race car. Change your race car to an old jalopy trying to go up hill; the car is really tired and old, so remember that it goes very slowly.

Some classes enjoy and can accept the responsibility for making the sounds of race cars and jalopies. You'll have to use your judgment about whether or not to encourage the sounds, which can be either productive or detrimental, depending on circumstances.

■ Now pretend that the fair is in town and you're going to go with your friends tonight to ride all the rides and eat all kinds of food. How excited are you? Really let your excitement show as you go home from school. Try it. Now, instead of going to the fair, you're going home, and you know you'll be in trouble

IMAGERY AND MOVEMENT

Much has been said about imagery and movement, specifically related to dance. We've all had the experience of asking children to "show a flower growing," only to discover that instead of exploring the movement possibilities available, the children were pretending to be flowers. Herein lies the pitfall of imagery: Concept development isn't pretending; it's understanding.

To be beneficial, the teaching of movement concepts and ultimately dance must first be involved with children learning a movement vocabulary and then relating it to other ideas (much like the development of movement skills before relating them to game play). This notion implies that we must talk about movement first and use images to lead to an understanding or enhancement of that movement. It precludes moving or dancing "about"

something (anger, fear, excitement, horses, etc.) or pretending to be something (a piece of fruit, a cowboy, flower, airplane, etc.).

Mary Joyce developed three useful phases regarding dance and imagery that can be easily applied to any creative movement (*First Steps in Teaching Creative Dance to Children*, 2nd ed., 1980, Palo Alto, CA: Mayfield):

1. Images that lead to movement: "Make your back curved like a banana."
2. Images that arise from movement: "You're in a curved shape. What else do you know that is curved?"
3. Images as a basis for movement: "What kind of movement might a banana do?"

Always remember to talk about the movement first and the image second.

because your mom told you not to take any more cookies from the cookie jar and you got caught taking the last two.

■ You're the fastest sprinter in the Olympics and are in the starting blocks waiting for the gun to go off. Go. Now you're a distance runner just about to start a ten-mile race; you have a long way to go, and you don't want to wear yourself out.

■ You're a mouse running from a cat. Now you're a hippopotamus with a full stomach trying to run.

Differentiating Among Time Words

Show me the difference among the words "dash," "waddle," "dart," and "crawl." First, dash. Go. Now, waddle. Go. Now, dart. Go. Next, crawl.

☐ Remember to change speeds with each word so the speeds are very clear. Let's try them again. Listen very carefully because I'm going to start calling them out faster and you'll have to change quickly from one to the other.

Other pairs of words can be used to elicit changes in time: creep/explode, pop/ sneak, gallop/totter, slither/stride.

ACTION WORDS

When you're teaching the effort concepts, action words help elicit many of the responses desired. For the exercise to be productive as well as exciting, students need to have more than a few, common words repeated over and over. Following are additional possibilities.

Single Action Words

Traveling Actions

Run	Hop	Creep
Dash	Skate	Sneak
Dart	Jump	Slither
Skip	Bounce	Crawl
Gallop	Slide	Step
Stamp	Kick	Stride
Whirl	Spin	Shuffle
Waddle	Totter	

Vibratory Actions

Shake	Wriggle
Rattle	Squirm
Vibrate	Snake
Gyrate	Whisk
Tumble	

Stopping Actions

Pause	Collapse
Stop	Slide
Freeze	Flop
Anchor	Crumple

Sinking Actions

Melt	Spin	Screw
Flop	Turn	Hammer
Drop	Slink	Spread
Collapse	Squash	Deflate
Pounce	Shrink	Crumple

Rising Actions

Evaporate	Spin	Swell
Float	Pop	Inflate
Rise	Grow	Lift
Turn	Blossom	

Nontraveling Actions

Flick	Squeeze	Contract	Jab	Stab	Relax	Lower
Jerk	Compress	Fold	Slash	Grip	Push	Drag
Twitch	Explode	Splatter	Chop	Release	Pull	Dangle
Writhe	Spread	Punch	Saw	Tense	Press	Drip

Sentences of Action Words

Run—freeze—skip	Slither—inflate—explode	Rise (turn)—twitch—skip
Dart—collapse—pop	Squeeze—jump—release	Gallop—stamp—screw
Grow—spin—deflate	Creep—pounce—explode	Jump—freeze—jab
Writhe—jerk—pop	Skip—pause—flop	Chop—whirl—slash

Descriptive Words (for use with action words)

Droopy	Excited	Light	Springy	Spikey	Square
Tired	Heavy	Tense	Carefree	Sharp	Angular
Happy	Strong	Floppy	Carefully	Rounded	Curvey
Greedy	Loving	Gentle	Fierce	Soft	Hard
Prickly	Spongy	Big	Small	Enormous	Tiny
Bubbling	Nervous	Unsure	Confident	Bold	Afraid

Nonsense Words

Snickersnack	Spelunk	Krinkle	Blump
Gallumph	Brip	Siczac	Crickcrock
Cavort	Bruttle-brattle	Swoosh	Snap-crackle
Flip-flop	Achoo	Kerumph	Wheezey
Grunch	Hic-up	Squizzog	

Source: From *Education Through the Dance Experience* by David Docherty, 1975, Bellingham, WA: Educational Designs and Consultants.

Combining Sport Skills and Time

Before beginning, I want you to think of your favorite television or sports character. Be sure you can tell me who it is when I ask because this is important. After you decide who your favorite character is, choose one action she or he performs that you really like. For example, if you choose a famous football quarterback as your favorite person, you might pick "throwing the bomb" as your favorite action. Think carefully to pick your person and action.

■ Now, on the signal you'll perform the action you choose as if it were on video set at a fast speed, such as a fast motion instead of slow motion. Repeat your fast-motion action four times, each time making the motion faster and faster.

■ Now do the same action as if it were in slow motion, just like instant replays.

□ Make sure there's a clear difference between your fast and slow motions. I should be able to tell just from watching which motions are fast and which ones are slow.

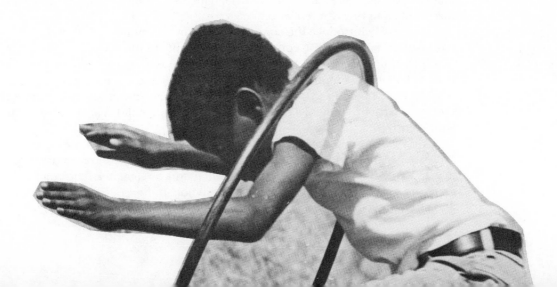

Continually Changing in Time While Traveling

As you're standing in your self-space, pick a point across the room you want to focus on. All the traveling you do will be directed toward that point. On the signal, slowly begin to travel around the point you've chosen, much like a lion stalking its prey. Gradually increase your speed so you're traveling at your maximum speed. Just before you reach the spot you've chosen, slow down, slowly circle, then suddenly pounce. The differences in the speeds at which you travel should be very clear. Thus your sequence should go like this: Pick a point to focus on, start slowly circling toward that point, gradually pick up speed until you're going really fast, then gradually slow down and suddenly pounce toward your spot.

■ Now that you have the idea, pick a new spot and practice your circling routine five times so that it's very good. Try to make it the best that you can because we're going to show some of them to the class. Slow should really be slow, fast really fast, and the pounce as quick as lightning.

To help clarify this activity, choose three or four children who are successfully completing it to demonstrate (they can all demonstrate at the same time). Reinforce the notions of gradually increasing speed and the sudden contrast of the pounce.

DEVELOPING THE CONCEPT OF FORCE

Force is the contrast of muscular tension. The extremes are strong and light, but there are obvious gradations between the extremes. Just as speed to a young child is "as fast as you can go," force often means trying to bat a ball as hard as possible, whether the situation calls for a bunt or an outfield placement. A preschooler is likely to use the same degree of force to throw a ball three feet as to throw it ten yards.

We usually introduce the concept of force by combining it with a skill that has been developed to the control level, preferably to the utilization level. For example, think of the child at a precontrol level who is learning to strike a moving ball. He is so fully concentrating his attention on making contact with the ball that the concept of force is an unnecessary and probably confusing thought. Hard and easy hits can come later, once the child is able to hit a ball consistently.

A dancer exemplifies the qualities of strong and light movement as he expresses aggression, strength, and power; the gymnast exemplifies the qualities in a free-floor exercise routine (tumbling on a large mat) as she combines firm and fine actions and balances in a demonstration of muscular control and strength.

ASSESSMENT GUIDE / Force

TASK   In your self-space, make a statue that shows a strong force. On the signal, change that same statue so that it shows a light force.

GUIDE   You'll know the children understand the concept of force when you observe that:

1. During strong force, all their body parts show muscular tension. During light force, their muscles are still firm but not tense.
2. They demonstrate the force quality asked for.
3. There's a discernible difference between their strong and light force qualities.
4. They don't hesitate when changing from one force quality to the other.

You'll know the children don't understand the quality of force when you observe that:

1. Only certain of their body parts display the force quality; others don't.
2. They don't demonstrate the force quality asked for.
3. There's no discernible difference between their strong and light force qualities.
4. They have to stop and think before displaying the force qualities.

TEACHING THE CONCEPT OF FORCE

This section provides suggestions for teaching children to understand the concept of force. Activities presented help youngsters develop an operational understanding of the strong (firm) and light (fine) actions of body parts and of the entire body. Actions of concentrated movement and muscular tensions are very tiring, so keep the activity periods short.

Activities Leading to Movement Concept Understanding

Exploring Force

In your own space, with your whole body make a statue that shows how strong you are. (A strong force is also called "heavy" or "firm.") Now practice the activity again, but think about making *every* muscle in your body strong, even your head, neck, stomach, back, hands, and feet.

■ Now make a statue that is very light, such as a ghost would be. Your statue should be so light that it would blow away if a strong wind came along. This is what is called a light force. Try a light shape again, such as a leaf floating through the wind.

■ When I beat the drum, change from a strong to a light statue and then back.

Traveling and Changing Force Qualities

This time you're going to travel around the whole space. But as you travel, try to be as strong as you can be. You're an indestructible and all-powerful force. Remember to make all your body parts strong, not just a few of them. No touching.

■ Now, as you travel, make yourself as light as can be, just as if you were floating away. All your muscles should be loose, not tight at all. Remember to make your whole body light, not just part of it.

Using Imagery and Force

This time you're going to use different images you know to help understand the force qualities. On the signal, think of yourself as a pat of butter left out on a hot day. All day long you sit in the hot sun, all weak and melted. Then suddenly someone puts you in the refrigerator, and in a little while you feel strong and solid again. Remember to make it clear with your whole body what it's like to be weak, and then make it clear with your whole body when you're strong again.

The imagery sequences you design provide experiences in extreme contrasts. Focus on the degrees along the continuum (the subtle changes) in conjunction with the actual skill, such as jumping and landing, or balancing.

OBSERVING DURING ACTIVITY

When concentrating on developing tasks, it's quite easy to forget to really look at the students and the responses they're making. A practical way to observe is, after you give a task and before saying anything to the class, to move to the outside of the area and observe for ten to fifteen seconds. You should quickly assess these three questions:

1. Are the children working safely without interfering with others?
2. If any equipment or apparatus is involved, is it being used within the context of the lesson?
3. Is the assigned task appropriate for the developmental level of the class and of interest to the class?

When you can answer yes to all three questions, look at the aspects you've determined to be important for the specific skill being practiced and extend or refine the task as appropriate.

Showing Contrasts of Force

Now you're going to show the force differences between things. On the signal I'll call out an idea; you show me what the idea looks like by moving either strong or light. Make it very clear which you are: strong or light.

Young children often equate the concept of strong force with the concept of size. Be careful to not pair all imagery examples as such—for example, big-firm or small-fine.

1. You're a bankrobber about to hold up the richest bank in the country; now you're the teller at the window that is getting held up; now you're the courageous person who comes in and stops the robbery and saves the teller.

2. You're going to show the life of Frosty the Snowman. First you're a single snowflake falling through the air; then you're several snowflakes that are beginning to stick together to make a shape; now you're the solid, sturdy snowman that can't be knocked over; and finally you're the snowman melting slowly as the sun comes out.

3. *Punch/flick.* Now we're going to use words to help us tell the difference between strong and light movements. The first two words are "punch" and "flick." I'll give you a story and you make the movements that go with it. One movement should be strong, the other light. Make each movement very clear. Pretending that you're a boxer, punch your opponent as hard as you can. Now, just flick a fly off your mother's freshly baked chocolate cake.

4. *Creep/pounce.* The words "creep" and "pounce" can help us learn strong and light movements. Let's try it. You're playing Hide-and-Seek; creep very quietly from your hiding place so no one will see or hear you. Now, you're creeping up to catch your runaway kitten. You've found her and are ready to pounce and grab her before she runs away again. Ready, pounce. Oops, you missed. Which movement was strong and which was light?

5. *Sneak/scare.* This time you're going to show light and strong actions when I use the words "sneak" and "scare." Let's pretend your brother has a letter from his girlfriend. You want to know what it says, so you sneak up behind him to find out. You can't read over his shoulder, so you figure if you scare him, he'll drop the letter and run. Go. You need to sneak, then scare.

6. *Float/collapse.* Have you ever seen a hang glider? It's like a big kite that floats through the air, but a person is floating with it, just as if he or she were attached to a kite. You're now a hang glider, sailing over the mountains. Go. Oh, no—all the wind suddenly died; your hang glider is crashing to the ground. You just collapse as you hit the ground. Make your light movements very light and your strong actions very strong.

7. *Glide/stomp.* You're a very good skater, and today you go roller skating. You're at the local roller skating rink gliding along having a grand time. Now something sticks to your skate; you don't fall, but you have to stomp

your skate really hard to try and get the object off. Clearly show the difference between your light and strong movements.

8. *Raindrop/thunderstorm.* You're a raindrop in a gentle spring rain, a rain that makes all the flowers bloom and the grass turn its greenest green. Now you're a raindrop in a bad summer thunderstorm—you know, a storm where the wind blows so hard you think the tress will fall down and the sky turns very dark. Remember to make it very clear which raindrop is strong and which one is light.

9. *Friends/foes.* Now you're going to show strong and light as you greet your friend and then as you meet an enemy. Pretend you're walking down the street and see an old friend. How would you greet her? Now play as if you've just seen the biggest bully in the school. How would you greet him? Which force was light and which one was strong?

10. Imagine what an ant trying to lift a rock feels like. Try hard; you're the only hope of the rock getting off the ground. Now you're a strong man trying to lift the same rock that the ant lifted. How are your actions different? Make sure that you really show the difference in how you use your muscles. One action should be strong and the other one light.

11. You're an Olympic weightlifter going for the gold medal; this is the heaviest weight you've ever lifted. As you pretend, remember to keep your entire body strong. Even show in your face that you're strong. Now you're lifting a five-pound bag of flour. How easy is it for you? Make your whole body light as you show this action. All your muscles should be loose, as if they're not being used at all.

DEVELOPING THE CONCEPT OF FLOW

Watch a very young child running down a hill. Her actions are unstoppable, almost out of her control, until she reaches the bottom. A batter's swing at a baseball, the smash a tennis player executes, a gymnast's giant swing on the high bar—all these are examples of free flow in movement. It seems that the performer is lost in the movement; the movement, not the performer, seems to control the situation.

Bound actions are stoppable, cautious, and restrained. The performer is in control at all times. Pushing a heavy object, traveling an angular pathway while trying to stay within boundaries, executing a slow cartwheel with a pause for a handstand before traveling on are all examples of bound flow.

ASSESSMENT GUIDE / Flow

TASK   Travel in general space using any bound movement you want. When the drum beats, change your movement from bound flow to free flow without changing your form of traveling.

GUIDE   You'll know the children understand the concept of flow when you observe that:

1. They demonstrate the correct aspect of flow.
2. They can change immediately from bound flow to free flow but take a few steps to change from free to bound flow.
3. Their bodies are very tense when the flow is bound; their bodies relax during free flow.
4. Their range of movement narrows when they demonstrate bound flow and expands during free flow.

You'll know the children don't understand the concept of flow when you observe that:

1. They have to stop and think before changing from one aspect of flow to the other.
2. They demonstrate the incorrect aspect of flow.
3. They stop free flow immediately or don't stop bound flow immediately.
4. They don't overtly display tension with bound flow.

TEACHING THE CONCEPT OF FLOW

This section provides activities that help children understand and demonstrate the difference between free flow and bound flow. The activities encompass a variety of movements that are important for both skill performance and safety. Music can greatly enhance the feel of bound or free flow.

Activities Leading to Movement Concept Understanding

Traveling and Flow

On the signal, travel around the room and pause the instant you hear the stop signal. *(Children tend to anticipate the teacher's signals. Make stop signals close together and frequent so this activity will be successful.)* I'm really looking for stops that happen suddenly, without you taking any extra steps. Freeze dead in your tracks. This kind of movement—jerky and stops a lot—is said to have *bound* flow. In other words, it doesn't flow very smoothly.

■ This time as you travel around the space, pretend you're completely free, such as an eagle soaring high in the sky, a prisoner who just was let out of jail, or a really happy person who has no cares in the world. Make your traveling seem as if it has no end; it could just keep going and going. This type of movement is said to have *free* flow. In other words, it doesn't stop, much like a balloon floating in the air.

Eliciting Flow Qualities

This time I'm going to give you some actions to help you practice bound flow. Pretend to do each action that I tell you, always showing the bound flow of what you're doing. Remember, bound flow can be stopped and is generally slow and sometimes jerky.

1. Press the floor with your hands and feet as you move. Make sure you keep a bound flow throughout the whole motion.
2. Pretend you're pushing a heavy box.
3. Now carry a glass of milk that is too full without spilling any of it.
4. Play as if you're pulling from the bottom of a well a full bucket of water on a pulley.

Challenging children to travel while balancing beanbags on their heads is one way to elicit bound flow.

■ Now I'll give you some actions that require free flow. Free flow can be harder than bound flow, so really concentrate on making your movements seem as if they could go on forever. Make it very clear that these are free movements and unstoppable.

1. Pretend to flick away a fly.
2. This time you're really mad at your brother. Slash your arms through the air to show how really mad you are.
3. You're cooking bacon on the stove and the grease starts to spatter; jerk your head and arms away so you won't get burned.

Following Flow Sentences

On the board are a number of sentences. The first one says "Walk, run, jump." On the signal, begin to travel, using the sentence as your guide. The words are clear; the commas mean to pause or hesitate, and the periods mean to stop. Make it very clear where your pauses are and when you stop. Repeat the action of the sentence three times.

Other possible sentences are: walk, sneak, pounce; leap, stamp, twist; creep, hop, flop.

■ What you just did was an example of bound flow. Now you're going to turn the same thing into free flow. This time, on the signal, you're going to follow the same sentences but without the punctuation marks—in other words, no commas and no periods or no pauses or stops. So you'll start at the beginning of the sentence and keep going all the way through; no one should know when you're going to change to the next action. Your action should just flow smoothly, one action leading to the next. When you get to the end of a sentence, just start over again. On the signal, let's start with the first sentence.

Children enjoy using interpretations of different punctuation marks, such as the comma, exclamation point, and question mark, as different ending shapes.

■ Now that you're so good at the sentences, you're going to make up one of your own. On the board is a list of words. *(Such words as "walk," "shrink," "gallop," "skip," "explode," "jump," "roll," and "hop" are good to use.)* Choose three of the words and make your sentence. Put punctuation in because punctuation is the key to when you stop or pause. Practice your sentence five times with the punctuation in it; then practice it five times without punctuation. Practice it very carefully because we'll show some of the sentences to the class. It should be obvious when the punctuation is and isn't in the sentence.

Practicing Flow Sequences

This time, there are two columns of words on the board, but no punctuation. You're going to join the words together to make a sequence. The first column of words reads "melt," "inflate," "slither," "shrink." On the signal, practice the words in the order you see them. It is your choice as when to change from one word to the next. Go.

- Now, do the second column of words: "jump," "spin," "stride," "pop."
- □ Which sequence gave you a bound feeling? Which one a free feeling?
- □ Now go back and practice each sequence three times, making it very clear each time which one is bound and which one is free.

Using Flow Conversations

Children beginning sequence work often need guidance in restricting the length of the sequence; generally two or three actions are appropriate for the initial sequence.

Now you're going to work with a partner and talk to your partner. The only catch is that neither of you can use your voice to talk. You're going to talk with your body. One of you needs to be bound and the other one free; go ahead and decide that now. Ready? This is how you'll talk: The partner who is bound will talk about being imprisoned and not being allowed to go out to see the world; the partner who is free will talk about how wonderful it is to roam and explore and run up and down the hills; in other words, what it's like to be free. Now, one of you start; with your body talk about your aspect. Keep your sentence very short. As you move, your partner listens or watches. After you make your statement, stop; your partner then answers with a statement and you listen. When your partner finishes, you again provide an answer. The whole conversation should go back and forth until each of you has moved five times. After you've completed the conversation once, go back and practice it twice more so that it's very clear who's free and who's bound. I know this is a bit hard to understand, so let me go over it one more time. You and your partner are going to talk about bound and free flow with your body actions, not your voices. Just as in any conversation, it's a give and take. One of you will make a short body action sentence and then the other one will answer. Each of you gets to talk five times and then ends it. After you've finished once, go back and practice two more times.

- □ Remember that two people can't talk at once, so listen when your partner is talking. "Still's" the word.

It really helps to find at least one group (hopefully more) doing the activity correctly and have them demonstrate. Be patient; the task will take time if the children are to really develop their conversations. Children should switch roles after sufficient time to practice the other aspect of flow.

DESIGNING SEQUENCES

Helping children learn how to design move-ment sequences is much like helping them learn how to design their own games (see Chapter 26). Following are several tips we've found helpful when beginning to have chil-dren design sequences.

1. It takes time.
2. Structure the sequence into a simple form that is easily remembered, e.g., a starting shape; a middle moving phase based on a specific aspect of movement; an ending shape.
3. Practice the starting and ending shapes separately before adding the middle movement.
4. Initially, provide a beginning signal, some time to practice (twenty to twenty-five seconds), and then an ending signal.

Source: Adapted from *First Steps in Teaching Creative Dance to Children,* 2nd ed., by Mary Joyce, 1980, Palo Alto, CA: Mayfield.

5. During the first stages, prompt the chil-dren during the movement aspect as to exactly what movements need to be included (change of level, speed, etc.).
6. Have children repeat their sequence sev-eral times. The middle movement aspect may vary slightly each time, but the begin-ning and end should remain constant.
7. In some way hold the children account-able for what they've created, for example, divide the class in half and have them present their sequence, present their sequence to another person, or write it down.

As the children's ability to design sequences increases, you can gradually relax some of these guidelines, but we've found these steps useful for both the students and the teacher when first beginning to create movement sequences.

Combining Time, Force, and Flow

The task sheet *(see Figure 13-2)* for today will allow you to practice combining the concepts of time, force, and flow. After you practice each challenge so that you feel it's as clear as you can make it, find a friend to watch you. If the friend feels you've done the challenge correctly, she or he signs her or his name in the blank; if not, you'll have to go back and practice some more. I'll walk around the class, and at any time I can ask you to show me any challenge you've marked off. If you have any questions, ask me.

APPLYING THE EFFORT CONCEPTS

We focus on concepts until the children have learned the basic terminology related to the effort qualities of movement. When the children are able to accurately demonstrate the differences between the extremes of each concept,

Name ——————————— Teacher ———————————

Time, Force, and Flow Task Sheet

Date	Who Watched	Challenge
		Find three body parts that you can move at a slow speed.
		Find three body parts (different from the ones in the first challenge) that you can move at a fast speed.
		Find four ways to move while showing free and light qualities.
		Find two movements that you can first make strong and slow and then make light and fast.
		Find any movement you want that combines two aspects of the effort concept (time: fast-slow, force: strong-light, flow: bound-free). After you finish, write down your movements and the concepts they included. Movement Concept ——————— ——————— ——————— ——————— ——————— ——————— ——————— ———————

Figure 13-2 Task sheet for time, force, and flow.

we no longer focus on the concept. Instead, we focus on how the concept relates to the performance of a particular skill: fast dribble, fluid roll, or light gallop. We want the children to learn the effort concepts so that they can apply the concepts to actual skill-learning situations.

The ability to use gradations of movement qualities distinguishes the inept performer from the skilled one, the sloppy movement from the polished one. An individual can learn to execute the basic requirements of a cartwheel, for example, so that it can be recognized as a cartwheel. But when that cartwheel is executed in a ragged, uneven, uncontrolled manner, it is clearly and easily distinguishable from a cartwheel performed by an experienced, trained gymnast. We teach children to apply the qualities of movement to their skill performances to help them become skillful movers.

Generally the concept of time (fast-slow) is easier for children to grasp than either the concept of force (strong-light) or the concept of flow (bound-free), so you may need to focus more on force and flow than on time. Time can be studied as an applied concept—fast and slow skips, rolling fast and rolling slow, accelerated and decelerated change of levels—before force or flow. The difference is that in teaching a concept, our observational focus is primarily on the children's ability to understand and apply the effort concept (Chapter 3). In contrast, when we use a concept as a subtheme, we know that the children already understand the concept from previous lessons, and therefore our teaching focus is primarily on the skill and how it can be executed by using varying movements.

READING COMPREHENSION QUESTIONS

1. How is a movement performed fast different from the same movement performed slowly?
2. How is a movement executed with a strong force different from the same movement performed with a light force?
3. How is a movement performed with a bound flow different from the same movement performed with a free flow?
4. Initially, the extremes, rather than the gradations, of the effort concepts are emphasized. Why?
5. When is slowness an important concept? List several movements.
6. What does the term *acceleration-deceleration* mean? Answer by using examples from the text or from your own experiences.
7. What does focusing on the movement quality of an image rather than on the image itself mean? This statement will help you: "Imagine that the floor is covered with peanut butter six inches deep."
8. When do you change from focusing on the effort concept to focusing on how the concept relates to the performance of a particular skill?
9. What is the purpose of teaching children to apply the qualities of movement to their skill performances?

C H A P T E R **14**

Relationships

Our lives are made up of relationships—to people and to objects—that occur not only in physical education classes but in everyday life. Driving to and from work in an automobile, maneuvering through a crowded aisle in a supermarket, or dodging around an icy spot on a sidewalk—all these activities involve complex, dynamic relationships. And each relationship involves several contextual variables (bodies, body parts, and objects) in simultaneous interaction.

The concept of relationship defines with whom or with what the body moves; it gives meaning to the interaction between individuals and their environment. The concept is divided into three major components: relationships of body parts, relationships with people, and relationships with objects and/or people. In turn, each of these constructs is defined by observable characteristics that can be taught to children. Figure 14-1 conceptualizes this idea, putting it in perspective with the other movement concepts and skill themes. The relationship category is in the right-hand side of the movement framework. The outermost ring defines the concept; the second ring presents the three components of the concept; and the third ring defines the aspects of the three components.

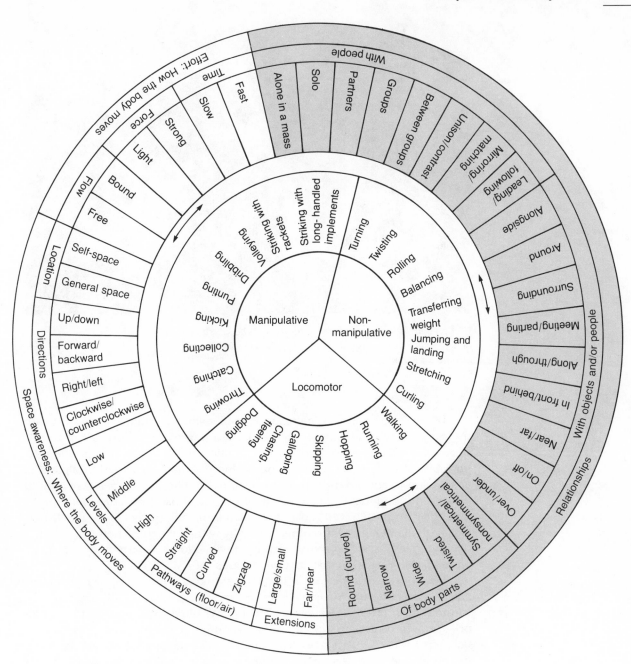

Figure 14-1 Movement analysis framework: Relationship concepts.

*"Touch ears with hands." Young children at the "I" stage
benefit from tasks designed to clarify the relationships
among body parts.*

When introducing the concept of relationships to children, we start with
the simplest relationships. Because many young children are still at the "I"
stage, the initial lessons focus on self-relationships, which include the relationships of body parts to one another and the movements of body parts to
change the relationship of those parts to make different shapes. As children
develop a functional understanding of the relationships among body parts,
we shift the emphasis to moving in relation to different objects. Finally, we
focus on relationships with others, initially with partners. When the children
develop the social and physical maturity needed to work with others, we focus
on relationships within and between groups.

Relationships as they occur in the areas of dance (for expressive purposes)
and in games and gymnastics (with a more functional intent) are typically
within the context of a particular situation. Within a given context, the appropriate emphasis is then placed on the dynamics of a specific purposeful relationship. In simpler terms, once the children have grasped the basic concepts,
we modify the emphasis on a relationship to suit the demands of a particular
movement situation.

When teaching the relationship concepts, it's sometimes easy to forget
that the purpose is to have the children actually *know* what each relationship

means. This analogy may help. Imagine that one of us [the authors of the book] is going to come and teach a class of your second-graders. Prior to teaching, we might ask if your children know the relationship concepts. If you said "yes," we'd assume that the children could make a symmetrical shape or a nonsymmetrical shape when asked to do so. Or we'd assume that the youngsters know the difference between mirroring and matching, over and under, around and through, etc. In this instance, "knowing" doesn't mean that the concepts were taught; knowing means that the children are able to show their understanding through their movement. In other words, the children have *functional understanding*.

Another illustration further makes this point. If one of us were going to teach a second-grade art class, we might ask the teacher if the children know their colors. If the teacher said "yes," we'd assume that the children know the difference among red, brown, black, orange, etc. We'd further expect that the children could readily use these colors in the lesson we taught. On the other hand, if the teacher said the children don't know their colors, we'd design our lesson to help the children learn their colors.

DEVELOPING THE CONCEPT OF THE RELATIONSHIPS OF BODY PARTS

Before children can focus on the relationships among body parts, they need to be able to identify specific body parts. Thus, it's essential that each child acquire a functional vocabulary of body part names. Tasks that can be used in teaching this vocabulary include

1. Pointing to the ceiling with the elbow (knee, nose)
2. Touching the floor with the wrist (waist, stomach)
3. Traveling with only the feet, hands, and seat (elbows and knees) touching the floor
4. Traveling around the room and on the signal stopping and touching heels (shoulders, heads) with another person

Once the children have learned the names of the body parts, lessons focus on making shapes (round, narrow, wide, twisted, symmetrical, and nonsymmetrical) and using body parts in relation to each other. For example, we might ask children to

1. Travel and stop in a twisted shape
2. Change from a symmetrical to a nonsymmetrical shape
3. Make a wide shape during flight
4. Move their feet so that they're higher than their head

"Point to the door with your elbow." A young girl responds to the teacher's challenge.

ASSESSMENT GUIDE / Relationships of Body Parts

TASK   Travel throughout the general space. On the stop signal, freeze in a twisted body shape with one elbow touching the floor. On the next six beats of the drum, gradually open up into a wide body shape. On the next six beats, slowly return to your original twisted position.

GUIDE   You'll know the children understand the concept of the relationships of body parts when you observe that:

1. One of their elbows touches the floor.
2. Their first body shapes are twisted and nonsymmetrical.
3. Their second body shapes are wide and symmetrical.

GUIDE   You'll know the children don't understand the concept of the relationships of body parts when you observe that:

1. One of their elbows doesn't touch the floor.
2. Their first body shapes aren't twisted and nonsymmetrical.

3. Their second body shapes aren't wide and symmetrical.
4. They have to stop and think for more than a few seconds about their body shapes before they make them.
5. There's no discernible difference between the two body shapes.

TEACHING THE CONCEPT OF THE RELATIONSHIPS OF BODY PARTS

This section provides suggestions for teaching children to identify and use different body parts and to develop an understanding of how different body parts can relate to one another. Suggestions for teaching the concepts of various body shapes and body part shapes also are presented. You can use any body parts for the activities given here, but with the tasks that require balancing, be careful to not use parts that will elicit balances that may be too complex for some students. For example, when using parts such as head and hands, make it clear that other parts can be used in conjunction with the head and the hands.

Activities Leading to Movement Concept Understanding

Identifying Body Parts

I'm going to call out different body parts. Touch the body parts I call out as quickly as possible when you hear them. Remember to pay close attention to what I'm saying because I may start to go faster or try to trick you. Ready? Remember, touch each body part as I call it out.

Body parts can include nose, arm, chin, ankle, ear, foot, elbow, temple, wrist, neck, shoulder, eyebrow, eye, teeth, cheek, leg, forehead, knee, thumb, mouth, side, hip, lip, earlobe.

■ This time, instead of just touching a body part as I name it, you'll have to touch whatever hand I call out to the different body parts I call out. This activity will be harder because you'll have to remember which is your right and which is your left. For example, if I say "right hand to left knee," touch your right hand to your left knee. Try to do this as quickly as possible, but be careful in deciding what body parts to use. Just to help you out, let's review right and left. Raise your right hand. *(Check to see that they're correct.)* Ready? Let's try it.

Body parts used can include left hand to right knee, right hand to left elbow, left hand to left shoulder, right hand to left knee, left hand to left foot.

■ This time you're going to play a game with finding body parts, similar to Simon Says, except you don't have to sit out if you miss. Here's how to play. I'll call out "Simon says to touch your toes" and you'll touch your toes. But if I don't say "Simon says," then you aren't supposed to do it. So if I just say "Touch your toes," you aren't supposed to touch your toes because Simon didn't say to do it. Pay close attention because the game will start to go very quickly. Remember that I'm watching to see if you touch the right parts and how quickly you can do it.

■ This time, instead of touching your hands to different body parts, you're going to touch two different body parts together. For example, I'll call out "knee to elbow" and you'll touch your knee to your elbow. You'll have to think hard on this one. Ready? I'm looking to see if you can get the correct different parts together.

Possible body part combinations can include knee to elbow, hands to waist, head to knees, foot to shoulder, knee to foot, elbow to wrist, back of wrist to back of knee.

Balancing While Using Different Body Parts

Place carpet squares on the floor, one square for each child.

Find a carpet square for yourself and sit on the square. I'll know that you're all ready when I see everyone seated on a carpet square. This time when I call out a body part, you should put that body part on the carpet square and make a shape with the rest of your body, leaving the one part that I called out on the carpet. So if I call out "elbow," put your elbow on the carpet and then make a shape with the rest of your body. When you make your shape, be sure to hold it very still so I can see what part is on the carpet and what your shape looks like. Ready? Let's try it.

☐ Shapes that you hold very still are called *balances*, almost like statues. Let's try this activity again; make your balances and shapes very clear and still.

■ Now you're going to balance on different numbers of body parts. I'll call out a number of parts; you balance by touching that number to the floor. Count your parts touching the floor very carefully because I'll be coming around and asking you how many parts are on the floor and which parts they are.

Four parts

Three parts

More than four parts

Two parts

One part

For each number, offer suggestions or hints, or have several students demonstrate the possible combinations of parts. Also mix up the order that the parts are called out in, and be sure to repeat each number at least three times.

Balancing on Matching and Nonmatching Parts

This time, instead of balancing on a certain number of parts, you're going to balance on parts that are alike and parts that are different. Parts that are alike are called *matching* parts. What parts do you have that are matching or alike? *(Children respond "hands," "feet," etc.)* Good; let's try to balance on some of those parts. First let's try an easy one: the feet. Now, how about the knees? Think up one of your own. Make sure that the parts you use are matching parts.

    ☐ Now pick one set of matching parts and make up a balance that you like and practice it until you can hold it very still. Be sure you know the name of the matching parts you're balancing on because I'll come around and ask some of you, just to make sure.

    ■ This time you're going to balance on different parts. *Different* parts are parts that don't match each other; they aren't alike. What are some possible combinations of different parts? *(Children respond "knee and elbow," "back and hands," etc.)* Let's try some. First, try the seat and the feet. Now try the shoulders and the elbows. What about the knees and the elbows? Now, make up one combination on your own.

    ■ Now pick one set of different parts and make up your own balance. Practice your balance until you can hold it very still. Be sure the different parts you're using are very clear because I might ask you what they are.

Traveling on Different Body Parts

This time, instead of balancing on different body parts, you're going to travel on different body parts. What body parts do we usually travel on? Let's start with the feet, just to get warmed up. Make sure to travel in all the space and to stay on your feet.

    ■ Now try something a little different: the hands and feet. Remember to travel with your hands and feet both touching the floor at some time. Ready? Make sure you actually go someplace, and be careful of others.

    ■ This time you're going to make up your own way of traveling using different body parts. As you do this, make sure that I can tell from just looking at you what body parts you're using for traveling; you should be using two different body parts to move around the room. Practice your new way of traveling until you can do it so it looks professional. Be very careful to watch where you're going and not touch anyone else.

Traveling and Freezing on Different Body Parts

You're going to travel around the space on your feet. When you hear the stop signal, touch the body part I call out to the floor. So if I call out "elbow" as you stop, touch your elbow to the floor. As you move, be very careful to stay in a space by yourself, so you don't touch anyone when you're trying to touch different body parts to the floor. This activity will start to go very fast, so touch the parts to the floor as quickly as possible, and make it very clear which part is touching the floor.

Body parts can include arm, ankle, foot, leg, side, hip.

■ When you travel this time, instead of touching body parts to the floor, touch the body parts I call out to one other person. So if I call out "heels," stop, touch your heels to the heels of one other person, and then freeze. As you do this, make the touching parts very clear; don't just stand beside the other person. To be safe, make sure as you touch that you stop first and then touch easily so no one gets hurt. The idea is to quickly and easily touch and then be ready to go again. Ready?

Body parts can include wrist, shoulder, forehead, knee, thumb, arm, ankle, foot, elbow, leg, side, hip.

Teaching Body Shapes

Today you're going to learn about different shapes you can make with your bodies. Everyone find a self-space so that you can't touch anyone else. The first shape you're going to make is a pretzel. All of you try to make a pretzel out of your body; hold very still. This shape is called a *twisted* shape.

■ Now, try a twisted shape on your own. As you do so, make sure your whole body is twisted, not just your arms and legs. Try to twist your stomach too.

■ The next shape is a circle. Try to make your whole body look like a circle. This is called a *round* shape.

■ Now try to make up a different round shape by yourself. Make sure that your whole body is making the round shape and that it is very round. Remember, round things have no bumps in them.

■ This time you're going to make a skinny shape. Try to make your body as skinny as possible, so skinny that if you turned sideways, no one would be able to see you. This is called a *narrow* shape.

■ Find another narrow shape by yourself. Make it as skinny as possible, as if you were trying to hide.

■ What do you think the opposite of skinny is? Fat, right. Make your body as fat as possible. This is called a *wide* shape.

■ Try another wide shape by yourself. Remember to get as wide as possible, as if you were trying to stop someone from getting around you.

■ This time pick your favorite kind of shape and make it, holding it very still. I'm going to come around and guess which type of shape it is, so make your shape as clear as possible. Your shape should be wide, narrow, round, or twisted.

■ Things are going to be a little harder this time. Still staying in your own space, you're going to make a wide shape. Then, when I give the signal, change

your wide shape to a narrow shape and hold it very still. The difference between the wide and narrow shape should be very clear. Make a wide shape and hold it. Now change that wide shape to a narrow shape.

■ Try it again—another wide shape; change to a narrow.

■ Now, a third.

■ This time pick the shape you liked the most and practice it until it changes very easily from wide to narrow. Work on it until it's your best and both shapes are very clear.

■ You thought the last activity was hard? This one is even harder! Think you can do it? You're going to change from a twisted shape to a round shape. So find your twisted shape. Got it? On the signal, change that twisted shape to a round shape.

■ Now, let's try another twisted to round shape. Go.

■ And a third twisted to round shape.

□ Make sure that your twisted is really twisted and your round very round. I should be able to easily tell the difference between the two shapes.

■ Now, pick the shape you liked the most. You need to practice your favorite one so that your move from twisted to round is very smooth, like a professional, and that your shapes are so clear the principal could easily tell the difference if he or she walked in.

Changing from One Body Shape to Another

You'll really need to be in your self-space for this activity, so make sure you're as far away from everyone else as you can be. Again you're going to change from one shape to another, but I'm going to give you drumbeats to help. You're going to move from a round shape to a wide shape, but instead of just doing it on your own, you'll have six beats of the drum to get from the round shape to the wide shape and then six beats to get back to your round shape. Listen now while I give you the beats of the drum. Does everyone understand? You'll start in a round shape and on the six beats of the drum open to a wide shape. You'll hold your wide shape very still, and then on the next six beats of the drum you'll return to your round shape. Let's try it. Find your round shape.

- Let's try it again; this time find different round and wide shapes.
- Now, let's do a third set of shapes.
- You're now going to practice one set of shapes four more times, so you can make it really good. Pick your favorite shapes. Remember as you move to make each shape very clear, and make sure that the movement goes with the beats of the drum.

Pick out one or two children who are succeeding with the activity and ask them if they'd like to show it to the class.

- You're going to make the shapes a little different this time. Instead of opening up on six beats and closing on six, you're going to open up on one quick beat and then close slowly on six. So the sequence will now go like this: Start in a round shape; on the beat, quickly open up to a wide shape and hold it still; then on the next six beats of the drum, slowly return to your round shape. Try it—round shape.
  - □ Again. Remember that you must open from the round to the wide shape very, very quickly, as if you were a flash of lightning.
  - □ One more time, and make the round and wide shapes clear enough so anybody could tell the difference. *(Pick out several children to show the activity to the rest of the class.)*
- Now practice your favorite shapes four times. Remember not only to make the quick sudden and the slow sustained but to make your round and wide shapes very clear. To help look really good, remember to hold the beginning and the end very still so that we all know when you started and when you finished.

Traveling and Freezing in Different Body Shapes

Instead of making shapes in your self-space, this time you're going to travel around the space and on the signal make the shape I call out. For example, if you're traveling and I call out "twisted," on the signal make a twisted shape. As you make your shapes, be sure they're very clear so that I can easily tell what they are. If I can't tell what they are, I'll have to ask you. As you travel, be careful of your classmates.

  - □ Let's see if you can make the shapes even better. Watch *(give the names of a boy and girl who are performing the activity correctly).*
- Now, as you stop to make your shape, try to do it as quickly as possible, almost as if you just froze in that shape when you stopped. Remember frozen shapes; don't fall over.

Making Symmetrical and Nonsymmetrical Shapes

You've already learned about wide, narrow, round, and twisted shapes. This time you're going to learn about two different kinds of shapes. The words

"Freeze in a low and wide shape." This task requires children to consider the relationship among body parts.

describing these shapes are hard, so listen carefully. First, find a body shape that looks exactly alike on both sides of your body; in other words, if you were cut in half, both sides of you would look alike. This is called a *symmetrical* shape.

■ Now try making another symmetrical shape. Remember, both sides of your body must look exactly alike. *(See Figure 14-2.)*

Figure 14-2 Symmetrical and nonsymmetrical shapes.

■ Now find a shape in which the two sides of your body don't look alike. In other words, if you were cut in half, each side would have a different shape. This is called a *nonsymmetrical* shape.

■ Do another nonsymmetrical shape. Remember, both sides must be different.

■ Since you now know the difference between symmetrical and nonsymmetrical, let's find three more balances of each shape. First do symmetrical; remember, both sides are alike. Try to make each of your balances very clear so I can tell without thinking what kind of shape it is. Practice your favorite symmetrical shape five extra times so you can show the class.

■ Now do nonsymmetrical shapes. Find three more nonsymmetrical shapes. Try to make the sides of your body as different as possible so no one could possibly confuse your shape with a symmetrical one. Once you've found three more nonsymmetrical shapes, practice your favorite one five extra times so you can show it to the whole class. *(Half the class demonstrates their favorite nonsymmetrical shape, and then the other half shows their favorite nonsymmetrical shape.)*

Creating Postcard Sculptures

You'll need museum postcards of statues, one postcard for every child. Children love to play the roles of statues and sculptors but tend to get silly during this activity. Warn them that no horseplay will be allowed. Also caution them to place others only in shapes they can hold without too much difficulty, so no one gets hurt.

You're going to pretend that you're sculptors who are creating great statues. To do this you'll need a partner. When I say "go," find a partner and sit beside your partner. I'll know you're ready when I see everyone seated beside a partner. Each set of partners has two postcards of statues; you're going to make each other into these statues. Decide which partner will be the sculptor first; the sculptor then decides which statue to make the partner into. The trick is to try and make each statue both symmetrical and nonsymmetrical, so it will be a little different from the postcard picture. First, make the statue just as it is on the card, as closely as possible to what you see. Then, if the statue is symmetrical, change it to nonsymmetrical; if it's nonsymmetrical, make it symmetrical. Mold each statue very carefully, and be sure you can tell me which statue is symmetrical and which is nonsymmetrical. After you make your statue, trade places with your partner.

■ This time you're going to design your own statues. You'll still need your partner. Go ahead and decide which of you is to be the sculptor first. Make your first statue symmetrical. The statue stays symmetrical until the signal. At the signal, move to someone else's statue and redesign it to suit yourself. On the next signal, move to another new statue and redesign it. Keep doing this until you're told to change. When you hear the change signal, change places with whatever statue you're with.

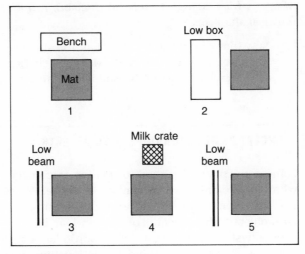

Figure 14-3 Equipment setups.

■ Let's practice once. Make your partner into a symmetrical statue. *(Allow at least one minute.)* Now, move to another statue and remake it, still into a symmetrical shape. Do you have the hang of it? *(Select several children for demonstration.)* Go to the next statue.

■ Now trade places with the statue you've just made. The activity changes a little this time; you're going to create nonsymmetrical statues. Ready? Without moving to a new place, form a nonsymmetrical statue out of your partner.

■ Change to a new statue and then change this statue to a nonsymmetrical shape. Remember: Nonsymmetrical means that both sides of the body are very different from each other.

■ Change one more time. Make this your best statue yet.

Building Body Shapes in the Air

You'll need boxes, benches, low beams, and milk crates set up around the space. Figure 14-3 is a typical equipment setup.

Now you're going to combine all the different kinds of body shapes that you've practiced so far. What you're going to do may be hard, but it'll be fun. Remember that as you work, all the rules for gymnastics apply. *(See Chapters 7 and 28 for establishing an environment for learning and for the rules for a gymnastics environment.)* Three or four of you will be at a piece of equipment at once. One at a time, you'll each jump off the equipment and make a shape in the air. I'll call out a shape, and each time you jump, try to make that shape in the air. Let's start with a wide shape. Make sure that you land on your feet after the jump, and don't crash to the ground. See if you can hold your landing as still as Mary Lou Retton.

After a while, change to narrow, twisted, round, symmetrical, and nonsymmetrical shapes.

☐ Now that you've been through all the shapes separately, you may practice them in any order you wish. Make the shapes so clear that I don't have to ask you what they are. Remember to land on your feet.

DEVELOPING THE CONCEPT OF RELATIONSHIPS WITH OBJECTS

Some concepts are studied in relation to objects; others have more meaning when they're practiced in relation to people. The concepts of on and off, along, through, over, under, around, and surrounding apply primarily to relationships with objects. The concepts of near and far, in front, behind, and alongside are generally studied as person-to-person relationships. The concepts discussed in this section can be studied as relationships to objects or to people. Because

Children travel cautiously through a narrow space; each child constantly monitors her or his relationship to the obstacle.

objects are more predictable (less dynamic) than children, however, we first focus on the concept of relationships with objects, then relationships with people.

It's interesting to note that children frequently identify a lesson by the object they related to rather than by the concept they studied. For example, after a lesson in which hoops were used to study the concepts of traveling over, under, and through, children might say, "Hey, that was fun! Are we going to play with hoops again tomorrow?" In time, however, children begin to understand and use the terminology that we use. For instance, a child might say, "It's easier to go over and under the hoop than to go through the hoop."

Within the context of a game or a dance lesson, specific terms are classified as objects. In dance, for example, wands, streamers, newspapers, or scarves are considered objects. Goals, boundaries, nets, and targets are objects with which the child learns relationship concepts within a game context.

ASSESSMENT GUIDE / Relationships with Objects

Note to Teachers. Each student will need a block and cane and a hoop, set up as shown in the accompanying illustration.

TASK   Travel *over* the hurdle, making sure you land in the hoop on the other side. Travel back *under* the hurdle, and move *around* the hurdle so that you end on the hoop side.

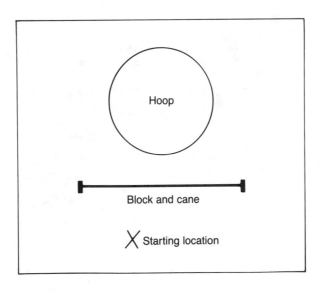

Hoop

Block and cane

X Starting location

GUIDE   You'll know the children understand the concept of relationships with objects when you observe that:

1. They go *over* the hurdle on the first crossing.
2. They land *inside* the hoop after crossing it.
3. They go *under* the hurdle after landing inside the hoop.
4. They travel *around* the outside of the hurdle after going under it.

You'll know the children don't understand the concept of relationships with objects when you observe that:

1. They don't do the above activities in the exact order given.
2. They don't appear to understand the terms over, under, inside, and around.

TEACHING THE CONCEPT OF RELATIONSHIPS WITH OBJECTS

The activities in this section will enhance the children's awareness and ability to function effectively in relation to the objects that exist in various physical activity contexts.

Activities Leading to Movement Concept Understanding

Traveling Over, Close To, Far Away, Inside

Each child will need a hoop or a rope. See Figures 14-4 and 14-5.

Figure 14-4 Construction of a hoop. Cut hoops from half-inch plastic air conditioner or water pipe. Make the connection with a dowel rod held in place with staples or tacks. You can also use special pipe connectors or fuse with heat to close the gap. For a 30-inch diameter hoop, you'll need 95 inches of pipe; for a 36-inch hoop, you'll need 113 inches of pipe; and for a 42-inch hoop, you'll need 132 inches of pipe.

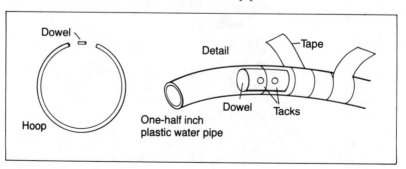

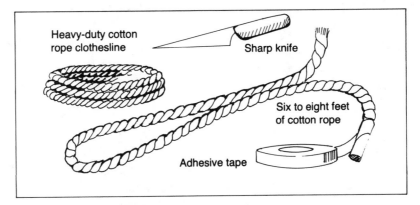

Figure 14-5 Construction of a rope. Use half-inch cotton rope. The cotton will eventually loosen up and give, so different shapes can be made with it. Single ropes should be from six to eight feet long. After you cut the ends of the rope, tape the ends to prevent fraying.

To warm up, travel *over* your piece of equipment in any way you want to. As you travel, make sure that you actually go over the equipment, not around it.

■ This time as you travel over your equipment, try to stay as *close* to the equipment as possible. Try to keep as much of your body as possible close to the equipment, not just one body part.

■ Now, instead of being close to the equipment, try to have as many body parts as possible as *far away* from the equipment as possible. Only the parts that are really used to support your body should be near the equipment.

☐ Make sure that your whole body is as far away as possible, not just the upper parts of your body.

■ The activity is a little harder now. Start on the *outside* of your equipment, put your weight down on your hands *inside* the hoop *(or a circle made with a rope)*, and then continue to travel over the equipment. Make sure that you shift your weight to your hands inside the hoop *(rope)* at some point.

■ These are all relationships that your body can have to equipment or other people. We can go over things, we can be close to things, we can be far away from things, or we can go inside things. Practice all four of these relationships on your own: over, close to, far away, and inside. See if you can find three ways to do each relationship. Be sure you know which ones you're practicing because I'll come around and ask you.

If you say you're going to come around and ask the children questions or see their work, Do It! Otherwise, the children will soon stop believing you.

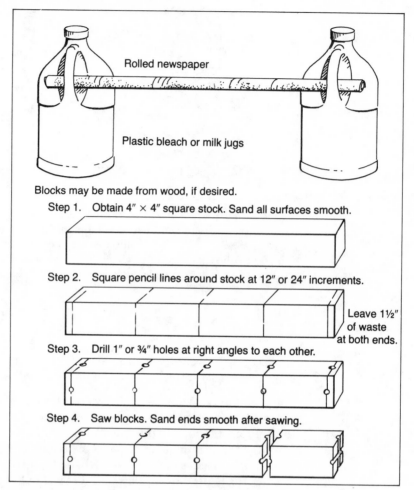

Figure 14-6 Construction of hurdles. Hurdles can be made from plastic bleach or milk jugs and rolled newspaper held together with masking tape. A more permanent type of hurdle can be made from wood and dowel rods.

Traveling over Equipment

You'll need a hurdle (see Figure 14-6) for each child in the class.

To begin, travel *over* the hurdle any way that you can; you can jump, use your hands and feet, or use only your hands. Whatever you do, make sure that you can land on your feet on the other side without falling down.

☐ This is called *going over* an object. Sometimes when we try to go over an object, we cheat and actually go around the side of it. Go back and practice going over the hurdle again, this time making very, very sure that you really do go over and not around.

Traveling Under Equipment

Now, instead of going over the hurdle, you're going to go *under* it. This will be hard because the hurdle isn't very far off the ground. You'll really have to scrunch up. Try to do it without upsetting the hurdle.

- Now, let's try going under in different ways. Sometimes go under feet first, sometimes head first, sometimes on your back, and sometimes on your stomach.
  - □ Be careful; always know where your body is, even those parts that you can't see.

Moving Close To and Far Away

One more activity. This time you're going to put part of your weight on your hands and bring your feet down in different places around the hurdle. To begin, bring your feet down very *close to* the hurdle. You may take your feet across the hurdle or simply leave them on one side; whatever you do, be sure your feet come down close to the hurdle.

- Now try bringing your feet down *far away* from the hurdle. Make sure that every time your feet touch the floor, they're far away from the hurdle.
- Now, as you work, your feet can be close to the hurdle or far away, but sometimes have your feet land close to each other, sometimes spread far apart from each other. Be able to tell me if your feet are close together or far apart when I ask you.
  - □ Remember, close together means almost so close that nothing could get between, and far apart means spread out so much that a person could crawl through.

Learning Onto/Off Concepts

Each student will need a low box or a milk crate.

You're now going to learn two more types of relationships: *onto* and *off*. I think you probably already know what these two ideas mean, but let's practice them just to make sure. Find at least three ways to get onto and off your piece of equipment. I'm really looking for very different ways to get onto and off the equipment.

- After you find three ways, practice the way you like best four extra times, so that you can show it to the class. Make it really special.
- I'm going to make the activity a little harder this time by combining different types of relationships. When I say "go," each of you get a hoop and place it on the floor beside your box.

Moving in relationship to a rolling hoop is a fascinating challenge for the skilled child.

Travel *into* the hoop before you travel *onto* and *off* the box. So your sequence will involve three different relationships: into, on, and off. Find three different ways to do this. Make them very different from each other. Go.

Ask several children who are doing the activity correctly and/or who've found very creative ways to accomplish the activity to demonstrate for the rest of the class. Be sure to use a variety of students so that the rest of the class has a number of ideas to base their work on.

■ Now you're going to make up a sequence of the relationships you practiced with the box and hoop. You must include the concepts of off, on, inside, and around in your sequence. Once you find a sequence that you really like, practice it until you can do it from memory and it looks the same each time.

Studying Over, Under, Around, In Front Of, and Behind Concepts

Each child will need a streamer, such as one used in rhythmic gymnastics. You can make streamers from two-inch-wide crepe paper or from surveyors tape cut into four- to ten-feet lengths.

Just to warm up, practice moving your streamer anywhere around your body. Remember to always try to keep the streamer in the air. To do this, you'll always have to keep the streamer moving; you can't let it stop or it'll touch the floor.

■ Now that you know how to keep the streamer in the air, try to make it go over, under, around, in front of, and behind different body parts, such as your head, legs, and trunk. As you do this, think about what relationship each position has to each body part. Remember, you must keep the streamer moving at all times.

■ Now you're going to pretend you're Olympic gymnasts. Make up a sequence in which your streamer goes over, under, or around three different body parts. After you make up a sequence that you like, practice it until it looks the same each time and you can do it from memory. It's very important that you remember exactly what you did because we're going to do something really special with it.

■ Do you remember your sequence? Now you're going to write it down on a piece of paper and exchange the paper with a friend. Your friend will try to do your sequence and you will try to do your friend's sequence just by reading the directions on the paper, so make it very clear which parts you went over, under, around, in front of, and behind.

■ Now practice your friend's sequence until you think you've learned it perfectly. When you think you're ready, ask your friend to watch you do the sequence. In a few minutes I'll ask for volunteers to show routines that clearly have all five of these concepts.

This series of activities is also very good for developing the concept of free flow.

Traveling Along Equipment

You'll need a number of low balance beams or benches set up around the room.

So far we've learned the relationships of on, off, over, in front of, under, and behind. Now we're going to learn the relationship of *along*. At your piece of equipment, each of you, one at a time, should travel along the bench by walking. Make sure that you travel from one end of the beam or bench to the other.

◻ This relationship of along means being on a piece of equipment and traveling from one part of it to another.

■ Now that you can walk on the beam, try some other ways. This time, slide. If you need help keeping your balance, spread your arms out to either side.

As children progress with learning traveling on or along equipment, you can increase the complexity of the activities by changing the locomotor pattern required for traveling. Patterns can include hopping, skipping, running, waddling. Before you change the pattern, be sure the children are able to advance safely to the next pattern. In other words, don't have them run on the balance beam before they can keep their balance at a fast walk.

■ This time we're going to be funny by combining two different relationships while you travel along the bench. Have some of your weight on the bench and some on the floor. For example, have one hand and foot on the bench and one hand and foot on the floor, or have both your feet on the bench and both your hands on the floor. The idea is to place part of your weight on the equipment and part on the floor. Make sure that I can tell where your weight really is.

■ Make up one way you like of traveling with part of your weight on the floor and part on the equipment and practice it, so you can show the class. Try to give your movement a name.

Going Over and Under the Obstacle Course

Set up an obstacle course using elastic or regular ropes placed at various heights around the room.

You can see that the whole room is now a giant maze. Your task is to go through the maze by going over or under the ropes. Everyone can move at once, but be sure to not touch anyone else as you find your way through the maze.

■ Now that you've gone through the maze at least once and think you're pretty good, I'm going to make the activity harder. This time, try to go over some of the high ropes that you went under and go under some of the low ropes that you went over. Be very careful to not touch anyone else, and try not to touch the ropes. This will take a lot of concentration—pretend the ropes are electric fences that will shock you if you touch them.

This is a good initial activity because you can set it up before class and then have the children help you take it down if you don't want to use it for the entire class. Kids really enjoy this activity.

Using Partners as Obstacles

Things are going to change a little this time. Instead of using equipment as obstacles, you're going to use partners. *(See Figure 14-7.)* To warm up, partner 1 freezes in any shape he or she likes and can hold still. Partner 2 finds as

Project Adventure in Hamilton, Massachusetts, has developed a number of initiative or group problem-solving activities that involve the use of relationships to objects, to other people, and to the environment. These activities are great fun, especially for older students, and develop the concepts of relationships in a myriad of enjoyable and beneficial ways. For more information about other activities, see *Cows' Tails and Cobras* by Karl Rohnke, Hamilton, MA: Project Adventure, 1977.

Figure 14-7 Using partners as obstacles.

many ways as possible to go over, under, around, and through the shape, without touching the obstacle. When partner 2 has found two ways to do each of the four movements, he or she changes places with the partner.

■ Now, partner 1 makes a shape and holds it while partner 2 finds three ways to go over that shape without touching it. Make sure you're actually going over the shape, not around it. After you've found three ways to go over the shape, trade places with your partner.

■ To make things a bit harder, this time as you cross the shape, try to match it. So if your partner is in a small round shape, you want to be in a small round shape in the air as you cross over your partner. Your partner on the floor makes three different shapes and then switches. I'll be watching to see how closely the two shapes match each other.

■ This time, instead of matching, you're going to try to look the opposite as you cross. So if your partner is in a round, curled shape, you want to be in a wide, spread-out shape. After you do this three times, trade places.

■ Let's make the activity even more difficult. Partner 1 forms a shape and partner 2 crosses the shape. Partner 2 now makes a shape for partner 1. Partners keep taking turns making shapes and crossing them. Every time you cross a shape, you immediately stop and form a shape for your partner to cross. Let's try it. Each partner should make three shapes and then stop.

□ Let's work on making the movement smoother so it flows together well. This time, cross the shape and smoothly and immediately go into your shape, as if you just flowed into it. The person getting up should begin movement as soon as her or his shape has been crossed. Partners should perform as if they can read each other's mind and are continually changing places.

□ It may help to plan your shapes ahead of time. This time, talk about your shapes first, so you know exactly what you're going to do. Remember, you must go over your partner, not around.

■ This will be the hardest activity yet. Each group of partners should mark off their own space. No one else can travel into this space, and the partners can't travel out of it. This is very important, so do it now. You must be able to show me the boundaries to your space when I ask.

■ Now that you have your space, here's what you'll be doing. Both of you will be traveling on your feet in your space. Suddenly, one of you will stop and make a shape; when this happens, the other person quickly travels over the shape, and then both of you continue traveling. Do this again, with the other partner making the shape. The whole movement is split second and unpredictable. No one knows when a shape will be made, and it is barely made before it's crossed. The action goes like this: Both of you travel, one of you stops and makes a shape, the other one crosses the shape, and you keep moving. The object is to perform this movement three times without breaking the flow of the movement or bumping into each other. Let's give it a try.

□ The secret to this exercise is to react as soon as you see your partner beginning to make a shape. You have to anticipate, somewhat like making an interception in football. Try again and see if you can move more smoothly, with fewer breaks and jerks.

DEVELOPING THE CONCEPT OF RELATIONSHIPS WITH PEOPLE

When children understand the concept of relationships with people, they have increased awareness of the interplay that occurs—in games, dance, and gymnastics—among the persons involved in the movement. Such interplay occurs, for example, when dancers converge and move around, between and beside each other; paired acrobats balance and flip each other; trapeze artists catch and throw each other; and soccer players work as a unit to advance a ball downfield.

Children often think of relationships to others simply as children working with other children. The term *relationships*, as we use it in physical education, is generally unknown to children. When teaching youngsters about relationships with people, we focus on alone in a mass, solo, partners, groups, and between groups. These relationships can occur in a variety of ways: Each child dribbles a ball in general space (alone in a mass); one child demonstrates a sequence before an entire class (solo); a child mirrors or matches the movement of a partner(s); children meet or part in a dance with a group to express an idea (groups); and individuals work with others as a team to accomplish a task against another team (between groups).

Alone in a Mass

This relationship occurs when all children move simultaneously, with no intent of observing one another. It's frequently seen in lessons that use a problem-solving or guided discovery approach. The children are indirectly relating to one another as they move throughout general space. In contrast to a solo relationship, the children say they feel they're truly on their own, even though they're surrounded by classmates. A child is alone in a mass when dribbling his or her own ball through general space. So too is each child when an entire class is running simultaneously to a predetermined location.

Solo

A solo relationship exists between an individual and the audience she is performing before and who is observing her. Examples are the pitcher on a baseball team, a featured performer in a ballet, and a gymnast. Because some children experience unpleasant pressure or tension when they're the center of attention, we make solo performances voluntary rather than mandatory. This is particularly important for the poorly skilled child, who often feels increased tension and pressure when asked to perform in front of an audience. On the other hand, some children enjoy the challenge of solo performances and actually seem to do better when watched by a group. The feeling experienced when moving and being observed by others is an interesting phenomenon and one that we want children to explore, but in a safe, nonthreatening environment. In all classes we discourage the children from laughing at or criticizing the performances of other children.

Partners

Partners are two individuals relating to each other through their movements. As children become increasingly skilled and socially mature, we introduce the partner relationship. Partner relationships include two dancers moving in synchronization to express harmony or peace, two people paddling a canoe, and two acrobats performing a routine together. Relationship concepts introduced as children work with partners (or groups) include

A child matches a partner's rocking movement.

1. Meeting and parting—traveling toward or away from a partner
2. Unison and contrast—both partners intentionally do the same thing (unison), or they intentionally do the same thing in different ways (contrast)
3. Leading and following—one partner leads, the other follows
4. Matching—partners are side by side and attempt to duplicate one another's movements instantaneously (to make the same movement at the same time)
5. Mirroring—partners face one another and form the reverse reproduction of the partner's movements, as if looking in a mirror

Groups

Group cooperative relationships occur when more than two children work together for a common purpose. These relationships include children working together to express an emotion in dance, to build a shape supporting one another's weight, or as a team trying to keep a ball from touching the floor, but without catching it.

As the size of the group increases, so too does the complexity of the relationship. A partner relationship involves being aware of one other child; a

A group of children work together for a common purpose.

successful group relationship necessitates an awareness of two or more children. The difficulty of decision making also increases proportionately with the size of the group. The concepts of meeting and parting, unison and contrast, and leading and following all become increasingly challenging as the size of a group increases.

We typically assign specific tasks to children in groups. This enables the children to develop the skills of moving in relationship to others before they try group tasks that require them to make decisions—such as those required when children make up a game or invent a sequence. Asking children who've had little opportunity to work in groups to make group decisions about their work has proven counterproductive. Once children become proficient at group

COMPETITION

Many intergroup relationships are competitive, with one group attempting to perform more skillfully than the other group. The emphasis on winning creates an intense emotional involvement that can produce disturbing feelings in some children. We talk with children about these feelings, which usually occur in competitive, predesigned team situations, and we explain to the youngsters how they can understand these feelings and deal with them effectively. Cooperative situations, in which children in a group work to accomplish a common goal, involve relationships that are easier for young children to handle.

Some might suggest that competitive relationships between groups are inappropriate for children. The affective and cognitive ramifications of competition include the feelings associated with winning and losing, false feelings of superiority or inferiority, and determination to beat an opponent. Our experience has been that competitive relationships, with many affective and cognitive ramifications, occur anyway, at recess or afterschool situations, so we're convinced that it's the teacher's responsibility to help children develop a healthy attitude about competitive situations.

It's important for children to understand that it's acceptable to choose to not participate in a competitive situation if they feel threatened or insecure. Similarly, children should understand that everyone makes mistakes in games, and that when they make mistakes, the other children are not unhappy with them as individuals but rather with the situation. These affective concepts aren't typically included in a discussion of relationships between groups. But it's in these types of relationships that we so often observe children developing the distaste and disaffection for physical activity that can endure for a lifetime if not dealt with effectively. And so we believe that it's important to discuss them.

relationships, however, they are challenged by the adventure and creative opportunities of group decision making.

Between Groups

This relationship occurs when two or more children relate to two or more children. It's the most complex of relationships because it involves not only being aware of one's own group but a responsibility to relate to another group. This relationship is extremely challenging, as demonstrated by the wide appeal of sports that match one team against another. We initially keep intergroup relationships small (three on a side) and try to allow choices about whether or not to participate in an intergroup relationship.

Between-group relationships can be competitive (two groups striving for a common goal) or collaborative (working with a group to outmaneuver another group). We usually begin with collaborative relationships and progress to more competitive relationships.

ASSESSMENT GUIDE / Relationships with People

TASK   With a partner, in a small space make a shape that mirrors the other person. The shapes can be as close together as you want, but they can't touch. On the signal, quickly pull away and form a shape by yourself and freeze. On the next signal, slowly come back together and make a shape that matches the other person. Do this twice; the first time one person is the leader and makes the shapes that are to be copied, and the second time the other person is the leader.

GUIDE   You'll know the children understand the concept of relationships with people when you observe that:

1. Their mirroring shapes mirror completely and their matching shapes match completely.
2. They actually pull apart as if they'd been a team.
3. They can meet without bumping into each other.

You'll know the children don't understand the concept of relationships with people when you observe that:

1. Their mirroring and matching shapes are incorrect.
2. They have to stop and think for more than several seconds before they can perform the required shapes.
3. They fall down or bump into each other when they meet.
4. You can't tell when they're parting or meeting. There's no clear pulling away and coming back together.

TEACHING THE CONCEPT OF RELATIONSHIPS WITH PEOPLE

The following activities are designed to improve children's ability to function successfully with other individuals and groups in a variety of situations.

Activities Leading to Movement Concept Understanding

Matching

Work with a partner. Partner 1 should make a shape, and partner 2 should try to copy it exactly. Try to make the shapes so alike that you look like twins. After five shapes, partners should change places, with partner 2 now making the shapes while partner 1 copies them. Work hard to make the shapes exactly alike.

■ These types of balances are said to *match;* they look alike as much as possible. Now you're going to make matching balances a little harder by playing Follow the Leader. On the signal, partner 1 leads by traveling; partner 2 follows. On the stop signal, you both stop, and the follower—partner 2—matches the shape the leader—partner 1—makes. As you make your shapes, try to match exactly what your partner does. Your whole body should do this, not just your trunk. After four turns, switch places. Be sure that when you're the leader you make a shape that your partner can actually do—not one that's too hard.

Traveling and Matching

Now you'll perform matching actions while traveling instead of being still. With your partner, make up five ways that you can travel and then perform the movements side by side at the exact same time, as if you're both part of a marching band that does everything alike.

◻ Now that you've figured out what your movements are, go back and practice doing them together so you do them at exactly the same time. It may help to count to yourselves as you move.

Mirroring

This time you're going to try something a little different. In your own space, partner 1 will be the leader and partner 2 the follower. The leader will make a balance, and the follower will then make the same balance, only opposite. For example, if partner 1 uses his right arm to do something, partner 2 uses her left arm. Make five statues and then trade places. Work very hard to make every part of the statue the exact opposite of what you see (it helps to face your partner). These types of actions are called *mirroring* actions because the effect is that of looking in a mirror.

Matching and Mirroring

This activity is to test how well you understand the difference between mirroring and matching. With your partner, make a matching balance. On the signal, change that balance so that you mirror each other.

It helps to have a group that is doing the activity correctly demonstrate it for the class.

■ With your partner, now try to find five more balances that you can change from matching to mirroring. I'm going to come around as you practice and ask to see at least one of your combinations, so be sure you know the difference. If you have questions, ask now.

Mirroring Opposite Movements

This time the activity will be harder. Instead of copying a still statue your partner makes, you're going to mirror your partner's movements. Remember that this is still in your own space and that there's no traveling. So if your partner moves her left arm down, you move your right arm up. Make four moves and change places. This is hard. Think about it.

■ This time, try to tell a story with your mirroring actions, such as a baby first seeing herself in the mirror, your mother putting on her makeup, or your father shaving. Practice your story until you can do it the same way three times in a row. Then we'll have the class try to guess what you're saying.

Traveling Alongside/Following

Though we haven't really discussed it, often you were practicing another type of relationship when you followed your partner around the space: *leading and following.* So far you've always followed from behind the other person; now let's try it differently this time, with you traveling alongside or next to your partner as you follow. One person is still the leader and the other the follower, but you both move as if you were a team of horses: beside each other. Each of you should take five turns leading and then switch places. This activity is harder, so you have to watch very closely what your partner does. Start out with very easy moves.

■ Now try to speed it up a little. Watch carefully. Try to follow exactly.

The leader must be aware of the follower's capabilities so that the leader challenges the partner but doesn't frustrate the partner with movements that are too difficult.

Following with a Group

This time you're going to try another type of following: from behind, with four or five of you in a group. The first person in line is the first leader and leads the group all over the room. Then on the signal, the first person goes to the end of the line and the second person becomes the leader; this change continues until everyone has had a chance to lead. The secret is to stay far enough apart so that you can see. The activity is just like Follow the Leader.

■ This time you're going to make the activity a little more challenging. I'm *not* going to give you the signal to change anymore. Your group will have to make up its own change signal, such as a hand clap. You'll start as you did before, with the first person leading. Then at some time the second person in line will give the change signal and at the same time start traveling a new way. When this happens, the whole line starts to follow the new leader and the old leader goes to the back of the line. The hard part is that you're going to do this without stopping the movement; the line must always keep moving. The same process continues until everyone has had a chance to be the leader. Remember, it's always the second person in line who gives the change signal.

Meeting/Parting

Now you're going to work with partners again. First you and your partner are going to work only with your hands while seated in your self-space. Very slowly, try to bring your hands as close to your partner's as you can without touching them. As soon as your hands are close, pull them as far away as you can without moving your body.

■ This relationship is called *meeting and parting*. To make it a little easier, I'm going to give you a drumbeat to go by. On the six slow counts of the drum, bring your hands as close as possible without touching them and freeze. Then, on a sudden loud beat, quickly pull your hands as far away as possible, as if you don't want them to touch poison.

■ Now try meeting and parting with your whole bodies. In a small space, use the six slow drumbeats to bring your bodies as close together as possible without touching and then freeze. On the sudden beat, quickly pull away. The secret is to pull away quickly, as if you were a flash of lightning, and then freeze very still.

■ The activity will be harder this time. You'll still have the same partner, but you both will be separated. You're all going to travel around the room, and on the beat of the drum quickly come toward your partner and freeze very close to each other, just for a few seconds, and then begin your traveling again. Do this every time you hear the signal. The secret is to always know where your partner is. Maintain eye contact.

■ This time, as you and your partner meet on the sound of the signal, come together as if you're greeting a friend you haven't seen in a long time; then, as you get right up to each other, you realize that you really don't know the person. It could be really funny.

Forming Cooperative and Collaborative Relationships

So far all our relationships with people involved how we moved with those people. You're now going to work on a few different types of relationships that involve not only how you move with people but how you think. In your group of four, you're going to travel in a line spread out across the field toward the goal. As you travel, throw the ball back and forth to each other, always staying the same distance apart. Imagine a marching band moving across the field but throwing a ball as they move. You may want to use the lines on the field to help you stay apart. The secret is that the receivers move slightly ahead of but not toward the passers and the passers throw the ball ahead of the receivers so that they don't have to come back to catch it. This type of relationship

When children begin to work with others in collaborative and competitive situations involving a manipulative skill, the skill level tends to deteriorate briefly if they're concentrating on the relationship. This should be expected and explained. The children, though, do need to have a certain level of manipulative ability before beginning these situations, or the activity will become very frustrating to them.

is called a *cooperative* relationship because everybody has to work together to make it work.

This idea works well if a lined field (such as a football field) is available and the children can follow the lines as guides.

■ Now you're going to change the cooperative relationship a little. You're still going to work with your group to move the ball across the field while staying the same distance apart, but two people who are going to try to steal the ball while it is in the air will be coming toward you. It will be really hard to resist the temptation to go close to your own players to try and help them, but remember you have two goals: to stay away from your teammates and to not let the other two people steal the ball. It really does help to stay away from the other people on your team.

   □ This is called a *collaborative* relationship because you have to work with the people on your team to keep the two other people from getting the ball. Let me give you a few more hints on how to make such a relationship work really well. First, when it's your turn to receive the ball, move slightly in front of the passer so the passer can easily throw the ball to you. Second, pass before the defender gets close to you; when you're free to pass, don't wait until the defender is so close that you're forced to pass.

As the children become more proficient with these activities, you may want to try manipulative skills other than throwing, such as kicking, passing, or striking.

Meeting and Parting in a Cooperative Group

This time, instead of meeting and parting with a partner, you're going to meet and part with a small group. Your group forms a group shape: Remember, close, but not touching. Then on the signal, suddenly leave, as if you're in a hurry, but take only a few steps and by yourself freeze into a shape you like. On the next signal, slowly come back to your group and form the same shape with which you started. To repeat, start with a group shape, on the signal quickly leave and form a shape of your own, and on the next signal return to the first group shape.

☐ Let's work on this activity with one series that you really like. Practice it so it works out the same each time. This will involve hard thinking. It may help to count your steps so you know exactly how far to move. It also helps to not laugh too much. Who knows, you could be stars!

Performing Solo

You're going to play a bunch of small dodgeball games—only six people in a group. Start with two people on the outside. When you get hit, do *not* sit out but become a thrower on the outside, so in the end there will be many throwers and one person in the middle. But I have another activity for you to think about while you're doing this. I want you to be able to tell what it's like to be in the middle, what all you have to think about, who and what you have to watch out for.

■ When you finish one game, just start another one. The last two players left in the middle are the first throwers in the next game. Remember to think about what it's like in the middle.

☐ Now you're going to write down your thoughts about what it was like in the middle. In case you're wondering, this is another type of relationship: a *solo* relationship, which means that there are many people around you, but it's each person for him- or herself. Write down what you thought.

After the youngsters have had some time to write, briefly discuss the feelings of being in a solo relationship when each child is the center of attraction. Point out that some people (probably the highly skilled) like being solo, but others (probably the lower skilled) prefer to not be solo.

APPLYING THE CONCEPT OF RELATIONSHIPS

The concept of relationships with objects and people is a beginning theme in the gymnastics and dance areas as the children are taught the concepts of over, under, in, out, alongside, and on. There the focus is on whether the child understands the concept rather than whether she or he can accomplish the skill involved. For example, you'd observe whether a child was actually jumping symmetrically over a hurdle rather than whether she or he was crossing without knocking it over. Once you're sure that the child understands the concept, you begin to focus on the skill. Once a concept has been learned, it can also be used for expressive purposes in dance situations.

We don't introduce the concept of relationships with objects in the games area until children have developed an adequate degree of manipulative skill. Children must learn to manipulate objects with some consistency before they can reasonably be expected to manipulate them in relation to objects or people.

If children are given tasks involving manipulative skills and relationships too early, they become frustrated and bored.

The concept of relationships with others is the last concept we introduce. Socially, children enjoy working near other children at a very young age, but often physically and cognitively they aren't able to function effectively in relationship to others. For example, children at the precontrol level don't possess enough skill to be able to consistently work with a partner—when such children are asked to throw an object back and forth to partners, only one out of three throws is likely to reach the partner. Therefore, you should deal with relationships with others as a *concept* when the children's skills are adequate and when they've matured enough socially so that their abilities are enhanced when they work with other children.

The strategy and challenge of working in groups and between groups are derived only when a skill has developed sufficiently so that the children are able to focus on the relationship while still performing the skill efficiently. There are no magical ages or times for introducing the different relationship concepts. Each teacher must reflect on information about the environment, the children, the skill, and personal ability as a teacher to determine the best time for introducing the concept of relationships.

READING COMPREHENSION QUESTIONS

1. List three examples each of relationships of body parts, relationships with objects, and relationships with people (total of nine examples).
2. What does the term *functional vocabulary* mean?
3. Define symmetrical and nonsymmetrical by listing examples of each concept.
4. We recommend that you teach the concept of relationships with objects before teaching relationships with people. Why?
5. What does the term *alone in a mass* mean? What does *solo* mean?
6. Solo performances and intergroup experiences aren't required; they're voluntary. Why?
7. Explain the difference between mirroring and matching.
8. What factors should you consider when making decisions about the most appropriate times to introduce the various relationships?

P A R T four

Skill Theme Development

Chapters 15 to 25 discuss the content of the skill themes we focus on in our physical education programs. Each chapter begins with an introduction to the skill theme; the introduction includes a discussion of the skill theme's characteristics and how the theme can be applied to teaching children. It's tempting to skip the introduction and get to the actual lesson ideas, but we recommend that you carefully read the introduction so you'll be able to adapt the skill theme to your particular needs. Obviously you'll change some of the ideas; an understanding of the skill as taught to children will help you make these adaptations.

The introduction is followed by an Assessment Guide, which helps the teacher determine where to begin with the class. Experienced teachers will use the Assessment Guides less than beginning teachers because they'll have a better idea of the children's levels of skill proficiency. As you use the Assessment Guides, keep in mind that they represent a gross estimate of proficiency levels for that skill. We certainly don't recommend grading children on the assessments. However, the guides do have the potential of letting you know how your children are progressing. And you don't have to use the Assessment Guides for all the children in all the classes you teach. Finally, you should devote only a minimal amount of time to using the assessments—the most important job is to help the children improve and develop, not to spend too much time testing children.

Where appropriate, many of the chapters also include Key Observation Points. The Key Observation Points remind you of what to look for when you're teaching; they're the key points the children should know about each skill. You should constantly emphasize the points as you refine the quality of the children's movement, to the degree that when children complete your program, they know the observation points because you've stressed them so much in your teaching. Each Key Observation Point is stated in a question format, along with illustrations of the correct/incorrect forms. We feel that this approach is closest to the way teachers observe when they're teaching. We suggest looking for an observation point one at a time rather than trying to observe three or four simultaneously. Regardless of the children's skill level, the Key Observation Points are constantly part of our observational focus (as explained in Chapter 9).

Each skill theme in Chapters 15 to 25 is arranged in a logical progression, from precontrol through proficiency levels. This progression is introduced by what we call a progression spiral, which outlines the content of each skill theme. Each line in the spiral corresponds to a section in the chapter that explains how to develop that idea.

As in the movement concept chapters (Chapters 12 to 14), the scripted text format helps you understand how a teacher might actually phrase the different tasks for development. You won't say things exactly the way we do, but our format is a helpful starting point. As you read, you'll notice that each section corresponding to the line in the progression spiral is preceded by a certain symbol: a solid box for extensions and applications and an open box for refinements.

We encourage you to change the suggested progressions and implied methodology to best suit your students' needs and your teaching goals. Our suggestions are certainly not prescriptions. The chapters in Part Four are ordered in the progression we'd use to organize our yearly plan (Chapter 5), but you should reflect on your situation and design the curriculum for *your* children.

Traveling

Children are first capable of changing the location of their bodies at about three months of age, when they turn over from their backs onto their stomachs. Unless seriously handicapped, they'll soon begin to crawl, then creep. At about one year, they'll take their first step. And by the time they enter school, they'll exhibit relatively mature walking and running patterns. Unlike other skills—such as throwing, catching, and striking—the basic locomotor patterns develop naturally in most children.

Most school-age youngsters, therefore, are beyond the precontrol level in walking and running. Nevertheless, the teacher's first task is to evaluate traveling performance to ensure that any youngsters who exhibit severely immature or inefficient patterns will receive remedial assistance. Most children attain a mature walking pattern through experience. Verbal clues from the teacher plus the modeling of the correct pattern will help children with inefficiencies. Continued deviations (e.g., toes turned out or in) signal the need for a thorough physical examination by a pediatrician.

Similarly, it's important to ascertain how many students can perform the fundamental locomotor skills that emerge from the walk-run pattern: hopping, leaping, sliding, galloping, and skipping. Young children need much practice of each skill when the skills are introduced, and they also need distributed practice of the locomotor skills throughout the primary grades. Young children, inexperienced in different locomotor skills, may not be able to give the correct locomotor response to a verbal command because they often lack cognitive understanding rather than motor performance. We've found that modeling is the best way for young children to learn these skills; the children follow the example of the teacher and other children who've mastered the skill. It's also important to name the locomotor skill each time you or others demonstrate it to the children.

By the end of grade two, we expect children to be able to execute the locomotor skills of hopping, leaping, sliding, galloping, and skipping in response to a verbal command. This expectation implies that children recognize the word and the action that the word represents and that they've mastered the skill.

WALKING

Walking is a process of alternately losing balance and recovering it while moving forward in an upright position. While moving forward, the body should display little up and down or side to side movement. The arms and legs move

When a class is challenged to travel about a general space, the teacher can observe individual children for possible inefficiencies.

in opposition. A mature walking pattern looks smooth and is accomplished in an easy manner.

When assessing the walking pattern of young children, look for the following inefficiencies:

1. Bouncy walk—too much vertical push
2. Excessive swing of the arms away from the sides
3. Failure to swing the arms at the shoulders
4. Feet held too close together so that the entire body looks jerky as the child walks
5. Feet held too far apart—duck walk
6. Toes turned out
7. Toes turned in—pigeon-toed
8. Head too far forward—body leaning forward before the lead foot touches the ground

RUNNING

During the earliest stage of running (at about twenty-four months), a child's new speed produces precarious balance. The child makes exaggerated leg movements. In particular, the knee of the recovery leg swings outward and then around and forward in preparation for the support phase. This knee action is accompanied by the foot of the recovery leg toeing out. These exaggerated movements gradually disappear as the legs become longer and stronger.

Most school-age youngsters are able to run at a relatively fast speed and are fairly successful at changing direction while running. In a mature running pattern (observed when children are attempting to run at maximum velocity), each leg goes through a support phase and a recovery phase, and the full sequence produces two periods of nonsupport. The essentials of the mature running pattern are:*

1. The trunk maintains a slight forward lean throughout the stride pattern.
2. Both arms swing through a large arc and in synchronized opposition to the leg action.
3. The support foot contacts the ground approximately flat and nearly under the center of gravity.
4. The knee of the support leg bends slightly after the foot has made contact with the ground.
5. Extension of the support leg at the hip, knee, and ankle propels the body forward and upward into the nonsupport phase.
6. The recovery knee swings forward quickly to a high knee raise and simul-

*From *Fundamental Motor Patterns*, 2nd ed., by R. L. Wickstrom, 1977, pp. 37–57, Philadelphia: Lea & Febiger.

taneously there is flexion of the lower leg, bringing the heel close to the buttock.

Use the following Key Observation Points to assess running patterns. The illustrations of the "correct" and "incorrect" patterns help you answer the questions you should ask yourself as you evaluate a youngster's performance.

KEY OBSERVATION POINTS / Running

LEG ACTION

Does the knee of the child's recovery leg swing forward and backward rather than outward, around, and then forward?

NO   YES

ARM ACTION

1. Do the child's arms move forward and backward in opposition to the legs without crossing the midline?

NO   YES   NO   YES

2. Do the child's arms stay close to the body throughout the action?

NO   YES

■■■■■■■ **TRUNK POSITION**

Does the child's trunk lean slightly forward?

NO   YES

■■■■■■■ **FOOT PLACEMENT**

Is the child's support foot approximately flat when it contacts the ground?

NO   YES

MATURE STAGE

When children are at the mature stage of running, do their runs look similar to the following sequence?

HOPPING

A hop is a springing action from one foot, in any direction, to a landing on the same foot (see Figure 15-1). The knee seldom straightens fully; the work of the ankle joint is primarily what accomplishes the push into the air and the absorption of the landing shock.

Figure 15-1 Hopping pattern.

LEAPING

A leap is an extension of a run—greater force is used to produce a higher dimension than a run (see Figure 15-2). A one-foot takeoff propels the body

Figure 15-2 Leaping pattern.

upward to a landing on the opposite foot. Arm opposition is the same as for the run. There's an emphasis on body extension for height or for distance. The landing leg bends to absorb the force of the body upon touching the floor.

SLIDING

A slide is a combination of a step and a run. The lead step is quickly followed by the free foot closing to replace the supporting foot (see Figure 15-3). The

Figure 15-3 Sliding pattern.

lead foot quickly springs from the floor into a direction of intended travel. The weight is primarily on the balls of the feet. The sequence is repeated for the desired distance. The same foot always leads in a slide, producing an uneven rhythm: step-close, step-close, step-close.

GALLOPING

A gallop is an exaggerated slide in a forward direction. The lead leg lifts and bends and then thrusts forward to support the weight. Quickly the rear foot closes to replace the supporting leg as the lead leg springs up into its lifted and bent position. The rhythm is uneven, the same as that of a slide.

SKIPPING

A skip is a combination of a step and a hop, first on one foot and then on the other foot (see Figure 15-4). The pattern has the alternation and opposition of the walk plus the same-sided one-foot hop. The skip has an uneven rhythm.

Figure 15-4 Skipping pattern.

LEVELS OF SKILL PROFICIENCY

In many schools, usually in communities where parents provide their preschoolers with a wealth of movement experiences, most five- and six-year-old children will already have mastered the traveling skills, and their classmates will be quick to catch on. However, we've observed some situations in which a number of the students were unable to perform many locomotor skills beyond walking and running. Such children need precontrol-level travel experiences so that they'll learn to:

1. Crawl along the floor
2. Creep on hands and knees
3. Walk along a line on the floor
4. Crawl underneath a low bar without touching it
5. Step over a low obstacle without touching it
6. Hop, leap, slide, gallop, or skip

Once youngsters can identify and perform the basic modes of travel relatively easily and efficiently, they're ready for control-level challenges. These challenges include several types of activities. First, the children can attempt variations of basic travel skills: walking at a low level, skipping backward, gal-

Children enjoy traveling at a low level.

The airborne sensation that results from combining a run and a leap is a thrill for children.

loping, changing direction on signal, and running in a crowded room without touching anyone. Next, the youngsters can try traveling rhythmically or expressively: skipping to the uneven beat of teacher's drum, running and leaping on the accented beat, walking as if on hot sand, and walking mechanically, like a robot.

Once children are easily able to perform a variety of locomotor skills and can use their travel abilities to carry out a primary objective, they're ready for utilization-level activities. At this point, an involvement in challenging situations can refine and expand the youngsters' repertoires of travel skills.

The children can combine two or more travel operations into a short sequence, such as run-jump-roll, or run-leap-turn in air-run. They can try to perform another skill while traveling: keeping a long ribbon from touching the ground by traveling swiftly, or striking a balloon and traveling to keep it up.

Children can improvise or plan in detail expressive travel for short dance phrases, focusing on:

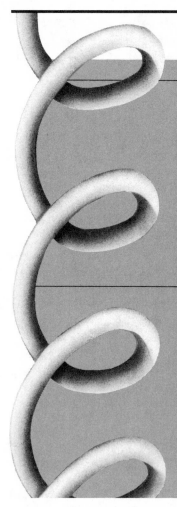

SKILL THEME DEVELOPMENT SEQUENCE

Traveling

Control Level

Performing slow motion replay
Traveling as water, steam, ice
Changing speeds to music
Traveling at different speeds
Playing Follow Me
Slidestepping
Traveling in different directions
Traveling an obstacle course
Leaping
Traveling in relation to others

Precontrol Level

Traveling through rope pathways
Traveling in confined spaces
Moving to rhythmical movements
Performing locomotor sequences
Running
Skipping
Hopping
Galloping
Sliding
Traveling in general space

1. The purpose, idea, or theme of the phrase—harmony, a battle, autumn
2. The pathway of travel most appropriate—straight, angular, curved, or symmetrical
3. The specific travel skills to be incorporated—running, leaping, collapsing
4. The travel qualities to be exhibited—smooth-flowing, jagged-jerky.

The youngsters can use effective travel skills and strategic pathways in dynamic game situations:

1. React quickly to a batted ball by charging forward, to the left or right, to collect a ground ball and throw accurately to a teammate
2. Run a planned pass pattern, using fakes and quick changes of direction to lose an opponent and receive a ball a teammate throws

When students consistently use a variety of travel skills and pathways

Traveling

Proficiency Level

Traveling in gymnastics
Traveling in games and sports
Performing rhythmical patterns: tinikling
Traveling to show tradition versus change
Depicting primitive tribes through travel

Utilization Level

Traveling to Tom Foolery rhymes
Traveling in bound and free flow
Traveling to express age: The Fountain of Youth
Performing rhythmical patterns
Shadowing
Traveling with a partner: matching pathways; changing speed and direction

effectively in game, dance, and gymnastics settings, they're ready to put all the elements together through participation in proficiency-level experiences:

■ Games: Youngsters play teacher- and/or student-designed games that demand alert and accurate performance of travel skills and strategic use of travel pathways.

■ Dance: Students and teacher work together to design dance studies. Specific travel pathways and locomotor skills are decided upon, practiced, revised, and refined. This process ends in a completed dance that clearly reflects the theme or idea that stimulated the study.

■ Gymnastics: Students and teacher cooperatively design travel patterns and select specific locomotor skills (as well as positions of stillness—balances) for individual or group gymnastic routines.

Our progression spiral on pp. 256–257 shows the sequence for developing the skill theme of traveling at the precontrol, control, utilization, and proficiency levels. Below is the Assessment Guide for traveling. Next, activities for developing proficiency at the four levels are fully described. As discussed in Chapter 4, you're encouraged to vary the method of organization to suit the objectives of the particular lesson.

ASSESSMENT GUIDE / Traveling

TASK   *Run* as fast as you can to the other side of the playing field; as you run back toward the starting line, zigzag through the marker cones.

Gallop to the other side of the playing field; *skip* back to the starting line. You don't have to zigzag through the cones.

Slide to the other side of the playing field, leading with your right foot; slide to the starting line, leading with your left foot.

Hop on one foot the distance to the second cone; return to the starting line by hopping on the other foot.

GUIDE   The children are ready for precontrol- or control-level tasks when you observe that:

1. They give an incorrect response for the locomotor pattern named.
2. They're unable to properly execute the skill, i.e., mature pattern.
3. They lose balance and/or bump into the cones when running the zigzag pattern through the marker cones.

The children are ready for utilization- or proficiency-level tasks when you observe that they're able to correctly execute the locomotor skill requested without losing their balance.

PRECONTROL LEVEL

The following activities are designed to acquaint children with the fundamental locomotor patterns and to help them develop mature and efficient travel skills.

Activities Leading to Skill Development

Traveling in General Space

On the signal, travel any way you wish in general space. Avoid colliding with others, and stop without falling when you hear the drum being hit.

- □ When you meet someone while traveling, you may have to move to the right or left to avoid a collision.
- □ If you're moving quickly when the signal to stop is given, lower your hips and spread your feet wide apart to stop without falling over. Keep both your feet in contact with the floor.

Sliding

Raise your right arm and point toward the far side of the blacktop. On the signal, use a slide step to travel across the area.

- □ Remember that your right foot will lead all the way across the field.
- □ When your left foot almost touches your right foot, with your right foot again step quickly to the side.
- □ Use light, springing steps, with your weight on the balls of your feet.

■ When you reach the far side, raise your left arm and return across the blacktop, leading the slide with your left foot.

Galloping

On the signal, gallop around the room.

- □ Remember that the same foot leads throughout the gallop.
- ■ Now lead with your other foot.

Hopping

Hop on one foot five times, and then hop on your other foot five times. Continue to alternate hopping on your right foot and then your left foot until you hear the signal to stop.

Skipping

Now that you can hop and gallop, try skipping. Skip throughout general space until you hear the signal to stop.

  □ Lift your knees high to touch your hands, which should be extended in front of you.

Developmentally, the progression for learning to skip is gallop, skip only on dominant side, then skip.

Running

Now that you can move without bumping others and stop on signal, try running throughout general space. Cover as much area as you can.

  □ Be sure your entire foot contacts the floor, not just your toes.
  □ Move your arms forward and backward as you run; don't let them cross your body in front of you. If you're having trouble, try running with your palms upward, thumbs outward; this helps you keep your elbows close to your side and keeps you from turning side to side.

  ■ Run quietly like a deer in the forest. Bend your knees so your landings will be soft.

Performing Locomotor Sequences

Think of your favorite locomotor movement that you've practiced. On signal, use that movement to travel in general space. I should be able to identify the locomotor movement by watching you travel.

Make out cards for each child in the class (or place slips of paper inside film cylinders). On each card or piece of paper, have a sequence of locomotor movements, e.g., walk, hop, gallop.

  ■ There are cards spread around the wall. When I say "Go," go get a card and bring it back to your space. Read your card. Each card contains a movement sentence: three locomotor movements separated by commas. What does a comma mean in your reading? Right—pause. After each locomotor movement you'll pause. Your sequence will be travel, pause; travel, pause; travel, freeze. Practice your movement sentence until you can do it the same way three times.

Children whose reading levels reflect ways to end a sentence enjoy freezing with an image of a period, exclamation, or question mark.

Moving to Rhythmical Movements

Listen to the drumbeat. I'll beat a cadence of one, two, three, four, and then you'll clap the same. Listen. *(Beat drum four times in even rhythm.)* Now clap. Walking and running are both even rhythms. Let's try again. Listen, then clap.

  ■ Let's walk the rhythm of the beat. Listen to the speed. *(Beat four times in even rhythm, slowly.)* Ready? Walk as I beat the drum. Clap as you walk.

You'll need to walk more quickly or slowly now, depending on the beat of the drum. I'll pause between each segment so you can hear the change in rhythm.

■ Now run to the beat of the drum. It's an even rhythm but a faster speed. Be sure you listen for the beat. Ready, go.

Traveling in Confined Spaces

Mark boundaries with masking tape, cones, etc. Reduce the boundaries for general space to half the normal amount.

Travel throughout general space with any locomotor movement except running. The space is smaller, so be careful to not bump into others as you travel.

■ Run in this reduced amount of space without colliding with another person.

Traveling Through Rope Pathways

Arrange an obstacle course, placing marker cones and ropes on the floor to form varying pathways of different widths for travel. See Figure 15-5.

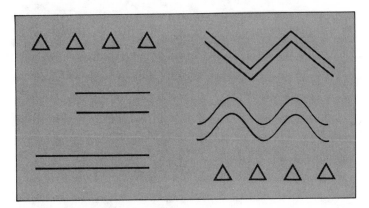

Figure 15-5 Traveling an obstacle course.

On the signal, travel around the cones and between the rope boundaries without touching them. I'll time you for thirty seconds. Try to finish with a perfect score—no touches.

CONTROL LEVEL

Here we describe experiences that help children expand their traveling abilities. The activities challenge youngsters to use different traveling patterns with other concepts, such as speed and direction.

Children seem to skip simply for the sheer pleasure they experience in doing so!

Activities Leading to Skill Development

Traveling in Relation to Others

Walk, skip, gallop, or hop throughout general space without touching anyone else. Remember, you may have to move to the right or left to avoid bumping into someone else. When I give the signal, stop quickly with both your feet on the floor.

■ I've selected music for each of our locomotor movements. The first is for skipping. Listen to the beat. Is it an even or uneven rhythm? Right, skipping is an uneven rhythm. Begin skipping when you hear the music. Stop when the music stops.

■ Now listen to the music for the gallop; it's also uneven. *(Pause, play music.)* Ready? Gallop.

■ The music for hopping is short and quick. Clap the rhythm. Is it even or uneven? Hop on one foot to the music.

■ I've saved your favorite locomotor movement until last. What is it? Running. Run quietly so you'll hear the music stop.

Children tend to practice only their favorite locomotor skill when the task is open. We find it helps to specify each skill in addition to "your choice" or "your favorite."

☐ Remember to lower your center of gravity and place your feet in a wider position to stop quickly.

Leaping

Who can remember what a leap is? *(Refer to Chapter 17, "Jumping and Landing.")* Right, it's taking off on one foot and landing on the other, with the body in the air between the takeoff and landing. Travel in general space by running. After running three steps, leap high in the air, and when you land, continue to run. Your travel will be: run, run, run, leap; run, run, run, leap. . . . Remember to land softly by bending your knee.

☐ Did you have your opposite arm forward while you were in the air?

■ I'm going to number you off in 1s and 2s. The 1s will be spread around the room in a curled shape close to the floor. The 2s will run throughout the room, leaping over the curled 1s without touching them. On the signal, the 2s will collapse to the floor in curled shapes. The 1s will count with me, "one, two, three," and then pop up and begin running and leaping over the 2s. *(Repeat the activity several times for endurance.)*

☐ Remember to take off on one foot and land on the other foot.

☐ To avoid collisions, be very sure you're aware of everyone else running and leaping.

Traveling an Obstacle Course

Set up an obstacle course using hoops, bamboo poles, low beams, etc. See Figure 15-6.

You've worked on various locomotor skills and on moving with control. Using a combination of a hop, skip, gallop, leap, walk, and slide, move through the obstacle course without touching other people, the hoops, or the bamboo poles.

Traveling in Different Directions

You've learned six directions. Let's name them together: forward, backward, right, left, up, and down. This time as you walk, run, or hop, change directions as you travel.

■ Begin walking forward. On the signal, change directions and walk backward. Exaggerate your movements so you look like a toy soldier or robot.

■ On the signal, run in a forward direction. When you hear the drum, slow

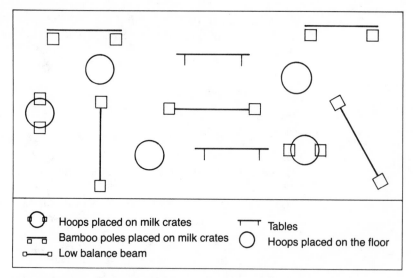

Figure 15-6 An obstacle course.

your speed and run to the side or backward. Take only a few steps; then continue running forward.

□ Watch out for others when you travel backward.

□ Keep your body centered over your feet for good balance and a quick change of direction.

□ Remember that widening your strides will let you change directions quickly.

■ Pretend you're going to draw a square with one foot. Hop forward, backward, to the right, and to the left to draw your square.

□ Stay facing the same wall all the time you're hopping.

Slidestepping

Use a slidestep to travel toward the far end of the field. On the signal, change the direction of your slidestep.

■ Using the slidestep, travel eight steps to the right, then eight steps to the left. Stop and balance on one foot. Repeat eight steps to the left, eight steps to the right. Stop and balance in a wide shape. Let's try that with some music (e.g., "Seven Jumps"). Remember to travel eight slidesteps to the left, eight to the right; stop and balance. Many folk dances use this slide skill.

Playing Follow Me

Select instrumental music with a strong beat, e.g., hoedown or country music.

We're going to practice our locomotor skills today; we'll combine the skills with rhythm and keeping the beat in self-space. This is called Follow the Leader, country western style. Spread throughout general space, facing me. I'll move to the right, the left, forward, and backward. You'll mirror my direction. So if I go left, you go right; if I go forward, you go backward. I'll hop, jump, gallop, slide, walk, and move in other ways. After each locomotor phrase, you'll stop in self-space and do such things as touch your hands to your heels, nod your head forward and backward, cross your knee, as in a Charleston, etc. You only need to watch and follow me.

Keep all activities in a count of eight—for example, eight slides to the left, eight slides to the right, stop, touch hands to heels in time with the music: one, two, three, four, five, six, seven, eight; gallop forward eight steps, gallop backward eight steps, stop, clap hands in time with the music: one, two, three, four, five, six, seven, eight.

Traveling at Different Speeds

Stack sheets of newspaper at the edge of the gymnasium.

Each of you will need one sheet of newspaper. After you get your sheet, unfold it and place it against your chest, holding it at your shoulders. On the signal, begin running; you'll no longer have to hold your newspaper. What will happen to the newspaper when you stop running? Ready, go.

■ Try running at different speeds, sometimes very fast, sometimes very slowly, to see if the paper will stay up.

■ After you lose the paper, swing your arms forward and backward close to your body as you run.

Changing Speeds to Music

Record music at 78, 33, and 16 rpm, or use a record player with variable speed control.

Listen to the music; it will start slowly and gradually increase in speed to a fast rhythm. Do you think you can run with a gradual increase and decrease in your speed? Match your running speed with the music. Begin slowly and gradually increase to your fastest speed; as the music begins to slow, decrease your speed to a jogging pace.

☐ Did you remember to lean slightly forward as you ran?
☐ Did you keep your elbows close to your body for maximum efficiency?

■ Remembering to lean slightly forward as you run and to keep your elbows close to your body, begin again. Listen to the music for your increase and decrease in speed.

Traveling as Water, Steam, Ice

Let's think about how water changes form as the temperature changes. At normal temperature, water is a liquid whose molecules are moving at a medium speed. As the temperature increases, the water molecules move faster and faster until the water is transformed into steam. As the temperature decreases, the molecules move slower and slower until they finally freeze, forming ice. Let's put this story into a creative dance. As I tell the story, you'll travel with changes in speed as the molecules increase their speed, decrease their speed, and freeze.

Performing Slow Motion Replay

Remember how the players move when a film is shown in slow motion or when the sports announcer replays a special segment from a game. I want each of you to think of your favorite moment in a sport. Is it when the quarterback breaks away to run for a touchdown, or is it when you scored the winning soccer goal? Perhaps it was the throw of the javelin at the Olympics or the relay team running at the track meet. Decide what kind of locomotor movement would portray your favorite moment. Combine your movements as in a slow motion replay. How would you begin—in what position? How will the replay end? Practice the segment until you can do it three times the same way, just like a replay. Remember, it's slow motion. We'll look at the movements when you're ready.

Other ideas for creative dance and travel include walking through a thick jungle, walking through a completely dark and haunted house, walking on the ledge of an eighty-story building, traveling across a high wire on a windy day, traveling during an earthquake.

UTILIZATION LEVEL

The activities in this section challenge children to travel in increasingly complex ways. Tasks are designed to develop the travel skills used in many dance, game, and gymnastics sequences.

Activities Leading to Skill Development

Traveling with a Partner: Matching Pathways

Stand back to back with a partner. When I say "Go," each partner travels in the direction he or she is facing. That is, each of you travels away from your partner. When you hear the drum, stop, turn around, and return to your partner with

MOONWALKING

A popular form of traveling is moonwalking, made famous by Michael Jackson. Children enjoy learning the basic steps and then creating their own styles of moonwalking.

Starting position: Stand on your left foot. Place the tip of your right foot on the floor. Put your weight on the ball of your right foot.

Glide your left foot along the floor to the back.

As your legs separate, let the heel of your left foot rise off the floor.

Lower the heel of your right foot to the floor as you come up on the ball of your left foot.

Put your weight on the ball of your left foot and glide your right foot back along the floor.

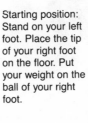

(continued)

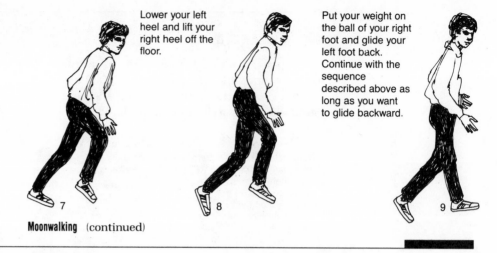

Lower your left heel and lift your right heel off the floor.

Put your weight on the ball of your right foot and glide your left foot back. Continue with the sequence described above as long as you want to glide backward.

7

8

9

Moonwalking (continued)

the exact pattern and locomotor movements you used before. *(See Figure 15-7.)* Return at the same speed you used to travel away from your partner.

■ Earlier you learned that there are three pathways. *(See "Space Awareness," Chapter 12.)* What are they? *(Ask for answers.)* All patterns are made up of those pathways or combinations of those pathways. This time as you travel away from your partner, be aware of the pathways you use. On your return, copy the same pathways.

■ Stand beside your partner. This time as you travel, use a slidestep to move away from your partner. Remember to return using the same pathway.

■ Select a partner and decide who's to be the first leader. When the follower says "Go," the leader travels across the field with a combination of straight, curved, and zigzag pathways. When the leader stops, the follower then travels the same pattern. The other partner then designs the pattern.

Figure 15-7 Traveling on pathways away from and toward a partner.

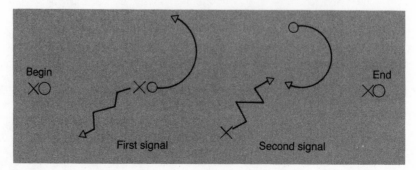

Begin
X O

First signal

Second signal

End
X O

You can make this activity a dance experience by adding music, such as "Dueling Banjos," with copy phrases. It can also be practice for patterns used in throwing and catching.

Traveling with a Partner: Changing Speed and Direction

Stand facing a partner approximately three feet apart; one of you is the leader, the other the follower. The leader slides to the right or left, changing directions quickly. The follower tries to stay directly across from the leader at all times. I'll give the signal each sixty seconds for you both to switch positions. Note that by adding dribbling a ball and defensive arm position to this pattern, we form an offensive-defensive drill in basketball.

□ Take quick short steps rather than a large stride.
□ Keep your weight on the balls of your feet for quickness.

Shadowing

Choose a partner whose speed and ability to change directions are very similar to yours. Partner 1 stands approximately two feet behind partner 2. When I say "Go," partner 2 travels quickly, changing directions with sharp turns to the right and to the left; partner 1 attempts to stay within an arm's distance at all times. When you hear the drum hit, stop without colliding or losing your balance. Partner 1 now stands in front, ready to be the new leader.

□ Watch out for others as you move quickly and change directions.
□ Keep your eyes on your partner's waist when you're the follower.
□ Remember, you're moving forward at all times.

This is excellent practice for dribbling skills. Give each partner a ball and repeat the task.

Performing Rhythmical Patterns

Scatter hula hoops around the room.

Jump in and out of your hula hoop with a four-four rhythm: two jumps in, two jumps out, or three jumps in, one jump out. Maintain an even tempo by clapping the four counts as you jump.

■ I'll clap the rhythm I want you all to use for your jumps: one, two, three, four. Let's all clap the rhythm together before we begin our jumps. *(Group practices with teacher as leader.)* Practice until you can match the rhythm three times with no mistakes.

■ Try your jumping pattern in and out of the hoop with the music *(e.g., "Jeremiah Bullfrog")*; remember, you may choose a three-one or a two-two pattern in and out.

Traveling to Express Age: The Fountain of Youth

Using combinations of locomotor movements, body language, and gestures, tell the story of an old, old person who discovers the Fountain of Youth. Let me set the stage for you. An old, old person is walking down the street. The person feels weary, tired, without enough energy to hold his or her head high. While walking down the street, the oldster sees a bottle in a gutter. An examination of the bottle reveals the words Fountain of Youth Juice. Puzzled, hesitant, yet desperate, the oldster takes a drink and then a few more. The transformation begins ... the old person is changed into an ecstatic youth who dances merrily down the street.

□ What type of movements would the old person use: jerky, smooth; slow, fast?
□ What body posture and what hand gestures would the old person assume?
□ How would the oldster approach the bottle?
□ Will the transformation occur quickly or be rather slowly executed?

■ Contrast the oldster's movements with those of the ecstatic youth: type of travel, speed, level, gestures.

Traveling in Bound and Free Flow

Here are two additional ideas for short dance phrases based on imaginary situations. First, a rag doll comes to life for a brief period of time. One interpretation is that the rag doll slowly comes to life with jerky, uncoordinated (bound) movements, falls over, and has trouble gaining control and balance; the doll gradually improves and is then running and leaping, turning in the air (free), and enjoying life. Then the doll suddenly stops, slowly walks back to the starting location, sits and sighs, freezes, and is a doll once again.

Second, a balloon filled with helium escapes from the hands of its owner, floats across the sky, leaks, and falls back to earth.

These types of dance experiences are often short, culminating the practice of travel patterns. Discuss with the children the travel qualities and movement concepts (space awareness, effort) appropriate for each activity. Each dance should have a clear beginning, rise to a climax, and then wind down to a conclusion.

Traveling to Tom Foolery Rhymes

Divide the children into groups of four. Write Tom Foolery rhymes on cards and place them around the room; you'll need enough cards for one per group. Some children may be able to write their own Tom Foolery rhymes.

In your group, make up a humorous sequence to the rhythmic pattern of the Tom Foolery rhyme written on your card. You decide the rhythm of chant and the locomotor patterns you'll use to accompany the rhyme. Travel around the room with your chosen locomotor patterns, chanting the rhyme as you go.

Here are the Tom Foolery rhymes:

> *Soft feet, gentle, quick run:*
> *Pit-a-pat, pit-a-pat, pit-a-pat,* jump back!

> *Swaying, rocking steps:*
> *See-Saw Mar-ger-y Daw,*
> *Jack shall have a new mas-ter.*
> *He shall have but a pen-ny a day,*
> *Be-cause he won't work an-y fast-er.*

> *Skipping:*
> *Here's a word to the wise:*
> *Don't get soap in your eyes!*
> *I hope the dope who thought up soap*
> *Has to eat it—I repeat it,* Eat it!

> *Bouncy jumps:*
> *Boinggg, boinggg, boingg, boingg, boingg,*
> *boingg, boingg,* bammmm!

PROFICIENCY LEVEL

The following activities let youngsters use their travel skills and knowledge of travel patterns to design and perform dance studies, gymnastics routines, and strategic game maneuvers.

Activities Leading to Skill Development

Depicting Primitive Tribes Through Travel

Dance can be a story without words. You're going to tell the story of primitive tribes through shapes and actions. *(Show children cave drawings of tribal dances.)* Use your imagination as you look at the drawings. How do you think these people lived? What was their work? What was home like for them—did they have a home? Now let's put your ideas into movement terms. At what level would the people move? Would their movements be flowing or sustained, jerky or smooth?

Divide the children into two groups.

Your dance will tell the story of two primitive tribes. Part 1 of your dance will show how the people live as a group. Show through your movements and gestures the life of a person in a primitive tribe. Part 2 of your dance will portray the two tribes discovering each other, their fear of the unknown, and their battle to defend their territory. In Part 2, each group begins with the movements portraying preparation for battle. The battle will consist of approach, attack (with no contact), and a retreat.

The following questions will help you design your movements for this dance story:

1. Will your travel be fast or slow when preparing for battle, approaching the enemy, retreating from the battle?
2. How can your gestures best represent the punching, jabbing, kicking, slashing actions of battle?
3. Will your travel be low, with angular actions, or high and smooth?
4. As you retreat from the battle, how will your travel show caution, fear, injury?

Excerpts from the songs "We Will Rock You" and "We Are the Champions" from the record album Queens' Greatest Hits *are excellent for this activity.*

Traveling to Show Tradition Versus Change

This is an advanced dance experience for children with a background in creative dance experiences.

Dance doesn't always tell a story. Sometimes dance is a study in form—the shapes we can make with our bodies, the spatial patterns we create as a group. *(Divide the class into two groups.)* Group 1 will represent tradition. The characteristics of tradition your body shapes and group travel can show might be a firm, solid shape, such as a square, the group forms; identical and simultaneous group movements; use of a small amount of space; and firm, sustained quality—control at all times.

Group 2 will represent the forces of change. The characteristics of change include individualized shapes, travel in different directions, use of a large amount of space, and a variety of movements. Working together as a group, design a dance that combines at least five shapes and three locomotor patterns to portray the characteristics of your group.

□ Remember that you'll have a beginning and an ending shape.
□ When we look at the tradition group, we should see oneness, sturdiness, caution; the shapes and actions of the change group should portray individuality, risk taking, and freedom.

Dance that tells a story can easily become only pantomine. Children will need guidance in avoiding exactly replicating gestures and using more total body movement and space.

DESIGNING FLOOR PATTERNS FOR DANCE STUDIES

The floor patterns created in dance experiences and the locomotor movements used are important components of creative dance. The patterns created as the dancer moves can tell the story, set the mood, or portray an idea. The various ways of travel used in dance and the patterns created aren't accidental; they're planned and carefully designed. When designing the travel pattern of a dance study, the teacher and children can focus upon the following concerns:

1. What idea stimulated the dance study? Was it a selection of music? A bull fight? A wiggly snake?

It's a good idea to have the children keep notes and diagram their pathways as they design them, for several reasons. First, the child will clearly visualize what the floor pattern looks like and be better able to evaluate its suitability for the dance. Second, children usually use several classes to put together a completed dance study and often fail to remember ideas they had in earlier classes. Third, when children finish a dance study, they take with them a written record of their accomplishments.

It's often beneficial to post several examples of pathways around the room on the walls, to give children an idea of what's expected. Another effective teaching aid is to post draw-

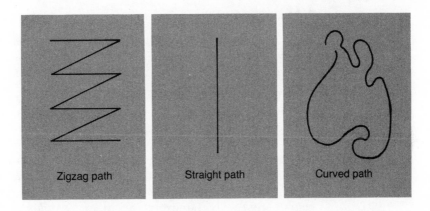

Zigzag path   Straight path   Curved path

2. What qualities are inherent in the theme of the dance or the selection of music? Is the tempo slow, moderate, or fast? Is the rhythm even or uneven? Is music harmonious? Vibrant? Mellow?
3. What pathway best expresses the feelings or emotions you sense? Advancing, attacking? Retreating? Collapsing? Gathering? Departing? Wavy? Angular? Jagged?

ings of locomotor skills and positions of stillness that the children have experienced. Rather than trying to diagram a sequence from memory, youngsters can look at these posters and select movements to incorporate along their floor patterns.

Even those of us with no artistic abilities can trace beautiful diagrams using an opaque projector!

Figure 15-8 Basic tinikling setup.

Performing Rhythmical Patterns: Tinikling

You'll need tinikling poles, which can be cut from bamboo or purchased commercially. Poles approximately twelve feet long will accommodate two persons tapping the poles and two persons jumping. Figure 15-8 shows the basic setup.

Tinikling is a rhythmical activity that involves coordinated stepping, hopping, jumping actions with the tapping of long bamboo poles. In the beginning position, the bamboo poles are approximately two feet apart; they're tapped down on the floor twice: tap, tap. The poles are then brought together for two counts: tap, tap. The pattern is repeated: apart, apart, together, together. This opening and closing position is maintained while dancers step or jump in and out without touching the poles. Let's do the action of the poles with our hands; clap the rhythm with me: out, out, in, in. *(Demonstrate with your hands apart, apart, together, together.)* This is the action we'll use for the bamboo poles for all our tinikling skills: out, out, in, in.

■ Divide into groups of four. Two persons clap the four-four rhythm; the other two persons practice the tapping action with the poles.

We find it helps to tape the ends of the poles where the children grip the poles, to prevent the bamboo poles from cracking and the fingers from being pinched.

■ You now know how to clap the four-four rhythm and to tap the bamboo poles to that rhythm. Now you'll learn the basic single-step pattern. *(Figure 15-9 shows single-steps. Have children stand beside a line made of colored tape on the floor. Their right sides should be toward the tape.)* Stand on your left foot; hop two times on your left foot. Step on your right foot between lines;

transfer your weight to your left foot between the lines. Hop on your right foot two times outside the lines. Repeat the action to the left. Clap the four-four beat as you hop.

■ Practice until you can perform the pattern four times with no mistakes. You'll then be ready to practice the single-step pattern with two persons tapping the poles.

   □ Remember, you step in as the poles tap apart.
   □ After you feel comfortable with the single-step pattern, try the double-step or hopping patterns. *(See Figures 15-10 and 15-11.)* When you're really good, you can create a new pattern with a four-four or three-four beat.

Students with advanced tinikling skills enjoy the action with four poles—two poles crossed over two poles—and the combination of basic tinikling actions with gymnastics stunts, e.g., cartwheels and walkovers between the poles as they move apart.

Figure 15-9 Tinikling: Single-step pattern.

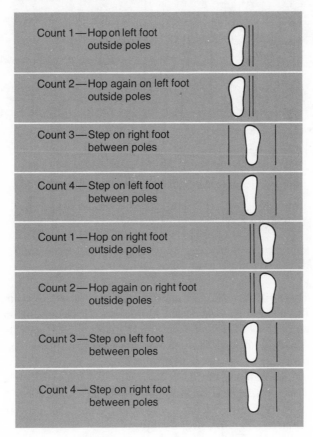

Count 1—Hop on left foot
outside poles

Count 2—Hop again on left foot
outside poles

Count 3—Step on right foot
between poles

Count 4—Step on left foot
between poles

Count 1—Hop on right foot
outside poles

Count 2—Hop again on right foot
outside poles

Count 3—Step on left foot
between poles

Count 4—Step on right foot
between poles

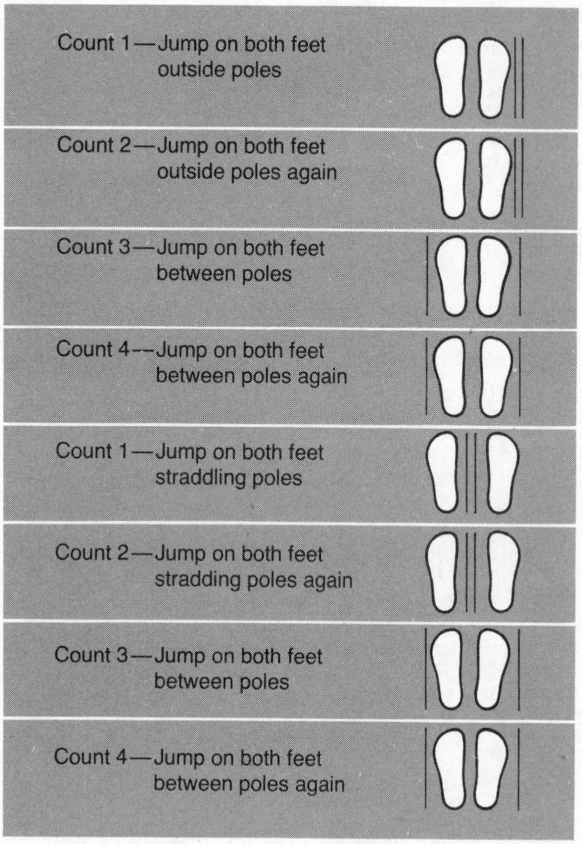

| Count 1—Jump on both feet outside poles |
| Count 2—Jump on both feet outside poles again |
| Count 3—Jump on both feet between poles |
| Count 4—Jump on both feet between poles again |
| Count 1—Jump on both feet straddling poles |
| Count 2—Jump on both feet stradding poles again |
| Count 3—Jump on both feet between poles |
| Count 4—Jump on both feet between poles again |

Figure 15-10 Tinikling: Double-step pattern.

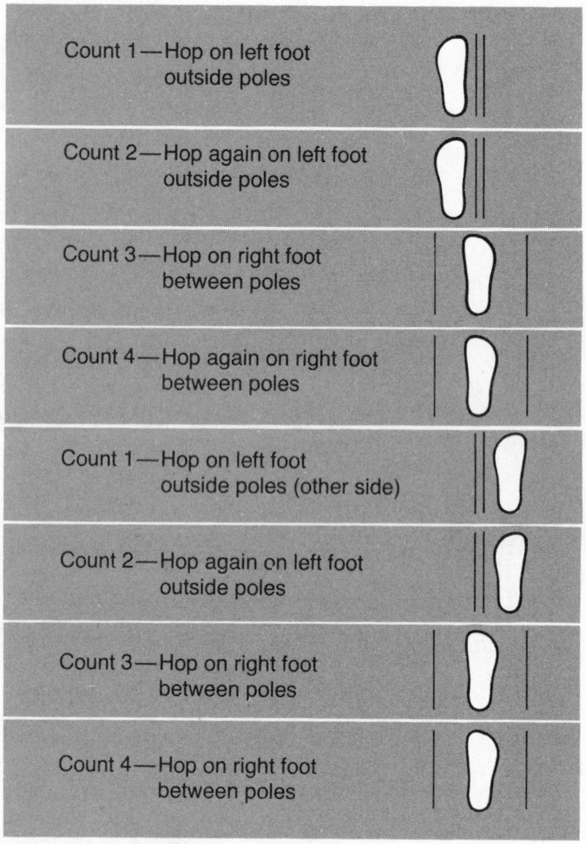

| Count 1—Hop on left foot outside poles |
| Count 2—Hop again on left foot outside poles |
| Count 3—Hop on right foot between poles |
| Count 4—Hop again on right foot between poles |
| Count 1—Hop on left foot outside poles (other side) |
| Count 2—Hop again on left foot outside poles |
| Count 3—Hop on right foot between poles |
| Count 4—Hop on right foot between poles |

Figure 15-11 Tinikling: Hopping.

TRAVELING IN GAMES AND SPORTS

The ability to travel in games is often what separates the skilled player from the average player. Many children can throw and catch accurately and with control while they're stationary, but they regress to a precontrol level when travel is added. Thus, traveling is an important part of the utilization and proficiency sections of the games skills chapters. Games-related tasks that incorporate traveling are discussed in Chapters 21 to 25: "Kicking and Punting," "Throwing and Catching," "Volleying and Dribbling," "Striking with Rackets and Paddles," and "Striking with Long-Handled Implements," and Chapter 16: "Chasing, Fleeing, and Dodging."

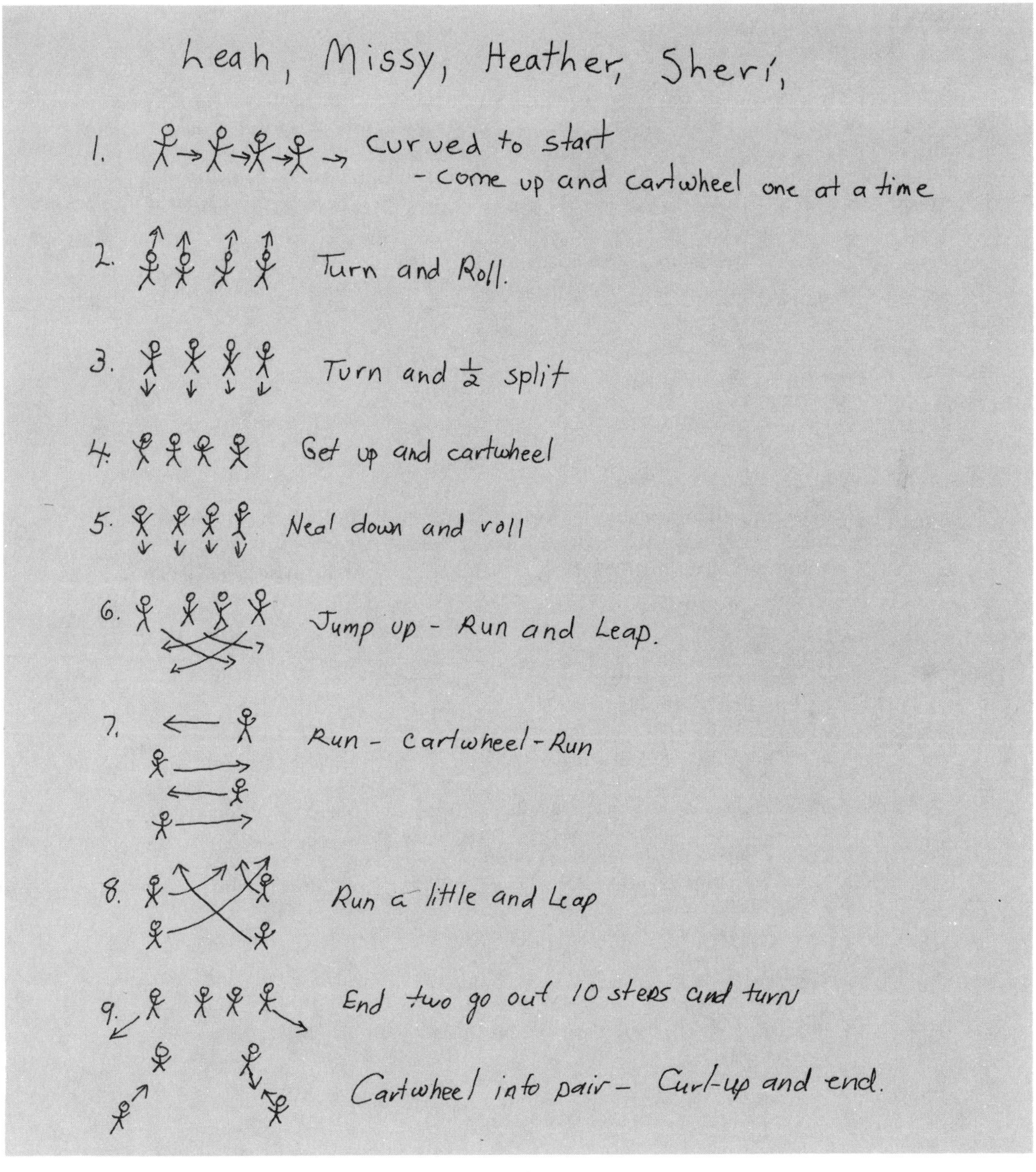

Leah, Missy, Heather, Sheri,

1. Curved to start
   - Come up and cartwheel one at a time

2. Turn and Roll.

3. Turn and ½ split

4. Get up and cartwheel

5. Neal down and roll

6. Jump up - Run and Leap.

7. Run - cartwheel - Run

8. Run a little and Leap

9. End two go out 10 steps and turn

   Cartwheel into pair - Curl-up and end.

Figure 15-12 Children's travel patterns in gymnastics.

ORIENTEERING

Orienteering is rapid travel over rugged terrain, guided only by a map and compass. This activity is becoming increasingly popular. The inclusion of orienteering in a curriculum obviously depends on the availability of the necessary components: compasses and a wooded area close to the school grounds.

Teachers who have access to these components will find a helpful article, "Orienteering," in the February 1978 issue of *Teacher,* pages 72 and 73. Ellsworth Boyd, the author, describes how orienteering can be taught in a school setting.

TRAVELING IN GYMNASTICS

Traveling in gymnastics supplies the buildup of force necessary for many Olympic stunts, e.g., handsprings, roundoffs, and aerial actions (see Figure 15-12). The floor patterns the travel creates form an important component of gymnastics routines. Travel in relation to gymnastics is discussed in Chapters 17 to 20: "Jumping and Landing," "Rolling," "Balancing," and "Transferring Weight," respectively.

READING COMPREHENSION QUESTIONS

1. What components of traveling are taught in a program of physical education for children?
2. What does naturally developing skill mean? List two examples.
3. Is a fundamental locomotor pattern the same as a naturally developing skill?
4. List the fundamental locomotor skills that emerge from the walk-run pattern.
5. What is a mature running pattern? Do all children have mature running patterns? Do all adults? Explain.
6. What is the difference among a hop, a leap, a slide, and a gallop?
7. What is orienteering? Why is it increasing in popularity?
8. Describe how travel is studied at the proficiency level in: games, gymnastics, and dance.
9. How can you use a Tom Foolery rhyme to stimulate different ways of traveling?
10. What is tinikling?

C H A P T E R **16**

Chasing, Fleeing, and Dodging

Since ancient times children have delighted in countless chasing, fleeing, and dodging games. Most of these games can be grouped into two categories: tag and dodgeball. In tag games, all free players flee or evade the touch of the chasing tagger. In dodgeball games, one or more players throw a ball to strike the fleeing or dodging players.

Physical education programs can build on the innate pleasure that children experience from playing these games. By providing a variety of challenging tasks and game situations, a teacher can help youngsters develop chasing, fleeing, and dodging skills (see our progression spiral, pp. 280–281). Experience suggests that it's best to focus on chasing, fleeing, and dodging skills after children have developed a working understanding of space awareness concepts and fundamental traveling skills.

Chasing, fleeing, and dodging activities are best played outdoors in large, grassy areas.

SKILL THEME DEVELOPMENT SEQUENCE

Chasing, Fleeing, Dodging

CONTROL LEVEL

Dodging and faking moves to avoid a chaser (Line Dodge; Freeze and Count Tag)
Dodging a thrown object without traveling (Glue Dodgeball)
Dodging stationary obstacles (People Dodge)
Maneuvering from a thrown object (Minidodgeball)
Dodging a thrown object (Call Ball)
Overtaking a fleeing person (Catch-Up Chase)
Dodging with quick changes of direction

PRECONTROL LEVEL

Dodging moving obstacles
Dodging in response to a signal
Traveling to dodge
Fleeing from a partner
Traveling to flee

CHASING

Chasing is traveling quickly to overtake or tag a fleeing person. In many game situations, the fleeing player is given a head start and allowed time to run away before the chaser can begin traveling. The fleeing player tries to avoid being caught or tagged. Thus, the chaser needs to be able to run at full speed and to react quickly to changes in the direction of the fleeing player's travel.

FLEEING

Fleeing is traveling quickly away from a pursuing person or object. In most game situations, the fleeing person tries to keep as much distance as possible between himself and the chaser. When the pursuer does close in, the fleeing player uses any maneuver possible to avoid being tagged or hit by a thrown object—the fleeing person dodges, changes direction quickly, or runs full speed. This continual demand on the fleeing player, to react quickly to emerging, threatening situations, is what makes tag and dodgeball games thrilling activities for children.

Chasing, Fleeing, Dodging

PROFICIENCY LEVEL

Using team strategy for chasing, fleeing, and dodging (Rip Flag)
Dodging in a game situation (Safety Bases; Pirate's Treasure)
Chasing and dodging simultaneously (Snatch the Flag)
Chasing and fleeing in a sport situation

UTILIZATION LEVEL

Dodging while manipulating an object
Dodging in a dynamic situation (Body Part Tag)
Dodging and chasing one person in a mass (Partner Dodge)
Dodging and chasing as part of a team (Octopus)

DODGING

Dodging is the skill of quickly moving the body in a direction other than the original line of movement. This includes any maneuver a person undertakes to avoid being touched by a chasing person or struck by a thrown object. Dodging may occur while a person is fleeing or stationary. Effective dodging actions include ducking, jumping, twisting, stretching, collapsing, and rolling.

LEVELS OF SKILL PROFICIENCY

We've found that most school-age children are familiar with a variety of tag and dodgeball games. But some youngsters whose chasing, fleeing, and dodging skills are at the precontrol or control level of proficiency have limited success in playing these games. That is, although many children can chase, flee, and dodge, they can't perform these skills effectively in dynamic game situations. In a game of tag, for instance, the child doing the chasing is often unable to overtake or tag any of the fleeing players and quickly tires of playing the game. In their classic study of children's games, Iona Opie and Peter Opie noted that chasing games were often plagued with arguments and ended prematurely in heated disputes.*

A teacher's initial task, therefore, is to help youngsters develop those skills prerequisite to becoming a capable chaser, fleer, or dodger in various game situations. In school situations where preschool youngsters' opportunities to play with other children are limited, a teacher may need to provide precontrol-level chasing, fleeing, and dodging activities, for example:

1. Running as fast as possible from one location to another
2. Traveling around a room and changing the direction of travel quickly when a signal is sounded
3. When a signal is given, quickly performing a designated dodging maneuver, such as jumping or collapsing
4. Running as fast as possible away from a partner; on the signal, running quickly toward a partner

Children who can competently perform a variety of quick, dodging maneuvers while running fast are at the control level. A teacher can provide challenging tasks designed to have these children keep their eyes focused on a target child and react quickly to the movements of that child by chasing, fleeing from, or dodging the target child. Such tasks include

1. Staying as close as possible to a fleeing, dodging partner
2. Chasing after a person who has been given a slight head start and is fleeing
3. Using a dodging maneuver to avoid being hit by a ball thrown by a partner
4. Trying to run across a field while dodging one or more chasers

When children can effectively dodge a thrown ball or chasing person and can react quickly and accurately to others' swift, darting movements, they're ready for utilization-level activities. Now the youngsters' chasing, fleeing, and dodging skills enable them to enjoy testing their abilities in ever-changing and complex game environments. Challenging activities include the following:

1. The players of one team flee and/or dodge the players of an opposing team while controlling an object (such as a football, Frisbee, or basketball).
2. One team chases down the members of an opposing team; that is, instead of fleeing their chasers, one team tries to run past them without being touched.

At the proficiency level, children are able to use chasing, fleeing, and dodging skills effectively in a wide variety of game contexts. Both the chasers and the fleeing, dodging players are skilled. At times the chaser gets the target; at other times the fleeing, dodging player escapes. Advanced chasing, fleeing, and dodging skills are evident in situations such as the following:

*Children's Games in Street and Playground, by I. Opie and P. Opie, 1969, New York: Oxford University Press.

Dodging a thrown ball requires agility as well as the ability to anticipate the path of a moving ball.

1. A runner in a football-type game darts quickly past the defense, dodging around the players who are chasing him.
2. A soccer player dribbles a ball past a defense player by faking one way and then traveling quickly in the opposite direction.
3. A defense player in a football-type game runs twenty to thirty yards to overtake an offensive runner heading for a score.
4. A basketball player races down court to score a lay-up even though a defense player is chasing right behind her.

In elementary school settings, children at the proficiency level enjoy playing teacher- and student-designed games in which chasing, fleeing, and dodging are the primary movements.

ASSESSMENT GUIDE / Chasing, Fleeing, Dodging

Note to Teachers. Mark several areas, each area approximately the size of a quarter of a basketball court.

TASK

With your group of six, you're going to play a tag game in the space marked around you. Two of you will be taggers; the other four persons will be dodgers. On the signal, the taggers will try to tag all the dodgers. If you're tagged, you must freeze until a free dodger crawls between your legs. Once you're freed, you can run again. On the stop signal, the game ends, and two different people in the group become taggers.

GUIDE

The children need precontrol- or control-level tasks when you observe that:

1. Dodgers are unable to stay within the boundaries to avoid getting tagged.
2. Dodgers simply run from the tagger to avoid being tagged, without dodging.
3. Taggers simply run after the dodger to try to catch the person and then quit, or they go to another dodger when they don't *immediately* succeed at catching the first one.

The children are ready for utilization- or proficiency-level tasks when you observe that:

1. The dodgers can stay within the boundaries and use a variety of twisting, turning, ducking, and speed-change maneuvers as well as running to avoid being tagged.
2. The taggers work together to catch the dodgers.
3. Taggers attempt to corner the dodgers and pursue them until they're caught, instead of giving up when at first they don't succeed.

PRECONTROL LEVEL

Activities at the precontrol level are designed to help children with limited movement experience who don't understand the concepts of chasing, fleeing, or dodging.

Activities Leading to Skill Development

Traveling to Flee

You've all played games in which you had to run away from someone trying to chase you. Today you're going to practice getting better at running away. This running away from someone is called *fleeing*. You're going to run as fast as possible against a set time. Here's how to play. First, everyone line up behind the line on this side of the field. On the signal, run across the field, then line up on the finish line and get ready to run back. You have to do all this in thirty seconds. Then you'll run again. So what I'm looking for is: on the signal, a run across the field and lining up on the finish line so you're ready to run back, all in thirty seconds.

> □ This time really run as if you think someone is chasing you. You'll be safe only when you're lined up on the finish line ready to run again.

Fleeing from a Partner

Stand about ten feet away from your partner. On the signal, walk slowly toward each other until you're as close as you can be without touching. Then, quickly jump backward, as if you're scared, and walk backward to your starting position, keeping a close watch on your partner.

> ■ This time you're going to do the activity a little differently because you seldom would move slowly to get away from someone. Try to move a little faster as you flee or go away from your partner. Just remember to not go so fast that you fall down.

> ■ Now, instead of walking away from your partner, try jogging. Remember to keep your eye on your partner and not go so fast that you fall down.

Traveling to Dodge

Place carpet squares, hoops, milk jugs, or ropes about the room on the floor.

On the signal, travel around the general space without touching anyone else or any of the objects on the floor. Everything is poison. Be sure to watch the other people as well as the objects.

> ■ This traveling to avoid something is called *dodging;* we learned a little about it when we studied space awareness. Now you're going to do the same thing again, but this time a little faster. A secret is to watch the nonmoving objects out of the corner of your eye and to carefully watch the moving people with your whole eye. Sometimes it also helps to change your speed a little to let other people go by. Remember, no touching and no falling down.

Dodging in Response to a Signal

Now you're going to become real sneaky. As you travel throughout the general space, when you hear the signal, pretend that you're going to go in one direction and then quickly change and go in a different direction. Be careful to not run into anyone else.

> □ What you just did is called a *fake* or a *dodge.* You're going to try to get really good at the maneuver; you never know when it might come in handy.

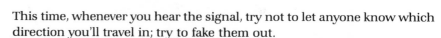

This time, whenever you hear the signal, try not to let anyone know which direction you'll travel in; try to fake them out.

■ Now, instead of me giving you the signal, you'll fake on your own. Whenever you come to an object or another person, pretend that you're going to go one way but go another. Really try to confuse the other person so they don't know where you'll be going. Make your move quickly once you decide which way you're going.

■ So far, most of your fakes have been made going forward. This time, try to go backward or sideways as well as forward.

☐ Here's one more thing that will help you make even better fakes. Go a bit faster, so that your moves happen in split seconds and are over with. The moves should be quick enough so that the other person doesn't even have time to react. Remember not to go so fast that you fall down.

Dodging Moving Obstacles

In this activity you'll act like a moving obstacle course. Half of you will start from one side of the room and half from the other. On the signal, try to walk to the opposite side of the room without touching anyone else. It really helps to spread yourselves out along the entire space so that you aren't bunched up in one place. Remember, no touching anyone else.

■ This time you're going to change the way you travel. You're going to cross the space with three body parts touching the floor. So you have to think about two things: not touching anybody else and having three body parts touch the floor. Spread apart and look up. Go.

■ Now you'll still travel across the space not touching, but you'll be at different levels, so you'll really have to think and watch for others. Everyone who has blue eyes will travel with his or her body parts high in the air; those with brown eyes will travel at a low level; and those with green or hazel eyes will travel at a medium level. Spread out. Go.

■ I'm really going to make it hard this time. You'll be traveling on your feet, but faster than before. First you'll go just a little faster, and then the speed will pick up. Never go so fast that you fall down or can't stop when you get to the other side. Let's try at a fast walk. Remember that the object is still to get to the other side without touching anyone else.

Begin slowly. Have the children walk. Gradually increase the speed as you observe the children traveling competently and without any collisions.

CONTROL LEVEL

The activities here are designed for those youngsters who chase, flee, and dodge with limited success. The tasks help children use their skills effectively in relation to an unpredictable and often equally skillful classmate.

Activities Leading to Skill Development

Dodging with Quick Changes of Direction

This time you're going to practice something very similar to what you did before. Travel around the general space. When you come close to another person, get as close as possible and then quickly dodge away and look for another person to approach. There should be a clear burst of speed as you dodge away from the person—as if you're trying to escape. Remember to watch out for other people.

  □ Dodging with speed as you just did is called *darting*. This time practice getting as close to the person you approach as you can before *quickly* darting away. Make the dart very clear.
  □ As you dart away, be looking for another person to approach; as you slow down, start toward the new person. Try to repeat the whole procedure five times without having to stop.

Overtaking a Fleeing Person (Catch-Up Chase)

With a partner you're going to play a chasing and fleeing game called Catch-Up Chase. On the first signal, partner 1 darts away from partner 2. After five seconds, another signal is sounded, and partner 2, who has remained still, chases after fleeing partner 1, trying to tag partner 1 before I blow the whistle in twenty seconds. For the next round you'll switch places. You must always stay inside the boundaries. So the game goes like this: Start together. On the first signal, partner 1 takes off running. On the second signal, partner 2 takes off and tries to catch partner 1 before the whistle is blown in twenty seconds.

  □ Now that you understand, I'll give you some clues to help you get better. If you're partner 1, the one fleeing, try to get as far away as possible in those first five seconds when partner 2, the chaser, can't run, and then use all the fakes and dodges you know to avoid being tagged. If you're partner 2, the chaser, always keep your eye on the hips of the person you're chasing and go at full speed; it helps if you can trap the runner in a corner, where escape isn't easy. Remember to never give up, even if the runner keeps getting away. Let's try it again. See if you can use all the moves you know.

This task is appropriate when the children have learned to travel in general space without bumping into one another. Initially, large areas make this an easier task for children because they're able to focus more on their partners and less on avoiding other children.

Dodging a Thrown Object (Call Ball)

Form youngsters into groups of four. Each group should have a foam, plastic, or yarn ball. Set up boundaries about twenty feet long on all four sides. Note that for all activities involving throwing a ball at another person, we recommend using dime store plastic balls, foam balls, or yarn balls. Red rubber playground balls are unacceptable because they're heavy, hard to throw, and can injure children.

To begin the game, one of you will be the thrower; we'll call you player 1. Now, player 1 tosses the ball straight up in the air and calls out the name of another player, who we'll call player 2. Player 2 then catches or collects the ball as quickly as possible while everybody else scatters within the boundaries. Player 2, after collecting the ball, shouts "Stop"; you other players must freeze where you are. Player 2 can take no more than three steps toward another player before throwing the ball in an attempt to hit that player. The dodging player may take only one step to try and dodge the ball. The player who was thrown at then becomes the thrower and the game starts over. Any questions? Remember to stay within your boundaries.

☐ This time I'm going to give player 2 some hints. As soon as you hear your name called, go quickly and get the ball, to prevent the others from running so far. Then make sure you take your three steps toward the *closest* person because you'll have a better chance of hitting that person. Let's try it again.

You don't have to penalize or eliminate a child who is hit by a ball because the challenge of avoiding being hit by the ball is motivation enough.

In some school yards we've observed classes of children playing a game popularly called Bombardment or Killer. As these names imply, the game can be dangerous. Typically, a class is divided into two teams, with a middle line separating each team. Each team throws a hard ball in an attempt to strike players on the opposing team; the teams often throw from close range and toward an unsuspecting child. We don't recommend this activity. There are many other dodge-type experiences you can plan that are safer, allow more children to participate, and are more apt to result in skill development.

Maneuvering from a Thrown Object (Minidodgeball)

You're again going to work on dodging. In each group of three, two of you will be throwers and one a dodger. The throwers should be about ten to fifteen feet apart, with the dodger in the middle. The throwers throw the ball *(plastic, yarn, or foam)* at the dodger, trying to hit the dodger below the waist. The dodger stays in the middle until hit. When hit, the dodger exchanges places with the successful thrower. This is really a minidodgeball game. Dodger, remember that one secret to staying in the middle is to always face the person who's throwing at you.

> ☐ Now some extra hints for the dodger: You can move quicker and not fall down if you keep your body low to the ground and your feet spread apart about shoulder width. Always stay on the balls of your feet; this enables you to duck, dive, jump, twist, turn, and run quickly so that there's less chance of you getting hit. Let's try it again. Dodgers, really make those throwers work hard.

Dodging Stationary Obstacles (People Dodge)

Place carpet squares on the floor, or mark X's on the floor.

Form into two groups, one group taggers, the other group dodgers. Taggers should stand on the X's *(or carpet squares)* marked on the floor and always have both feet on their X's *(or carpet squares)*. The dodgers should start on one side of the room and try to get to the other side of the room without being tagged. After five runs, switch places. If you get tagged, try to figure out how you can avoid being tagged next time.

> ☐ Remember as you try to cross the tag zone to surprise the taggers. Use the dodges and fakes that you've learned.

> ■ Now you're going to find the activity a little harder. If you're tagged, you must freeze right where you're tagged and become a tagger. Dodgers, this will get really hard at the end, so be on your toes.

Dodging a Thrown Object Without Traveling (Glue Dodgeball)

This dodgeball game will probably be different from any that you've ever played before and will really test your skill as a dodger. There will be six people to a group; four will be dodgers and two will be throwers. As in a regular dodgeball game, the people on the outside try to throw to hit the people on the inside; a person who's hit trades places with the throwers. However, in this game, the dodgers must stay in the squares marked inside each playing area. *(Figure 16-1 shows the setup.)* At all times, the dodgers must keep one foot in their assigned area. They can pivot, duck, bend or stretch but can't move from that area, as if they're glued to that one spot and have to dodge without running away.

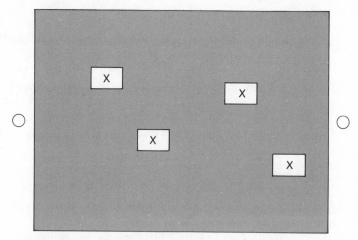

Figure 16-1 Setup for Glue Dodgeball. X = dodgers; O = throwers.

Dodging and Faking Moves to Avoid a Chaser (Line Dodge)

Mark out lines on the floor (see Figure 16-2 for the setup) and have red arm bands for the chasers.

This tag game has different rules than most tag games. You must always stay on the lines marked on the floor. You may go backward, sideways, or forward so that you can keep the tagger in view, but you have to stay on the lines. If you're tagged, you must stand on one foot until you count out loud to thirty; then you can come back into the game. There are four chasers who'll be wearing red arm bands so you can identify them.

Figure 16-2 Setup for Line Dodge.

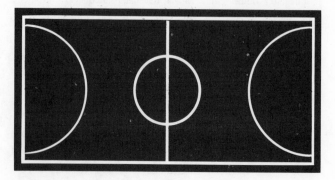

Dodging and Faking Moves to Avoid a Chaser (Freeze and Count Tag)

Each group will need a space approximately the size of a quarter of a basketball court.

This chasing and fleeing game will really make you work hard. You can't be slow or you'll be caught. There will be six of you in each group, and your group will be in a space that has clear boundaries. Make sure you know where those boundaries are. Two people will start out as chasers—you decide who they'll be. The other four players are runners. On the signal, the chasers have one minute to try and catch all the runners. If tagged, a runner has to freeze and then count to ten out loud before starting to run again. The object is for the taggers to catch all the runners at the same time. After the first minute, change taggers and play again. Remember, the taggers have to try to catch everyone, and no one can go outside the boundaries.

  ▢ While you rest, let me give you a few extra hints. The taggers need to work as a team; it may help to talk about your plan before you start. Runners, you have to try some different things to avoid being caught, such as changing direction quickly, varying your speed, or maybe even ducking and rolling to avoid the taggers. Let's try it again.

UTILIZATION LEVEL

Children at the utilization level are ready to test their skills in increasingly complex and gamelike situations. In these activities, children will have to frequently fake and dodge quickly in reaction to the deceptive movements of others.

Activities Leading to Skill Development

Dodging and Chasing as Part of a Team (Octopus)

Divide the class into two groups. Place tape or chalk marks on the floor to designate where the members of one team must place their feet. Place these marks approximately an arm's length apart. Figure 16-3 shows the setup.

To play this game, half of you will be taggers, and you must stand on the marks on the floor. You can't move either of your feet from your mark. The other half of you are dodgers. You'll begin at this end of the room and try to travel through the taggers without being touched. After you dodgers make it to the other side of the room, return around the outside of the room, and keep trying to get through the taggers until you hear the stop signal. On the stop signal, switch places. Dodgers, this activity is really tricky, so think carefully and catch the taggers off guard; for example, when the taggers reach one way to touch some-

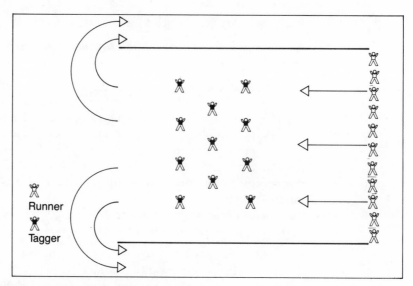

Figure 16-3 Setup for Octopus.

one else, go around the other side; or change your speed, so you have time to maneuver around taggers; or change the level at which you travel.

■ This time things are going to be a little harder for the taggers. Instead of just tagging the dodgers, the taggers have to tag the left knees of the dodgers with their right hands. *(You can change these directions to several combinations of body parts, for example, right hand-right knee; left hand-right knee; left hand-right elbow.)*

Dodging and Chasing One Person in a Mass (Partner Dodge)

For this tag game, you and a partner are on opposite teams. One of you is a tagger and the other one a dodger. On the signal, the taggers will spread out inside the boundaries, and the dodgers will line up on this side of the field. On the next signal, the dodgers will try to get to the other side of the field without being touched by their partners, the taggers. The trick is that each dodger can be tagged only by the partner. When the dodgers get to the other side, they return to the starting line by going around the outside of the field and continue to travel across the space until they hear the stop signal. On the stop signal, trade places with your partners.

    □ While you rest, I'll give the dodgers some hints. First, remember to use all the quick fakes that you've learned, such as taking a quick step to the left and then running to the right. Also, you can use teammates' bodies as obstacles or blockers to help avoid your tagger, but remember to not push anyone. Let's try it again.

Dodging in a Dynamic Situation (Body Part Tag)

This game is called Body Part Tag. The object is to tag the runners on a named body part if you're a tagger or, if you're a runner, to avoid being tagged on the named body part. There are ten of you in a group, eight runners and two chasers. Chasers, try to touch the runners on the body part I call out. Any runners that you tag, must freeze. The tagged runners can be unfrozen if they're tagged by a free runner on a body part other than the tagged part. The taggers will have one minute to try and catch all the runners. At the end of one minute, start again with two new taggers. You must stay inside your boundaries. Get ready; "shoulders." Go.

□ Now that you know how to play, here are a few hints. Taggers, you must make a plan and work together to try and tag everybody. It helps to go after one person and corner one person at a time. Now, dodgers, you have to be quick—you might try ducking, stopping, and starting, and changing speeds in combination with just running. Ready?

Dodging While Manipulating an Object

On the floor or the pavement, mark boundaried areas approximately the size of a basketball key circle.

The object of this game is to dribble a ball and at the same time try to take a ball away from someone else. Here's how it works. Each of you in your circle *(two or three)* will be bouncing a ball. As you bounce the ball, you'll be trying to knock the other players' balls out of the area while keeping your ball from being knocked away. The secrets are to (1) keep your body low while using a quick bouncing action and (2) keep your body between your ball and the players trying to get at it. If your ball gets knocked out, just go get it and start again.

□ A third secret is look at the other players while you're bouncing your ball so you can see what's going on.

PROFICIENCY LEVEL

Children at the proficiency level are ready to use their skillful chasing, fleeing, and dodging abilities in a variety of complex and ever-changing game situations. In the activities here, two teams of players are required to chase, flee, and dodge one another.

Activities Leading to Skill Development

Chasing and Fleeing in a Sport Situation

You'll need enough flag belts for all the youngsters.

Utilization level: Children enjoy the thrill and excitement of chasing, fleeing, and dodging while manipulating an object.

Each group of six will be divided into two teams, with three players on each team. One team will start with the ball. Each team will wear different colored flag belts. On the signal, a player on the team with the ball, team 1, tries to pass or run the ball from its goal to team 2's goal without the ball touching the ground or team 2 grabbing the flag of the player with the ball. Members of team 1 should always move *toward* the goal they're trying to get, not go backward. They should also try to go as fast as possible but use whatever fakes are needed to get downfield.

◻ This time I'll give some help to the taggers, team 2. You need to make a plan about how to catch the runners on team 1 and then work together to catch them. One plan might be for each team member to choose an opposing player to guard and then to stay as close to that person as possible.

Chasing and Dodging Simultaneously (Snatch the Flag)

This game pits each player against every other player. The object is to snatch the flag off another player's belt without losing your own flag and while staying within the designated boundaries. If your flag is pulled off, another player can put it back on and you can keep playing. You *can't* put your own flag back on. You've really got to watch all the other players and move to stay out of their way. Remember all the turning, twisting, and jumping dodges.

This game should start with groups of about six children. As the children become more proficient, you can increase the size of the groups.

Dodging in a Game Situation (Safety Bases)

Mark off a large boundaried area, and place hoops—safety bases—within the area. Figure 16-4 shows the setup.

This is another tag game, called Safety Bases. The object is for one team of runners, team 1, to cross the space without being touched by a team of taggers, team 2. Team 1 begins at one end of the field; the taggers on team 2 begin at the other end. On the signal, the runners try to cross the field without being tagged; the taggers try to stop any runners from getting across the field. The runners are safe—can't be tagged—when they're in any of the hoops. The runners have about two minutes to cross the field. After two turns, you'll switch places. The safety bases will help, but use them wisely, only as a last resort when you're about to be tagged; don't just stand in them the whole time.

Dodging in a Game Situation (Pirate's Treasure)

Mark off a square playing area. Place a hoop in the center of the area, with a beanbag inside the hoop. Figure 16-5 shows the setup.

This chasing, fleeing, and dodging game is called Pirate's Treasure. The object is for the free players to try and steal the treasure, which is in the beanbag, from the middle of the space and return it to the outside of the space without being tagged by the pirate who is protecting the treasure.

There are five players on each team: one pirate, and four sailors trying to get the treasure. The pirate's job is to protect the treasure from the sailors. On the signal, the sailors have two minutes in which to steal the treasure and get it to the outside of the square without being touched by the pirate. If the sailors

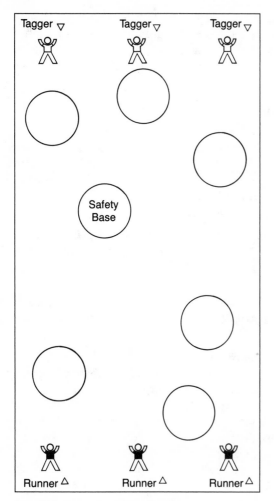

Figure 16-4 Setup for Safety Bases.

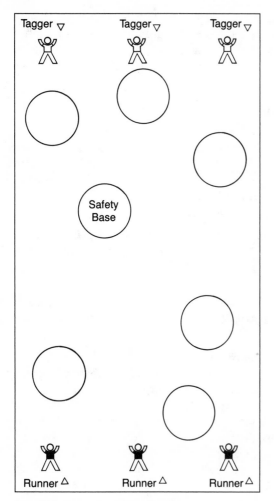

Figure 16-5 Setup for Pirate's Treasure.

get the treasure to the outside or the two-minute limit is reached, a new pirate tries to protect the treasure and the game starts over. It helps if the sailors work together and make a plan to steal the treasure. One player may try to fake the pirate out of position while another sailor steals the treasure. It also helps if the pirate stays very near the treasure *(but the pirate can't go in the hoop with the treasure)* and closely watches all the sailors.

Using Team Strategy for Chasing, Fleeing, and Dodging (Rip Flag)

Each team member has to wear a flag belt with two flags on it. Each opposing team member has a different color flag.

The name of this game is Rip Flag. The object is to see how many of the other team's flags you can get without losing your own. There are four players on a

In many primitive tribal games, the tribes believed that the chaser was evil, magic, or diseased and that his touch was contagious. Although today's games are a far cry from fleeing possible death, one has a hard time believing otherwise when observing the intensity and all-out effort children fleeing a chaser display!

team. One team begins at each end of the space. On the signal, both teams move into the playing area, and each team tries to snatch as many flags as possible from the other team's belts while preventing the other team from stealing their own flags. On the next signal, all play stops and the teams return to their sidelines and count how many flags they were able to steal.

□ The real secret to this game is to always keep moving. It also helps to work with your teammates to decide whose flag you'll go after and when.

READING COMPREHENSION QUESTIONS

1. List the differences among chasing, fleeing, and dodging.
2. Describe four effective dodging movements.
3. What are the characteristics of each of the four levels of skill proficiency for chasing, fleeing, and dodging?
4. Rank the following tasks by placing the number 1 in front of the easiest (most basic), the number 2 in front of the next more difficult, and so on.
   (   ) A defensive player in a football-type game pursues an offensive runner.
   (   ) You travel around the room. On a signal, you change directions as quickly as possible.
   (   ) You stay as close as you can to your partner, who'll try to get away from you.
   (   ) One team chases the members of an opposing team.
5. What is a fake? Give several examples of when a fake might be used.
6. Why do you use large areas when introducing the chasing, fleeing, and dodging skills?
7. As a teacher, what do you look for when helping a child who is learning to dodge a ball? List at least three questions.
8. What is your observational focus when you're teaching fleeing? List at least three questions.
9. When a child is tagged during a tag game, what is one alternative to eliminating the child until a new game begins?
10. Killer (also called Bombardment) is a game that has been played for years in elementary schools. What is the authors' reason for not recommending it?

17

Jumping and Landing

Jumping is a locomotor pattern in which the body propels itself off the floor or apparatus into a momentary period of flight. As an isolated maneuver or in combination with other basic patterns, jumping—particularly the flight phase when the body is unsupported in the air—is a fascinating body action.

A jump is performed for one of two reasons: (1) to raise the body vertically (straight up) for height or (2) to raise the body with a forward momentum to travel over a distance. Children who learn to effectively jump for height and distance are prepared for a multitude of game, dance, and gymnastics activities in which the performer needs to be a skilled jumper.

FUNDAMENTAL JUMPING PATTERNS

Wickstrom* suggested that infants are developmentally capable of performing a jumping action when they're approximately twenty-four months old. He described the types of jumps preschool children achieve in terms of progressive difficulty:

Fundamental Motor Patterns, 2nd ed., by R. L. Wickstrom, 1977, p. 63, Philadelphia: Lea & Febiger.

Jump down from one foot to the other.

Jump up from two feet to two feet.

Jump down from two feet to two feet.

Run and jump from one foot to the other.

Jump forward from two feet to two feet.

Jump down from one foot to two feet.

Run and jump forward from one foot to two feet.

Jump over object from two feet to two feet.

Jump from one foot to same foot rhythmically.

It's safe to assume that, within an average class of young children, some will be incapable of performing one or more of these jumping tasks. Initial

Young children often jump up and down like bouncing balls, enjoying the sensation of propelling the body off the ground for a momentary period of flight.

"Make a wide shape in flight."

observations will probably reveal a wide range of jumping abilities. Typically, kindergarten students are at the precontrol level. Their jumps usually achieve little height or distance, and they jump on two feet to ensure that they maintain their balance. Children at this level seem to be jumping merely to enjoy the sensation of momentarily losing contact with the ground and the challenge of maintaining balance upon landing. A teacher can build on this natural fascination by providing learning activities that progressively lead children toward the mature performance of jumping and landing in different dance, game, and gymnastic situations (see our progression spiral, p. 301).

The fundamental jumping pattern consists of the following five basic variations:

1. Two-foot takeoff to a one-foot landing
2. Two-foot takeoff to a two-foot landing
3. One-foot takeoff to a landing on the same foot (hop)
4. One-foot takeoff to a landing on the other foot (leap)
5. One-foot takeoff to a two-foot landing

SKILL THEME DEVELOPMENT SEQUENCE

Jumping and Landing

PROFICIENCY LEVEL

Vaulting jumps
Hurdling jumps
Jumping, dancing, and imagery
Jumping as part of a dance creation
Jumping with a springboard
Jumping with a partner to mirror/match actions

UTILIZATION LEVEL

Jumping to an accented beat
Throwing and catching while jumping
Jumping on a bench
Jumping to throw
Jumping to catch

CONTROL LEVEL

Jumping and landing task sheet
Jumping over, on, off equipment using buoyant and yielding landings
Jumping over equipment using buoyant landings
Jumping using buoyant and yielding landings
Jumping a self-turned rope
Jumping a turned rope
Jumping in rhythmical sequences
Jumping rhythmically
Performing jumping sequences and making body shapes
Traveling, jumping, and body shapes
Jumping to form a body shape during flight
Jumping over low obstacles: hoops; hurdles

PRECONTROL LEVEL

Jumping over a swinging rope
Landing on one foot
Jumping for height
Jumping for distance
Jumping and landing: basic patterns

However, the specific actions of the body in performing a jump vary according to the purpose or intention, for example, jumping to catch or jumping to dismount from apparatus.

LEVELS OF SKILL PROFICIENCY

When we begin to focus on jumping, we have children think of the skill as three successive phases:

1. Takeoff: Actions of the body as it's propelled off the ground
2. Flight: Actions of the body while it's off the ground and in the air
3. Landing: Actions of the body as it reestablishes contact with the ground

We present tasks designed to have the children discover and experiment with the five possible takeoff and landing combinations. Children begin to sense which takeoff procedures cause the highest jumps as opposed to those that cause the longest jumps. They find that actions of the legs, arms, torso, and head during the flight phase influence the trajectory of the jump. And they come to recognize the unique giving action of the ankles, knees, and hips in absorbing the shock of landing.

The two Key Observation Points illustrate the correct and incorrect forms for the takeoff, flight, and landing phases as well as illustrating the mature stage. The Key Observation Points for jumping for height and landing starts on the next page; see p. 306 for the second Key Observation Points: jumping for distance.

Once children can accurately perform the five basic jumping variations using vigorous takeoffs and balanced, controlled landings, they are ready for control-level challenges. At this point we place more emphasis on the flight phase of children's jumps. For example, they can begin to explore bodily actions in flight such as:

Jumping and making a wide body shape

Jumping and gesturing with an arm (for example, punching)

Jumping and twisting the hips

Jumping and turning clockwise

Low apparatus is used to create new jumping situations, such as:

Jumping over a hurdle

Jumping onto a milk crate

Jumping through a hoop

Jumping from a table

When children can repeatedly jump to fulfill a variety of objectives and their jumps continually exhibit a mature pattern, then utilization-level tasks are appropriate:

Jumping on an accented beat

Performing a series of light, gentle leaps

Jumping to catch a ball

Jumping to mount or dismount apparatus

Jumping to a hanging support (for example, ropes)

Performers at the proficiency level are able to jump high enough to carry out complex maneuvers in the air and to use a variety of jumping actions to express a feeling, idea, or attitude. Examples of proficiency-level performances include

Jumping and throwing a ball to a target

Hurdling

Leaping reception of a football against an opponent

Standard patterns of jumping (for example, long jump, high jump)

KEY OBSERVATION POINTS / **Jumping for Height and Landing**

TAKEOFF

1. Do the child's hips, knees, and ankles flex in a crouch as the child prepares to jump?

2. Do the child's arms extend vigorously forward and then upward upon takeoff, reaching full extension above the head at liftoff?

FLIGHT

Does the child's body extend fully in the air during the jump—especially the arms?

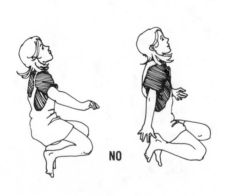

LANDING

1. Do the child's ankles extend in preparation for landing?

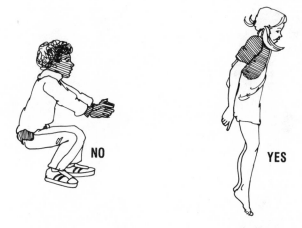

2. Do the child's hips, knees, and ankles flex to absorb the shock of landing?

MATURE STAGE

When children are at the mature stage of jumping for height, do their jumps look similar to the following sequence? The hips, knees, and ankles flex in a preparatory crouch. The jump begins with a vigorous forward and upward lift

by the arms. The thrust is continued by forceful extension at the hips, knees, and ankles. The body remains in extension until the feet are ready to retouch, and then the ankles, knees, and hips flex to absorb the shock of landing.

Source: Fundamental Motor Patterns, 2nd ed., by R. L. Wickstrom, 1977, Philadelphia: Lea & Febiger.

KEY OBSERVATION POINTS / Jumping for Distance

TAKEOFF

1. Do the child's arms extend vigorously forward and then upward upon takeoff, reaching full extension above the head at liftoff?

NO

YES

2. Are the child's hips, knees, and ankles fully extended at takeoff? Is the takeoff angle at 45° or less?

NO   YES

FLIGHT

Does the child bring the legs forward and the arms downward in preparation for landing?

LANDING

1. Do the child's heels contact the ground first?
2. Are the child's knees flexed and the arms thrust forward at the moment of contact?

MATURE STAGE

When children are at the mature stage of jumping for distance, do their jumps look similar to the following sequence? The arms extend vigorously forward and then upward upon takeoff, reaching full extension above the head at liftoff. The hips and knees are extended fully, with the takeoff angle at 45° or less. In preparation for landing, the arms are brought downward and the legs thrust forward until the thighs are parallel to the surface. The center of gravity of the body is far behind the base of support (feet) upon foot contact, but at the moment of contact the knees are flexed and the arms are thrust forward to maintain the momentum to carry the center of gravity beyond the feet.

ASSESSMENT GUIDE / Jumping and Landing

TASK Run, jump using a one-foot takeoff, and turn in the air so that you land on one foot facing the opposite direction without falling over or moving your foot.

GUIDE The children need precontrol- or control-level tasks when you observe that:

1. They're unable to take off on one foot when they jump.
2. They're unable to land balanced on one foot without moving their foot.

The children are ready for utilization- or proficiency-level tasks when you observe that they complete the task as explained: one-foot takeoff, 180° in the air, landing on one foot without moving the foot or losing balance (i.e., falling down or using their hands to maintain balance).

PRECONTROL LEVEL

The following activities provide a variety of jumping experiences that lead to the ability to use jumping patterns and land without losing balance. Children should be able to distinguish between actions that result in going high and those that result in going far.

Children can learn to land safely by jumping off low benches or milk crates onto grass or a mat.

Activities Leading to Skill Development

Jumping and Landing: Basic Patterns

Place four stacks of ropes against one wall. There should be a rope for each youngster.

Look around and you'll see four stacks of ropes. Walk to the stack nearest you and select a rope. Place the rope in a straight line in your self-space. Jump over the rope, taking off on two feet and landing on two feet.

□ Try to be as high as you can when you're over the rope. Swing your arms— hard! Push off your toes—strong!

■ Stand alongside your rope. Try to jump from one end of the rope to the other. Don't forget to swing your arms and push with your toes.

■ Arrange your rope in a shape different from a straight line—a circle, a rectangle. Jump into the rope, taking off on one foot and landing on two feet. Bend your knees when you land so that your landings are very quiet.

■ Let's try a hop. A *hop* is taking off on one foot and landing on the same foot. Hop into and out of your rope.

■ See if you can hop into and out of your rope three times without touching your other foot to the ground. Then see if you can do the same thing on the other foot.

Jumping for Distance

Place your rope on the floor far away from others. Jump as far as you can without running. This is called a *standing long jump*.

  □ Be sure to bend your knees and swing your arms as you get ready to jump.
  □ When you land, are you landing on your heels first? Are your arms swinging forward just as you land so that you don't fall backward?

Place one strip of masking tape on the wall for each child.

Get a piece of tape off the wall; lie on the floor with your feet touching the rope, and place the tape by the top of your head. If you're having trouble, ask a friend to help. The distance from the rope to the tape is how tall you are. Try to jump your height. If you jump farther than your height, move the tape to where your heels first touched the ground when you landed.

■ Now try running and jumping. Take off before you get to the rope. You should be able to jump farther this way. Be sure to bend your knees when you land. Move the tape each time you jump farther than you did before.

Jumping for Height

Hang streamers at various heights above a rope stretched along the playground.

Jump to see if you can touch the streamers hanging over the rope. Be careful of others.

  □ Are you crouching as you jump? Are you swinging your arms high and hard? Are you pushing off strongly from your toes?

■ Use a one-foot takeoff. Use a two-foot takeoff. Which takeoff works the best for you?

■ Now run and jump and try to touch a streamer. Be sure to swing your arms hard over your head. *(The teacher or a child demonstrates.)*

Landing on One Foot

Practice taking off on two feet and landing on one foot. Bend your knee as you land so that you don't lose your balance.

■ When you can land balanced on one foot, practice running and then jumping from two feet to one foot. Once again, be sure to bend your knee when you land so that you don't fall over.

■ When you're able to land twice in a row without losing your balance, see if you can do the same thing when you land on the other foot.

■ Taking off on one foot and landing on the opposite foot is called a *leap*. When you hear the drumbeat, practice a leap. Try to stay in the air for a long time when you leap.

■ When leaping gets easy for you, try jogging around the grass. When you hear the drumbeat, leap and then keep jogging. Swing your arms hard so that you can get high into the air as you leap. When you bend your knee, your landings will be softer.

Jumping over a Swinging Rope

In your groups of three, you're going to take turns jumping over a swinging rope. Two of you will gently swing the rope while the other person jumps. After ten jumps, trade places.

□ One hint: Take little jumps that barely get you off the floor.

CONTROL LEVEL

At the control level we encourage children to practice both long and high jumps until their landings are balanced and controlled. We also provide opportunities for exploring variations in the flight phase of the jump and jumping in relation to different rhythms.

Activities Leading to Skill Development

Jumping over Low Obstacles: Hoops

Each child should have a hula hoop on the floor.

Jump over your hoop. As your feet touch the ground, freeze your body and hold perfectly still. Remember that to freeze without falling over you'll have to bend your ankles, knees, and hips as you land. Think of sinking into the floor, as if the floor were a sponge.

■ If you're really good with jumping and freezing using two feet to take off and two feet to land, try to use one-foot takeoffs and one-foot landings. Practice until you can land without falling at least three times in a row.

Youngsters at the control level enjoy running and jumping over low obstacles.

■ Once you're able to jump over hoops by using two feet to take off and two feet to land and one foot to take off and one foot to land, practice the other three jumps that you've learned. Remember what they were? They were taking off on two feet and landing on one foot, taking off on one foot and landing on two feet, and taking off on one foot and landing on the opposite foot. Each time you land, remember to bend your knees, ankles, and hips so you don't fall over after landing. Remember to stick your feet to the floor as if you had glue on your feet.

Jumping over Low Obstacles: Hurdles

Each child should have a hurdle (cones and paper or rope). See p. 224.

Jump over your hurdle using a two-foot takeoff and two-foot landing. Try to be high when you cross the top—remember to push off with your toes.

□ When you can jump over the hurdle without knocking off the crosspiece, practice making your landings really quietly. As you land, pretend the floor is a sponge that you sink into. Bend your ankles, knees, and hips as you touch the floor.

■ Now as you jump over the hurdle, try to use all the other jumps that you've learned. Try the easiest ones first and then the harder ones. Practice each jump at least three times after you're able to do it without falling and without knocking the cane off the hurdle's crosspiece. Remember: *quiet* landings.

Jumping to Form a Body Shape During Flight

Each child should have a hurdle or rope in a shape on the floor in a personal space.

Jump over your equipment and form a narrow body shape while you're in the air. A narrow body shape is very skinny. Remember to make all the parts of your body skinny, not just one part. Practice your shape until it's as skinny as it can be.

■ Now think of five more skinny body shapes that you can make while you're in the air. Practice all the shapes until they're the best you can do. I'll come and ask each of you to show me your best shape, so be ready. Remember to not fall over on your landings; your feet should stick as if you had glue on them.

■ This time you're going to jump using wide body shapes in the air. A wide shape is very big and spread out, like a wall. Remember as you jump to make your whole body wide in the air, not just part of it. Practice your shape until it's as fat as it can be.

■ Now that you know what a wide shape is, think of five more wide shapes you can make when you jump. Let them be really different, even weird. Practice all the shapes until they're the best you can do. I'm going to ask some of you to show your wide shapes, so work hard. Don't forget to stick as you land. *(Pinpoint several children who are using wide shapes.)*

■ This time you're going to learn some new names for body shapes. First you're going to make symmetrical shapes in the air. A *symmetrical* shape looks exactly alike on both sides. For example, if I were to cut your body in half from head to toe, you'd look the same on both sides. At your equipment, practice at least five different symmetrical jumps. Be sure that they look exactly alike on both sides of your body.

■ This time you're going to do nonsymmetrical jumps. In a *nonsymmetrical* jump, both sides of your body really look different. So if I were to cut you in half, one arm might be up in the air and the other one out to the side, or one leg might be going forward and the other one backward. In other words, one side shouldn't look like the other one. In your space, find five different non-symmetrical jumps you can do in the air.

■ Try to do wide, symmetrical jumps. Find three that you really like and practice them. Remember, you still need to stick on your landings.

■ Now try to find three narrow, symmetrical jumps. After you do that, find three wide, nonsymmetrical jumps and three narrow, nonsymmetrical jumps. I'm going to ask some of you to show your jumps to the class, so make them the best that they can be.

Traveling, Jumping, and Body Shapes

As you travel around the room, each time you hear the drumbeat make the kind of jump that I've called out. The jump may simply be wide, or it may be narrow and nonsymmetrical. You'll have to be alert to what I'm saying as well as watching out for others. Remember to make your shapes as clear as you possibly can.

Performing Jumping Sequences and Making Body Shapes

Make out a card for each child in the class. On each card list a sequence of body shapes, e.g., wide, wide symmetrical, narrow nonsymmetrical, narrow symmetrical. Each card should contain at least four different body shapes.

There are cards spread out along the walls. When I say "Go," each of you should get a card and bring it back to your own space. Study your card; there are four body shapes listed on it. You're going to make up a sequence of jumps that show those body shapes in the air. To do this, you'll first travel a bit and then jump, showing the first body shape; then you'll travel again and jump and show the second body shape listed; you'll travel again and jump using the third body shape; you'll travel one more time and jump showing the last body shape. So your sequence should be like this: travel, jump; travel, jump; travel, jump; travel, jump, freeze. Repeat the sequence enough times so that you can do it the same way each time. Memorize it. When it's memorized, show the sequence to a friend.

Jumping Rhythmically

Each child has a carpet square.

Inside your carpet square, jump while keeping beat with the drum. You'll have to listen carefully because the drumbeat will change at different times. To do this without losing the beat, take little jumps so that your feet barely leave the floor. In other words, you'll be almost bouncing on your toes.

Have a record or tape of the sounds of tools and machines.

■ This time, instead of a drumbeat you'll hear the sounds of different machines and tools that you're familiar with. Staying inside your carpet square, take little jumps, keeping time with the tool and machine sounds you hear. The sounds will change often, so be alert and take little bouncy jumps on your toes. It helps to keep your head up when you're jumping rather than watching your feet. Remember to make sure that your feet leave the floor each time you hear a sound.

■ Again the drumbeat will guide your jumps. As you hear the slow beat, take big high jumps. When you hear the quick beat, take small jumps. This maneuver involves careful listening, so be prepared to change at any time. Make sure that you have clearly big jumps on the slow beats and really little jumps on the fast beats.

Jumping in Rhythmical Sequences

This time you're going to travel and then jump and then travel again, always keeping the same rhythm. To begin, you'll all practice the same travel/jump pattern, which will go like this: run, run, leap/run, run, leap. As you move, all say together "run, run, leap" so you can stay together. Let's practice saying that and keeping the same tempo before beginning to move. *(Practice saying the phrase in tempo.)* As you jump and run this time, remember to stay with the voices; everyone should be jumping at the same time if you're all together.

■ Now instead of saying the phrase, you're going to clap it as you go. You'll have to remember what to do on your own.

■ Now that you can follow the phrase that I designed for you, you're going to make up your own and follow it. Your phrase should contain two traveling actions followed by one jumping pattern. You should repeat the sequence three times before coming to a stop. Practice the whole thing until you think that it's the best you can do. As you begin, it helps to say to yourself what you're supposed to be doing, just as you did in the previous activity. When you think you know it, go to clapping instead of saying it. When you're really good, practice doing it with no noise at all. Remember, two traveling actions followed by one jumping action, repeated three times. You must keep the same rhythm throughout each part of the sequence. *(Pinpoint several children who've created an interesting sequence—they don't have to be the most skilled children in the class.)*

Jumping a Turned Rope

Children have to be in groups of two or three, with a long rope or a long rope attached to a fence post, pole, or chair. Mark a box on the floor at the approximate center of the rope.

At your ropes, two people will turn and one person will try to jump and stay in the box marked on the floor. After fifteen jumps, trade places.

□ One key to doing this activity well is the turners. Turners, make sure that you turn the rope in large, slow, smooth turns that barely touch the floor each time.

JUMPING ROPE

Jumping rope is an American pastime that children enjoy tremendously. Although young girls have traditionally been more interested in and more adept at jumping rope, the popularity of Jump Rope for Heart and the movie *Rocky* have caused many boys to become jump rope fanatics.

In a typical class of first year students, some children will already be experts—they'll be able to demonstrate rope jumping tricks that many adults can't perform. Other children, however, won't be able to jump rope even once without faltering. Thus the teacher needs to assess the rope jumping abilities of all the students to determine how to begin with each class.

In our teaching, children follow a skill progression of jumping rhythmically without ropes, jumping over long ropes turned by others, and then jumping using individual ropes. At first, youngsters need to practice buoyant jumping in time to an even pulse sounded by the teacher on a drum, for example. As you observe children jumping in cadence to a steady beat, you can let them begin to jump over long ropes turned by classmates.

Once children are able to jump five to ten times over a long rope without a miss, they can begin to practice jumping with individual ropes. Each child should have a rope of an appropriate length. To determine the correct length, have each youngster stand with both feet on the middle of a rope and lift the ends of the ropes. The rope is the right length for that child if the ends reach to chest (armpit) level.

Once children are able to jump individual ropes five to ten times, their rope jumping skills can be further developed through frequent,

Jumping rope is a favorite pastime of children.

repetitive practice. For instance, once or twice a week let children jump rope at the beginning or end of a learning session. As the youngsters' abilities improve, they will enjoy attempting jump rope routines set to music or to popular rope jumping rhymes such as

Teddy bear, Teddy bear, turn around.
Teddy bear, Teddy bear, touch the ground.
Teddy bear, Teddy bear, say your prayers.
Teddy bear, Teddy bear, say goodnight.
Teddy bear, Teddy bear, turn out the light.

□ Jumpers, it helps if you watch the turners' hands and the rope in their hands rather than looking down.

■ When you can successfully jump the rope by starting in the middle, try to start from the outside: run in and jump. The only thing I'll tell you is that the turners need to turn the rope so that they're turning it toward you.

□ Start your run as soon as the rope touches the floor and is on its way back up. This should get you in in time to make the next jump.

Jumping a Self-Turned Rope

Have enough ropes so each child has a personal rope.

Practice jumping your rope by turning it forward over your head.

□ If you're having trouble, bring the rope over your head and stop it on the floor in front of your feet; then jump the rope. As you become successful, start going a little faster and not letting the rope stop so much.

■ If you can jump forward fifteen times without missing, turn the rope backward and try to jump it. Again, start slowly and speed up the rope as you feel comfortable.

Jumping Using Buoyant and Yielding Landings

Jump three times in a row on two feet, pausing between each jump. This is called a *yielding* landing. Be sure to bend your knees when you land.

■ This time, jump three times in a row using a two-foot takeoff and a two-foot landing without pausing between each jump. Again, remember to bend your knees as you land. This is called a *buoyant* landing. You should spring up quickly after each jump.

■ Now jump two times in a row, the first time with a buoyant landing and the second time with a yielding landing. Make sure that your landings are clearly different so that I can tell which one you're doing simply by watching.

Jumping over Equipment Using Buoyant Landings

Set up pairs of hurdles around the room. Place the pairs one after the other so that the children can jump one hurdle and then the other one.

Jump over the first hurdle in front of you and use a buoyant landing to start the jump over the second hurdle.

□ Practice this activity until you seem to just pop over the second hurdle. Remember, this is a quick, springy landing, with your feet barely touching the floor. Your knees should just barely bend before you're off again.

Jumping on and off Equipment Using Buoyant and Yielding Landings

Set up boxes, benches, milk crates, and other similar equipment around the room.

Jump onto a piece of equipment and use a buoyant landing to quickly spring off into another jump to the floor. You should barely touch the equipment before you're off again and back on the floor, almost as if you were on a spring-board: no stopping between jumps.

■ This time, jump on to the piece of equipment using a yielding landing, hold still for a few seconds on top of the equipment, and then jump to the floor using another yielding landing. Remember that on this jump your knees should really bend and you should be able to hold still when you finish.

■ This time on the signal, jump high, turn in the air, land balanced, and freeze. Again, use yielding landings.

■ Now, jump high, turn in the air, and upon landing collapse to the floor, curl, and freeze. Remember to use your arms to help you turn in the air.

■ Try this one: jump high, turn in the air, and upon landing collapse to the floor, curl, and freeze for an instant, and then quickly resume traveling. Make your moves very smooth so that they really go together and you know exactly what you're doing and what comes next. Use your arms to help you get up in the air. Strive for a yielding landing.

■ So far I've made up all your jumping and traveling patterns. On your piece of paper *(pass out paper to the youngsters)*, write down a jumping/traveling pattern that you'd like to do yourself. After you've written it down, practice it until it goes smoothly and you know it by heart. Make sure that you always begin and end in the same place, which is one way you know you're doing the same thing each time. I should be able to tell what you're doing by watching you. If I can't, I'll ask you.

Jumping and Landing Task Sheet

Each child will need a jumping task sheet, similar to the one in Figure 17-1.

This task lets you test the jumping skills you've practiced so far. Whenever you've practiced a challenge and think you can do it correctly, ask a friend to watch you. If your friend thinks you've done the challenge well, the friend signs her or his name on the sheet next to the challenge.

UTILIZATION LEVEL

At the utilization level, we provide contexts that help children use jumping and landing in combination with other movements, with complicated rhythms, and as a means for expression. We make the manipulative activities more dif-

Name _____ Teacher _____

Jumping Task Sheet

Verification	Challenge
	I can jump starting on two feet and landing on two feet.
	I can jump from two feet to one foot.
	I can jump from one foot to the other foot.
	I can hop from one foot to the same foot.
	I can jump from one foot to two feet.
	I can jump, turn in the air, and land without falling.
	I can jump off a box and land without falling.
	I can jump off a box, turn in the air, and land without falling.
	I can run and jump over a block and cane and land without falling.
	I can turn a jump rope myself and jump 15 times without missing.
	I can
	I can
	I can

Figure 17-1 Task sheet for jumping and landing.

ficult by the objects the children throw. Start with beanbags. Then as children improve, switch to whiffle balls, foam footballs, and, for the highly skilled, tennis balls.

Activities Leading to Skill Development

Jumping to Catch

One child stands on a low bench, chair, or milk crate. A partner tosses a yarn or a plastic ball so that the child must jump to catch.

Jump from your bench *(chair, crate)*. Catch the ball in the air. Be sure to use your arms to jump high. Your partner should stand close and begin the throw as soon as the jump begins. Switch after three jumps.

- See how many times in a row you can jump and catch. It counts only if you catch the ball before you land.
- If this activity is getting easy for your partner, sometimes throw the ball so that your partner has to reach to the left or right to make the catch.
- Now, you and your partner decide who's going to throw and who's going to catch. The catcher is going to catch the ball while in the air. The thrower must throw so that the catcher is forced off the ground to catch, which means that the ball has to be thrown to a point above where the catch will actually be made. Throwers, it helps to pick a spot on the wall *(or a tree or telephone pole)* to aim at. Remember to swing your arms to help you get high off the ground. Try both one- and two-foot takeoffs. Switch with your partner after five throws. *(Both partners are on the ground for this task.)*
- As this activity gets easier, practice running, jumping, and catching in the air. This will involve a good throw from your partner. It works best if you can jump straight up *(vertically)* rather than traveling a long way in the air *(horizontally)*. At first, run and jump from right to left and then from left to right.
- When you're able to make at least three catches in a row, run away from the thrower—that is, start close and run from your partner as you might in a football game.

Jumping to Throw

One child stands on a low bench, box, or milk crate. A partner stands several feet away.

Jump from the bench *(box, crate)* and throw the ball to your partner before you land. Try to throw the ball so that your partner can catch it easily. Switch after four jumps and throws.

- Pick a target, such as a target on the wall *(or a basketball backstop, a hoop, or a stationary partner)*. Jump and throw the ball to the target. Be sure that you keep looking at the target as you throw.
- Start close to the target. When you hit the target five times in a row, move farther away from the target. It counts as a successful throw only if you hit the target and make your throw while in the air.

■ As this activity gets easier, try running, jumping, and throwing to the target.

□ When you jump, be sure to jump straight into the air so that you'll be more accurate.

Jumping on a Bench

You'll all work one at a time on the bench. First travel on the bench to the middle; then take off and land on two feet on the bench. To help stay on the bench, focus your eyes on the end of the bench. Be sure to spread your arms and land with your knees bent.

■ When you're able to do this activity several times without falling off, practice landing on only one foot. Hold your balance on the bench before your other foot comes down on the bench. Try to hold your balance for two or three seconds. Be sure to bend your knee and use your arms for balance.

□ Don't forget to keep your eyes on the end of the bench.

■ Design a sequence along the bench that includes at least two different jumps. For example, hop on one foot along the bench, jump and turn so that you land facing the opposite direction, and travel back to the start using small leaps. At first, your jumps won't be very high, but as you get better, you'll want to make them higher. Practice your sequence until you can do it three times in a row without falling off.

Throwing and Catching While Jumping

Mark off the boundaries of a court with a rope or net. The size of the court is determined by the space available: The larger the court, the more difficult the game.

The game you're going to play will give you a chance to practice throwing and catching while jumping. The object is to have the ball touch the floor on the opposite side of the net. Here are the rules:

1. There are three players on a team.
2. There is one team on each side of the rope *(or net)*.
3. A player must be off the floor when the ball is thrown or caught.
4. At least two players on your team must touch the ball before it is thrown back over the rope *(net)*.
5. Points are scored when the ball lands out of bounds, the ball hits the floor in bounds, a player throws or catches the ball while that player's feet are touching the ground.

This game can also be played cooperatively: Both teams work together to see how many times the ball can cross the rope or net without breaking any of the rules. A point is scored each time the ball crosses the net. A good score to aim for is ten throws in a row across the net without breaking a rule.

In games, children use the ability to jump while catching a rebounding ball.

Jumping to an Accented Beat

Each child should have a hoop.

When I beat the drum, jump into and out of your hoop every time you hear the drumbeat.

■ Now take off on two feet and land on two feet. As the drumbeat gets faster, be ready to jump by having your knees bent and your arms flexed. Try to land on only the balls of your feet, which means that your heels won't touch the ground.

■ Take off on one foot and land on the same foot. Be sure to bend your knee

Children at the utilization level can experience a variety of ways to jump onto and off apparatus.

when you land. Try to keep up with the beat—it's going to get faster and faster. When one leg gets tired, change to the other leg.

■ Listen as I beat the drum. The first beat is louder than the others. This is called an *accented* beat. Use one- or two-foot takeoffs and landings, but jump on only the accented beat. The first beat will be accented; the next three beats will be unaccented.

PROFICIENCY LEVEL

At the proficiency level, dynamic dance, game, and gymnastics activities are designed to help youngsters use, refine, and enjoy their jumping abilities. Jumping is almost always in relation to objects or other people (or both), and children use jumping for both expressive and functional purposes.

Activities Leading to Skill Development

Jumping with a Partner to Mirror Actions

Place two pieces of equipment (benches, tables, or vaulting boxes) about fifteen feet apart, with a large mat on the floor between them.

You and your partner are going to mirror each other's jumps. *Mirroring* means that you face each other and copy the other's movements, as if you were looking in a mirror. Therefore, if your partner uses her left arm, you'll use your right arm. To start, decide which of you will be the first leader. The leader makes up the first jump and shows it to the partner. Then you both face each other and do that jump at the same time, mirroring each other exactly. This activity will be hard at first because you'll have to take off at the same time, jump the same height, and do everything exactly together. Start with some easy jumps and then go to harder ones. Each person takes three turns as leader and then switches. Again, make your jumps so that they look like a reflection of your partner's. It helps to count before you start so that you're able to begin your jumps at the same time. *(Pinpoint several pairs who are mirroring jumps accurately.)*

■ As you get better at mirroring your partner, you may want to include such actions as gesturing in the air, turning in the air, or rolling when landing. This will really take a lot of work; you may want to count out everything before you do it.

Jumping with a Partner to Match Actions

Now that you've become very good at mirroring a partner's actions and jumps, you're going to try matching jumps. *Matching* means that you do the same thing at the same time; thus, if you're facing your partner, your actions look the opposite of his. For example, if you use your right leg, then your partner must also use his right leg. Again, decide which of you will be the first leader. The leader makes a jump and faces the partner; the two of you then try to match jumps. Again, it helps to count so that you both begin at the same time. Take three turns as leader and then switch. Start out with easy jumps.

■ Once you've become quite good at matching jumps with your partner while facing each other and standing still, try traveling a short distance together and then at a set point do matching jumps in the air. This activity will be hard. You must pick a starting point, count exactly how many steps you'll travel before you jump, and then jump and land. First, by yourself practice the traveling by itself, then the jump by itself, and then combine the traveling and jumping. Finally, try to do the task with your partner. The sequence is travel, jump, land, freeze—all movements exactly matching those of your partner's. You two should look like twins.

■ To the sequence you just made up, add a second traveling action and a second jump. Remember to always stay exactly with your partner; side by side is easier than following in front and back.

Jumping with a Springboard

You'll need springboards or beat boards for this task.

Using the nearest springboard, run, jump using a two-foot landing on the board, spring up high, and land on two feet. Remember that to do this you'll really need to push down hard with your feet and knees as you contact the springboard. Spring up, not out, and use your arms to help pull you up.

   □ Now that you're going higher with the jump, concentrate on the landing. You still want a quiet, soft landing; however, for stability, not only bend your knees when landing but spread your feet slightly apart as you land. You want your body to be slightly behind your feet as you land.

■ As you become good at going off the springboard and landing without falling over, add a turn in the air as you jump so that you end up facing the place where you started.

   □ Remember to bend your knees and spread your feet apart when you land.

■ When you're able to do this activity, try a complete 360° turn in the air before you land. To get all the way around, you'll have to throw your arms up and around in the direction that you want to turn.

Jumping as Part of a Dance Creation

Now you're going to use jumps to make up a dance. The main actions of the dance will all use different jumps. First think of a theme for your dance, such as a fight. If you use that idea, your jumps will contain such gestures as punching, slashing, jabbing, protecting, and retreating.

   In groups of no more than four, think of what you want your dance to say. Once you've decided the theme, try to put together a series of jumps that express that idea. You'll be using your jumps and other movements to tell a story. It may be that you all move at the same time, or that two of you move and then the other two move. Your dance needs to have a definite beginning and a definite end, with at least six different jumps in the middle. Try to make the dance look really professional. This will take a while to do; I'll be available to help each group as they work. When you've finished, toward the end of class we'll show the dances to the rest of the class.

Jumping, Dancing, and Imagery

Jumps can be used to create a dance about the things around you *(the flight of a bird, the leaves in the wind, etc.)*. This time you're going to make up a dance that uses one of these things as its main idea. Jumps will communicate that idea to your audience. You must decide in your group of no more than four what natural thing you'd like to communicate in a dance using jumps. After you've decided, begin to develop your dance, keeping the following ideas in mind:

1. The actions you're demonstrating should clearly portray your theme.
2. The starting location of each person should be clear.
3. The dance should rise to a climax and then wind down to a conclusion.
4. The jumps and gestures you're using to communicate your ideas should be the most effective ones you can create.
5. The pathways used in the dance should be clear.

At the end of class, we'll show all the dances you want to the class.

Hurdling Jumps

Set up a series of hurdles children can run between before they jump again. Have stopwatches available at the starting lines.

In this activity you'll be *hurdling,* which is sprinting over barriers (hurdles) placed along the way. Begin behind the first hurdle and run to the end of the line of hurdles. Each time you come to a hurdle, jump it and keep going. Start your jump *before* you reach the hurdle by extending your front leg upward and forward. Try to get over the hurdles by barely clearing them rather than jumping really high over them. Run to the end of the line, come back to the first hurdle, and start again.

Use low barriers at first, to allow youngsters to focus on proper technique without worrying about clearing the obstacles. Once children begin to exhibit quality hurdling actions, you can gradually increase the height of the barriers. Milk crates spread apart with bamboo poles supported between them are satisfactory barriers.

■ As you feel you're getting better at hurdling, time yourself and see if you can improve each time. You can use one of the stopwatches available at the starting line of each row of hurdles.

Vaulting Jumps

Set up a vaulting box (Figure 17-2), a horse without pommels, or other pieces of equipment as obstacles. At each obstacle place a card that illustrates various vaulting possibilities.

Vaulting is transferring weight from the feet to the hands and back to the feet again. The many obstacles set up around the room are for you to jump and vault over. Your run to the equipment should be light, with your weight on the balls of your feet. Always use a two-foot takeoff, and plant your hands firmly on the equipment about shoulder width apart. Remember to push with your hands as your body centers over the equipment. Always land on two feet.

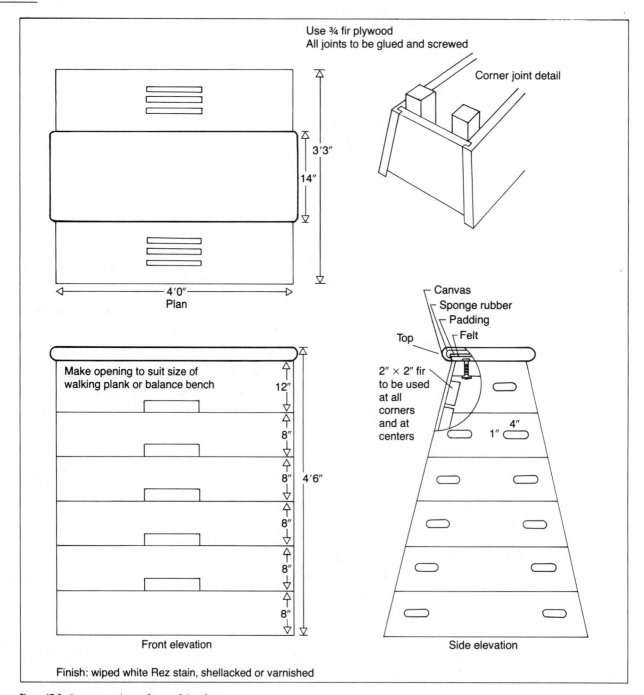

Use ¾ fir plywood
All joints to be glued and screwed

Corner joint detail

3'3"

14"

4'0"

Plan

Make opening to suit size of
walking plank or balance bench

12"

8"

8"

4'6"

8"

8"

8"

Front elevation

Canvas
Sponge rubber
Padding
Top
Felt

2" × 2" fir
to be used
at all
corners
and at
centers

4"

1"

Side elevation

Finish: wiped white Rez stain, shellacked or varnished

Figure 17-2 Construction of a vaulting box.

VAULTING POSSIBILITIES

A vaulting box, a horse without pommels, or a sturdy table can serve as vaulting apparatus. For safety, place mats adjacent to any vaulting apparatus; we also highly recommend placing trained spotters (students or teacher) at vaulting locations. A spotter shouldn't help children perform a skill they're not yet capable of; spotting is only a measure to prevent serious injury from a fall. Because spotting techniques differ for each skill, you should consult a gymnastics text before attempting to spot students.

Vaulting with a Curled Body Shape

As children take off, they place their hands on the apparatus, shoulder width apart. They then bring their legs up between their arms in a squatting position and jump forward to the mat.

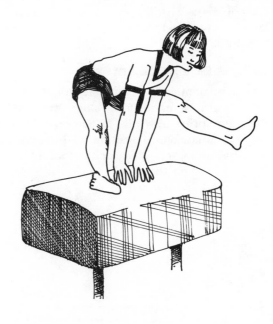

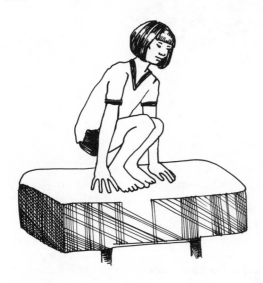

Vaulting with a Wide Body Shape

As children reach the takeoff board, they spring high and put both hands on the apparatus. At the same time, they spread their legs far apart, landing in a standing position. This is an advanced vault, to be attempted only by those successful at side vaults.

Vaulting with Legs Extended Outward

As children propel themselves upward from the takeoff board, they place both hands on the apparatus, shoulder width apart. They quickly shift their weight to one hand. They lift the other hand from the apparatus, bring their feet together horizontally, and move their

(continued)

body over the obstacle under the nonsupporting hand. Then the children push off from the apparatus with the supporting hand and land on two feet with their backs to the apparatus.

Vaulting with the Body in an Inverted Position

This is recommended only for students who can perform a handspring along the floor. Children spring from the takeoff board and come to a handstand position, keeping arms straight and locked. They tuck in their heads and fully extend their bodies over the apparatus to land on the mat.

Vaulting Possibilities (continued)

READING COMPREHENSION QUESTIONS

1. Name the two basic reasons for performing jumps.

2. What are the three phases of a jump?

3. List in order of difficulty the five different takeoff and landing patterns for jumping.

4. What does a precontrol jump look like?

5. What are the characteristics of jumping and landing at each of the four skill levels? For example, what does a utilization-level jump look like?

6. What is the focus of the jumping and landing activities for the precontrol and proficiency levels? (The introductory text to each section will get you started.)

7. Describe a low obstacle that children can safely practice jumping over.

8. What is the difference between a buoyant landing and a yielding landing?

9. Describe a sequence for teaching young children to jump rope.

Rolling

Children find the sensations of rolling—dizziness, loss of perception, and not knowing where or how you'll finish a roll—fascinating. The feeling of not knowing where you are or where you'll end up that is characteristic of a child's first attempts at rolling is both intriguing and perplexing. And so a child loves to roll. As a child becomes adept at rolling, the fascination of traveling upside down is augmented by pleasure in being able to roll in different directions and at various speeds while doing different rolls.

Rolling is the act of transferring weight to adjacent body parts around a central axis. In physical education classes, rolling is generally dealt with in a gymnastics sense, as a transference of weight. In gymnastics, safety through rolling is a skill introduced early to help children avoid crashing to the floor when they lose their balance. In the dance and games areas, rolling is dealt with briefly, to increase the children's range of movement and to enhance expressive abilities (see our progression spiral, on the next page).

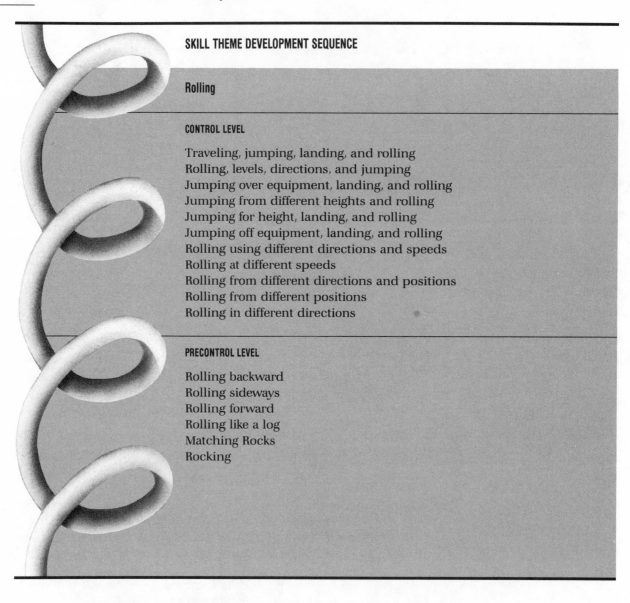

SKILL THEME DEVELOPMENT SEQUENCE

Rolling

CONTROL LEVEL

Traveling, jumping, landing, and rolling
Rolling, levels, directions, and jumping
Jumping over equipment, landing, and rolling
Jumping from different heights and rolling
Jumping for height, landing, and rolling
Jumping off equipment, landing, and rolling
Rolling using different directions and speeds
Rolling at different speeds
Rolling from different directions and positions
Rolling from different positions
Rolling in different directions

PRECONTROL LEVEL

Rolling backward
Rolling sideways
Rolling forward
Rolling like a log
Matching Rocks
Rocking

LEVELS OF SKILL PROFICIENCY

The precontrol level of rolling is characterized by rocking actions from head to feet on the back and stomach. At this level, children are challenged when asked to perform actions such as rocking back and forth like a rocking chair or rolling in a stretched position like a log. Rolling, initially in a forward direction rather than from side to side, is also studied at the precontrol level. When a child first begins to roll, the hands and arms may be of little use. This child

Rolling

does "get over," but the whole body usually uncurls in the middle of the roll and the child lands sitting down.

At the control level, the child is able to execute rolls that go over the head (as opposed to over the shoulder), using the arms and hands to push while staying curled. Tasks such as the following can be presented to children:

1. Changing the direction of the rolls—backward, sideways, forward
2. Changing the speed of the rolls—fast or slow
3. Rolling from different positions—starting from low or standing positions and different balances (on one foot, two feet, three body parts)

4. Combining jumping, landing, and rolling
5. Traveling and rolling

At the utilization level, children are able to roll in different directions while staying curled; the arms are a functional part of the roll, and children can end their rolls on their feet. Children at this level begin to combine several different concepts along with the task of rolling, such as

1. Rolling with something in their hands
2. Rolling after catching an object
3. Diving and rolling
4. Rolling on or over low equipment
5. Combining rolling with other locomotor forms as an expressive movement

Rolling is a skill that fascinates children.

When children can roll fluidly from any position and rolling has become an almost natural reaction to a fall, they can function at the proficiency level. At this level, appropriate tasks include

1. Rolling after flight from a high object so that the entire action is fluid
2. Rolling along high and/or narrow equipment (such as a regulation balance beam)
3. Striking or catching in an off-balance position and rolling to recover and maintain the action (for example, a save in volleyball)

Children who master the skill of rolling are able to comfortably and safely participate in activities that involve the risk of being off balance and falling because they possess sufficient recovery techniques. This skill also gives children a fluid way to connect different balancing actions and to change direction and/or speed in a dynamic, unpredictable situation.

When introducing the skill of rolling, we prefer to have one mat for each child. When we don't have a mat for each child, we try to use as many mats as possible. We've found that a good ground rule for any rolling situation is to have only one child on the mat at a time. This does *not* mean that the other children must stand in line and wait; they can stand around the mat and roll, in turn, as soon as the mat is empty. Sometimes we set up learning centers to prevent long waits in line. Grassy areas or carpeting can also serve as appropriate areas for practicing rolling.

The following Key Observation Points show the correct and incorrect forms for rolling. Observe children carefully to help them overcome any problems with rolling.

KEY OBSERVATION POINTS / Rolling

1. Do the child's hands and arms receive the body weight evenly at the beginning of the roll without the body collapsing to one side?

NO

YES

2. Does the child's head slide through as the weight goes from the hands to the upper back and leave the mat as soon as the shoulders touch?

NO

YES

3. Do the child's arms come off the mat as soon as the shoulders touch?

NO

YES

4. Does the child's body stay curled and the roll end on the feet?

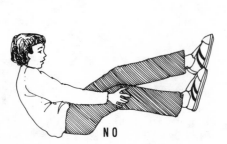

NO

YES

5. When children are at the mature stage of rolling, do their rolls look similar to the following sequence?

ASSESSMENT GUIDE / Rolling

TASK   From a box or bench, jump, make a 180° turn in the air, land on your feet holding completely still, and roll backward, coming to your feet after the roll.

GUIDE   The children need precontrol- or control-level tasks when you observe that:

1. They're unable to roll backward or they roll over one shoulder instead of their head.
2. They fall upon landing from the jump.
3. They land on their feet from the jump but crash into the roll.
4. They land on their knees instead of their feet when finishing the roll.
5. They extend their body during the roll.

The children are ready for utilization- or proficiency-level tasks when you observe that they complete the task as stated: they make a 180° turn, land and keep their balance, lower themselves down to a smooth backward roll that goes straight over their head and shoulders, stay tucked and round, and finish on their feet.

PRECONTROL LEVEL

The ability to arch or round the body is an important prerequisite to rolling. Once children are able to curve their bodies, they learn that rocking and rolling actions can be used for traveling and transferring weight.

Rolling while on equipment is a more demanding challenge than rolling on the floor.

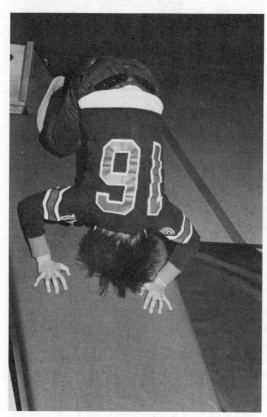

Children discover the difficulty of rocking when not in a round shape.

Activities Leading to Skill Development

Rocking

In your own space, you're going to pretend you're a rocking horse. But this rocking horse can do special things. First, you're going to rock on your back. To rock on your back, you must make your back round because flat things can't rock.

■ Now your special rocking horse is going to rock on its stomach. Remember to make that stomach round so you can rock smoothly.

■ Now you're going to do something that no rocking horse has ever done: you're going to try to rock on your side. Can you make your side round? Try it.

■ Your rocking horse is getting warmed up, so let's see if it can go faster. Try to go fast in each position that you just rocked. Rock so fast that your rock takes you up onto your feet. Remember to stay round.

■ Now for a really hard one. This time, when you're rocking on your back, try to rock so fast that you can make your feet touch the mat over your head. For you to do this, your body will really have to be round.

■ Now see if you can keep rocking on your back without stopping, almost as if you can't stop. It helps to use your hands and arms.

Matching Rocks

This time you're going to play a game called Matching Rocks. You and your partner will be side by side. On the signal, you'll start to rock on your back. The challenge is to rock the same way and at the same time as your partner so that you look like twins.

- This time change to rocking on your stomach.
- Now see if you can find two other rocks that you and your partner can make match.

Rolling Like a Log

Now you're going to try something different; you're going to roll sideways, like a log. Sometimes go fast, as if you were going downhill, sometimes go slowly, as if you were rolling on flat land. Try to make your rolling really smooth. See if you can roll in a straight line without going off the side of the mat.

Either you or a child who can do a log roll can demonstrate.

- □ I've noticed that some of your rolls were a bit bumpy. Here are two helpful hints: make sure you stretch your body out as much as you can, and stretch out your arms above your head.

Rolling Forward

Now you're going to try to roll forward over your head. See if you can roll as smoothly as possible. Remember, flat tires can't roll, and you don't want your head to bump. Try to come to your feet when you finish. *(See Figure 18-1.)*

- □ This time as you roll, try to make both your arms help you the same amount.
- □ I think some of you may get really bad headaches if we don't change a few things. As you roll this time, try to tuck your chin all the way down to your

Figure 18-1 Hand positions on forward roll.

If children keep their chins close to their knees as they roll, they'll be able to stay in a round shape.

chest, and push off with your arms so much that your shoulders and the back of your neck touch the mat first, instead of your head. Imagine that there's paint on the top of your head; try not to get it on the mat.

☐ One last thing: try to make your body stay like a ball all the way through the roll. Make the roll really smooth, with no bumps.

Rolling Sideways

Instead of rolling forward, you're going to roll sideways, but in a curled position. Try to keep your body curled the whole time so that there aren't many bumps.

This is a good time for a demonstration.

☐ It helps to use your hands to help you push off the mat, so make sure they aren't wrapped around your legs.

Rolling Backward

When trying to roll backward, children often get stuck and roll no further, usually because the children:

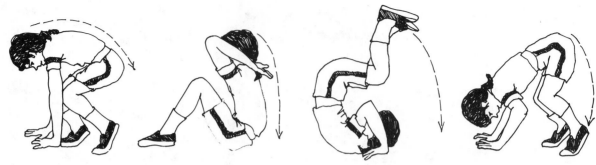

Figure 18-2 Hand positions on backward roll.

1. *Make a flat rather than a round shape (knees move away from the chin), so they find it virtually impossible to roll*
2. *Fail to place their hands in the proper position and thus are unable to push with the force needed to complete the roll*

Practicing to overcome these two critical errors will enable children to roll backward.

Now you're going to do a roll in a third direction: backward. You almost did this a while ago when you rocked so hard that your feet came to the mat over your head. At a mat, in your own space, practice rolling backward. Just as before, try to keep your body as curled and as round as you can—flat tires can't roll backward.

□ Now you want to make it look better. Make sure that you use your hands back by your shoulders, with your fingers pointing toward your shoulders like this to help you go over. *(Demonstrate the correct hand placement; see Figure 18-2.)* Also think about keeping your tight ball shape all the way through the roll.

□ One last thing with the backward roll: this time, see if you can roll so that at the end of the roll you land on your feet instead of your knees.

This is a good time to use teaching by invitation or intratask variation to let children practice the rolls they need to work on.

CONTROL LEVEL

Children must be able to roll in different directions and from different positions if they're to perform other movements safely. At the control level, rolling is studied as an automatic response to a fall. In addition, children learn that rolls are useful for connecting various balances.

Activities Leading to Skill Development

Rolling in Different Directions

You worked on rolls that went in different directions. Right now you're going to practice rolling in all different directions: backward, sideways, and forward. I'll be looking for three things: (1) rolls in each of the three directions; (2) a tight, round body throughout the roll; and (3) the use of your hands to help you roll. Remember as you work that only one of you rolls on the mat at a time; however, as soon as the person ahead of you is finished, you can roll. I should see no lines, just people rolling from all places around the mat.

☐ This time I'm going to add one thing more to what I want to see. Each time you roll, try to end up on your feet, not your knees or seat.

Rolling from Different Positions

Most of you have been starting your rolls from a low position, close to the mat; this time you're going to try to start your rolls from a lot of different positions: kneeling, squatting, or even standing. Remember, you must keep your body round regardless of the positions you start from, and the first body part to receive your weight must be very round or you'll look like a flat tire again. Try four rolls from each of the positions.

Smaller mats are adequate for introducing children to rolling; larger mats can be used for rolling in sequences and in relation to apparatus.

▫ Let's practice this a little more. This time pick the position that was the hardest for you. Practice rolling from that position until you can do it with ease. If the standing position was the hardest for you, remember to lower yourself down to the mat very slowly, with your arms and hands leading, so that your arms gradually take your weight. If you go too fast, sometimes your arms don't have the time or the strength to support your weight and you crash.

Rolling from Different Directions and Positions

Now you're going to combine the two things you've done: rolling in different directions and rolling from different positions. Start rolling backward from a sitting position.

- Now roll forward from a standing position.
- Next, roll backward from a kneeling position.
- Now roll sideways from a squatting position.
- On your own, practice as many ways to roll as you can think of, but always be able to tell me the direction of your roll and the position you're rolling from.

  ▫ Just a little reminder: your roll will be smoother if you contact the mat slowly and softly, gradually letting your body absorb the force.

- Now that you've practiced on your own, find three direction-position combinations that you like and practice them until they're very smooth and flowing. Be able to tell me what direction and position you're using, and then we'll show part of them to the rest of the class.

Rolling at Different Speeds

Do you remember when you worked on traveling at different speeds? Now you're going to roll at different speeds; sometimes you'll roll fast, sometimes you'll roll slowly, and sometimes you'll roll at a medium speed. Your arms will be your brakes and your accelerator, so be sure to use them. I should be able to tell which is a slow roll and which is a fast roll just by watching.

- Now, I'm going to test you. I'll call out a speed and you roll at that speed. I'll be watching to see if you *really* roll at the speed I call out.

Rolling Using Different Directions and Speeds

Now here's another combination. Want to guess? This time it's directions and speeds. This means that sometimes you roll backward at a fast speed and sometimes at a slow speed. Practice on your own. I should see all three directions: backward, sideways, and forward combined with all three speeds: fast, medium, and slow. That means that there's a total of nine different ways you can roll; practice them all. I'm going to ask to see some of the differences after a while, so be sure you can show me your differences in speed and direction.

You'll need two bags: one containing index cards with a speed category on each card and the other bag containing index cards with a direction on each card. The number of cards in each bag should equal or exceed the number of children in the class. You'll also need paper and pencils for the children.

You're now going to draw your speeds and directions out of a bag. On the signal, one at a time come and draw one card from each bag. One card will have a direction written on it and the other card will have a speed written on it. The two cards together will give you the direction and speed you're supposed to practice. After you practice, I'm going to let groups show their rolls.

■ Now for the hardest rolling task yet. Imagine you're in the Olympics and you're going to do three rolls in a row. This is called a *sequence*, which means that you do all your rolls without getting up. You do a roll, finish it, pause for just a second and do the next roll, and so on until you're finished. Let's start with this sequence: forward, fast; backward, slow; forward, fast. The sequence is written on the board in case you forget what needs to be in it.

■ Now make up your own combination. Practice it until it flows together well. When you finish, come to the side of the room, get a piece of paper and a pencil, and write down what you did. You can use the example that I put on the board as a guide to tell you how to write it. Practice your combination three more times, then write it.

Jumping off Equipment, Landing, and Rolling

Place a low box or milk crate at every mat the children are using for rolling. You can sometimes get milk crates from the local dairy. Make low boxes by filling soft drink cartons with flat newspaper and taping heavily over the outside of the box.

You're now going to jump off a box *(crate)*, land, and then roll. There's a box *(crate)*, at the end of your mat. One at a time, jump off the box *(crate)*, land on your feet, and then roll. Go slowly at first until you get the hang of it. Always be sure to land on your feet. The next person can go as soon as the person in front gets off the mat. Don't rush, but go quickly.

□ Some of the rolls are beginning to look sloppy. Remember to keep them round, and *slowly* let your body absorb the force as you come to the mat instead of crashing down. Go practice again—thinking about the jump *and* the roll.

■ It's getting harder. This time change the direction of your jump. Sometimes jump backward, sometimes sideways, and sometimes forward; then roll in any direction you want. If you aren't sure about jumping backward, just try stepping off until you get used to it. Remember to keep your body round when you roll.

■ We're going to change the activity again. This time you'll still jump off in different directions, but you'll roll in the same direction as the jump. So if you jump sideways, you roll sideways; if you jump backward, you roll backward. Make sure you always land on your feet after your jump, before you roll.

Jumping for Height, Landing, and Rolling

This time, instead of changing directions, you're going to practice jumping higher off the boxes *(crates)*, still landing and rolling. Do you remember when we worked on jumping? What do you do to make your jump go higher? Right— you bend your knees and throw your arms up as if you were reaching for the sky. To warm up, just practice jumping high off the box *(crate)* and landing on your feet. If you fall on the landing, you know that you're jumping too high.

■ Now add a roll after your jump and landing. Everything should be in control. If you're falling on your landing or crashing into your roll, you'll know that you're jumping too high. Try it: high jump, land, and roll.

■ So far most of what I've been seeing are jumps, lands, and rolls in forward directions. Go back and add different directions to your high jumps. The rules about falling down and crashing into rolls still apply. If you fall down or crash, jump a little lower.

Jumping from Different Heights and Rolling

Set up different stations around the room with boxes and benches of varying heights; see Figure 18-3. On the floor, mark arrows from station to station.

We're working at stations for this task, which will give you practice jumping from objects of different heights. This is how the activity works. There will be five of you at each station. On the signal, you'll begin to practice jumping, landing, and rolling from the equipment at your station. On the next signal, stop and rotate to the station the arrow on the floor points to and then start all over again. Remember, you're practicing jumping, landing, and rolling from the equipment that's at your station.

□ Use your hands and arms for balance when you land from the jump by placing them out to your sides. Remembering how Mary Lou Retton did it in the Olympics may help you control your rolls a little more.

Jumping backward from the equipment is difficult for some children, as well as scary. Have the youngsters first step backward if they're hesitant or fearful.

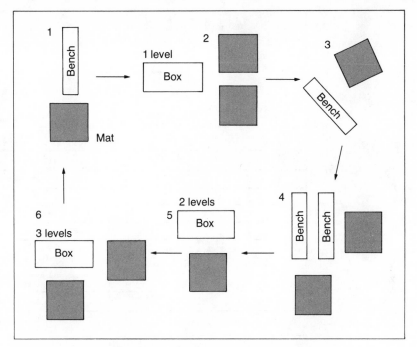

Figure 18-3 Stations to facilitate jumping, landing, and rolling.

Jumping over Equipment, Landing, and Rolling

At each station have a hurdle and a mat; see p. 224 for hurdle construction details.

Your job now is to jump over the hurdle, land, and roll. Remember, just as in jumping off objects, you must land on your feet before you roll. Keep your rolls round and smooth.

■ This time begin to change the direction of your jump. Sometimes try to jump sideways and backward as well as forward. You can roll in any direction you want. Remember, land on your feet before you roll.

■ Now change the direction of the roll after the jump as well as the direction of the jump. So if you jump backward, roll backward. Controlled jumps and round rolls are our goal.

■ You can also change the speed of the jump and roll. This time practice mixing up the speeds of the jump and the roll. In other words, I might see a slow motion jump with a fast roll or a fast jump and a fast roll. Make whatever speed you use very clear. Always land on your feet; if you fall, you're going too fast.

Verification	Challenge
	I can roll forward, coming up to my feet.
	I can roll sideways, coming up to my feet.
	I can roll backward, coming up to my feet.
	I can jump, land, and roll forward.
	I can jump, land, and roll sideways.
	I can jump, land, and roll backward.
	I can jump over a block and cane, land, and roll, coming back to my feet.
	I can roll over the block and cane without knocking it over.
	I can jump, land, change directions, and roll.
	I can jump, twist in the air, land, and roll without falling down.
	I can jump off a box, land, and roll without falling down.
	I can jump off a box in different directions, land, and roll.
	I can jump off a low box, make different body shapes in the air, land, and roll.
	I can jump off a box, twist in the air, land, and roll without falling down.
	I can

Name _____   Teacher _____

Rolling Task Sheet

Figure 18-4 Task sheet for rolling.

Rolling, Levels, Directions, and Jumping

Each child will need a task sheet similar to the one in Figure 18-4.

Today I'll give you the chance to test yourself and see how well you can do the rolls you've been practicing. I'll also give you time to practice the rolls that have been hardest for you. Each of you has a task sheet. Your challenge is to do all the tasks on the sheet. When you think you can do something well, have a friend watch you; if the friend thinks you did the challenge correctly, the friend puts his or her initials on the sheet. The area has been set up so that there's space to practice each challenge.

Traveling, Jumping, Landing, and Rolling

Now you're going to use only the mats, but you're going to jump, land, and roll at your mats all on your own. Practice jumping, landing, and rolling in different directions at your mat. Remember, you can start or end at any place around the mat, so there should be no lines.

■ This time begin to travel around the outside of the mat. When the mat is empty, take a little jump, land, and roll. You'll almost be jumping from a moving position, but not quite. You'll travel, jump, pause, and roll, so you really come to a short stop before you roll. If you crash, you're going too fast. One on the mat at a time.

■ Here's a new challenge. Instead of just jumping this time, try jumping over the corners of the mat, land, and roll. Remember to practice all the different jumps you learned: one foot to the other, one to the same, two to one, one to two, and two to two.

■ Now I'll challenge you even further. As you jump the corners of the mat, add a twist or turn in the air before you land. You still have to land on your feet before you roll. Make sure you twist or turn in the air, not on the ground after you land. Arms out to your sides will help you balance when landing.

UTILIZATION LEVEL

Children at the utilization level can develop the ability to incorporate rolling actions into other activities, such as rolling to connect locomotor movements or catching and rolling. They can also learn to precede a roll with a dive and to perform a roll with varying degrees of effort (quickly or slowly; with much or with little tension).

Activities Leading to Skill Development

Jumping, Landing, and Rolling: Follow the Leader

We're going to play a fun game now. It's like Follow the Leader, except it uses jumping, landing, and rolling. The leader starts out by jumping the corners, landing, and rolling, and then two people follow, doing exactly what the leader did. After leading three times, the leader trades places with a follower and the game starts again. The secret is to stay behind the leader far enough so you can see what's being done and not run into anybody else. Include different directions and jumps in your game.

The leader must be sensitive to the followers' capabilities and not ask them to do tasks that are beyond their skill levels.

Playing Busy Mat

This is another game, called Busy Mat. It'll really give you a workout, so get ready. The object of the game is to always have someone rolling on the mat while the others are traveling around the outside of the mat. As soon as one person finishes rolling, another person should start. The timing should be split second. Everyone should always be moving either on the outside by jumping and landing or on the mat by rolling. Let's do a practice round.

If students aren't able to safely decide who is to roll when, specify the order in which they'll roll before they begin.

  □ The secret to playing this game well is to be a mind reader: you have to try to guess what everyone else is doing and when they'll be doing it. See if you can get your timing so that there are bare misses, as if you're almost going to collide but really don't.

Practicing Touch and Go Rolls

Now you're going to practice making your jumps, landings, and rolls more professional. You've been coming to a clear stop after landing and before rolling. Now you're going to roll with no hesitation. Your feet should barely touch the floor and you're into the roll. Your roll just flows, but your feet still have to hit the floor before you roll. To do this, you'll really have to bend your knees upon landing, let your arms absorb your weight, and make sure your shoulders are round.

  □ It helps if you try to make your jumps so that you land a little off balance and you're falling into the roll. Try to make it smooth, as if you're rolling to save yourself from crashing. No stopping—just touch and go.

  ■ Make sure you sometimes change the direction of your land and roll, making it backward or sideways as well as forward, and still keeping your touch-and-go actions.

Rolling over Equipment

Set up mats around the room, with hurdles at each mat.

This is really a new task, but you were almost doing it with the last activities. A hurdle is at each mat. Place your hands on the other side of the hurdle and try to roll over the hurdle without touching it. You'll really have to raise your seat up in the air and push off with your legs. As you do that, really tuck your head so your weight lands on your shoulders.

☐ You may have already discovered that your arms really have to give when your feet leave the floor. Bending your arms a little as you push off helps you let yourself down softly.

Rolling on Equipment

Set up a number of benches and tables around the space, with mats under them.

At your piece of equipment, get on it any way you like and practice rolling along the top of it; then get off any way you want. Try to stay on the equipment and not fall off. If you fall off a lot, you may want to go to a wider piece of equipment. Be certain to push evenly with both your hands.

☐ I realize that this task may be difficult, but try to keep your rolls as smooth and round as possible, along the equipment. Also try to finish your entire roll on the equipment and not roll off the end.

■ This time when you roll on your equipment, try to roll in a different direction, either sideways or backward. Keep it smooth and slow.

■ Next, try to change what your legs do during the roll. You might want to extend them as you finish the roll or finish with them wide apart; the secret is to keep your back round and go slowly.

■ Now you're going to make up a sequence using all you've practiced. First figure out how you want to get on the equipment; you don't have to get on by rolling. When you're on the equipment, roll along the equipment and then get off any way and roll after your dismount. The sequence will go like this: get on, roll along, get off, roll on the mat. Practice on your own until it looks the same each time you do it. *(See Figure 18-5.)*

Figure 18-5 Child's rolling sequence.

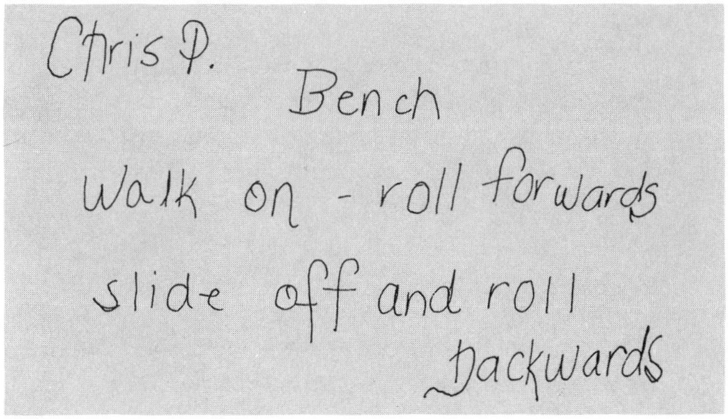

Chris P.

Bench
Walk on - roll forwards
slide off and roll
backwards

□ As you practice, work toward making everything flow together so that it's smooth, like a masterpiece.

□ Practice your sequence three more times, just to make sure that it's really in your memory. When you finish, come over and write it down.

Traveling and Rolling Between Pieces of Equipment

This next activity is similar to what you just did. As you can see, there are two pieces of equipment at each station. Your task now is to get on the first piece of equipment, roll one way on it, travel to the second piece of equipment without touching the floor, roll a different way on the equipment, jump to get off, and roll on the mat. The sequence goes like this: get on, roll, travel across, roll another way, jump off, roll. Practice these ideas.

□ Now pick one sequence that you really like and practice it until it's smooth and fluid. There should be no breaks, and you shouldn't have to stop and think about what comes next. Make sure you land on your feet after you jump off before you roll.

Rolling to Express an Idea

This time you're going to roll to express an idea. You're going to pretend and tell a story by rolling. The first thing you're going to tell is being scared. Here's how it works. Your partner will come close to you and pretend to scare you, without using words. You're so scared that you fall down and roll backward trying to get away. Make sure that your roll really shows that you're afraid; it should be a very stiff roll. After two turns, switch places with your partner.

The following two tasks are best performed outside in a soft grassy area.

■ You're going to tell a desert story this time. Have any of you seen those old westerns on television where tumbleweeds go blowing across the desert, with nothing stopping them? Well, you're going to be a tumbleweed, just blowing and rolling all over the desert. Remember, a tumbleweed is loose and bouncy as the wind just bumps it along.

■ Instead of being a loose piece of tumbleweed, this time you're going to be a seed. The wind is blowing you all over; you're bouncing all around. Suddenly, the wind stops and you sprout roots and start to grow. When you start to grow, remember the ideas we talked about earlier about rising and spreading. Your sequence goes like this: wind blows you around, the wind stops, you send out roots and grow into a big tree or flower.

Throwing, Catching, and Rolling

This next series of tasks is best performed outside on a soft grassy area. It can be performed inside if you use a very large mat or the space is completely covered with smaller mats. You'll need beanbags for each set of partners.

With your partner, throw and catch the beanbag. Throw so that your partner has to really stretch to catch the beanbag. Remember to make your partner stretch; you have to throw at a point *away* from her.

■ Now that you're stretching to catch, as soon as you catch the beanbag, roll in the direction you had to stretch in to catch it. Keep the beanbag in your hand as you roll. Remember the whole sequence: stretch to catch, catch, and then roll.

■ Now for just a little while practice throwing and catching the beanbag to yourself. Throw to yourself so that you have to jump to catch the beanbag in an off-balance position and then roll to break the fall from being off balance. The hardest part is throwing so that you force yourself to be in an off-balance position.

□ Try to make the movement so that you have to roll after the catch, whether or not you want to. Try it again, really trying to force the off-balance position so you have to roll.

□ One last thing: each time after you roll, come back up to your feet with the beanbag still in your hands, so that you could get rid of it if you wanted to.

■ Now go back to working with your partner. Try the same task. Throw so that your partner has to first catch the beanbag in an off-balance position and then roll after catching it. Catchers, make sure you're really off balance and have to roll to recover your balance or so that you won't be hurt. Throwers, really force the catchers off balance when they catch.

Successful throwing and catching with partners depends on throwers' ability to throw so that they're actually forcing catchers to be off balance or to move to catch. Before exposing children to these ideas, make sure they're at the utilization level of throwing and catching.

Throwing Frisbees and Rolling

Have a supply of Frisbees for each set of partners.

For this task you'll be throwing Frisbees. With a partner, throw a Frisbee back and forth so that your partner has to stretch in different places to catch it. The catcher should roll in the direction of the fall. Throwers: really try to make your partner stretch. Catchers: make your rolls smooth and come up on your feet.

Rolling, Balancing, and Rolling

You worked on balancing before; now you're going to combine balancing and rolling. At your mat, practice rolling forward into a symmetrical balance. Try to roll right into the balance so that there's no pause between the roll and the balance.

SAFETY PRECAUTIONS FOR AERIAL ROLLS

For any activities that require rolls from an aerial position, certain safety precautions should be taken:

1. Precede the activity with tasks involving nonaerial rolls over objects.
2. Many children like to attempt aerial rolls before they're ready. Don't allow or encourage children whose rolls display any of the following characteristics to practice rolls from an aerial position:
   a. Rolls that display any uncurled body parts—that is, rolls that aren't totally round

   b. Rolls in which the child's arms collapse and the child hits the mat suddenly and with a great deal of force
   c. Rolls in which the child lands on his or her head
3. Never force a child to attempt rolls from an aerial position before the child personally feels ready and wants to try.
4. These are good activities for using intra-task variation and teaching by invitation because they let children practice what they need and want.

□ I've noticed that some of you tend to stop after the roll and before the balance. Really concentrate on rolling right into the balance.

■ Most of you are balancing on very stable body parts, such as knees and hands. This time, try some body parts that aren't quite so stable and see if you can still balance.

■ Now try rolls from different directions—backward and sideways—and still roll straight into the balance. Hold it still. To help hold your balance, shift a little of your weight backward, just as you get balanced.

■ Now that you're so good with this activity, we're going to add to it. The beginning will still be the same—roll and then balance—but then you'll roll out of your balance and end on your feet. So the sequence should be: roll, balance, roll. Make sure there's a clear balance before the second roll. Find three different ways that you can do this task.

Diving over Low Obstacles to Roll

Set up stations around the room with different pieces of low equipment—hurdles, rolled-up mats, boxes stuffed with newspaper. Have a mat at each station. Figure 18-6 shows the setup.

This task is much like the one in which you rolled over hurdles. To warm up, let's start by rolling over a hurdle. Practice placing your hands on the opposite side of the equipment at your station and rolling over the equipment. Remember to really get your seat up into the air and push with your legs. Also make

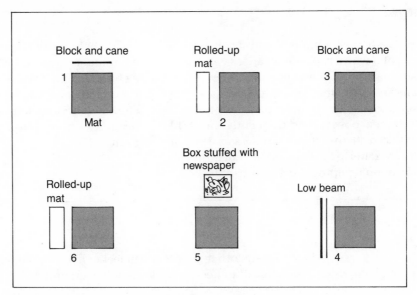

Figure 18-6 Equipment setups for aerial rolls.

sure you give with your arms so you can let your body down slowly. The sequence is: get your seat up, push with your legs, and give with your arms. Go.

■ Now you'll have a choice. If you can roll over the hurdle and each time land softly and roll smoothly, you may want to try to get off the ground for a brief second before you roll. This will be a dive-type roll or a roll from an aerial position. You'll have to push hard with your legs and almost jump as you take off. You then land on your hands and give immediately with your arms so that you're able to tuck your head and roll smoothly. Try this from a standing position. If you don't feel you want to try this, keep practicing rolling over the equipment as you have been.

If you see any children attempting these rolls when you feel they shouldn't be, vary their task so that they don't try something before they're ready.

□ It's very important that you really give with your arms on these rolls so you can lower yourself gently into your roll.
□ It helps if you start to reach out a couple of feet beyond the equipment as you bring your hands down, instead of trying to roll right on the other side of the equipment.
□ One other point: make sure that you're really in the air when you cross the equipment; your feet must be off the floor before your hands touch

The question of spotting—physically assisting a child with a skill—often arises with gymnastics activities. Our experience in our programs and with other programs is that spotting often encourages children to attempt a skill before they're ready, and frequently the child won't even attempt the skill unless assisted. If skills are developed progressively, children will perform on equipment with no spotting.

If, because of the nature of a skill or the equipment on which it is performed, we feel a child might fall, we often find it sufficient to have someone stand beside the student as the student practices, to break any fall that might occur. We rarely physically help a child perform a skill.

on the other side. You will feel when your feet are off the floor, but just as an extra check, have a friend watch and see if she or he can tell when it happens.

Rolling onto Equipment

Around the room, set up benches or low boxes with mats beside them.

Now you're going to use a roll to get onto a piece of equipment. First, simply stand at the end of your equipment and use a roll to get onto the equipment. You can get off any way that you like. Make sure that you're actually using a roll to get onto the equipment, not getting on the equipment and then rolling.

☐ It helps to move very slowly and make your roll very round so that you can control your roll and make sure you have no "unround" places in your roll that might hurt you or make you fall.

■ Now I'm going to add to your task. At the equipment, use a roll to get onto the equipment, travel any way that you want while on the equipment, jump to get off, land, and roll. Again, make sure that you're actually using a roll to get onto the equipment.

Rolling off Equipment

This task should be preceded by initial tasks of rolling over equipment. To do this activity successfully, children must be able to absorb their body weight with their arms.

This time you're going to practice using a roll to get off equipment. To practice, get on your equipment any way you want and lie down with your hands over the edge of the equipment. When you're ready to get off, place your hands on the floor about two feet out from the equipment and gradually lower yourself off the equipment and into a roll.

◻ The secret to this task is to lift your body up a little with your arms and really tuck your head as you begin the roll.

■ If you feel comfortable with rolling off the equipment from a lying position and can do it smoothly six times in a row without crashing to the mat, try rolling from other positions, such as kneeling or sitting. You always have to have smooth, controlled rolls.

At this point, some children may want to attempt or be capable of attempting rolls off equipment from a standing position. The criteria for attempting rolls from an aerial position apply; see the box on p. 354.

Rolling onto and off Equipment

This time you're going to combine rolling on and off equipment. You're going to make a sequence by rolling onto the equipment, traveling along it, and then rolling to get off. You may choose any rolls and any form of traveling that you like as long as the sequence is smooth and you're able to do it with round rolls.

◻ Practice your sequence until it flows smoothly from one part to the next and you can do it from memory.

■ Now I'm going to make your sequences a little harder: there must be one change of direction somewhere in the sequence. So practice the same thing you just did, but some place in it show a change of direction.

■ One more addition: keep everything the same, but in the middle, when you're traveling across the equipment, add a balance, hold it still, travel to the end, and roll off. So what you've added is a balance in the middle. You should know by now that I'd come up with something like this!

Rolling from an Aerial Catch

At various places around the room, set up boxes, with a mat at each box.

There will be one thrower and one jumper at each box. The jumper jumps off the box to catch the beanbag that the thrower throws while the jumper is in the air. The jumper should catch the beanbag, land feet first on the mat, then roll while holding onto the beanbag. This task will really take some concentration. Catchers, you need to time your jump so that you can catch the beanbag in the air, land on your feet, and be able to roll without crashing. After five turns, switch places.

◻ As you practice, make sure that the body part you first put on the mat to roll on is round, so you can roll smoothly.

■ As you get better at doing this task, gradually have the thrower throw the beanbag farther away from you so you have to jump farther out to catch it.

Rolling over Higher Objects

This task must be preceded by other tasks to develop the skill of rolling from an aerial position. See criteria on p. 354. Around the space, set up medium-high hurdles—eighteen inches to two feet high—with a mat at one side of each hurdle.

At each hurdle, practice diving over the hurdle and rolling when your hands touch the mat on the other side. To do this, you'll really need to give with your arms as soon as they touch the mat and tuck your head quickly.

□ The key is to begin to tuck your body while you're in the air so you can go straight into the roll as soon as your hands touch the mat.

At this stage in youngsters' development, it's extremely difficult for children to roll backward over an object, so we don't stress this movement.

PROFICIENCY LEVEL

At the proficiency level, children can learn to perform a roll as a part of another action. They're also ready to learn to roll spontaneously when a situation that calls for a roll (e.g., a recovery in volleyball, a fall from a high piece of equipment) occurs.

Activities Leading to Skill Development

Rolling onto High Equipment

Around the room, set up a variety of high equipment: high boxes, regulation beams, and tables. Place mats under and around each piece of equipment.

At your piece of equipment, roll onto the equipment, travel along it any way you want, and then roll to dismount. Remember to begin with slow movements, and make sure that the parts that are going to absorb the force are round and give with the action.

■ Now as you do the task, try to change the rolls a bit. You may want to change the direction of the roll so that sometimes you go backward, sometimes forward, sometimes sideways. Still keep those parts round and the movement slow.

■ I'm now going to add to your sequence: roll onto the equipment, connect two locomotor actions on the equipment with a roll, roll to dismount. Also, there must be two changes of direction. Try to make the whole sequence flow together without breaks. Practice it until you can do it from memory. The sequence is written on the board in case you forget it.

Arriving on Equipment and Rolling

These tasks must be preceded by early tasks in jumping and landing (see Chapter 17). Set up climbing ropes in the gymnasium. Place boxes, beams, and tables near the ropes, and surround each piece of equipment with mats.

Your task now is to play Tarzan. You're going to swing onto the piece of equipment from a climbing rope, roll on the equipment, travel along the equipment, and then roll off. I know you're thinking that this can be dangerous. Yes, it can be, but to make it less dangerous, when you first begin, make your swings slow and not from very far away, almost as if you were just stepping from the rope. Only as you really get better can you swing from a farther distance. To be able to do this task, you'll need to land at the *end* of the box so you'll have room to do everything. First practice just landing on the end of the box, then add the rest.

■ Now that you can land on the box, add the rest of the sequence: roll, travel, roll off. Remember that you have to absorb a lot of force with your legs as you land on the box, so bend your knees, squat down low, and move your arms to the side for balance.

Diving and Rolling

Before attempting any of the following tasks, see criteria regarding rolling from an aerial position on p. 354. At various places around the room, set up high equipment—boxes (two to three feet high) or cones suspended between chairs. Have mats at each piece of equipment.

■ Dive over the equipment and roll as soon as your hands touch the mat. Remember to give with your arms and tuck your head. It helps to start to curl your body while you're still in the air.

Diving for Distance and Rolling

Place a double set of low hurdles at each mat.

For this task you'll add distance to your dive and roll rather than height. Starting with the hurdles, about two feet apart, dive over them and roll. Make sure that your arms and shoulders absorb the force and that your head is tucked. You can keep moving the hurdles farther apart and make longer dives as long as it's safe and I see you being able to absorb the force and roll smoothly.

Rolling over Partners

This time you're going to roll over a partner. Partner 1, make a low-level shape and hold it still; partner 2, dive over partner 1's shape and then roll. Partner 2, as soon as you've dived and rolled, freeze and make a low-level shape for partner 1, who's now ready to dive and roll. This exchange of places is continuous, and the action doesn't cease until each partner has performed five rolls. Let's practice.

■ Now that you're getting it, try diving so that sometimes you must roll in different directions.

□ Now you're going to work to make your dives and rolls look better. Try to make them flow into each other. When you dive and roll, go straight into your low-level balance; your partner is already moving as soon as your hands touch the floor. Make the whole timing split second.

■ This time you're going to make a performance out of the whole sequence. You need to practice a sequence that involves at least four dives and rolls each, until you can do it from memory and it has no stops or breaks in it. The sequence flows, and you're proud enough of it to show it to someone else.

Balancing and Rolling on Equipment

Spread tables, benches, and beams throughout the room, with mats under all the equipment.

At your equipment, practice mounting the equipment, balancing on the equipment, rolling out of the balance, and dismounting. Make sure your rolls out of the balances are going in the direction that seems natural for the balance, not necessarily the easiest way for you. Create five balances and rolls out of the balances.

■ Now, keep the same balances, but for each balance find at least one more roll, going in a different direction than the first roll. Thus you should have two rolls out of each balance, each roll going in a different direction.

Rolling to Meet and Part

You're going to work with the idea of meeting and parting. There will be five people in each group. Each group starts by spreading apart from each other and coming together by traveling on their feet. When you get together, make any group shape that you want and hold it still for a few seconds. Next, each of you leave your group by rolling away and freezing in a shape by yourself.

You need to plan your rolls so that all of you come together at the same time to form the group shape and you know exactly when to roll away.

□ The only thing that I can say to help you improve your work is that you really want to concentrate on making it flow smoothly so no one has to stop and think about it. You should know it by heart, even if you have to count to remember when to do things. It helps you all if you try and tell a story with your moves; that way it'll make more sense to you.

At the proficiency level in rolling, the emphasis turns from the roll to the flow and smoothness of the movement. Children should already have a high level of motor development in their rolls; refinement is now the goal.

Striking and Rolling

This next series of tasks is best performed outside on a soft grassy area.

In a space by yourself, strike a plastic ball with any body part so that you fall off balance when you strike and have to roll in the direction that you're falling. Make sure that you really strike the ball before you roll, and roll in the direction that you're falling, not some other direction.

□ Try to make your strike, fall, and roll one fluid movement so that it seems very natural for you to do it. You'll really have to have your body parts round.

■ Try to strike the ball so that you have to roll in directions other than forward, such as backward and sideways.

■ Now work with a partner. The partner throws the ball to you; you try to strike the ball back to your partner, roll, and be ready for the next throw. The thrower should always throw the ball so the striker really has to reach for it. After five strikes, change places.

□ You really need to watch the ball carefully and react quickly. To be ready for the next strike, you must roll up to your feet after each strike; you can't hesitate at all.

Rolling, Catching, and Throwing

This is a really tough task. Your partner will throw you a ball so that you have to stretch and roll to catch it. Your job is to try to throw the ball back to your partner as you begin the roll. The secret is to keep your eyes open and try and catch with your throwing hand. Remember, you must throw as you begin the roll, not after you've rolled. After five times, switch places.

Playing Hot Potato

Across a well-defined grassy space approximately fifteen by twenty feet, draw a line across the middle for each group of four.

You're going to play a game called Hot Potato. There will be two of you on a team. Your space is one side of the line across each square. The game goes like this: you throw the ball across the line, trying to make someone on the other team catch the ball while off balance. The person who receives the ball must roll as he or she catches the ball and get rid of the ball by throwing it to a partner or to the other team before completing the roll. Each group works to see how long it can keep the ball going before someone misses. This really requires quick reaction and recovery; you can't be lazy.

READING COMPREHENSION QUESTIONS

1. Define *rolling* and *rocking.*
2. How is rolling used in dance and in games?
3. In what way is rolling a safety skill?
4. What are the characteristics of rolling for each of the four skill levels? For example, what does a control-level roll look like?
5. What are sufficient recovery techniques?
6. What problems does a child usually encounter when rolling backward?
7. Using the chart on p. 32, list the major concepts that are used as subthemes with rolling.
8. At what level of skill does rolling become natural and fluid rather than hesitant and jerky?
9. Name three major observational foci at the precontrol level.

19

Balancing

Webster's dictionary defines balance as "stability produced by even distribution of weight on each side of the vertical axis," which is also "an aesthetically pleasing integration of elements." There's no extraneous motion, no flagrant waving of arms to maintain position, no near topple or wobble from side to side. The center of gravity is clearly over the base of support.

The elementary school child attempting to do a headstand, walk a beam, or ride a skateboard encounters different types of static and dynamic balance challenges. Among the key teaching concepts in providing balance experiences are:

1. It's easier to balance over a wide base of support than a narrow base.
2. The center of gravity should be aligned over the base of support for stationary balance (see Figure 19-1).
3. Extensions to one side of the body beyond the base of support necessitate extensions in the opposite direction for counterbalance.

Static balance involves maintaining a desired shape in a stationary position; gymnastics balances, headstands, and handstands are examples. Dynamic

Figure 19-1 Center of gravity over base of support.

balance involves maintaining an on-balance position while moving, starting, or stopping. Dynamic balance occurs in weight transference, jumping, throwing, catching, and all forms of travel. Balance as a concept is discussed in Chapters 15, 17, 20, and 22 as it applies to learning specific skills.

LEVELS OF SKILL PROFICIENCY

At the precontrol level, children sporadically achieve balance; it's often more coincidental than intentional. Activities at this level are designed to introduce weight bearing and stillness as prerequisites to balance. Appropriate tasks include using different body parts as bases of support, using wide bases to balance, and maintaining stationary balances.

The child at the control level is ready to focus on holding stationary supports for several seconds, balancing on smaller bases, and maintaining inverted balances. Appropriate tasks include:

1. Supporting weight on combinations of body parts (for example, head or hands)
2. Momentarily supporting weight on hands alone

Children can be challenged to balance on a variety of body parts.

3. Balancing on narrow bases or in inverted positions
4. Holding stationary balances on various types of large apparatus

The child at the utilization level is ready to study balancing on equipment and in dynamic situations, combining balance with locomotion and weight transference. Appropriate tasks include:

1. Combining stationary balances with actions on benches, tables, and beams
2. Balancing nonsymmetrically
3. Locomotion into handstands and back extensions
4. Moving from an on-balance to an off-balance position

Balance at the proficiency level is characterized by tasks that focus on maintaining balances on inverted and narrow bases. Children practice moving rapidly into and out of stationary balances; dynamic balances on high, narrow equipment; and contrasting balance-time factors on the floor and on apparatus. Appropriate experiences include:

1. Extensions away from the body when balanced on a narrow base
2. Partner and group balances

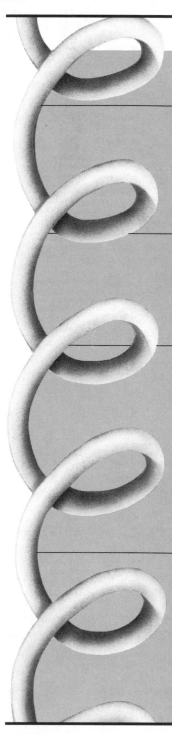

SKILL THEME DEVELOPMENT SEQUENCE

Balancing

PROFICIENCY LEVEL

Performing apparatus sequences that combine stationary balances and traveling with movement concepts
Balancing on hanging ropes
Transferring onto and off equipment with weight on hands
Balancing while supporting the weight of a partner

UTILIZATION LEVEL

Performing sequences that combine stationary balances and traveling on mats
Performing inverted balances on equipment
Traveling into and out of balances

CONTROL LEVEL

Balancing on stilts
Balancing on boxes
Balancing symmetrically and nonsymmetrically
Doing kickups
Performing inverted balances
Balancing sequence
Traveling while balanced
Traveling on large apparatus
Balancing with a partner
Balancing on boards

PRECONTROL LEVEL

Performing stationary balances on equipment
Traveling on low gymnastics equipment
Balancing in different body shapes
Moving off balance
Balancing on a wide base of support
Traveling and stopping in balanced positions
Balancing on different body parts
Balancing on different bases of support

3. Rapid turns, twists into balanced position
4. Mounts on apparatus into an inverted balance
5. Dismounts (from apparatus) that conclude with landings in balanced, stationary positions

The sequence for developing the skill theme of balancing at the precontrol, control, utilization, and proficiency levels is shown in our progression spiral on the opposite page.

ASSESSMENT GUIDE / Balancing on Feet

TASK   Stand on one foot with your eyes closed for five seconds. I'll count "one thousand one," "one thousand two," etc.

GUIDE   The children are ready for precontrol-level tasks when you observe that:

1. They're unable to stand on one foot without losing their balance, i.e., placing both feet on the floor.
2. They're unable to maintain their balance without extraneous movements of their arms, such as waving and flapping.

The children are ready for control-level tasks when you observe that they're capable of standing on one foot with their eyes closed for five seconds without losing their balance or moving their arms extraneously.

ASSESSMENT GUIDE / Balancing on Hands

TASK   Assume a front-back stance (one foot in front of the other) with your feet; lean forward and place your hands shoulder width apart on the mat. Kick your legs upward so that you're momentarily taking your weight on your hands only.

GUIDE   The children are ready for control-level tasks when you observe that:

1. They're unable to kick their legs into a stretched, vertical position higher than their trunk.
2. They're unable to maintain their weight on their hands for three to five seconds.

The children are ready for utilization- or proficiency-level tasks when you observe that they're able to take their weight on their hands in a stationary balance with their legs stretched toward the ceiling and their trunk aligned over their hands for three to five seconds.

ASSESSMENT GUIDE / Balancing and Traveling on Gymnastics Equipment

TASK   Stand on the *low balance* beam; place the beanbag on your head. Walk the length of the balance beam with the beanbag balanced on your head; when you reach the other end of the beam, walk backward four steps.

GUIDE   The children are ready for precontrol-level tasks when you observe that:

1. They lose their balance and step off the beam as they're walking.
2. They're unable to keep the beanbag balanced on their heads as they're walking.
3. They're unable to walk the balance beam without extraneously waving and flapping their arms.

The children are ready for control-level tasks when you observe that they're capable of walking the balance beam with beanbags on their heads without losing their balance or dropping the beanbags.

PRECONTROL LEVEL

Tasks at the precontrol level are designed to give children experiences in supporting weight on different body parts, establishing steady bases of support, and maintaining static balances. Children should move from balances that seem coincidental toward being able to choose and maintain simple balance positions on appropriate body parts.

Activities Leading to Skill Development

Balancing on Different Bases of Support

Place carpet squares or small mats throughout general space, with sufficient room between mats for children to work without bumping others.

Balance on different bases of support on your mat. Your base of support is the body parts that are holding you in the balance. See how many body parts can be bases of support. Hold each balance as you count to yourself three seconds—"one thousand one," "one thousand two . . ."

□ Remember that a gymnastics balance requires muscular tension if you're to hold the shape without falling over.

■ Try different combinations of body parts as you create your balances.

■ Let's list all the body parts you've used as bases of support for your balances. *(List on the chalkboard or flipchart as children give responses.)* Do you see some body parts listed as bases of support that you didn't try? Take a few minutes to try all the combinations.

□ Remember, when I look at the balances, I shouldn't see your arms waving and you falling over. Hold each balance very still for three seconds.

Some children will watch others in class, often the more skilled students, and attempt to copy their balances. This can result in injury to the less skilled. A reminder from the teacher to the group and/or to the less confident students concerning what we're looking for eliminates this potential problem.

Balancing on Different Body Parts

Now I'll name the body parts that I want to be the bases of support. First, hand(s) and feet.

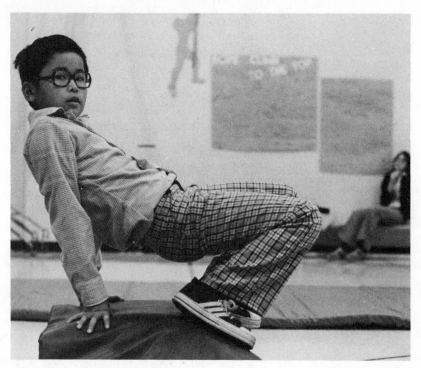

Balancing on four body parts.

■ Be creative in your balance. Although you're all using the same base of support, the gymnastics balances may be very different.

□ Challenge yourself. Make your balance as difficult as possible for your skill.

Additional body parts to use as bases of support include feet and head, knees and elbows, stomach, base of spine, and shoulders in combination with other body parts. Sometimes children attempt to balance on body parts that aren't appropriate for supporting weight. Don't let youngsters balance in unsafe positions that could result in stress or injury.

■ From all the balances you've done today, choose three of your favorites, each showing a different combination of body parts as bases of support. Practice until you can hold each balance three seconds without moving or losing your balance. When you've completed your practice, show your three balances to a neighbor and ask him or her to name the base of support for each balance.

Young children enjoy labeling on a large stick figure the body parts that can serve as bases of support.

Traveling and Stopping in Balanced Positions

Travel through general space any way you choose. On the signal, stop and create a gymnastics balance with two feet and one hand touching the floor.

☐ Remember to hold your balance stationary without tottering on or off balance.

■ Travel again, but this time stop balanced on three body parts other than the ones you just used. Think which three parts you're going to use before traveling. Ready? Go.

■ This time, change your way of traveling. If you ran before, now skip or gallop. On the signal, stop and create a balance with four body parts as a base of support. Think of the four parts before traveling. Ready, Go.

For additional travel, have children balance on five body parts and then two body parts.

■ Remember the balance you created with four bases of support? Think of the balance you created with two bases. Now you're going to make a sequence of two travels and two stationary balances. Your sequence will be: travel, stop, balance on two body parts. I'll give the signal for travel and then you stop. You'll decide the ways you're going to travel; use the balances you just did. Practice your sequence until you can do it exactly the same three times.

☐ Remember that the balance should be a clear, still shape with no movement.
☐ Try to move very smoothly into each balance.

■ After you've completed your two-part sequence and feel good about the travel and the balances, create a larger sequence by adding other ways to travel and additional balances, for example, three bases, five bases. How about going from five bases of support to one base, with travel between balance?

The image "long enough to take a picture of it" helps children know how long to hold a balance.

Balancing on a Wide Base of Support

On the mat *(ground)* create a four-part balance on your hands and lower legs; have your hands under your shoulders and knees and your legs apart approximately the same distance as the width of your hips. This wide base of support creates a very stable balance. It would be difficult for me to try to push you over.

■ Now move your hands toward each other and your legs together until they touch. Your base is the same, but it's now very narrow. What would happen if I tried to push you over now?

■ Now balance on your two feet and two hands with your feet and hands shoulder width apart. Then balance with your hands close together and your feet touching. Which balance is easier to hold still?

■ Balance on different bases of support, changing each balance from a wide to a narrow base. Remember, decreasing the base of support decreases your stability.

Moving off Balance

Balance on two hands and your lower legs *(that area from your knees to your feet)*. Raise your right arm and your left leg off the floor and slowly extend them away from your body. Your base has changed, but your balance should still be fairly stable.

■ Return to your four-point balance. Now raise your right hand and your right leg and extend them outward. What happens to your stable balance now? Right—you lose your balance.

■ Remember, body parts must move in opposite directions to counterbalance; this keeps your center of gravity over your base of support.

Balancing in Different Body Shapes

Create a gymnastics balance on a wide base of support. You create a wide shape by extending your free body parts outward from your trunk; free body parts are those body parts not being used as bases of support.

☐ Remember that a certain amount of muscular tension is necessary for a good gymnastics balance.

■ Create a new wide base of support. Be sure you can hold it stationary for three seconds.

■ I'm going to put on some background music for a few minutes. Create three balances that show wide shapes; each balance should have a different base of support. Challenge yourself with a level of difficulty that tests your skills. When the music stops, I'll look at your three wide-shape balances.

Soft, background music helps self-conscious children become more at ease in creating balances and doing work that is perhaps new to them. A good record album is Sea Gulls, *Educational Activities, AR584.*

■ Now let's create gymnastics balances that show narrow shapes—thin, like a piece of spaghetti. Create narrow shapes by holding your body parts close to each other. Create a thin shape, balanced on your feet and hands.

☐ Remember that the balance is more difficult to hold when the base is narrow.

■ Now create a narrow balance on the base of your spine. Stretch your legs and arms outward to counterbalance.

■ Create two new narrow balances, one at a low level, the other at a medium level. *(See Chapter 12.)*

- You can create a curled (*round*) body shape by curling your spine forward or arching your spine backward. Free body parts may be tucked close to the body, or they may be added to the curled image by bending in the curve. Create a curled gymnastics balance on your chosen base of support.

  - Remember to hold your balance three seconds.

- Create a curled-shape gymnastics balance in which the spine curls forward; slowly change into a curled-shape balance with your spine arched backward.

- Stand in a balanced position, with both feet as bases of support for your weight. Create a twisted shape by turning your body to the right or the left without moving your feet. Now balance, using your left foot and the lower portion of your right leg as bases of support. Create a twisted shape by rotating your trunk to the left or the right.

- You create a twisted shape when the base of a body part or your total body remains fixed and the extension of that body part rotates, that is, turns to the left or the right. Create twisted shapes by rotating your trunk, arms, legs, neck, ankles, and wrists.

- Balance on three body parts. Create a twisted shape by rotating free body parts, for example, arms, legs, trunk, neck. Create two more twisted-shape balances on various bases of support.

Children at the precontrol level often confuse twisting with crossing arms and/ or legs. Your modeling will help them understand the twisting action.

- Think of all the balances you've done today. They represent four shapes: wide, narrow, curled, twisted. Review the balances you did; choose your favorite balance to show each shape. On each signal, show me your favorite wide, narrow, curled, and twisted shape.

- Using stick figures, draw each of your four shapes; label the body shape of each figure.

Traveling on Low Gymnastics Equipment

Arrange jump ropes, low balance beams, two by four-inch planks, low, narrow benches, and tape pathways on the floor. See Figure 19-2.

Travel *on* the different pieces of equipment without losing your balance.

  - Extend your arms outward to help keep your balance.
  - Focusing on one spot at the end of the rope, beam, or bench in front of you helps you remain more stable as you travel.
  - Be sure to stand tall—head up, shoulders back—as you walk.

- After you feel comfortable traveling forward on the equipment, try some of the following activities:

1. Travel backward.
2. Walk with your arms above your head.

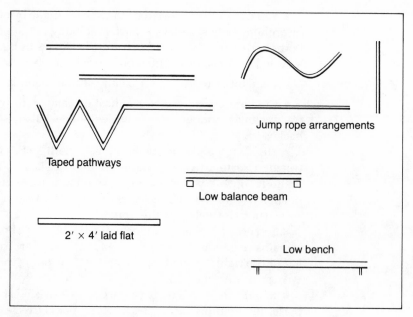

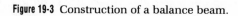

Figure 19-2 Equipment arrangement for traveling.

Figure 19-3 Construction of a balance beam.

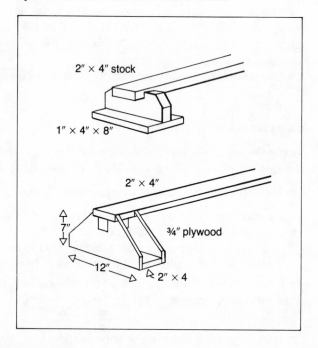

3. Walk with a beanbag on your head.
4. Catch a ball or a beanbag a friend tosses to you.
5. Toss a ball to a friend who's standing beside the equipment.

Performing Stationary Balances on Equipment

Figures 19-3, 19-4, and 19-5 give information about constructing a balance beam, a balance bench, and a wooden sawhorse, respectively.

Scattered throughout the gymnasium are various pieces of gymnastics apparatus: low tables, boxes, benches, climbing frames, low balance beams, and sawhorses. *(On the playground, the equipment will be low balance beams,*

Figure 19-4 Construction of a balance bench.

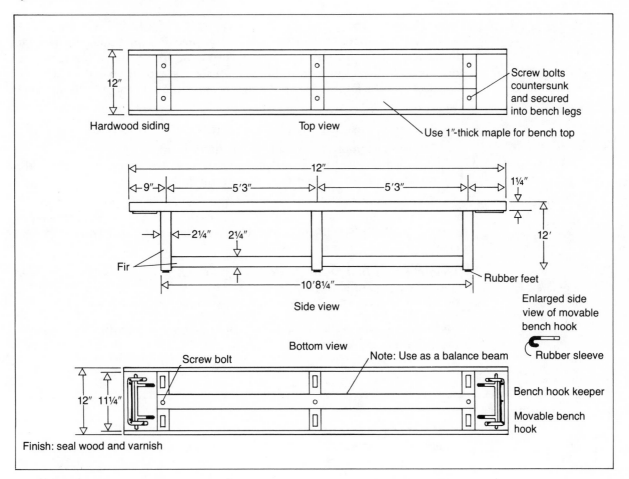

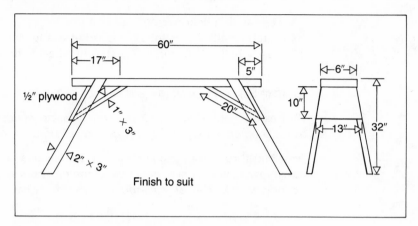

Figure 19-5 Construction of a wooden sawhorse.

jungle gyms, horizontal ladders.) Select the piece of apparatus you want to begin work on. Spend a few minutes exploring the apparatus until you're comfortable on this new surface and height. Perform stationary balances at different places on the apparatus: on the top, near one end, in the middle, on a low rung, underneath.

- Perform at least three gymnastics balances on the apparatus.
  □ Remember to hold each balance for three seconds.
  □ Move slowly on the apparatus as you create the balances because the surface is quite different from that of the floor.

- After you create three balances on the first piece of apparatus, move to another piece and create three new balances. If there are already six persons working on that piece of apparatus, choose a different piece; you can return later.

When children first begin this type of gymnastics, they may not be able to move independently from apparatus to apparatus. We've found it best in the beginning to assign the children to groups and rotate the stations.

- Continue rotating to the various pieces of apparatus until you've created three balances on each piece.

CONTROL LEVEL

Experiences at the control level focus on balancing on increasingly smaller bases of support, holding the body in inverted positions, and learning to maintain the stillness and control of a balance. These experiences begin to provide ingredients for a movement repertoire of balances that may be included in sequences involving traveling and other balances.

Activities Leading to Skill Development

Balancing on Boards

Arrange square, rectangular, and circular balance boards throughout the area. See Figure 19-6.

Balance on a balance board without falling off or letting the edges of the board touch the ground.

Figure 19-6 Construction of a balance board.

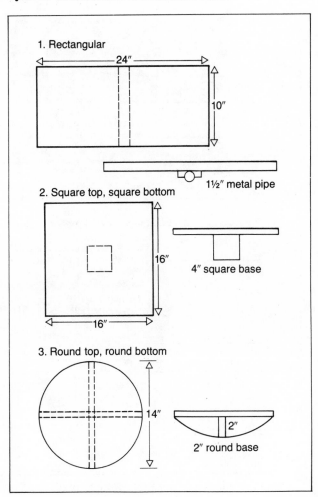

Balance board activities may be written in the form of a task sheet. Younger children enjoy drawing the smile face for completed tasks; older children can record the date of successful completion.

Name _Melissa_____

Homeroom _4b_____

Balance Board Task Sheet

Draw a smile face beside those activities you can successfully complete.

I am able to:

_____☺_____ Balance on the board standing on two feet

_____☺_____ Sit in a balance position on the board

_____ Change from a standing to a sitting position on the board without losing balance

_____ Raise my hands high above my head while standing on the board

_____ Balance on the board standing on one foot

_____ Catch a ball tossed to me by a friend

_____ Toss a ball to a friend without losing my balance

New ideas by me:

_____ clap my hands 3 times

_____

_____

- ☐ You may want a partner to stand in front of the balance board to help when you first step up; place your hands on your partner's shoulders for support.
- ☐ Standing with your feet shoulder width apart makes balancing on the board easier.
- ☐ Remember to extend your arms to the sides for balance.

Write additional tasks on flip charts or task cards near the balance board.

- ■ When you can stand on the board for five seconds without the support of your partner and without losing your balance, you're ready to try the tasks written on the chart:

1. Slowly move your arms above your head. What happens to your center of gravity? *(Right—it moves upward.)*
2. Slowly move from a standing to a squat or low curl position. Which is more stable? Why is the low position more stable? *(When working on large apparatus, remember that we're better balanced when the center of gravity is low.)*
3. Catch a ball thrown by your partner; toss the ball to your partner.

Balancing with a Partner

Working in groups of four, create a balance statue in which each person partially supports another. The statue should represent the four basic shapes; one person will balance in a wide shape, one in a narrow shape, one curled, and one twisted.

- ■ After you make the body-shape statue, convert it to a movable monster by moving as a unit in either self-space or general space.

Traveling on Large Apparatus

In open space, arrange large apparatus: benches, tables, beams, commercial gymnastics equipment.

Travel forward and backward on the large apparatus.

- ■ Sometimes travel with your center of gravity close to the apparatus, that is, lower your hips. Sometimes travel with your center of gravity high; for example, walk on your tiptoes with your body stretched toward the ceiling.
- ■ Walk forward the length of the beam or bench; make a half turn and walk forward again. The secret to the turn is to take your weight on the balls of your feet and then pivot and quickly drop your heels so they make contact with the beam.
- ☐ Remember to focus your eyes on something stationary.
- ■ Practice turning both clockwise and counterclockwise while traveling forward and backward.

■ Walk to the center of the apparatus and lower your hips into a squat position. Execute your turn in this low-level position.

Traveling While Balanced

Travel on the apparatus using a series of gallops, hops, or skipping steps. You'll probably want very little height when you perform these skills on the apparatus.

■ Travel across the apparatus on four body parts.

■ If you're comfortable doing forward rolls on the mats, try rolling forward across the apparatus. Pretend you're executing the skill in slow motion; tighten your abdominal muscles for control.

Each task should be performed on each piece of apparatus.

Balancing Sequence

Design a sequence that combines traveling and balancing on your favorite piece of apparatus. Choose either sequence A or sequence B.

Sequence A: Create a sequence of traveling combined with balancing on different bases of support. Your sequence must contain three balances with different bases and at least two travels.

Sequence B: Create a sequence of traveling combined with balancing in the basic body shapes. Your sequence must contain the four basic shapes—wide, narrow, curled, twisted—and at least three travels.

Practice your sequence on the floor and then on the apparatus. When you have the sequence memorized, let a friend watch it to see if the bases of support or shapes are clear and the travels smooth. I'll watch it when you're ready for me to do so.

Performing Inverted Balances

Balance with your head and two feet as your base of support.

□ Anytime you perform an inverted balance involving your head, it's important to distribute your weight equally among all body parts serving as your base of support.

■ When performing these balances, concentrate on taking your weight equally on the following bases:

1. Head and knees
2. Head, hands, one foot
3. Back of head, shoulders, arms

■ Balance on your head and hands with your knees resting on your elbows. *(See Figure 19-7; other inverted balances are shown in Figure 19-8.)*

Figure 19-7 Inverted balance on head and hands.

■ Balance on your head and hands with your trunk and legs extended toward the ceiling. The secret to the headstand is to form a triangular base with your weight equally supported on your head and hands; keep your abdominal muscles tight; and stretch toward the ceiling with your legs.

■ For some of you it'll be easier to extend your legs upward from the tripod position, whereas others of you will be more successful starting with your weight on your hands, head, and one foot, then kicking your free leg upward.

☐ Remember to keep your body in a straight, stretched position. Pretend your toes are attached by a string to the ceiling and stretch.

■ If you overbalance and begin to fall over, push with your hands, tuck your chin, and roll out of the balance.

Doing Kickups

Place one foot in front of the other *(front-back stance);* lean forward and place your hands on the floor shoulder width apart, fingers pointing forward. Using your back leg as a lever, kick both your legs upward so your weight is supported on your hands only. When taking the weight on your hands, remember to *stretch* your trunk and legs toward the ceiling; keep your shoulders directly over your hands when you begin to kick your legs upward; and keep your head in line for good balance.

With practice, the success rate for balancing on hands is very high; but practice must be massed and distributed.

■ Practice counting seconds as you balance on your hands.

Balancing Symmetrically and Nonsymmetrically

Balance on the base of your spine with your arms and legs extended outward. Create exactly the same shape on both sides of your body.

Figure 19-8 Inverted balances.

■ Keeping the same base, change your free body parts, keeping both sides symmetrical. That is, both sides should look the same.

■ Balance on your chosen base of support. Create a symmetrical shape. Now change to a nonsymmetrical shape—the sides look different—while balanced on that same base.

■ Balance on your shoulders, back of head, and arms. Create a symmetrical shape with your legs. Change to a nonsymmetrical shape and then back to a symmetrical one.

A nonsymmetrical balance.

Balancing on a narrow base while extending arms outward in a symmetrical balance.

■ Repeat this three-part symmetrical, nonsymmetrical, symmetrical sequence; slowly change your legs into the different shapes. This smoothness in transition is an important component of gymnastics sequences.

Balancing on Boxes

Stack milk crates and boxes against the wall. Stuff boxes with newspaper or computer packing materials and tape the boxes so they'll support the weight of the children.

You and your partner will each need a crate or box. You can work side by side in a matching sequence, or face each other and perform a mirroring sequence. Design a partner sequence of symmetrical and nonsymmetrical balances on the milk crate and box. Your sequence must contain the following:

Three symmetrical and two nonsymmetrical balances

A minimum of three different bases of support

At least one inverted balance.

□ Many of the balances that were easy for you to perform on the floor or mat will be more difficult on the crate and box because of the added height and the size of the surface.

□ Remember, your sequence should represent a double image. Not only should your balances match your partner's, but the transitions between balances should also match. Move the same way, at the same speed.

Nonsymmetrical balances on equipment.

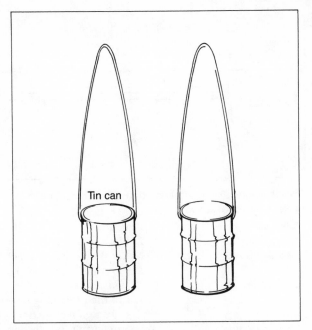

Figure 19-9 Construction of tin can stilts. (1) Two holes are cut in the top sides of the cans. (2) Rope is strung through the holes and tied together inside each can. (3) Children put each foot on a can and pull on the rope with their hands.

Balancing on Stilts

Children first experiencing this type of dynamic balance will develop confidence on tin can stilts before progressing to regular stilts. You can make tin can stilts from discarded rope and large cans from the school cafeteria. See Figure 19-9. Place marker cones around the gym.

Walk forward on the tin can stilts. You'll have to take smaller steps than you would when walking normally.

- Walk backward.
- Walk around the marker cones.

   After you've mastered walking on the tin can stilts, you're ready for the higher wooden stilts. *(See Figure 19-10.)* It's easier to mount the stilts from an elevated position, such as on a step or chair.

- Walk forward, backward, and sideways.
- Walk around the marker cones.
- Shift your weight to one stilt; lift your other leg and swing it around.
- Jump forward with small steps.

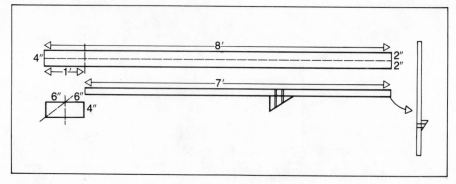

Figure 19-10 Construction of wooden stilts. (Each board makes one set of stilts.)

Materials
  One board, 2" × 4" × 8'
  Nails or bolts

Directions
  1. Cut twelve inches from one end of the board.
  2. Cut the twelve-inch board in half.
  3. Cut the six-inch board diagonally in half for the steps.
  4. Cut the remaining seven-foot board lengthwise to make two two-inch by seven-foot poles.
  5. Nail or bolt the steps to the poles.

UTILIZATION LEVEL

Activities at the utilization level include balancing in dynamic environments and transferring weight into stationary, still balances on various bases of support. Tasks that involve sequences of movement, on the floor and on apparatus, are particularly important and valuable. It's important for children to be able to make decisions about the combination of movements and to be able to select and invent ways for one movement to move smoothly into another.

Activities Leading to Skill Development

Traveling into and out of Balances

Rock backward into a shoulder stand; hold the balance for three seconds, and then roll either forward or backward.

Children functioning at the utilization level in balancing should also have mastered rolling forward and backward.

■ Balance in a headstand for three seconds and then press with your hands and roll forward.

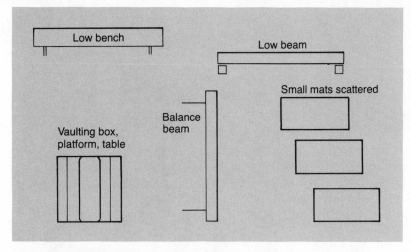

Figure 19-11 Large equipment for balancing.

■ Balance with your weight on your hands, slowly lower yourself to the mat, and roll forward. Remember to tuck your chin and curl your back.

■ Roll backward. When your hips are vertically above your head, forcibly extend your legs upward and push against the mat with your hands so that you're in a handstand. You may have to shift the placement of your hands once you're in the handstand.

■ Transfer your weight from your feet to your hands; pause in the handstand and then make a quarter turn and transfer your weight back to your feet.

Performing Inverted Balances on Equipment

Balancing in an inverted position on a piece of apparatus is quite different from balancing on the mats or floor because the position of your hands is often quite different and the surface much smaller. You'll want to perform these balances on the low bench and low beam several times before you try them on the higher, more narrow vaulting box and other apparatus. *(See Figure 19-11.)*

■ Balance on your shoulders, back of your head, and arms. Stretch your legs upward. *(Box, bench, tables.)*

■ Balance on your head and hands in a tripod position. Remember that your weight is equally distributed on your head and hands; this is even more important on equipment.

■ Balance on your head and hands with your legs extended toward the ceiling.

■ Balance on your hands only.

Balancing on equipment in an inverted position.

Performing Sequences That Combine Stationary Balances and Traveling on Mats

Sequence work at this level is for students who are proficient in balancing and transferring weight. Previous work in developing sequences plus experiences with levels, directions, and inverted balances are essential. Place large mats together to form an area twelve by thirty feet.

Create a sequence that combines stationary balances and travel. Your sequence should cover the length of the mat as well as the four corners. Your sequence must include the following:

1. A minimum of four balances, each with a different base of support
2. A minimum of three travels, with a change of direction and levels
3. At least two inverted balances

☐ All gymnastics routines have a beginning and an ending shape.
☐ Contrasts in time of actions—some fast, some slow—and changes in the force concept—some powerful, some delicate—will add interest to your sequence.

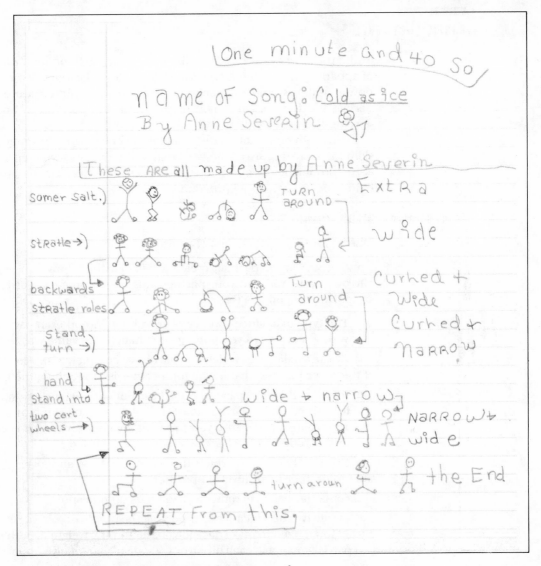

Figure 19-12 Child's sequence to music, showing use of rolling, weight transfer, balance, and concepts of narrow, wide, curled, and directions.

■ Tomorrow we're going to practice doing your routine to music. If you like, bring a cassette tape of a song from home, or I'll have several here. Your task will be to make up a routine to the music and then diagram the sequence so that it can be repeated exactly the same each time. *(See Figure 19-12 for an example of a routine.)*

PROFICIENCY LEVEL

At the proficiency level, balance is studied on the floor and on various pieces of apparatus in combination with time and force factors to express contrast in power, stillness, and excitement in sequences. Children are encouraged to perfect the flow of their movements from one position to another and to develop their use of focus and full extension.

Although often not readily available, such activities as unicycling, skating, skiing, and surfing are challenging dynamic balancing experiences for children at the proficiency level. Sometimes these experiences can be provided during field trips or afterschool programs.

Activities Leading to Skill Development

Balancing While Supporting the Weight of a Partner

Working with your partner, create a balance that shows one wide and one narrow shape. You and your partner must be helping each other by partially supporting the other's weight.

- □ The type of balance you perform will depend on each partner's weight— who's heavier; are you both approximately the same weight?

- ■ Create a balance in which one partner is completely supporting the weight of the other partner; that is, the top partner isn't touching the floor.

- □ If you're the base partner, your bases of support, for example, arms and legs, should be no farther apart than the width of your hips and shoulders. Top partner, make sure you put your weight over the arms or hips, *never* in the middle of the back, which is unsupported.

- ■ Create a balance in which the base partner is supporting the weight of the top partner in an inverted position.

- □ For better balance, remember to focus on one spot.

- ■ Create two new balances supporting the weight of your partner. *(See Figure 19-13.)* You'll need to make decisions based on the weight of both partners: will you partially support each other, or will one of you totally support the partner?

- □ Be sure you can hold the balance stationary for five seconds.

- ■ Draw your two balances on a sheet of paper and post them at our partner balance center.

Transferring onto and off Equipment with Weight on Hands

Balancing on your hands on the apparatus, make a quarter turn and transfer your weight from your hands to your feet on the mat.

- ■ Before you try the skill on the apparatus, practice on the floor to be sure you'll turn to the right or to the left.

- □ Stretch your trunk and legs to maintain balance and stillness.

Figure 19-13 Student-created balances supporting a partner.

□ Bend your knees to absorb the force of the landing; hold your head and shoulders erect to maintain your balance as you land.

Balancing on Hanging Ropes

On a hanging rope support your weight with your hands, your hands and your legs, and one hand. Create each of the basic shapes—wide, narrow, curled, twisted—with your free body parts. *(See Figure 19-14.)*

Creating a balance on a hanging rope.

Figure 19-14 Balances on hanging ropes.

☐ Before you perform the balance in an inverted position, be sure you can support your body weight in the balance with your head upward.

■ Create a series of symmetrical and nonsymmetrical shapes while supporting your weight on the rope.

Performing Apparatus Sequences That Combine Stationary Balances and Traveling with Movement Concepts

Select a piece of equipment and design a sequence that combines stationary balances and travel. The sequence is to be ninety seconds long; you can select the music. Your sequence must include a

1. Mount onto the apparatus
2. Series of stationary balances and travels on the apparatus
3. Dismount from the apparatus

■ You can add excitement and interest to your sequence by a turning, twisting action on the apparatus and in the dismount; by changing levels and directions; by using very slow, controlled movements and very quick, sharp movements; by performing inverted balances. Practice your sequence as if you were preparing for the Olympics. When you've completed and timed it with the music, show it to a friend and then to me.

Children enjoy having their sequences videotaped for their review and for their parents to see.

READING COMPREHENSION QUESTIONS

1. In your own words, define *balancing*. Be sure to include the meaning of *base of support* and *center of gravity*.
2. Draw or diagram (stick figures are best) the three key teaching concepts that are emphasized in providing balance experiences.
3. What is the difference between a static balance and a dynamic balance?
4. What are the characteristics of balancing for each of the four skill levels? For example, what does a precontrol-level balance look like?
5. List five concepts or skills typically used as subthemes with balance.
6. List five different pieces of equipment that children can use to practice balancing. Include a task you might use with each piece of equipment.
7. What does *inverted balance* mean?
8. How is transfer of weight typically combined with balancing to present challenging tasks to children at the utilization and proficiency levels?

Transferring Weight

To travel—walking, running, leaping, rolling, stepping, springing, sliding—is to transfer weight on hands, on feet, on different body parts. The infant creeping on trunk and elbows is transferring weight, as is the toddler shifting weight from side to side as he begins to walk unassisted, the gymnast performing a walkover, the Russian dancer executing a series of rapid mule kicks, the athlete poised to shift her weight to fake an opponent, and the dancer collapsing to the floor in an expression of grace and control. Locomotion is transfer of weight.

Probably the most common form of weight transfer is that from foot to foot. In its simplest form this is walking. At an advanced level—and when combined with the stretching, curling, twisting actions of flips, layouts, and full body twists—the transfer of weight from foot to foot demands extraordinary kinesthetic awareness, muscular strength, and control.

LEVELS OF SKILL PROFICIENCY

Children at the precontrol level are still trying to achieve control of their bodies when they transfer weight to different body parts. They enjoy traveling on body

Children at an advanced level can transfer weight using various body parts.

parts other than their feet, and they enjoy exploring apparatus. Activities at the precontrol level include:

1. Traveling on specific body parts (such as feet and seat or hands and feet)
2. Transferring weight by sliding, slithering, or creeping

Children at the control level are ready to transfer their weight onto specific body parts, such as the back for rolling actions and the hands for inverted balances and travel. Activities at the control level focus on:

1. Stretching, curling, twisting into transfers
2. Transferring weight following step and spring takeoffs
3. Transferring weight onto and off equipment using different body parts
4. Transferring weight from feet to hands

Children at the utilization level are ready to transfer their weight onto their hands for travel and balances, for spring takeoffs, and for handsprings. At this level, weight is also transferred by rolling. At the utilization level, the child tries movements that combine the transfers onto specific body parts with stretching and twisting. Challenging activities include:

1. Stretching, twisting actions (for example, a cartwheel) on apparatus
2. A stretched layout prior to mounting apparatus (for example, onto a vaulting box)

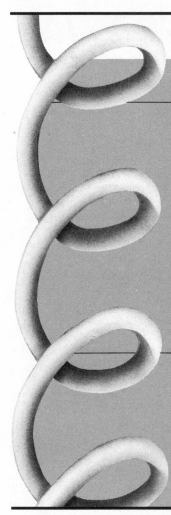

SKILL THEME DEVELOPMENT SEQUENCE

Transferring Weight

CONTROL LEVEL

Transferring weight to hands and forming a bridge
Transferring weight to hands by stepping: cartwheels
Transferring weight to hands and twisting
Transferring weight to hands, followed by rolling
Transferring weight to hands: walking
Transferring weight from feet to hands
Traveling off of low apparatus
Traveling onto low apparatus
Traveling over low apparatus
Making spring/step takeoffs with sequences
Performing spring/step takeoffs onto crates
Performing step/spring takeoffs
Stretching, curling, twisting into transfers

PRECONTROL LEVEL

Transferring weight from feet to back
Transferring weight across mats
Transferring weight from feet to combinations of body parts
Transferring weight from feet to hands
Transferring weight from feet to other body parts without traveling
Traveling on body parts other than feet
Traveling on body parts

3. Mounting apparatus by using inverted positions
4. Traveling on apparatus with curling actions

Children proficient in transferring weight enjoy the transfer from foot to foot with aerial actions between the contacts. They combine stretching, curling, and twisting with flight onto, off, and over apparatus. Tasks appropriate for children at the proficiency level include:

1. Aerial flips in free floor exercise
2. Piking (bending while in the air) and twists off apparatus

The progression in gymnastics is from mats on the floor to low apparatus with a large surface to higher apparatus with a narrow surface. Our progression spiral presents the full spectrum of weight transfer, from the precontrol level through the proficiency level. Alternative ways of further developing the ideas are discussed in Chapter 6.

Transferring Weight

PROFICIENCY LEVEL

Dismounting from bars
Dismounting from apparatus by transferring weight from hands to feet
Using hands only with stretching, twisting actions
Using a springboard for vaulting

UTILIZATION LEVEL

Combining weight transfer and balances in sequences
Combining skills on mats
Transferring weight on bars
Transferring weight from feet to hands
Transferring weight by rolling
Transferring weight along apparatus
Transferring weight over apparatus
Transferring weight onto bars
Transferring weight to head and hands on apparatus
Transferring weight onto large apparatus

ASSESSMENT GUIDE / Transferring Weight

TASK   Assume a front-back stance (one foot in front of the other). Lean forward and place your hands shoulder width apart on the mat. Kick your legs upward so that you're taking your weight on your hands only. Maintain your weight on your hands for three to five seconds and then transfer your weight back to your feet and assume your original position.

GUIDE   The children are ready for precontrol- and control-level tasks when you observe that:

1. They're unable to kick into the inverted position with their legs extended toward the ceiling.

2. They're unable to hold their weight on their hands without "walking" on their hands to maintain their balance.

3. They're unable to hold their weight on their hands for three to five seconds.

The children are ready for utilization- and proficiency-level tasks when you observe that they're able to transfer their weight to their hands only, hold the position for three to five seconds, and return to their feet in the original position.

PRECONTROL LEVEL

Tasks at the precontrol level are designed to provide experiences traveling on various body parts, transferring weight onto and off small apparatus, and developing an awareness of the body parts best suited for weight transfer.

Activities Leading to Skill Development

Traveling on Body Parts

All travel involves transfers of weight. When you walk, hop, skip, or gallop, you transfer your weight from foot to foot. *(See Chapter 15.)* Let's review some of those locomotor movements. Travel throughout general space with a skip or gallop.

□ Move smoothly as you travel.

□ What body parts are you transferring your weight onto—from what to what?

■ Hop on one foot. Do you transfer weight to different body parts when you hop? No, you move on one foot only.

Traveling on Body Parts Other Than Feet

Now travel on body parts other than your feet. Travel throughout general space on your feet and hands.

■ Sometimes travel with your feet and hands touching the floor at the same time. Sometimes travel by transferring your weight from your feet to your hands to your feet.

■ Travel with any combination of body parts you choose.

Transferring Weight from Feet to Other Body Parts Without Traveling

Scatter individual mats or carpet squares throughout general space.

Transfer your weight from your feet to your back and return to your feet with a rocking action. *(See Chapter 18.)*

■ Lower your weight slowly to a squat position; curl your spine so you transfer your weight to your rounded back.

□ Your action from your feet to your back to your feet should be one fluid motion, not three separate actions.

Transferring Weight from Feet to Hands

Transfer your weight from your feet to your hands to your feet, momentarily taking your weight on your hands only.

■ Begin in a squat position with your hands and feet touching the floor. Transfer your weight to your hands only by kicking your feet in the air. After you're comfortable taking your feet off the floor, begin to kick your feet higher in the air each time.

□ The key to taking your weight on your hands is strong arms and shoulders. Kicking your feet only a few inches off the mat will help you develop these muscles.
□ Your hands should be shoulder width apart.

■ Stand at the end of your mat with one foot in front of the other. This is a front-back stance. Step forward and then transfer your weight from your feet to your hands and then back to your feet.

□ When you assume the front-back stance, lean forward so your weight is over your forward foot.
□ Kick upward with your back leg.

Transferring Weight from Feet to Combinations of Body Parts

Transfer your weight from your feet to other combinations of body parts. Always return to your feet. *(See Figure 20-1.)*

Transferring Weight Across Mats

Scatter small mats (or carpet squares or ropes stretched on the floor) throughout general space.

You've been transferring your weight from your feet to other body parts and bringing your feet back down to where you started. Now you're going to transfer your weight from your feet to other body parts to travel across the mats or ropes. Begin at one end of the mat *(or carpet square or one side of the rope)* and finish on the other side. Travel across the mat *(square; rope)*, transferring your weight from your feet to your hands and back to your feet.

Figure 20-1 Transfer of weight from feet to other body parts.

■ Begin in a squat position with your feet on the floor and your hands on the other side of the square (*rope*) or relatively close to your feet on the mat. Transfer your weight to your hands and bring your feet to the floor on the other side of the mat (*square; rope*).

□ This is more difficult than bringing your feet down in the same place as you did before; you must stay on your hands longer.

■ Stand at the side of your mat *(square; rope)* in the front-back stance. Extend your arms upward. Step forward with your lead foot and transfer your weight to your hands. Bring your feet to the floor on the opposite side of your mat *(square; rope)*.

□ Stretch your legs toward the ceiling as you travel.

□ If you stretch your trunk and legs as you transfer your weight to one hand and then to the other, you'll begin to do a cartwheel.

Transferring Weight from Feet to Back

Transfer your weight from your feet to a rounded back. As you rock back to your shoulders, push with your hands to roll backward across the mat.

□ Remember to push hard with your hands so you don't get your neck stuck.

□ Rolling backward is a weight-transfer skill. What body parts do you transfer to in a backward roll? Feet to what? To feet.

■ Think of the forward roll. When you do a forward roll, you transfer your weight from your feet to what? Now travel across the mats, transferring your weight, as in a forward roll.

Chapter 18 has procedures for teaching children how to roll forward and backward. Those skills should be taught prior to or in connection with weight-transfer skills.

CONTROL LEVEL

Tasks at the control level are designed to help children transfer their weight to specific body parts—for example, from feet to back, to hands, to head and hands—so they can travel or balance.

Activities Leading to Skill Development

Stretching, Curling, Twisting into Transfers

Balance on one foot. Bend at your waist and extend your arms forward and your free leg backward. Stretch your arms forward until you're off balance; transfer your weight to your hands and then to your curled back and roll forward.

Transferring weight onto and off equipment using different body parts.

■ Balance on your knees and one hand. Extend your free arm under your body, twisting your trunk until your weight transfers to your shoulder and new bases of support.

■ Balance in a shoulder stand with your weight on your shoulders, upper arms, and head, with your legs stretched toward the ceiling. Twist your legs and trunk, bringing your feet to the mat behind you in a new balance.

■ Balance on your chosen base of support. Twist until you're momentarily off balance; transfer your weight onto a new base of support.

■ Balance on your chosen base again. This time use a stretching or curling action to transfer onto a new base of support.

□ When you first begin transferring weight by stretching, curling, or twisting, you must move slowly to maintain control and avoid injury.

Performing Step/Spring Takeoffs

Approach your mat from a distance of about ten feet. Just before you reach the mat, use a two-foot takeoff to spring high in the air; land softly in the center of the mat.

□ The spring takeoff in gymnastics is very similar to the approach on the diving board.

□ Remember to extend your arms upward for added height.

□ Be sure to bend your knees when you contact the mat to absorb the force of your landing.

Before practicing spring and step takeoffs in weight transfer, children should be at the control level of jumping and landing.

□ Focus on a stationary object and keep your shoulders erect for good balance when you land.

■ Approach the mat, spring off your two feet, make a quarter turn, and land in a balanced position. Now try the turn in the opposite direction.

■ When you're comfortable with a quarter turn, try a half turn. Remember to practice both clockwise and counterclockwise turns.

The spring takeoff is used for gymnastics skills requiring power, for example, aerial flips, handsprings, vaulting. It's a jump for height, as in a basketball jump ball.

■ Approach the mat. Using a step takeoff, land on your two feet in the center of the mat.

The step takeoff is used for gymnastics skills requiring slow control, for example, walkovers and cartwheels. It's the takeoff needed for a lay-up in basketball.

Performing Spring/Step Takeoffs onto Crates

Arrange milk crates throughout general space; place them against mats to prevent them from sliding.

Approach the crate from a distance of from ten to fifteen feet. Using either a spring or step takeoff, land in a balanced position on the crate.

□ Bend your knees for a soft landing.

□ Keep your head and shoulders up to prevent overbalancing and falling off the front of the crate.

■ Practice each takeoff until you can transfer your weight onto the crate in a balanced position three times.

■ Approach the crate, use a spring takeoff, and transfer your weight to your feet and hands on the crate.

■ Approach the crate, use a step takeoff, and transfer your weight to your hands only on the crate.

Making Spring/Step Takeoffs with Sequences

Approach the crate and use either a step or spring takeoff to transfer onto the crate.

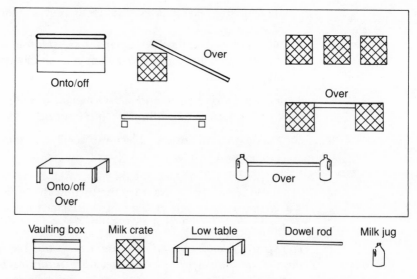

Figure 20-2 Equipment setups for transfer of weight in relation to small equipment.

■ You'll have to decide what body parts you're going to use as bases of support on the crate before you decide whether to use a spring or step takeoff.

■ Create a series of four balances by transferring your weight to different body parts on the crate. *(See Chapter 19.)*

■ Transfer off the crate either by kneeling on the crate and placing your hands on the mat and rolling off or transferring your weight from your feet on the crate to your feet on the mat. When you jump, make a shape in the air or turn while airborne.

Children working at the upper control level will begin to transfer their weight off milk crates and low equipment by using their hands only, for example, handstands, cartwheels.

Traveling over Low Apparatus

Arrange milk crates, benches, low tables, hurdles, hoops, and milk jug/rolled newspaper rods throughout general space (see Figure 20-2).

Travel *over* the various pieces of low equipment by transferring your weight from your feet to your hands to your feet. At the hurdles and at the newspaper rods, place your hands on the mat on the other side of the hurdles or rods and then transfer your weight over, landing on your feet. At the benches and milk crates, place your hands on the equipment, take your weight on your hands only, and land on your feet on the opposite side of the equipment.

□ Keep your fingers pointing forward when you place them on the mat or equipment; don't rotate your wrists outward.

■ As you become comfortable taking your weight on your hands, kick higher toward the ceiling, stretching your legs and trunk.

Traveling onto Low Apparatus

Use the benches and low tables to practice transferring your weight onto equipment. Practice transferring your weight from your feet to your feet and hands on the equipment by springing off your two feet and landing on your hands and feet.

☐ Land softly on the equipment by first taking your weight on your hands and feet and then lowering your total body onto other body parts. Don't jump onto the equipment.

■ Practice until you can land on the equipment without losing your balance.

■ Sometimes spring off your two feet with a small jump; sometimes use a front-back stance and step into the transfer.

■ Transfer your weight onto the equipment by momentarily taking weight on your hands only.

☐ Be sure your hands are firmly planted on the equipment so you won't slip when you transfer your weight to your hands only.

☐ Extend your legs toward the ceiling and stretch to maintain the balance on your hands.

Youngsters can travel over, under, and through apparatus, transferring weight to a variety of body parts.

Traveling off of Low Apparatus

Transfer your weight *off* the bench, table, or crate by assuming a kneeling position, placing your hands on the mat, and rolling forward.

- □ Slowly lower your weight to the mat.
- □ Tuck your head on your chest, contacting the mat with your upper back.
- □ Remember to keep your back rounded for a smooth roll.

Although specific tasks for transferring weight with large apparatus aren't listed until the utilization level, children at the precontrol and control levels need exploration time on large apparatus to become familiar with the equipment and to gain confidence moving on it.

Transferring Weight from Feet to Hands

Transfer your weight from your feet to your hands. Balance on your hands momentarily, and then bring your feet down to their original place.

Transferring weight to travel along equipment.

- □ Remember to point your fingers forward.
- □ Reach downward, not forward, with your hands.
- □ Stretch your legs toward the ceiling; tighten your stomach muscles to maintain balance.

- ■ Use a step action to transfer your weight to your hands; try to have your shoulders directly over your hands when you kick your legs up.

- □ If you begin to overbalance, push with your fingertips to maintain balance.
- □ If you begin to lose your balance completely, twist your trunk so you do a quarter turn and bring your feet to the floor.

- ■ Practice until you can balance for three seconds on your hands. Transfer your weight back to your feet in their original position.

Taking their weight on their hands for brief periods of time should be introduced to children early in the elementary school years. Children need frequent practice to achieve control-level mastery of transferring weight to and balancing on hands.

Transferring Weight to Hands: Walking

When you're comfortable balancing on your hands for three seconds, try walking on your hands.

- □ Focus on your hands to help you balance as you move.

Transferring Weight to Hands, Followed by Rolling

Transfer your weight to your hands with your body stretched toward the ceiling. Slowly lower your weight to your spine and roll forward.

- □ Be sure your inverted balance is steady before you lower your weight to the mat.
- □ Remember to keep your back rounded for the roll.

Transferring Weight to Hands and Twisting

Transfer your weight to your hands, twist your body a half turn, and bring your feet to the floor so you're facing the opposite direction.

- ■ While you're balanced on your hands, slowly walk on your hands a half turn to face the opposite direction.

Transferring Weight to Hands by Stepping: Cartwheels

Using a step action, alternate transferring your weight to your feet and to your hands, returning to your feet in a step action, as in a cartwheel.

□ You can begin the cartwheel by facing the mat or by standing sideways with one shoulder toward the mat, but facing the mat is easier. *(Teacher or child demonstrates.)*

□ Stretch your legs toward the ceiling; tighten your trunk muscles to hold your body in alignment.

□ Keep your legs in a straddle position in the air.

□ Remember that your weight transfers momentarily from your foot to your foot, to your hand, to your hand, to your foot, to your foot.

□ Feet and hands should be placed in a straight line, not a curve.

□ The cartwheel is one fluid movement from beginning to end—no pauses.

■ Practice leading with both your right and left sides so you can do a cartwheel in either direction.

■ Transfer your weight to your hands, as in the cartwheel. While you're balanced in the inverted position, bring your feet together, twist a half turn, and bring your feet down quickly to face the opposite direction, as in a roundoff.

Children discover many ways to transfer weight across large apparatus.

Transferring Weight to Hands and Forming a Bridge

Using a step action, transfer your weight to your hands with sufficient force to continue the forward motion. Your feet should remain in the steplike stance as they move upward over your hands. Bring your feet together just prior to contacting the floor; you're then balanced in a "bridge," with your feet and hands supporting your weight. Push with your hands to return to a standing position. *(Teacher or child demonstrates.)*

□ Bend your knees slightly just prior to contacting the floor so your feet are under your body, not extended outward.

■ Keep your legs in the steplike stance throughout the transfer. As your feet contact the surface, push with your hands to continue your transfer to a standing position. This transfer with no pause is a *walkover.*

Children won't master gymnastics tasks in only one or two thirty-minute lessons. A station format (see Chapter 6) provides opportunities for distributed practice of these skills.

UTILIZATION LEVEL

Tasks at the utilization level are designed to teach children to transfer their weight onto, over, and from large apparatus. Transfer is now combined with stretching, curling, and twisting, with increased periods of time in aerial moves. There's also emphasis on the development of more complex sequences involving weight transference.

Activities Leading to Skill Development

Transferring Weight onto Large Apparatus

Have large apparatus—benches, tables, vaulting boxes, balance beams, parallel bars, large climbing frames—around the gym.

Transferring weight onto large apparatus in gymnastics usually includes an approach to build momentum, a spring or step takeoff, and the transfer onto the apparatus. Approach the apparatus from about fifteen feet. Using a spring takeoff, transfer your weight from your feet on the floor to your feet and hands on the apparatus *(box, beam, table).*

□ A strong spring takeoff is very important because of the increased height of this apparatus.
□ To maintain balance, keep your head and shoulders erect.

■ Transfer your weight to your feet and hands in a tuck position.
■ Transfer your weight to your feet and hands in a straddle position.

■ Transfer your weight to your feet and hands in a "wolf" position: one knee bent, one leg straight.

Transferring Weight to Head and Hands on Apparatus

Approach the apparatus and use a spring takeoff to transfer your weight to your hands and head on the apparatus *(box, beam, table)*.

 ▫ Push hard with your legs on the takeoff for sufficient height and time for the transfer.
 ▫ Remember to take your weight first on your hands only and then on your head and hands.

■ Approach the apparatus from the sides as well as the front. Practice both spring and step takeoffs to transfer your weight to various body parts on the apparatus.

 ▫ Remember that you'll need a spring takeoff for power and/or height; a step takeoff is a slower way to transfer weight.

Many of the precontrol- and control-level tasks with low apparatus can be repeated for large apparatus. This is good practice because it enables children to comfortably adjust to the increased height and more narrow surface of large apparatus.

Transferring Weight onto Bars

■ Standing under the apparatus, use a spring takeoff to transfer your weight to your hands on a high bar. Hanging on the bar, pull up with your arms as you swing your legs over a lower bar and balance in a sitting position *(parallel bars, climbing frame)*.

■ Approach the apparatus with a series of steps. Using a spring takeoff, grasp the bar with your hands and jump up, balancing with your hands and upper thighs on the bar. Swing one leg over the bar so you can straddle the bar.

 ▫ To lift your body above the bar, push hard with your arms as you jump.
 ▫ Keep your head up and your shoulders erect to prevent overbalancing.

■ Approach the apparatus with a series of steps. As you step under the bar, grasp the bar with your hands and kick your rear leg forcefully upward, to bring your hips to the bar. Assume a pike position by bending your legs; a *pike* is a bend of the body while the body is in the air. The momentum of the leg kick will cause your body to circle the bar. Balance on your hands and upper thighs on the bar.

 ▫ Keep your arms bent throughout the circular action, pulling the bar close to your body.

■ Approach the apparatus from the back, front, and side; practice both spring and step takeoffs to transfer your weight to various body parts on the bars.

 ▫ Remember to always keep a firm grip on the apparatus.

At the utilization and proficiency levels, many skills closely reflect Olympic-style gymnastics. Encourage children to be creative in designing new skills and in combining skills for sequences.

Transferring Weight over Apparatus

See Chapter 17, "Jumping and Landing," for the vaulting skills appropriate for the utilization level.

Transferring Weight Along Apparatus

Use stationary bars, tables and benches of various heights, vaulting boxes, balance beams, and a stage.

Many of the gymnastics skills you learned to do on the floor and on low equipment can also be performed on large apparatus. You'll probably want to do the activities on the floor, concentrating on each movement, before trying them on the large apparatus.

Transferring Weight by Rolling

Standing on the apparatus, transfer your weight from your feet to your hands and your curled back for rolling *(beam, bench, box, table)*.

- ☐ The position of your hands will be quite different than when you're rolling on the floor. Place your thumbs and the sides of your palms on top of the beam or the apparatus, with your hands and fingers on the sides of the equipment. This provides a steady grip and constant awareness of the width of the surface and the direction you're rolling in.
- ☐ Your head *must* be tucked when rolling on apparatus.
- ☐ Remember to roll slowly; you're on a much higher, narrower surface.
- ☐ When rolling backward on the apparatus, place your head to the side and roll backward over one shoulder.
- ☐ Extend your hands above your head to hold onto the sides of the apparatus.
- ☐ When rolling backward on large apparatus, it's easier to transfer your weight from your curled back to one bent knee with one leg extended. With this narrow shape, it's easier for you to balance on the small surface of the apparatus.

Transferring Weight from Feet to Hands

Tape lines on the gym floor.

Practice a cartwheel on a tape line on the floor until you can do it perfectly three times. Now transfer your weight from your feet to your hands in a cartwheel on the low bench.

- After you're comfortable doing a cartwheel on the bench, try it on the beam.
  - □ Move slowly and with control.
  - □ If you feel off balance or unable to complete the weight transfer after you're inverted, push with your hands to move your body away from the beam or bench and transfer your weight to your feet on the floor.

Teaching by invitation or intratask variation is very effective when working with transferring weight on apparatus. Permit only those children who are clearly ready to practice inverted weight transference along apparatus.

- Transfer your weight from your feet to your hands, as in a walkover on the bench or beam.
- Transfer your weight from your feet to your hands, slowly execute a half turn, and bring your feet down on the apparatus surface facing the opposite direction.
- Create three ways to transfer your weight while moving along the apparatus. Consider changes in levels and directions of travel.

Transferring Weight on Bars

Transfer your weight to different body parts as you move from bar to bar on the parallels or other climbing apparatus.

- Circle the bar with your body curled, in a pike position.
- Use twisting actions to move your body off balance and into the transfer.
- Remember to make some transfers on the bars quickly, others slowly.
  - □ Your thumbs should be curled around the bar in the direction you're to move—forward or backward.

Combining Skills on Mats

Travel the length of your mat, transferring your weight from your feet to other body parts, in various sequences.

- Perform slow movements and then very quick movements, for example, the contrast of a walkover and a handspring.
- Do movements that show strength and then movements that demonstrate slowness and smooth control.
- Perform twisting, turning actions, for example, a roundoff, weight on your hands, a 360° turn on your hands.
- Use combinations of actions, for example, weight on your hands, lower body into a forward roll.
- Travel the length of your mat combining a balance, a jump, a roll, and a hands/feet action.
- Travel the length of your mat, transferring your weight from your feet to your hands, add a roll, and finish in a balance.

Combining Weight Transfer and Balances in Sequences

Gymnastics routines on mats and apparatus are combinations of weight transfers and balance. Children at the utilization and proficiency levels of balance and weight transfer are ready for sequences involving combinations of skills and travel. Figure 20-3 is an example of the assignment plus guidelines.

Figure 20-3 Sample assignment for proficiency-level sequence.

```
                                        Name:_____


                           Final Project:  Gymnastics

         Grade 6:  (a) mat sequence, (b) equipment sequence
         Alone; with a partner: mirror, side by side

         1.  Beginning

             A.  Approach:

                 distance, starting point, pathway

                 walk, run, leap, roll, walkover, cartwheel

                 other_____

             B.  Takeoff:

                 spring, step

         2.  Development of sequence:  Mix in any order for interest.

             A.  Balances:

                 minimum of four body shapes/four different bases of support

             B.  Actions:

                 minimum of three

                 stretch curl; twist turn

             C.  Transfers:

                 movement

                 feet to hand, back, head/hands

                 (headstands, cartwheels, rolls, etc.)

             D.  Inversion:

                 minimum of two

         3.  Ending shape or dismount

             A.  Music selection:  ninety seconds

             B.  On back side of page, list the progression of section 2;
                 illustrate it if you wish.
```

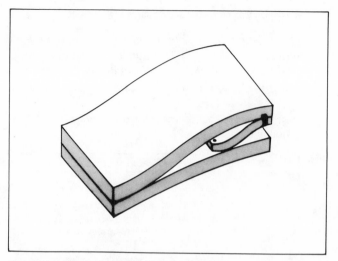

Figure 20-4 Springboards may be purchased from gymnastic companies (Nissen, Gym Master) or made from plywood and heavy-duty springs.

PROFICIENCY LEVEL

Tasks at the proficiency level are designed so that children focus on increasing the horizontal and/or vertical distance of the weight transfer. The activities can include intricate maneuvers (twists, curls) of the body and its parts as weight is transferred from and received by different body parts.

Activities Leading to Skill Development

Using a Springboard for Vaulting

A springboard is recommended for hands-only transfers over the vaulting box. See Figure 20-4.

Build up speed as you approach the vaulting box. Using a two-foot takeoff from the springboard, transfer your weight to your hands only on the box. Travel over the box in the inverted position, landing on your feet on the other side.

- □ The approach and spring takeoff should provide sufficient momentum to carry your body over the box with ease.
- □ Remember to bend your knees when you land on the mat, to absorb the force.

Dismounting from apparatus with a stretching or twisting action.

Using Hands Only with Stretching, Twisting Actions

Approach the box with a series of running steps, to build momentum. Using a spring takeoff, transfer your weight to your hands only on the box. As your body becomes airborne off the box, use a twisting action with your body stretched to turn in the air. Land on your feet facing the opposite direction.

Dismounting from Apparatus by Transferring Weight from Hands to Feet

Transfer your weight from your feet to your hands on the apparatus *(beam, bench, table)*. Push your body away from the apparatus and land in a balanced position on your feet beside the apparatus.

□ Hold the inverted balance momentarily before you push for the dismount.

■ Stand in the middle of the apparatus and face the end you're going to dismount from. Use a step action to transfer your weight from your feet to your alternate hands, as in a cartwheel. Land on the mat at the end of the apparatus.

□ Be sure your final hand position is near the end of the apparatus so you'll clear the apparatus when you dismount.

■ Dismount from the apparatus by transferring your weight to your hands, executing a twisting action in the air, and landing after completing a quarter or half turn.

□ Twisting actions in the air require sufficient momentum to easily carry the body through all phases of the dismount.

Dismounting from Bars

Transfer your weight to your hands only on one of the bars. Hold the inverted balance momentarily, and then push away from the bars and land in a balanced position on the mat.

□ It's very important that you bend your knees when landing, to absorb the force of dismounting from this height.
□ When you first practice this skill, hold the bar with one hand until you're balanced on your feet.
■ Transfer from the bars with one aerial twisting action.
■ Transfer from the bars by executing circular actions around a bar before dismounting to your feet on the mat.

READING COMPREHENSION QUESTIONS

1. List several examples of weight transfer.
2. What is the most common example of weight transfer?
3. Children at the precontrol, control, utilization, and proficiency levels are ready for what types of weight-transfer experiences?
4. Which relationship concepts are typically used as subthemes in the study of weight transfer?
5. What does the question "Do the feet come down with control?" mean?
6. What are weight-transfer tasks at the utilization level designed to do?
7. What is a spring takeoff?
8. List five examples of large gymnastics apparatus.
9. Describe the typical progression in gymnastics.
10. What are the parts of a weight-transfer sequence at the proficiency level?

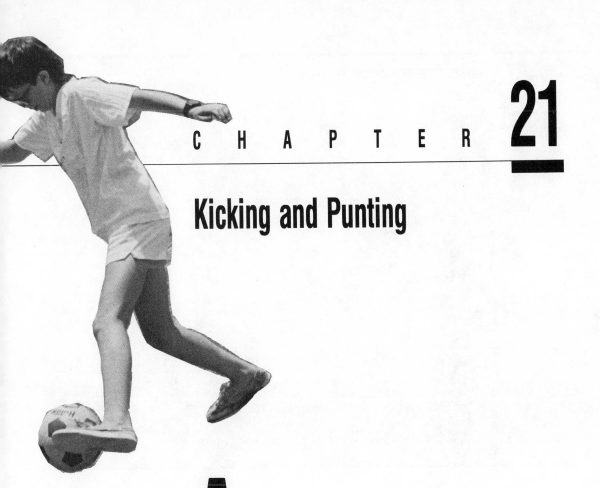

Kicking and Punting

A young boy kicking a stone along the sidewalk as he walks home from school, a neighborhood game of Kick the Can, kickball on the school playground at recess, an aspiring athlete practicing the soccer dribble, and the professional punter—all are executing a similar movement: the kick. This movement requires accuracy, body control, point of contact, force, and direction. Some children seem to perform the kick with intense concentration, others effortlessly.

We try to give children a variety of opportunities to practice kicking so that they'll develop a foundation of kicking skills that they can use in different situations. We emphasize the development of mature kicking patterns by focusing on experiences designed to elicit such patterns. For example, kicking for distance leads to the development of a mature kicking pattern, but this isn't true of kicking for accuracy.

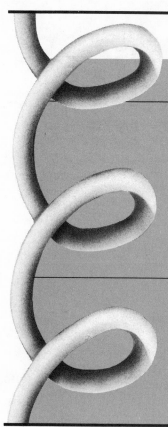

SKILL THEME DEVELOPMENT SEQUENCE

Kicking

CONTROL LEVEL

Keeping It Perfect: Zero, Zero
Dribbling around stationary obstacles
Traveling in pathways
Starting and stopping
Tapping the ball along the ground (Soccer Dribble)
Kicking to a partner
Kicking to targets
Kicking to a distance zone

PRECONTROL LEVEL

Tapping the ball along the ground and moving with it
Kicking a rolling ball from a stationary position
Kicking on the ground, in the air
Approaching a stationary ball and kicking
Kicking in the air
Kicking a stationary ball from a stationary position

LEVELS OF KICKING SKILL PROFICIENCY

Children at the precontrol level of kicking are challenged by the task of making contact with a stationary ball. Once the children begin to consistently make contact with a stationary ball, we challenge them to kick the ball for distance. Appropriate precontrol tasks include:

1. Running to kick a stationary ball
2. Kicking a ball the teacher (or an older child) has rolled
3. Tapping a ball along the ground while moving behind it

At the control level, children are introduced to contacting a ball with different parts of the foot—inside, outside, back, and front. They're also given challenges that involve dribbling with either foot, at various speeds, and in different directions. Appropriate control level activities include:

Kicking

PROFICIENCY LEVEL

Playing Cone Soccer
Playing Alley Soccer
Playing Soccer Keep Away
Playing minisoccer
Kicking at a moving target
Kicking at small stationary targets

UTILIZATION LEVEL

Playing two on one soccer
Playing one on one soccer
Passing to a partner in general space
Kicking to a traveling partner
Kicking to a partner from various angles
Playing Soccer Golf
Traveling, kicking for a goal
Performing a continuous tap/dribble with change of direction
Changing directions: tap/dribble

---

1. Sending a ball along the ground or through the air to a partner
2. Kicking toward a target
3. Making quick kicks
4. Starting/stopping, changing directions with the soccer dribble

Children at the utilization level of kicking are able to kick for both distance and accuracy. They enjoy and learn from the challenge of one on one Keep Away situations (trying to prevent another child from getting the ball) that combine the skills of tapping a ball along the ground with the skills needed to dodge an opponent. Dynamic game situations enjoyed at the utilization level can involve:

1. Kicking a ball to a target while on the run
2. Kicking for accuracy while trying to maneuver around an opponent
3. Differentiating between high and low kicks

One youngster tries to keep the ball away from his partner using only his feet—no touching.

Children who've reached the proficiency level in kicking enjoy group participation with more players, more complex relationships, and the excitement of strategy development. Sample tasks include:

1. Kicking for a target against defense
2. Gamelike situations
3. Kicking at moving targets

The entire spectrum of kicking experiences, from precontrol through proficiency, is represented in our progression spiral on p. 418. The tasks are stated in terms that imply a direct approach (Chapter 4), but teachers are encouraged to vary the approach according to the purpose of the lesson and the characteristics of the class.

The following Key Observation Points illustrate correct and incorrect ways of kicking along the ground and in the air. Ask yourself the questions as you observe the youngsters in action.

KEY OBSERVATION POINTS / Kicking Along the Ground

SOCCER DRIBBLE

Does the child contact the ball for the dribble behind the ball, not on top?

NO   YES

DRIBBLE/KICK FOR DISTANCE

1. Does the child make contact with the instep (shoelaces) of the foot, not with the toes?

NO   YES

2. Is the child's trunk inclined slightly backward for the kick?

NO   YES

KEY OBSERVATION POINTS / Kicking in the Air

1. Is contact below the center of the ball, not on top?

NO   YES

2. Is the child's kicking foot extended for contact on the shoelaces, not on the toes?

3. Does the child's kicking leg bend in preparation for the kick and follow-through after contact?

4. Does the child's trunk incline slightly backward for the kick?

MATURE STAGE

When children are at the mature stage of kicking, do their kicks look similar to the following sequence? The approach to the ball involves one or more steps, with the distance just prior to the kick covered with a leap. The kicker is airborne in the approach. The knee of the kicking leg is slightly flexed due to the leap just prior to kicking. The trunk is inclined backward prior to and during contact. The momentum of the kick is dispersed by hopping on the support leg and stepping in the direction of the object that was struck.

Sources: Adapted from "Developmental Sequence of Kicking," mimeographed materials, by V. Seefeldt & J. Haubenstricker, presented at the University of Georgia, Athens, June 1978; *Fundamental Motor Patterns*, 2nd ed., by R. L. Wickstrom, 1977, Philadelphia: Lea & Febiger.

ASSESSMENT GUIDE / Kicking

Note to Teachers. Arrange a series of marker cones as shown in the accompanying diagram. Leave six to eight feet between each cone. Place two cones fifteen feet away in a target position.

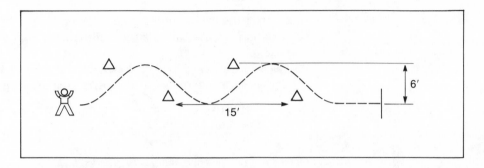

TASK   Zigzag between the cones, tapping the ball gently with either foot. After you complete the foot dribbling around the cones, tap the ball to the kicking line. Without stopping, kick forcefully toward the target so the ball travels between the target cones.

GUIDE   The children are ready for precontrol- or control-level tasks when you observe that:

1. They're unable to tap the ball around the cones without bumping the cones or losing control of the ball—it rolls away from them.
2. They're unable to kick for the goal as a continuation of the traveling—they have to stop and then kick.
3. They're unsuccessful at three attempts at the goal.

The children are ready for utilization- or proficiency-level tasks when you observe that they're able to tap the ball (soccer dribble) around the cones, travel fifteen to twenty feet to the kicking line, and kick successfully to the target without pausing or hesitating.

PRECONTROL LEVEL

At the precontrol level, we want children to be able to make consistent contact with a stationary ball. When they're able to do this, we progress gradually to kicking a ball rolled by a skilled roller and tapping a ball gently along the ground.

Activities Leading to Skill Development

Kicking a Stationary Ball from a Stationary Position

Place the balls for kicking approximately ten feet from the wall around the gymnasium.

Stand behind a kicking ball. Use your instep (shoelaces) to kick the ball to the wall. Kick it hard!

- ▢ Contact the ball behind the center so it travels forward at a low level.
- ▢ Kick hard so the ball hits the wall with enough force to rebound back to you.
- ▢ Place your nonkicking leg alongside (not behind) the ball.
- ▢ Center your weight over your nonkicking leg for good balance.

Place a series of two-inch colored tape markers on the walls of the gym, approximately three feet above the floor.

Children need many opportunities to practice kicking.

■ Kick the ball so it contacts the wall below the tape line. *(Teacher or child demonstrates.)*

■ Practice kicking with both your right and your left foot until you can kick three times in a row with each foot.

Kicking in the Air

Stand behind a kicking ball. Contact the ball with the instep of your foot—your shoelaces, the Velcro closings—to send the ball to the wall.

□ Contact below the center of the ball will cause the ball to travel upward rather than at a low level.

□ Your nonkicking leg should be beside the ball when contact is made.

□ Bend the knee of your nonkicking leg slightly for good balance.

□ This aerial kick from stationary position sends the ball a greater distance than the low, along-the-ground kick.

■ Now try kicking with your other foot.

After a couple of years, the eight-and-a-half-inch inexpensive plastic balls become partially deflated; they can't be inflated. These half-life plastic balls are excellent for kicking. We mark them with a large K so children know which balls are for kicking, which ones for dribbling. Playground and kickballs can also be partially deflated for beginning practice and for use indoors.

Approaching a Stationary Ball and Kicking

Place the balls for kicking approximately ten feet from the walls around the gym, as shown in Figure 21-1.

Figure 21-1 Arrangement for the approach and kick of a stationary ball.

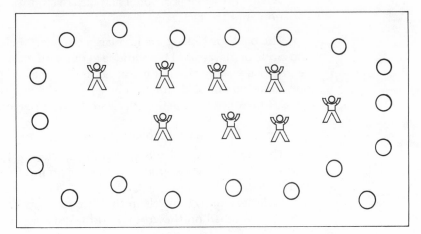

Stand five to six feet behind the kicking ball. Approach the ball and use the instep of your foot to contact the ball, sending it forward to the wall.

- □ Remember to contact with the top of your foot, not your toes.
- □ Contact the ball directly behind, not on the top.
- □ Immediately after you kick the ball, take a small hop on your nonkicking leg and then step forward in the direction of the kick; this hop-step checks your forward momentum.

■ The balls for kicking are scattered around the edge of the gymnasium. Begin traveling in general space, avoiding collisions with others or the balls on the floor. On the signal, approach the ball nearest you and kick it toward the wall. Quickly retrieve the ball you kicked and place it about ten to twelve feet from the wall. You're now ready to move again. Ready? Travel in general space.

- □ Remember to listen for the signal to kick.
- □ Approach the ball on the run; the kick is an extension of your travel.
- □ At the moment of contact, your eyes should see your foot kick the ball— watch the ball, not the wall.

■ Alternate kicking with your right foot and your left foot so you'll be skilled at using both feet.

Kicking on the Ground, in the Air

You worked on kicking with the upper part of your foot, focusing on the correct movement pattern. Let's name the four things we need to remember for good kicking:

1. Run to kick the ball; don't pause or hesitate.
2. Your weight should be balanced over your nonkicking leg.
3. Make contact with the instep of your foot.
4. When you kick hard, you'll actually rise off the ground and take a small hop after the kick.

■ The balls for kicking are in a large circle on the playground. Stand inside the circle of playground balls and face outward. *(See Figure 21-2.)* You're going to practice kicking along the ground and in the air. There's enough space for you to kick as hard as you can. After you kick, retrieve the ball and quickly bring it back to your starting place so the next person can kick.

- □ Remember, you're stationary, the ball is stationary.
- ■ The first kick will be along the ground. Ready? Kick.
- ■ Now, kick along the ground with your nonpreferred foot. Kick really hard. Ready? Kick.
  - ■ Kick the ball so it travels in the air away from the circle.
  - ■ Place the ball on the ground and take three to four steps back from the

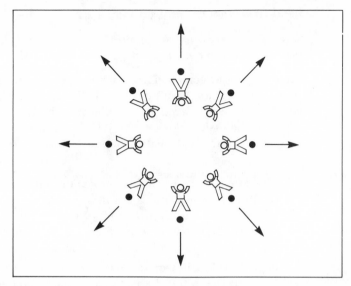

Figure 21-2 Circular pattern for distance kicking.

ball. Approach the ball with three to four running steps and then kick the ball along the ground *(in the air)*.

   □ These running steps help build the momentum for a more forceful kick.

Numbering the balls 1, 2, 3, 4, etc., eliminates confusion about which ball belongs to whom.

Kicking a Rolling Ball from a Stationary Position

Stand approximately ten feet from a partner; one of you will need a ball for kicking. Partner 1 rolls the ball along the ground; partner 2 kicks the ball so it travels back to partner 1.

   □ Keep your eyes on the ball from the time it leaves your partner's hands until your foot contacts it for the kick.
   □ Kick only hard enough for the ball to travel to your partner.

   ■ Practice the kick along the ground with both your right foot and your left foot; practice the kick in the air with your preferred foot. Sometimes in game situations you'll want to kick along the ground, so make contact directly behind the ball. When you want the ball to go in the air, contact the ball below the center of the ball. *(Teacher or child demonstrates.)*

   □ Remember to use your instep, not your toe.

The focus at the precontrol level is contacting the ball and developing the correct skill pattern, not accuracy.

Tapping the Ball Along the Ground and Moving with It

Space five to six hula circles on the floor around the gym; within each circle place four to five balls for kicking.

On the signal, select a ball from a circle, scatter throughout general space, and stand with one foot resting on the ball. *(Visually scan the room to make sure children are well spaced.)* Begin traveling through general space, tapping the ball with the inside of your foot. When you hear the signal, quickly place one foot on top of the ball, slightly behind center to stop the momentum. Ready? Go.

 □ The contact area is the inside of your foot. The amount of force is a light tap. Your feet are turned out like a duck's.
 □ Keep the ball within three to four feet of your body as you tap and travel, to allow you to trap the ball quickly on signal.
 □ Alternate tapping with your right foot and your left foot.

■ Begin traveling in general space, tapping the ball in the soccer dribble you just learned. Try to travel and tap the ball with alternate feet without letting the ball get away from you or colliding with another person. Ready? Begin.

 □ Remember that the ball should stay within three to four feet of you at all times.
 □ Don't be in a hurry; you should be able to trap the ball at any time.

■ Now dribble in general space and see if you can make it for thirty seconds without your ball touching anyone else's ball. Ready? Go!

As children improve, you can increase the time to forty-five seconds and then a minute.

CONTROL LEVEL

At the control level we provide a variety of kicking experiences that include kicking for accuracy, kicking in different directions, and partner relationships. We encourage use of different parts of each foot and greater control of speed and direction.

Activities Leading to Skill Development

Kicking to a Distance Zone

Arrange marker cones or plastic milk cartons at ten-foot intervals across the playground; number the cones consecutively so the children can see the numbers when they're at the kicking line. See Figure 21-3.

Place the ball you're going to use at the kicking line. Approach the ball from about five to six feet. Kick the ball so it travels as far as possible through the

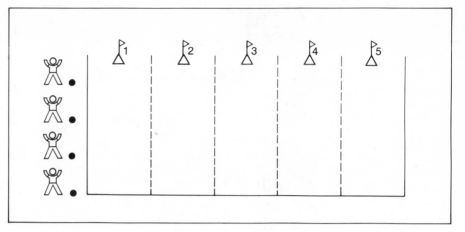

Figure 21-3 Numbered distance zones.

air. Note the number of the zone in which the ball first contacts the ground. Kick five times, trying to improve your distance.

- ☐ Remember to run to the ball.
- ☐ Contact the ball with your instep so the ball travels through the air.

■ Now try to kick the ball so that it lands in the same zone three times in a row.

Kicking to Targets

Arrange a series of various targets of different heights throughout the gymnasium. See Figure 21-4.

Spaced around the gym are targets for kicking—suspended hoops, marker cones to kick between and to hit, ropes hung between chairs for kicking over, tape squares on the wall.

■ I'll assign you to a station; at that station practice kicking at the target. Place the ball at the kicking line. Approach the kicking line with two or three steps prior to making contact. After your turn, retrieve the ball and return to your group to wait your next turn.

■ Continue practicing at your station until the signal is given to change to another kicking station.

- ☐ Focus on the ball, not the target, until it leaves your foot.
- ☐ Remember to kick with the instep of your foot.

■ Here's what you'll do at the different stations. At the hoops, kick the ball through the circle. At the large and small marker cones, kick the ball hard enough to make the cone fall over. At the rope between the chairs and the rope

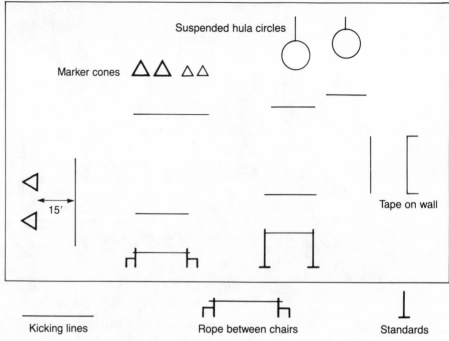

Figure 21-4 Targets for kicking.

stretched between the standards, kick the ball so it travels over the rope. At the marker goals, kick the ball along the ground between the cones. At the tape square, kick the ball so it touches the wall inside the square.

Weighted jugs, cones, or tape marks on the wall can serve as goals. Vary the width of the goal according to individuals' abilities.

Kicking to a Partner

Stand approximately fifteen to twenty feet from your partner; face each other across the playground. Each set of partners has one ball. Kick the ball along the ground to your partner so she can stop it with her foot without moving from her self-space.

- □ Try to contact the ball directly behind the center so the ball will travel along the ground.
- □ Remember, when trapping the ball, place your foot slightly behind the ball, above the center back.
- □ Always stop the ball before you kick it to your partner.

■ Practice until you can kick five times to your partner so she traps the ball without moving from her self-space.

The force required to kick a ball for accuracy is initially different from that required to kick for distance.

□ Watch the ball, not your partner.

■ When you're comfortable with your skill and can kick accurately five times, take a large step back and repeat the task. Practice at different distances to determine your maximum distance for accuracy to a partner.

Tapping the Ball Along the Ground (Soccer Dribble)

Travel throughout general space, kicking the ball along the ground three to four feet in front of you as you go.

■ Alternate the tap/kick between your right foot and left foot.

□ You may tap with the inside or the outside of your foot; however, most often you'll probably use the inside of your foot for a controlled dribble.

- Begin traveling through general space, dribbling the soccer ball as you go. Gradually increase your speed, keeping the ball within three to four feet of you at all times. Increase and decrease the speed of your travel, adjusting the force of your kick as you increase and decrease speed.

Starting and Stopping

Begin dribbling in general space. When you hear the signal, quickly trap the ball. Maintain a balanced, ready position *(weight centered over support leg)* so you can move again quickly. Ready? Begin.

This activity provides practice in stopping the ball quickly. Frequent signals will be needed: ten seconds of dribbling, stop, one minute of dribbling, stop, etc.

- Travel through general space, dribbling as you go. Each time you meet another person, stop the ball quickly with your foot, execute a quarter turn, and continue dribbling. The ability to stop and start quickly is an important offensive skill that helps you maintain control of the ball and avoid your opponents.
- Test your dribbling skills with a two-minute activity. On the signal, begin dribbling in self-space. Each time you hear the drum or meet another person, stop quickly, trap the ball with one foot, execute a quarter turn, and continue dribbling. Your goal is to stop/start for two minutes without losing control of the ball or bumping another person or the ball he or she is dribbling. The signal at the end of the two-minutes will be a double drumbeat.

Traveling in Pathways

Tape various patterns on the gym floor, or spray paint the patterns on the grass.

Travel through the formations using the soccer dribble; travel at the speed at which you can control the ball. In other words, you'll be able to trap the ball at any time. You'll find combinations of straight, curved, and zigzag pathways; be sure you travel each pathway.

Dribbling Around Stationary Obstacles

Scatter marker cones or milk jugs throughout general space.

Tap/dribble the ball throughout general space, alternating contacting with your right foot and your left foot. Avoid bumping into the cones with either the ball or your body. Travel in zigzag and curved pathways to avoid the obstacles.

- Your visual range must now include the ball you're dribbling, other people, the balls they're using, and the obstacles.

Dribbling a ball around obstacles requires intense concentration.

□ Remember, keep the ball within three to four feet of you at all times.

■ Tap/dribble in general space. Each time you approach an obstacle, trap the ball, execute a quarter turn to either the right or left, and continue dribbling.

■ Vary the speed of your travel—sometimes approach a cone very quickly, sometimes slowly.

■ Tap/dribble in general space. As you near a cone *(jug)*, tap the ball gently with the inside of your right foot, passing the ball to the left of the cone *(jug)*. Quickly continue the dribble.

■ Tap/dribble in general space. As you near a cone *(jug)*, tap the ball gently with the inside of your left foot, passing the ball to the right of the cone *(jug)*.

■ Tap/dribble in general space. As you near the cone *(jug)*, tap the ball gently with the outside of your right foot, passing the ball to the right of the cone *(jug)*.

■ Tap/dribble in general space. As you near a cone *(jug)*, tap the ball gently with the outside of your left foot, passing the ball to the left of the cone *(jug)*.

To master passing methods, children need practice in each method. Exposure only will result in children using only their favorite or easiest method.

■ Each of you has one-hundred points. On the signal, begin to tap/dribble in general space. If the ball you're using contacts a cone, you must subtract ten points from your score. If you collide with another person, subtract twenty-five points. Try to complete the activity with one hundred points.

□ Be careful—you can end up with a negative score!

Keeping It Perfect: Zero, Zero

Thus far in our tap/dribble study you've practiced dribbling with control, trapping with one foot, avoiding obstacles, changing the speed of your travel, and tapping the ball to the right or the left, as in passing. The game of Keeping It Perfect: Zero, Zero will give you a chance to test these skills.

Each of you has a perfect score of zero. The object of the game is to still have the perfect score at the end of the two minutes of activity. On the signal, begin to tap/dribble in general space. You may travel at any speed you choose, increasing and decreasing your speed as you wish. When you hear the drum, trap the ball immediately; I'll give a verbal "go" for you to continue.

■ You earn negative points if you:

1. Don't trap the ball within two seconds of the drumbeat (-1)
2. Bump into another person or the ball they're dribbling (-1)
3. Bump into a marker cone (-1)

The key is control. Ready? Go.

You can use this activity to focus on specific skills. For example, in the first two minutes, children are to travel in general space (control); in the second two minutes, they are to travel in each area of the gymnasium (speed); in the third two minutes, they are to zigzag around as many cones as possible (passing, accuracy).

■ At the end of each two minutes, stop, rest, and calculate your scores. Remember, a perfect score is zero.

UTILIZATION LEVEL

At the utilization level, the focus is on providing experiences for applying kicking skills in unpredictable situations of increasing complexity. Performing skills on the move and in relation to an opponent are important challenges. A great degree of accuracy and control are desired at this level.

Activities Leading to Skill Development

Changing Directions: Tap/Dribble

Begin traveling in general space, tapping the ball three to four feet in front of you as you go. When you're comfortable with your control of the dribble, tap the ball ahead of you, run quickly beyond the ball, tap it gently with your heel, quickly turn, and continue the dribble.

- □ Be sure you run beyond the ball to tap the front of it; contact on top of the ball will cause you to fall to the floor!

Performing a Continuous Tap/Dribble with Change of Direction

Mark a large rectangular area on the playground so children can practice skills on a rough surface.

You learned to change the direction of the ball by tapping it to the right or left with the inside or outside of your foot. And you just learned one method of changing direction front to back. Travel within the boundaries on the playground using changes of direction to avoid contact with others and to avoid crossing the outside boundaries. Your task is continuous dribbling. Ready? Begin.

- ■ Challenge yourself in the following ways:

    Approach a boundary quickly; use the heel tap to change the direction of the dribble at the last moment, to prevent crossing the boundary.

    Purposely approach the other persons; use a pass to the right or left to avoid contact with them.

    Gradually increase the speed of your travel to determine the maximum rate you can travel with a controlled dribble and frequent changes in direction.

Traveling, Kicking for a Goal

Scatter milk jugs as obstacles throughout general space. Place marker cones for goals around the outside boundaries. See Figure 21-5.

Travel at your own speed and tap the ball while avoiding obstacles and other people. On the signal, travel quickly to an open space and kick for the goal. Retrieve the ball; begin dribbling again, listening for the signal to kick for the goal.

- ■ Practice dribbling around obstacles and kicking for the goal on your own; I won't give the signal for the kick.

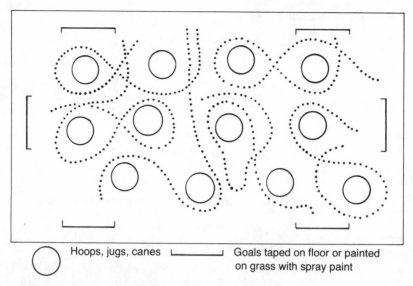

Hoops, jugs, canes   ⌐____⌐   Goals taped on floor or painted on grass with spray paint

Figure 21-5 Room arrangement for combination dribble and kick with varying degrees of force.

Playing Soccer Golf

The game of Soccer Golf involves the skills of dribbling in pathways, kicking for a goal, and kicking over a low height. The playground is arranged as a golf course. *(See Figure 21-6.)* Your task is to complete the course with the least amount of kicks. There are boxes to dribble around, zones to zigzag through, hula hoops to kick into, and poles to kick over. Count your kicks as you proceed through the course. When you finish the course, begin again, trying to lower your score.

To decrease waiting time, have the children begin at different holes on the course rather than having everyone start at the first hole.

Kicking to a Partner from Various Angles

Select a partner and stand approximately fifteen to twenty feet from that partner. Review your skill of kicking along the ground so your partner can trap the ball without moving. Take three to four steps to the right so you're at an angle to your partner. Kick the ball from this position so it travels directly to your partner. Kick with the inside of your right foot and the outside of your left foot until you can kick four out of five times directly to your partner with each foot.

■ Move to the left three to four steps from your original position. Kick the ball to your partner from this angle. Practice the kick with the inside of your

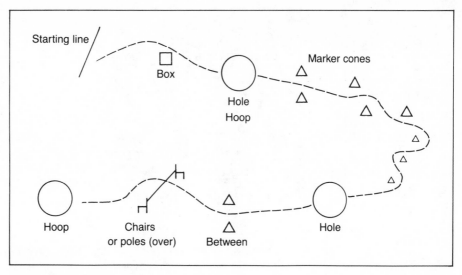

Figure 21-6 Soccer Golf.

left foot and the outside of your right foot. Then practice with the outside of your left foot and the inside of your right foot.

■ Position yourself at different angles in relation to your partner and practice kicking to your partner from these positions. The ability to kick at different angles is important in passing the ball to teammates and in kicking for a goal in games.

□ Be sure you practice with both your right foot and your left foot.

□ Remember to practice with both the inside and the outside of each foot.

Kicking to a Traveling Partner

Arrange sets of partners at one end of the playing field, approximately fifteen feet from each other. One of the two partners has a ball for kicking. See Figure 21-7.

Travel the length of the playing field, passing the ball to each other as you travel.

□ Kick the ball along the ground, not in the air.

□ Pass to your partner while you're on the move; don't stop to execute the kick.

□ When you're receiving the pass, remember to slow the momentum of the ball with a trap before you tap.

□ Remember to pass the ball ahead of your partner so he can continue jogging without having to pause or stop.

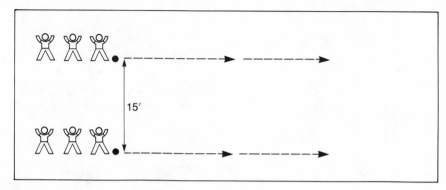

Figure 21-7 Kicking to a traveling partner.

The second set of partners may begin their travel/pass when the partners in front of them are one-third the distance of the field, or you may signal when each set of partners is to begin traveling.

Passing to a Partner in General Space

Travel in general space, dribbling and passing to your partner. All other players will be traveling and passing at the same time, so it is important that you be aware of others and passing in open spaces. Ready? Begin.

- ☐ To avoid other people, remember to trap the ball momentarily or change the direction of the dribble.
- ☐ Your partner may no longer be directly across from you each time you pass. Pass to your partner wherever she is: to the left or the right, in front or in back of you.
- ☐ Because your partner will be at varying distances from you when you pass the ball, adjust the force of each kick to each distance.

Playing One on One Soccer

Select a partner whose tap/dribble skills are very similar to your skills. Cooperatively decide the boundaries for your area; a small area provides more practice. Partner 1 begins to travel and dribble the soccer ball within that area; partner 2 attempts to gain possession of the ball by using her feet to trap the ball or tap it away.

- ☐ Contact the ball, not the person.
- ☐ Gain possession of the ball; don't kick it away.

■ If you gain possession of the ball, begin your dribble as the offensive player; your partner will be the defense.

If partners are unmatched in skill, give a signal for the change from offense to defense. That is, each time partner 2 gains possession of the ball, she will give it back to partner 1, who continues to tap/dribble until the signal to switch positions is given.

■ Within your area, set up two marker cones *(or milk jugs)* as a goal. Partner 1 will tap/dribble until within scoring range *(ten to twelve feet of the goal)* and then kick for the goal. Partner 2 will attempt to gain possession of the ball, using his feet only. After each kick for the goal, switch positions.

■ You may want to design a game using the skills of the soccer dribble and kicking for the goal. Work cooperatively with your partner to decide the rules of the game, scoring, boundaries. Can you think of a name for your game? *(See Chapter 26.)*

Playing Two on One Soccer

Form groups of three; two of you will be offensive players, and one of you will be a defensive player. The two offensive players will tap/dribble and pass to each other within the boundaries of your soccer area. The defensive player will attempt to gain possession of the ball by intercepting passes or tapping the ball away on the dribble.

■ Each team will have possession of the ball *(offense)* for two minutes. See how many goals you can score within that interval.

■ The offensive team must execute at least two passes before attempting a kick for the goal.

 □ Remember, soccer is a noncontact game.

 □ The emphasis is on control of the ball, not kick and chase.

PROFICIENCY LEVEL

At the proficiency level, we give children opportunities for using the skill of kicking in group games and for learning the strategy of offensive/defensive participation. Children play self-designed games, or the teacher chooses the games. These games involve relationships that are made increasingly complex by the number of players and types of strategies required.

Activities Leading to Skill Development

Kicking at Small Stationary Targets

Place marker cones six feet apart to serve as a target. Place a line for kicking fifteen to twenty feet from the target. See Figure 21-8.

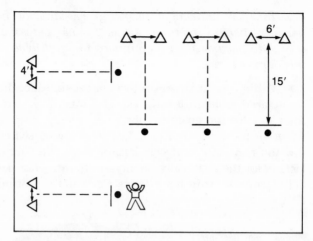

Figure 21-8 Kicking at small targets.

Each person will have ten kicks at the goal; mentally record your score. After each person has kicked ten times, move the cones closer together until they're three feet apart. Each person then kicks ten times at this target. Compare this score with your score for the six-foot target.

Kicking at a Moving Target

Suspend a hoop from a rope hanging from a frame, wall bars, or outdoor playground equipment. Partners may also hold the hoops for each other.

Partner 1 starts the swing of the suspended hoop or moves back and forth with the hoop she is holding in her hand. Partner 2 then kicks at the moving target, attempting to kick the ball through the moving hoop. After five trials, partners should change places.

Playing Minisoccer

Set up milk jugs and marker cones as goals.

Form groups of six to eight persons to play this soccer-type game. The milk jugs and marker cones are the goals. Cooperatively decide the rules, scoring, and the boundaries. I'll place only one limitation on the game: each member of the offensive team must dribble the ball before making a kick for the goal. *(See Chapter 26.)*

Playing Soccer Keep Away

The object of Soccer Keep Away is to keep the ball away from the opponents using the tap/dribble and passing skills you've been practicing. The game is

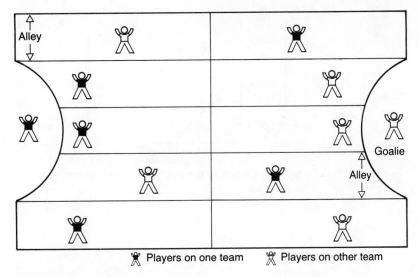

Players on one team   Players on other team

Figure 21-9 Alley Soccer.

played with two teams, three to six people on each team. To start, one person throws the ball *(two hands, overhead)* in from the sideline. Play continues with the ball being dribbled and passed as the other team attempts to gain possession by trapping, intercepting, or gaining control of the dribble.

Playing Alley Soccer

This game and Cone Soccer are for children at the proficiency level. Since all the children in a class are rarely ready for games of this type at the same time (see Chapter 26), youngsters not at the proficiency level can be practicing different types of kicking.

Divide the playing field into five equal alleys; see Figure 21-9. Place marker cones six feet apart at each end of the field.

Alley Soccer is an activity that uses dribbling, passing, and kicking for a goal. Each team has six players—one player for each alley plus a goalie. Players may travel the length of their alley but can't cross into another alley. Your task is to dribble, avoid the opponent in your alley, pass to teammates, and kick for the goal. At regular intervals, I'll give the signal to rotate alleys; this rotation will allow each of you to play each position.

Playing Cone Soccer

Place a marker cone at either end of the playing area, see Figure 21-10. Spray paint (or use marking dust) a circle ten feet in diameter around each cone.

Cone Soccer emphasizes dribbling, passing, and kicking for accuracy. The object

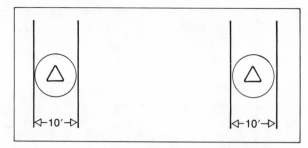

Figure 21-10 Cone Soccer. Dimensions of the playing area may be adjusted to the size of the available area and the number of players.

of the game is to kick the ball, knock over the other team's cone, and protect your own cone. No one is allowed inside the circle to kick or to defend. If one team makes body contact, the other team gets a free kick on the spot; everyone must be three feet away for the free kick. The game can be played with two to six people per team.

A good way to divide teams for equal skill is to ask children to select a partner and then place the selected partners on opposite teams (see Chapter 14).

LEVELS OF PUNTING SKILL PROFICIENCY

Punting is a form of kicking; a ball is released from the hands and kicked while it's in the air. This is a difficult skill for children to master. Because the punt involves a complex coordination of body movements—moving the body forward, dropping the ball accurately, and kicking it before it reaches the ground—we've found it best to introduce the punt after children have practiced other types of kicking.

When children first try to punt, they toss the ball up and then kick it with their knee or leg rather than their foot. Often the novice punter may try to contact the ball after it bounces. We give children at the precontrol level round, lightweight balls and challenge them to contact the balls with their foot before the balls touch the ground. At this level we emphasize dropping the ball rather than tossing it and moving forward to make contact rather than standing in one place.

When children continually contact the ball with their feet before the ball

Punting is a difficult skill for children to master.

hits the ground, we begin to provide control-level experiences to expand the basic skill. Such experiences include:

1. Punting for distance
2. Punting for height
3. Punting different types of balls
4. Punting for accuracy

At the utilization level, experiences are designed to combine punting with other factors. Appropriate activities include:

1. Punting to a partner
2. Catching and punting within a limited time

At the proficiency level, children are able to punt in relation to unpredictable, dynamic situations, such as might occur in a football or a rugby game.

Ideas for varying the contexts in which punting skill can be practiced are presented in our progression spiral on p. 446. As in previous chapters, we encourage you to alter the method of organization, as suggested in Chapter 4. Study the following Key Observation Points to check youngsters' punting skills.

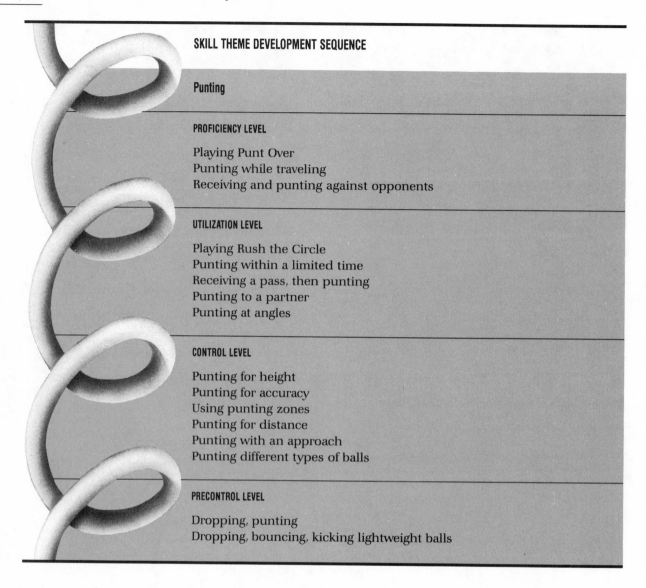

SKILL THEME DEVELOPMENT SEQUENCE

Punting

PROFICIENCY LEVEL

Playing Punt Over
Punting while traveling
Receiving and punting against opponents

UTILIZATION LEVEL

Playing Rush the Circle
Punting within a limited time
Receiving a pass, then punting
Punting to a partner
Punting at angles

CONTROL LEVEL

Punting for height
Punting for accuracy
Using punting zones
Punting for distance
Punting with an approach
Punting different types of balls

PRECONTROL LEVEL

Dropping, punting
Dropping, bouncing, kicking lightweight balls

KEY OBSERVATION POINTS / Punting

1. Does the child drop the ball rather than toss it in the air for the punt?

2. Is the child's kicking foot extended for contact on the instep (shoelaces) rather than with the toes?

3. Does the child make contact at the right height for a 45° angle of flight rather than too soon or too late?

MATURE STAGE

When children are at the mature stage of punting, do their punts look similar to the following sequence? The child makes a rapid approach of one or more steps that culminates in a leap just before contact. If a leap does not precede contact, the forward momentum may be enhanced by a large step. The ball is contacted at or below knee level as a result of the ball having been released in a forward and downward direction. The momentum of the swinging leg carries the punter upward off the surface and forward after contact.

Sources: Adapted from "Developmental Sequence of Punting," mimeographed materials, by V. Seefeldt & J. Haubenstricker, presented at the University of Georgia, Athens, June 1978; *Fundamental Motor Patterns*, 2nd ed., by R. L. Wickstrom. 1977, Philadelphia: Lea & Febiger.

ASSESSMENT GUIDE / Punting

TASK   Standing behind the kicking line, punt (drop and kick) the round ball so it travels through the air and lands within the target zone.

Note to Teachers. If the first trial isn't successful, give children a second attempt. The accompanying diagram shows the target zone, which is twelve by twenty feet wide.

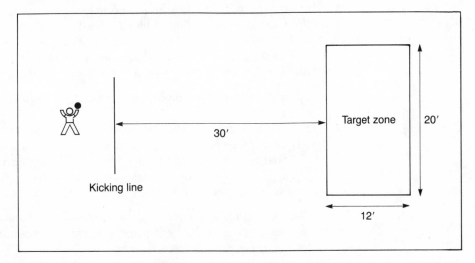

GUIDE   The children are ready for precontrol- or control-level tasks when you observe that:

1. They're unable to contact the ball before it touches the ground.
2. The ball travels straight up or back over their heads.
3. The ball travels forward but not far enough to land within the target zone.
4. The aerial flight is at such a left or right angle that the ball doesn't land within the target zone.

The children are ready for utilization- or proficiency-level tasks when you observe that they're able to punt the ball so it travels forward and lands within the target zone.

PRECONTROL LEVEL

At the precontrol level, we focus on giving children repeated opportunities for dropping a ball, contacting it before it touches the ground, and sending the ball in the intended direction. The goal is for children to consistently contact the ball with their feet before the ball hits the ground.

Activities Leading to Skill Development

Dropping, Bouncing, Kicking Lightweight Balls

Position the balls for kicking around the perimeter of the gym, approximately fifteen feet from the walls.

Stand behind a kicking ball and face the wall. Hold the ball with both hands at waist height. Take one step forward on your nonpreferred kicking foot and then swing your preferred kicking leg forward as you drop the ball. Let the ball bounce one time, then contact it with the top of your foot, sending the ball forward through the air. Quickly retrieve the ball and get in position to wait for the next kicking signal. *(Teacher or child demonstrates.)*

- □ Extend your toes downward to provide a large, flat surface for contact with the ball.
- □ Contact the ball with your instep—your shoelaces or the Velcro closing.
- □ Your preferred kicking foot is usually the same as your preferred hand, that is, the hand you throw a ball with, the hand you write with.
- □ Remember to drop the ball; don't toss it up.
- □ Keep your eyes on the ball until it leaves your foot.

This task lets the teacher observe the drop and ascertain the child's ability to visually track a ball. At this time we aren't concerned about where the ball travels or how much force is used.

Dropping, Punting

Place the balls for kicking around the gym, about twenty feet from the wall.

Stand behind a kicking ball and face the wall. Hold the ball in both your hands at waist height. Take a step forward on your nonpreferred foot. Release the ball from your hands as you swing your kicking leg forward, contacting the ball before it touches the floor. This drop-kick action is called a *punt*.

- □ Remember to point your toes *(extend your foot)* so the ball will travel forward.
- □ It's most important to watch the ball until you see it leave your foot.
- □ Lean slightly backward when you punt to counterbalance the forward swing of your kicking leg.

At a height of four to six feet, suspend stretch ropes between standards or across chairs.

- ■ Stand approximately ten feet behind the rope. Punt the ball so it travels over the rope. Retrieve the ball and kick from the opposite side of the rope.

- ☐ If you're having trouble contacting the ball for the punt, let it bounce one time before kicking it.
- ☐ Remember, keep your eyes on the ball until it leaves your foot.
- ☐ Remember to drop the ball, not toss it.

Children who are having difficulty can practice punting a balloon to help them understand the concept of dropping, not tossing, the object to be punted.

CONTROL LEVEL

At the control level, children need opportunities to punt different types of balls to develop increasing distance and consistency. We focus on one factor at a time rather than a combination of factors. For example, distance is emphasized and then accuracy.

Activities Leading to Skill Development

Punting Different Types of Balls

Around the playing field, place a variety of balls: foam, deflated rubber, plastic, foam football.

Practice punting with the different types of balls. Some are heavy, some are light; all are of a different shape. Practice with each type until you can punt successfully three out of five trials.

- ☐ For a successful punt, contact the ball before it touches the floor, and kick so the ball travels forward through the air.
- ☐ Remember to extend your kicking foot to provide a solid kicking surface.
- ☐ Hold the football with one end facing the direction the ball is to travel.

Punting with an Approach

Select the type of ball you feel is best for your punting. Take a series of quick steps forward. As your kicking leg moves from back to front for the contact with the ball, slightly hop on your supporting leg so you're actually airborne for the contact.

- ☐ Your last step before contact will probably be a large one, almost like a leap.
- ☐ Your weight should be balanced over your support leg.
- ☐ Remember to lean backward to counterbalance the forceful forward swing of your kicking leg.
- ☐ Quickly straighten your kicking leg at the moment of contact. *(Teacher or child demonstrates.)*

■ Practice until you can successfully punt three times in a row. When I watch your punting action I should see the following:

1. A series of quick steps
2. Your body airborne for contact
3. The ball being dropped, not tossed
4. Your instep making contact with the ball

Punting for Distance

Have colored jugs the children can use for markers.

Punt the ball as far as possible. Place a colored jug at the spot where the ball first touches the ground and then try to punt beyond the jug. Each time you better your distance, move your marker to that spot.

□ Remember, the 45° angle of flight is best for distance. To achieve that angle, properly extend your foot and make contact with the ball at the right moment.
□ If you contact the ball too high and/or if your toes aren't extended, the flight will be high and lofty rather than forward.
□ For increased power on the punt, concentrate on straightening your leg when you contact the ball.

■ Each time you punt, try to make the ball travel slightly beyond your previous best. Always strive to punt farther.

When a new factor (distance) is added, children may modify their kicking patterns. Some individuals may need verbal clues, for example, "drop the ball" or "move forward for contact."

Using Punting Zones

Use colored tape, spray paint, marker cones, or colored streamers to mark a series of target zones; each zone is approximately fifteen feet long. Target zones (see Figure 21-11) may be numbered, color coded, or named for professional teams, states, etc.

Approach the kicking line with a series of steps; punt the ball for maximum distance. Mentally note the zone the ball first lands in. Retrieve the ball and get ready for another turn.

□ Remember to keep your eyes on the ball until it leaves your foot.
□ The kick is a continuation of the approach; don't run, stop, kick.

A key component in punting for distance is practice. Consistently marking the zones for short to long distance each time they're used lets children check themselves against their previous best.

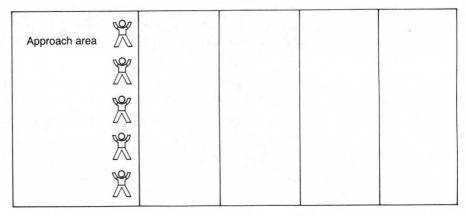

Figure 21-11 Punting zones.

Punting for Accuracy

We previously used the target zones in punting for distance. Now we're going to focus on accuracy. Can you consistently make the ball land in a particular area? Practice your punting from behind the kicking line to review the skill and to determine the zone that is your best distance. Try to consistently punt the ball so it lands within that zone.

■ Test yourself. Punt the ball five times, attempting to make the ball land within that zone each time.

■ Punt the ball so it lands within the first target zone.

■ Choose a zone midway between the first target and your best distance. Punt the ball so it lands within this target zone.

■ Practice each of your selected zones until you can successfully punt three out of five balls into that zone.

□ Don't forget to approach the kicking line with a series of steps.

□ The amount of force you need depends on the distance to be covered; adjust your power. Don't always kick "as hard as possible."

Punting for Height

Sometimes you want the ball to travel in a high, lofty aerial position rather than at a 45° angle, to adjust the forward distance of the punt. Punt the ball so it travels as high as possible.

□ Contact the ball directly underneath so it travels upward.

□ Time the drop of the ball and the swing of your kicking leg so you contact the ball close to waist height.

■ Punt the ball high in the air; see if you can catch it before it touches the ground.

Because of the hazards of running to catch while looking up, this activity must be done in a large outdoor field space. If such a space is unavailable, some children can practice punting for height while others practice punting for distance.

■ Select one of the first three target zones as your target area. Punt the ball so it travels in a high, lofty aerial pathway to that zone.

Students highly skilled in punting for accuracy will enjoy the challenge of smaller targets, such as hoops.

UTILIZATION LEVEL

At the utilization level, we provide punting experiences in dynamic situations. This encourages children to use punting skills in combination with other factors, such as time and accuracy. Relationships with a partner may be stressed by focusing on punting so that a partner can catch the ball or punt shortly after receiving a throw from a partner.

Activities Leading to Skill Development

Punting at Angles

Using spray paint, marker dust, or milk jugs, divide the target zone area lengthwise (see Figure 21-12).

Practice punting into the different target zones—to the right and to the left of where you're standing

■ Select a target zone and practice until you can consistently punt the ball into that zone. Then select a zone on the opposite side.
■ Practice until you can select a target zone, tell a partner which one you've chosen, and then punt three out of five balls into that zone. How about five out of five?

Punting to a Partner

Using the target zones as a measure of distance, tell your partner where to stand for the two of you to punt to each other; choose a distance at which both of you have been successful. Punt the ball so your partner can catch it without moving more than a couple of steps.

☐ Remember, you're punting to your partner, not beyond him or to the right or to the left of him.

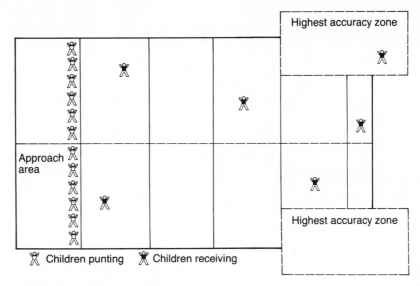

Figure 21-12 Punting at angles.

- Punt so your partner can catch without moving from her self-space.
- From behind the kicking line, practice punting to your partner in each of the target zones: near/far, right/left angles.
  - □ Punt some balls high and lofty, others at a 45° angle.

Receiving a Pass, Then Punting

Select a partner with whom you can work well independently. Separate to a distance from which you can both throw and catch successfully. Partner 1 throws the ball to partner 2, who receives the pass and punts the ball across the playing field. You're attempting to punt as quickly as possible after receiving the pass. Alternate positions—passer and punter.

- □ Remember to drop the ball, not toss it up.
- □ Take a couple of steps before punting, even though you're punting quickly after the pass.
- □ If you're using a football, be sure it's in the proper position (*end toward/away from you*) for the punt.

With children throwing, catching, and punting, space awareness can be a safety factor. We've found it best to organize this activity with all passes and punts traveling in the same direction, i.e., across the playing area or end to end— not a mixture of directions.

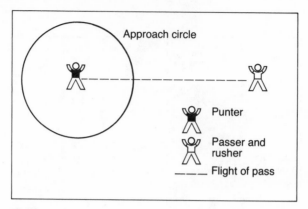

Figure 21-13 Partner pass and rush punting.

Punting Within a Limited Time

Partner 2 throws the ball to partner 1. As soon as partner 1 receives the pass, partner 2 begins to count "one alligator, two alligators, three alligators." When partner 1 receives the pass, he punts it across the playing field as quickly as possible, trying to complete the punt before partner 2 counts "three alligators." Partner 1 retrieves the ball and switches positions with partner 2.

□ Follow all the proper steps, even though you're punting quickly.

Playing Rush the Circle

Use spray paint or marking dust to draw a ten-foot-diameter or larger circle on the playing field. Draw a passing line approximately fifteen feet from the edge of that circle (see Figure 21-13).

Select a partner whose throwing/catching skills are similar to yours. The punter will be positioned inside the circle; the passer will be approximately twenty feet away, behind the passing line. The passer throws the ball from behind the passing line. When the punter receives the catch, the passer runs toward the circle, trying to reach the circle before the punter can kick the ball. The punter punts the ball as quickly as possible when he receives the pass. In other words, the punter tries to punt the ball before the passer reaches the circle.

□ Punters, keep your eyes on the ball for the punt, not on the rusher.
□ Remember the approach and airborne hop for the punt.

Some children will enjoy developing point systems and minigames for each task. Others will be content to practice the skill in the changing situation.

PROFICIENCY LEVEL

Punting experiences at the proficiency level will lead to the ability to punt accurately and for distance in dynamic and unpredictable situations. The relationships will be more complex. Emphasis is on punting while traveling and on working with others in game situations.

Activities Leading to Skill Development

Receiving and Punting Against Opponents

Working in groups of three, two partners will assume the offensive positions of passer and punter. The other player will be the defense, attempting to block the punt. Offense: Partner 1 throws the ball to partner 2 from approximately twenty feet. Partner 2 punts the ball down the playing field. Defense: Rush the offensive, from the twenty-foot distance of the passer, to tag the punter before she releases the kick. You can't begin the rush until the punter receives the pass.

  □ Remember the importance of the approach steps, even under the pressure of the rush.

  ■ Alternate positions until each person has been the punter, the passer, the defense.

Punting While Traveling

Run with the ball the distance of two target zones, then quickly punt the ball. Focus on the accuracy of contacting the ball for forward travel.

  ■ Focus on the accuracy of the ball landing in a specific zone.
  ■ Focus on punting for maximum distance.

Playing Punt Over

Use spray paint or marking dust to outline the playing field into target zones, each zone ten feet long. The last zone on each end is the end zone. Teams may choose to use footballs or playground balls.

You can play Punt Over in groups of four or six. The object of the game is to punt the ball over your opponents so it lands in the end zone. Here are the rules:

  1. Play begins with the punting team in their first zone; one person punts the ball toward the opposite end zone.
  2. If the opponents catch the ball, they advance forward one zone before they punt.

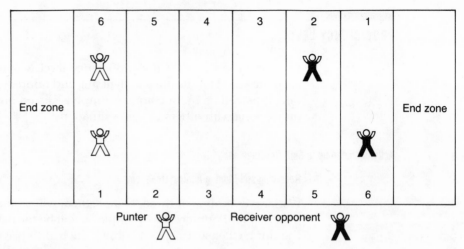

Figure 21-14 Punt over.

3. If the opponents retrieve the ball short of the end zone, they punt from that spot.
4. The game consists of alternate punts; the number of points awarded for landing in the end zone corresponds to the zone from which the ball was punted (*See Figure 21-14.*)

The groups decide cooperatively:

1. If the defensive team catches the ball on the punt, can they run to the opposite end zone to score?
2. Can you rush the punter after the punter has received the pass?

READING COMPREHENSION QUESTIONS

1. What is the difference between a kick and a punt?
2. What is a mature kicking pattern? What is a mature punting pattern?
3. What kicking tasks lead to the development of a mature kicking pattern?
4. Describe appropriate kicking tasks for each of the four levels of skill proficiency.
5. At the precontrol level, why do you number the balls?
6. Where does a child's foot need to contact the ball so that it travels into the air, along the ground?
7. What experiences do children have at each of the four skill levels when they're learning to punt a ball?
8. What is the outcome when a child makes contact with the ball too soon in a punt? What happens when the child makes contact too late?

Throwing and Catching

Throwing and catching go together just as nicely as soup and a sandwich. The two skills, however, are opposite in movement focus and unusually difficult for young children to master.

Although throwing and catching are complementary, we've learned that children have limited success in combining throwing and catching in game situations unless each skill has been given specific attention and developed in appropriate practice situations. It is important that the teacher be certain that children can throw *and* catch with relative success before progressing to the utilization and proficiency levels. Activities at those levels—throwing to a running partner or trying to prevent an opponent from catching a ball—require mature throwing and catching skills. Too often teachers neglect catching, feeling it isn't that important. But as anyone who has ever watched a professional baseball game knows, catching is a skill, a skill that often determines whether a game is won or lost.

459

LEVELS OF THROWING SKILL PROFICIENCY

Throwing is a basic movement pattern performed to propel an object away from the body. Although throwing style (overhand, underhand, sidearm) and purpose may vary, the basic pattern remains consistent:

1. An object to be sent away is grasped with one or both hands.
2. In a preparatory phase, momentum builds for the throw.
3. The actual propulsive phase—the release of the object—is performed.
4. In a follow-through phase, the body maintains control and balance while using up the momentum of the throw.

The physical educator in an elementary school setting will observe a wide range of throwing abilities among a class. Initially, the teacher should focus on ascertaining each child's skill level. When the youngsters manipulate objects such as beanbags or yarn balls, the teacher can observe individual children for significant developmental characteristics (see the following Key Observation Points for throwing as a guide).

KEY OBSERVATION POINTS / Throwing

1. Does the child take a forward step on the foot opposite the throwing arm?

NO

YES

2. Do the child's hips and spine rotate so that they can uncoil in forceful derotation?

NO   YES

3. Is the child's elbow flexed and held away from the body and extended on the backswing?

NO   YES

After making a gross assessment of each child's development in throwing, the teacher has a basis for structuring appropriate instructional tasks. (See our progression spiral for throwing and catching activities on p. 466.)

For children at the precontrol level, the first tasks are designed to provide a multitude of throwing experiences. Many of these experiences are designed to elicit distance throws, in which children use more mature throwing patterns.

We expose children at the control level to various contexts so that they use throwing actions in different but relatively static situations:

1. Throwing fast/throwing slow
2. Varying the distance of throws
3. Throwing under/throwing over (a net or other obstacle)
4. Tossing a beanbag at a target
5. Throwing a yarn ball through a hoop
6. Throwing a foam ball into a basket

When children begin to focus primarily on hitting a target, they sometimes regress and use inefficient throwing patterns. Generally, longer throws elicit mature throwing patterns. Thus, it's a good idea to vary distance, sometimes fostering success at hitting the target, other times enhancing the development of a mature throwing pattern.

Once the children are able to perform smooth throwing actions in a variety of static contexts, they're ready for utilization-level experiences. At this level, children are given tasks that encourage refinement of skills and an increase in the breadth of throwing abilities. Appropriate activities include:

1. Throwing accurately while running
2. Throwing at a dodging target (for example, a partner)
3. Throwing at a goal while off the ground
4. Throwing a Frisbee accurately

Children are at the proficiency level of throwing when they're able to effectively throw in the unpredictable contexts of gamelike situations and are ready to study throwing as it's used in the relatively complex and changing environments that characterize sports. Appropriate tasks include:

1. Throwing a ball at a target (for example, basketball goal) as an opponent attempts to block and deflect the throw
2. Throwing a ball to a partner so the ball can be caught without being intercepted by an opposing player
3. Making several accurate throws in a row (as in bowling and basketball free throw shooting)

LEVELS OF CATCHING SKILL PROFICIENCY

Catching is the receiving and controlling of an object by the body or its parts. Initially, a young child's reaction to an oncoming object is to fend it off, to protect herself—often by using the whole body rather than the arms and hands. Typically, a ball bounces against the young child's chest as the remainder of the body scrambles to surround it and still maintain equilibrium.

Children's catching abilities, like their throwing skills, vary immensely. The teacher who plans learning sessions in which young children manipulate soft, textured objects (such as beanbags, foam balls, or yarn balls) can observe for the developmental characteristics of catching (see the following Key Observation Points for catching as a guide).

KEY OBSERVATION POINTS / Catching

1. Are the child's elbows flexed rather than extended in preparation for making the catch?

NO   YES

2. Does the child make the catch with the hands alone rather than by trapping the ball against the body?

NO   YES

3. Are the child's elbows extended as the catch is made so the child can absorb the force of the ball?

4. Do the child's eyes track the ball into the hands?

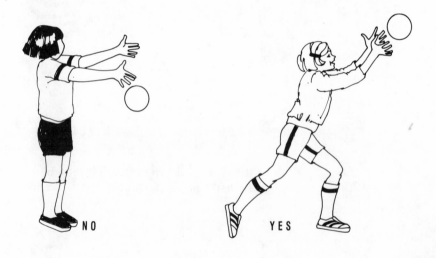

Our progression spiral for throwing and catching (p. 466) has activities the teacher can expand while leading children from the precontrol to the proficiency level. Initially, children need experiences that repeatedly challenge them to accurately manipulate their arms and hands into position to receive an object. When focusing on the catching performances of children at the precontrol level, we find that many of these youngsters have difficulty throwing an object accurately to themselves or a partner; and an inaccurate throw is

Throwing and catching complement each other and are taught together.

difficult to catch. We've found it helps to teach the skill of throwing before teaching the skill of catching. Older, more skilled children serving as teacher aides can gently and accurately throw a ball to children who are at the precontrol level. And children can work with partners. For example, one child stands on a chair with a ball held in an outstretched hand and drops the ball to the partner, who is positioned directly below, ready to catch.

Children at the precontrol level experience greater success when soft, textured, relatively large balls are used. The primary task is for the child to catch a ball thrown directly to him.

Children at the control level need opportunities to develop the skills used when catching with the right and left hands, at either side of the body, and at various levels. Appropriate tasks for children at this level include:

1. Catching in different places around the body
2. Catching objects thrown to different levels
3. Moving one step in any direction to catch
4. Catching with the right hand and the left hand
5. Catching with an implement

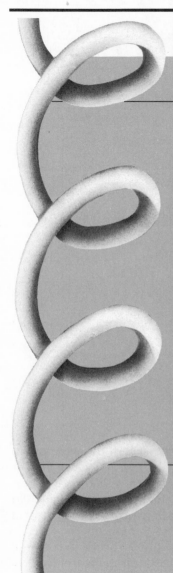

SKILL THEME DEVELOPMENT SEQUENCE

Throwing and Catching

CONTROL LEVEL

Throwing and catching over a bench with a partner
Throwing and catching over a net with a partner
Throwing and catching with a partner
Throwing for distance
Throwing a ball against a wall and catching the rebound
Catching with a scoop
Throwing a Frisbee
Throwing backhand to a target
Throwing to high targets
Throwing underhand to hoops
Throwing underhand at targets
Throwing at can targets
Throwing at a stationary target
Catching in different places around the body
Throwing an object to different levels and catching it
Bouncing a ball to self and catching it
Throwing overhand, underhand, and sidearm
Throwing sidearm
Throwing underhand
Throwing overhand

PRECONTROL LEVEL

Tossing to self and catching
Catching from a skilled thrower
Catching a rolling ball
Throwing at a large target
Throwing a yarn ball against the wall

When children are consistently able to catch a variety of objects with one or both hands, they're at the utilization level and can begin to use their catching skills in dynamic, unpredictable situations. Appropriate tasks include:

1. Catching a passed football while traveling
2. Catching a kicked soccer ball
3. Catching a rebounding ball

Children at the proficiency level are ready to learn to catch in changing

Throwing and Catching

PROFICIENCY LEVEL

Playing passball
Playing European handball (modified)
Playing four-person football
Playing Frisbee Football
Playing half-court basketball (modified)
Playing Hitting the Pin
Playing Keep Away
Throwing to avoid a defender
Running the bases
Tagging a base runner: Run Down
Playing Frisbee Stretch

UTILIZATION LEVEL

Throwing while in the air
Catching to throw quickly to a target
Catching to throw quickly to a partner
Playing Frisbee Golf
Performing a target backaway
Throwing for distance and accuracy
Throwing to a moving target
Throwing to make a partner move to catch
Throwing on the move
Throwing and catching while traveling
Moving to catch

environments. Experiences for children at the proficiency level challenge them to catch an object while traveling in relationship to other players. Appropriate activities include:

1. Losing a defender to catch a ball
2. Catching a rapidly thrown or hit ball that bounces against the ground
3. Catching a ball with one hand while off balance or in the air
4. Catching a ball that someone else is trying to catch

This youngster moves one step to her right—ready to catch.

ASSESSMENT GUIDE / Throwing and Catching

Note to Teachers. String a rope from a height of eight feet; supply a tennis ball. A number of students can perform the task if you use a longer rope and several tennis balls.

TASK   Throw the ball over the rope and catch it before it hits the ground on the other side of the rope. For this assessment, no special type of throw is required—that is, you can throw underhand or overhand.

GUIDE   Children who are unable to catch the ball will benefit from tasks at the pre-control and control levels. Students who are able to catch the ball twice in a row are ready for tasks at the utilization and proficiency levels.

PRECONTROL LEVEL

Instructional tasks at the precontrol level give children opportunities to repeat-edly throw and catch. Emphasis is on throws made directly to the children, enabling them to experience success in catching.

Activities Leading to Skill Development

Throwing a Yarn Ball Against the Wall

Place carpet squares about twenty feet from the wall, one square for each child. See Figure 22-1 for construction of a yarn ball.

Throw the ball against the wall as hard as you can. Use the hand you hold your pencil with. Watch how I throw. *(Demonstrate.)*

- ▫ When you throw, your side should be toward the wall, so if you walked straight ahead, you'd walk along the wall, not toward it. *(A demonstration may be necessary.)*
- ▫ When you throw, be sure that your hip (belly button) moves away from the target so that your body winds up or coils like a spring.
- ▫ Step with the opposite foot from your throwing hand.

Some children have a hard time remembering which foot to step with to achieve opposition. To help these children, place an old wrist sweatband around the appropriate foot as a reminder to step with your opposite foot. You can also use a large loose-fitting rubber band for this purpose.

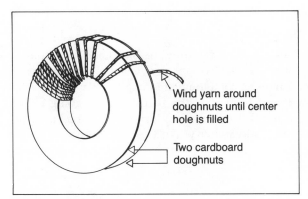

Wind yarn around doughnuts until center hole is filled

Two cardboard doughnuts

Figure 22-1 Construction of a yarn ball.

1. Cut two "doughnuts"—rings made from cardboard—with a diameter one inch larger than you want the diameter of the yarn ball to be. The center hole of each doughnut should be about one inch in diameter.

2. Cut several ten-foot lengths of yarn. Rug yarn is excellent, but any heavy yarn will do. A one-ounce skein will make two three-inch balls.

3. Place one doughnut on top of the other. Wind yarn around each doughnut (through the hole and around the circle) until the cardboard is covered and each hole is full of yarn.

4. Slip scissors between the doughnuts at the outer edge, and cut the yarn all the way around.

5. Slip nylon string between the doughnuts, making a circle around the yarn in the middle. Pull tight, and then make a strong knot.

6. Pull the doughnuts off, and fluff the ball. You can trim any longer strands of yarn to make a smoother, rounder ball.

     □ Your arm is extended from your body so that your elbow is almost straight when you let go of the ball.

     ■ This time move three steps farther away from the wall. When you throw, try to remember these cues: sideways, coil, opposition, elbow. You can think about only one cue each time you throw rather than trying to think about all four cues at the same time.

Throwing at a Large Target

In various places around the room, suspend several large targets (old sheets work well). Attach the top of the sheet to a broom stick or dowel and weight the bottom of the sheet with heavy washers. Attach a rope to both ends of the rod in the top of the sheet and then hang the rope from a basketball goal or the rafters.

Now you have a target to aim at. This kind of target will soak up your ball; your ball won't come bouncing back to you. Your job is to throw at the target as hard as you can and try to make the target move. Remember as you throw to step forward on the foot opposite the hand that is holding the ball.

A student teacher once used this idea but embellished it with his own creativeness. It was Halloween, so on the target he painted the school, a full moon, and a witch flying over the school on a broom stick. Did the children ever throw hard to try and hit the target once there was a little colored paint and a semblance of a drawing to aim at! You don't have to be an artist—a little tempera paint, a little imagination, and a good story to tell the children are all that it takes.

Catching a Rolling Ball

With your partner, you're going to practice catching the ball. Each pair should be in their own space and seated on the floor about five feet away from each other, with legs spread apart. Partner 1 rolls the ball to partner 2, who catches it with his or her hands. Partner 2 then rolls the ball back. I'm going to be watching to see if you use your hands to catch and don't trap the ball against your body. You'll know you're a good catcher when you can always stop the ball with your hands.

Catching from a Skilled Thrower

You'll need help for this task, for example, from the classroom teacher, the principal, older students who've earned a reward, parents, or even grandparents. This activity is a wonderful way to actively involve others in the physical education program. You'll also need a yarn ball for every set of partners.

The catching abilities of young children vary.

For this task you'll have a "big" partner. You and your partner will stand about four to five feet apart in your own space. Your big partner will throw the yarn ball to you so you can practice catching it using just your hands. When you catch the ball, throw it back to your big partner, who'll then throw it to you again. For you to become as good a catcher as your big partner, you must try to catch the ball using only your hands and not let the ball get stuck against your stomach or chest. Remember: hands only.

☐ Watch the ball so closely that you can see the different colored pieces of yarn as they come toward you.

☐ To be a good catcher you must use your hands, but you must also use them a certain way. If a ball is coming to you at a height higher than your shoulders, keep your thumbs together and fingers pointed upward to catch it. If the ball is coming to you so that it'll be below your waist, keep your fingers together and pointed toward the ground. Remember—ball above the waist, thumbs together; ball below the waist, fingers together. *(Demonstrate.)*

The teacher can assess catching abilities by observing the youngsters while they toss and catch yarn balls.

Tossing to Self and Catching

In a space by yourself you're going to practice tossing and catching by yourself. Choose a yarn ball or a beanbag. I'll especially look to see if you're catching with your hands and if your eyes are following the ball or bag all the time, which is called *tracking*.

- □ Toss the ball or bag very close to your body, close enough so the ball or bag doesn't go very high over your head or very far out from your stomach.
- □ Remember the fingers together and thumbs together rule. If the ball or bag goes low, your fingers should be together and pointed toward the floor. If the ball or bag is at a middle level, your thumbs should be together. Watch me.
- □ One thing we haven't talked about yet that really makes good catches is what your hand and arm do after you make the catch. To be a good catcher, you should absorb the force of the catch or make quiet catches. The trick is to "give" with the ball or beanbag as you catch, so that your hand meets the yarn ball or beanbag high in the air and gradually sinks down with it.

If this happens, the ball or beanbag will just float down with your hand and you'll never be quite sure when it really came to rest in your hand. Give it a try—soft catches.

■ If you can toss and catch the yarn ball or beanbag five times in a row, keeping it very close to your body, now toss it just a little farther away and see if you can still catch it. Each time keep in mind the hints: watch, reach, give.

■ This is your challenge for the day. See if you can toss and catch the ball or beanbag ten times in a row without moving more than one step from your space. It helps to keep the tosses close to your body.

For children at the precontrol level, the emphasis is on providing many throwing experiences. Varying the context too early (for example, placing children in gamelike situations) causes children to use immature throwing patterns in an attempt to achieve the results called for.

CONTROL LEVEL

Children at the control level are ready to focus on catching at different levels, catching at different places around their bodies, and using either hand to catch. Throwing experiences are designed to help the children learn to throw for accuracy and with varied degrees of force and to throw a variety of objects.

Activities Leading to Skill Development

Throwing Overhand

In your own space at the mark, practice throwing at the wall. Throw overhand as hard as you can. I'm going to be looking to see if you're throwing so your arm comes up just past your ear and follows through so that it slaps the target—if the target were close enough. In case you haven't guessed, this is called an *overhand* throw.

◻ Remember the cues: sideways, coil, opposition, elbow.

Throwing Underhand

This time, instead of throwing overhand, you're going to practice throwing almost as if you were bowling. You're going to throw to the wall, but instead of your arm coming by your ear, it'll come just past your knee. This is called an *underhand* throw. *(Teacher or child demonstrates.)*

◻ To make the ball go straight toward the target, when you let go make sure your hand is pointing right at the wall.

Throwing Sidearm

Now you're going to try another different throw. Instead of throwing overarm or underarm, you're going to practice throwing from the side, in a sidearm movement. To do this, your arm will come around from the side of your body. *(Demonstrate.)* Your tendency will be to keep your arm straight as you throw, but that's wrong; your arm should bend at your elbow as it comes around the side. In other words, this task is really a throw, not a fling. Let loose of the ball just before your hand is facing straight at the wall.

Throwing Overhand, Underhand, and Sidearm

Now that you know the names for the three different kinds of throws, you're going to practice the throws on your own. You can practice the throws in any order you want, but make sure that you practice each one at least fifteen times.

□ With each throw that you practice, to make it the best throw possible, step on the foot opposite your throwing arm. I'll be watching for that each time you throw.

■ Here's some more practice. Pick out the throw you're having the most trouble with. Practice only that throw until you can hit the wall ten times in a row. After you can hit the wall ten times with the throw you found the most difficult, pick another throw you're having trouble with and practice it until you can hit the wall ten times in a row. When you can hit the wall ten times in a row with all three throws, take three giant steps back and try again.

Bouncing a Ball to Self and Catching It

You're going to practice catching this time so you can get used to catching a ball that's coming down toward you. In your own space, bounce the playground ball *(or tennis ball)* so that it barely goes over your head and try to catch it as it comes down, before it hits the floor. Remember to use your hands to catch and don't trap the ball against your body.

□ It helps to watch the ball all the time. You should be able to see the ball as it goes into your hands.

■ If you can catch the ball six times in a row, bouncing it the way that you have been, try bouncing it a little higher and still catch it using only your hands. If you have to start using your body to catch the ball again, you know you're bouncing the ball too high.

Throwing an Object to Different Levels and Catching It

This task is to give you more practice catching. In your own space, throw a beanbag *(or yarn ball)* up in the air and catch it. To warm up, throw the object at about head level. Remember to watch the object all the time.

■ Now that you're warmed up, practice throwing the object about arm's length over your head and catching it. This makes catching a little more difficult because there's more force involved.

  ▫ One thing you need to remember here is the idea of soft catches. It's harder to catch from higher throws, so concentrate on meeting the object high *(little fingers together)* and letting it float down.

■ Once you're able to catch the object ten times in a row using soft, quiet catches, you're ready to throw it a little higher still, maybe five feet over your head. Always remember that you must still be able to catch quietly at each level you throw to. If you can't, then you know you're throwing too high and need to bring the throw down a little.

Catching in Different Places Around the Body

You practiced catching an object that goes to different heights; now you're going to practice catching an object that goes to different places around your body. Standing in your own space, throw the beanbag so you have to reach in different places around your body to catch it. This may mean catching it to the sides sometimes, or behind your head. See how many different places you can find to catch the beanbag from without leaving your self-space.

  ▫ Most of us don't like to practice places that are really hard. This time as you practice, pick out two places that you tried to catch and had the hardest time with. Practice those two places until you can catch the beanbag four out of five times.

■ Remember what we worked on before this activity: soft catches. Sometimes we forget about the soft catches. This time practice your same catches in new places around your body, but always try to see that the catches are as quiet as possible. Absorb the force.

■ I'm going to make this task a little harder still. It's easy to catch the beanbag when it's fairly close to your body, but now I want you to practice catching the beanbag so you have to reach to catch it. Really stretch so you feel you're almost going to fall over. It helps to think of keeping one foot glued in place all the time. You stretch from that glued foot because the foot can't move.

  ▫ Don't forget as you're stretching to catch to still try to catch in different places. So the task should be: stretch and reach to catch in different places around your body.

  ▫ One last thing to remember—soft catches. So now there're three things to do: (1) stretch to catch, (2) find different places to catch, and (3) keep the catches soft. *(Pinpoint several children who are doing all three tasks.)*

The success of the previous tasks depends a great deal on the child's ability to throw so that she or he has to stretch. It helps to practice stretching without the throw or simply throwing away from the body. If the students aren't catching on as you think they should, look and see if the reason is the throw.

Throwing at a Stationary Target

Place targets on the wall for each student to aim at. Paper plates with faces and pictures on them make good targets; a carpet square for each child will help them maintain their spacing.

This time you're still going to throw at targets. You'll have to keep your eyes on the target. Each of you has a target in your own space. See how often you can hit it.

- ☐ You must watch the target so you know where the ball is going. Throughout your entire throw, keep your eyes focused on the target.
- ☐ As you throw, don't forget to step forward on the foot opposite your throwing arm. This point is really easy to forget as you start to concentrate more on aiming rather than on throwing.

Youngsters often become so enthralled with hitting the target that they rush their throws and move closer and closer to the target. You can tape lines on the floor (or spray paint on grass) to designate a minimum throwing distance from the target. Encourage the children to slow down and be accurate.

Throwing at Can Targets

Stack tin cans on a bench or other object so that each student has a can target to throw toward. Use carpet squares as starting lines.

With a partner, you're going to practice throwing at the tin cans stacked on the bench in front of you. Stand behind the throwing line as you throw. To start, one of you is the thrower, one of you the stacker. The stacker stands far enough behind the cans so he doesn't get hit if the cans get hit but close enough so he can pick them up quickly if they do. After six throws, trade places. The secret is in the stacking: The faster you stack, the faster the game goes.

- ■ If you can knock the cans over two times in a row, move your carpet square back three giant steps and try throwing from the new distance.
- ☐ With this task, it's really important that you watch the target all the time. If you take your eyes off the cans, even for a second, you're more likely to miss.

When several children are aiming for one target area, we always try to have a throwing area for each child or group or pair of partners, to maximize the number of throwing opportunities.

Throwing Underhand at Targets

On the floor, set up targets such as Indian clubs or a two-liter bottle (such as a soft drink bottle) weighted in the bottom with dirt or sand for every child. Four- to six-inch playground balls work well with this task.

You're going to practice throwing at targets on the ground by using an underhand throw. Each of you has a "pin" to aim for. Using an underhand throw, try to knock the pin over. If you knock it over twice in a row, move one giant step back and try again.

☐ Remember that your hand follows through right to the target.

When you let the children determine the distance from the target, you'll find that they'll be close enough to hit the pin most of the time. As the youngsters improve, you'll notice them gradually moving farther away from the target.

Throwing Underhand to Hoops

You'll need a hoop and beanbag for each pair of children.

This time you're going to practice throwing so your beanbag lands in the hoop that's in the middle of your space on the floor. Throw the beanbag so it lands inside the hoop. Move one giant step back each time the beanbag lands in the hoop. Your partner will collect the beanbag and throw it back to you. After five throws, switch places. Remember: The best way to do this is to throw underhand.

Throwing at a target.

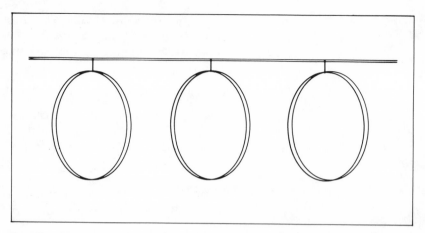

Figure 22-2 Hoops suspended from rope.

■ A game you can play is called Around the World. Start in one place and try to hit the hoop. If you hit the hoop from that place, move to the next spot and try to hit it from there. If you miss, your partner gets a chance to toss. Whenever you miss, trade places with your partner. You can keep adding new spots to throw from as you get better.

□ Remember: Watch the target and follow through with your hand.

Throwing to High Targets

Across the space, string ropes with hoops attached to them; the hoops will be the targets (Figure 22-2). String some of the targets at chest height; string others at a height over the heads of the children.

You're going to be aiming at a high target or goal. This task will give you good practice for basketball later on. Decide how far away from your goal you want to stand. For this task you'll use your overhand throw.

□ When throwing at a target, remember to watch the target at all times. Give it a try.
□ Remember the cues for overhand throwing: sideways, coil, opposition, elbow.

■ This time you're going to test yourself. Pick a place to stand, and see how many throws in a row you can throw through the hoop. When you make eight out of ten goals, move to a new spot and try for eight out of ten goals again.

Throwing Backhand to a Target

In the ground, put in sticks (similar to horseshoe poles), and have plastic deck rings for each child.

Reed and Sophie, who were five years old, were playing a game in which they threw a ball under their legs to knock over a pile of tin cans. Reed placed her head a bit too far under her legs and inadvertently fell into a forward roll as she released the ball. With an expression of sheer excitement, Reed announced that she'd discovered the "flip throw."

Try to throw the ring so it goes over your stick. This activity is a little different from anything you've done before, so start very close. The throwing action is also different; instead of throwing overhand or underarm, you're actually throwing sort of backward—sidearm using a flick of your wrist away from your body toward the stick. *(A demonstration by the teacher or skilled child is necessary here.)*

■ If you can ring the stick six times in a row from where you're standing, move back a couple of steps and try it again.

Throwing a Frisbee

Now you get to practice throwing a Frisbee. The action involved is similar to the one you just did with the ring: a flick of the wrist to make the Frisbee fly. *(A demonstration is essential here.)* Practice throwing the Frisbee toward your partner and have her throw it back to you. Don't worry about aiming—just try to throw to the general area where your partner is. You'll know you're getting better when the Frisbee flies flat *(not tilted)* each time you throw it.

■ Now try to throw the Frisbee so it goes fairly close to your partner. Start off pretty close together and slowly move farther apart as you improve.

Catching with a Scoop

You'll need plastic scoops and beanbags for each child. See Figure 22-3.

In your self-space, practice throwing the beanbag up with your hand and catching it in the scoop. To be a good catch, the beanbag must stay in the scoop and not bounce out. Again, it helps to keep your eyes on the beanbag at all times and give with the scoop to absorb the force. One of the important things about catching is giving with the beanbag as you catch it so that the catch is quiet. Practice making quiet catches with your scoop.

■ Now your partner will throw the beanbag to you and you'll catch it with the scoop. The partner shouldn't be very far away to begin. After seven throws, trade places.

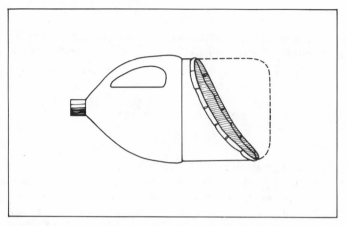

Figure 22-3 Plastic scoop. You can make scoops for throwing and catching by cutting the end and part of the side from large plastic jugs that have grip-type handles. For protection, place tape over the cut edges.

Catching with a scoop is an exciting challenge for a child at the control level.

A baseball glove is an implement that can be used to catch an object, but generally we prefer not to use gloves in our program. When children bring their own gloves to school, there are problems. Many children prefer to not share their gloves with children who don't have gloves. We also have a hard time justifying the expense of purchasing gloves for a physical education program. In the schools we've taught in, we've always wanted other equipment that needs to be purchased and is more important than baseball gloves.

- The idea of giving with the beanbag as you catch it has changed a little with a partner throwing to you. Instead of giving down, as you did when you caught from a throw you made yourself, you have to give down and back. *(A demonstration by the teacher or a skilled student is very useful here.)*

Throwing a Ball Against a Wall and Catching the Rebound

You need enough wall space so that children can spread out and not be in each other's way as they throw and catch. Carpet squares are helpful reminders for the children.

At your carpet square, throw the ball against the wall and catch it on the return.

- As the ball bounces off the wall, try to position your body so that you're behind the ball, not to the side of it. This means moving your feet quickly to get to a new position.
- Another way to have a better chance of catching is to catch the ball at stomach or chest level. *(A demonstration here helps clarify the idea.)*

■ As you practice now, sometimes throw the ball hard and sometimes soft so that you have to move to different positions to catch it. Remember, you want the ball to come up to your stomach or chest.

■ Let's make this a little harder. Try to catch the ball before it bounces twice. If that's still too easy, try to catch the ball before it bounces once. This means that you have to move quickly to get to the ball to catch it. It helps if you throw the ball hard so that it rebounds a good distance off the wall.

On the ground, draw a line approximately five to six feet from the wall. On the wall, draw another line, about two to three feet off the ground.

■ Now throw from behind the line on the ground so the ball hits the wall above the line on the wall. Catch the ball as it rebounds before it hits the ground. Give it a try.

■ We'll make a game out of it this time. I'll time you for one minute. Count

Throwing a ball against a wall and catching the rebound.

to yourself how many times you can hit the wall above the line and catch the ball in the air on the rebound. Remember the number because we'll do it again so you can try to improve your score.

Throwing for Distance

You'll need a large outdoor field. Each group of partners will need a bucket of about ten tennis balls. Often you can get old tennis balls from parents who play tennis. A good idea is to send parents a note at the beginning of the year asking tennis players to save old tennis balls and then collect them on a regular basis. It doesn't take long to accumulate more balls than you need. You'll also need beanbags or soft drink bottles to mark where the balls landed.

You're going to practice throwing long distances. It helps if you've played the outfield in baseball. Throw each tennis ball as far as you can. With markers, your partner will mark your farthest throw and collect the balls. Each time, try to beat your last throw. After you've thrown all your balls, trade places with your partner.

□ There are several secrets to throwing a ball a long way. One of the most important is the principle of *opposition*—stepping forward on the foot opposite the hand that is throwing the ball. When you threw short distances, sometimes you could fake it and not do this, but to throw long distances, you *must* step forward on the opposite foot. Another secret to throwing long distances is *trunk rotation*—turning your hips and upper body back toward your throwing arm before you throw, as if you were making a spring with your body that will uncoil as you throw. This gives you more power. *(Demonstrate.)* This time as you practice, concentrate on coiling before you throw.

Throwing and Catching with a Partner

Throw and catch so that your partner doesn't have to move to catch the ball. To begin, you need to be about ten feet apart. Remember that the key is to watch the ball at all times. You'll probably want to start with an underhand throw.

- We all tend to forget sometimes, but always try to catch the ball with your hands, not trap it against your body.
- It isn't nice to make your partner move all over the place to have to catch the ball—this is a "be nice to your partner" game—so practice the things you learned about aiming. When you let go of the ball, your hand should be aimed right at your partner.
- Try to make *sympathetic* throws, which are throws that have enough force behind them to get there but not so much force that they can't be caught.

■ If you and your partner can make ten throws and catches from the place where you are now without missing, then both of you move back two giant

Time-out temporarily removes a child who was off-task (see Chapter 8) from throwing and catching activities.

steps and practice from there. Do the same thing as before: good throws so your partner doesn't have to move more than a step in either direction to catch.

■ From wherever you're standing, see how many throws and catches you can make without a miss. To count, the ball must be caught, not just batted back to your partner.

■ This time we'll play a game called One Step, which goes like this: Each time you and your partner make a catch, both of you move back one giant step; if you miss, you both move toward each other one giant step.

If children are relatively close to one another, don't expect mature throwing patterns. However, as the distance between partners increases, you should start observing mature patterns.

Throwing and Catching over a Net with a Partner

Set up nets or ropes around the space at various heights. Have beanbags and yarn balls on hand.

With your partner, choose a net *(rope)* that you want to practice throwing and catching over and a beanbag or yarn ball. After you've chosen your net *(rope)*, begin throwing and catching. Try to throw so that your partner doesn't have to move more than one step in either direction to catch the bag or ball.

◻ This is an easy task for catching against your body instead of using your hands because the object is coming from over your head, so take extra care to catch it with your thumbs together. *(A demonstration may be needed here.)*

◻ Throwers, it'll really help your partner if you put an arch on the object when you throw it. That will give her time to react to the bag or ball and get under it for catching.

◻ Remember when you were throwing against the wall and you always had to have quick feet to move your bodies behind the ball? This is the same thing, except your body has to be behind and under the object so you have a better chance of catching it.

■ See how many throws and catches you and your partner can make without missing. Watch the object closely. Use sympathetic throws.

Throwing and Catching over a Bench with a Partner

Each pair of children will need an eight-inch playground ball and a bench or table.

Bounce the ball so that it travels over the bench and your partner catches it. Your partner shouldn't have to move more than one step in either direction to catch the ball.

> ◻ In this task, the secret to throwing and catching is in the bounce. The ball has to bounce on your side of the bench in order to travel over the bench so that your partner can catch it in the air. To travel over the bench on a bounce, the ball has to bounce a little closer to the bench than to you. If you bounce the ball too close to the bench, it'll simply crash into the bench, so experiment to find the best place.

■ As you bounce the ball over the bench, sometimes bounce it with one hand and sometimes with two hands.

■ Try to keep the ball going back and forth as long as you can, using the bounce throw over the bench. To do this, you'll have to go back to the quick feet we talked about before. Remember, this is a throw and catch, not a volley, across the bench.

UTILIZATION LEVEL

Throwing tasks at the utilization level are designed to help children learn to throw while traveling, to throw accurately at moving targets, and to jump to throw. Catching experiences include catching while traveling, while in the air, and in gamelike activities that require the ability to catch while moving in relationship to various objects and/or people.

Activities Leading to Skill Development

Moving to Catch

You're going to practice throwing so that you have to move to catch. Each of you has to be in a self-space with a lot of extra space around you so you don't run into anyone else. To begin, toss the ball so that you have to move just one step to catch it—the ball is just barely out of your reach. Practice this in all places around your body: forward, backward, and sideways.

> ◻ Make sure that your throw is just right. That means that it's far enough away from your body so that you have to move to catch it.
> ◻ After you've practiced getting your throws just right, go back to concentrating on the catching. To have the best chance of catching an object, you must be under or behind it. This means that you have to move your feet quickly to get under and behind the ball.
> ◻ I see some people catching at the same place; try to catch at different places, especially toward the back of your body.

This task must *be performed in a large area, such as a full-sized gymnasium, or preferably outdoors in a large open space.*

Children at the utilization level profit from jumping to catch.

This task will take a lot of concentration on your part, not only to catch the ball but to make sure you don't run into or hurt others. It's fun, but it must be done with a great deal of safety. You practiced moving one or two steps to catch the ball; now you're going to practice moving a long way to catch. Throw the ball away from you so that you have to move several steps to catch it. Make the catch and then throw again so you have to move to catch the ball. Your throws should always be catchable. In other words, don't throw so far that there's absolutely no way you can ever catch the ball. Start out with throws that make you move only a few steps and then try longer throws. Remember, if at all possible, you should be under and behind the ball to catch it.

■ After each successful catch, see if you can throw the ball a little farther the next time. In other words, see how far you can really move to make the catch.

Throwing and Catching While Traveling

You practiced throwing that makes you move to catch, but you were standing still when you threw. Now you're going to throw and catch while moving. To

Throwing and catching on the run.

begin, toss the yarnball *(beanbag)* in the air and catch it while you walk around the space. You must be very careful while you do this and use two sets of eyes: one to watch the ball and the other to watch out for other people so you don't run into them.

    ☐ Usually when people first travel and throw and catch at the same time, they begin by throwing, walking, stopping, and catching and then moving again, almost as if they hadn't stopped—but you know they really did. Now as you travel, really concentrate this time to never stop the walking. See if you can actually throw and catch as you move so you're doing two things at once.

    ■ If you can catch the ball almost all the time when you're walking, throwing, and catching, try slowly jogging as a way of traveling. Still watch closely so you don't run into each other.

    ■ This time try skipping as you throw and catch.

Throwing on the Move

Set up relatively large, stationary targets for every two children. Possible targets are a hoop hanging from a basket, a tire hanging from a tree, or a target placed at a backstop. A large space is necessary for this task.

With a partner, you're going to practice throwing at a target while you're running. Run across in front of your target and try to throw the ball through or into the target. Your partner will give the ball back to you so you can run again. After four throws, trade places.

□ As you throw at the target, you'll be more successful if you throw the ball in a straight, direct pathway, not an arched, curved pathway.

□ Sometimes when people perform this task they tend to run, stop, and then throw. What you really want to be doing is throwing as you run, so the throw seems to just flow out of the run as you keep running afterward. This time, have your partner watch you closely as you run and throw. Her task is to tell you whether you stop and throw or throw on the run. Sometimes we can't feel what we're actually doing.

Throwing to Make a Partner Move to Catch

With your partner, throw back and forth so that your partner has to stretch or move a few steps to catch. The idea is to not make your partner miss but to really force him or her to catch by stretching or moving so he or she can practice difficult catches.

□ The thrower really has a difficult job here because she has to throw away from her partner—to where her partner isn't. Our senses all tell us this is stupid, but we still have to do it. It helps your partner if she gives you a target to throw toward, such as an outstretched hand. Better still, on the floor or wall pick a spot just beyond your partner's reach and aim for that. That way, you somewhat avoid aiming at your partner and you're better able to make your partner reach.

□ Catchers, your job isn't easy either. If you're going to get behind the ball, you have to react as soon as you see the ball leave your partner's hands. So be quick on the draw and get there—the quicker the better.

□ An activity you practiced a long time ago needs thinking about again. As you start your catch, stretch your arms out in front of you so you have time to pull the ball toward the center of your body as you catch it and absorb the force. Your arms can actually extend toward the ball as you're moving.

Throwing to a Moving Target

You're going to practice throwing the ball to your partner, who's moving. Your ultimate goal is to throw so that your partner doesn't have to stop moving or turn around to catch the ball. The thrower remains still; the catcher runs away from the thrower. The thrower throws the ball to a point already decided upon so the runner can catch the ball without stopping. After six tries, trade places.

◻ This task is hard because you're really throwing to an empty space, not a person. You're trying to have the ball and the person meet in the same space at the same time. To do this, you must throw the ball to a space in front of where the receiver is running, a spot he hasn't reached yet, so that when the receiver does get to that place, the ball and the receiver will both arrive at the same time. If you don't do this, the ball will go behind the receiver. This movement is called *leading the receiver.* Concentrate on calculating exactly where the best space will be for the receiver to catch the ball without having to stop running.

▪ Instead of your partner running away from you, change so that your partner is running across in front of you. The space to throw the ball is still in front of the runner; the runner is simply coming from a different direction. Decide ahead of time where you're going to try to give the runner the ball.

▪ There's one more way to practice this idea. This time, the runner must be coming toward the thrower. Again, the space is in front of the runner so that the runner doesn't have to stop or turn around to catch the ball.

▪ Up until now each set of partners decided where the catch was to be made. Now practice *without* deciding ahead of time where you'll throw the ball. This means that the thrower will have to be very accurate with the throws and the catcher will always have to be on the alert to catch the ball whenever and wherever it goes.

◻ To successfully catch on the run, you have to do two things at once. First, you must know where you're going and how you're going to get there. Do this as you start on the run while watching the passer as you go. Second, as you run, and especially as you begin to receive the ball, you must track the ball all the way into your hands. Watch the ball closely, and be sure you have a good grip on it before you really take off running again.

Throwing for Distance and Accuracy

The object of this task is to practice throwing accurately to someone far away. You and your partner need to start throwing and catching about ten yards apart. Throw so your partner doesn't have to move to catch the ball. Remember as you throw to watch your target—your partner—the entire time. You want the ball to go straight to your partner.

◻ Think back to when you practiced throwing for distance. Four factors helped increase the distance you could throw a ball: sideways, coil, opposition, elbow. As you throw this time, concentrate on using these four principles. Your partner will observe and tell you if you miss one of the cues.

◻ Another important point when throwing for distance and for accuracy is the angle at which the ball travels through the air. You don't want the ball to travel in a very arched pathway in the air. If it does, it takes a long time to get to the target, and it uses up much of its force going up instead of out. The best pathway for the ball to travel in is about halfway between straight up and the ground, at a 45° angle. This time as you practice, see if you can find the halfway pathway. *(A demonstration helps here.)*

☐ Another key to success is watching your partner all the time. Be very sure you know where your target is.

■ If you can throw successfully ten times to your partner who's ten yards away, each of you back up two giant steps and try again. Each time you can successfully make the throws ten times, back up another two giant steps. Try to find your maximum distance.

Performing a Target Backaway

Place stationary targets in various locations around a large space. Targets can be placed against baseball backstops, trees, or playground apparatus.

The task now is to try to hit the target from far away. Start close enough so you know you can hit the target. When you hit it three times, back up about five yards and throw again. After five successful throws, back up again. See how far away you can get and still hit the target.

☐ Don't forget that it helps to turn your hips before you throw a long distance so you have more power behind your throw. This time concentrate on coiling tightly before you throw.

☐ The other thing you need to remember is to watch your target the entire time. It helps to know exactly where you're throwing.

■ See how many throws out of ten you can make right to the target.

Playing Frisbee Golf

You'll need a Frisbee for each student and a Frisbee golf course. Use a hula hoop tied between two chairs or a hoop suspended from a tree as a target. The distance and angle of the target from the starting line can vary, depending on the amount of space available. We use a range of 50 to 150 yards. Trees, playground apparatus, fences, or backstops can be used as obstacles to throw over or around. (For a detailed analysis of Frisbee skills, write for Frisbee: Flying Disc Manual for Students and Teachers, *International Frisbee Disc Association, P.O. Box 970, San Gabriel, CA 91776.)*

The name of this game is Frisbee Golf, a form of golf in which you use a Frisbee instead of a golf club and ball. The object is to throw a Frisbee for distance and often around obstacles, eventually placing it through a target hoop. You want to use as few throws as possible. Here are the rules:

1. All players make their first throw from behind the starting line.
2. Players make the second throw and all throws after that from the landing spot of the previous throw. Players are allowed to take one step in throwing.
3. Players count how many throws were needed to place the Frisbee through the hoop.

Catching to Throw Quickly to a Partner

Sometimes it's necessary to throw very quickly after you catch a ball, much as baseball players do when they're trying to make a double play. With your partner, you're going to practice throwing quickly after catching. Your partner will throw you the ball and you throw it back as quickly as possible, like a hot potato. The throw to your partner needs to be accurate as well as quick. To begin, one of you practices the quick throws; the other one is a thrower and the target. After seven throws, switch places.

- □ The throw can occur faster if you move toward the ball as it is coming to you and at the same time begin to face the direction in which you're going to throw. *(A demonstration is beneficial here.)*
- □ In reality, you're combining two skills into almost one movement. The catch and throw should flow together into one movement, as if the catch is simply moving into the throw. As you practice this time, concentrate on making a smooth movement, with no stops or jerkiness.
- ■ When most of the throws go directly to your partner, back up a few steps and try the task again.
- ■ Now to make the task even harder, try to catch the ball with one hand and throw it with the same hand. This is almost as if you don't ever want to really hold the ball. You need to get rid of the ball quickly. You may want to use a beanbag for this task.

Catching to Throw Quickly to a Target

Set up fairly large (two × two-foot) targets in various places around the area.

With your partner, you're going to practice catching and then throwing quickly to a target. This skill is used in the game of team handball, for example. Your partner throws you the ball; you catch it and quickly throw it to the target. You're trying for a quick throw so that no one can block your shot. After six times, switch places.

- □ Make the catch and the throw simply flow into one smooth movement, with no stop between the catch and the throw.

■ See how many throws out of ten you can make land in the target. Remember: quick throws only; ones that stop don't count. Your partner is the judge.

Many of the throwing and catching skills at the utilization level can be transformed into gamelike situations for children. Some children at this level enjoy practicing in nongame contexts, while others are interested only in practicing if the skill is used in a gamelike situation. Generally, these are the children who continually want to know, "When do we get to play the game?"

Throwing While in the Air

Sometimes when you throw, you need to be in the air. This type of throwing is harder than throwing when you're on the ground. To start, run a few steps, jump in the air, and throw the ball to your partner while you're in the air. Make the throw as accurate as possible.

□ Often when people practice this task they aren't in the air when they think they are. Sometimes people run, throw, and then jump; sometimes they run, jump, land, and then throw. It's hard to tell exactly what you're doing without some help, so your partner's job is to watch you very carefully to see if you're really in the air as you throw. For now, your partner takes the place of the teacher—your partner must tell you exactly what he or she saw.

□ After you get in the air on the throws, sometimes the throws will go all over the place. As you throw, make sure that your upper body is facing the target you want to throw to, in this case, your partner.

□ To work on accuracy, you must follow through toward your target after you throw the ball. Your hand should go straight toward the target.

PROFICIENCY LEVEL

Experiences at the proficiency level include throwing and catching in relation to an opponent who attempts to prevent the throw or the catch. These tasks foster development of consistent degrees of accuracy and distance in throwing. Children learn to catch a variety of objects while traveling rapidly and suddenly changing direction and level.

Activities Leading to Skill Development

Playing Frisbee Stretch

This game is called Frisbee Stretch. You'll need a partner. The object is to throw the Frisbee so that your partner has to stretch to catch it. The scoring is: If the Frisbee is caught, that counts as one point. If the body is stretched a long way while reaching to catch the Frisbee, that counts as three points. I'm going to throw a few to Mary. Let's watch to see how many points she'll get for each of her catches. *(Select a skilled catcher and throw, or have someone else throw, the Frisbee so that the catcher has to stretch to make the catch.)*

▫ Remember to try to anticipate the flight of the Frisbee and to move your feet so that you can be in a position to stretch to catch.

▫ You may want to change the way you score the game. You can work together to see how many points you can make; or you may want to play against your partner. Remember, though, that you'll have to make good throws if your partner is going to have a chance.

Tagging a Base Runner: Run Down

This is a baseball-type game whose object is to tag out a base runner. There are three in the game. You'll need to decide how far apart to place your two bases. The two rules are simple:

1. Two players stand on bases spread apart. *(Distance will depend on the players.)* On the signal, one player who begins in the middle attempts to reach either base without being tagged by a base person possessing the ball.
2. The base runner must run every third throw.

Change positions when the runner gets tired or the runner is out. Be certain that you all get lots of chances to throw and to run.

▫ Focus on catching the ball and quickly transferring the ball to your throwing hand. In this game, the faster you can throw the ball, the better your chance of getting the runner out.

Running the Bases

The object of Running the Bases is to throw a ball around the bases twice before a runner can circle the bases once. Here are the rules:

1. There are four players to a team.
2. The fielding team places a player at each base—first, second, third, and home plate.
3. The player at home plate *(the catcher)* begins with the ball. On the signal, two runners try to run the bases before the fielders throw the ball to each base twice.
4. If the runners travel the bases before the fielders throw and catch the ball twice, they score a run. If all the fielders throw and catch twice before the runners circle the bases, it's an out.
5. After three outs *or* when all runners have had a chance to run the bases twice, the teams switch roles.

Adjust the distance between the bases according to the throwers' ability and the runners' speed.

□ Remember when you throw to keep your eyes focused on your target—most likely the chest of the person you're throwing to.

Throwing to Avoid a Defender

In this task you'll practice throwing to someone who's being defended. One of you is a thrower, one a receiver, and one an interceptor. Thrower, get the ball to the receiver. Use quick moves, and get rid of the ball whenever you have a chance. Receiver, move so that you're in an open space to receive the ball *(zigzag pathways)*. Once you're in an open space, things must happen quickly because the interceptor won't let the space stay open long. Interceptor, guard the receiver and try not to let the receiver make the catch. Don't forget that you're not allowed to touch the receiver. After five throws, switch places.

□ Throwers, remember to lead your receivers so they can keep running after they get the ball.
□ Catchers, remember to watch the ball until it actually touches your hands.
□ Interceptors, remember to focus on the hips of the person you're guarding, not on the person's head or feet.

Playing Keep Away

This game is called Keep Away. In a group of three, one of you will be trying to take the ball away from the other two. Here are the rules:

1. Decide your boundaries and mark them off with cones.
2. You can only catch the ball in the air.
3. If you get the ball, trade places with the person who threw it.
4. You may run with the ball, but you can't keep it for longer than five seconds.

□ The secret to playing this game is to never stand still. If you don't have the ball, you should be moving so that you can get to an open space so that the thrower can send you the ball.

Playing Hitting the Pin

You'll need two pins and one ball for each group of six students. For the court setup, see Figure 22-4.

The name of this game is Hitting the Pin; the object is to knock over the other team's pin. Here are the rules:

1. There are two or three players on each side.
2. Players can take only two steps when they have the ball; then they must pass the ball to a teammate or shoot at the pin.
3. No players are allowed in the goal area.
4. If the ball touches the ground, the last player to touch the ball loses possession. The other team begins play at that location.

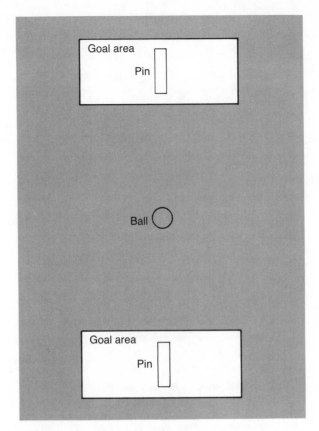

Figure 22-4 Setup for Hitting the Pin.

Playing Half-Court Basketball (Modified)

This is a basketball game with one exception: no dribbling or running with the ball. Here are the rules:

1. There are three players on each side.
2. When a player has the ball, the player must shoot it to the basket or pass it to a teammate. No dribbling or steps are allowed.

Have the children focus on traveling, with changes in direction, when they don't have the ball. When they receive the ball, have them focus on getting rid of it quickly—to a teammate or toward the goal.

Playing Frisbee Football

This game is called Frisbee Football. The object is to catch the Frisbee in the other team's goal area. *(Figure 22-5 shows the setup of the playing field. Instead of a Frisbee, you may use a ball or a beanbag.)* Here are the rules:

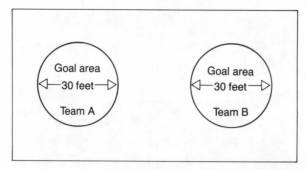

Figure 22-5 Frisbee football. There are no boundaries other than the two goal areas, each of which is thirty feet in diameter. Generally, the farther apart the goal areas can be placed, the more interesting is the game.

1. There are two to four players on each team.
2. When a player has the Frisbee, he or she can take no more than three steps before passing it to a teammate.
3. A point is scored when a player catches the Frisbee in the opposing team's goal area.
4. If the Frisbee touches the ground, the team that touched the Frisbee last loses possession. The opposing team puts the Frisbee in play from that location. There is no out-of-bounds.

As you observe, you may see a need to stop the game and ask the children to practice throwing to a partner who's traveling or to reduce the difficulty by having the children practice two against two or two against one. The emphasis needs to be on leading the partner with the throw. Once children are successful at the easier task, you can put them back in the game again.

Playing Four-Person Football

This football game has just throwing and catching, no running with the foam football. You try to throw the ball to your partner, who's being guarded by someone on the other team. Here are the rules:

1. There are two players on a team.
2. Each team has four chances to throw and catch the ball in an attempt to move the ball from their goal line to the opposing team's goal area.
3. When on offense, one player is the thrower. He or she may not move forward. The thrower tries to accurately throw the ball downfield to her or his teammate, the receiver.
4. When on defense, one player tries to stay with the receiver to block or intercept the ball. The other player remains at the location where the play

starts. That player counts aloud, "One alligator, two alligators," up to "five alligators," and then rushes the thrower, trying to touch the thrower or block the thrower's pass.

5. A play is over when the ball touches the ground or when a defensive player touches the offensive player who has possession of the ball.

You'll have to adjust the playing area so that it's possible for the children to throw the ball on a fly into the other team's goal area. This will depend to some extent on the type of ball the children use. For starters, try a distance of twenty yards from the midfield to the goal area.

Playing European Handball (Modified)

This game is a little like soccer because there's a goalie, but the ball is thrown rather than kicked. *(A five-inch diameter playground ball works well in this game.)* The object is to throw the ball through the other team's goal. *(See Figure 22-6.)* Here are the rules:

1. There are three or four players on a team.
2. Players must stay out of the semicircle.
3. The goalie must stay in the semicircle. She or he tries to collect the ball, to prevent it from going through the goal.
4. A player who has a ball can bounce it, pass it to a teammate, or throw it toward the goal. Once a player stops bouncing the ball, he or she must pass or shoot it; she or he can no longer dribble it.

Playing Passball

This game is a little like football. The object is to pass a ball to someone on your team who's in the other team's goal area *(see Figure 22-7)*. It helps to

Figure 22-6 Modified game of European handball. Goals can be made of stacked tires; semicircles can be spray painted on the ground.

Figure 22-7 Passball. The dimensions of the field may be adjusted according to the children's ability.

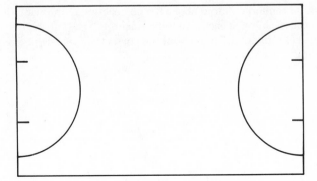

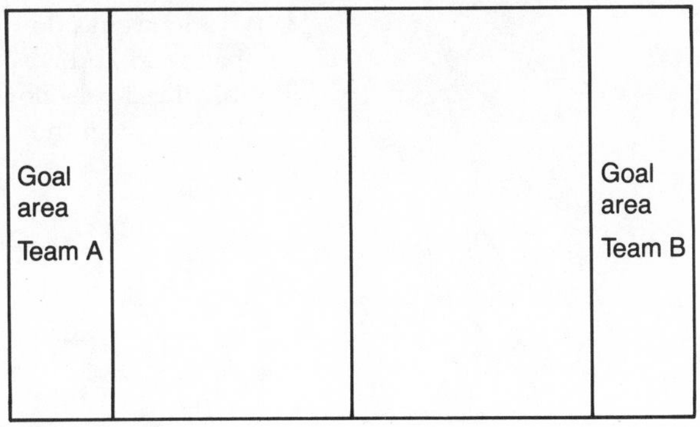

Goal area Team A

Goal area Team B

decide the type of pathways the receivers will be running before each play: straight, curved, or zigzag.

Here are the rules:

1. There are three players on a side.
2. Spray paint a line across the middle of the field. The quarterback must remain behind this line, and no defensive player may cross the line.
3. The offensive team has three plays or attempts to have successful pass completions. Then the teams switch roles.
4. A point is scored each time a receiver catches the ball. Two points are scored when a receiver catches the ball in the end zone.
5. After each play, the ball is again placed at midfield.
6. No player may purposely bump or block another.
7. All players rotate to different positions after each play.

READING COMPREHENSION QUESTIONS

1. Name the three styles of throwing. What type of task encourages children to practice overhand throws?
2. What does the term *trunk rotation* mean when throwing a ball?
3. What does throwing in a static context mean? Describe an example of a task that includes throwing in a static context and an example of a task that includes throwing in a dynamic context.
4. Why do we focus on throwing before catching?
5. Name two characteristics of an individual at the utilization level in catching.
6. What does tracking a ball mean? How can a teacher tell if a child is tracking a ball appropriately?
7. Rank the following tasks by placing the number 1 in front of the easiest (most basic) task, the number 2 in front of the next more difficult task, and so on.
   (   ) Play the game of passball.
   (   ) Toss up a beanbag and try to catch it with a plastic scoop.
   (   ) While running, throw a ball to a partner who's also running.
   (   ) Toss a yarn ball high in the air so you have to travel to catch it.
   (   ) Throw and catch with a partner.
8. What four cues do we use to remind children about the correct way of throwing a ball overhand? Explain the meaning of each cue (refinement).
9. What three cues do we use to remind children about the correct way of catching a ball? Explain the meaning of each cue (refinement).

Volleying and Dribbling

For our purposes, we define volleying as striking or giving impetus to an object by using a variety of body parts—for example, hands, arms, head, or knees. Dribbling is a subdivision of volleying. Although our discussion here is divided into two separate sections—volleying and dribbling—when teaching, you can develop dribbling and volleying together. Volleying is almost exclusively a game skill, used in such sports as soccer, volleyball, handball, basketball, and speedball.

LEVELS OF VOLLEYING SKILL PROFICIENCY

Children at the precontrol level of volleying are still struggling to achieve the hand-eye coordination required to contact the ball. They're rarely able to intentionally direct the flight of a ball when contact is made. Appropriate activities for children at this level include:

Striking an object upward.

1. Striking balloons in the air
2. Striking balloons with different body parts
3. Developing an underhand striking pattern

At the control level, children are able to strike a ball continuously (letting it bounce) in their own space. They're able to control the amount of force that they put into the volley so that they can control the ball in their own space. At the control level, children begin:

1. Volleying balls with different body parts
2. Striking a ball using the overhand and underhand patterns
3. Striking over low nets and lines on the floor with partners

At the utilization level, children can also control the direction as well as the force of their strikes. They're able, with a variety of body parts, to produce a level surface with which to strike the ball. The children can also combine several different concepts with the skill of striking. Children at the utilization level have mastered the basic skill patterns and can concentrate on:

1. Continuously volleying with body parts
2. Playing wall and corner handball games
3. Volleying over a high net

When children are able to strike an object and simultaneously focus on the activity around them, they're able to function at the proficiency level. Appropriate tasks include:

1. Volleying with different body parts while traveling
2. Striking to targets
3. Playing competitive games involving different striking patterns

We focus on volleying as a major skill in many of our game situations. Efficient striking patterns are generally the last of the fundamental manipulative patterns to develop because of the fine perceptual and motor adjustments that the child must make. Once the child does begin to strike an object, the range of possible activities is enormous. Our progression spiral for volleying on p. 502 indicates activities at various levels. The text ideas include suggestions for children at the different levels, and a range of activities within each level, stated rather directly. Remember though that we encourage you to modify the suggested organizational structure to satisfy your objectives (Chapter 4).

ASSESSMENT GUIDE / Volleying

Note to Teachers. Mark a line on the wall approximately three feet above the floor. Mark the second line seven feet from the floor so it's directly above the three-foot line. A dotted line of plastic colored tape works well; a continuous line of tape isn't necessary.

TASK Stand eight to ten feet from the wall (you can mark a line on the floor). Drop the playground ball so it bounces one time; then strike the ball with your open palm so the ball travels to the wall and hits between the tape marks. After the ball bounces one time on the floor, strike it again to the wall. The pattern will be: strike ball with palm, ball hits wall, ball bounces on floor, strike ball again, ball hits wall.... Try to keep the pattern going at least five times. You can hit with either hand or with both hands.

GUIDE The children are ready for precontrol- or control-level tasks when you observe that:

1. They're unable to strike the ball between the tape marks.
2. They catch the ball each time rather than continuously hitting.
3. They're unable to hit the ball five times in a row.

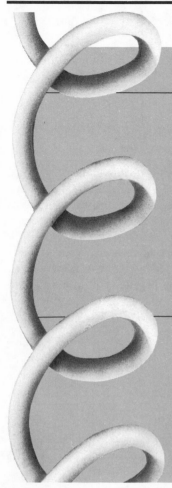

SKILL THEME DEVELOPMENT SEQUENCE

Volleying

CONTROL LEVEL

Playing one-bounce volleyball
Striking over a low net
Playing Four Square, Two Square
Volleying game: child-designed
Striking the ball over a line
Volleying underhand to the wall
Volleying overhand to the wall
Playing Keep It Up
Volleying to a partner
Striking a ball upward continuously
Striking a ball noncontinuously with different body parts

PRECONTROL LEVEL

Striking a variety of balls
Striking the ball to the wall
Striking with an underhand pattern
Striking with different body parts
Striking the balloon forward
Striking balloons in the air

The children are ready for utilization- and proficiency-level tasks when you observe that they're capable of striking the ball between the tape marks five times without breaking the pattern.

PRECONTROL LEVEL

It's important for each child to be able to strike a ball with his or her hands so that the ball stays within a particular space. At the precontrol level, we work toward control so that children don't have to run after the ball to retrieve it after each strike.

Volleying

PROFICIENCY LEVEL

Playing modified volleyball
Playing team line volleyball
Volleying in a line formation
Spiking
Playing over the line
Playing against the wall
Striking downward with force
Striking to a target
Serving overhand over the net
Striking with different body parts while traveling

UTILIZATION LEVEL

Serving underhand over the net
Playing competitive three on three
Volleying three on three
Volleying continuously to a partner
Volleying over a net
Playing corner handball
Playing handball with a partner
Striking to the wall varying levels, force, body position
Volleying with a volleybird
Playing Aerial Soccer
Volleying with the foot
Striking a ball continuously with different body parts

Activities Leading to Skill Development

Striking Balloons in the Air

Balloons are excellent to use with younger children because they float slowly, providing more time for visual tracking. They don't work well on windy days outside, however. Beach balls and punch balls also work well.

Strike the balloon upward so it stays in the air. Try to keep the balloon from touching the floor.

■ Strike the balloon high above your head. Practice striking with both your right and left hands so you'll be equally good with each hand.

Striking a balloon upward while traveling.

       □ Tap the balloon gently directly underneath so it travels up, not out at an angle.

    ■ On the signal, begin striking the balloon upward. Try to keep the balloon in the air until you hear the signal to stop; I'll time you for thirty seconds.

    ■ This time, try to keep the balloon in the air for thirty seconds without moving from your self-space. Remember to tap the balloon directly underneath so it travels up, not out.

Striking the Balloon Forward

Strike your balloon in the air so it travels forward. You'll have to contact the balloon in back to make it travel forward.

       □ Tap the balloon gently so it moves in front of you as you walk forward.

       □ What happens if you strike the balloon too hard? Does it go forward? Sometimes too much force isn't good—tap gently for control and direction.

Striking with Different Body Parts

Keep the balloon in the air by striking it with different body parts. How many different body parts can you use to tap the balloon upward? Head, elbows, knees, feet, shoulders. . . .

- □ Remember to strike under the balloon to direct it upward.

- ■ Count how often you can tap the balloon before it touches the floor. Don't use the same body part two times in a row. Try this combination: hand, head, knee, elbow.

Striking with an Underhand Pattern

Strike the balloon with both hands so it travels upward.

- □ Strike the balloon with an open palm; don't toss it upward.
- □ Remember to contact the balloon directly underneath.
- □ Use only enough force to send the balloon four or five feet above your head.
- □ Move your feet quickly so you can hit the balloon without having to reach too far.

- ■ Practice until you can do this underhand skill five times, never leaving your self-space.
- ■ Strike the balloon upward continually. Try to keep the balloon going so it doesn't hit the floor.

- □ Be sure your hands are directly under the balloon when you contact it.
- □ Bend your knees so your flat palms are under the balloon.

Striking the Ball to the Wall

Stand five to six feet from the wall. Bounce the playground ball one time and then strike it with your open palms so it travels to the wall. As the ball rebounds from the wall, let it bounce one time and then catch it. *(See Figure 23-1.)*

- □ Use an underhand action to strike the ball.
- □ Contact the ball slightly below center and behind so it travels slightly upward to the wall. *(Select two children using the correct pattern to demonstrate for the class.)*

- ■ Practice until you can execute the pattern drop, hit, bounce three times. Remember to catch the ball after each movement.

Striking a Variety of Balls

Provide a variety of balls: beach balls, Nerf balls, plastic balls. Encourage children to practice their skills with each type of ball. Repeat the underhand striking skills with each type of ball.

Figure 23-1 Underhand striking pattern.
1. Hold ball in one hand, with feet in the front-back stance.
2. Let ball bounce once. Bring hitting arm back so it's ready to hit.
3. As ball bounces back, hit it with open palm, from underneath and slightly back.

CONTROL LEVEL

At the control level, children learn to volley a ball in various directions and at various levels. They use different body parts, and relationships to other people and to objects begin to be important. Children at this level still find that it helps to let the ball bounce between strikes or to use their hands between strikes so that they gain control over their volleying. We've found that when children are ready, they often eliminate the bounce themselves.

Activities Leading to Skill Development

Striking a Ball Noncontinuously with Different Body Parts

Strike the beach ball upward with different body parts: feet, elbows, upper thigh, shoulder, head.

- □ Remember to make contact directly under the ball to send it upward.
- □ Bend your legs to get under the ball; extend your legs when you contact the ball to help the ball travel upward.

- ■ Contact the ball with your upper thigh so the ball travels directly upward, not forward. Catch the ball after each volley.

- □ Keep your upper thigh level as you contact the ball; bend your other leg to provide the force for the volley.

Striking to different levels using different body parts.

■ Practice until you can do three single volleys, with a catch after each, without moving from your self-space.

■ Practice with both your left and right legs so you're equally skilled with both legs.

■ Contact the ball with the top of your foot so the ball travels directly upward, to a height slightly above your head. Catch the ball after the tap.

□ Extend your toes so the top of your foot provides a flat surface for the contact.

□ Use only a slight tap; you aren't kicking for distance.

□ Keep your eyes focused on the ball until it contacts your foot.

□ Keep your weight centered over your supporting foot, with your knee slightly bent for good balance.

■ Practice with each foot until you can volley three times with each foot. Remember to catch the ball after each tap.

■ Contact the ball with your head, where your hair meets your forehead, sending the ball upward and forward. Step forward to catch the ball after the volley.

　□ Remember to bend your knees to get under the ball; extend them with a slight jump when you contact the ball.

　□ Tighten your neck muscles at the moment of contact to provide a firm, stable surface for the volley.

■ Practice this skill until you can execute three volleys correctly with your head. The ball should travel forward and upward; catch the ball after each volley.

Striking a Ball Upward Continuously

Volley the ball upward with your hands above your head so the ball returns directly to you.

　□ Use your fingertips to contact the ball.

　□ Remember to bend your legs to get under the ball; extend your arms and legs on contact.

■ Toss the ball upward and then volley it one time two to three feet above your head.

■ Toss and then volley the ball upward two times.

■ Toss and then volley the ball from medium level; that is, let the ball drop until it's three to four feet from the floor before you volley.

　□ Again, move your feet quickly to get under the ball.

Volleying to a Partner

Stand three to four feet from a partner. Using the overhand skill you just learned, volley the ball back and forth to your partner. Try to keep the ball in the air as long as possible.

　□ Remember, the skill is a quick tap, not a catch/throw.

Playing Keep It Up

Keep It Up is a group game designed for practice of the overhead volley. The game may be played with any number of teams. The more teams you have, the less children there will be per team, which means increased participation for each child.

The object of the game Keep It Up is to see how many times your team can volley the ball before it touches the ground. The rule is that a player can't hit the ball twice in a row. See if you can break your own record. Count out loud.

Volleying Overhand to the Wall

Place tape lines on the floor, about six feet apart.

Stand approximately four feet from the wall. Toss the ball slightly above your head and then volley it to the wall with both your hands.

- Contact the ball slightly below center back so it travels forward and upward to the wall. Use your fingertips.
- The volley is a tap action, not a catch and throw; strike the ball quickly.
- Use your legs to provide the power for the volley; extend *(straighten)* them as you contact the ball. *(Select two children who are contacting the ball with their fingertips and using their legs for the force of the volley to demonstrate the key concepts in the skill.)*

■ Practice until you can execute three overhead volleys to the wall without catching the ball or letting it drop below your height.

■ Count the number of volleys you can hit to the wall above the tape line. Remember, the volley must be with two hands; don't catch the ball.

Volleying Underhand to the Wall

Place tape lines on the floor, about three feet apart. Have vinyl, beach, or playground balls for the children.

Stand approximately six to eight feet from the wall. Using an underhand action, strike the ball with your open palm so the ball travels to the wall. Let the ball bounce one time after the volley and then catch it.

- Keep your striking arm extended as you strike the ball.
- Step forward on your opposite foot as you contact the ball.
- Contact the ball just below center back so it travels slightly upward to the wall.

■ Using the underhand action, strike the ball with your open palm so the ball contacts the wall above the tape mark. Continue the volley after each bounce. The pattern will be: strike ball with palm, ball hits wall, ball bounces on floor; strike ball, ball hits, ball bounces. . . .

- Try to always be in position to hit the ball. Anticipate where the ball will bounce, move quickly, and be balanced for the contact.
- When the ball returns to your right side, contact it with your right hand. When it rebounds to your left side, contact it with your left hand.

■ Count the number of volleys you can make without a mistake. A mistake is two bounces on the rebound or a volley that hits the wall below the tape line. Remember to practice with each hand.

Striking the Ball over a Line

Place tape lines on the floor, about five feet apart.

Select a partner to practice underhand hits with. Stand approximately three feet from the tape line so you're facing your partner across the line. Using the underhand action, strike the ball so it crosses the line and bounces on the other side. Your partner then contacts the ball so it returns to you.

- ◻ You can hit with one hand or both, but try to always use the underhand action.

- ▪ Cooperate with your partner to see how many times you can strike the ball back and forth over the line.

- ◻ Remember, when building a cooperative score, strike the ball so your partner can get a good return hit—not too much force, good placement.

Volleying Game: Child-Designed

You've practiced striking the ball against the wall and over a line. In both situations you used an underhand volley, striking with your open palm. Now your task is to design an original game for two partners or a small group to provide practice for these skills. *(See Chapter 26.)* You can design your game so it can be played against the wall or over a line. Remember, the focus is the underhand volley. You'll have to decide the following:

1. Will your game be against the wall or over a line?
2. Will the game be cooperative or competitive?
3. Will you keep score?
4. How does a player score a point?
5. Will the game be played with a partner or in a small group? *(Not more than three.)*
6. What are the boundaries?
7. What are the rules?

Record your game on a piece of paper so you can refer to it later and others in the class can learn how to play it. You don't have to give your game a name if you don't want to. *(See Figure 23-2.)*

Children not experienced in designing games will need more direction from the teacher and less opportunity to make decisions; for example, the teacher decides whether the game is against the wall or over a line, whether the game is cooperative or competitive.

Playing Four Square, Two Square

Four Square (four persons) and Two Square (two persons) are games for practicing the underhand volley. Mark off squares on the floor and assign players to the squares. See Figure 23-3.

Stand outside your assigned squares. Serve the ball by dropping it and hitting it underhand from the bounce. The server can hit the ball to any of the other three courts. The player receiving the ball must keep it in play by striking the

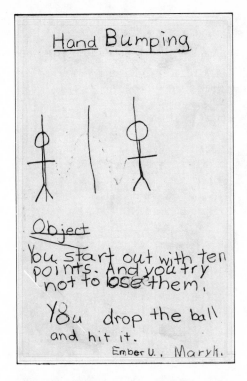

Hand Bumping

Object
You start out with ten points. And you try not to lose them.

You drop the ball and hit it.

Ember U., Mary H.

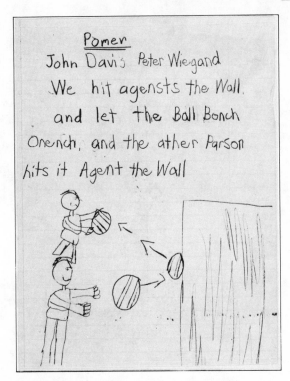

Pomer
John Davis Peter Wiegand
We hit agensts the Wall, and let the Ball Bonch One nch, and the ather Parson hits it Agent the Wall

Figure 23-2 Child-designed games against the wall (Don't Bounce Count; Power) and over a line (Hand Bumping).

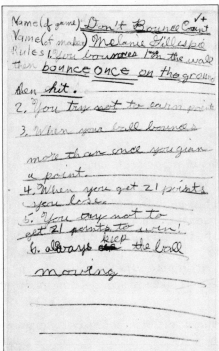

Name (of game) Don't Bounce Count
Name (of maker) Melanie Gillespie
Rules 1. You bounces 1° on the wall then **bounce once on the ground**, then **hit**.
2. You try not to earn point
3. When your ball bounces more than once you gian a point.
4. When you get 21 points you lose.
5. You try not to get 21 points to win!
6. always keep the ball moving

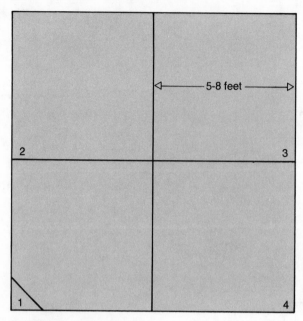

Figure 23-3 Four-square court.

ball with an underhand hit to any square. Play continues until one player fails to return the ball or commits a fault. Faults include hitting the ball sidearm or overhand, stepping in another square to play the ball, catching the ball, and letting the ball touch any part of the body other than hands.

☐ Remember to move your feet quickly to stay in position to get to the ball.

Striking over a Low Net

Arrange nets at varying heights throughout the gym. You can lower standard nets or improvise nets from ropes. See Figure 23-4.

You practiced the underhand hit against the wall and over a line on the floor. Now you're ready to use the same skill for sending the ball over a net to a partner. The server bounces the ball one time and then sends it over the net with the underhand volley; the partner returns the volley after the ball bounces once. Practice a few minutes to adjust to the height of the net and to your partner. When you're ready, keep a collective score of how many hits you make before making a mistake.

☐ Get in position each time *(quick feet)* for a backward/forward swing with your striking arm.

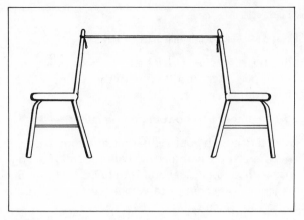

Figure 23-4 Construction of a net. Suspend a rope between two chairs.

- □ When you contact the ball, step forward on the foot opposite your contact arm.
- □ Use your left as well as your right hand.

Playing One Bounce Volleyball

Divide children into equal numbers (three to four per team) of players on each side of a low net.

A player begins the game by bouncing the ball one time and striking it over the net with an underhand serve. The receiving team may let the ball bounce one time before hitting it back. Only one bounce is permitted before the ball is volleyed back over the net; however, any number of players may volley the ball before it crosses the net. The serving team scores a point when the receiving team fails to return the ball over the net within bounds or when the ball bounces more than once.

UTILIZATION LEVEL

For continuing skill development, children must develop consistency and accuracy. They should be able to use various body parts and to move in relationship to other people and objects. Strategic placement skills in a relatively stable situation are developed at the utilization level.

Activities Leading to Skill Development

Striking a Ball Continuously with Different Body Parts

Volley the *(beach or vinyl)* ball from your knee to your foot by striking it with your upper thigh and then with the top of your foot. Catch the ball after the volley from your foot.

  ▫ Remember to keep your contact surface—thigh and foot—as flat as possible.

  ■ Practice with your right knee and foot as well as your left knee and foot.

  ■ When you're comfortable with the volley from your knee to your foot *(three times with no mistakes)*, add your head; that is, volley the ball from your head—this is called *heading*—to your knee to your foot or from your head to your foot to your knee.

  ▫ For this task, don't send the head volley too far forward.

Volleying with the Foot

Volley the beach ball with your foot, keeping the ball in the air for several contacts. Use the inside, outside, top of your foot, and your heel to strike the ball upward.

  ▫ Strike the ball with enough force to send it upward as high as your knee.

  ■ If this is easy, change to a vinyl or playground ball.

  ■ On the signal, begin your foot volley. I'll give the count each ten seconds; keep the ball in the air as long as possible.

Playing Aerial Soccer

Aerial Soccer is played with a six-inch woven bamboo ball (or one of similar size, weight, and texture).

Practice your skills of heading, instep and toe kicking, and foot-to-head taps with the soccer ball. When you feel comfortable with your individual skills of Aerial Soccer and can keep the ball aloft for at least ten seconds, you can play a game of Aerial Soccer with a partner or in a small group. The ball must stay aloft at all times. You decide the following:

  1. Is the game to be cooperative or competitive?
  2. How many will be in the group? *(Not more than six—three on three.)*
  3. Will you play in self-space or travel in general space?
  4. The boundaries.

This game was observed at Regents Park in London, England. It's exciting for observers to watch and challenging for highly skilled soccer players.

Volleying a ball with the head.

Volleying with a Volleybird

Volleybirds are flat-bottomed shuttlecocks that have been used in Taiwan for centuries. The volleybirds are volleyed with different body parts, including hands, thighs, the instep of the foot, and the inside and outside of the foot. Because the volleybirds are flat-bottomed, they can also be caught on different body parts. Young children find these relatively slow moving and brightly colored "birds" very attractive. You can order volleybirds from Learning Toys, Inc., 1395 Marietta Parkway, Suite 234, Marietta, GA 30067.

See how many times in a row you can strike the volleybird before it touches the ground. Start with one of your hands; then try your other hand. Other body parts you can use are your thigh, the instep of your foot, the inside or outside of your foot.

■ Make up a sequence that uses three different body parts. See if you can repeat the sequence without a miss.

Striking to the Wall Varying Levels, Force, Body Position

Strike the ball to the wall between the three- and seven-foot tape marks so the ball contacts the wall at different levels. Strike the ball so it sometimes hits the wall at a high level, just below the seven-foot mark, and sometimes at a low level, just above the three-foot mark.

■ Vary your striking action; sometimes use an underhand strike, sometimes an overhead one.

■ Vary the amount of force you hit the ball with. Sometimes hit the ball hard so it rebounds far from the wall; sometimes use just enough force to get the ball within the tape zones. How will the ball rebound this time? Right—close to the wall.

■ Strike the ball from different positions in relation to your body. Contact the ball while it's high over your head, close to the floor, on your right side, on your left side. Being able to contact the ball from different positions is important in game situations when you don't always have enough time to get in position.

Playing Handball with a Partner

Your target is the area between the three- and seven-foot tape marks. Try to strike the tennis ball to the wall so your partner can't return the shot. Challenge your partner to a game of fifteen points.

■ Each time you select a partner, both of you should agree on the rules, including the outside boundaries, type of hits, how to keep score, number of bounces permitted on the rebound.

Playing Corner Handball

Challenge a partner to a game of corner handball. This is basically the same game as wall handball, but now you have two corner walls for the play area. Use a tennis, racquet, or playground ball.

Volleying over a Net

Arrange nets at seven-foot heights. Provide a variety of beach balls, eight-inch plastic balls, and volleyballs.

Select a partner; stand on either side of the net and face each other. Partner 1 tosses the ball over the net; partner 2 volleys the ball back over the net to partner 1 with the two-hand overhead hit. Partner 1 catches the ball and then tosses again. After ten tries, partner 2 tosses and partner 1 volleys.

□ Remember to move into position under the ball, bend your knees, and position your hands overhead so you're ready for the contact.

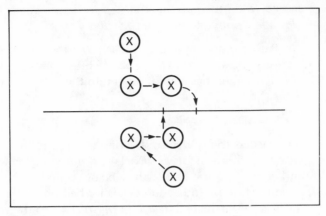

Figure 23-5 Three on three volleys: two patterns.

- ▢ Contact the ball with your fingertips; extend your arms upward. *(Demonstrate.)*
- ■ Hit the ball so your partner can catch it without moving from self-space.

Volleying Continuously to a Partner

Partner 1 tosses the ball slightly above partner 2's head and then volleys it over the net to partner 2; partner 2 volleys the ball back over the net. Continue the overhead volley.

- ▢ Remember to use a quick tap on the ball, not a catch/toss action.
- ▢ Keep your hands in *front* of your forehead to prevent illegal hits.

Volleying Three on Three

Divide the class into groups of six; each group of six subdivides into a group of three on each side of the net. See Figure 23-5.

Use only the overhand volley to hit the ball in the air three times on your side of the net. On the third contact, volley the ball over the net to the other team. Each team volleys the ball three times, sending it over the net on the third hit.

- ■ Rotate positions so you hit the ball from different places.
- ■ Work cooperatively to keep the ball in the air as long as possible. Remember: three hits per side, one hit per person.

Playing Competitive Three on Three

Challenge the other team to a three on three game. Rather than cooperating to keep the ball in the air, use strategies to outscore the other team. Points are scored when the ball hits the floor or lands out of bounds. *(Have two teams play a few points to explain the rules.)*

☐ Rather than just hitting the ball over the net, direct it to a certain location.
☐ Vary the amount of force on the hit. Sometimes send the ball just over the net; sometimes send it deep into the back court.

Serving Underhand over the Net

You learned the underhand action of striking the ball with your open palm, swinging your arm forward/backward, stepping forward on your opposite foot, and contacting the ball slightly below center and back. Now you're going to learn the underhand action of a volleyball serve. Stand ten to fifteen feet from the wall; serve the ball *(beach or plastic ball)* to the wall; your target is the area just above the seven-foot tape line.

☐ Hold the ball in your nonserving hand with your arm extended. Don't toss the ball; swing your serving arm backward and then forward.

■ I'll walk around and observe the underhand action of your serve. When it's correct and you feel successful, select a partner for practice over the net *(rope)*. Partner 1 stands ten to fifteen feet from the net and serves the ball over the net. Partner 2 retrieves the ball and then serves it back over the net.

■ After you feel successful serving over the net, your partner will select a position on the court and stand in that spot. Serve the ball *to* your partner so your partner can catch without moving from self-space.

PROFICIENCY LEVEL

Children at the proficiency level should be able to move consistently and accurately in relation to others and be able to react effectively to increasingly dynamic and unpredictable situations. They can simultaneously focus on volleying and on the activity around them.

Activities Leading to Skill Development

Striking with Different Body Parts While Traveling

Travel the length of the gym, volleying the ball with different body parts as you go.

☐ Don't catch the ball at any time—keep it moving.
☐ Don't let the ball touch the floor until you've traveled the length of the gym.
☐ Remember, you're moving, the ball is moving.

■ Select a partner and travel throughout general space, volleying the ball back and forth with different body parts; both of you should always be moving.

■ Vary the level of the volley. Sometimes volley high; sometimes volley low.

Serving Overhand over the Net

You learned an underhand striking action that can be used as a serve in volleyball. However, when you watch a skilled volleyball team, you'll notice they serve with an overhand striking action. The opponents have less time to get ready for this serve because it travels in a less arched path. Stand fifteen to twenty feet from the net and face a partner on the opposite side of the net. With your nonstriking hand, toss the ball slightly above your head. Contact the ball directly behind center with the heel of your other hand so the ball travels just above the net to the opposite side. Your partner will retrieve the ball and then serve it back to you. *(Demonstrate.)*

  □ The action for the overhand serve is a direct forward/backward "punching" motion.
  □ Your striking arm is raised so your hand is at head height for the punching action.
  □ Your feet are in a front-back stance, as in the underhand serve.
  □ To produce force on the serve, transfer your weight to your forward foot as you extend your striking arm quickly.

■ Tell your partner where to stand in the opposite court. Serve the ball to your partner so she can catch it without moving from her self-space.

Striking to a Target

Divide the court on one side of the seven-foot net into four areas, using tape or chalk to mark divisions (Figure 23-6). Number each of the four target areas.

Stand behind the designated serving line, fifteen to twenty feet from the net. Using either the underhand or the overhand striking pattern, practice serving the volleyball into each target area.

■ Practice serving to each target area until you can successfully serve four out of five tries to each area.
■ Stand behind the serving line. Verbally call the number of the zone you're going to serve to. Strike the ball to that zone.

Striking Downward with Force

Standing ten to fifteen feet from the wall, begin striking the ball between the tape marks, using the underhand pattern. After several hits, strike the ball on top so it travels downward to the wall, contacting the wall just above the bottom tape line.

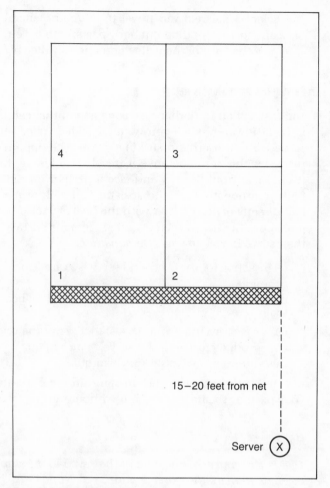

Figure 23-6 Target areas for serving.

□ Contact the ball with your hand slightly cupped. *(Demonstrate.)*

□ Contact the ball with force to send it quickly downward. *(Demonstrate.)*

■ Practice a pattern of three underhand hits followed by a downward hit with force.

Playing Against the Wall

Challenge a partner to a handball game against the wall. Throughout the game, use a combination of forceful downward strikes and underhand hits.

Playing over the Line

Challenge the same partner to a competitive two-square game. Use the forceful downward striking to create situations that move your opponent out of position and thus make it more difficult for him or her to return the ball.

Spiking

Spiking is hitting the ball downward in volleyball. It takes a lot of practice to learn to spike effectively, so we're going to start practicing. You'll need a partner. Partner 1 throws the beach ball or plastic ball straight into the air. Partner 2 jumps into the air and with an overhand hit tries to hit the ball when it's overhead. Here's how it looks. *(Teacher selects two children to demonstrate.)*

- ☐ The secret to spiking is to time your jump so you contact the ball as high as possible so that the ball goes downward.
- ☐ Bend your elbow and then straighten it out as you hit the ball. *(Demonstrate.)*

■ When you and your partner can spike the ball consistently *(four out of five times)*, move over to the rope *(net)*.

The rope or net should be slanted so the children can select an appropriate height. See Figure 23-7.

■ Now try to spike the ball over the net and into the area marked by the cones *(an area about twenty by twenty feet)*.

Figure 23-7 The slanting net, helpful when children are learning to spike the ball.

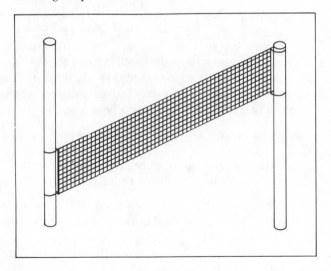

□ For the best spiking, your partner should toss the ball well above the rope *(net)* so that it'll land almost on top of the rope *(net)* if you don't spike it.

Volleying in a Line Formation

Arrange the class in groups of four. Each group of four is in a line formation facing the wall approximately three to four feet away from the wall.

The first person in your line volleys the ball to the wall so it contacts the wall above the upper tape line. After the volley, the first person moves quickly to the back of the line. The second person volleys the ball to the wall, moves quickly to the back, etc. The objective is to keep the volley going. Don't let the ball touch the floor or touch the wall beneath the tape mark.

□ Remember to use your fingertips for the contact.
□ Move into position under the ball with your legs and arms bent, ready for the volley.

Playing Team Line Volley

Remaining in your group of four, face another team of four, with approximately ten feet between the two leaders. Team members should line up behind the leaders. One leader tosses the ball to the leader of the other team; that leader then volleys the ball back and quickly moves to the end of the line. This game is very similar to the volley against the wall: Each person volleys and then moves to the end of the line. The objective is to keep the volley going between the teams.

Playing Modified Volleyball

Divide the class into teams of four or six, depending on space available. Place an equal number of children with comparable skills on each team. The size of the court in relation to the number of players is a crucial element. Don't expect children to cover the amount of space per person that adults do in volleyball. A beach ball or plastic ball works best.

The game begins with a serve from the back boundary line; you'll have two chances to serve the ball successfully over the net. In a regulation volleyball game, the ball may be hit only three times on a side; we'll decide as a class if we want three hits per side or unlimited. *(Discuss; vote.)*

□ Remember, you score a point only if your team is serving.
□ A serve that touches the net is no good; the ball in play is still good if it touches the net.
□ Although not an official rule, try to use the skills you learned: two-hand volley. Use one hand only for a spike.

□ A skilled volleyball game shows set, set, over or bump, set, over, not single hits back and forth over the net.

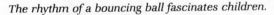

DRIBBLING

Dribbling is striking downward, generally with the hands. Basketball and speedball are the traditional sports in which dribbling is used. Dribbling a ball on the floor or ground, as in soccer, could have been included in this chapter, but because it's also a kicking skill, it's included in the kicking and punting discussion (Chapter 21).

LEVELS OF DRIBBLING SKILL PROFICIENCY

Our progression spiral for developing the skill theme of dribbling, from the precontrol to the proficiency level, is shown on p. 524. At the precontrol level of dribbling, children strike the ball down once with the whole palm of their hands; the hand is kept rigid rather than flexed. After one bounce, the child typically cannot control the ball when it rises again because the hand and arm move in opposition to the ball rather than in unison with it. Tasks that are appropriate at this level include:

The rhythm of a bouncing ball fascinates children.

SKILL THEME DEVELOPMENT SEQUENCE

Dribbling

PROFICIENCY LEVEL

Using Harlem Globetrotters' dribbling/passing routines
Playing small-group basketball
Dribbling and throwing at a target
Playing Dribble/Pass Keep Away
Dribbling and passing in game situations
Dribbling and passing with a partner
Playing Dribble Tag
Playing Now You've Got It, Now You Don't
Dribbling against opponents—group situations
Starting and stopping; changing directions quickly while dribbling

UTILIZATION LEVEL

Dribbling against an opponent: one on one
Dribbling around stationary obstacles
Dribbling in different pathways
Dribbling while changing directions
Dribbling and changing speed of travel

CONTROL LEVEL

Dribbling and traveling
Dribbling in different places around the body while stationary
Dribbling with the body in different positions
Dribbling continuously while switching hands
Dribbling at different heights

PRECONTROL LEVEL

Dribbling with one hand
Striking down (dribbling) continuously with both hands
Striking a ball down and catching it

1. Bouncing the ball with both hands
2. Bouncing the ball with one hand
3. Bouncing a ball in self-space and trying to keep it going
4. Dribbling with the other hand, staying in self-space

When children can repeatedly bounce the ball with either hand and remain in self-space, they're functioning at the control level. Appropriate tasks include:

1. Dribbling at different heights
2. Dribbling continuously and switching hands
3. Dribbling and traveling

At the utilization level, children can successfully dribble with either hand and no longer have to look at the ball. They dribble with their fingers, and the wrist is relaxed. Appropriate tasks include:

1. Dribbling around obstacles
2. Dribbling in different pathways
3. Dribbling while changing directions

When children reach the proficiency level, dribbling seems to be almost automatic. They're able to focus on the strategy of a particular situation that involves dribbling. Appropriate tasks at this level include:

Children need a variety of dribbling activities so they'll be able to control a ball in different situations.

1. Starting and stopping, changing directions quickly while dribbling
2. Dribbling to keep the ball away from an opponent
3. Dribbling in game situations

Dribbling is a skill normally developed for a basketball situation. We focus on it as one aspect of striking rather than as a basketball skill. Children enjoy working with bouncing balls. Remember, though, that dribbling—like striking upward—is one of the last fundamental skills to develop because it requires fine hand-eye coordination.

ASSESSMENT GUIDE / Dribbling

TASK   Begin dribbling in self-space (allow fifteen seconds for self-space dribble); on the signal, begin dribbling in general space without losing control. Stop and catch the ball quickly on the signal.

GUIDE   The children are ready for precontrol- or control-level tasks when you observe that:

1. They're unable to continuously dribble without catching the ball.
2. They're unable to dribble in self-space without losing control of the ball or moving out of self-space.
3. They're unable to travel and dribble without losing the ball.
4. They can only walk slowly and dribble with control.

The children are ready for utilization- and proficiency-level tasks when you observe that they can dribble in self-space and combine traveling with dribbling while maintaining control of the ball.

PRECONTROL LEVEL

At the precontrol level, we give children opportunities to strike a ball down repeatedly without losing the ball from self-space. The children should use their fingers and a flexed wrist action rather than holding the whole hand rigidly. Relatively light balls—eight-inch plastic playground balls—that bounce true (they aren't lopsided) are best for introducing children to dribbling. Be careful when inflating balls: Too much air equals too much bounce for control.

Activities Leading to Skill Development

Striking a Ball Down and Catching It

Bounce the ball down in front of you so it rebounds directly up to you.

- Bounce the ball with two hands.
- Bounce the ball hard enough so it will rebound slightly above your waist height. Too much force makes the ball bounce over your head; with insufficient force, the ball won't come back up.
- Place your fingertips directly on top of the ball and push down. A push out will make the ball bounce away from you.

Striking Down (Dribbling) Continuously with Both Hands

Bounce the ball down with both your hands so it rebounds up and then push down again so the bounce continues. This continuous bounce is called a *dribble*.

- Push the ball with your fingertips, not your flat palm.
- Stand with your feet shoulder width apart to avoid bouncing the ball on your feet.
- Practice until you can dribble the ball five times without losing control of it.

Dribbling with One Hand

Figure 23-8 Dribbling a ball.

Dribble the ball with one hand, like a basketball player. *(See Figure 23-8.)*

- You can move your feet slightly to avoid dribbling on your toes, but stay close to your self-space position.
- Stand with your knees bent, leaning *slightly* forward to create clear space for dribbling.
- Remember to push the ball directly down.
- Push hard enough on each contact for the rebound to reach waist height.
- Count the number of times you can dribble without losing control: Catch the ball, bounce it on your toes, move it out of your space.
- On the signal, begin dribbling with one hand. Continue dribbling in self-space until the signal to stop is given.
- Dribble the ball with your other hand. Let's review the clues for success:

1. How high should the ball rebound?
2. How do you keep the ball from traveling forward and away from you?
3. How do you avoid dribbling on your toes?

Have children repeat each task with their nondominant hand throughout all levels of skill. The proficient basketball player is equally skilled with each hand.

CONTROL LEVEL

At the control level, children learn to dribble and travel at the same time. They'll also be able to dribble in different places around their bodies and vary both direction and pathway.

Activities Leading to Skill Development

Dribbling at Different Heights

Staying in your self-space, dribble the ball with your preferred hand. Continue dribbling until you hear the signal to stop.

- □ Remember to push the ball down, not out, to stay in self-space.
- □ Push the ball with enough force to make it bounce at a height between your shoulders and your waist. Maintain a steady push so the ball rebounds the same height each time.

■ Dribble the ball at a low level so it bounces only to your knees. Keep your body in a standing position; don't kneel or squat down to the floor.

■ Dribble the ball so it rebounds to a height between your waist and your knees. This medium-height dribble is the one most often used in games and the one we'll concentrate on throughout our work.

■ On the signal, begin dribbling the ball at waist height. Continue dribbling at this height until you hear the drumbeat; don't move from your self-space area.

- □ Maintain a steady force so the height will be consistent.
- □ Remember to keep your toes out of the way by standing with your feet shoulder width apart. Move your feet slightly if you need to.
- □ Begin dribbling the ball; raise your head and continue dribbling without looking at the ball. Your peripheral vision enables you to look straight ahead and still see the ball. Your peripheral vision is your ability to look to your side and straight ahead at the same time. This is extremely important in game situations involving dribbling.

Dribbling Continuously While Switching Hands

Begin dribbling with your preferred hand. After several dribbles, switch to your other hand and continue dribbling. Don't catch the ball; simply switch from dribbling with one hand to the other hand.

- □ Dribble the ball in front of you whether you're dribbling with your right or your left hand; twist your upper trunk slightly to bring your right or left hand over the ball. *(See Figure 23-9.)*

■ Begin the dribble with your preferred hand. Dribble five times and then switch to your other hand. Continue to switch after each five dribbles per hand.

Dribbling the ball at a low level.

Figure 23-9 Dribbling changing hands.

□ Remember that the ball should bounce no higher than your waist and no lower than your knees.

■ On the signal, begin dribbling with your preferred hand. Each time you hear the drumbeat, switch hands. Continue to dribble and switch hands on each drumbeat until you hear the signal to stop.

□ Remember to stay in your self-space.

Dribbling with the Body in Different Positions

Assume a kneeling position balanced on one knee and one foot, with your body at low level. Dribble with one hand while you maintain the balanced position.

□ Because you're dribbling at a lower level, you'll need less force.

■ Dribble while in a squat or tuck position balanced on both feet at low level.

■ Balance in different positions, dribbling with one hand. Create three different positions in which you can dribble with either your right or your left hand.

■ Begin dribbling in a standing position. Continue to dribble as you change your position to low level—a kneeling or squatting position. Continue changing body positions while maintaining the dribble. Changing body positions without stopping the dribble requires a high level of control. *(Choose several children to demonstrate the combination of body positions they can assume while dribbling.)*

Dribbling in Different Places Around the Body While Stationary

Standing in self-space, dribble the ball in different places around your body: on your right, on your left, behind your legs.

  □ Bounce the ball six to twelve inches from your body so you won't lose control as you dribble in the different places.

  ■ Begin dribbling with your right hand; after several dribbles, bounce the ball under your right leg and continue the dribble with your left hand.

  □ For this skill you'll have to dribble the ball outside your right *(left)* leg rather than in center front.

  □ When you bounce the ball under your leg, place your hand slightly on the side of the ball rather than directly on top for the push, to direct the bounce to the side.

  ■ Practice the skill from right to left and from left to right until you can execute it in both directions.

  ■ Dribble the ball directly in front of your body; bounce the ball between your legs from front to back. Can you dribble between your legs from back to front?

  ■ Put together a dribbling sequence of all the ways you can dribble in self-space: in front, to the side, in back, around your body, between your legs. Change levels as you go; assume different positions balanced on different body parts.

Dribbling and Traveling

Travel throughout general space, dribbling the ball as you go.

  □ Travel only as fast as you can control both your movement and the ball.
  □ Remember to keep your head up; watch where you're going.
  □ Push the ball slightly ahead of you as you dribble and travel.
  □ When you combine traveling and dribbling, the ball is on the side of your body rather than directly in front of you.

  ■ Begin dribbling in general space. When you hear the drumbeat, stop in self-space and continue the dribble. The second drumbeat is the signal to travel again. The pattern is: drumbeat, travel with dribble; drumbeat, stop with continued dribble; . . .

  ■ Each of you has one hundred points. On the signal, begin dribbling in general space. If you lose control of the ball, subtract ten points; if you collide with another person, subtract twenty-five points. I'll time you for sixty seconds; you're trying to keep all one hundred points. Ready? Begin.

■ Begin dribbling in general space; each time you meet someone, switch hands and continue to travel/dribble.

UTILIZATION LEVEL

At the utilization level, we provide children situations in which they must dribble with either hand, without looking at the ball. Obstacles may be provided, and the children should learn to vary the force of the bounce.

Activities Leading to Skill Development

Dribbling and Changing Speed of Travel

Travel throughout general space, maintaining a controlled dribble at all times. Sometimes travel very fast, sometimes slowly.

■ Begin moving through general space with a slow, steady walk. As you're walking and dribbling, focus your eyes on a spot on the floor fifteen to twenty feet away. Without stopping your dribble, move as quickly as possible to that spot. When you arrive, stop your travel but continue the dribble. Visually select another spot and repeat the sequence. The ability to change speeds and maintain a continuous dribble is a very important offensive skill in basketball.

□ Remember to push the ball ahead of you as you travel.

■ Stand beside a partner whose dribbling skill is very similar to yours. Partner 1 begins the travel/dribble throughout space, changing from fast to slow speeds at will. Partner 2 attempts to stay beside partner 1 at all times. Both of you will dribble continuously. When the signal to stop is given, rest for ten seconds, and then partner 2 becomes the leader.

Dribbling While Changing Directions

Dribble throughout general space, changing directions as you go: travel forward, backward, to the right, to the left. Travel slowly when you first begin the travel/dribble with a change of directions. Maintain the dribble during all the direction changes; don't stop and start again.

Traveling backward and dribbling isn't easy because the ball must move toward the body and often hits the feet. Children will develop this direction last and should be made aware of the difficulty of dribbling backward.

■ Begin dribbling in general space, traveling in a forward direction. Each time you hear the drumbeat, quickly change the direction of your travel and continue the travel/dribble.

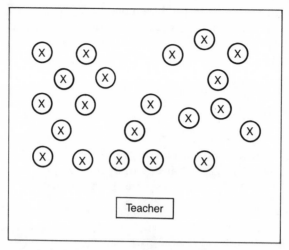

Figure 23-10 Formation for practicing dribbling and moving in the directions the teacher suggests.

☐ Remember that the wall you're facing when you begin will be the wall you'll face throughout your travel/dribble.
☐ When you travel to the left, dribble with your right hand; when you travel to the right, dribble with your left hand. You may choose either hand for the forward/backward dribbling.
☐ We talked earlier about keeping our heads up when we dribble. Why is this so important when practicing the travel/dribble with changing directions? Right—other people are traveling and moving in different directions. You must be aware of others as well as yourself.

Arrange children in scattered formation, approximately three to four feet apart, all facing the same direction. See Figure 23-10. Position yourself at the front of the group facing the children.

■ Begin dribbling in self-space; keep your head up—eyes focused on me. On the first signal, I'll point to your left; dribble with your right hand as you slidestep to your left. When you hear the next signal, stop your travel but continue to dribble. I'll then point forward; travel backward as you dribble. Stop on the signal. Each time the signal is given, change the direction of your travel: right, left, forward, backward.

Children need both verbal and visual directional signs as well as audible signals (via drum or whistle) for change of directions. The children will mirror your visual clues.

☐ All your travel will actually move within a five- to six-foot-square space.

☐ Use the slidestep when you move to the right or the left because this is the most efficient way to move to the side if you've covering a short distance.

Dribbling in Different Pathways

Dribble throughout general space, traveling in straight, curved, and zigzag pathways.

■ Travel in a straight pathway as you dribble. Each time you meet another person or hear the drum, turn quickly to your right or left and continue to travel/dribble in a straight pathway.

■ Follow the straight lines on the gym floor (or playground) as you travel/dribble.

■ Travel in a series of curved pathways as you dribble. If you curve to the left, dribble with your right hand; if you curve to the right, dribble with your left hand. Always keep the ball on the outside of the curve.

■ Travel/dribble throughout general space, quickly moving from side to side in a zigzag pathway.

■ Travel/dribble in a straight pathway. On the signal, quickly zigzag to miss an imaginary opponent and then continue dribbling in a straight pathway.

■ Stand approximately three feet behind a partner; each of you has a playground ball. Partner 1 (in front) travels/dribbles throughout general space,

Figure 23-11 A child's pathways map.

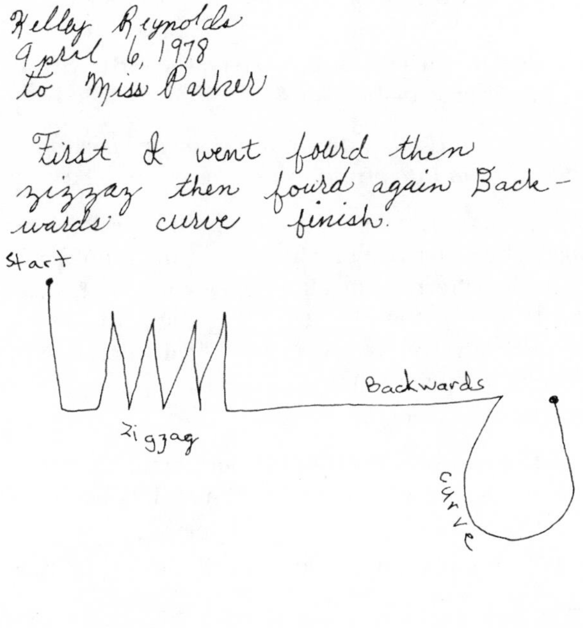

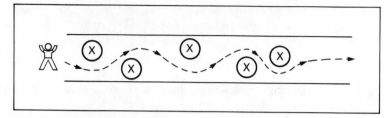

Figure 23-12 Dribbling around obstacles.

changing pathways. Partner 2 *(in back)* attempts to stay three feet behind the leader/partner at all times. *(Give each partner several chances to be the leader.)* Design a traveling/dribbling strategy to move from the center of the gym *(or outdoor blacktop)* to the end line. Design the strategy using combinations of pathways to outwit imaginary opponents. *(See Figure 23-11.)* Practice the traveling/dribbling strategy until you can do it three times exactly the same way. If I were to place five opponents in a zone defense, could you still execute your strategy?

Dribbling Around Stationary Obstacles

Set up marker cones or milk jugs throughout general space. Vary the space between cones; place some three feet apart, others five to six feet apart.

Travel/dribble throughout general space, dribbling around the obstacles.

- □ Always keep your body between the ball and the obstacle as you're dribbling. This skill will be very important later when the obstacles are people trying to take the ball away from you.
- ■ See if you can dribble sixty seconds without bumping into a cone or another person—heads up.

Using colored tape, divide the floor or blacktop into a series of alleys. Divide the children into groups, one group per alley.

One person in your group will be the dribbler; he'll stand at one end of the alley. The other persons in your group should arrange themselves in a zigzag obstacle pattern in the alley. *(See Figure 23-12.)* The dribbler attempts to dribble the length of the alley, avoiding the obstacles and staying within the side boundaries. The obstacles try to gain possession of the ball. Obstacles can stretch and pivot but can't move from self-space; obstacles can touch only the ball, not the dribbler.

- □ Here's a hint for the dribbler: Remember to keep your body between the obstacle and the ball. You'll have to switch hands as you zigzag down the alley.
- ■ Each person in the group will have equal turns as the dribbler.

Dribbling Against an Opponent: One on One

Select a partner who dribbles while traveling as well as you or slightly better. On the signal, partner 1 begins dribbling while traveling toward the end line; partner 2 attempts to gain possession of the ball by tapping it away. Neither partner should foul the other by bumping, pushing away, or reaching in. Partner 1 attempts to keep possession of the ball for thirty seconds; if partner 2 gets the ball, she gives it back. At the end of thirty seconds, partner 2 will dribble and partner 1 will try to take away. Ready? Begin.

■ Select a partner whose dribbling skills are similar to yours. Each of you will have a playground ball. On the signal, each partner begins dribbling while attempting to take the ball away from the other person. Remember: You're dribbling *and* trying to gain possession from your partner—and your partner is trying to get the ball from you.

PROFICIENCY LEVEL

Children at the proficiency level seem to dribble without thinking about it. They're able to change direction, speed, and pathway at will. They're challenged by situations that involve other children as partners or as opponents who make the situation increasingly unpredictable.

Activities Leading to Skill Development

Starting and Stopping; Changing Directions Quickly While Dribbling

Begin dribbling in general space. Travel slowly at first, and then gradually increase your speed until you're moving quickly while maintaining the dribble. On the signal, quickly stop both your travel and the dribble.

☐ To stop in a balanced position, remember to bend your knees and lower your body.
☐ The ability to stop both your travel and your dribbling at the same time will keep you from traveling violations in basketball.

■ Begin dribbling throughout general space. On the signal, stop quickly in a front-back stance, maintaining the dribble. Pivot by reversing the way you're facing; turn on the balls of your feet. Continue your travel/dribble.

Dribbling Against Opponents—Group Situations

Divide the children into two groups, with equal numbers in each group. Give each child a playground ball for dribbling. Space should be fairly confined; for example, twenty-five children need the space of half a basketball court.

On the signal, begin dribbling throughout general space. As you dribble, try to take the ball away from someone else while not letting anyone take away the ball you're dribbling. *(Give signal to begin, time youngsters forty-five seconds, give signal to stop.)*

When the activity is a game situation with competing skills, it's best if you divide children into groups, thus placing equal skills in each group.

Playing Now You've Got It, Now You Don't

Divide children into two groups.

Each team stands on opposite side lines of the gym *(or blacktop)* and faces each other. Each member of team A has a playground ball for dribbling. On the signal, team A players begin dribbling toward the opposite sideline. Team B, without playground balls, begins moving forward, trying to take away the balls. If a team B player gains possession of the ball, she dribbles toward the opposite sideline. When players from team A or team B make it over their goal line, they stay there until all playground balls are behind one of the sidelines. Team B is now given all the playground balls, and the game begins again.

Playing Dribble Tag

Give each child a playground ball for dribbling. Designate two or three children to be "it."

On the signal, everyone will begin dribbling in general space. The players who are "it" will try to tag you as you're traveling and dribbling; the "its" also are dribbling. You're caught if

1. You're tagged by an "it"
2. You lose control of the ball

If you're caught, stand and hold the ball above your head. You'll be free to travel if a player who is dribbling touches you.

- Each two minutes, we'll rest for ten seconds while I appoint new "its."

Dribbling and Passing with a Partner

Arrange the children in two lines approximately ten feet from each other at one end of the gymnasium or blacktop. Partners are across from each other; one partner has a playground ball for dribbling and passing.

Partner 1 will dribble eight to ten times and then pass to partner 2, who has been traveling forward. Partner 2 receives the pass, dribbles as he travels forward, and then passes back to partner 1. Partners continue to travel/dribble and pass the length of the gymnasium.

□ Remember to begin dribbling as soon as you receive the pass; in basketball it's a traveling violation if you take a step before the dribble begins.
□ Pass to your partner on the move; don't stop your travel.

■ Select a partner and scatter throughout general space, approximately fifteen feet from your partner. Each set of partners will have a playground ball for dribbling and passing. On the signal, begin traveling, dribbling, and passing to your partner. *(Allow two minutes of activity and then rest for ten seconds.)*

□ Remember, if you have the ball, you must dribble when you travel.
□ Be aware of where your partner is and where other players are located; control the dribble.

Dribbling and Passing in Game Situations

Working in groups of three, two of you will dribble and pass while the third player tries to steal the ball. We'll rotate the interceptor every two minutes.

□ This is a no-contact game; don't foul the person with the ball.

You need advanced skills to dribble while successfully avoiding an opponent.

Playing Dribble/Pass Keep Away

Working in groups of four, two of you will dribble and pass while the other two try to gain possession of the ball either by intercepting a pass or stealing the ball on the dribble.

- ▫ Remember to keep your body between the ball and your opponent when you're dribbling.

Dribbling and Throwing at a Target

Use colored tape to mark a four-foot square target on the wall at each end of the gymnasium, approximately seven feet above the floor.

Beginning at the center of the gymnasium, travel/dribble toward the end wall. When you're within ten to twelve feet of the target, throw the ball, trying to hit the wall within the target square. Collect the ball, quickly move to the side, and return to midcourt.

- ▫ Throw at the target while you're still on the move; don't stop and then throw.
- ▫ You're permitted one step after you stop dribbling before you must release the ball.

- ■ Select a partner who will serve as a defense. Partner 1 dribbles toward the end wall and attempts to score by hitting the target; partner 2 tries to gain possession of the ball on the dribble and block the throw to the target. Change partner roles after each travel/dribble.

- ▫ Remember to use a variety of pathways toward the goal to outwit your opponent.
- ▫ Keep your body between the defense and the ball when you're dribbling.

- ■ Practice the dribble/target activity with an offensive partner. Combine dribbling and passing to a partner as you travel toward the target. Alternate the throw to the target between partners.

- ▫ Avoid a traveling violation—don't take extra steps after the dribble.

- ■ You and your partner join with two other partners for a two on two activity of dribbling, passing, and throwing at a target.

Place targets around the walls as space allows. Place targets on both side and end walls to provide maximum activity.

Playing Small-Group Basketball

If you're comfortable with your skills of dribbling, passing, and throwing at a target, you may want to play a small-group basketball game. The maximum number of players on a team is three. Match the skills on your team so the game will be a challenge for everyone; it's no fun if the score is a runaway.

- Before we begin the team play, let's think of all the skills we need for being successful in basketball: spatial awareness, throwing, catching, traveling, dodging, dribbling, shooting at a target. Within your group, discuss what you need to know about each skill to be successful in basketball.

Using Harlem Globetrotters' Dribbling/Passing Routines

You can have four, five, or six persons in your group. Put together a series of dribbling and passing skills in a Harlem Globetrotters' routine. Design the floor pattern, ways to travel, individual tricks, and partner or group skills. Practice your routine until you have it memorized and in time with the music. We'll then look at each routine. *(Good music is "What's New Charleston," from* A Fitness Experience, *KIMBO.)*

READING COMPREHENSION QUESTIONS

1. Discuss the difference between volleying and dribbling.
2. Name five body parts that can be used to volley a ball.
3. What is the primary focus of the tasks at the precontrol level of volleying? What is the teacher trying to accomplish before moving on to the control level?
4. List four different types of balls that can be used to practice volleying at the precontrol level.
5. What does the phrase "strike the ball with a level body part" mean? What does the phrase "meeting the ball at a right angle" mean?
6. Rank the following tasks by placing the number 1 in front of the easiest (most basic) task, the number 2 in front of the next more difficult task, and so on.
   - (   ) Striking a ball to different levels
   - (   ) Striking a ball with two hands
   - (   ) Striking a ball to outwit an opponent
   - (   ) Striking a balloon
   - (   ) Striking a ball to a partner
7. Give one example of a repeatable sequence of striking that uses a minimum of three different body parts.
8. Explain the meaning of the phrase "the location of hit determines the direction of travel."
9. Give two examples of dynamic and unpredicable situations related to the skill of volleying.
10. What characterizes each of the four skill levels of dribbling?
11. What does it mean to keep one's hand relaxed and flexible as opposed to flat and stiff when dribbling?

Striking with Rackets and Paddles

Children learning to strike with a racket or paddle must coordinate many familiar skills into one new one. They must learn to accurately toss or drop the object to be contacted, visually track the object while they're traveling to an appropriate location, and contact the object at exactly the right moment. And simultaneously they must adjust to the weight and length of the implement. A successful striker must coordinate *all* these variables.

Because striking with an implement is a complex skill, we teach this skill after children have been introduced to the skill of striking with body parts, specifically the hand (see Chapter 23).

LEVELS OF SKILL PROFICIENCY

The difficulty of striking with an implement increases with the length of the implement. Children at the precontrol level benefit from practicing first with short-handled, lightweight implements. Balloons, which travel slowly, expedite visual tracking and eye-hand coordination. Appropriate tasks for children at the precontrol level include:

1. Striking a balloon with a lightweight paddle or hose racket
2. Striking a suspended ball
3. Tossing a ball or object upward and hitting it
4. Dropping an object and contacting it underhand
5. Dropping a ball and contacting it after a bounce

When children are able to strike a ball consistently in these contexts, they're ready for control-level experiences, which include contacting a rebounding ball a number of times in succession, sending the object in a desired direction, and varying the force of the contact. Other appropriate control-level activities include:

1. Striking a ball at a target
2. Sending a ball high enough to travel over a net

Children at the utilization level are able to contact a ball repeatedly without a miss (bouncing it up or down with a paddle or racket) and send a ball or other object various distances and in different directions. The youngsters are now ready to apply these skills in dynamic situations, such as moving into various positions to contact an object at different places around the body and returning shots to a partner. The skill of striking is now used in activities such as:

1. Striking with a variety of rackets and objects
2. Continuously hitting to a rebound wall
3. Striking cooperatively with a partner for high scores
4. Striking with overhand, forearm, backhand, and underhand strokes

When the children have attained the proficiency level, they demonstrate a mature pattern of striking: both body and implement control while traveling and an ability to select the most effective type of striking when responding to a partner. Experiences at the proficiency level center around game situations. Fast-moving, quick-reacting patterns of striking are required in both cooperative and competitive games. Appropriate activities include:

1. Playing cooperative or competitive games
2. Offensive-defensive movements involving others

Our progression spiral on p. 542 presents ideas for developing the skill of striking with rackets and paddles from the precontrol through the proficiency levels. The following Key Observation Points illustrate correct striking with rackets and paddles.

SKILL THEME DEVELOPMENT SEQUENCE

Striking with Rackets and Paddles

CONTROL LEVEL

Striking a ball rebounding from a wall
Striking an object to send it over a net
Striking through a target
Varying the force of the hit
Sending an object in the desired direction
Striking an object in the desired direction
Striking a ball upward with both sides of the paddle
Striking a ball upward or downward for more than one contact
Striking upward continuously
Striking downward continuously

PRECONTROL LEVEL

Striking a ball straight upward
Striking a self-tossed object or dropped ball
Striking a suspended ball
Striking a balloon with a lightweight paddle
Balancing objects on paddles

KEY OBSERVATION POINTS / **Striking with Rackets and Paddles**

1. Does the child take a forward step on the foot opposite the striking arm?

NO   YES

Striking with Rackets and Paddles

PROFICIENCY LEVEL

Playing self-designed racket games
Playing Badminton Volleyball
Playing Minitennis doubles
Playing aerial net games
Playing Minitennis
Playing Racket Four Square
Playing Corner Ball
Playing Wall Ball

UTILIZATION LEVEL

Playing Racket Call Ball
Striking in various aerial pathways in gamelike situations
Striking overhead over a net
Striking overhead
Striking to different places around a partner
Striking at different positions in relation to the body
Hitting cooperatively and continuously with a partner

2. Does the child's body coil and rotate forward as the child swings the racket?

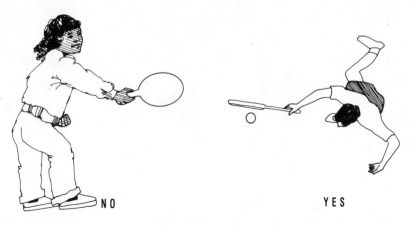

NO   YES

3. Does the child draw the racket back and then swing it forward along a full arc?

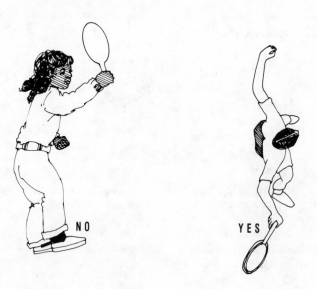

MATURE STRIKING PATTERNS

When children are at the mature stage of striking with rackets and paddles, do their strikes look similar to the following sequence? In the preparatory phase, weight is shifted to the back foot, the trunk rotates 45° to 90°, the hip

and trunk are cocked, and the racket is drawn back. This is followed by movements that occur in such quick succession that they seem almost simultaneous: The weight shifts, the body rotates forward, and the racket is swung forward along a full arc (an arc around the body).

Source: Adapted from *Fundamental Motor Patterns*, 2nd ed., by R. L. Wickstrom, 1977, Philadelphia: Lea & Febiger.

ASSESSMENT GUIDE / Striking with Rackets and Paddles

TASK   In your own space, try to strike the ball against the wall at least five times in a row. The ball can bounce once before you hit it.

Note to Teachers. Each child will need enough space so he or she can hit against the wall and not interfere with another child; a wooden or plexiglass paddle; and a tennis ball.

GUIDE   The children are ready for precontrol- or control-level tasks when you observe that:

1. They're unable to continually strike the ball, or they have to stop the ball before returning it to the wall.
2. The ball and/or the children are unable to stay in the designated space.
3. The swings are short and choppy.

The children are ready for utilization- or proficiency-level tasks when you observe them completing the task as explained: They continually keep striking the ball within the boundaries of their space and their strokes are smooth and encompass a full range of motion.

PRECONTROL LEVEL

At the precontrol level, we provide experiences for the children to use lightweight paddles to contact balls, shuttlecocks, and other objects. These objects are often suspended from ropes at various heights to make the task easier.

We recommend balloons at the precontrol level because the flight of a balloon is longer and slower than that of a ball and so the child has more time for visual tracking. Heavier balloons, although a bit more expensive, are more durable than inexpensive, lightweight balloons. They also tend to be less erratic during flight and consequently are easier for children to strike successfully.

Activities Leading to Skill Development

Balancing Objects on Paddles

Each child will need a paddle and balloon. Ethafoam paddles are best because they are lightweight and easy to control.

You're going to practice a new skill now. To warm up, just try to balance a balloon on a paddle. As you do this, try to keep the balloon in the middle of the paddle. Always watch the balloon.

☐ Keeping your paddle flat will help you do this. *Flat* means even or level. Pretend that you're balancing a full glass of milk on the paddle and you don't want any of the milk to spill.

■ The balloon was fairly easy to balance, but this time we're going to make it a little harder. Instead of a balloon, balance a ball on your paddle. Try to keep the ball on the paddle as long as you can. Concentrate and watch the ball closely.

■ If you're really good at keeping the ball on the paddle so that it doesn't fall off very often, try rolling the ball around on the paddle while still making it stay on. At times you'll really have to do some fast work to keep the ball on the paddle!

Volleybirds (badminton shuttlecocks with flat bottoms; see Chapter 23) work well with precontrol children. The youngsters learn to keep the paddle flat as they walk around carrying the volleybird on the paddle and then attempt to catch the volleybird on the paddle.

Striking a Balloon with a Lightweight Paddle

Each child will need a nylon hose or ethafoam paddle and balloon. See Figure 24-1. When children first begin striking balloons with paddles, it helps to tie (use string) the balloon onto the paddle's handle. This saves much chasing time and makes it easier for children to remain in their self-space.

In your own *(indoor)* space with your paddle and balloon, strike the balloon up in the air. Find out how to keep the balloon in the air.

☐ The secret is to watch the balloon and the paddle very closely. You should see the balloon touch the paddle.
☐ I've noticed that the balloon seems to be leading some of you all over the room. This time try very hard to strike the balloon and concentrate on staying in your self-space. Don't let the balloon lead you around.

■ Now I have a challenge for you. While you stay in your own space, see how many times you can strike the balloon before it touches the floor. Make sure that you strike the balloon with your paddle flat right in front of you so the balloon doesn't go back over your head.

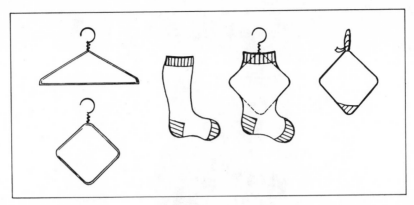

Figure 24-1 Construction of nylon hose rackets. Lightweight rackets can be made from old coat hangers, nylon socks (or stockings), and tape.

1. Grasp the handle and the bottom of the hanger.
2. Pull in opposite directions until the hanger is the desired shape.
3. Put one sock over the hanger from bottom to handle.

4. Bend the sharp edge of the handle down and wrap the excess sock around the handle.
5. Tape or tie the end of the sock around the handle.

To increase the length of nylon hanger rackets without substantially increasing the weight, tape a rolled-up newspaper to the handle.

How many times can you strike an object before it touches the ground?

Youngsters at the precontrol level benefit from practice with short-handled, lightweight rackets.

■ Before, you tried to stay in your own space while you were striking the balloon. This time you're going to do the exact opposite. Practice keeping the balloon in the air in front of you while traveling slowly forward. It helps to strike the balloon just a little forward as you travel.

Striking a Suspended Ball

Students will need balls suspended from string (see Figure 24-2) and paddles.

In your own space you have a ball that is hanging from a string. This time, instead of striking an object up in the air, your task is to strike the object so that it travels straight forward. Make sure you strike the ball with the face of your racket, as if you were trying to spank the ball.

Suspend balls above shoulder height for this task; place carpet squares or other markings on the floor behind each ball.

■ To strike the ball now, stand on the carpet square and strike from that position.

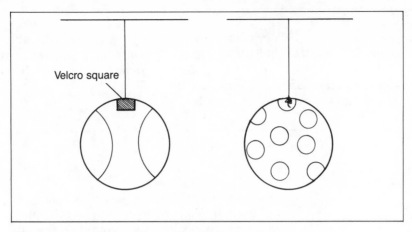

Figure 24-2 Suspending balls on strings. Glue a Velcro square to a string and tennis ball, to enable the ball to drop from the string when the ball is struck; or knot string or elastic into the hole of a plastic whiffle ball. Balls can be hung from climbing apparatus, traveling rings, and between volleyball game standards, and they can be attached to walls in the corners of the gym.

Striking a suspended ball is an effective form of practice for many children.

Attach a small bell to a ball, or place a metal gong, loose plastic jugs, or similar sound-producing objects on a wall as targets. Young children enjoy the auditory feedback from a jingle bell or a metal gong when contact is made.

A tennis ball can be attached to a rope with small squares of Velcro so the ball will detach and travel when contacted.

☐ Some of you aren't hitting the ball very hard. This time really try to hit the ball hard. It helps to step through with your front foot as you strike the ball and to twist your trunk around, so that all your body weight is behind the strike. Pretend you're really mad and want to slam the ball down hard.

For this task, move the carpet squares to a position beside the suspended balls and lower the balls to waist height.

■ We've changed things a little this time. Your carpet squares are now on the side of your ball. Try to strike the ball from this position so that it will travel straight forward.

☐ You really want to make the ball go very far forward, so I'm going to give you a few suggestions. As you strike the ball, step forward on your front foot *(opposite foot)* and make the paddle follow the ball even after the ball has been hit.

At this point, children should be striking on their preferred sides. When the children begin to strike consistently, challenge them to strike on the opposite side of their bodies (for example, backhand).

Striking a Self-Tossed Object or Dropped Ball

Before, you had to strike a balloon with a paddle. This time it's going to be a little harder; you're going to strike a ball with a paddle. You'll use the same action you used to strike the balloon, but a ball makes the task harder. To begin, try to strike the ball down with the paddle as you would if you were dribbling a basketball. Strike the ball only once, catch the ball, and do the task again. Don't try to keep the ball going; just try to hit it so that you're able to stay in your same space.

■ This time instead of trying to hit the ball down, try to strike it up in the air. If you keep the ball close to you and don't hit it very high, you can control it better. Again, just hit the ball up once and catch it and then do the task again.

□ I'll tell you the secret to both types of striking: keeping your paddle very level. If you can do this, the ball will tend to stay where you are and not fly all over the room.

■ Now that you've practiced for a while, choose whatever way you want to strike the ball—up or down—and practice that way. Remember, catch the ball each time before you strike again.

Striking a Ball Straight Upward

Each child will need a nylon hose paddle and a lightweight ball.

In your self-space, hold the ball at shoulder height and your racket at your waist or lower. Then release the ball and try to contact it so that it goes straight up before it touches the floor. Make sure that you drop the ball, not toss it.

□ You need to think about one thing: Don't start to swing your paddle forward until the ball has been released. If you start sooner or later than that, you'll miss the ball.

For this task, each child will need a wood, ethafoam, or plexiglass paddle (see Figure 24-3) and a shuttlecock or volleybird.

Figure 24-3 Construction of short-handled paddles. Short-handled paddles can be cut with a jigsaw from one-half-inch finished plywood or from one-fourth-inch plexiglass. Sand plywood edges until they're smooth, and wrap the handles with fiberglass tape. Each paddle should have a wrist string for safety.

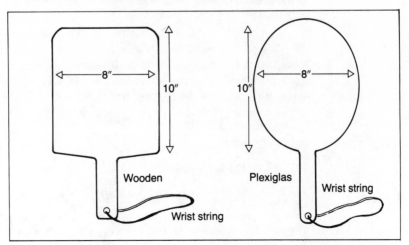

Although wooden and plexiglass paddles are very good for learning to strike, they do present a safety problem. Recently a new paddle made of ethafoam has become available. The paddle is made with both short and long handles; we prefer the ethafoam paddles whenever the children are working in close spaces or in groups.

■ This time you're going to do the exact same thing as before but with different equipment. Hold the shuttlecock or volleybird at shoulder height and the racket at waist level. Drop the object and try to strike it so that it travels straight up. You'll have to concentrate on timing your swing because the shuttlecock or volleybird doesn't fall as fast as the ball.

□ One secret to all striking is to *always* watch the object you're trying to hit. You should see it hit the paddle. This time try to follow the shuttlecock or volleybird very closely with your eyes all the time.

CONTROL LEVEL

Experiences at the control level are designed to help children go beyond just contacting the ball. At this level children learn to control the direction, force, and aerial pathway of an object. One of the first cues we give children when beginning striking activities is "watch the ball." This is hard for many youngsters because so much else is going on around them. To help children focus on the ball, paint a bright dot or letter on it and direct their concentration toward this mark.

At the control level, we introduce children to a variety of striking implements and to objects with various surfaces, lengths, and types and degrees of bounce, including Ping-Pong paddles, racket ball paddles, paddleball paddles, badminton rackets, tennis rackets, paddleballs, tennis balls, racket balls, rubber balls, shuttlecocks, Ping-Pong balls. (At the utilization and proficiency levels we continue to provide a variety of striking implements and objects.)

Activities Leading to Skill Development

Striking Downward Continuously

Each student will need a wooden paddle and a dead tennis ball.

In your own space, try to strike the tennis ball down with the racket so that the ball keeps going. Make sure you keep your arm out away from your body so the ball doesn't bounce on your foot.

□ Make sure that the paddle is flat when you hit the ball. If it is, the ball will come straight back up to you.

■ Now you have to keep the ball going and also keep all the bounces below your waist.

■ I'm going to time you to see how many strikes you can get in one minute. These strikes don't have to be below the waist. Ready? Go.

Striking Upward Continuously

Each student will need a wooden paddle and a dead tennis ball.

You're going to strike a ball so it travels up in the air. You don't have to keep the ball going—just try to strike it. Remember to really hit the ball, not just let it hit your paddle. This task will be harder.

□ This time as you try to hit the ball up in the air, watch it so closely that you can see the seams in the ball as the ball contacts the paddle.

■ See how many times in a row you can strike the ball without losing control of it. Try to use just the right amount of force on the ball to keep it going. Too much force will send the ball across the room, and with too little force, the ball will just die on your paddle.

Striking a Ball Upward or Downward for More Than One Contact

Each child will need any kind of racket and a lightweight ball.

Now that you've hit the ball down to the floor and up in the air, you're going to combine both tasks. One time hit the ball into the air, and the next time hit the ball to the floor. Keep the ball close to you, and try not to hit it very hard. The objective is to see how well you can control the ball.

■ This time things are even more difficult. You're still going to hit the ball to the floor one time and in the air the next time, but you're going to walk around the space as you do it. Watch the ball carefully, and watch the other people out of the corner of your eye.

You can make this task more difficult by changing the form of locomotion to skipping, hopping, etc., by varying the speed, or by placing obstacles for the children to travel around.

Striking a Ball Upward with Both Sides of the Paddle

This time, try to strike the ball with both sides of your paddle, sometimes using the top side and sometimes using the bottom side. Remember, no matter what side of the paddle you use to strike with, the ball always has to go up.

■ To make the activity a little harder, try to strike the ball while it's in the air with both sides of the paddle on both sides of your body. This means that you'll use the top side of your paddle on the side of your body you usually use and the bottom side on the other side of your body.

■ See how many times you can keep the ball going to both sides of your body without missing.

Striking an Object in the Desired Direction

The children will need a shuttlecock and a racket.

Facing the wall and in your own space, drop the shuttlecock and try to strike it with your racket so it goes straight ahead. This strike is a little like an underhand throw; you're actually striking the shuttlecock from underneath, not from the side.

❑ Some of your strikes are going back over your head instead of straight forward. The trick to making the shuttlecock go forward is to contact it before your racket gets above your waist. Try it.

■ This time you're going to strike balls instead of shuttlecocks, so the task will be a little harder. Begin with the same idea: try to strike the ball with the racket so that it goes straight forward toward the wall. Remember, contact the ball before your paddle gets above your waist.

Remind the children to step into the ball so it's contacted at a point slightly in front of the forward foot. You can suggest the angle of the swing with the verbal clue of "drawing a line"—straight, left, right—with the swing.

❑ Here's one tip that'll really make you look like a pro. As you bring your paddle forward to hit the ball, you know you're really in control if the paddle just brushes against your hip as it comes forward. See if you can do this.

For this task, be sure there are a variety of targets on the wall in front of each child.

■ As you face the wall in your own space, you'll see a number of targets on the wall in front of you, some of them straight in front of you and some off to either side. Try to strike the ball so it sometimes goes to the right of you, sometimes to the left. You don't have to hit the target—use the targets as guides to tell you when you're really able to strike the ball to the right or to the left.

❑ When trying to strike an object so it goes to the right or left, bring the paddle back in the same direction that you want to hit the ball. In other words, if I want to hit the ball to my left, I bring my paddle back so that I can aim it to my left.

■ Keep practicing for a little while longer. The objective is to hit three balls in a row to where you want them to go.

■ This time I'm going to challenge you. I'll call out a direction—right or left—and you hit the ball to that side of your body. Think you can do it?

Sending an Object in the Desired Direction

Each student will need a tennis ball and a wooden paddle. Tape or paint circles on the wall in the following pattern:

O   O

O

O   O

For this task you're going to hit the ball against the wall, into the circles. To begin, don't try to hit the ball continuously. Each time, just catch the ball and start over again, aiming for a different circle.

Varying the Force of the Hit

This task is best taught outside on a large field. Each child will need a number of objects to strike, after which each child collects the objects.

Standing on the line, so that you're all facing the same direction and won't hit anyone else, practice striking the objects, changing the amount of force that you use for hitting. Sometimes use a lot of force, sometimes not very much force. Each time, make sure that you use the proper swing and follow-through, no matter what amount of force you use. Use up all your objects and then go collect them.

■ This time you're going to play a game with yourself. First, strike an object to as far away as possible. Take a marker and mark the place that your object fell. Be sure that you can see the mark from the striking line. Now try to hit an object so that it's halfway between the striking line and your far object. Practice until you feel as if you've really figured out just exactly the right amount of force to use. Then see if you can hit the spot three times in a row.

■ After you've done this task three times in a row, hit another object as far as you can, mark it, and try the same thing all over.

For this task, you'll need objects such as hoops for targets; use one object for every two students.

■ You'll be working with a partner this time. Each group of partners has a hoop that is on the floor. Now, instead of seeing how far you can strike, you're going to try to strike your object so it lands in or hits your target. First, start close, and then after you can hit the target three times, move back a few steps and try again. Your partner will keep the balls from rolling all over the place. After you get six hits, switch places with your partner for six hits and then switch back.

    □ Sometimes you'll do well from a close position but seem to miss more when you get farther away. Don't worry—that happens to all of us. But a couple of hints will help. First, remember to change the force of your hit in relation to how far away you are from the target. If you're far away, it takes a lot of force, but if you're close, only a little force. Second, the position of the face of the paddle makes a difference: If you're close, the face should be pointed slightly upward.

    ■ Now you're going to make a game out of striking into hoops. Place three hoops on the floor, one about three feet away from you, one six feet away, and one ten feet away. One partner will try to strike so that the object lands in each hoop; the other partner will collect the object after the hits. Then the partners switch places. You can make up any other rules that you wish, but you both need to practice striking into all three hoops.

Striking Through a Target

From the ceiling, suspend a hoop to about shoulder height for each group of two.

At your hoop, one of you will bounce the ball on the floor and then try to strike it through the hoop. The partner will catch the ball and return it to the striker. After ten strikes, change places.

    □ This activity is harder than some of the other things you've done because the hoop tends to move and is a bit higher. You really have to watch closely and aim for the middle of the hoop so that even if the hoop moves a little bit, you'll still have a chance of getting the ball through the hoop.

    ■ Now that you've practiced by first letting the ball bounce, try it without letting the ball bounce. In other words, just drop the ball and hit it before it hits the ground and try to make it go through the hoop.

Striking an Object to Send It over a Net

Around the space, set up nets about three feet high.

With your partner at your net, strike the ball across the net. Your partner won't hit the ball back to you; he'll catch it and throw it back. After ten hits, change roles. It helps to bounce the ball on the floor once before you hit it across the net.

    ■ This time use three different striking patterns to hit the ball across the net: sidearm swing, overhead swing, and underhand swing. Take ten practices

*Children at the control level benefit from repeatedly
striking a ball against a wall.*

with one swing and then switch; take ten practices with another swing and
then switch; take ten practices with the third swing and then switch. Ready?
Three different ways of striking, ten practices each.

■ You can practice any way of striking you want this time, but try to pick a
spot on the opposite side of the net and hit the ball to that spot, as if you were
aiming for a target. Ten practices each, then switch.

*So that children in every group have their own net to work over, simply suspend
a rope between two chairs. This way you can set up nets of different heights
and lengths at various places around the space.*

Striking a Ball Rebounding from a Wall

Each child will need wall space.

Now you're going to have a chance to strike the ball against a wall. In your
space, about six feet from the wall, practice striking the ball against the wall
with a sidearm strike, called a *forehand* grip. *(See Figure 24-4.)* When you hit
the ball, you should be slightly behind and about an arm's length to the side
of the ball.

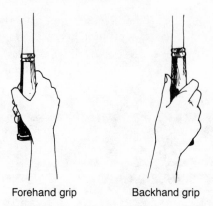

Forehand grip   Backhand grip

Figure 24-4 Examples of forehand and backhand grips.

■ Here comes the challenge. See how many times you can strike the ball against the wall and let the ball bounce only once before hitting it again. If you miss, just start counting over.

▫ This time try to keep the ball going, but always try to contact it at waist height. This means you have to bend your knees if the ball is lower than your waist or let the ball drop down if it's higher than your waist.

■ Now I'm going to make the activity a little harder for you. Hit the ball to different places on the wall, always trying to be ready to hit it when it comes back to you. In other words, you'll have to figure out where the ball is coming when it bounces off the wall and be behind it so you can hit it again. Remember, hit different places on the wall.

▫ Sometimes it's impossible to get behind the ball so that you can hit it on the easy side. When that happens, you have to hit the ball on the opposite side on your body and turn your hand slightly on your racket. This is called a *backhand* grip. *(See Figure 24-4.)*

For this task, mark a line on the wall, approximately three feet from the ground.

■ This time the challenge is really hard. You need to see how many times

---

For many beginning teachers, the idea of teaching striking is almost overwhelming because of the complexity of the skill. If you feel this way, remember these three points

about striking and leave the other aspects until later:

1. Focus on the ball.
2. Step forward on the opposite foot.
3. Stand sideways to the target.

in a row you can hit the ball above the line on the wall. The ball can bounce only once on the ground between hits. Ready? Go.

For this task, mark a line on the ground five feet from the wall space being used.

■ This time you can do what you've wanted to do for a long time: hit the ball as hard as you can. But I have some rules. First the ball must land behind the line marked on the ground; second, you're allowed only one bounce to hit the ball back, to prevent you from hitting the ball so hard that you can't get to it.

UTILIZATION LEVEL

Experiences at the utilization level enable children to strike with an implement, not as an invariant skill, but in dynamic environments that involve partners and striking from different positions in relation to the body.

Activities Leading to Skill Development

Hitting Cooperatively and Continuously with a Partner

With your partner, in a space by yourselves, see if you can strike the ball back and forth to each other. The ball can bounce in the middle, but remember to get ready to hit the ball again after each hit.

☐ Remember that you're working with your partner, so you always want to try to hit the ball so your partner can hit it back. This means easy hits, ones that don't go very hard or fast.

☐ Sometimes when we start working with partners we forget things we already know, like stepping into the hit. This time, think about taking that step as you hit.

☐ Remember when you worked on hitting the ball on both sides of your body? I see some of you running around so you don't have to use your backhand. This time practice trying to hit the ball on both sides of your body by changing your grip rather than moving your body all over the place.

You can modify this task or make it more complex by having the children practice it against the wall, over a net or a line on the floor, or across a table or bench.

Striking at Different Positions in Relation to the Body

This time your partner is going to throw rather than hit to you. Partner 1 will throw the ball to partner 2 so that it bounces once before it reaches partner 2.

Partner 2—the hitting partner—then tries to hit the ball straight back to partner 1—the thrower—regardless of where the ball has been sent. Partner 1 then catches the ball and throws to a new place. After ten throws, switch places. The first time, always throw the ball to your partner's right side. The next time, always throw it to your partner's left side. Right—now don't mix up the two sides.

▫ Sometimes you seem to get all crowded up to the ball when it comes to places you have to move to get to. Think about moving your feet so that your body is at least an arm's distance away from the ball as you hit it. *(Demonstrate or ask a child to demonstrate.)*

■ This time, don't let your partner know which side you're going to throw the ball to. Hitters, as soon as you see the ball leave the thrower's hand, adjust your position so that you can return the ball. Ten throws and change.

In the beginning stages of striking a ball sent by a partner, children benefit from having the ball tossed consistently to their preferred or nonpreferred side. This way they can progress to adjusting the preparatory stage according to the direction of the oncoming ball.

Striking to Different Places Around a Partner

Each set of partners will need a space approximately ten by twenty feet.

With your partner, strike the ball back and forth, each time hitting it to an opposite side of your partner's body. In other words, once you'll hit to the left, the next time to the right. Make sure that your racket follows through in the direction you're sending the ball. Try to keep the ball going for as long as possible.

▫ As you send the ball back to your partner, try to really place the ball so that it's going to your partner's opposite side; don't just hit the ball back.
▫ Some of you are getting lazy. After each time you hit the ball, remember to return to the center of your space and get ready to hit the next ball.
▫ For some of you, one side of your body isn't as good as the other side. When you use the side that isn't as good, really think about stepping forward, extending your arm as you hit the ball, and following through with your paddle in the direction that you want the ball to go. *(The teacher or a student should demonstrate.)*

■ As you practice now, see how long you can keep the ball going, but almost try to make your partner miss.

At this point we often observe a regression to an immature striking pattern, and frustration, because a successful hit depends a great deal on the other child's hit. Remember: Children are individuals. Rarely will an entire class be ready for this task at the same time!

Striking Overhead

Each child will need wall space.

Stand about ten feet from the wall. Toss the ball higher than your racket can reach in the air and then stretch to hit the ball when it's at its highest point. In other words, you throw the ball up, and when it reaches the very top of the throw, the point where it won't go up any farther and hasn't started to come down, you hit it so it goes against the wall. Don't try to hit the ball back when it bounces off the wall; just catch it and start over.

  ❑ If you throw the ball too high, you'll never be able to hit it. The secret is to throw the ball just above the top of your paddle, just barely, so that if you really reach and stretch, you can hit the ball.

  ■ Now that you've caught on to this idea, try to make the ball go down so that it hits about three feet from the bottom of the wall. To make it go down like that, the face of your racket must point slightly down as you hit the ball. Give it a try. Remember to watch the ball contact the racket so that you can see what you're doing.

For this task, mark a line on the wall, approximately three feet above the floor.

  ■ This time you have a target to aim for. Try to strike overhead again, but have the ball strike the wall just above the line. Watch your racket contact the ball so that you can tell which direction your racket face is pointed.

Striking Overhead over a Net

Each set of two youngsters will need balls, paddles, and a net.

You're going to practice hitting overhead again. Stand at the back of your court area, with your partner on the other side of the line. The partner with a paddle and some balls should throw the ball in the air just above her or his reach, including the reach of the paddle, and then hit the ball down and over the net. This is like a tennis serve, only everything is smaller. The nonhitting partner should collect all the balls as they're hit. After ten times, switch places.

  ❑ One thing that will really help you do this task is to think about stretching as you try to hit the ball. You want to throw the ball so that it's just out of your reach over the end of your racket and your whole body has to reach to hit it. *(The teacher or a student should demonstrate.)*
  ❑ Another thing that helps is throwing the ball so that it's slightly in front of your body and then contacting it when your racket is beginning to face down. If you hit the ball when your racket is facing up, the ball will go up.
  ❑ As you begin to hit more balls over the net and in the court, start to try to hit the ball a little harder. But don't attempt this until you can get ten hits in a row over the net and into the court.

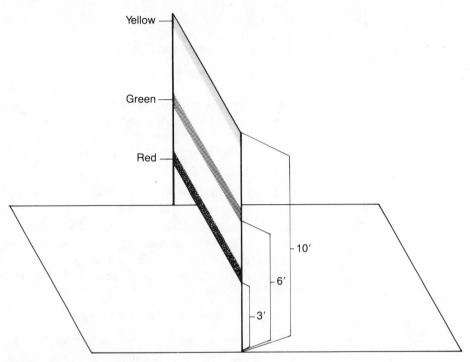

Figure 24-5 Setup for aerial pathways.

Striking in Various Aerial Pathways in Gamelike Situations

Hang different-colored pieces of yarn above each other, at three feet, six feet, and ten feet, so that children can use them as nets. See Figure 24-5.

Using a shuttlecock or volleybird and an underarm swing, try to make the object go over the lowest piece of yarn. After five tries, switch with your partner.

- Now try the middle piece. Five times each, then switch.
- Now the highest piece. For this one you're really going to have to use a big underarm swing to get the object over the net.
- This task will be difficult. Try to keep the shuttlecock or volleybird going with your partner, but this time, on the first hit, make it go over the low piece of yarn; on the next hit, make it go over the middle piece; on the third hit, make it go over the top piece. Then start over and reverse the order. Practice until you can do the sequence one time all the way through.

Playing Racket Call Ball

This time you're going to play a game with striking. You need no more than five people in a group to play. Here are the rules:

To be accomplished both safely and effectively, striking activities require a great deal of space. Unfortunately, many indoor facilities in elementary schools don't have such spaces available. If this is true at your school and there aren't any outdoor alternatives, you can have two activities going simultaneously in the space available. Often this involves striking activities taking place against the walls and activities that require less space, such as balancing or weight transference, occurring in the center of the space or on a stage area.

1. One person stands in the middle of a circle.
2. The person in the middle hits a ball with an ethafoam paddle straight up in the air and calls out the name of another person in the group.
3. The person whose name is called out must run to the middle of the circle and hit the ball up in the air before it bounces and call out another student's name.
4. The caller takes the place of the person whose name was called out.

□ Now that you've had a little time to try this out, I'll give you some hints about how to play. If you hit the ball really high in the air, it'll be very hard to control when it comes down and the game won't run smoothly because you're always chasing the ball. So you'll want to try hitting the ball at a lower level and have the players in close until you get the hang of it. Then you can gradually start to hit the ball higher and have the players move farther apart.

The complexity of any striking situation can be increased by the type of racket used. A light, short-handled racket is the easiest for a child to master; a heavy, long-handled racket is the most difficult. As children begin to master the skills of striking with rackets, we gradually change the type of racket used to continually make the task more difficult.

PROFICIENCY LEVEL

Experiences at the proficiency level encourage children to enjoy the challenge of striking with short-handled implements in game situations. These activities involve partner or opponent relationships, spatial strategy, and the varied use of effort qualities.

Activities Leading to Skill Development

Playing Wall Ball

Today you're going to play Wall Ball. The objective of this game is to hit the ball against a wall so your opponent is unable to return it. Here are the rules:

1. There are two people to a game.
2. Each player has a racket or a paddle.
3. One ball is used.
4. You may score only when you serve.
5. The ball may be returned either after one bounce or before the bounce.

The courts are marked on the floor. *(See Figure 24-6.)* To start play, partner 1 serves the ball against the wall and partner 2 tries to return it. Each time partner 1 hits the ball, it's partner 2's job to try and return it. You get points when you serve; if you fail to return the ball when it's your serve, the other partner gains the serve.

□ Now that you've been playing Wall Ball a while, let's see if you can really become a good Wall Ball player. Here are some hints. First, after you hit the ball, move quickly back to the center of the court so that you're ready for the next hit. It will thus be harder to catch you out of position. So now as you play, concentrate on moving back to the center of the court after each hit.

□ Second, use different types of strikes each time, to try and mix up your opponent. For example, sometimes use long strikes; other times use short strikes. This might also mean sometimes using a wrist action in your strikes and sometimes drawing a line to swing *(a swing that travels along an imaginary line to the target).* Now try different types of strikes as you play— mix them up. *(The teacher or a student should demonstrate.)*

Figure 24-6 Setup for Wall Ball.

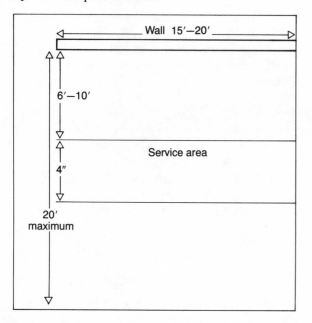

Figure 24-7 Setup for Corner Ball.

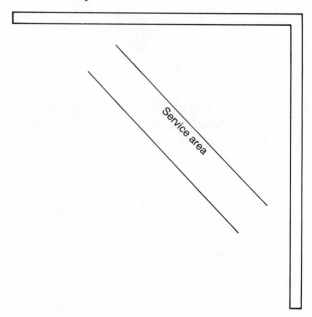

Playing Corner Ball

This game is very much like the last game that you played, except it's played in a corner instead of just flat against the wall. *(See Figure 24-7.)* As you might guess, the game is called Corner Ball. All the same rules as Wall Ball apply: two players, points won only when you serve, hit the ball either after one bounce or before it bounces. Go ahead and get used to playing in the corner.

□ As you may have found out, Corner Ball is a little harder to play than Wall Ball because the corner makes the ball do funny things. As you practice this time, hit the ball into the corner and try to make it bounce off the corner so that your opponent can't return the ball.

□ Now that you've practiced using the corners, go back to practicing mixing up your hits to the wall. Sometimes use wrist action, sometimes make corner shots, sometimes make long shots. Remember that no matter what shot you use, always return to the center of the court so you have a better chance of hitting the next shot.

Wall Ball and Corner Ball can be played cooperatively instead of competitively. That is, children may prefer to see how many hits they can make without a miss.

Playing Racket Four Square

Set up four square courts, each court fifteen by fifteen feet, labeled A, B, C, and D. Each group of four students will need foam paddles and a ball.

This game is called Racket Four Square. Here are the rules:

1. There is one person in each square.
2. You must hit the ball to another square.
3. The ball can't be hit to the person who hit it to you.
4. You must hit the ball after its first bounce.
5. The person who misses the ball goes to square D, and everyone else moves up a square.

□ To play this game well, you must always be ready to hit a ball coming from any direction. To do this, it helps to be in the ready position, which means carrying your weight on the balls of your feet with your knees slightly bent and holding your racket in front of your body at about waist level. If you do this, you'll be better able to return any ball hit to you.

□ Another helpful hint is to stay near the back corner of your square so you can always move forward to hit the ball *(which is the easiest way to move)* and are always able to see the ball. If you get caught up close to the middle of your square, your opponents can easily hit the ball behind you and you'd never be able to get it.

Playing Minitennis

For every two children, set up a low net on a surface that allows the ball to bounce. Mark off a court at each net area.

The objective of this game is to send the ball over the net so it bounces within the court and the opponent hits the ball before it bounces twice. Here are the rules:

1. Play begins with an overhead strike behind the end line.
2. The ball can bounce no more than once on each side of the net.
3. You may hit the ball before it bounces.

You may or may not keep score; the choice is yours. If you decide to keep score, decide on how you'll do so before you start to play.

☐ As you hit the ball, remember to strike with the racket fully extended away from your body. This means that your arm is straight out; your elbow is slightly bent, and your arm is *not* close to your side. This position gives you better control of the ball and enables you to better aim the ball to where you want it to go.

Playing Aerial Net Games

You'll need solid rackets, paddles or badminton rackets and shuttlecocks, tennis balls or volleybirds. String a net between the children's shoulder and head height. String one net for every pair of children. Mark off a court at each net with a serving line. See Figure 24-8.

The objective of this aerial net game is to send the object over the net so that the opponent can return it before the object touches the floor. Here are the rules:

1. Play begins with an underhand strike behind the serve line.
2. Aerial strikes continue until the object touches the floor or goes out of bounds.
3. If you like, you can make up your own way of changing serves and keeping points.

☐ Here are a few hints to make you really good at this game. Just as in Wall Ball and Corner Ball, you need to mix up your hits. And now you have more ways to mix them up. Sometimes make the hits go long, sometimes short—in other words, sometimes use a little force, sometimes a lot. You'll also want to change where you place the object: sometimes in the middle, sometimes down the sideline. So now as you play, really concentrate on mixing up your shots—never let your opponent know what you're going to do.

☐ Don't forget the wrist action that you practiced before; it can help you outsmart your opponent.

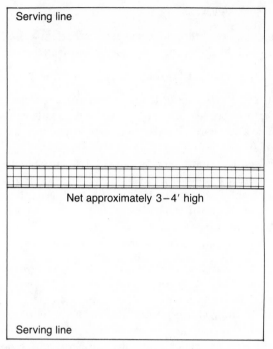

Serving line

Net approximately 3–4' high

Serving line

Figure 24-8 Court setup for aerial net games.

- Strike the object without running all around, no matter where around your body the object comes. I've seen some of you running all around the court and the object so you don't have to hit the object when it's on the nonracket side of your body. We call this action *dodging your backhand.* It isn't a very smart thing to do. You'll be a better player if you learn to hit the object just where it comes: the right or left side of your body, overhead, or down low. Practice making all those shots—don't avoid them. Thus your goal this time is to not avoid any shots because they aren't exactly where you want them.
- Now just one hint to help you have more accurate serves. As you serve, make sure that your swing starts in the front, goes to the back, travels forward again, and is close to your body, almost brushing your leg as it comes forward.

Aerial net games using a shuttlecock can be played with regular tambourines, with old ones that are discarded from rhythm band because the jingles have been lost, or with tambourines with rubberized heads. Children enjoy the sound made when the shuttlecock strikes the tambourine.

Playing Minitennis Doubles

Each group of four will need tennis balls, wooden paddles, and a net. The court is made up of four equal squares, with the net running down the center.

This game is called Minitennis. Here are the rules:

1. There are two people on each team.
2. Team A serves underhand and diagonally to team B.
3. The two teams hit the ball back and forth across the net until one team misses.
4. When the team serving misses, the other team takes over serving.
5. When the receiving team misses, the serving team keeps serving.
6. The serve always begins in the back right-hand corner behind the line, alternates to the back left-hand corner on every consecutive serve, and then back to the right.
7. The ball may be hit before it bounces or after one bounce.

   □ The trick to playing this game well is to cover all the empty space on your side of the net so your opponents don't have anywhere to hit the ball. This takes some planning on your and your partner's part so you know where each other should be and what to do when one person moves to a new spot. The standard way to do this is for one partner to play up and the other partner to play back; both partners move from side to side as necessary.

Playing Badminton Volleyball

Each group of six will need badminton rackets or paddles, shuttlecocks, and a net.

You're going to play Badminton Volleyball. Here are the rules:

1. There are three players on each team.
2. A player near the back of the court serves underhand to the other side of the net. The opponents hit the shuttlecock twice on their side of the net and then return the shuttlecock back over the net.
3. The shuttlecock must be hit twice by two different players on each side of the net before it's returned.
4. The shuttlecock must be hit before it touches the ground.
5. When the serving team misses, the other team scores.
6. You can keep score any way you want or not at all.

   □ The hard part of this game is that two people have to hit the shuttlecock before it crosses the net. This means you have to position yourself so you can hit the shuttlecock after the first person hits it. The best way to do this is to make sure that someone is positioned close to the net so he or she is able to hit the shuttlecock just before it crosses the net. You may want to establish some positions on your team to make sure that this happens.

Playing Self-Designed Racket Games

Today you're going to combine all that you've practiced into a game. You'll make up your games yourselves. In groups of no more than six, make up a game that involves striking with a foam racket. You can have whatever rules you want as long as you include these two: (1) The game must involve striking with foam rackets, and (2) everyone in your group must be playing at the same time. In other words, nobody sits out and waits for a turn. Remember, groups of no more than six, striking with foam rackets, and everybody plays. Go.

☐ After you've made up your rules and started to play your game, make sure you know your rules so that you can tell somebody else how to play your game. At the end of class, I'll ask you to write down your game.

Now is a good time to have students write down their games and actually play them again another day or teach them to another group. This forces the children to think about how to play the game.

READING COMPREHENSION QUESTIONS

1. Students at the precontrol level benefit from striking an object suspended from a string. Describe three different ways to suspend objects.
2. What types of striking implements and objects are recommended for students at the precontrol level?
3. Give two examples of invariant tasks for striking with rackets and two examples of dynamic tasks. (See Chapter 26, pp. 616 to 617, if you're not sure of the meaning of the terms *invariant* and *dynamic*.)
4. How does a teacher know when a child is ready to be challenged to "see if you can strike the ball on the opposite side of the body" (i.e., backhand)?
5. Describe the position of a child's arms and feet when the child is striking with a racket or paddle.
6. What characterizes each of the four generic levels of skill proficiency of striking with rackets and paddles?
7. What does a paddle facing forward (square face) look like? What does a paddle facing upward (open face) look like? What happens when an object is struck with a paddle held in each position?
8. What does it look like when children run around the ball instead of striking the ball on the opposite side of the body? Describe a task that would help them learn to not run around the ball.
9. A child swings a racket so that it remains at waist height throughout the swing. What direction does the ball travel if the child strikes the ball too early in the swing? Too late in the swing?
10. What is the major difference between Wall Ball and Corner Ball? Which of the two games is more difficult to play? Why?
11. Design six tasks related to striking with rackets or paddles. Rank them in order from the easiest to the hardest. Be certain to include at least one task from each skill level. Use a different striking implement or object for each task.

CHAPTER 25

Striking with Long-Handled Implements

T he skill of striking is used in many games. In this book, striking is divided into various categories: kicking and punting, volleying and dribbling, striking with rackets, and striking with long-handled implements. This division allows us to cover in some detail the gamut of striking activities. The basic action in all striking is the same—giving impetus to an object with a hit, punch, or tap—although often the purpose and the equipment differ.

This chapter focuses on striking with three specific long-handled implements: golf clubs, hockey sticks, and bats. These implements are swung in horizontal or vertical planes, although the underlying challenge of coordinating hands and eyes when striking with a long-handled implement remains constant. Because each swing has distinctive characteristics, each implement is covered separately in the Key Observation Points and/or Assessment Guides. Each swing involves striking away from the body, but the motor skills differ in relation to the purpose of the task.

Generally, striking is the last fundamental motor pattern learned because of the complexity of the hand-eye coordination involved. Children may possess a mature striking pattern before they're able to consistently make contact with the ball.

A sidearm pattern is used when striking a ball with a bat, to keep the bat at the same distance from the ground and in a horizontal plane throughout the swing. (See Key Observation Points on pp. 574 to 576 for striking sidearm with a bat.) In contrast, a swing with a hockey stick or golf club uses a more vertical arc, what is referred to as an underhand swinging pattern because in many ways it resembles the movement used to throw a ball underhand. (The Key Observation Points for striking with a golf club are on pp. 577 to 579.)

We don't introduce children to striking with long-handled implements so that they'll become experts at golf, tennis, or hockey. We provide children opportunities to practice striking patterns they're likely to use in a variety of contexts throughout their lives. This rationale can be fully appreciated when watching an adult trying to strike with a long-handled implement. If that individual has had no previous experience with a particular striking pattern, the results can be disastrous. Frustration will result, and ultimately the person may abandon the sport. Our emphasis is on giving children a variety of movement opportunities rather than on perfecting the technical aspects of a particular swing. Specific opportunities to refine and perfect different swings are provided at the secondary level or in private instruction.

Most long-handled implements are designed for adults. Because children aren't "regulation size," they find it difficult to manipulate implements of official size, length, and weight, so we use lightweight, plastic implements in our programs, or we make implements that match the sizes of the children. This prevents the children from learning poor habits when they try to use equipment that is too heavy or too long.

LEVELS OF SKILL PROFICIENCY

Initial striking tasks at the precontrol level include:

1. Striking a stationary object with a hockey stick or golf club
2. Striking a ball off a batting tee with a plastic bat
3. Traveling slowly while striking an object with a hockey stick
4. Striking a suspended object

When children are able to consistently make contact with an object (control level), they then become able to succeed at more difficult tasks, such as:

1. Traveling while striking an object (beanbag, puck, ball) and changing direction
2. Traveling with an object and changing speed while using a hockey stick
3. Striking a pitched ball
4. Using a hockey stick to propel an object while traveling along different pathways
5. Traveling, stopping, and controlling the ball (or puck)

SKILL THEME DEVELOPMENT SEQUENCE

Striking with Long-Handled Implements

CONTROL LEVEL

Throwing a ball in the air and striking it—bats
Striking a pitched ball—bats
Striking, varying force and distance—golf
Striking to a partner, varying distance and force—hockey
Striking stationary objects, varying distance and force—hockey
Striking to a stationary partner—hockey
Striking to a target (Around the World)—hockey
Striking in different places around the body—hockey
Striking to a large stationary target—hockey
Traveling in different pathways, directions, and speeds—hockey
Traveling and changing pathways and directions—hockey
Traveling, striking, and changing pathways with a partner—hockey
Traveling and striking while changing pathways—hockey
Traveling while changing speed and direction—hockey
Traveling, stopping, and controlling the ball—hockey

PRECONTROL LEVEL

Traveling slowly while striking a ball—hockey
Striking a ball on the floor while traveling slowly—hockey
Striking suspended objects—bats
Striking off a batting tee—bats
Striking to targets—hockey
Striking a stationary ball on the floor—hockey
Striking for distance—golf
Striking a stationary ball on the floor—golf or hockey

6. Throwing a ball up to self and striking it
7. Striking to a stationary partner
8. Striking a ball for distance with a golf club

At the control level, the tasks typically include only one variable besides striking.

When children can control a ball in the space around them (whether they're stationary or traveling) and their striking pattern is in the appropriate phase, they're functioning at the utilization level. Appropriate tasks include:

Striking with Long-Handled Implements

PROFICIENCY LEVEL

Playing Half Rubber
Playing One-Base Baseball
Playing Six-Player Teeball
Playing Minihockey
Striking to a teammate to avoid others in a dynamic situation—hockey
Playing Whiffle Ball Golf
Directing the pathway, distance, and speed of an object (Call Your Hit)—
   bats
Directing the pathway, distance, and speed of an object—golf
Keeping It Moving—hockey
Passing and receiving on the move—hockey
Striking to dodge an opponent—hockey

UTILIZATION LEVEL

Striking from a stationary position to a moving target—hockey
Directing the air pathway of the object struck—bats
Directing the air pathway of the object struck—golf
Playing Hockey Bowl
Playing Hoop Golf
Striking to distant targets of various sizes—golf
Striking and dodging stationary objects—hockey
Batting combining force and open spaces
Striking a pitched object, varying the distance—bats
Hitting to open places—bats
Directing the placement of an object—bats

1. Propelling an object while traveling and dodging stationary objects
2. Striking a ball consistently for distance and accuracy, at targets of different sizes, with a golf club
3. Directing the pathway of a pitched or rolled ball using a bat or hockey stick
4. Striking for distance
5. Passing to a traveling partner

When children reach the proficiency level, many possess mature striking patterns, and striking becomes a skill that can be used in dynamic situations. At this point, children are able to incorporate previous experiences into situations that involve strategy and split second decisions. Appropriate tasks include:

1. Traveling while propelling an object and dodging other children
2. Positioning the body to strike an oncoming object to an open space while traveling and while stationary
3. Striking with a golf club to targets in a strategic situation
4. Passing and receiving an object while moving and dodging other children

Striking skills may be the last to develop. But once children have developed the ability to consistently strike objects with long-handled implements, they can participate in many fascinating activities. The tasks in this chapter are organized according to their relative difficulty. This organization method more nearly fits the reality of the typical elementary physical education setting and also enhances the development of the skill of striking with long-handled implements. If you choose to develop a whole sequence of lessons around one particular striking pattern, each task is labeled as to its pattern. Be reminded though that some tasks relate to previous activities that may not necessarily have been designed to develop the same pattern.

Our progression spiral for developing the skill themes of striking with hockey sticks, bats, and golf club is on p. 572.

KEY OBSERVATION POINTS / Sidearm Striking with a Bat

1. Does the child swing the bat in a horizontal plane?

NO   YES

2. Does the child take a forward step and follow it quickly with hip, trunk, and arm rotation?

NO   YES

3. Do the child's wrists uncock with contact?

NO   YES

Mature Stage

When children are at the mature stage of sidearm striking, do their strikes look similar to the following sequence? A forward step is taken, followed quickly by hip, trunk, and arm rotation. The forward movement of the trunk stops before

contact, but the whipping rotation from the shoulders and arms continues. The pushing motion of the right arm (left arm, if the child is left-handed) and uncocking of the wrists are the final significant forces.

Source: Adapted from *Fundamental Motor Patterns*, 2nd ed., by R. L. Wickstrom, 1977, Philadelphia: Lea & Febiger.

KEY OBSERVATION POINTS / Striking with a Golf Club

1. Is the child's left arm (for right-handed children) kept firm at the top of the backswing?

NO   YES

2. Is the child's weight shifted to the back foot at the top of the backswing, with both knees remaining bent?

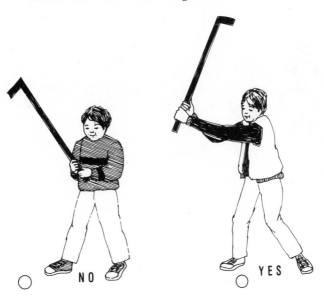

NO   YES

3. Is the child's weight shifted to the forward foot as the swing begins?

NO   YES

Mature Pattern

When children are at the mature stage of underarm striking, do their swings look similar to the following sequence? The joints are cocked—weight is shifted

to the back foot, the hips and trunk rotate away from the ball, the implement is raised up and behind the back shoulder, and the wrists are cocked. The body weight is then shifted to the forward foot. There is a forward rotation of the hips and spine, a downward swing of the forearm, and uncocking of the back arm and wrists. The forward arm stays straight throughout the swing.

Source: Fundamental Motor Patterns, 2nd ed., by R. L. Wickstrom, 1977, Philadelphia: Lea & Febiger.

ASSESSMENT GUIDE / Striking with Long-Handled Implements: Bats

Note to Teachers. Each set of partners will need a whiffle ball and a plastic bat.

TASK Work with a partner. One of you will be a fielder, the other a batter. The batter throws the ball up and hits the ball in the air to the fielder. After five turns, switch places.

GUIDE The children are ready for precontrol- or control-level tasks when you observe that:

1. They're unable to contact the ball.
2. They hit the ball so that it travels on the ground.

3. The batters stand and face the fielder to hit the ball rather than having their sides face the fielder.

4. The body and bat move as a unit to hit the ball. (See the Key Observation Points.)

The children are ready for utilization- or proficiency-level tasks when you observe that:

1. They consistently contact the ball.
2. The ball consistently travels in the air to the fielder.
3. The batters have their side to the fielder when preparing to strike the ball.
4. They shift their weight from the back foot to the front and rotate their bodies as they hit. (See the Key Observation Points.)

ASSESSMENT GUIDE / Striking with Long-Handled Implements: Golf Clubs

Note to Teachers. Position children so they have ample space in which to swing a golf club and not hit anyone. Mark a field with targets at various points on the field. Each child will need a golf club and several plastic golf balls.

TASK   From your own space, pick a target and try to hit the golf balls so they land within five yards of the target. After you've used one target, pick another one and try to do the same thing.

GUIDE   The children are ready for precontrol- or control-level tasks when you observe that:

1. They can't hit the ball within a five-yard range of the designated target.
2. They consistently miss the ball.
3. Their swings are short and choppy, nonflowing.

The children are ready for utilization- or proficiency-level tasks when you observe that:

1. They consistently hit the ball to the designated target.
2. They use a full swing to hit the ball. (See the Key Observation Points.)

ASSESSMENT GUIDE / Striking with Long-Handled Implements: Hockey Sticks

Note to Teachers. You'll need a series of five obstacles set up approximately four yards apart, as shown in the accompanying diagram. No more than five children should be at each series of obstacles.

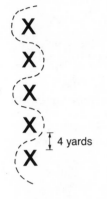

4 yards

TASK   On the signal, begin to dribble through the obstacles, keeping the ball close to your hockey stick. Whenever you hear the next signal, you should be able to stop with the ball close to your stick. You may start through the obstacles as soon as the person in front of you passes the first obstacle, but be sure to look up so that you don't run into anyone else.

GUIDE   The children are ready for precontrol- or control-level tasks when you observe that:

1. They're unable to keep the ball within twelve inches of the stick as they travel.
2. They're unable to stop with the ball next to their stick.
3. They're constantly looking at the ground as they strike the ball.
4. They push the ball as they dribble instead of striking it.

The children are ready for utilization- or proficiency-level tasks when you observe that:

1. They look up as they strike the ball.
2. They're able to stop the ball with the stick on signal.
3. The ball is no more than twelve to eighteen inches from the stick as they dribble.
4. They tap the ball with short strokes.

PRECONTROL LEVEL

At the precontrol level, we give children experiences that help them adjust to the additional length of the implements and the greater demands on their hand-eye coordination. They learn to strike a stationary object with a bat, golf club, and hockey stick, and they begin to be able to control a ball with a hockey stick while traveling.

All activities at this level need to be done with various-sized balls. For beginners, yarn balls or large plastic balls are easier because they're larger and/or don't roll as fast as other balls. For tasks that involve traveling, plastic pucks

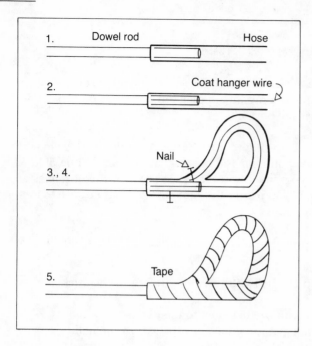

Figure 25-1 Construction of a golf club or a hockey stick (design by Tom Trimble, University of Georgia).

Materials

    Hardwood dowel rod, ⅝" × 3'

    Garden hose or rubber tubing, ⅝" (inside diameter)

    Roll of electrical or adhesive tape (one roll is
       enough for at least twelve sticks)

    Two flat-headed nails, ⅝"

    Coat hanger

Directions

1. Cut an eighteen-inch-long piece of the garden hose and slip it approximately three-and-a-half inches onto the dowel.

2. Insert a piece of coat hanger wire into the hose so that it butts up against the bottom of the dowel and extends almost to the end of the hose.

3. Bend the hose so that the ends meet on the dowel rod. You can form the hose at whatever angle is desired.

4. Use two nails to secure the hose to the dowel. One of the two nails can be used to attach the bottom portion of the hose, bent in half, to the top portion.

5. Use tape to further support the hose or the dowel.

are easier to control initially if the lesson is being taught on a smooth wood or tile floor. Until children become skilled and responsible, we recommend using plastic balls. The flight of the balls won't be as true, but safety is an important consideration.

Activities Leading to Skill Development

Striking a Stationary Ball on the Floor—Golf or Hockey

This task is best accomplished in a large outdoor space but can be adapted for indoor space. Each child will need a golf club (see Figure 25-1) or a plastic field hockey stick. Long-handled street hockey sticks aren't appropriate. The striking action being taught is that of a golf swing.

The first thing you're going to do is practice hitting a ball with a golf club *(hockey stick).* You're going to pretend that you're putting a golf ball. You just want to hit the ball so it goes a little ways, not very far at all. Find out what it takes to hit the ball a little ways.

■ Now that you've practiced, here's another task. See how far you can hit the ball with the golf club *(hockey stick).* To begin with, that's all I'll tell you—see how far you can make the ball go. I'll give you a safety reminder though. All of you are lined up so that you're hitting in the same direction so you won't hit anyone else. You have five balls each; hit all the balls and then wait for the signal before collecting them. So this is how it works: Hit your five balls as far as you can, wait for the signal to collect them, start over.

- To make balls go a little ways, you probably just tapped the ball lightly. Here's a hint for making the balls go farther when you hit them: Always make sure you're standing to the side of the ball when you go to hit it, so you can get a full swing and put a lot of power behind the hit.
- This time I want you to take a good look at how you're holding the club. To make things work the best, the hand you don't write with should be near the top of the club, and the hand you write with should be just under that hand. *(See Figure 25-2.)* With this grip your arms will swing more smoothly and powerfully.
- Using your whole body in the swing, not just your arms, will also make the ball travel farther. Pretend you can twist like a spring—your feet stay put while the upper part of your body turns away from the ball. Then as you start to hit the ball, your whole body uncoils and *wham*, all that power is behind the ball. Try it—twist up and then let loose as you hit the ball. *(Demonstrate.)*
- If you twist hard enough and you really swing with all your might, you'll feel as if your back foot should take a little step forward. That's a good sign; that's exactly what should happen. Try to swing so hard this time that your back foot takes a step forward. Remember, this should happen because you're twisting and untwisting your body so much and swinging so hard that your back foot goes forward—not just because I told you your foot would. I'll be looking to see if your swing makes your foot go forward or you do it just because I said so.
- Make sure your knees are bent—the whole time. If you straighten your legs, you may completely miss the ball. Knees bent. *(Demonstrate.)*

Figure 25-2 Golf club grip.

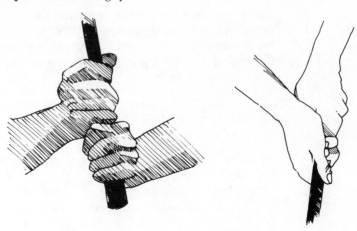

There is much concern over the use of hockey sticks and related skills in the elementary school. With the increased popularity of street and ice hockey has come the advent of hockey sticks being raised above the shoulders on both the backswing and the follow-through. Because elementary school physical education classes are usually crowded, there can be injuries from raised hockey sticks. We've successfully reduced the chance of such injuries by not letting youngsters raise their hockey sticks higher than their waists on *any* stroke. This restriction doesn't significantly alter the striking action; in fact, it encourages the correct field hockey striking action while at the same time providing a much safer environment for learning skills involving striking with hockey sticks.

Striking for Distance—Golf

Set up markers (to be used for measuring) at various distances from where the children are hitting. Each child should have a plastic golf club.

This time you're going to get to test how far you can hit the ball. The markers set up on the field will help you remember how far you hit the ball each time. Each time, see if you can hit the ball a bit farther than the last time by remembering all the hints you just learned and using them.

Striking a Stationary Ball on the Floor—Hockey

Each child will need a plastic hockey stick and a lightweight ball.

Your task is to hit the ball against the wall with the hockey stick. Each time the ball comes back to you, stop it any way you want and then strike it again. See what you have to do to make the ball go straight to the wall in front of you and not off to the side.

▫ One important part of working with hockey sticks is safety. Hitting someone else can be dangerous, but there's an easy way to prevent this from happening: When you strike, *never* bring the stick above your waist, both before and after hitting the ball. This is an important *rule* when working with hockey sticks.

It's good to demonstrate here what both the hockey stick coming above the waist and not *coming above the waist look like.*

▫ There are several differences between working with a hockey stick and a golf club. With a hockey stick, instead of hitting the ball from the side, you hit it from behind, as if you were walking up to it and hitting. So practice hitting this ball from behind, not turning sideways to hit it. The movement is almost like an underhand throw or as if you were bowling. *(Demonstrate.)*

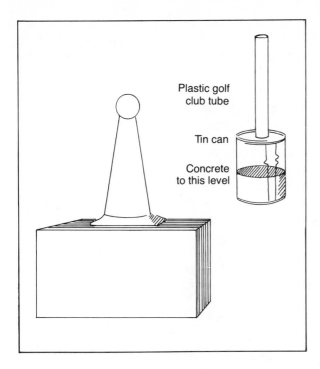

Figure 25-3 Construction of a batting tee. The easiest way to make a batting tee is to use a large (thirty-six-inch) traffic cone, which is high enough for young children. Increase the height by placing the traffic cone on a cardboard box. A batting tee can also be made out of a tin can and a plastic tube.

Materials

Large tin can (available from the school cafeteria)
Plastic golf club tube (obtained from a sporting goods store)
Sack of ready-mixed concrete (1/10 to 1/8)

Directions

1. Place the golf club tube into the tin can.
2. Add water to the concrete mix, and fill the tin can approximately half full.
3. After a few minutes, when the concrete begins to harden, make sure that the golf club tube is not leaning to the side. Once the concrete dries, the batting tee is ready to use.

You can vary the heights of the batting tees by shortening the plastic golf club tubes before inserting them into the cans. We try to have batting tees of three different heights.

Striking to Targets—Hockey

In front of each child, mark a target on the wall near the floor.

Your challenge is to see how many times in a row you can hit the target in front of you. Remember to stop the ball each time it comes back to you before hitting it again.

Striking off a Batting Tee—Bats

This task is best performed outside in a large open space. For at least every two children, preferably every child, you'll need whiffle balls and bats and batting tees (see Figure 25-3).

This time, with a plastic bat you're going to hit a whiffle ball off a tee. See how far you can hit the ball. You're all lined up facing the same way so you won't hit each other. Hit all the balls in your box, and then wait until I give the signal before collecting them. Remember: Hit as far as you can.

☐ Something that I haven't told you is how to hold the bat. *(See Figure 25-4.)* Hold the bat near the end. The hand you don't write with should be right at the end of the bat, and the hand you do write with should be

Batting tees are helpful for children at the precontrol level who are unable to strike a moving ball and for children at the utilization level who are practicing ball placement.

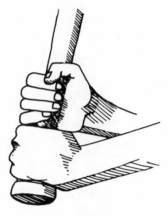

Figure 25-4 Batting grip.

just above that hand, so close that your two hands almost touch. This time, look at your hands and keep checking to make sure they're in the right position.

☐ To help hit the ball farther, make sure you're standing to the side of the ball when you try to hit it, not behind it. Also make sure that you're far enough away from the ball to really stretch the bat and your arms out as you hit the ball. A good way to figure out how far this distance should be is to stand beside the ball and face it and hold the bat with both hands and stretch your arms and the bat out; the right distance is where the end of your bat is about four inches past the ball.

☐ This time you're going to think about your swing. Your bat should start back above your back shoulder—this will give you more power—and then you swing forward. The bat should stay fairly level throughout the whole swing; you don't want to swing down so much as you want to swing forward. So now when you practice, concentrate on swinging forward and level.

☐ Remember that we talked before about twisting your body when you were striking so you could get more power behind the hit. You're going to do the same thing here. Still standing to the side of the ball and facing the ball, with your feet about shoulder width apart, practice twisting or coiling your body toward your back shoulder so that you can get a spring action when you start to untwist and hit the ball. As you start to bring the bat forward, your body will begin to untwist and you should receive extra power. *(Demonstrate.)*

□ If you're really twisting *(coiling)* and swinging hard, your front foot will feel as if it should take a step forward just to help you keep your balance. This is good. So try to do the task so your front foot has to go forward as you finish the hit. If you do this, you'll know that you're using your whole body to strike the ball.

□ One last hint: Don't ever take your eyes off the ball. You really don't need to watch the bat at all. All the time keep your eyes glued to the ball, so much that you see the bat hit the ball and then follow the ball way in the field after you hit it.

□ When striking with a bat, the important cues are coil, step, level, watch. *(Demonstrate as a reminder.)*

Striking Suspended Objects—Bats

Around the practice area, suspend whiffle balls from string. See Figure 24-2, p. 549.

This task is a little harder than the last one. Instead of hitting balls that don't move off batting tees, you're going to hit balls that are hanging from strings. To begin, simply try to hit the ball.

□ Try to remember all the things you practiced when you were hitting the ball off the tee. Stand to the side of the ball, facing the ball. Bring the bat behind your back shoulder *(coil);* take a little step forward with your front foot *(step)*. Now untwist and swing the bat level *(level);* watch the bat actually hit the ball *(watch)*. Try to hit the ball hard.

□ One thing that we didn't work on before is uncocking your wrists as you hit the ball. The pros call this *breaking your wrists*. This action gives your hit a little more power. *(Demonstrate.)*

□ Something you all need to remember as you strike is to shift your weight from your back foot to your front foot and to take a step forward when you start to lose your balance. It isn't good to spin around in a circle as you hit the ball.

□ One last thing to practice. Remember to be far enough away from the ball so that the end, not the middle, of your bat strikes the ball.

■ This time you're going to have a little contest with yourself and the ball on the string. See how many times you can strike the ball in a row without missing. Now you can't do this without stopping the ball after each hit, so the rules are: Strike the ball, stop it from moving, and then strike it again. See how many times you can do this in a row.

Learning to swing level by practicing with a ball suspended on a string.

To enhance striking practice, tie plastic balls onto heavy string and then tie the suspended balls to a rope stretched across the practice area.

Striking a Ball on the Floor While Traveling Slowly—Hockey

In your own space *(or inside a hoop),* use the hockey stick to move the tennis ball around in as many ways as possible without leaving your self-space. The trick is to keep the ball moving and not let it go out of your self-space. This activity will take a lot of fast reactions and quick moves.

- □ One way to keep the ball inside your self-space is to use both sides of the hockey stick. In other words, if the ball goes on one side of your body, use the side of the stick; if the ball goes on the other side of your body, use the other side of your stick. *(Demonstrate.)*
- □ Remember the grip: The hand you don't write with should be near the top end of the hockey stick and the other hand below, toward the blade. When you're trying to move a ball in a small space as you are now, it helps

Figure 25-5 Hockey stick grip.

*if your bottom hand is even farther down the stick so that you have more
control of the ball. (See Figure 25-5.)*

■ This next task I'm going to ask you to practice is harder. Most of us like to
strike the ball with the hockey stick on the same side of our body as the hand
we write with. This time, practice striking the ball on both sides of your body
so that you can use the opposite side of your body as well as your preferred
side. What would happen if you were in a game and the only way to score was
to strike the ball on the opposite side of your body? Go.

  □ A lot of us want to look down and keep checking on the ball as we move
  it around. Well, that's all right for beginners, but what would happen if you
  looked down while you were trying to move the ball on a field with other
  people? Your task now is to still try and move the ball around in your own
  space, but only watch it out of the corner of your eye. The rest of the time,
  try to look up so you can see everybody else in the class. This is called
  using your peripheral vision.

■ Now for the real test. You're to keep moving the ball around in your own
space and I'm going to hold up a certain number of fingers. You have to tell
me how many fingers I'm holding up. You'll have to keep looking up because
I'll change the number of fingers often.

■ We all sometimes tend to move the ball from side to side and forget moving
it backward and forward. This time I want you to concentrate on moving the
ball backward and forward. You'll have to move your feet quickly to keep from
stepping on the ball and falling down. Try it: backward and forward instead
of side to side.

Traveling while manipulating a ball with an implement.

Traveling Slowly While Striking a Ball—Hockey

You're now going to begin to move around the entire space while striking the ball with the hockey stick. To begin, go slowly. Your task is to travel around the entire space while striking the ball and not touching anyone else. Try it.

□ The secret is to keep the ball very close to your body and the hockey stick. If the ball goes too far away, you won't be able to control it. Soft hits help.

□ Sometimes when you try so hard to keep the ball close to the hockey stick you end up pushing it with the stick rather than striking it. This time work on really striking the ball, but with little, short, light taps so the ball stays close to the stick. You'll know when you're pushing the ball instead of striking it by watching. If your stick always stays next to the ball and is always touching it, then you're pushing. If your stick leaves the ball a little bit each time after you touch it, then you're striking. Remember, this time work on striking.

□ Be sure to watch the ball out of the corner of your eyes and watch where you're going. Concentrate on watching where you're going this time by looking up occasionally.

■ This time as you move around the room, I'm going to hold up different numbers of fingers. Tell me how many fingers I'm holding up. You'll have to look often because I'll change the number of fingers often and try to trick you.

CONTROL LEVEL

At the control level, children begin to develop mature striking patterns that are used in increasingly complex contexts. Traveling while striking or tapping an object along the ground is combined with a single variable, such as changing direction or speed. The children also practice striking a pitched ball and striking a golf ball for distance.

Activities Leading to Skill Development

Traveling, Stopping, and Controlling the Ball—Hockey

Each student will need a plastic hockey stick and a ball.

Before, you practiced traveling around the room keeping the ball close to you. This time you're going to do the same time, but with something added. Whenever you hear the signal, stop the ball, using only your stick, and wait for the signal to go again. Stopping the ball using your stick will take some careful moving. You'll have to absorb the force of the ball with the stick, just as you do in catching. You'll have to *give* with the ball by bringing the stick back a little bit when you're trying to stop the ball. This is kind of like catching with the stick. *(Demonstrate.)*

■ This time try going a little faster and doing the same thing. Move around the space, striking the ball with the hockey stick, and on the signal stop the ball using the stick and wait for the next signal. I'll know you can really do this if I always see the ball close to your stick and all balls stopped on the signal, without you having to chase them all over the room.

■ Now I'm going to change the task a little. Again you should move around

the entire space striking the ball, but on the signal, instead of stopping the ball, stand still and keep moving the ball in your own space until you hear the signal to travel again. This is called *controlling* the ball. You'll know you're really good at this when as soon as you hear the signal you can stop and start moving the ball around in your self-space without first having to chase the ball across the floor.

When first working with this idea, some children may have to be reminded to slow down. The purpose is to travel with the object, not to hit and then chase it.

■ You're going to play a little game with the stopping this time. Every time you come near another person, stop the ball still and then start again. This is as if you don't want anyone else to come near your ball, so you're going to protect it; the only way you can protect it is by stopping it still.

Traveling While Changing Speed and Direction—Hockey

Things are getting more complicated. You're still going to move around the room and stop the ball on the stop signal, but you're also going to change direction and speed as you move. Whenever you hear a drumbeat, change your speed and the direction you're traveling in. For example, if you're traveling forward quickly and hear the change signal, start traveling either backward or sideways more slowly. The next time you hear the change signal, start traveling in another direction and at a different speed. As you travel in other directions, you'll know you're in control of the ball if it's always close to your hockey stick and you don't have to run to chase the ball across the floor.

■ Each time you come near other persons, change your direction and speed to stay out of their way. This is one way of protecting the ball from another player, so you need to be able to change direction and speed quickly whenever another player comes near. It helps to slow down and control the ball as you practiced before you actually begin to change direction. Moving one hand down the stick a little will help control the ball.

■ You'll play a different game this time. As you move, I'll call out the changes in direction and you change according to what I call out. You'll have to pay close attention because I'll start out slowly and then speed up the changes as you get going. You can tell if you're really in control if you can make all the changes while always keeping the ball close to your hockey stick.

Traveling and Striking While Changing Pathways—Hockey

Tape or mark various pathways on the floor. The more pathways, the better.

You're going to practice something new this time: changes in pathways. Do you remember pathways—straight, curved, and zigzag? Again you're going to move around the entire space, but whenever you come to a pathway on the floor, try to follow it exactly. Once you finish one pathway, travel to another and follow it. Remember as you follow the pathways to be sure you're striking the ball, not pushing it along.

   □ With a zigzag pathway you need to almost stop the ball and then start again at each corner. This is a stop and go action.

Traveling, Striking, and Changing Pathways with a Partner—Hockey

Another way to practice striking while traveling in different pathways is to work with a partner. You're going to play Follow the Leader. The leader travels in different pathways—curved, straight, and zigzag—as the follower tries to stay close behind, copying the exact pathways the leader makes. Leaders: As you begin, make easy pathways. The object is not to lose your partner but to practice striking while traveling in different pathways. On the signal, change positions as leaders and followers.

   ■ This time the following is going to be a little harder. Instead of staying right behind the leader, the follower is going to watch while the leader moves in a short pathway sequence. When the leader stops and freezes, the follower moves, copying the pathway of the leader until she catches up with the leader. When the follower catches up, the leader takes off again. This is sort of like a game of cat and mouse: Just as soon as you think you've caught someone, they slip away again. As you move, remember that the purpose of this task is to practice different pathways, so include them in your movements. After five turns as a leader, switch places.

   □ To be able to change directions quickly, you must keep the ball close to the stick.

Traveling and Changing Pathways and Directions—Hockey

This task is actually a combination of two other things you've done; it's the real test of what you know. By yourself, make up a sequence of traveling and striking moves that involves two changes of direction and two changes of pathways, such as straight backward and zigzag forward. Practice your sequence until you can do it from memory three times without stopping. Each time the sequence should look the same. Then we'll all share the sequences.

Traveling in Different Pathways, Directions, and Speeds—Hockey

Each child will need a plastic hockey stick and a ball.

This is a self-testing task. The task sheet lets you practice traveling in different pathways, directions, and speeds while striking a ball. *(See Figure 25-6.)* Practice the tasks one by one. When you think you can do a task well, have a partner watch you. If your partner thinks you did the task successfully, the partner signs your sheet. I'll check to see how you're progressing.

Name_____ Class _____

Task Sheet for Striking

Verification	Task
	I can dribble a ball with a hockey stick in a straight pathway, keeping the ball close to the stick.
	I can dribble a ball with a hockey stick in a curved pathway, keeping the ball close to the stick.
	I can dribble a ball with a hockey stick in a zigzag pathway, keeping the ball close to the stick.
	I can dribble a ball with a hockey stick around four cones set up about four feet apart, keeping the ball close to the stick.
	I can dribble a ball with a hockey stick through the cones and while running, keeping the ball close to the stick.
	I can dribble a ball with a hockey stick while traveling sideways.
	I can make up a sequence including two pathways, two changes in speed, and two different directions. I have written my sequence below.

Sequence:

Figure 25-6 Task sheet for striking.

Striking to a Large Stationary Target—Hockey

This task is intended for use as one of a series of stations (see Chapter 6). Each child will need a target. Tape marks on the floor in front of each target to designate the spot from which the children are to practice the task. An easy way to tape is to tape one color mark approximately six feet away, another color approximately ten feet away, and a third color mark about twelve feet away.

At this station your task is to practice striking the ball to the target. You want a full hit, no soft little tap into the goal. To make sure things are safe, I have a rule for this activity. Each time the ball comes back to you, be sure to stop it so that it's completely still before you strike it again. To begin, you need to practice striking at the target from the mark closest to the target.

Often you don't have enough official targets for each child in the class, but you want each child to have practice opportunities without waiting. This is when improvisation and resourcefulness become paramount. Possible targets include an X marked on the wall; sports pictures laminated and taped to the wall; holiday characters (witches, ghosts, the Grinch that stole Christmas, etc.) taped to the wall; milk crates turned on their sides (be sure you get permission from the dairy because some milk companies frown on losing their crates); two cones or other objects to mark the space; or trash cans or ice cream containers turned sideways.

- ☐ It's hard to get much power behind your swing if your elbows are close to your body or the ball is too close to your feet. Check these two things. First, the ball should be about eighteen inches in front of your foot on the hitting side of your body. Second, when you're hitting the ball, be sure your elbows aren't touching your sides or stomach; you need to see air between your elbows and your body as you hit. The cues to remember are ball forward, elbows out.
- ☐ Don't forget when first striking at targets to watch the ball all the way through *and* the target at the same time. This time concentrate on watching the ball from beginning to end. You should see your hockey stick contact the ball while looking at the target out of the corner of your eye. After you hit the ball, watch it all the way to the target.

Striking in Different Places Around the Body—Hockey

Now you're going to practice striking from other places around your body. You're still working at your target and at the closest mark to your target. To begin, place the ball about eighteen inches in front of the foot you haven't been using and try to strike the ball to the target from that position. *(This task can be another station, or it can be used as a later lesson.)*

Use street hockey sticks or sticks that have two flat sides. Field hockey sticks, with one flat and one rounded side, won't work, and the skill of hitting on the opposite side of the body with a field hockey stick is too complex for most students to learn at this point.

- ■ This task isn't as easy; it's almost like the backhand. Do the same thing as you do with the backhand: Turn your stick so that you're using the other side of it, the back side. Practice again, this time using the back side of your stick.
- ■ So far you've worked on the two sides of your body. Now you're going to practice in all kinds of places around your body. It's up to you to find places around your body from where you can strike the ball toward the target. Find

one place and practice it for a while; then find another place and practice. Try to find at least five different places where you can be successful.

□ Just a reminder: To be successful, the blade of your hockey stick must be flat and pointed toward the target or the ball will miss the target.

Striking to a Target (Around the World)—Hockey

Place five tape marks in a semicircle on the floor in front of each striking mark. This task is also appropriate as one of a series of stations (see Chapter 6).

This time the striking is going to be a game. Have you ever played Around the World in basketball? This game is going to be Around the World in striking. As you see, there are five tape marks on the floor in front of you. You must hit the ball to the target from each tape mark. You can start on either side, but go to the next mark only when you can hit the target from the mark before it. If you make it through once, go back and try again. This is a kind of mini Around the World because you won't really move from your spot; you're hitting from different places around your body instead of moving around to different places to hit.

Striking to a Stationary Partner—Hockey

You and your partner should be about six to seven feet apart. Strike back and forth to your partner. Try to hit straight to your partner so that she or he doesn't have to move. You hit the ball to your partner; your partner stops the ball completely still and then hits it back. Remember to strike easily so that your partner is able to stop the ball. This is called a *sympathetic* hit.

□ Make the blade of your hockey stick flat and follow through straight to your partner. *(Demonstrate.)*
□ You need to work on stopping the ball so that it doesn't bounce all over the place. Remember when you learned to catch so the ball didn't hurt your hands? It's the same idea when stopping a ball with a hockey stick: You have to give a little bit with the ball or absorb the force so the ball doesn't go flying all over the place. With the hockey stick, this means bringing the stick back a little bit as you try to stop the ball. Work on this as you try to stop the ball this time. *(Demonstrate.)*

■ Before you worked with a partner you practiced hitting the ball to different places. Now you're going to do that with a partner, and the partner is going to be a target for you to aim at. The partner who is to receive the ball will put his hockey stick out in one place and hold it still; the partner hitting the ball will use the stick as a target and try to hit it without the receiving partner having to move the stick. Change roles each time.

■ With your partner, see how many times you can hit the ball back and forth without a miss. Remember, you must stop the ball before you return it to your partner. If you miss, just start counting all over. If you get to ten, let me know.

Striking Stationary Objects, Varying Distance and Force—Hockey

Each student needs a space against the wall. Mark a target on the wall; mark lines on the floor to indicate different distances. For this setup, see the task in Striking to a Large Stationary Target, pp. 594 to 595.

When you worked on striking to targets before, you always hit from the closest line to the target. Now you're going to start moving back a little at a time. Start at the closest mark. When you can hit the target five times in a row without missing, move back to the next mark. When you hit the target from that spot five times without missing, move back again. So if you hit the target four times and then miss, start your counting over.

Striking to a Partner, Varying Distance and Force—Hockey

You and your partner should start hitting back and forth from a distance of about six feet apart. Each time stop the ball before you send it back to your partner. After you hit successfully to your partner ten times and your partner is able to stop the ball, move back two steps each and then start again. When you're successful ten times in a row, move back again.

- □ Shots that come from farther and farther away become harder to stop. This time focus your attention on stopping the ball without it bouncing all over the place. Really think about absorbing the force of the ball by giving with the hockey stick.

Striking, Varying Force and Distance—Golf

This task is best accomplished outside in a large space. Each child will need a golf club and a plastic ball.

You're going to be practicing by yourself in a place that is facing away from everyone else. With your golf club, try to see how far you can hit the ball.

- □ You create more power if you use a full swing to hit the ball. Make sure you bring the club behind your shoulder as you start your swing, and don't forget to turn your hips. *(Demonstrate.)*

Striking a Pitched Ball—Bats

This task is best accomplished outside where children have plenty of space. Mark both a pitcher's square and a batting box for each group of two. It further helps to mark each batter's box with "neat feet" in the correct batting position. See Figure 25-7. Each pair needs one plastic ball and a bat.

Before, you hit a ball off a batting tee or from a string. This time you're going to practice batting a ball that's pitched. With your partner, start by one of you being the pitcher and the other person the batter. The pitcher stands on the

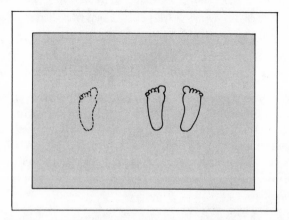

Figure 25-7 "Neat feet" for a right-handed striking action. You can easily make "neat feet" by painting them in the correct position on a rubber mat. Challenge the children to move their left foot to the position of the dotted foot as they swing.

pitcher's square and pitches the ball to the batter. The batter stands on the batter's square and tries to hit the ball. The batter's square has a secret help in it: pictures of feet that show you exactly where to stand so you have the best chance of hitting the ball. Just try to hit the ball so it doesn't have to go far. After ten hits trade places.

- ☐ As you try to hit the ball, make sure you watch the ball all the time. You should see the ball leave the pitcher's hand, see your bat strike the ball, and then see the ball go into the field.
- ☐ Make sure your swing is smooth and occurs without stopping. As you swing the bat, think about keeping the bat going without stopping.
- ☐ Try to swing level so you'll have the best chance of hitting the ball solidly.
- ☐ Don't forget to step with your front foot. Remember the cues: coil, step, level, watch.

Throwing a Ball in the Air and Striking It—Bats

This task is best done outside where there's plenty of space. Each child will need a plastic bat, a ball, and a carpet square.

You're going to practice hitting a ball you throw into the air yourself. In your own space, on a carpet square, facing away from everyone else, practice throwing the ball up into the air and then hitting it with the bat. You must have both your hands on the bat when you hit the ball, so you'll have to work quickly. *(Demonstrate.)*

- ☐ Remember to keep your arms away from your body.
- ☐ Keep checking the position of your hands on the bat. Make sure that the

hand you write with is the top hand on the grip, with your other hand underneath the writing hand.

Mark lines on a field. Each child will need a number of whiffle (or tennis) balls and a plastic bat.

- Now we're going to add something that you worked on before: striking to different distances. This involves using different amounts of force to hit the ball. There are a lot of lines on the field; you can use them to judge how far you hit the ball. Each time you hit a ball, see how far you can make it go. If you hit it over one line one time, try to hit it over the next line the next time you hit.

- Pick out a line you know you can hit the ball past. Try to hit the ball past that line five times in a row. After you've practiced at one line, pick another line and try again.

Children enjoy having a field marked off at different distances so it's very clear where they're aiming.

UTILIZATION LEVEL

At the utilization level, we give the children situations in which they learn to consistently strike objects with long-handled implements. There are a variety of contexts, particularly those that involve more than one variable in an unpredictable or changing environment.

Activities Leading to Skill Development

Directing the Placement of an Object—Bats

Each child should have a partner; each pair needs a batting tee, a plastic bat, and a ball. This may also be one of several stations.

Before, you practiced hitting the ball different distances; this time you're going to practice hitting the ball to different places. To start, one person will be at bat, and the partner will be in left field. The batter first tries to hit five balls to left field, aiming for her or his partner. If everything works correctly, the partner shouldn't have to move very far to catch the balls. After the first five hits, the partner moves to center field and the batter tries to hit the next five balls to the partner. The batter then tries to hit the next five balls to right field. Then switch places. You'll know you're really good when your partner doesn't have to move to catch the balls.

- Remember to change your stance so you're facing the way you want the ball to go. For example, if you want the ball to go to right field, point your front foot slightly toward right field.

■ This time the fielder is going to make it harder. After every hit, the fielder moves to a new position and the batter tries to hit the ball exactly to the fielder. The fielder can choose any place to go. After ten hits, trade places.

Hitting to Open Places—Bats

This task is best done outdoors in a large area. Children should be in groups of three or four. Each group needs a batting tee, a plastic bat, and a ball.

In your group you're going to play a game. Instead of hitting to where the fielder is, you're going to hit to where there aren't any fielders. One of you will be at bat, and the other people will be spread out in the field. The batter bats the ball off the tee and tries to make it go to spaces where there are no fielders. To make it fair, the fielders can't move until after the ball has left the tee. The batter's goal is to try to get a base hit: The ball has to hit the ground before anyone touches it. After ten hits, trade places.

■ You're going to hit a pitched ball and still try to make it go where there are no fielders. One of the fielders will become the pitcher. All pitches must be easy so they can be hit. The batter will try to hit to the outfield and make the ball hit the ground before a fielder can touch it. The batter gets one point for each ball that lands untouched. After ten hits, switch places.

Striking a Pitched Object, Varying the Distance—Bats

This task is best accomplished outdoors in a large space. Pair the children, who'll need a plastic bat and a ball.

This time you're going to practice hitting a pitched ball different distances. To begin, one of you will pitch and the other person will hit. Batter, your task is to sometimes hit the ball short so it lands near the pitcher; other times hit it long so it goes to the outfield. Try to decide ahead of time where you want the ball to go and then hit it there. After ten hits, switch places.

■ Now to show how good you are, call out where the ball is going—short or long distance—before you hit it. Do this ten times and then switch places.
■ This game will change a little from the last one. Instead of the batter calling out where the ball is to go, the pitcher calls out where the ball is to be hit. The batter changes places with the pitcher after five hits.

Batting Combining Force and Open Spaces

Children need to be in groups of four or five in a space large enough to let them bat a ball without interfering with others.

In your group, one of you will be the pitcher, one of you the batter, and the rest fielders. You're now going to combine hitting different distances and hit-

Working as partners: one child pitches a ball, the other strikes it with a bat.

ting to open spaces. The pitcher will pitch ten balls to the batter who tries to hit the balls to where no one is standing. Some hits need to be short and others long, but all hits should be to empty spaces.

Striking and Dodging Stationary Objects—Hockey

Set up an obstacle course of cones and hoops or other equipment. Each child will need a hockey stick and a ball.

You've traveled while dodging objects. This time you're going to do it while striking a ball with a hockey stick. Your task is to travel throughout the space, striking the ball with the hockey stick. Try not to let the ball get away from you. Don't touch any of the obstacles or other people. Freeze on the signal and have the ball with you.

□ Do you remember a few of the things you worked on when you were dribbling with your feet—the keys to success? They still apply here. Keep the ball fairly close to the stick so the ball doesn't go all over the place and you spend all your time chasing it. This means striking the ball with short little taps, not pushing it. Concentrate this time on keeping the ball close.

□ Now that you have the ball close to your stick, the next thing to work on is looking up as you go, so you can see where you're going and avoid bumping into anyone. Watch the ball out of the corner of your eye.

■ As practice for looking up, you're going to play the counting game again. I'll keep holding up a different number of fingers and you tell me how many I'm holding up while you're striking the ball around the space.

■ This time when you hear the drumbeat, change directions. For example, if you're traveling forward, go backward or sideways. The next time you hear the signal, change directions again. Practice going in all three directions.

■ You've all been going at fairly slow speeds. This isn't always good in game situations, so you're going to practice going at different speeds. Each time you hear the signal, change the speed at which you're traveling. Make the change clear—so if you're going slow, it's very obvious that you've speeded up. The rules are still the same: no touching, and you must be able to stop on the signal and have the ball with you.

Striking to Distant Targets of Various Sizes—Golf

Set up targets of various sizes at different distances from the striking spot, like a driving range. Each child will need a plastic golf club, a number of plastic balls, and a carpet square.

This task is like target practice. There are a lot of targets set up on the field and you have a number of balls. See if you can hit the targets from where you're standing. After you hit all your balls, wait until the signal before collecting them.

■ Now as you practice, see how many times in a row you can hit the target you're trying for.

□ Remember the cues: coil, watch, follow-through.

Playing Hoop Golf

Spread hoops and other targets of various sizes around a field. Place targets at different distances apart. Each child will need a plastic golf club and a ball.

This is like a golf course, but there's no order to it. Strike the ball from hoop to hoop, using as few strokes as possible. You may want to go back and do the same hoop over again and see if you can make it in fewer strokes. Be careful to not get in anyone's way.

How far can you hit the ball?

Try to strike the ball into the hoop using as few strokes as possible.

□ Be sure to vary the length of your strokes to adjust for the different distances between the hoops: short swings for short distance, long swings for long distance.
□ Don't forget to keep your knees bent.

Playing Hockey Bowl

Set up pins (two-liter soft drink bottles work fine) for every two children, and mark a line away from the pins, to create a lane as in a bowling alley.

This game is called Hockey Bowl. Your task is to strike the hockey ball from behind the line and see how many pins you can knock down. After three hits, or when all the pins have been knocked down, whichever happens first, trade places.

■ The first time you can knock all the pins down three times in a row, move back three steps and try it again. If you still want to make the task harder, take away some of the pins so you have a smaller target to aim for.

Directing the Air Pathway of the Object Struck—Golf

Each child will need a plastic golf club and a ball. Set up the space with obstacles of varying heights. Possible obstacles are blocks and canes, cones, boxes, cones on top of boxes. Carpet squares mark the starting point.

When I say "Go," find an obstacle to practice at. Two of you may be at one obstacle. Your task at the obstacle is to see if with the golf club you can gently lift the ball off the ground so it travels over the obstacle in the air. You may want to start at some of the lower obstacles and then move on to the higher ones. You can change obstacles whenever you like, but there can never be more than two people at an obstacle.

□ The whole face of the club needs to be under the ball. Think of trying to get a piece of pie out of a pie dish—you really have to get underneath or you'll lose part of it. Be sure to bend your knees so the club face remains low.

Directing the Air Pathway of the Object Struck—Bats

Children should be in groups of three or four. Each group has one batter and a pitcher, with the rest of the group being fielders.

Do you remember the game where the pitcher told the batter which field the batter was to hit the ball to? This game is similar, but the pitcher calls out either line drive, pop fly, or grounder, and the batter has to hit that kind of ball. After five hits, switch places.

Striking from a Stationary Position to a Moving Target—Hockey

It's best to use a large, open, grassy space. Children work with partners.

You practiced striking a ball to a partner before, but then you were always standing still. When you're in a real game, how often are you able to pass to a partner who's standing still? Not very often. You're going to practice striking a ball to a partner who's moving. One of you will be the passer and the other one the receiver. The passer stands still and the receiver starts to run down-field, away from the passer. When the receiver is about five yards away, the passer sends the receiver the ball. The receiver should collect the ball on the run and then keep going for a few more steps. Take five turns and then switch positions.

About a year ago I was at a party and the hosts set up a croquet game. Adults and children alike were intrigued, and bingo, the light hit: This is a striking game. Do you remember? Croquet is a fun activity to add as a special treat and ties together the ideas of striking at targets and varying force and distance really well. No croquet sets you say? You'll be amazed how many families have croquet sets at home that they're willing to let you use (or sometimes even give to you). I just acquired an antique croquet set that was on its way to Goodwill. Give croquet a try sometime!

- ☐ Send the ball slightly in front of the receiver. This maneuver is called *leading the receiver* and helps the receiver collect the ball without having to stop or turn around to get it.
- ☐ Now some tips for the receiver. First, try to time your run so you don't have to stop and wait for the ball. This may mean slowing up or speeding up a bit, but it helps.
- ☐ Receivers have a better chance of collecting the ball if they try to collect it with the entire flat surface of their stick. Your stick should almost touch the ground, with the blade positioned so the ball will hit it. *(Demonstrate.)*
- ☐ Here are three hints to help prevent the ball from bouncing off the stick. First, spread your hands apart more on the stick so they cover more area. Second, make sure you receive the ball with your stick vertical and away from your body so you have more time to absorb the ball. Third, relax your grip a little as the ball touches the stick so the stick can give a little with the ball. The cues are hands apart, stick vertical, relax your grip. Try it.

■ You've been passing to the same side so far. Now try passing to the other side so the receiver has to receive on the opposite side of his or her body. This will seem awkward at first, but stick with it. Ten passes and then switch.

PROFICIENCY LEVEL

At the proficiency level, children are given situations that facilitate development of the ability to strike with implements while focusing on the strategy and outcome of the action and on the skill. The focus at this level is the attainment of consistency and accuracy while standing still or moving.

Activities Leading to Skill Development

Striking to Dodge an Opponent—Hockey

Several children will need hockey sticks and balls; other children will be obstacles, holding hockey sticks in their hands. See Figure 25-8.

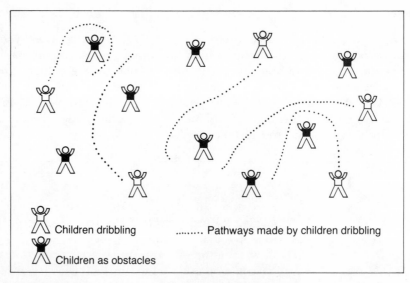

Figure 25-8 Arrangement for dribbling and dodging activity.

This is a dodging game. We've played games like it before, but without equipment. To begin, those of you with blue on will be the obstacles; the rest of you will be dodgers. Obstacles, find a self-space and stand there. Dodgers, try to cross the room without coming near an obstacle. The obstacles have the right to steal the ball if it comes within their area. Their area is that space they can reach while keeping one foot glued to the floor. The goal of the dodgers is to get to the other end of the space without having the ball stolen. The group gets five tries and then switches places.

☐ When you get involved in a game situation, sometimes you forget all the things you've learned. Dodgers, remember the moves that help you get around the obstacles: changing pathways, changing speeds, and changing directions. Use those three skills to help you dodge without losing the ball.

■ You're going to change the game a little this time. Instead of all the dodgers having their own ball, they're going to have one ball. Their job is then to get the ball to the other end, as a team. The obstacles still have the same rule: They can take the ball only when it comes into their area. Four tries and then switch places.

☐ For this task the strategy is a bit different. You still have to change pathways, directions, and speed, but at times you have to do it without the ball. When you don't have the ball, the secret is to move to an open space, where no one can guard you; as you move, have the person with the ball pass to you. So essentially you've also added the skill of receiving on the move as well as dodging.

Try to keep the ball away from a partner.

■ Now that you have the idea, let's form into groups of six. Two people are dodgers, four are obstacles. Switch every time so you all get a turn.

Passing and Receiving on the Move—Hockey

This task is best accomplished outside in a large grassy area. Children will need to be in pairs, with one ball for each pair. Each child should have a hockey stick.

With your partner, travel in the same direction, side by side, about twenty feet apart. As you're traveling, pass the ball back and forth by using the hockey stick. The key to this task is that you both must always be moving forward. When you get to the end of your area, turn around and come back.

□ Remember to pass a little in front of your partner. Because you're so close together, this won't take a lot of force, but it does involve good placement. Make sure you lead your partner with the pass.

□ Now for the receiver. Sometimes we forget to give a little when we get the ball and so lose control of the ball. As you contact the ball, relax your grip just a bit and give with the ball, so you can control it and send it back immediately.

■ This is a test this time. See if you can get at least six passes back and forth between the beginning and end of your space.

Keeping It Moving—Hockey

A group of our children made up this game. Youngsters enjoy it, but because the game is so fast and intense, it doesn't last very long.

This time you're going to play a game called Keeping It Moving. There will be four players on a team. Use four cones to mark out a space about five yards by five yards. One person begins by passing the ball to another player. That player passes it to someone else, and so on. The object is to never let the ball stop moving and never let it go out of bounds. The secret here is for all players to keep moving so they're ready to get the ball when it comes to them and so there's always someone to send the ball to.

Directing the Pathway, Distance, and Speed of an Object—Golf

Set up boxes of various heights in the entire space; on the back side of the box, place a hoop on the floor. Each child will need a golf club and a ball. This is an appropriate station task (Chapter 6).

The task is to hit the ball with the golf club so the ball travels over the box and into the hoop. Once you're able to do this five times in a row standing close to the box, back up three steps and try it again.

- □ To do this well, be sure to bend your knees. Don't try to lift the ball; hit down on the ball so it goes into the air.
- ■ When you succeed, move to a new place and try again.

This is a good time to have children design their own games using the striking skills they've acquired. See Chapter 26 for details about how to help children design their own games.

Directing the Pathway, Distance, and Speed of an Object (Call Your Hit)—Bats

For this game you use a plastic bat and ball. Here are the rules:

1. There are five people on a team: one batter, a pitcher, and three fielders.
2. To start, the batter is at bat, the fielders in the field.
3. Before the pitcher pitches the ball, she or he calls out a distance, a pathway, and a speed. The batter has to hit the ball as called out.
4. The batter changes after five hits.
5. Each player keeps her or his own score—one point for every ball that is hit as it was called out.

Playing Whiffle Ball Golf

You'll need a whiffle ball golf course. See Figure 25-9.

The game you're going to play is called Whiffle Ball Golf. It's played just as

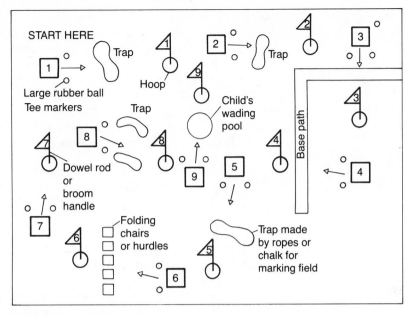

Figure 25-9 Whiffle Ball Golf course.

regular golf is played. The objective is to get the ball to land in the hoop with as few shots as possible. Each of you will start at the hole I assign you and then go to the next higher-numbered hole. Each hole has a tee area to start from; this area is marked with big rubber balls. This guarantees that everyone starts from the same place. When you get to hole 9, go to hole 1. Keep score by counting the shots it takes you to go around the entire course.

One of our students made the sensible suggestion that we use tires as the holes on the golf course, so the ball won't roll out so easily. Old tires are easy to obtain.

Striking to a Teammate to Avoid Others in a Dynamic Situation—Hockey

The children need to be in groups of three in a fairly well-defined space.

In your group of three, you're going to play a game similar to Keep Away, only this time with hockey sticks and balls. Two of you will be offensive players; one of you will be a defensive player. The two offensive players are going to try to get the ball to the other end of your playing space while still maintaining their control of the ball as the defensive player tries to steal the ball. After the offense tries three times to go up and down the space, one offense person trades places with the defensive player. You must stay in the boundaries of your space.

◻ To be successful, the offensive players have to use each other. The player without the ball has to keep moving until she can get into a position where she's unguarded so the ball can be passed to her. The player with the ball has to be aware of where the other player is moving and anticipate when she'll be open so the ball can be sent just as she arrives in the open space—not too soon and not too late. If both of you stand still, the defensive player has an easy job.

◻ Defensive players will be able to steal the ball best when they play between the two players but closest to the player without the ball. *(Demonstrate.)*

Playing Minihockey

This game is called Minihockey. The objective is to hit the ball into the opponent's goal. Here are the rules:

1. There are two or three people on each team.
2. The players on the teams decide the boundaries and width of the goal—only one right now.
3. Use milk crates, cones, or boxes for goals.
4. The game starts with one team getting the ball first.
5. Make up your own form of scoring (if you want to keep score).
6. Make up any more rules you need.

Everyone must be playing—no standing around.

◻ One thing that many of you tend to forget in game situations is to keep moving and stay open for a pass from another player. If I'm close to another player, there's no way he can pass to me, so I must stay away.

▪ We're going to change the game a little this time. Instead of one goal on each end of the field, there will be two.

Playing Six-Player Teeball

This game is called Six-Player Teeball and involves the skills of striking, throwing, and catching. The objective is to place a batted ball, catch and throw, and run bases. Here are the rules:

1. There are three players on each team.
2. The batter strikes the ball from the tee and tries to run the bases.
3. The fielders try to catch or collect the ball and throw it to one another so that all three players catch the ball before the batter completes running the bases.
4. Each player on a team bats, and then the teams switch places.

◻ One hint to help this game go better: The fielders must throw the ball quickly when they get it. It may even help if you have a plan of who throws the ball to whom.

During the class, we focus on each child's individual improvements rather than on class or individual competition. Many children (and faculty!) enjoy voluntary tournaments, after school or at lunch time.

Playing One-Base Baseball

You're going to play One-Base Baseball. *(See Figure 25-10.)* The objective is to get to the base and back before the pitcher gets the ball. Here are the rules:

1. There are three or four people on each team.
2. The batter bats and tries to run to the base and back to home plate before the pitcher gets the ball again.
3. Each person on a team bats, and then the teams trade places.

- ☐ Have you figured out the one secret to this game? It's hitting the ball to open spaces. If you hit the ball to where someone is standing, you don't stand a chance of getting to the base and back before the pitcher gets the ball.

Playing Half Rubber

This game, called Half Rubber, is really just for fun. It's basically played like baseball. Here are the rules:

Figure 25-10 Setup for One-Base Baseball.

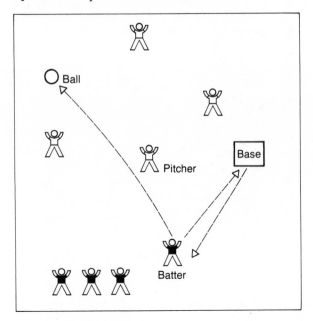

1. There are three or four players on each side.
2. Use a three- or four-inch solid rubber ball, cut in half, as a ball and a broom handle as a bat.
3. The rest of the rules are up to you.

This activity is fun, although extremely difficult. For years we played it on the beach, and it's a challenge to master, but it can be done! Kids love to try it!

READING COMPREHENSION QUESTIONS

1. What basic action is used in striking with any long-handled implement?
2. What is a sidearm pattern? What is an underhand swinging pattern? Which swings are used with which implements?
3. What is the purpose of introducing children to striking with long-handled implements?
4. What can be the long-term result when children try to swing implements that are too heavy or too long?
5. What are the observable characteristics of individuals at each level of skill proficiency in striking with long-handled implements?
6. Describe a mature striking pattern for striking a ball with a bat and with a golf club.
7. Why do we recommend that children initially practice striking using yarn or plastic balls?
8. What does a level swing look like when the player is attempting to strike a ball with a bat?
9. Describe two examples, one for bats and one for hockey sticks, of contexts that are unpredictable or changing.
10. What do the terms *give* and *control* the ball with a hockey stick mean?

P A R T five

Games, Dance, and Gymnastics

Chapters 26 to 28 cover games, dance, and gymnastics, respectively. Although Parts Three and Four contain ideas for these movement forms, we think it's important to understand the different forms and ways a teacher might combine skill themes and movement concepts in games, dance, and gymnastics. Many of the ideas in these chapters are appropriate for children at the utilization and proficiency level who've acquired the basic forms of a particular skill and are ready to combine several skills as they begin to focus on more complex combinations, heightened quality, and dynamic environments. The emphasis in our teaching, however, remains skill development rather than the form of a particular movement and a set of rituals. We're more interested, for example, that children actually learn to use appropriate

613

manipulative skills in gamelike situations than that they learn the rules for many different games. Nevertheless, as our children advance and improve, they'll benefit from the challenge of combining skill themes and movement concepts in the fascinating and interesting formats of games, dance, and gymnastics.

C H A P T E R **26**

Teaching Games

All too often when it comes to the physical education of children we steal away this world of the child by dictating games to them. We do this under the assumption that it is good for all children to learn about our major sports through lead-up games involving kickball, dodgeball, Newcomb, line soccer, steal the bacon, and the like. Most of these games, however, are characterized by large groups, lack of participation, elimination, and stress on winning. Those who are not ready because of interest, motivation, strength, size or skill often turn to a search for stimulation in activities other than the game. These symptoms can be seen when children begin daydreaming, playing with dandelions in the grass, shoving, pushing, pulling, or looking for mischievous action with a friend.

Peter Werner

Games are probably the easiest subject to teach. Unlike dance and gymnastics, games are self-propelling because once students grasp the basic concepts of a game, they require little teacher intervention, except for resolution of misunderstandings and arguments.

The ease with which a subject can be taught shouldn't be the primary determinant of the content of a physical education program. The current and future needs and interests of the children in the program are the key factors to consider when planning an overall program. The instructor who teaches children to play games successfully and effectively does more than simply provide opportunities for children to play games. The successful teacher must create a variety of learning opportunities, including situations in which the children play games and situations in which they practice skills. The children in such programs acquire a foundation of movement skills that enables them to participate successfully in a broad variety of games and sports. Once children have acquired the prerequisite game skills, sport becomes an attractive leisure-time alternative for them throughout their lives.

For the remainder of this chapter to communicate our intended message, it's crucial, at the outset, that you understand completely how we use the term *game* and the differences between our use and the traditional use of the word. Throughout the book we use *games* to refer to the activities (usually manipulative activities) that children in elementary schools typically play. Activities that use the same basic skills but have standardized rules and procedures (such as football, basketball, and baseball), we call *sports*. Sports activities are designed primarily for adults, and, to be enjoyed, they require a level of technical expertise many children will never aspire to (Williamson, 1982). In their common form, sports activities are inappropriate for most children.

GAME EXPERIENCES

Children need practice experiences that will lead to the acquisition of game skills and strategies as well as an enjoyment of games. We organize game lessons into three types of experiences based on the children's skill levels: invariant game skill experiences, dynamic game skill experiences, and games-playing experiences (Barrett, 1977; Figley, Mitchell, & Wright, 1977).

Research suggests that a child has little chance of being able to actually use basic skills in a changing or dynamic situation unless he or she first practices the skills in an open, changing, or dynamic setting rather than in an unchanging situation (Arnold, 1978; McKinney, 1977; Schmidt, 1977). The skill acquired by a child who throws and catches a yarn ball with a partner may minimally transfer to the skill of throwing and catching used in, for

example, baseball or basketball. For this reason, as soon as a child displays a minimum level of mastery in an invariant, unchanging situation, it's necessary to create situations which are progressively and increasingly complex and in which skills are used as they occur in game settings. If the child doesn't display a minimum level of mastery, however, frustration again can permeate the experience.

To determine the appropriate time to switch from invariant skill experiences to dynamic situations, the teacher classifies the children's abilities according to the generic levels of skill proficiency (see Chapter 4). When children reach the utilization level of skill proficiency, they're usually ready for dynamic game skill experiences. This does *not* mean that you never return to invariant game skill experiences (think of how many Olympic-caliber athletes practice basic skills for hours daily); it means that you can gradually make the invariant skills more complex so that they approach an increasingly open situation.

Invariant Game Skill Experiences

The first experiences we give children involve basic skills in a closed or unchanging situation. Such experiences allow the pupils to gain control of an object using a specific motor pattern (Rink, 1985). The experience is structured so that the task is as identical as possible each time—the experience is invariant in that the child isn't required to predict the flight of a ball or the movement of an opponent, for example. Such experiences are appropriate for a child who is at the precontrol or control level of skill proficiency and would have difficulty executing a skill in a dynamic or open situation. As a child's proficiency in a skill increases, you can increase the difficulty of the tasks while retaining the relative predictability of the skill. For example, when a child is learning to throw a ball to hit a stationary target, you can increase the distance to the target. If the child is learning to run and leap over a low obstacle, increase the height of the obstacle.

When a child who isn't able to perform a basic

Kicking a ball at a target from behind a designated line is an example of invariant game skill experience.

Dynamic Game Skill Experiences

When children have learned to perform skills successfully under relatively static conditions, they need and are challenged by opportunities to practice skills in circumstances similar to actual sports situations (utilization level). Shooting a basket with no opposition is a different skill from that needed to make a basket immediately after stopping a dribble or when guarded by an opponent. Children should be exposed to many experiences that relate to a variety of sports. Not only do we expose children to experiences from sports played in America, we also attempt to expose the youngsters to game-type experiences that require different combinations of skills which have no apparent relationship to any sports we're familiar with. Such experiences encourage children to develop techniques and applications of skills in unique situations because no doubt they'll experience games that have yet to be invented and that require skills and abilities yet unheard of.

Dribbling a ball past a defender into a goal is a skill experience similar to dribbling in a game situation.

skill consistently (precontrol level) is placed in a game that requires that skill and the ability to perform it in a dynamic or changing situation, the results are often counterproductive. A child in that situation often fails and becomes frustrated because of continuing inability to execute the prerequisite movements of the game. The child may then become a self-proclaimed, permanently terminated games player or a teenager or adult who vows to never again play in a game situation. And the other children are frustrated when an unskilled player interrupts the flow and their enjoyment of the game.

Rink's (1985) progression suggests that dynamic-type game skill experiences actually involve two aspects of skill development: (1) the combining of more than one motor skill into cooperative relationships and (2) the ability to use skills in simple offensive and defensive relationships. When viewed in this manner, the progression from invariant game skill experiences to dynamic game skill experiences to actual games-playing experiences is quite logical and developmental. For example, within dynamic game skill experiences, a child first practices dribbling and shooting a basketball while at the same time passing off to a partner and then practices the same skill with one person acting as a defensive player. The implication of this progression is that as the child slowly becomes more adept at using a motor skill or combination of motor skills, the child is simultaneously learning games-playing strategies to accompany the skill.

Providing experiences that require children to use game skills is different from teaching games. You can create practice opportunities that simulate the way skills are used in games but don't include scoring and control or limit competition. For example, ask children to try to keep a ball away from a partner using only a dribble (hand or foot), or to work in a group of three to keep a ball moving in the air without actually catching the ball. These tasks approach the dynamic situations of games and sports.

Games-Playing Experiences

We try to acquaint children with many different types of games-playing experiences. These activities can help children experience the enjoyment, satisfaction, excitement, and sense of accomplishment that can occur from a developmentally appropriate game.

Some skill development results from playing games, but game playing isn't the most efficient way for all children to improve the motor skills used in games. Thus it's useful to distinguish between lessons in which the primary purpose is to improve skills (invariant and dynamic game skill experiences) and lessons in which the primary purpose is to develop enthusiasm for and a playing knowledge of a variety of games (games-playing experiences).

Lessons devoted to skills acquisition are punctuated by a number of starts and stops. The teacher continually refocuses or redefines the tasks, giving individuals and groups feedback in an attempt to enhance the quality of their movements.

The games-playing environment is somewhat

Nettie Wilson (1976) conducted a study to determine the number of throwing, catching, and kicking opportunities in the game of kickball, as played by third- and fourth-grade children under the direction of a classroom teacher. She found:

1. Less than one-half of the game was actually spent using the criterion skills.
2. The average number of catches attempted in the kickball games was slightly more than two—35 percent of the children never caught the ball. Of the children who didn't catch the ball, 83 percent were girls.
3. The average number of throws made in the kickball games, excluding those made by the pitcher and catcher, was slightly more than one—52 percent of the children never threw the ball at all during the entire game, and 67 percent of those who never threw the ball were girls.

COMPETITION/COOPERATION

Some children love to compete; others prefer (and seem to learn better in) games that encourage cooperation. We attempt to respect each child's preference by giving choices, trying never to place an entire class in a competitive situation. Instead, we let children choose between two or more games or ask them to make up their own games. The teachers heighten or lessen the degree of competition. Teachers who constantly shout out the score, post team won and lost records, and reward the winners (thereby punishing the losers) place an emphasis on competition for which some children aren't ready. If you don't believe us, talk to the thousands of adults who were unskilled as children and yet were placed in highly competitive situations. They can describe, in vivid detail, the feelings of being picked last, shouted at for dropping a ball, and ridiculed for "letting the team down." Such distasteful experiences usually have lasting and negative influences on the individual's willingness to participate in sports.

different, however. The enjoyment and satisfaction derived from playing games frequently are products of playing a game without interruption. In the limited time most of us have to teach our classes, there's hardly enough time for skill practice and

Skill acquisition lesson: Teacher challenges children to dribble a ball through an obstacle course.

game playing in a single lesson. Try to observe the types of skill work that children need as they're playing games, and focus on those needs during later classes. Try not to stop or interfere in the children's games to teach skills unless the game has become unsatisfying and boring because of lack of ability. Adults prefer not to be interrupted during a game, even by someone who wants to provide feedback. Children share this feeling, and teachers must respect it if they want to create positive attitudes toward games.

One implication often drawn from the progression of invariant, dynamic, and games-playing experiences is that until children are exceedingly proficient with dynamic game skills and approaching the proficiency level of skill development, they shouldn't play games. This contention is only partially true. Although we don't advocate that children at the precontrol and control levels play games, we encourage application, self-testing, and dynamic game skill experiences. Children conceive of many of these types of experiences as games. In other words, children are playing games in their own minds; what is different is our adult conception of what a game is. Thus all children can play "games," depending on who is calling the activity a game.

I would like to contrast the richness of children's natural play with the stultifying rigidity of play that is organized by adults. No better example can be found than that of the Little League, for what boys, left to their own devices, would ever invent such a thing? How could they make such a boneheaded error as to equate competition with play? Think of the ordinary games of boys—in sandlots, fields, parks, even stickball in the street. They are expansive and diverse, alternately intense and gay, and are filled with events of all kinds.

Between innings the boys throw themselves on the grass. They wrestle, do handstands, turn somersaults. They hurl twigs and stones at nearby trees, and yell at the birds that sail by. A confident player will make up dance steps as he stops a slow grounder. If an outfielder is bored, he does not stand there pulling up his pants and thumping his glove, but plays with the bugs in the grass, looks at the clouds. . . . There is almost always a dog on the field, and no part of the competition is gayer or more intense than that between the boys and the dog, who when he succeeds in snapping up their ball, leads them off in a serpentine line that is all laughter and shouts, the dog looking back over his shoulder and trotting with stiff legs, until finally he is captured and flattens his ears as they take back their ball. No one has forgotten the score or who was at bat. The game goes on. The game goes on until darkness ends it, and the winners can hardly be distinguished from the losers, for by then everyone is fumbling the ball and giggling and flopping on the grass.

George Dennison,
The Lives of Children

GAME LESSON DESIGNS

There are at least five types of lesson designs a teacher can use to structure games-playing experiences for the children's variety of skill levels: predesigned, modified predesigned, teacher-designed, teacher/child-designed, and child-designed games (Riley, 1975).

Predesigned Games

Predesigned games are those described in textbooks or learned in a methods class and taught to the children without modification. The textbooks imply that such games will be appropriate as well as interesting and exciting for your pupils. Brownies and Fairies; Duck, Duck, Goose; Red Rover; Four Square; and Snatch the Bacon are well-known predesigned games.

Predesigned games are easy to teach because they require little preparation or teaching skill. The teacher selects a game and explains it to the children. When the children understand the game, they start to play, and the game continues until the lesson ends or the teacher changes to another activity.

Unfortunately, few predesigned games are appropriate for all the children in a class. A few skilled or popular children often dominate such games, while others are minimally involved, both physically and emotionally. You may occasionally have a situation in which a particular predesigned game is appropriate for a class or group of children. Usually, though, you'll find that, while many of the ideas in a predesigned game are worthwhile, you have to modify the structure of a game to match the game to the abilities and interests of different children.

There are exceptions to the inappropriate-

When I first started teaching. I was looking for games that were recommended for first grade children and did not require a great deal of game skill. Brownies and Fairies, a simple running and chasing game, was prescribed in one text as appropriate for six-year olds. The first time the game was played, two children fell down and bloodied their knees when they tried to run in a crowd of children. They could run without falling by themselves. But when they were placed in a dynamic situation that involved both running and dodging, they were unsuccessful. They probably forgot that experience many years ago—once their knees healed. I haven't.

ness of predesigned games. Several authors (Friends Peace Committee, 1976; Fluegelman, 1976; Morris, 1980; Orlick, 1978a; Wasylik, 1982) specifically designed alternatives to predesigned games, to meet the developmental needs of the majority of students in a group. These alternatives involve the restructuring of the inappropriate aspects of a game while still retaining the basic tenets of the original game. In essence, the games presented are modified predesigned games.

Modified Predesigned Games

Modifying a predesigned game requires greater planning and organizing ability than picking a game from a book. The chances increase that a game will be more appropriate for a particular class when a teacher modifies a predesigned game. You might decide to narrow or widen the playing area; require that different skills be used in the game (e.g., throwing instead of kicking or volleying), or change a rule to make the game less complex (e.g., allow two tries instead of one).

During the lesson, the instructor may use the same teaching skills required to teach a predesigned game—explaining the game and intervening only when that's necessary to keep the game going. Evaluating the game is more complex. You'll have to decide, after observing the children, whether the game should be modified further or is satisfactory as currently structured.

Teacher-Designed Games

Sometimes a teacher can't find a game appropriate for a particular class, and modifications of predesigned games don't seem effective. In such a situation, the teacher may design a game that satisfies a specific goal. Designing a game places a greater demand on a teacher's creative abilities than do either of the game lesson structures already discussed.

The teacher needs to understand the children's skill abilities and interests and be able to use this knowledge to design a game form that the children will find interesting and enjoyable. For example, a teacher could design a game to focus on striking a ball with a bat. The object would be to strike a pitched ball and then run around a cone and back before the other players catch or collect the ball and touch the home base with the ball. If the children used rather narrow boundaries and played in small groups, they would be assured of more striking, throwing, and catching opportunities than if they played the standardized nine-per-side version of softball. The teacher could design the game to be played by two teams or design it so that each child goes back "to the field" once she or he hits the ball and runs around the cone. Parts Three and Four include additional ideas that can be used when designing games for children. Once you've created the game, the teaching skills used are virtually identical to the skills needed

Children enjoy playing a modified game of soccer.

cessfully teach a modification of a predesigned game.

Each of the three game lesson structures discussed places the responsibility for selecting or designing a game on the teacher. One advantage of these games structures is that the children spend most of the time—once the game has been explained and organized—playing the game. But the children don't contribute to the design of the game, nor do they have anything to say about whether they would like to continue playing the game as is or change the game to make it better. The two game lesson structures now discussed involve the children in the design of the game. They require more advanced teaching skills if they're to be effective.

Teacher/Child-Designed Games

When the children and the teacher design a game together, the teacher presents the purpose of the game and the restrictions. The children and the teacher then work cooperatively to decide the rules, scoring, and equipment to be used.

You'll find that it's wise to stipulate that, once the game has begun, only the team with the ball (or the advantage) can stop play to suggest a change. (Unless the children are restrained by this rule, they're likely to stop the game and suggest a change every time the other team gains an advantage.) After a brief discussion of the proposed change, the class votes, with the majority decision prevailing. If a rule needs to be made to ensure safety, offer solutions to be voted on, or ask the children to propose a solution.

One example of a teacher/child-designed game is Magladry Ball, named by the children after their school. The teacher was concerned about the children's inability to travel and pass a ball or other object to a teammate who was also traveling, particularly when an opponent attempted to intercept or prevent the pass from being made. After

Chapter 26   Teaching Games   **623**

describing the purpose of the game, the teacher imposed two restrictions: Children couldn't touch each other, and once the ball (object) touched the ground, it was automatically in the possession of the team that didn't touch it immediately before the object hit the ground. The object of the game was to throw the ball (beanbag, Frisbee) through a hoop suspended from a goal post by a rope at either end of a field. Once the game began, children made decisions about how long one child could remain in possession of the ball (object); what type of ball (object) to play the game with; boundaries, violations, and penalties; and scoring.

Teacher/child-designed games evolve slowly, and you may spend several lessons creating games that children are excited about and enjoy playing. Once the time and effort to create a game have been spent, the children will want to have opportunities to play it.

The instructor in a teacher/child-designed game serves as a facilitator, enhancing and expanding ideas rather than imposing personal ideas on the children. The teacher helps the children modify the games, offers suggestions, and manages a group of eager, charged-up children who are anxious to get the game going again. This isn't an easy task, and it often takes some time to master this approach.

Child-Designed Games

The underlying assumption of the first four game lesson structures is that the entire class is playing the same game together (even though, in actuality, you may have children playing several games at the same time). With child-designed games, however, we assume that a number of games are being played simultaneously and that few, if any, are identical. Such an environment is a far more complex one in which to teach. The teacher is assisting groups of children to develop different games and is also responsible for observing a number of different games and assisting or staying away when appropriate.

Child-designed games have some definite advantages. Children in groups of similar skill ability (given a choice, children typically choose to be with others of similar ability) are allowed to design games that are interesting and exciting to them. These may be cooperative or competitive, active or passive, depending on the children's intent.

You may consider it a disadvantage that some children take a great deal of time to design games. Children who've had little experience in designing their own games may spend as much as half of a lesson seriously working out the way they want a game to be played, perhaps without ever actually playing the game. But you'll find that as students gradually become more adept at designing games, playing time increases substantially. One way to increase the time the children are active is to suggest structure—purpose, boundaries, rules—when children are beginning to design their own games. As the children learn to make decisions about their games, you can decrease the amount of imposed structure (Chapter 4).

Most children enjoy participating in the design of their own games. But the children must be ready—they must be able to function successfully in a small group (two or three is an appropriate number) when playing a game they know before they can begin to design games. Some teachers, even of younger children, can use child-designed games from the time they begin teaching and have exciting, successful lessons. But when a teacher—even one who believes in the philosophy represented by child-designed games—tries to have children design their own games before the children (and the teacher) are ready, the outcome can

A true game is one that frees the spirit—the true game is the one that arises from the players themselves.

Peter Opie and Iona Opie,
Children's Games in Street and Playground

THE FAMILY CIRCUS   By Bil Keane

6-28
Copyright 1978.
The Register and Tribune
Syndicate, Inc.

"We made it up ourselves. You don't need nine
guys on a team, or grownups, or uniforms. . . .
It's like baseball, only better!"

be a disaster. Start with the design that you think is most appropriate to a class and situation and proceed from there.

THE BEST GAME DESIGN?

The ecology of the particular teaching situation determines which game design is best. When selecting a games-playing lesson design for a class, consider the purpose for playing the game, the skills required, the children's interests and abilities, the playing area and equipment available, and your skills as a teacher. We try to very carefully match the skills required in games-playing experiences to the children's skills. Nothing is so counterproductive as having children participate in games for which they don't possess the necessary

prerequisite skills. If the teacher has closely assessed the children's skill level, well-matched games-playing situations can be discovered and/or designed to ensure the children's success and pleasure. Also, as many children as the situation will allow must be involved in actively playing a game. We've found that groups no larger than eight facilitate this idea. This implies that more than one game may be played simultaneously. Sometimes two games going on simultaneously are better than one because then twice as many children can actively participate. And three games are usually better than two for the same reason. Some games are better with more participants; others can be played with fewer children. However, several games going on at one time can be uncomfortable for many of us because we feel out of control. If this is true for you, we suggest you begin slowly; start with a class you're confident with, and have only two concurrent games being played. As you feel more confident with your role in the new situation, gradually add a few more games.

Gradually, each class begins to need less teacher monitoring of games, and the teacher becomes more effective at delegating responsibility. When this happens, the teacher can begin to design lessons that offer children a choice between two different games played simultaneously. Remember, the children will need to have played both games if they're to make informed, responsible choices. You can expand the selection to three or four games as the children become more adept at decision making (Chapter 4).

RESEARCH ON CHILD DEVELOPMENT

The research on child development (Piaget, 1962) and the development of reasoning (Kohlberg & Mayer, 1972) further supports placing children in game situations designed to accommodate their skills, interests, and abilities. Before the age of eight, children are in the egocentric stage. They have a

personal conception of reality; the world centers around self. There's no sense of obligation to rules, no desire to check for accuracy. "I" am right at all times. Whatever meets the needs at the present time is what is true. Following rules is fine if it serves the purpose at the time. The concept of cheating doesn't exist since rules constantly change to fit the child's needs. At this stage the child feels completely understood by all and that everyone is in agreement with what the child wants or does. Imagine placing twenty-five youngsters in a traditional group game when each child thinks he or she is completely understood and in agreement with all!

Piaget (1962) described the game play of the young child (from the child's viewpoint) as a situation in which everyone plays the game as each understands it, with no concern for "checking" on others. Nobody loses and everybody wins at the same time because the purpose is to have fun (Piaget & Inhelder, 1969).

Children between eight and eleven have a strong social need. To be a part of the group, to belong, is extremely important to children in the upper elementary years. In the early phases of this stage, however, children still have strong egocentric tendencies. Group interaction is desired, but so too is the desire to cling to the comfortable self-centered view. The earlier "absolute" view is now confronted with the viewpoints of others, viewpoints perhaps not in agreement with one's self.

How many children do we see get upset and leave the game when things don't go their way or they're asked to sacrifice self for the good of the team? Cooperative game situations with small groups of children can facilitate establishing the child as a member of the group and foster acceptance of differing points of view.

Students entering the higher level of cognitive development, ages eleven and above, begin to create strategies and mentally test their abilities. They enjoy group activity and respect the physical and mental skills of others in the game situation. The game no longer rules the group; the game is made for the use of the group—to be adapted as needed.

A FINAL THOUGHT

During the past few years, much has been written about the inappropriateness of adult versions of sports for children (Orlick, 1978b; Thomas, 1977; Tutko & Bruns, 1976). The child who seeks sport experiences can find them outside the school. Most communities in the United States offer adequate sports in junior and senior high school, in after-school programs, and in programs sponsored by youth agencies.

Physical educators have a responsibility to provide instruction for all children, to help them become skillful games players who enjoy participating in games and are eager to play games on their own time. We must do more than produce a few good athletes. In a successful physical education program, all the children improve their games-playing skills and are eager and excited about playing games.

SUMMARY

Because games are self-propelling, they're easier to teach than dance or gymnastics. Ease of teaching, however, is an educationally unacceptable rationale for curricular decision making. Teachers need to provide children with appropriate experiences that lead to the development of games-playing skills. We give children experiences that involve invariant game skills, dynamic game skills, and games playing.

Invariant game experiences focus on skill acquisition in a predictable, closed environment where the movement is essentially the same each time. Dynamic game experiences require the children to use game skills in unpredictable, open situations where they must focus on more than the execution of a particular skill. Games-playing experiences are designed to expose the children to the joy and satisfaction that can be found in games. These experiences can be divided into five categories of games: (1) predesigned, (2) modified predesigned, (3) teacher-designed, (4) teacher/child-designed, and (5) child-designed.

The teacher's work is more complex when children are encouraged to help create their games. But the enthusiasm generated when children do invent their own games makes this process worthwhile.

READING COMPREHENSION QUESTIONS

1. What is the difference between games and sports?
2. Games are organized into what three types of experiences? Define the purpose of each experience.
3. What happens when we place children in dynamic situations before they're ready?
4. When is it appropriate to move children from a static to a dynamic situation? Why is such movement necessary?
5. How are situations that require children to use games skills different from actual games?
6. What is one difference between a games-playing lesson and a skill-development lesson? What role should a teacher take in each lesson?
7. Identify five types of games-playing lesson designs. What are the advantages and disadvantages of each type? How does the role of the teacher change with each type?
8. What abilities must teachers possess to design their own games?
9. What teacher and student characteristics must be established before attempting to have children design their own games?
10. What two major considerations must be taken into account regardless of what games-playing lesson design is used?

REFERENCES

Arnold, R. K. (1978, November–December). Optimizing skill learning: Moving to match the environment. *Journal of Physical Education and Recreation*, 84–86.

Barrett, K. R. (1977, September). Games teaching: Adaptable skills, versatile players. *Journal of Physical Education and Recreation*, 21–24.

Dennison, G. (1969). *The lives of children.* New York: Random House.

Figley, G. E., Mitchell, H. C., & Wright, B. L. (1977). *Elementary physical education: An educational experience.* Dubuque, IA: Kendall/Hunt.

Fluegelman, A. (Ed.) (1976). *The new games book.* Garden City, NY: Doubleday.

Friends Peace Committee. (1976). *For the fun of it! Selected cooperative games for children and adults.* Philadelphia: Nonviolence and Children Program. Available from 1515 Cherry Street, Philadelphia, PA 19102.

Kohlberg, L., & Mayer, R. (1972). Development as the aim of education. *Harvard Educational Review, 42*(4), 449–496.

Mauldon, E., & Redfern, H. B. (1981). *Games teaching* (2nd ed.). London: MacDonald & Evans.

McKinney, D. E. (1977, September). . . . But can game skills be taught? *Journal of Physical Education and Recreation,* 18–21.

Morris, G. S. (1980). *How to change the games children play.* (2nd ed.). Minneapolis: Burgess.

Opie, P., & Opie, I. (1969). *Children's games in street and playground.* New York: Oxford University Press.

Orlick, T. (1978a). *The cooperative sports and games book: Challenge without competition.* New York: Pantheon.

Orlick, T. (1978b). *Winning through cooperation: Competitive insanity, cooperative attitudes.* Washington, D.C.: Acropolis.

Piaget, J. (1962). *Play, dreams, and imitation in childhood.* New York: Norton.

Piaget, J., & Inhelder, B. (1969). *The psychology of the child.* New York: Basic Books.

Riley, M. (1975, February), Games and humanism. *Journal of Physical Education and Recreation,* 46–49.

Rink, J. (1985). *Teaching physical education for learning.* St. Louis: Mosby.

Schmidt, R. (1977). Schema theory: Implications for movement education. *Motor Skills: Theory into Practice, 2,* 36–48.

Thomas, J. R. (Ed.). (1977). *Youth sports guide for coaches and parents.* Washington, D.C.: Manufacturers Life Insurance Company and the National Association for Physical Education and Sport.

Tutko, T., & Bruns, W. (1976). *Winning is everything and other American myths.* New York: Macmillan.

Wasylik, K. (1982). *Volleyball developmental model.* Ottawa: Canadian Volleyball Association and Coaching Association of Canada.

Werner, P. (1979). *A movement approach to games for children.* St. Louis: Mosby.

Williamson, T. (1982). A critical look at the games curriculum. Reflecting on the teaching of games. *Bulletin of Physical Education, 18*(1), 23–33.

Wilson, N. (1976). The frequency and patterns of selected motor skills by third- and fourth-grade girls and boys in the game of kickball. Unpublished master's project. Athens: University of Georgia.

C H A P T E R **27**

Teaching Dance

One of the great values in the education of children comes from the experience of making their own forms to express, to communicate, to enjoy. Each child is unique in his individualism and in his environment. He needs a chance to say what he is, how he feels, what his world means to him.

Ruth L. Murray

Dance is probably the hardest teaching area for the same reason that games teaching is the easiest. Most teachers have an extensive background in games playing, but few teachers have experience as dancers. And most of us do teach best what we know best. Many teachers, because of their limited background in dance, omit dance altogether or have only a few dance experiences in their programs.

None of the authors of this book is a dancer, yet each of us has learned to give children exciting, interesting, and educational dance experiences. In fact, dance has become one of the most enjoyable areas for most of us to teach because of the children's enthusiasm and excitement about dance. We're convinced that individuals who've had a minimum of formal training in dance can learn to teach successfully.

THE PURPOSE OF DANCE IN ELEMENTARY SCHOOL

One of the keys to providing children with successful dance experiences is to develop an understanding of dance and its purpose in an educational program. When we teach games, our purpose isn't to produce varsity athletes. Similarly, when we teach dance, our purpose isn't to train children to become professional dancers. Few, if any, physical education teachers have the expertise to train children to become professional dancers, and few children want to dance professionally. Dance experiences in physical education classes should give children:

1. The ability to use their bodies to express feelings and attitudes about themselves and others

Many children are enthusiastic and excited about dance.

2. A sense of self-satisfaction that can be derived from effectively using one's body as an instrument of expression
3. Enjoyment and appreciation of dance as a worthwhile experience for all, not for just a few
4. An appreciation of dance as an art medium that can have value for both the participant and the spectator
5. The ability to interpret and move to different rhythms

When children begin school, many are still in tune with their bodies as an instrument of expression. The task of the teacher of young children is not so much to teach them how to use their bodies as instruments of expression as to enhance the body's expressive abilities that young children already possess. By helping children at an early age to become aware of how they use their bodies for expressive purposes, we can help each child avoid a mind-body dichotomy. We're able to help children develop an increasing awareness of their bodies as instruments of expression. Too many of us, once we're able to communicate verbally, no longer use our bodies as tools for communication.

DANCE FORMS

Expressive or creative dance is easier for most teachers to teach to younger children. Certainly it isn't impossible to involve older children in creative dance experiences that they'll find enjoyable and educational, but it generally takes a skilled,

THE MOVEMENT MOVEMENT

When we are children most of us can run and tumble and roll in the grass. We can yell and laugh and cry. We can sing our inner songs and dance our personal dances. Our feelings are visible in our actions. When we're unhappy, we stomp and mope. When we're happy we turn cartwheels and splash in puddles. Our imaginations have a direct line to our arms and legs. We can take giant steps and be giants. We can flap our arms and they will fly us away over houses and mountains. We can do all of this and more, for a while.

And then, somewhere between five and twenty, we stop.

We stop running just for the fun of it. We stop letting out the shouts and belly laughs. We stop looking at the treetops and start walking the city sidewalks staring at the pavement. We begin, somewhere along the line, to "keep a stiff upper lip," to put "starch" in our spines, to speak softly and when spoken to. Our behavior becomes "acceptable" and, in the process, we are cut off bit by bit from ourselves and therefore from each other. If my impulses can't get through to me, how can I possibly share them with you? As we lose touch with our bodies our heads take over and begin to monitor our actions, to restrict our responses until the simple interaction of children becomes an elaborate and inaccurate communication system between Brain A and Brain B.

Jules Feiffer pictures one of these disconnected, clever heads floating around complaining about its headless, funny-looking, malfunctioning body. "It's lucky," Feiffer's head says, "that I need my body to carry my head around . . . otherwise . . . out it would go."

Too drastic.

We can fit our heads back onto our bodies. We can rediscover the links between the headbone and the toebones. We can regain the freedom to spread our arms out wide; to run and shout without feeling awkward or embarrassed. We can learn to fall down, jump up, and bend over without breaking. We can unlock the sounds of our sadness and our joy. We can tune in to the beat of our pulse and stamp our feet to our inborn sense of rhythm. We can explore the sounds and the gestures of our feelings and our dreams. We can reclaim our bodies and our voices; free them to rediscover our inherent sense of balance and design; and use them to show each other who we are and what we hope to be.

"The Movement Movement," by Ken Jenkins, in *California Living: The Magazine of the San Francisco Sunday Examiner and Chronicle*, Jan. 25, 1976, p. 19.

---

self-confident teacher to introduce creative dance to older children who've had little or no previous creative dance experience. Our major emphasis in teaching dance to children is on creative or expressive dance. We have nothing against folk, ethnic, or square dances—we enjoy them ourselves. We've found, however, that creative dance is easier and more enjoyable for both the children and the teacher when it's taught to the younger pupils. As children enter secondary school and become more interested in partner dances, they can begin to learn more of the cultural dances that are an important part of a society's heritage.

Children in the upper grades may find it interesting to learn a dance that is representative of a particular topic they're studying in the classroom, for example, the culture of Greece or the pioneer period in American history. Older children also enjoy creating folk dances from all the patterns and skills learned in previous dances.

Some teachers include clogging, breakdance, and various folk dances in their programs. The following resources can supply information about teaching these dance types:

National Clogging & Hoedown Council, P.O. Box 1648, Durham, NC 27702

Appalachian Clogging & Hoedown, The Carper, Bailey, Steele Travelers, Bill Carper, 1537 4th Avenue, Charleston, WV 25312

R. H. Hipps and W. E. Chappell, *World of Fun* (1970). Available from United Methodist Church, P.O. Box 871, Nashville, TN 37202

THE CONTENT OF EXPRESSIVE DANCE

The movement framework, depicting the interaction of skill themes and movement concepts (Chapter 3), is used as the foundation for expressive dance experiences for children. The majority of skill themes categorized under locomotor skills (walking, running, hopping, skipping, and galloping) and nonmanipulative skills (turning, twisting, rolling, balancing, transferring weight, jumping and landing, and stretching and curling) are used in expressive dance. Virtually all the movement concepts (Chapter 3) are used to heighten and expand the child's ability to express feeling and emotion through movement (see Table 27-1).

The focus in expressive dance is not on simply executing a particular movement—a turn or a balance—but on performing the movement so that it communicates the message the child intends it to. Once children are able to perform turns efficiently, they can begin to experiment with different qualities of turning. Slow, hesitant turns or fast, sudden turns are two possibilities. Eventually

TABLE 27-1 / Overview of the Content and Rationale of Teaching Expressive Dance to Children

We want children to acquire:	By learning a movement vocabulary of:	That can be used to express emotions and thoughts such as:	Stimulated by catalysts such as:

An ability to use their bodies as a means of expression	Movement concepts
	    Space awareness
	    Effort
		Friendship
		Warmth
		Anger
			Sounds
			Music
			Poetry

The sense of self-satisfaction that can be derived through expressive movement	Relationships	Unhappiness Peace	Art History
	Skill themes Locomotor	Hostility Joy	Motion pictures Personal experiences
An enjoyment and appreciation of dance	Nonmanipulative	Satisfaction Harmony	
An ability to interpret and move to different rhythms			

Source: Adapted from "Educational Dance," by K. R. Barrett, in *Physical Education for Children: A Focus on the Teaching Process,* by B. Logsdon et al., 1977, Philadelphia: Lea & Febiger.

The quality of a movement communicates the message.

these qualities of turning can be used to express inner feelings or attitudes. For example, slow, hesitant turns might be used to depict sadness or uncertainty; sudden, quick turns could be used to express anger, frustration, or perhaps joy. Turning, by itself, communicates little. It's the quality of the turn that communicates a message, just as it's the quality of any movement that is expressive. This is the reason why it's so important to give children a movement vocabulary if they're to become expressive movers.

IMAGERY

Imagery is the use of a creative stimulus as a catalyst for movement. Many people believe, inaccurately, that imagery provides the content of dance. The content of expressive dance is movement; imagery is a helper. Asking children to use imagery as the content of expressive dance is similar to asking children to write a story when they have a vocabulary of only fifty words. One or two extraordinarily intelligent pupils might do well. Most,

however, would fail miserably because they hadn't yet acquired the tools needed for successful story writing.

The same principle can be applied to expressive dance. Children must be provided with the tools of dance, the ability to use a variety of movements effectively. Only when children have developed these skills can they successfully combine the movements into dances that express what they want to communicate. Movement vocabularies, however, aren't acquired through imagery, as the following example illustrates.

A teacher focusing on the concept of slow, heavy movement may ask children to travel as if the floor were coated with six inches of peanut butter. But using the peanut butter image without first teaching the concept of slow and heavy travel is of little value. Children who are adept at such movements at the beginning of the class will remain adept. Those individuals who were unable to travel slowly and heavily might move in the desired manner when stimulated by the image of a peanut butter floor, but they won't have acquired a functional understanding of slow, heavy movement as a concept that can be transferred to other movement situations. In short, imagery can be useful as a reinforcer for certain movements, but imagery by itself doesn't enhance the quality of children's expressive movement.

DANCE EXPERIENCES

Dance experiences for children can be classified into two types: rhythmic and creative. In rhythmic experiences, children are taught about different rhythms, to develop awareness of rhythm and the ability to move in relation to various beats. In creative experiences, we devise situations that invite children to insert their own ideas into the lesson. Many rhythmic experiences involve a correct response. Creative experiences have no right or wrong answers; the children are asked to provide interpretations or responses to a particular problem or situation.

Rhythmic Experiences

Initially, rhythmic experiences for children at the precontrol level are very basic and used to reinforce the movement concepts and themes the children are already studying. For example, ask the children to move body parts (head, feet, knees) to a simple beat you produce by playing on a rhythm drum, tambourine, or wood block. Or ask the children to skip three beats in one direction and then change to skipping in a different direction on the fourth beat. This experience focuses on the skill theme of skipping and the movement concept of direction. Enhance awareness of body parts by asking children sitting on the floor yoga style to bounce their heads up and down four times to the right, four times to the left, and four times straight ahead in accompaniment to a beat. A record with an obvious beat heightens the children's enjoyment of this type of experience. Shakers and drums, such as those illustrated in Figure 27-1, can also be used. Appendix 1 at the end of this chapter lists records that are suitable for various kinds of movement and rhythmic experiences.

The teacher challenges a class to lead the rhythmic movement with their elbows.

Once children have grasped the basic concepts of rhythm and are able to respond correctly to different beats, they'll enjoy experiences that involve a group response to a given rhythm. These control-level experiences are designed to involve the children in remembering a sequence of movements or actions performed to a rhythm. Several pieces of equipment are useful for teaching rhythmical group routines: Chinese ribbons, jump ropes, lummi sticks, and parachutes. Examples of routines to music and appropriate records are included in Appendix 2 at the end of this chapter. Dribbling to music is described in Chapter 23, "Volleying and Dribbling." Rhythmical group routines are excellent for promoting physical education at school assemblies, PTA programs, and community functions (Chapter 31).

DRUMS

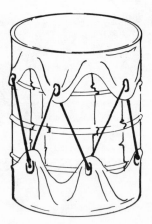

Tin can drum

Remove the top and bottom of any size tin can. Cut two circles, about an inch larger in diameter than the tin can, from an inner tube. Punch about six small holes around the edge of each rubber circle. Place one circle over each end of the can. Tighten by lacing strong string or nylon cord through the holes. Bells or bottle caps may be added for additional sound.

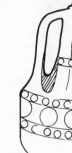

Bleach (or milk) jug drum

Screw top of jug and secure with tape or glue. Hit with dowel rod. The children can decorate the jug with paint or colored tape.

CLACKER

Cut two pieces of board to the same size. Drill holes in one end of each board and join the boards with nylon cord or wire. The children can decorate the boards.

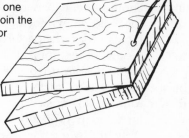

SHAKERS

Tube shaker

Cover one end of an empty paper towel tube with heavy paper or aluminum foil. Fill with small round stones or dried beans. Then cover the other end. The children can decorate the shaker.

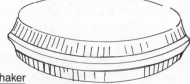

Pie pan shaker

Place small round stones or dried beans in an aluminum pie pan. Staple another pie pan of the same diameter onto the top of the first pan.

Balloon shaker

Pour sand, rice, beans, or a combination of these ingredients into a balloon. Partially inflate the balloon and tie the end.

Cup shaker

Partially fill a paper or plastic cup with small stones, beans, or bottle caps. Tape another cup on top of the filled cup.

Figure 27-1 Easy-to-make rhythm instruments.

Jumping rope can be a rhythmic dance experience.

The amount of time a teacher has to spend on these routines depends to a great extent on how often physical education is scheduled. Teachers whose classes meet twice a week, for example, typically spend more time on mastery of the basic skills involved in the rhythmic experience, e.g., rope jumping, ball handling.

Utilization- and proficiency-level experiences focus on children creating new lummi stick routines, designing individual and partner jump rope routines, and using ball-handling skills in routines to music, e.g., Harlem Globetrotters. Children at these levels of rhythmic experiences will com-

bine various movement qualities and patterns with their manipulative skills, e.g., floor patterns, directions, levels, phrases, and variations in rhythm: double time, half time, and so on.

As is true in creative dance, it isn't sufficient for the teacher to say, "Today we're going to design a jump rope routine. Find a partner and get started." As teachers, we provide guidelines for the routine. We tell the children the limitations we're imposing, such as the number of persons in a group, the length of the routine, the minimum number of skills to be included, and the music to be used (if this is a teacher decision). Children also need to know the necessary inclusions in the routine that are to be group decisions, for example, directions, pathways, floor patterns, and levels, as well as basic skills to be performed.

One of the most difficult parts of child-designed rhythmic or folk dance experiences is the time factor, that is, the matching of the length of the routine to the length of the music. Children often need guidance in choosing to add skills, repeat phrases, or repeat the entire routine.

Creative Experiences

Creative and rhythmic experiences in dance aren't separated in our program; many of the creative experiences are performed to rhythm. In fact, it isn't uncommon for us to switch the focus several times during a lesson, sometimes focusing on the rhythm of the movement, other times focusing on

If the teacher selects the music, there is maximum participation by the children during class since all can practice to the same music. If each group of children selects the music, there is greater variety of music but limited practice time.

A child travels to the rhythmic pattern played on a rhythm drum by a classmate.

the expressive qualities of the movement. When concentrating on rhythmic experiences, the primary focus is on the children's ability to move to the rhythm. In contrast, creative experiences are intended to provoke creativity and expression. Creative experiences for children are designed to evoke the expressiveness and lack of body inhibition so characteristic of the young child.

At the precontrol level, experiences are designed to help children develop sensitivity and awareness to movement by focusing on fundamental body actions and travel skills. Stretching, curling, bending and skipping, galloping, and leaping are movements frequently used with precontrol children. Initially it's a good idea to focus on giving children opportunities to explore a wide range of movement possibilities. Once this has been

accomplished, shift the emphasis to the spatial quality of the movements. For example, have the children do a complete, full stretch or a very tight curl, and use the movement concepts to enhance the children's sensitivity to the potential of movement. The primary emphasis, however, is still on the movement rather than the body's expressive or communicative possibilities.

At the control level, begin to clarify for children the expressive and communicative aspects of movement. The focus now centers more on the effort and relationship concepts (Chapter 3). Through these concepts, movement is explored as a tool for expressing an idea, attitude, or feeling. Movement is no longer studied primarily as an entity in and of itself; it's viewed as a medium of expression. Challenge the children to structure their movements to an imposed beat or rhythmic pattern, or have them verbalize how their movements feel and describe their emotional reactions to classmates' expressive movements.

Children at the utilization level have learned to efficiently perform the movements studied at the precontrol level and to modify the movements intentionally by focusing on different movement concepts. At this level, children can begin to structure their communicative movements into organized forms. This structuring is often termed *sequencing* or *phrasing*.

It's usually a good idea to narrow the focus of a sequence or phrase to one, two, or at most three skills and concepts. When youngsters at this level are given too many possibilities, they're often unable to decide where to begin. The ability to move, however, combined with a working knowledge of movement concepts, enables pupils to elicit varying and qualitative responses to a single challenge.

DANCE MAKING

Dance making—structuring several sequences or phrases into a whole—is the focus at the proficiency level. The idea behind a dance can be stim-

EXPRESSIVE AND COMMUNICATIVE ACTIVITIES

Time

Travel or gesture in slow motion.

Travel to an externally imposed beat or rhythmic pattern, such as a handclap or drumbeat.

Rise and sink suddenly or slowly.

Force

Travel or perform nonlocomotor actions to a strong beat.

Travel or perform nonlocomotor actions to light, gentle, delicate music.

Freeze in a strong, dramatic pose.

Youngsters explore the expressive possibilities of partner formation.

A child freezes in a strong pose.

Flow

Combine two travel skills, such as running and leaping, always moving smoothly.

Display hesitant, jerky, mechanical flow to create the illusion of being a robot.

Feel and observe the differences in combining a step with a turn, first with smooth, continuous flow, then with pauses (stillnesses) interspersed between each step and turn.

Relationships

Experience the sensation of matching, mirroring, or shadowing the movements of a partner.

Explore the expressive possibilities of group formations—for example, sculpture for the city park, or a mountain range.

Experience the feeling of contrasting the movements of a partner—for example, as one partner rises the other sinks, or one partner travels in a geometric path (square) while the other travels in a random path.

SEQUENCE ACTIVITIES

- Design a sequence that combines light, gentle, delicate leaps with smooth, fluent, step-turns interspersed with dramatic stillnesses.
- Combine appropriate travel skills and gestures with the rhythmic patterns of several Tom Foolery rhymes.

- Have groups of children organize into group formations and then continually transform themselves into different formations.
- Design a sixty-second phrase depicting the plight of a caravan of lost travelers crossing the Sahara.

---

ulated by an infinite variety of sources, such as machines, natural phenomena (flowers, snow flakes), sculpture, music, poetry, or painting. There are additional ideas for the development of creative dance experiences in the movement concept chapters (12 to 14) and skill theme chapters (15 to 25). Appendix 3 at the end of this chapter is a listing of dance and rhythm ideas found throughout the book.

Design of Dance

We've found it valuable to have upper grade children view the dance-making process as composed of the following procedures:

1. Selection of the purpose, idea, or theme of a dance
2. Identification of appropriate movements and movement concepts to express the intended idea, attitude, feeling, or theme
3. Design of a powerful opening statement for the dance
4. Design of a series of actions rising to a climax
5. Design of the portion of the dance that is to be the climax or peak of the action
6. Design of the resolution or concluding statement of the dance

The possibilities for dance making are infinite. Two examples illustrate how dances can be designed to portray different emotions or thoughts.

The first is an abstract dance contrasting tradition with the forces of change. One group arranges itself as a solid square facing in one direction. Symmetrical movements prevail. Actions are firm, sustained. The other group is scattered widely, facing in random directions. Nonsymmetrical movements, free use of space, and variety are used.

The second dance is based on the theme of freedom. Joyous, vibrant movements prevail. Free use of space, meeting, and parting are appropriate. Displays of strength, courage, or pride are also suitable.

Evaluation of Dance Making

The evaluation of dance making is a continual process that results in constant refinement and revision. Children need to be satisfied with the final product. Evaluation examines all movement skills and concepts the teacher and children have incorporated into the dance. Considerations include:

- Beginning location and pathway of each youngster—how the children choose to locate themselves at the beginning of the dance and the pathway they choose to express various feelings
- Selection of travel skills (leaping, skipping) and the quality with which they're performed—whether the children are using a variety of

(text continues on p. 641)

CHILDREN DESIGNING THEIR OWN DANCE: A DESCRIPTION OF A PROCESS

One of the goals in teaching dance is to work with children so that they learn to design dances to express feelings or thoughts that are important to them. This description of the process of creating a dance tells how one teacher worked with a group of upper grade children, assisting them to create their own dance. The description is intended to reveal the process of creating dances; it isn't presented as a predesigned dance to be taught to other children.

Background

The population of the community in which the children in this class lived was predominantly black. The eight children in this group wished to create a dance that expressed pride and respect for their Afro-American heritage.

We began by using several methods to develop an outline for the dance:

1. One student wrote a short paper describing what he considered the most important events in the movie *Roots*.
2. The school librarian provided several sources of information. Individual students read and outlined these sources for the remainder of the group.
3. Several students interviewed teachers and classmates about their family backgrounds. They also asked people to describe what emotions they had about their heritage.

Without question, the movie *Roots* had the biggest influence in determining the students' conception of black history. The pride and courage of Kunta Kinte and his descendants were the qualities the children wanted most to exhibit in their dance.

An Outline of the Dance

After gathering and reviewing this information, we discussed a sequential outline for the dance. It was agreed that:

1. We'd begin by depicting, in some way, the period of slavery.
2. The arrival of freedom would be expressed. Interestingly, the children didn't want this portion of the dance to be happy or exhilarating, for several reasons. They felt that blacks were always free, despite slavery; that many freedoms were long in coming; and that the struggle for equality continues today.
3. Upon arrival of freedom, it was important to display the pride and courage of Afro-Americans in overcoming many injustices, both as individuals and as a people.
4. The conclusion of the dance would be spiritual, exhibiting respect and thankfulness to God for blessing a cherished people.

Creation of the Dance

Children focused on each section of the dance before putting it all together. For each portion the youngsters needed to decide upon and write on paper the

1. Beginning location of each dancer
2. Sequential travel pathway of each dancer or of the entire group
3. Expressive qualities they intended to exhibit in their movements
4. Sequence of specific gestures and travel skills incorporated to express desired qualities

Once the group could perform one section to the teacher's and their own satisfaction, work was begun on the next phase of the dance.

(box continues on next page)

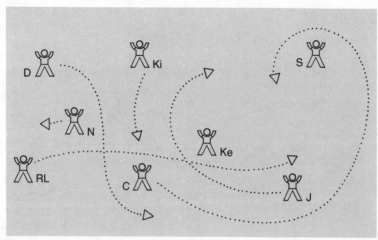

Travel Pattern for "Freedom"

Travel pathways
   Random: dancers weaving in, out,
     and around one another
Qualities
   Smooth, wavy, uncertain, looking to
     others for help
Actions
   Wavy gesturing of arms, held
     upward for protection or reaching
     out
   Hips smoothly waver
   Slow stepping, with changes in
     direction and levels

Slavery

After discussing the accumulated information, the children agreed to begin the dance by exhibiting the qualities and actions of field slaves laboring under a hot sun.

Freedom

This phase of the dance was the most difficult for the children. After experimenting with several ideas, the youngsters asked if they could select music to serve as background for the dance. They thought that if they had appropriate music as a stimulus, they'd be able to solve their dilemmas. After listening to several cuts from the *Roots* soundtrack album, the children unanimously agreed that the words and slow pulse of the song "Many Rains Ago (Oluwa)" was perfect for their purposes. They

Travel Pattern for "Gathering Again: Strength, Pride, Confidence"

Travel pathways
   All dancers suddenly and simulta-
     neously gather in the middle with
     a run, leap, and turn
Qualities
   Strong, confident, proud, smooth,
     and fluent
Actions
   Smooth, fluent leap and landing,
     when dancers grasp each other's
     hands overhead and freeze into a
     stillness

decided to express freedom by simply putting down their tools and slowly and smoothly beginning to interweave with one another, making eye contact with others for the first time. This was intended to express changed circumstances, in which they were free and proud but still struggling. During this phase, the youngsters' facial features exhibited fear and uncertainty about the future. The travel pattern was random.

Gathering Together: Strength As a People

To express their solidarity and pride as a people, the children's random travel began to be directed toward the center of the room where they gathered one by one, grasped one another's hands tightly, and formed a strong, unified statue.

From this point the youngsters were able to complete their dance with little teacher suggestion or intervention.

Dispersing: Strength As Individuals

Youngsters dispersed from center stage with new vigor and traveled along definite travel patterns.

Gathering Again: Strength, Pride, Confidence

Children leaped to center of room, where suddenly and simultaneously they clasped hands with one another overhead and formed a statue.

Respect and Thankfulness to God

From the statue position, youngsters slowly bowed and traveled to semicircle formation. Slowly they dropped to their knees, and then slowly they raised their hands and heads upward.

Conclusion: We Are Strong and Proud

Youngsters slowly bent to curled position. . . . Suddenly and simultaneously they rose on knees to grasp one another's hands to form a statue as a final statement of strength and pride.

travel skills and executing them clearly and precisely as intended with the desired impact
- Relationship of the children to one another—whether the children are reacting to each other with sensitivity and whether the timing, strength, and speed of their responses are appropriate
- Flow of the dance—how the parts of the dance are connected to give a unity of expression

THE PROCESS OF TEACHING DANCE

Teaching creative dance is different from teaching functional movements. A functional movement is performed correctly or incorrectly, and the teacher's task is to guide the child toward an appropriate execution. Dance movements, performed to express an idea or emotion, are more difficult to define clearly, and so the teacher's task is different.

Because the child is trying to express feeling or attitude, observation and feedback are also more complex. In games and gymnastics, the purpose of a movement is obvious; this isn't true in creative dance. When teaching dance, the teacher initially encourages, expands, and embellishes rather than correcting or refining. As the teacher comes to know the children and understand them as individuals, and as the children begin to trust the teacher, the children will seek sensitive and supportive feedback from the teacher. Remember, though, that human expression is very fragile and easily misinterpreted. Nothing stifles expression more quickly than insensitivity or lack of understanding. The teacher of creative dance needs to be constantly aware of how easily creativity is threatened.

THE AWFUL BEGINNING: A TRUE STORY, UNFORTUNATELY

I looked across the desk at my big girl. She'd come for help in planning her semester schedule.

"Look," I said, "you have some electives. Why don't you take a course or two for fun? You've worked hard and really should take something outside your major that will be pleasurable."

"Like what?" she asked.

My eyes scanned the college schedule of courses. "Like Dr. Mann's Creative Writing or Dr. Camp's Painting for Beginners or something like that."

She threw back her head and laughed. "Who me? Paint or write? Good grief, Dad, you ought to know better than that!"

"And this," I thought, "is the awful ending."

It was not always like this. I remembered an early golden September day when I went to my garage studio and gathered together my easel, paintbrushes, and watercolors. I sensed someone was watching me and looked up from my activity to see her framed in silhouette in the doorway. The breeze and the sun tiptoed in the gold of her curls. Her wide blue eyes asked the question, "Whatcha doin'?"

"I'm going to the meadow to paint," I said. "Want to come along?"

"Oh, yes." She bounced on her toes in anticipation.

"Well, go tell Mommy and get your paints." She was off but returned in no time carrying the caddy I had made to hold her jars of paint and her assortment of brushes.

"Paper?" she asked.

"Yes, I have plenty of paper. Let's go."

She ran down the hill before me, pushing aside the long soft grasses of the meadow. I watched closely for fear of losing her golden top in the tops of the goldenrod. She found a deserted meadowlark's nest and we stopped to wonder at it. A rabbit scurried from under our feet. Around us yellow daisies and goldenrod nodded in friendly greeting. Above, the sky was in infinite blue. Beyond the meadow, the lake slapped itself to match the blue of the sky.

On the lake, a single white sailboat tipped joyously in the breeze. My daughter looked up and saw it. "Here!" she said.

Trusting her wisdom as I always did, I set up our easels. While I deliberated over choice of subject and color, she had no such problem. She painted with abandonment and concentration and I left her alone, asking no questions, making no suggestions, simply recognizing uncontaminated creative drive at work.

Before I had really begun, she pulled a painting off her easel.

"There!" she said. "Want to see?" I nodded.

I cannot describe the sense of wonder that flooded over me as I viewed her work. It was all there—that golden September day. She had captured the sunlight in her spilled yellows, the lake in her choppy, uneven strokes of blue, the trees in her long, fresh strokes of green. And through it all, there was a sense of scudding ships and the joyousness of wind that I experience when I sail, the tilting and swaying of the deck, the pitching of the mast. It was a beautiful and wondrous thing and I envied her ability to interpret so honestly, so uninhibitedly, so freshly.

"Are you going to give it a name?" I suggested.

"Yep! Sailboats!" she responded, as she taped another sheet of paper to the easel.

There wasn't a single sailboat in the picture.

She began school the following week. One dreary November day she came into my study with a sheet of paper in her hand.

"Daddy," she asked, "will you help me draw a sailboat?"

"Me? Help you draw a sailboat?"

My eyes turned to the wall where her golden September painting hung in a frame I had made for it.

"Me? Help you draw a picture of a sailboat? Why, sweetheart, I could never paint a picture like the one over there. Why don't you paint one of your own?"

Her blue eyes looked troubled.

"But, Daddy, Miss Ellis doesn't like my kind of painting."

She held up her sheet of paper in the middle of which was a dittoed triangle.

"Miss Ellis wants us to make a sailboat out of this."

And that was the awful beginning!

James A. Smith

You don't have to be a dancer to be a successful teacher of children's dance. The following thoughts may help those who are searching for ideas that will help them develop effective programs of creative dance, even though they're inexperienced, both as dancers and as teachers of dance.

Don't Call It Dance!

Children who've had little exposure to creative dance experiences often react negatively to the prospect of studying dance. Children in the upper grades have been known to express their hostility to the idea with groans, frowns, sighs, and even emphatic refusals to participate. This resistance can be understood when you realize that too often, children in the upper elementary grades have had few opportunities to move creatively. Too often even those few opportunities have been poorly presented. Children have been forced, for example, to participate in uninteresting, unstructured forms of dance that had no purpose or reason for involvement that was apparent to the children.

Children enjoy practicing meeting and parting relationships as groups.

When that has happened, children have turned away from the joy of dance instead of becoming excited about creative movement. The teacher who, initially, avoids the word "dance" can involve the children in enjoyable, challenging movement experiences before they realize they're dancing. As the youngsters' awareness that dance can be exciting and stimulating grows, the stigma attached to the word "dance" will disappear.

Begin Gradually

The first experiences of a class with creative dance needn't last for an entire class session. A few minutes at the beginning or end of a class are often sufficient to introduce creative movement concepts—and simultaneously build your confidence as a creative dance teacher. One idea that we've found particularly effective can be used as a conclusion to an active lesson. Ask the children to lie on the floor, close their eyes, and use only their fingers (toes, arms, legs, elbows) to move to music. Short segments of lively music are most effective. With their eyes closed, children are less inhibited. The teacher, with eyes open, sees the creative dance potential that seems to be an inborn characteristic of the young child.

Start with a Cooperative Class

Some classes are more agreeable to work with than others. Select a class that is generally cooperative as the first one to which you'll teach creative dance. You don't need to start dance programs with all your classes at the same time. Instead, pick one class that you feel comfortable with. As your confidence builds, start dance programs in other classes. Use the first class as a testing ground for your ideas.

Use Props

Creative dancers derive great pleasure and satisfaction from focusing on how they can move their bodies. In contrast, immature dancers often feel insecure when asked to focus on how they're moving. Props can serve as catalysts, redirecting the child's attention and so reducing self-consciousness. The use of such props as scarves, ropes, hoops, newspapers, balloons, dowel rods, stretch nylon, and even shadows can effectively divert the attention of uncertain children from their bodies. For example, when attempting to duplicate the light, airy movements made by a floating sheet of newspaper, the child's attention is focused on moving as the newspaper does, rather than trying to travel lightly. As confidence builds, the children's attention can be gradually focused to their own movements.

Start with Exciting Movement Experiences

Fast, vigorous, large movements are attractive and appealing to young children. A lesson that focuses on running, leaping into the air, landing, and rolling evokes the exuberance associated with speed and flight. Gradually the teacher can begin to focus on the quality of the leaps, the effectiveness of the landings, and the use of gestures while in flight.

Dance to the Music

One of the most devastating experiences for poorly skilled children occurs when a teacher plays some music and simply says "Go ahead and dance to the music." This can be a terrifying experience for youngsters with little background or confidence in creative movement, children who haven't yet acquired a vocabulary of functional movements. The challenge "Move to the music" can be appropriate later, when the children are putting together movements they've acquired.

A FINAL THOUGHT

One instructor's initial attempts at teaching creative dance are still vivid. She recalled teaching to a second-grade class an entire lesson that focused on running, jumping, and turning to different rhythms. Afterward she remarked to a friend that it was the best workout the children had experienced the entire year and added that she was going to teach another lesson because of the physical fitness benefits. After another lesson was received as enthusiastically as the first, she was struck with the realization that the reason the children had been so actively involved was that they were totally immersed in the exciting atmosphere that was generated by exploring fast and slow turns, acceleration and deceleration leading into jumps. The children loved creative dance.

The physical education instructor who doesn't offer creative movement experiences is being professionally irresponsible. You may be more qualified to teach gymnastics or games. But you'll always be teaching some children who might eventually choose creative dance as their primary form of participation in the motor domain. Depriving children of opportunities to experience creative movement is no more acceptable than eliminating all opportunities to practice throwing and catching. You may have to devote much time and work to developing a successful program. But any teacher, even one who has little background in creative dance, can provide children with effective creative movement experiences.

SUMMARY

Teachers who lack experience and educational background in dance find it difficult to teach dance to children. But any teacher who's willing to try new and possibly unfamiliar ideas can learn to successfully teach children's dance. Children look forward to and enjoy dance experiences that are presented appropriately.

Because of the ages and abilities of children in elementary schools, we've found creative or expressive dance to be the most successful. Creative dance is also consistent with the nature and characteristics of young children, who are already adept at fantasizing and expressing their thoughts and feelings through movement.

The content of expressive dance is derived from the movement concepts and the majority of locomotor and nonmanipulative skill themes. The initial emphasis is on executing particular movements. As children learn to perform these skills efficiently, the emphasis shifts to varying the quality with which the movement is executed.

Children should have both rhythmic and expressive dance experiences. In rhythmic experiences, the focus is on moving in relation to different rhythmic beats. In contrast, creative dance experiences focus on expressive interpretation by children as they expand their movement vocabulary for communicating feelings and moods.

Through a process of trial and error we've discovered numerous techniques that help make dance lessons for children both interesting and educational. For example, we suggest that teachers initially avoid the word "dance" because it has negative connotations for some children. Inexperienced dance teachers may find it helps to begin by teaching dance to one cooperative class. Using props and designing lessons that are vigorous and action-packed are also strategies that help excite children about dance.

READING COMPREHENSION QUESTIONS

1. What should dance in the elementary school provide for children?
2. Identify two dance forms. Where does each form fit into a curriculum and why?
3. What skill themes and movement concepts generally appear in dance content?
4. What is the focus of expressive dance?
5. What is the role of imagery in dance? What must children possess before they can effectively use imagery?
6. Expressive dance can be classified into what two types of experiences? What is the primary focus of each experience, and how does the purpose differ at each proficiency level?
7. What is sequencing?
8. What is dance making? What procedures must be included in dance making?
9. How can you evaluate dance making?
10. What cues do the authors give for starting to teach creative dance?

REFERENCES

Barlin, A. L. (1979). *Teaching your wings to fly*. Santa Monica, CA: Goodyear.

Boorman, J. (1969). *Creative dance in the first three grades*. New York: McKay.

Carroll, J., & Lofthouse, P. (1969). *Creative dance for boys*. London: MacDonald & Evans.

Docherty, D. (1977). *Education through the dance experience*. Bellingham, WA: Educational Designs and Consultants.

Fleming, G. A. (1976). *Creative rhythmic movement*. Englewood Cliffs, NJ: Prentice-Hall.

Fleming, G. A. (Ed.). (1981). *Children's dance*. Reston, VA: AAHPERD.

Joyce, M. (1980). *First steps in teaching creative dance* (2nd ed.). Palo Alto, CA: Mayfield.

Joyce, M. (1984). *Dance technique for children*. Palo Alto, CA: Mayfield.

Murray, R. L. (1975). *Dance in elementary education* (3rd ed.). New York: Harper & Row.

Russell, J. (1975). *Creative movement and dance for children*. Boston: Plays, Inc.

Slater, W. (1974). *Teaching modern educational dance*. London: MacDonald & Evans.

Smith, J. A. (1972, April). The awful beginning. *Today's Education*.

Appendix 1

APPROACHING DANCE THROUGH MUSIC: A LIST OF SOURCES

Slow, Smooth, Delicate, or Flowing Music

"Love Theme from St. Elmo's Fire"—
David Foster. Atlantic LP 81261-1
(7-89528/45 rpm).

Easy flowing, gentle, turns in
motion.

"Theme from E.T. (The Extra
Terrestrial")—John Williams. MCA
LP 6109 (MCA 52072/45 rpm).

Smooth and gentle flowing motions,
delicate, expressive motions.

Evergreen—A Sound Odyssey.
Realistic (Radio Shack), Fort Worth,
TX 76102. Catalog Number 50-1007.

Slow, smooth, delicate, and flowing;
leaps, turns, sinking, rising, and
delicate expressive motions.

Chapter Two—Roberta Flack.
Atlantic Recording Corporation SD
1569.

Smooth, flowing turns, gentle leaps.

"Morning Has Broken"—Cat Stevens
(from *Teaser & the Firecat*) Motown
Record Corporation 8555-S.

Dance study of the life cycle of a
flower.

Carole King Tapestry. A & M Records
SP 77009.

Sustained rising and sinking.

James Taylor's Greatest Hits. Warner
Brothers Records BS 2979.

Fluent leaps with turns in flight;
relaxed abdominal breathing after
strenuous work.

Gay, Lively, Locomotor Music

"Flashdance . . . What a Feeling"—
Irene Cara. Casablanca Records 811
440-7/45 rpm.

Exciting and expressive locomotor
movements; leaping, aerobic
experiences.

"Theme from The Greatest American
Hero"—Joey Scarbury. Elektra
E-47147-A/45 rpm.

Expressive light but lively
movements.

"St. Elmo's Fire (Man in Motion)"—
John Parr. Atlantic LP 81261-1
(7-89541/45 rpm).

Explosive movements in locomotor
patterns.

"Part-Time Lover"—Stevie Wonder.
Tamla 1808TF/45 rpm.

Lively locomotor pattern that may be
repeated with skips, gallops,
rhythmic patterns.

"A Fifth of Beethoven"—Walter Murphy and the Big Apple Band. Private Stock Records PVT 1169/45 rpm.

Lively expressive patterns, disco-type movement.

"California Strut"—Walter Murphy and the Big Apple Band. Private Stock Records PVT 1170/45 rpm.

Lively rhythmic patterns.

Earl Scrugg's Nashville Rock. Columbia Records CS 1007.

"Loraderojosp III Breakdown"— Children vigorously move one body part to music (elbow, finger, tongue).

Country Boy—Lester Flatt. RCA Records APL1-0131.

"Feudin' Banjos"—Dance study based on the concept of question/answer.

Dueling Banjos/Reuben's Train—Eric Weissberg and Marshall Brinkman. Warner Brothers Records GWB0309.

"Dueling Banjos"—Partners contrast or match movements. "Reuben's Train"—Exciting locomotor patterns (slide, skip, gallop).

Rhythm and Blues (Simple Underlying Beat; A Range of Qualities)

"Give It All You Got"—Chuck Mangione. AM Records LP-SP-3715 (AM-2211/45 rpm).

Body shapes and changes in direction with a flowing movement.

Roots/Soul Sounds of a Proud People. Kent Records KST-700.

Change of direction or body shape on the accented beat.

Turn on Your Love Light. London Records SHL 32044.

"Bright Lights, Big City"—Creative dance study based on the theme of "cool members of a street gang."

Jazz (Exciting, Vibrant, Moody)

"Part-Time Lover"—Stevie Wonder. Tamla 1808TF/45 rpm.

Exciting, quick change of motion and levels; pivots, turns, vibrant movements.

"Eye of the Tiger"—Survivor Scotti. Brothers LP FZ 38062 (ZS5 02912/45 rpm).

Exciting, expressive movements, aerobic in style; changes in direction or levels with repeating rhythmic patterns.

"Maniac"—Michael Sembello. Casablanca Records 812516-7/45 rpm.

Expressive rhythmic patterns, changes in direction, aerobic-style rhythmic movements.

Honey in the Horn—Al Hirt. RCA Records LPM-2733.

"Java"—Ideal for exciting locomotor movements with quick stops or changes in level or direction.

Feels So Good/Maui-Waui—Chuck Mangione. A & M Records SP-6700.

Exciting, high leaps with turns in flight—sudden, fluent pivot turns concluding in dramatic body shapes.

Television Themes (A Range of Qualities)

"Miami Vice Theme"—Jan Hammer. MCA 6150/LP (MCA 52666/45 rpm).

Quick, sharp movements, changes in direction.

"Theme from Magnum P.I."—Mike Post. Elektra E-47400-A/45 rpm.

Strong beat with smooth, flowing expressions.

"Theme from The Greatest American Hero"—Joey Scarbury. Elektra E-47147-A/45 rpm.

Jumping, landing, slow-to-fast expressive movements.

TV Hits, Volume II. Pickwick International SPC-3566.

"Nadia's Theme"—Smooth, fluent sequencing of travel skills and balances.

Hit TV Shows, Volume II. Peter Pan Records 8197.

"Hawaii Five-O"—Vibrant, exciting locomotor combinations. "Little House on the Prairie"—Light gentle gallop, skip, leap.

Music from the Movies (A Range of Qualities)

"Eye of the Tiger"—Survivor Scotti. Brothers LP FZ 38062 (ZS5 02912/45 rpm).

Creative exciting movement patterns; aerobic activities; traveling patterns.

"A Fifth of Beethoven"—Walter Murphy and the Big Apple Band. Private Stock Records PVT 1169/45 rpm.

Strong beat; sinking, rising, leaping, rhythmic patterns.

"Titles"—Vangelis (from *Chariots of Fire*). Polyar LP (S) 1-6335.

Smooth, flowing, with strong expressive movement patterns, dance experiences.

"Theme from E.T. (The Extra Terrestrial)"—John Williams. MCA LP 6109 (MCA 52072/45 rpm).

Smooth, expressive movements; creative rhythmic dance patterns.

"Flashdance . . . What a Feeling"—Irene Cara. Casablanca Records 811 440-7/45 rpm.

Live, vibrant, rhythmic patterns with expressive movements.

"Love Theme from St. Elmo's Fire"—David Foster. Atlantic LP 81261-1 (7-89528/45 rpm).

Smooth and flowing; builds movement patterns that rise and fall.

"Georgetown"—David Foster. Atlantic LP 81261-1 (7-89528/45 rpm).

Smooth, flowing, expressive movements.

"St. Elmo's Fire (Man in Motion)"—John Parr. Atlantic LP 81261-1 (7-89541/45 rpm).

Exciting, expressive patterns; sharp movement such as changing direction and jumping.

"Maniac"—Michael Sembello. Casablanca Records 812516-7/45 rpm.

Dance patterns with aerobic benefits; many patterns that involve quick movements.

West Side Story. Columbia Records OL 5670.

"The Rumble"—Two groups use fighting gestures (punch, kick, slash, jab) in creating a dance; music is also appropriate for a creative dance based on "The Bull Fight."

Original Soundtracks and Music from the Great Motion Pictures. United Artists Records UAS 3303.

"How the West Was Won"—Exciting locomotor patterns, combining jumps with other travel skills. "Lawrence of Arabia"—Heavy, hot, tired, lethargic movement; creative dance, crossing the desert.

The Big Gun Down. United Artists Records UAS 5190.

Creative dance based on idea of battle—two primitive tribes, the bull fight, crossing the desert.

The Graduate. Columbia Records OS 3180.

"Sounds of Silence"—Lends itself to sustained, light, or gentle movements.

Born Free. MGM Records SE-4368.

Creative dance based upon theme of freedom—exciting, joyful movements, free use of space, free to meet and part with others.

"Roots Medley/Many Rains Ago"—Quincy Jones & Orchestra (from *Roots*). A & M Records SP-4626.

Creative dance based on the theme of black history—slavery, arrival of freedom, continued struggle, strength and pride, family strength, unity as a people.

"Theme from Summer of '42" and "Brian's Song"—Peter Nero & Orchestra. Columbia Records ZSP 156095.

Smooth, fluent, delicate movements. By changing speed to 78 rpm, abstract dance creations become possible—e.g., PinBall Mania.

For a Few Dollars More—Hugo Montenegro & Orchestra. RCA Records 447-0799.

Mystery, intrigue, imminent danger.

Star Wars. 20th Century-Fox 2T-541.

Abstract floor and air patterns; "Robots!"

Godspell. Arista Records SP 3300.

"Day by Day"—Joyous, vibrant movements—for example, turning with eyes focused upward and arms spread outward.

Electronic Music

"Miami Vice Theme"—Jan Hammer. MCA 6150/LP (MCA 52666/45 rpm).

Quick and vibrant motions.

The In Sound from Way Out—Perrey-Kingsley. Vanguard Recording Society VSD-79222-B.

"Jungle Blues from Jupiter"—Stop and go, change direction or level. "Visa to the Stars"—Study of slow motion or loss of gravity.

Switched On Bach. Columbia Records MS 7194.

Lends itself nicely to study of sudden, jerky gestures; creative dance based on idea of electrocution.

Halloween Sound Effects

Chilling, Thrilling Sounds of the Haunted House. Disney Records 1257.

Creative movement: Alone in a haunted house—scared expressions, hesitant, nervous travel; jumping in reaction to a creak or howl.

The Sounds of Halloween. A & M Records SP 3300.

Creative movement: Lost in a mob or caught in the midst of a hurricane.

Music for Parachute Activities, Routines, and Creative Movement Experiences

Most music that is flowing, smooth, and expressive, with a strong underlying beat, is very good for parachute activities. Many movie themes and television themes are excellent, for example, "Flashdance . . . What a Feeling," "Theme from Magnum P.I.," "Theme from E.T. (The Extra Terrestrial)," "Give It All You Got," "California Strut." Parachute shapes and activities are created through dance expressions and a variety of movement experiences.

Music for Rope Jumping

Rope jumping is a rhythmical, challenging, aerobic, and developmental experience when music is used with a strong beat that generates energy. Musical categories such as Disco, Electronic, Country, Movie and Television Themes, and Mild Rock (current Top 40) are recommended. Suggestions:

"Double Dutch Bus"—Frankie Smith. WMOT Records W58 5356/45 rpm.

"Eye of the Tiger"—Survivor Scotti. Brothers ZS5 02912/45 rpm (LP FZ 38062).

"Jump (For My Love)"—Pointer Sisters. Planet Records YB-13780/45 rpm (LP BXL1-4705).

"Swingin' "—John Anderson. Warner Brothers Records 7-29788/45 rpm (LP SP-3715).

"Part-Time Lover"—Stevie Wonder. Tamla 1808TF/45 rpm.

"St. Elmo's Fire (Man in Motion)"—John Parr. Atlantic 7-89541/45 rpm (LP 81261-1).

"Miami Vice Theme"—Jan Hammer. MCA 52666/45 rpm (MCA 6150/LP).

"Theme from Magnum P.I."—Mike Post. Elektra E-47400-A/45 rpm.

Other Sources of Music

A variety of physical education records—square dance albums, ethnic dance records, tininkling activities, basic rhythms, and music from around the world—are available from educational companies such as:

Educational Records, Inc.
Freeport, NY 11520

Kimbo Educational Records
Box 246
Deal, NJ 07723

Appendix 2

TEACHER-DESIGNED GROUP ROUTINES

Lummi Sticks

Lummi sticks for elementary age children are usually twelve inches long and one inch in diameter. They may be made from rolled newspaper sealed with tape, or cut from broom and mop handles or dowel rods. Each child needs two sticks. The routine that follows is designed in two parts. First, children learn the basic patterns without tossing the sticks; then they work with a partner to add tossing and catching the sticks in the rhythm of the pattern.

- Music: "Hey, Look Me Over," *Perceptual—Motor Rhythm Games*, Educational Records, Inc., Freeport, NY 11520
- Additional music: *Rhythm Stick Activities*, Educational Records, Inc., Freeport, NY 11520

5-C   Lummi Sticks   Congolian
Leslie Parrett + Melinda Johnson   Routine

1. Down together Down together, Cross Touch Cross
touch, flip, flip.

2. Touch Touch Touch, hit, Touch, Touch Touch
hit.

3. flip flip, Cross Cross, flip flip, Cross Cross

4. Down touch, Side touch, Cross touch,
flip flip.

5. toss Toss, down Together, down together, cross, cross,
flip flip.

6. Down together flip flip, Down together flip flip.
Repeat

Student-Designed Lummi Stick Routine, to Be Performed with a Partner

Basic Patterns

Pattern 1: Hold sticks together vertically, one in each hand. Tap sticks down, tap sticks together, extend right hand forward. Tap down, tap sticks together, extend left hand forward. Repeat entire pattern two times.

Pattern 2: Hold sticks vertically, one in each hand. Tap both sticks down, tap them together, extend right hand, extend left hand. Repeat pattern four times.

Pattern 3: Hold sticks horizontally, with front tips extending toward the floor. Touch the edge of the sticks to the floor, and then half-flip the sticks, catching the sticks in your hands. Hold sticks vertically for one count. Repeat pattern 2. Touch edge of sticks to floor, half-flip the sticks, hold sticks one count. Then repeat pattern 2: Tap down, tap sticks together, extend right hand, extend left hand. Repeat entire pattern four times.

Pattern 4: Hold sticks horizontally on each side of your body. Touch the edge of each stick on the floor, and then half-flip the sticks. Bring sticks to in front of you and perform pattern 3: Side touch, flip; front touch, flip; tap down, tap together, extend right hand, extend left hand. Repeat entire pattern four times.

Pattern 5: Hold sticks horizontally on each side of your body. Touch side front, side back, side front. Bring the sticks to in front of your body; touch front, cross your arms over, touch on opposite side, uncross arms and touch. Repeat pattern 2: Side, touch front, back, front; front, side, cross, side. Tap down, tap together, extend right hand, extend left hand. Repeat entire pattern four times.

Tossing to a Partner

Children sit facing a partner, approximately three feet from the partner. Patterns are the same basic patterns, except that instead of an extension of the arm, the stick is tossed to the partner, who catches it.

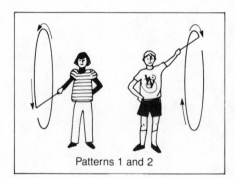

Patterns 1 and 2

Pattern 3

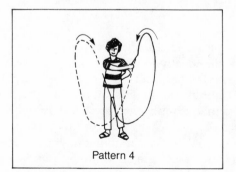

Pattern 4

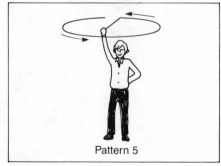

Pattern 5

Chinese Ribbon Patterns

Chinese Ribbons

Chinese ribbons or streamers are eight to twelve feet long and made of plastic. Crepe paper can be used, but it doesn't withstand children's practice or rough handling. Attach each streamer to a twelve-inch dowel rod with either an eyelet and screw or a swivel hook and nylon fishing line.

In time with the music, the streamers are twirled in front of the body, to the side, or over the head. The following patterns represent a combination of skills suited for control level:

> Four-count introductory phrase
>
> Pattern 1—right side eight times
>
> Pattern 2—left side eight times
>
> Pattern 3—front eight times
>
> Pattern 4—figure eight eight times
>
> Pattern 5—overhead sixteen times

- Music: "Sidewalks of New York," *Rope Jumping and Ball Handling*. Bowman Records, Inc.
- Additional music: *Chinese Ribbon Dance*. Twinson Company, Los Altos, CA

Musical Parachute

Children sit around the parachute and face clockwise. They hold the parachute in their right hands. The children are numbered 1 and 2, with the 2 being behind the 1, who is the partner.

Start the introductory music ("Pop Goes the Weasel"). The children stand up on the first "pop," still holding the parachute with their right hands only.

The children march clockwise in time with the music until they hear "*Pop goes the weasel*," at which point the 1's let go of the parachute and walk under the chute and behind their partners. Now the 2's are in front.

Students march clockwise. On the next "pop," the 2's let go of the chute and go under the chute and behind their partners. Now the 1's are in front again.

Children now skip clockwise. On the "pop," the 1's go under the chute and behind their partners.

The children continue skipping. On the "pop," the 2's go under the chute and behind their partners.

Students now face the center of the circle, holding the parachute with both their hands. Using the slidestep, they travel clockwise. On the "pop," children stop, then repeat the slidestep counterclockwise. They stop again, raise the parachute high in the air, and bring it back to the tuck position; they don't let go of the chute.

Youngsters wait for the next "pop," at which point they raise the parachute high in the air, walk forward three steps, and then pull the parachute down behind them so they're "in the cave."

Students wait quietly in the cave. When they hear the final "pop," they come out of the cave.

- Music: "Pop Goes the Weasel," *Rope Jumping and Ball Handling.* Bowman Records, Inc.
- Additional music: *Parachute Activities with Fold Dance Music.* Educational Records, Inc., Freeport, NY 11520.

Jump Rope

Jump rope routines at the control level should be relatively short and include only the basic jumps that everyone in class can do. As a rhythmic experience, a group jump rope routine involves executing the jump rope skills correctly, staying in rhythm with the music, and staying in time with others in the group. Here is an example of a jump rope routine for children at the control level:

The children place their ropes in a V shape on the floor, so they can stand inside the V and jump outside the V.

Start with a six-count introductory phrase. Then have the children execute six double jumping jacks. Starting inside the V, they clap thighs twice and clap hands above head twice. They jump outside the V as they clap overhead, inside the V as they clap thighs: out, out, in, in.

The children then pick up their ropes and step over the rope so it is behind them, ready for the first skill (four counts).

They jump the rope using two-foot jumps, eight times.

Next, they hold both handles of the rope in their right hands and execute eight double side swings. They turn the ropes in a forward circle on each side of their bodies.

Then they open the ropes and jump twelve times, using the step-jump skill.

Children again hold handles in their right hands. This time, they twirl the rope overhead like a helicopter (sixteen counts).

Finally, they quickly place the ropes in a V on the floor and stand inside (four counts). Then they execute six double jumping jacks.

- Music: "Frog Went Courting," *Honor Your Partner,* Square Dance Associates, Freeport, NY 11520.
- Additional music: *Jump Aerobics,* Kimbo, Long Branch, NJ 07740.

Appendix 3

DANCE AND RHYTHM IDEAS

Teaching Gymnastics

> If gymnastics is to be for everyone, including the handi-
> capped child, then all children cannot be asked to do the
> same gymnastic movement at the same time, in exactly the
> same way, for clearly some children are going to be under-
> challenged and some are going to be overchallenged.
>
> Andrea Boucher

Gymnastics move-
ments are fascinating to children. Climbing trees,
balancing on logs, swinging from limbs, and
maneuvering through playground apparatus are
all responses to the same question: "How well can
I avoid falling down as I explore different challenges?" The skills of balancing and transferring
and supporting weight on different body parts and
combinations of body parts are intriguing to children for at least three reasons.

First, these accomplishments are easy to measure. Children know that they did something today
that they couldn't do yesterday or last week. Second, the feedback children receive about the success of the attempt to defy gravity is instant and
self-revealing. Children don't have to rely on others

to determine whether they've been successful.
Third, children naturally find many of the possibilities in gymnastics on their own; in dance and
games they're typically introduced to possibilities
by outside sources, such as a coach or teacher or
television.

Many gymnastics movements are referred to
as *self-testing*. For children, especially younger ones
who still find it difficult to work with other children, the challenge of testing themselves in appropriate environments designed by a teacher is exciting and enduring.

In recent years—primarily because of television coverage of gymnastics featuring Mary Lou
Retton, Bart Conner, and other members of the
1984 United States Olympic medal-winning gym-

In educational gymnastics, we aren't training children to become competitive gymnasts. We don't have the time, and most physical education teachers don't have the expertise. And not every child wants to be a competitive gymnast. We give children gymnastics experiences to teach them to maneuver their bodies effectively against the force of gravity, on both the floor and apparatus.

Rather than giving children a relatively narrow gymnastics program focused specifically on learning to execute a series of predetermined stunts, we attempt to provide them with a foundation of

How well can I defy the force of gravity?

The joy of gymnastics can be instantaneous.

nastics team—interest in gymnastics has increased. Young children watch these exceptional performances by skilled gymnasts and are fascinated by the speed and difficulty of these gymnastics movements. In years past, most children were introduced to this sport in physical education classes. Today, most children are introduced to Olympic gymnastics through television.

THE PURPOSE OF GYMNASTICS

Educational gymnastics (as taught in physical education classes) and Olympic gymnastics aren't the same; they're related but have different purposes.

THE LITTLE GYMNAST

*Come with us, now, to a very nice place where little
children swing on rings.
Where laughter is king—and happiness queen—and
everyone likes who they are.*

On a little green island called Mercer, in
a big blue Washington lake surrounded by trees,
is a wonderful building assembled by people
who think it's important for children to play.
And learn. And find out what they can do.

The building is called the Jewish Community Center, and children come from miles
around to follow a Pied Piper of a man named
Robin West.

Robin grew up in South Africa and then
went to college at the University of Saskatch-
ewan in Canada. Now he teaches movement,
tumbling and gymnastics to hundreds of boys
and girls in the United States. One of his favorite classes is "kiddie gymnastics," for little
gymnasts, four to six.

Most four-year-olds already know how to
run, jump and play when they come to their
very first day of kiddie gymnastics. But in no
time at all, Robin can open their eyes to
hundreds of new ways to move, swing, roll,
bend and balance their bodies with success.

"Success for everyone" is the motto in kiddie gymnastics. It's such a simple motto—so
easy to follow—that sometimes even Robin and
the children's parents must stop to remind
themselves of its magic.

A child is a butterfly in the wind. Some
can fly higher than others; but each one flies
the best way it can. Why compare one against
the other? Each one is different. Each one is
special. Each one is beautiful.

In kiddie gymnastics, everyone flies and
nobody fails. There's plenty of praise for the
attempt well-tried. To balance on a beam for
the very first time is discovery. To be praised
and applauded for the very same motion is
joy.

In just a few short weeks the children in
Robin's class have learned to move with a confidence, poise and imagination that surprises
and pleases both themselves and their parents.

But they've also learned something else
along the way. You can see it in their eyes when
they tug so gently on Robin's bushy black beard.
You can see it in the way they lie on their back-
sides and stare at the ceiling and giggle. It's as
if they've learned something deep and exciting about themselves.

"I'm me . . . I'm special . . . I can try."

"If I make a mistake, it's all right. I'll start
over . . . I'll learn . . . I'll get better."

"Look at my friend. I'm helping him stand
on his head. He's special, too."

"We're good. We're children. We're okay."

Dan Zadra

gymnastics experiences that increases their skills
and introduces them to the types of activities that
are characteristic of gymnastics.

The children can gain specialization in specific skills elsewhere. For example, children interested in gymnastics can enroll in programs sponsored by youth agencies; others can join school
programs available at the secondary level. Some
elementary schools offer programs before and after
school for children who want additional practice
in gymnastics.

Specialization in physical education class can

lead to education of a few while the majority are left behind. Educational gymnastics programs should be designed to assist all children, regardless of ability, to improve their gymnastics skills—to become better able to control their bodies in the variety of planned and unplanned encounters they'll have, as children and as adults, with the force of gravity.

This doesn't mean we exclude all Olympic stunts from our gymnastics curriculum. Children at the utilization and proficiency levels with the body control and background of gymnastics experiences often use Olympic stunts as a response to a gymnastics task. When children use a handstand, walkover, cartwheel, and so on, the maneuver should be properly identified as such. Other children may ask help in learning a specific stunt or in perfecting one they've seen and are practicing on their own. The teacher's guidance is very important in these instances. As teachers, we can assess the child's skill level and the difficulty of the stunt. If there's a match, we can give the verbal clues and/or assistance for the child to learn the skill correctly and safely.

THE CONTENT OF EDUCATIONAL GYMNASTICS

Educational gymnastics is divided into floor experiences and apparatus experiences. Floor experiences are movements, executed on grass, mats, or carpeting, that don't require equipment to enhance the challenge. Apparatus experiences involve moving in relation to one or several pieces of equipment (tables, benches, beams, bars, vaulting boxes, and playground apparatus). Initially the majority of gymnastics lessons are devoted to floor practice, but once children have become sufficiently skilled on the floor, a larger percentage of the lessons are devoted to apparatus experiences. Many movements performed on the floor are replicated on apparatus, but executing a balance or a roll is more difficult on apparatus.

One of the first objectives is to have children learn to keep their bodies rounded.

Floor Experiences

With children at the precontrol level, the initial focus is on placing body parts close together and maintaining round shapes. Once children have learned to curve their bodies and body parts and keep them rounded, they can focus on rolling in different directions. Children at the precontrol level can also learn to transfer weight to different body parts, to balance on different body parts, and to travel on lines or ropes on the floor.

Control-level experiences include rolling from standing positions and traveling and rolling. Non-

Inverted balances are introduced at the control level.

symmetrical balances and inverted balances are also introduced. The concept of stillness is studied as an interesting contrast to rolling or as a goal for a particular type of balance. Children are challenged to begin simple combinations of two related skills, for example, moving from a two-part balance into a three-part balance without using the body parts from the two-part balance.

More advanced and increasingly complex sequences of movements are enjoyable and challenging to utilization-level children who've developed control over movements executed singly. Transferring weight from feet to hands, exploring "almost off" balance, and taking part or all of a

partner's weight are other tasks appropriate for children at this level.

The concepts of acceleration and deceleration, strong and light, bound and free are stressed with children at the proficiency level. These children have learned to perform some gymnastics movements with relative ease and enjoy the challenge of focusing on the quality of the execution. Matching or mirroring the movements of a partner, repeating sequences of several gymnastics movements, and experiences that involve several children supporting each others' weight are all proficiency-level gymnastics experiences on the floor.

Apparatus Experiences

As children become skillful at floor work, we introduce them to experiences on apparatus. Balance beams, parallel bars, side horses, vaulting boxes, and still rings are Olympic gymnastics equipment. Some elementary schools have this official gymnastics apparatus, but many elementary school programs use benches, tables, chairs, hoops, the edge of a stage, blocks and canes, climbing ropes, and climbing frames to provide gymnastics expe-

Rolling on a bench is a challenge for a utilization-level student.

Children are encouraged to explore apparatus.

Children enjoy creating symmetrical body shapes while in flight.

riences on apparatus. Unofficial equipment is often more compatible with the children's abilities. And children have fewer preconceived notions about what is expected when they work with an unfamiliar piece of equipment.

You can introduce the children to a piece of apparatus by encouraging them to explore the equipment, never forcing a child onto a piece of apparatus. A child at the precontrol level can start by walking along a low beam or bench, jumping from a chair or low table, hanging from a climbing rope, or traveling along a climbing frame. Obstacle courses designed from available equipment—tables, benches, chairs, hoops, ropes, blocks, and canes—are also challenging to children at this level as they learn the concepts of under, over, along, and through.

Children at the control level, while continuing to explore apparatus, can begin to focus on different ways to move in relation to the equipment. They can try different ways of traveling along a beam, hanging from a bar or rope, jumping from a table or chair, or traveling from side to side on a climbing frame. As children develop the ability to function with relative ease and security on apparatus in a variety of ways, you can begin to chal-lenge them to transfer skills that they learned on the floor to the apparatus.

Children at the utilization level can try different ways to get onto equipment, vaulting over equipment, and forming shapes in flight while moving from apparatus to the floor. Experiences that involve supporting weight on different body parts, nonsymmetrical balances, and inverted balances are also appropriate for children at this level.

When children reach the proficiency level, they should continue to focus on increasingly demand-ing balances, shapes, ways of traveling, and ways of supporting body weight. As with gymnastics experiences on the floor, the children should be encouraged to focus on the quality of their move-ments as they practice repeating movements exactly and combining movements into sequences that flow together smoothly and fluently.

OUTDOOR PLAY EQUIPMENT AS GYMNASTICS APPARATUS

Outdoor playground equipment can serve as gym-nastics apparatus in schools that have no indoor

GYMNASTICS NOTATION

Steve Sanders, Director of the Children's Movement Center in Atlanta, Georgia, devised a gymnastics notation system while working with students at the Walker School in Marietta, Georgia. His purpose for developing the system was twofold. First, he viewed such a system as a way of enhancing the children's movement vocabulary so that they'd better understand the meanings of the terms in the movement analysis framework. Second, he wanted to enhance the amount of thought and creativity that went into the student's work in building gymnastics sequences.

The notation system, inspired by Rudolf Laban's notation in dance, uses a symbol for each framework element most frequently used in gymnastics. For example, middle level is represented by ——□——, movement in a backward direction is represented by ◁——▷, a

roll is represented by 〰〰〰 , and a movement performed at a slow speed is represented by • • • • • • • . In a written description of a gymnastics movement, the skill is listed first and the movement concept(s) are written underneath the skill.

Notation of Routine

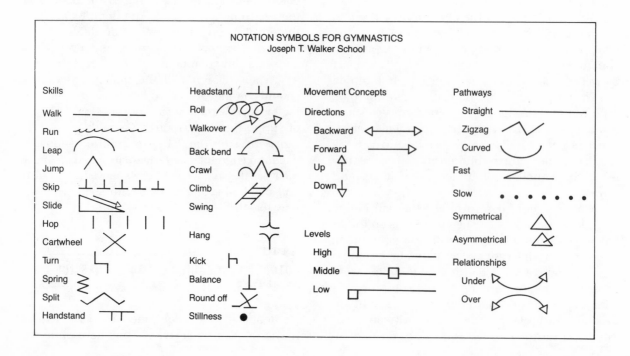

NOTATION SYMBOLS FOR GYMNASTICS
Joseph T. Walker School

Example of Gymnastics Notation and Routine

Student starts routine by running very fast, executing a forward roll, balancing on one foot, and skipping to the balance beam. Routine is continued by student mounting the beam and then performing a forward roll, two jumps, and a cartwheel. Next, the student dismounts from the beam. The student ends the routine by performing a backward roll and balancing on one foot.

equipment and/or indoor physical education facility and as an additional avenue of exploration for children who've experienced indoor gymnastics. Children at the precontrol and control levels can focus on body control on various pieces of equipment. Children at the utilization and proficiency levels will be challenged by the complexity of structure, the number of bars, the distance between bars, and the variety of levels on playground equipment. Horizontal ladders, parallel bars, jungle gyms, monkey bars, and telephone pole balance beams can be used for rolling, balancing, and transferring weight on apparatus. (See Chapters 18 to 20 for these activities.)

Playground equipment can be used effectively to teach different body shapes while balancing.

Very often the key to successfully teaching gymnastics on the playground is the positioning of the playground equipment: grouping versus isolated pieces of equipment. If the playground equipment is grouped, several pieces can easily accommodate a class of twenty-five to thirty children. But if the playground arrangement is such that instruction to the group on various apparatus as well as to individuals isn't possible, cable spools and milk crates can be added to supplement large apparatus.

Children's work on playground apparatus should begin with a study of the proper use of the equipment—the acceptable and unacceptable activities on the apparatus—and correct ways of getting on and off the apparatus. In early fall, let the children explore the various pieces of apparatus; this will lead to questions from the children and class discussions about what is permitted during both physical education class and recess. Any safety rules needed should be developed cooperatively by teacher and students; the rules may vary for younger and older children.

The use of playground equipment in physical education class will lead to increased use of that equipment during recess, which may make classroom teachers uncomfortable with children on the equipment. However, a booklet of the rules established for physical education class and for recess will help the classroom teacher be more at ease. The use of apparatus during physical education can be very different from the use of apparatus during recess; it's our responsibility to be sure children understand the difference.

THE PROCESS OF TEACHING EDUCATIONAL GYMNASTICS

Teaching gymnastics is different from teaching either dance or games since apparatus is used and because of the self-testing nature of gymnastics. Successful educational gymnastics teachers are able to match interesting and challenging tasks to the children's ability levels. This is a teaching skill learned only with time and practice.

Some teachers avoid gymnastics because they're concerned about the safety of the children and are afraid that children might be injured. Remember, though, that injury is always a possibility in physical education classes. When gymnastics experiences are presented sequentially and in an appropriate environment, gymnastics is no more dangerous than any other physical education activity. The following ideas will help create successful and safe gymnastics experiences for children.

Vary the Task

When all the children in a class are expected to perform the same skill the same way, two things are likely to happen. Many of the children in the class will be bored because they can already perform the task successfully. Some of the children will be frightened because the task is too difficult for them and they know it. When you offer children some choices about how they'll perform a task, each child can select an appropriate level of activity. For example, it's unlikely that all the children in a particular class will be able to do a handstand. Some children may not be strong enough to support all their body weight on their hands; some won't be able to land safely if they lose their balance. Instead of telling the entire class to do a handstand, you could tell the children to find a way to place some or all of their weight on their hands. An instruction that allows for individual differences in ability affords all children an opportunity for success.

Gymnastics Environment

An appropriate environment in gymnastics is one in which safety is emphasized. Encourage children to be responsible for their own safety. Explain that you can't be everywhere in the gym or at every station on the playground. Stress that if they don't think they can do something, they shouldn't do it

Children are encouraged to be responsible for themselves.

Hanging inverted balances are more easily accomplished on some playground equipment.

or they should ask you for help. Games of I Dare You and Follow the Leader are inappropriate in gymnastics classes. When you encourage children to be responsible for themselves, you'll find that they rely less on you and more on themselves to determine what is appropriate. The development of self-reliance should be one of the goals in teaching gymnastics.

Spotting

Spotting—the practice of physically assisting children as they perform a movement—isn't com-

monly used in educational gymnastics classes. Children who depend on such help are likely to be unsure and even afraid unless a teacher is nearby. And, conversely, spotting encourages children to attempt movements they may not be ready for. We've observed a number of programs, including our own, in which children have progressed to a relatively high level of skill proficiency without any spotting.

Demonstrating

Some teachers feel that because they aren't skilled gymnasts themselves, they won't be able to teach gymnastics effectively. Certainly a thorough background in a teaching area is an asset in teaching. But even teachers who aren't skilled gymnasts can provide children with appropriate gymnastics experiences. In educational gymnastics, the instructor doesn't need to be able to correctly demonstrate a skill because the children are never expected to perform the same skill the same way. If you want to give children additional ideas or to emphasize a particular movement quality or concept, you can invite some of the more proficient children to demonstrate for the rest of the class. This technique has the added advantage of reinforcing those children who are working especially well.

Moving Equipment

In some situations, if the teacher had to move the gymnastics equipment alone, gymnastics would never be taught. Gymnastics apparatus is heavy, cumbersome, and difficult for one person to move. You can devote some time during each of the first few gymnastics apparatus lessons teaching the children how to move the equipment. Once they learn to maneuver apparatus safely and efficiently, a gymnastics environment can be set up or taken down in a short time. It's wise to have the children follow a few simple rules when they move equipment:

1. An adequate number of children (as determined by the teacher) must be present before equipment can be moved.
2. Children are to lift the equipment together and lower it together, being careful of their toes and fingers.
3. Each piece of apparatus has its own storage space to which it is to be returned after the lesson has been concluded.

Children need several lessons (some classes will need even more) to learn how to handle the apparatus efficiently. Once the children learn to maneuver the equipment, their help saves much time.

One technique to reduce management time is to teach children early to transport apparatus safely and efficiently.

Children skilled on the floor move on to apparatus.

Stations

One of the most effective ways to organize a gymnastics lesson is to divide the children into groups (once they're able to work this way) and set up stations (learning centers) in different parts of the teaching area (Chapter 6). Each group works on a different skill and uses different equipment. Sample tasks could include jumping from a table or chair onto a mat, landing and rolling; traveling different ways along a bench or beam; climbing a rope; practicing putting weight on hands; and vaulting over a table.

This method of organization allows the use of various pieces of equipment and eliminates long lines. When the children have learned to function successfully in this environment, you can write tasks on poster boards and tape them to the wall near each station. Since children usually read far faster than teachers talk, this will increase practice time.

Club Gymnasts

Because of the increased interest in gymnastics, some children in your classes may be studying gymnastics independently, perhaps in a club or recreation program. Most of these club gymnasts are more skilled than the other children—many are at the proficiency level in many skills—and so provide an interesting dimension to gymnastics lessons. The other children will look to the club gymnasts as models and sources for new ideas. Although you won't be teaching Olympic gymnastic skills, you certainly can encourage the club gymnasts to practice the skills they've learned elsewhere. The presence of club gymnasts in a gymnastics class results in an interesting blend of child-created gymnastic skills and Olympic gymnastic skills.

A FINAL THOUGHT

Teaching educational gymnastics is, in some ways, more difficult than teaching Olympic gymnastics. In Olympic gymnastics the desired outcomes are clear—the teacher wants the children to learn to execute predetermined skills in specific ways. The desired outcomes of educational gymnastics are less easily defined. The skills to be learned aren't predetermined, nor are they to be executed in one correct way. Instead, the teacher helps the children to improve their abilities to move in relation to the force of gravity, to learn self-confidence and self-reliance in interpreting tasks and determining the best ways to execute skills. Often it's more difficult for a teacher to share decisions with children than it is for the teacher to make the decisions. You'll find, however, that the process of sharing decisions in educational gymnastics can be exciting for you the teacher and rewarding for the children, regardless of their gymnastics abilities.

Some of the children who are working on gymnastics at an outside club or program may come to class with gymnastics skills that exceed your teaching knowledge and ability. Since you're responsible for the safety of all the children, the activities of these club gymnasts may cause you some uneasiness.

If you explain your concern to these children, you'll find that they appreciate your candidness. Tell these young gymnasts that you're working to learn about the movements they're practicing. Assure them that once you're skilled enough to help them practice appropriately and safely, you'll be delighted to have them resume practice in class.

This approach makes it clear that you aren't criticizing but instead are respecting their proficiency. Students will, in turn, respect you for acknowledging your limitations and seeking their cooperation, and teacher-student rapport will be enhanced.

SUMMARY

Because of the self-testing nature of gymnastics, most children are fascinated by the challenge of attempting to defy the force of gravity. It's important to distinguish between educational gymnastics and Olympic gymnastics. Educational gymnastics focuses on enhancing each child's ability to more effectively maneuver his or her body against the force of gravity. Olympic gymnastics emphasizes the learning of specific gymnastics stunts, usually for the purpose of entering individual or team competition.

Many gymnastics movements are learned on the floor (mats) first and then practiced on apparatus. Gymnastics apparatus can be purchased, or equipment available in schools—such as tables, chairs, and benches—can be adapted to serve the same purposes.

Because of the increased likelihood of injury in gymnastics, it's important to establish an appropriate learning environment so that children avoid games like Follow the Leader or I Dare You. Gymnastics tasks can be presented in ways that allow for individual differences, and this should be done so that children aren't tempted to try movements they aren't ready for.

READING COMPREHENSION QUESTIONS

1. Why do children find balancing, transferring weight, and supporting weight on different body parts fascinating skills?
2. What are the purposes of Olympic gymnastics and educational gymnastics?
3. What are the two types of experiences in educational gymnastics? Describe each type.

4. What activities are taught at the different levels of skill proficiency for both types of educational gymnastics experiences?
5. How are children introduced to equipment?
6. What are the considerations in teaching gymnastics?
7. Why is it important to vary the task in gymnastics?
8. Why is teaching Olympic gymnastics somewhat easier than teaching educational gymnastics?

REFERENCES

Boucher, A. (1978). Educational gymnastics is for everyone. *Journal of Physical Education and Recreation, 49*(7), 48–50.

Cameron, W. McD., & Pleasance, P. (1971). *Education in movement—gymnastics.* Oxford: Blackwell.

Carroll, M. E., & Garner, D. R. (1984). *Gymnastics 7–11: A lesson-by-lesson approach.* London: Falmer Press.

Holbrook, J. (1974). *Movement activity in gymnastics.* Boston: Plays, Inc.

Kirchner, G., Cunningham, J., & Warrell, E. (1970). *Introduction to movement education* (1st ed.). Dubuque, IA: Brown.

Mauldon, E., & Layson, J. (1965). *Teaching gymnastics.* London: MacDonald & Evans.

Morison, R. (1969). *A movement approach to educational gymnastics.* London: Dent.

O'Quinn, G. (1978). *Developmental gymnastics.* Austin: University of Texas Press.

Parent, S. (Ed). (1978, September). Educational gymnastics. *Journal of Physical Education and Recreation,* 31–50.

Williams, J. (1974). *Themes for educational gymnastics.* London: Lepus Books.

Zadra, D. (1976, June). The little gymnast. *Young Athlete Magazine,* 8.

Physical Fitness and Mainstreaming

Chapters 29 and 30 focus on two important aspects of a physical education program for children. Our emphasis in Chapter 29, "Physical Fitness in Children's Physical Education," is on children developing the important cognitive understanding related to the hows and whys of physical fitness. There simply isn't enough time in most regularly scheduled physical education classes to help children improve their physical fitness, so we discuss teaching children how they can improve their fitness on their own at home, before and after school. The fitness concepts are tied in with the AAHPERD Health-Related Fitness Test so that both the children and the teacher have an accepted means for measuring needs and progress in cardiovascular efficiency, muscular strength and endurance, flexibility, and body composition.

Chapter 30, "Mainstreaming Children with Handicapping Conditions in Physical Education," gives the teacher practical information about teaching children who are hearing- or vision-impaired, on crutches, in wheelchairs, or handicapped in other ways. We emphasize effective ways for meeting the needs of these special children in physical education rather than merely describing the causes and characteristics of handicaps.

Physical Fitness in Children's Physical Education

Intelligence and skill can only function at the peak of their
capacity when the body is healthy and strong.

John F. Kennedy

Many people
view fitness as synonymous with physical education, but we believe it's an integral part of physical
education, a product of a quality physical education program. Elementary school children are
usually transported to school in cars or buses. They
go home to electronic games and television. The
advantages of high technology have been accompanied by a decrease in active lifestyles, changes
in families' eating habits, and less physical work
for children and adults. We're seeing a decrease in
physical fitness among elementary age children,
and these same children are showing increases in
conditions associated with heart disease in adults
(Gilliam, 1979). Gilliam's research with children eight
to ten showed that even children in competitive
sports, with the exception of track and swimming,

don't experience the level of physical activity needed
to develop strong, healthy hearts. In addition to
the increased presence of risk factors for heart disease among children, the rate of obesity has
increased; the incidence of childhood obesity is
calculated as between 20 and 30 percent (Humphrey, 1979). An estimated 80 percent of these children will remain obese throughout their lives
(Winick, 1980). Vigorous activities are important
because they can help decrease body fat and the
risk factors associated with cardiorespiratory
disease.

This chapter is an overview of physical fitness
for elementary age children. We discuss the components of physical fitness and principles of training for children, delineate the place of fitness in
the elementary physical education curriculum,

summarize the principal tests used for assessing the fitness levels of children, and cover the use of such tests.

PHYSICAL FITNESS: A DEFINITION

Physical fitness is the capacity of the heart, blood vessels, lungs, and muscles to function at optimum efficiency. In previous years, fitness was defined as the capacity to carry out the day's activities without undue fatigue, but we're now recognizing that this condition may not be sufficient for healthy hearts and lungs. Optimum efficiency is the key.

Physical fitness includes both health-related and skill-related components. Health-related fitness focuses on factors pertaining to a healthy lifestyle and the prevention of health problems. Skill-related physical fitness focuses on specific fitness components associated with games and sports. The health-related components are cardiovascular efficiency, muscular strength and endurance, flexibility, and body composition. The skill-related components include agility, balance, coordination, power, and speed. Although all the fitness components are integral parts of our planned lessons in physical education, the health-related components are the focus of this chapter.

CARDIOVASCULAR EFFICIENCY

Cardiovascular efficiency is the entire body's ability to undergo vigorous exercise for a long time. Children who are physically fit have sufficient endurance to participate in vigorous activities without undue fatigue—they'll show only a slight increase in blood pressure. These children can participate longer and play harder than those less fit. Gilliam's research showed that cardiovascularly fit children are less likely to have cardiorespiratory disease as they grow older. Cardiovascu-

lar efficiency is developed through vigorous physical activities—jumping rope, jogging, swimming—and planned activities that allow maximum participation and that increase heart rate for extended periods of time. Cardiovascular efficiency can be promoted in physical education classes through such activities; see Chapters 15 to 17, 22, 23, and later in this chapter for ideas.

MUSCULAR STRENGTH AND ENDURANCE

Muscular strength is the amount of power a muscle can produce; muscular endurance is the muscle's ability to produce that power for a long duration. Children who are normally active and healthy possess sufficient leg strength for participation in activities. However, today there's growing concern over the upper trunk strength of children and adolescents. Less physical chores and less outdoor work at home coupled with an increase in sedentary activities have produced a generation of youngsters often described as excellent in the fine motor skills of joysticks and keyboards but very weak in arm and shoulder strength. Lack of strength in the back and abdominal muscles is associated with poor posture and with lower back problems in later life. The vigorous physical activities that develop cardiovascular endurance also develop muscular strength and endurance in the legs. Upper arm and shoulder strength and abdominal strength are enhanced through activities that focus on supporting weight on hands, transferring weight involving hands, gymnastics balances requiring muscular tension, stretching actions of the trunk, and challenging activities on gymnastics and playground equipment (see Chapters 19, 20, and later in this discussion).

FLEXIBILITY

Flexibility is the ability to use joints fully; it's the capacity of a joint to move through its potential range of motion. Very young children are extremely flexible, seemingly capable of moving their bodies in innumerable positions, literally tying themselves in knots. With few exceptions, children remain flexible throughout their elementary school years. Lack of flexibility in adults is a contributing factor to chronic low back problems, a leading cause of absenteeism among the work force.

Flexibility can be increased through stretching the muscles, tendons, and ligaments. Activities that emphasize extending the range of motion, such as dance and gymnastics, help children attain and maintain flexibility. Activities that promote stretching actions and extending the range of motion are incorporated into the skill themes of transferring weight, rolling, and balancing within stretching, curling, and twisting actions. See Chapters 18 to 20 for appropriate tasks.

Flexibility is specific to each joint; therefore, we try to carefully select activities that will increase flexibility in various muscle groups, that is, the legs, lower and upper back, and shoulders. Children benefit from being taught the concept of specificity and exercises to enhance each muscle group, so they develop a cognitive understanding of the relationship between individual exercises and the specific muscle group they enhance.

Children involved in competitive athletics may experience a lack of flexibility in certain muscles as other muscles are emphasized for the particular sport. All stretching actions should emphasize a static stretch, in which the joint or muscle is slowly moved to its stretching point and the position held, rather than bouncing to force the body into position. As mentioned in Chapter 13, slowness of movement is a difficult concept for children to grasp yet a most important one.

BODY COMPOSITION

Body composition is the amount of fat cells compared to lean cells in the body mass. Lean body mass is the nonfat tissue of muscles, bones, ligaments, and tendons. Body composition is measured by skinfold thickness. Skinfold thickness remains relatively constant until age seven, after which it gradually increases until puberty. For girls, the gradual increase continues throughout adolescence; for boys, the percentage of body fat levels off or decreases.

A certain amount of body fat is essential for good health, but an extremely high or low amount of body fat is unhealthy. With the nation's emphasis on leanness, children often have misconceptions about fatness versus leanness in body composition. Children also confuse body weight and body composition. Lean muscle mass actually weighs more than the same amount of fat tissue; therefore, body weight can't be used to determine body composition.

A person's percentage of body fat is determined by heredity, nutrition, and level of activity. Increased activity can decrease body fat; however, best results are obtained through a combination of activity and diet. Body composition is a fitness component that can't be changed in a short period of time; adjustments in nutritional habits and lifestyle must be carefully planned and continued for a long time. These changes require the involvement of not just the child but the child's family. It isn't enough to guide the child into healthy nutritional habits for school lunch and active participation during physical education and recess. To be successful, the nutrition/lifestyle package must be carried out at home as well as at school. We try to be extremely sensitive of parents' perceptions, emphasizing nutrition and activity for healthy living and trying to avoid the negative assessment of the family's lifestyle and eating habits.

PRINCIPLES OF FITNESS TRAINING

The components of fitness, both the health- and the skill-related ones, are developed through the principle of overload—exercising more today than yesterday and more tomorrow than today. Levels

Children enjoy learning how to take their pulse to determine how fast their hearts are beating during different activities and during periods of nonactivity. Young children won't be concerned with target heart rate but will be very inquisitive about the difference between rest-ing and active heart rates. We've found it best to count the pulse for six seconds, multiply by ten, and then add a zero to determine heart rate per minute. Children will need guided practice locating their pulse in their neck or wrist and counting during the timed period.

of fitness are increased by changes in the intensity, duration, and frequency of exercise. Running faster, farther, longer, and more often subjects the cardiovascular system, for example, more often to an increasing "load" and enables that system to adapt to higher performance levels.

Intensity is how hard you have to work (exercise) to improve fitness. To produce gains, exercise must be strenuous enough to require more exertion than normal. Increasing the heart rate, stretching muscles beyond their normal length, and contracting muscles against resistance (isometric exercise) increase intensity.

Duration is how long you must exercise to improve your fitness. Fifteen minutes is considered the minimum time for exercise to be effective. Duration is enhanced by maintaining your target heart rate for fifteen minutes, holding the static stretch for at least fifteen seconds, and increasing the number of repetitions in muscular endurance exercise (isotonic exercise).

Frequency is how often you must exercise to produce gains in your physical fitness. Frequency overload is attained by performing cardiovascular and flexibility activities and exercises at least three times per week. Muscular strength exercises should be performed every other day to permit muscular growth.

Resting heart rate is the number of times your heart beats per minute when you're still, lying down, or resting comfortably. Target heart rate is the heart rate you must attain (and maintain for fifteen minutes) to produce gains in cardiovascular efficiency.

Corbin (1983) developed ranges of target zones for beginners in aerobic activities. If the resting heart rate is below 50 per minute, the target heart rate (target zone) to aim for is 135 to 140. For a heart rate of 51 to 70, the zone is 140 to 145. And for a resting heart rate of 71 and over, the zone is 145 to 150 beats per minute.

FITNESS IN THE CURRICULUM

Research has shown that children can be trained in the components of fitness if (1) exercises are maintained at a rate of intensity high enough to produce desired results, that is, Olympic-style training schedule, and (2) diversified programs of physical education are replaced with programs of just physical fitness a minimum of three times per week. Both these concepts, however, are in direct opposition to our beliefs about activity programs for children.

Caution must be used in involving children in intensive training programs or distance running because short-term gains may be outweighed by long-term detriments, for example, bone growth damage and lack of interest and motivation in later years.

Programs of strenuous calisthenics for children can result in "winning the battle but losing the war." We may develop fitness in children for the period of time they're under our control, but the negative feelings associated with the forced activity often lead to negative feelings toward activity and exercise that continue into adulthood.

We try to present vigorous activity as an enjoyable experience so that children develop a positive attitude toward an active lifestyle. We also try to provide children and their parents with a sufficient knowledge of fitness and training concepts to be wise consumers of commercial fitness items, package programs, and health spas. As teachers, we can help children and their parents choose sports and activities to attain and maintain fitness and have fun doing so. We can also help students set realistic physical fitness goals for themselves. Fitness is a personal matter; its goal is self-improvement toward healthy living. Within our elementary physical education curriculum we can teach basic concepts of fitness, design our lessons to promote the fitness components, and help children build a repertoire of exercises for their personal use.

THE AAHPERD HEALTH-RELATED FITNESS TEST

The two most commonly accepted tests used to measure physical fitness are the AAHPERD Health-Related Physical Fitness Test and the skill-related AAHPERD Youth Fitness Test. The Health-Related Fitness Test measures four components: abdominal muscular strength and endurance, lower back flexibility, cardiovascular efficiency, and body composition. Here we discuss how the Health-Related Fitness Test measures each component, the concepts behind each component and how they relate to elementary school children, and some exercises and activities for each component.

Measurement of Abdominal Muscular Strength and Endurance

Abdominal muscular strength and endurance are measured by a student's performance of modified sit-ups. The student lies on a mat on her or his back with knees flexed, feet on the floor, heels approximately twelve to eighteen inches from buttocks. The arms are crossed on the chest, and fingers are extended over the collarbone. A partner holds the student's feet (Figure 29-1). The student curls to a sitting position, touching arms to thighs (Figure 29-2). The student's hips shouldn't lift off the mat when the curling action begins; the arms and hands must remain in contact with the chest throughout the sit-ups.

Figure 29-1 Starting position for sit-ups.

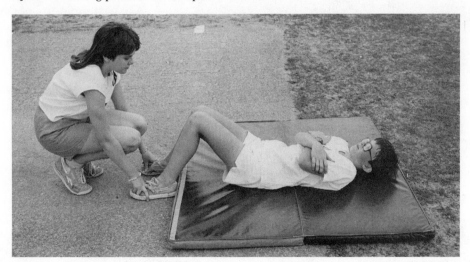

Figure 29-2 Curl position for sit-ups.

The student returns to the mat; the return is complete when the midback contacts the mat. The student's score is the number of sit-ups completed in sixty seconds.

Concepts. The following muscular strength and endurance concepts are important for elementary age children:

- Muscular strength is specific: Different muscles require different exercises.
- Abdominal strength can be improved through sit-ups and other exercises that develop the abdominal muscles.
- Abdominal strength exercises should be performed carefully so that the student can concentrate on the abdominal muscles.
- Good abdominal strength helps prevent lower back disorders in adulthood.
- Poor posture is often the result of poor muscle tone.

Exercises and Activities. Muscular strength and endurance can be increased through exercises that emphasize specific muscles. The following exer-

cises are designed specifically to strengthen abdominal muscles:

- Wall push (see Figure 29-3): Stand with your back against a wall, your feet only a few inches from the wall. Your knees should be slightly bent, with your arms at the sides of your body. Pull in your abdomen and press your shoulders, small of back, and buttocks against the wall. Hold the position for five seconds.
- Untimed sit-ups (see Figure 29-4): Lie flat on your back, with your knees bent and your arms crossed on your chest. Gradually perform sit-ups; aim for twenty-five.
- Sit-up variations
  - □ Extend your arms forward. Shake your hands and arms as you curl up.
  - □ Extend your arms forward. Clap your hands on the floor as you curl back to the mat.
- Thigh curl (see Figure 29-5): Lie flat on your back, with your legs and arms extended. Place your hands on top of your legs. Raise your trunk and slide your hands on your legs until your hands reach the top of your knees. Return to the beginning level; perform the thigh curl a total of ten times.

Figure 29-4 Unassisted version of an untimed sit-up.

Figure 29-3 Correct position for a wall push.

Figure 29-5 Performance of a thigh curl.

Many exercises can be done at home, as the child awakens; as the student is getting ready for the school day; while the youngster goes to school; while the child studies; or during the time the child watches television. The following exercises are designed to improve muscular strength in the arms, legs, and back as well as in the abdominal areas:

- Wake-up time
  - □ Before getting out of bed, tighten all the muscles in your body, rest your muscles, then tighten them again—hard! Can you tighten one part of your body at a time?
- Getting ready
  - □ While you're wringing out the washcloth, squeeze and twist it as hard as you can. What does this movement strengthen?
  - □ After putting on your shoes, lift both your feet and legs up and down from a sitting position. How many times can you do this

without stopping? Can you hold both legs in the air for thirty seconds?
- Going to school
  - □ Hold a heavy book in one hand and see how many times you can lift it up and down by bending your elbow. Try lifting the book while keeping your arm straight.
  - □ On the bus, put your feet underneath the seat in front of you and tighten your leg muscles to make them straight and stiff.
- Studying
  - □ Hold the sides of your chair and pull as hard as you can, but don't bend your back.
  - □ How hard can you push down on the desk with your hand and arm? Push and hold for thirty seconds.
- Television time
  - □ Lie on your side and lift one leg up and down in the air. Can you do each leg for a whole commercial?
  - □ On your back, try to raise your legs, arms,

Figure 29-6 Student performing the sit and reach test.

and back off the floor at the same time. Hold that position. Can you raise your legs, arms, and chest while on your stomach?

☐ Lie on your back. Place a pillow between your knees, and try to curl up in a ball so that your nose touches the knees. How many times can you do this during one commercial?

Measurement of Lower Back Flexibility

Lower back and hamstring flexibility is measured by the student's performance of a sit and reach exercise (see Figure 29-6). The student should remove his or her shoes and sit with feet shoulder width apart and flat against the testing box (see Figure 29-7), with knees fully extended. Arms are extended forward, with hands on top of each other, palms down. The student reaches forward four times and holds the maximum reach on the fourth trial. This stretch is held for one second while the reach is recorded.

Place your hand on the student's knees to pre-vent flexing of the knees. Students will have difficulty reaching evenly with both hands; place a rubber band around their hands to heighten their awareness. Let students warm up by stretching before they take the test. The score is the number

Figure 29-7 Sit and reach measurement apparatus. *Source: Health-Related Physical Fitness Test Manual,* Reston, VA: AAHPERD.

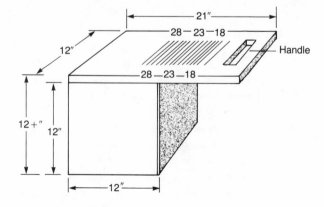

of centimeters the student reaches without flexing the knees or reaching unevenly with fingers.

Place the testing box against the wall to prevent it from sliding. We've found it helps to place one hand on the box, approximately the distance you think the student can reach; ask the student to touch your hand with their fingers. This fosters a gentle stretching action as opposed to a harsh bounce.

Concepts. Improved flexibility allows more efficient movement and prevents muscle injury. The following flexibility concepts are important for elementary school children to know and understand:

- Flexibility is very joint specific; you may have excellent flexibility in your upper trunk but very poor flexibility in your lower back.
- You must continue exercise to maintain flexibility; a large percentage of flexibility is lost in a relatively short amount of nonexercise time.
- Stretching exercises increase flexibility.
- Perform stretching slowly, *without* bouncing.

- Good hamstring flexibility helps reduce chances of developing lower back problems in adulthood.
- Doing stretching exercises reduces the chance of injury in sports, such as pulled muscles.

Exercises and activities. The following exercises are designed to increase flexibility:

- Trunk and shoulder extensions: Slowly extend both your arms overhead as high as possible and hold them for ten seconds.
- Trunk and shoulder rotation (see Figure 29-8): With your right arm at shoulder level, look and slowly turn to your left; hold ten seconds. Repeat the movement in the opposite direction.
- Inner thigh stretch (see Figure 29-9): Sit on the floor with your legs spread apart and extended. Slowly lean forward with one arm on each side of one leg and hold the position. Repeat the exercise on the other leg.
- Lying knee pull (see Figure 29-10): Lie flat on your back with your legs extended and arms straight at your side. Bring your left knee to

Figure 29-9 Student performing the inner thigh stretch on the right leg.

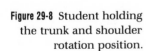

Figure 29-8 Student holding the trunk and shoulder rotation position.

Figure 29-10 The lying knee pull exercise.

your chest, grabbing under the knee with both your hands. Pull and hold your knee for five seconds. Repeat the exercise with your right leg. Remember to keep your extended leg straight and on the floor.

- Wake-up time
  □ Stretch all your body in all different directions; then wiggle like Jello on a plate.
  □ Lie on your stomach and then reach back and grab your feet with your hands. Try to make a bowl shape with your body by raising up your chest and legs and rocking on your stomach.
- Going to school
  □ Keep one arm straight and swing it in a big circle from the front of your body to the back. Hold on tight to your books.
  □ Shake your leg each time you take a step. If you're wearing long socks, try to shake them down to your ankles. The vibration of the skin and muscles will help loosen you up.
- Studying
  □ Hold your hands together behind your chair, keeping your arms straight. Can you feel which muscles are being stretched?
  □ Let your head fall to one shoulder, and then roll it around to the other shoulder. Be limp, but don't fall asleep.
- In the kitchen or den
  □ Stand about three feet from the kitchen counter or a table. Lean over and hold onto the edge of the counter or table. Can you keep your legs straight and your feet flat on the floor?
- Television time
  □ Lie on your back with your legs together. Lift your legs up and over your head so that your feet touch the floor above your head. Try to keep your legs straight.
  □ Sit on the floor and pull your feet up to your body with the bottom of your feet together. Hold on to your feet; then use your elbows to push your knees to the floor. Next, try to touch your chest to your feet. What do you feel stretching this time?

- Family time
  □ Sit facing a partner with your legs spread apart and your feet touching your partner's feet. (If you're doing this exercise with your father or mother, your feet may only touch their ankles because their legs are much longer.) Hold hands; one partner leans back and slowly pulls the other partner so that he or she is stretching. Take turns stretching your partner.

Measurement of Cardiovascular Efficiency

Cardiovascular efficiency is measured by either the one-mile run for time or the nine-minute run for distance. The nine-minute run is easier to administer and minimizes class time spent on testing.

The nine-minute run may be on paved surface, jogging track, or playground. The running path should be clearly indicated and distance zones marked. On the signal, students begin the nine-minute run on the designated course (see Figure 29-11). Instruct students to run as far as possible before they hear the signal to stop. Students may walk, but the objective is to cover as much distance as possible.

An important key to successfully administering the nine-minute run is scoring. Three methods have proven successful:

1. One half the class begins the run together; the remaining half serves as partners and counts laps.
2. Code the number of laps by marking a student's hand with washable marker as the student completes each lap. Younger children enjoy the marks becoming a smile-face as they complete each lap; for example, mark a circle for one lap, one eye for a second lap, the second eye for a third lap, etc.
3. Give each child a Popsicle stick each time one lap is completed.

Since students will be at different distances when the signal to stop is given, the zones within

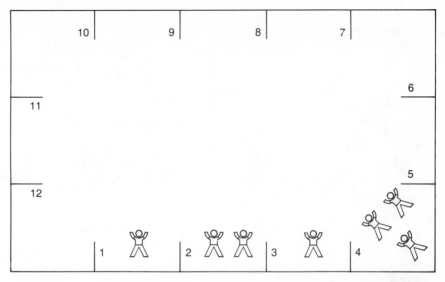

Figure 29-11 Top: Distance zones for the nine-minute run. Bottom: Students lined up, ready to run.

the laps must be marked. Students must be given directions concerning what to do when the stop signal is given to ensure they receive credit for the number of zones completed.

Concepts. Children need an understanding of the following cardiovascular concepts:

- The heart is a muscle that benefits from **exercise**, as do other muscles.
- Vigorous physical activity increases **cardiovascular efficiency**.
- Being on an athletic team doesn't **automatically** increase cardiovascular efficiency; **active**

Jumping rope is fun for beginners and for students with advanced skills.

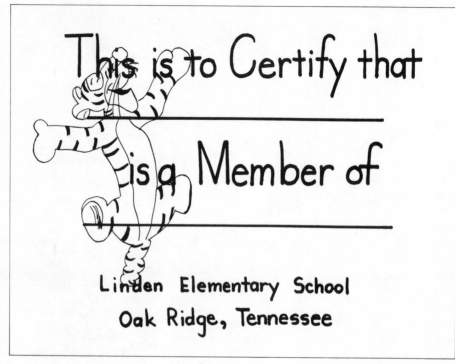

Jump rope certificate.

participation for an extended period is necessary.

- Cardiovascular efficiency contributes to feeling good and being healthy.
- Cardiovascular efficiency helps prevent cardiorespiratory diseases in adults.
- You can calculate your heart rate by counting your pulse.
- The heart rate increases during exercise.

Exercises and Activities. In-school activities such as jumping rope and jogging can provide daily and enjoyable vigorous exercises for children. Jump rope clubs can be organized at different skill and interest levels. Clubs may include Tigger the Tiger—basic jumps forward and backward, Dolphin Club—jumping for speed, Jimmie Cricket—tricks, Kanga and Roo—group jumping, and the E.T. Club—Jump Rope for Heart. Jump Rope for Heart, sponsored by the American Heart Association and AAHPERD, has contributed significantly to improved cardiovascular efficiency for children. Instructional booklets and information on organizing jump rope teams are available from local chapters of the American Heart Association. Jump rope clubs can be organized to meet before school, after school, or during recess. Many schools award certificates for participation in the activity.

Jogging clubs can also meet before school, after school, or during recess, depending on the teachers' and students' schedules. The following guidelines are helpful for organizing a jogging club:

- Obtain written parental permission for each child's participation.

- Teach children the correct foot placement for jogging: feet pointing straight ahead; landing flat-footed or on the heel first.
- Remind children in the beginning that jogging is *not* running at top speed or racing with others. Hands should be held loosely, not clenched in fists.
- Distance should be built up gradually; the teacher will have to set the upper limits.

Children may enjoy names for their jogging clubs, such as Red Roadrunners and Jogging Jaguars. Wall displays can depict the number of miles each child has completed, such as the Snoopy/Woodstock Club pictured here. The main wall display shows Snoopy in sweatpants for his morning jog. Each child in the club has a Woodstock with her or his name on it. Stick-on numbers on the cafeteria or hallway wall indicate the number of miles completed; the child posts her or his Woodstock near the number that corresponds to the amount of miles completed. Classroom teachers, parent volunteers, the physical education teacher, or the child can do the record keeping. Each child's monthly chart (see Figure 29-12) shows the number of laps completed per day; cumulative laps/miles are recorded across the chart.

Family jogging or vigorous walking can contribute to both the child's cardiovascular efficiency and the fitness of the entire family. Thirty minutes of walking daily is an excellent beginning activity for the family. Family jogging can begin with a two-minute jog away from home and walking back, with a gradual increase in time and distance. The goal is cardiovascular efficiency, not Olympic training.

Additional cardiovascular activities include:

- Wake-up time
  □ Before getting out of bed, lie on your back and kick your legs up in the air. Keep kicking them as fast and as long as possible, or move them in a circular motion, as if you were riding a bicycle.
- Getting ready
  □ Stand in front of the mirror and pretend

The jogging club provides opportunities to improve cardiovascular fitness.

you're boxing with yourself. How quickly can you swing and punch? How long?
- Going to school
  □ Walk, skip, ride a bicycle, or even jog to school or the bus stop.
  □ If you ride in a carpool, run to the car before mom or dad get there, and then count the number of times you can jump up and down before they arrive.
- Family time
  □ Put on some upbeat music and dance. See who can move around the most, longest, and best.

Month _November_

Previous total _____ laps _____ miles __5__

Name _____ Homeroom _____

Number	Date																														
of Laps	1	2	3	4	⑤	6	7	⑧	9	10	11	⑫	13	14	⑮	16	17	18	⑲	20	21	㉒	23	24	25	㉖	27	28	29	30	31
30				＼			＼													＼					＼						
29																															
28																															
27																															
26																															
25																															
24																															
23																															
22																															
21																															
20												＼			＼				＼												
19																															
18																															
17																															
16																															
15																						＼				＼					
14																															
13																															
12																															
11																															
10																															
9																															
8																															
7																															
6																															
5																															
4																															
3																															
2																															
1																															

Figure 29-12 Daily jogging chart.

Measurement of Body Composition

The skinfold measure indicates the amount of body fat. Two skinfold sites, the triceps and the subscapular, are used for the test because they're easy to measure and highly correlated with total body fat.

The triceps measure is taken on the right arm halfway between the elbow and the shoulder, with the skinfold parallel to the longitudinal axis of the upper arm (see illustration). The subscapular measure is taken one-half inch below the inferior angle of the

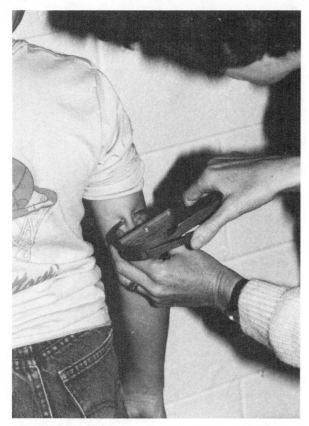

Skinfold measure taken on the site of the triceps of the right arm.

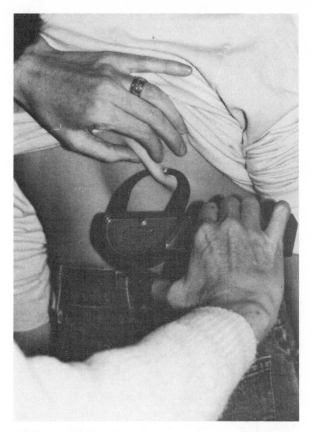

Skinfold measure taken on the site of the subscapular.

scapula in line with the natural cleavage of the skin (see illustration).

Following is the proper procedure for administering the skinfold test:

1. Grasp the skinfold between your thumb and forefinger, being careful to grasp the "fat" layer, not muscle or skin only (see Figure 29-13).
2. Grasp the skinfold with the caliper one-half inch above or below your finger/thumb hold.
3. Release the tension of your finger/thumb grasp while releasing the grip of the caliper, enabling the caliper to exert tension on the skinfold.
4. Record the measure to the nearest 0.5 millimeter.

It's often difficult to obtain an accurate tricep reading for obese children and children with highly muscular arms, such as competitive swimmers. In these cases, take three readings for each student to ensure accuracy.

The skinfold measures are very personal; the results should be confidential. Record the measures without verbal comment or display. Conduct the subscapular measure in private because the student's shirt or blouse has to be lifted. We've found it best not to tell students their scores for the skinfold. The measure is difficult for young children to interpret, and individual differences among students can lead to misconceptions, negative self-feelings, and in some instances extreme dieting among children. The best interpretation of

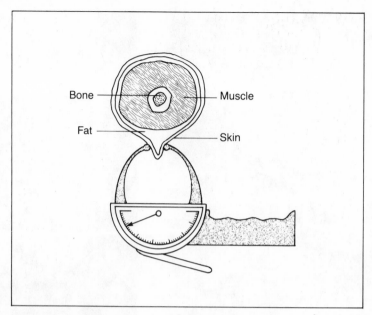

Figure 29-13 Skinfold caliper pinch of skin and underlying subcutaneous fat. *Source: Health-Related Physical Fitness Test Manual*, Reston, VA: AAHPERD.

the skinfold measure can be obtained after a three-year testing period. Results may then be communicated to parents regarding increases or decreases in body fat, natural growth patterns, and comparison to norms. (The national norms as well as further details and testing manuals for both the Health-Related and Youth Fitness tests are available from AAHPERD, 1900 Association Dr., Reston, VA 22091. The health-related norms are calculated for ages five to seventeen; the skill-related norms begin at age nine.)

Development of a fitness profile reflecting testing results over time is the recommended method of communicating all fitness results to parents and counseling students for improvements in needed areas.

Concepts. It's difficult for children to understand the

When first learning to use calipers, it helps to practice with coworkers before measuring the children. Two persons can measure the skinfold of a third person and record the results on paper. Compare readings; if there are differences of more than three millimeters, review procedures and continue practicing until

comparisons are within one millimeter. Caliper prices range from $9.95 for a Fat-O-Meter or Fat Control Caliper to approximately $150 for the Lange or Harpenden calipers. Calipers should give reliable measurements and be sturdy enough to test hundreds of elementary students.

concept of body composition. Emphasis should be on the following concepts:

- Body composition is affected by heredity, nutrition, and lifestyle.
- A certain amount of body fat is essential for protecting bones and organs and for proper functioning of the body.
- Body fat (fatty tissue) is *not* the same as body weight.
- Good nutrition is essential for good health and total fitness.
- Vigorous physical activity can help decrease the percentage of body fat.

Exercises and Activities. The activities that contribute to a decrease in body fat are the same as those that promote cardiovascular efficiency. At home, family activities are very important for improving this component of fitness.

THE SKILL-RELATED AAHPERD YOUTH FITNESS TEST

The skill-related Youth Fitness Test includes modified sit-ups and the following exercises:

- Pull-ups or flexed-arm hang for upper arm and shoulder strength
- Thirty-foot shuttle run to measure agility
- Standing long jump to measure muscular strength in the legs
- Fifty-yard dash as an indicator of speed and power
- Six-hundred-yard walk/run to measure endurance

USE OF FITNESS TESTS

Physical fitness tests can be used to culminate a unit and to motivate students and as diagnostic screening instruments. We strongly advocate using the physical fitness test for screening purposes. If the physical fitness test is to be used as a diagnostic tool, administer the test in early fall; test results can then be used to help plan the yearly curriculum and to establish remedial programs for individual students. We recommend that students who score below the twenty-fifth percentile be given remedial fitness programs, an individualized educational plan (IEP) for their area(s) of weakness. The physical education teacher can counsel the student individually on ways to improve fitness. Students can report to the gymnasium or physical education teaching area during recess or before or after school to work on specific areas of weakness. Exercise programs can be developed for use at home, and parents can become active participants with the child. The child can monitor personal progress. When the IEP is developed, it's important that the exercises be carefully taught to the student and that only the recommended exercises be used.

Whether the physical fitness test is used as a screening tool in the fall or as a culminating experience for children, it should be an educational endeavor. Each test item is carefully explained, with emphasis on the particular component being tested. All too often, children do poorly on a test item because they haven't understood the directions. Allow sufficient time for practice, so children will understand the proper techniques and stretch their muscles. The purpose of the test is for the children to do their personal best, not to trick students. We recommend not recording test scores below grade two. Younger children can take the test as an educational experience, but their characteristics don't lend themselves to maximum output and extended concentration on a subject that is of more interest to the teacher than to the children.

A key to successful testing is management of the time involved. Physical fitness testing can take an exorbitant amount of time. Carefully planning the testing and class organization can reduce the time to the necessary minimum. We've found it best to structure the study of the theme in games,

Recording fitness scores and percentiles can be time-consuming. The Campbell Soup Company, in cooperation with the President's Council on Physical Fitness and Sports, developed a computer program to convert raw scores to percentiles and print a Fitnessgram for each student. The Fitnessgram can save teachers time in scoring test results and communicating results to parents. Write to Fitnessgram, Institute for Aerobics Research, 12200 Preston Rd., Dallas, TX 75320, for information.

gymnastics, or dance so that children can independently work while the teacher is involved in the scheduled fitness testing. Thus children can continue their study of the theme, their completion of the project, or their refinement of skills.

The focus of elementary physical education is the child; the focus of physical fitness should also be the child. No child should be asked to give more than his or her personal best. Therefore, do *not* compare scores. And fitness scores should not be used for grading. The goal of physical fitness in the elementary school should be, in the words of Chuck Corbin, "feeling good, looking good, being healthy, enjoying life."

INCORPORATING PHYSICAL FITNESS

Teaching the important physical fitness concepts is an important part of the physical education curriculum, but it doesn't happen by chance; it must be carefully planned. During the process of planning the daily lesson, keep in mind the components of fitness and the muscle groups involved in the activities outlined for the children. Not all lessons will lend themselves to incorporating fitness into the theme of study. Other types of activities that can be used to teach physical fitness concepts are dance aerobics, fitness circuits (Chapter 6), and activities to enhance the specific fitness components.

Dance aerobics is similar to continuous cal-

isthenics, except that various dance steps are added. A typical routine combines exercises for flexibility, muscular strength, and endurance with dance steps, jogging, or other locomotor movements. The aerobic routine needs to be sufficiently long and intense to attain the target heart rate. A number of videotapes that lead the children in the routines are now for sale. You may want to suggest that your school librarian obtain several of these tapes for use throughout the school.

A fitness circuit can be set up around the perimeter of the gymnasium or playing field. Exercises and activities at each station focus on different muscle groups and fitness components; cardiovascular activities may be incorporated into the stations or performed as a total group. You need a sufficient number of stations to permit all students to be actively involved (Figure 29-14). There can be rotation between stations after a given number of repetitions or on signal from the teacher after a predetermined amount of time. Children enjoy doing the exercises to recorded music, rotating each time the music stops.

Fitness parcourses are permanent outdoor fitness circuits. There are commercial parcourses, or parents and teachers can build them as a PTA project. A typical parcourse includes stations for exercising various muscle groups. At each station is a large sign or laminated poster with a graphic representation of the exercise and the number of suggested repetitions for both a beginner and an experienced participant. Parcourse stations are often set up around a jogging track to suggest car-

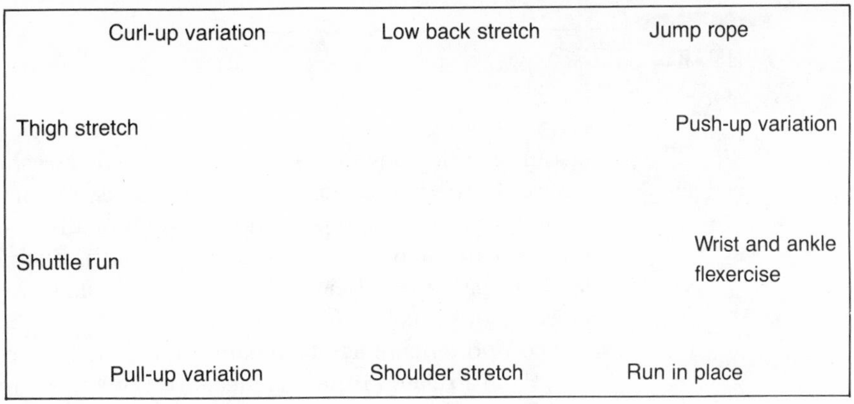

Curl-up variation	Low back stretch	Jump rope
Thigh stretch		Push-up variation
Shuttle run		Wrist and ankle flexercise
Pull-up variation	Shoulder stretch	Run in place

Figure 29-14 Fitness circuit.

diovascular activity, such as walking and jogging, as well as muscular strength and endurance and flexibility workouts. Parcourses are excellent opportunities for community and family involvement in physical fitness at the school environment after the normal school day ends as well as fitness for students during recess on non–physical education days.

Many traditional games and activities can be adapted for large group fitness. Examine the game carefully to be sure all students can participate. Teacher-designed activities may also be used to focus on specific fitness components. Following are examples of teacher-designed or -adapted large group fitness activities.

- *Here, There, Everywhere (cardiovascular efficiency):* When the teacher calls, "Here," students run toward the teacher. When the teacher calls "There," students run where the teacher is pointing. When the teacher calls, "Everywhere," students run freely in general space.
- *I See (cardiovascular efficiency, flexibility, muscular strength):* Children are in scattered formation facing the teacher. The teacher speaks in loud voice, "I see." The children answer in chorus, "What do you see?" The teacher responds, "I see all students moving in any direction without touching anyone." Children respond to this signal until the teacher says, "I see. . . ." Children stop and answer, "What do you see?" Teacher responds with a new challenge: locomotor skills, push-ups, bend and stretch, and twisting actions. Make each challenge focus on a different muscle group and fitness component.
- *Heart Hustle (cardiovascular efficiency):* Construct a series of color-coded exercise/activity cards. Place them blank side up on a table. Students select a card and perform the activity pictured on the card. At the end of the timed interval, the students return the cards to the table and select a different color. Possible activities include rope jumping, stationary running, speed walking, free-form dancing.
- *Magic Cars (cardiovascular efficiency, leg strength):* Scatter carpet squares around the room. Students place their hands on the carpet square that is to be their magic car. On the signal, they begin traveling around the room by pushing the carpet square. When the teacher calls, "Red light" or stops the music, all cars must stop and the children sit down. Children rest for a few seconds and begin travel again. This is an excellent cardiovascular activity.

SUMMARY

Physical fitness is the capacity of the heart, lungs, and muscles to function at optimum efficiency. Research in recent years has shown a relationship between a lack of fitness and adult health problems, including degenerative cardiorespiratory diseases. The potential for such health problems can be seen in even children of elementary school age. Health-related fitness focuses on those factors related to a healthy lifestyle: muscular strength and endurance, flexibility, cardiovascular efficiency, and body composition. Skill-related fitness adds the components of agility, balance, coordination, power, and speed.

Health-related fitness is measured by the sit and reach test for lower back and hamstring flexibility, timed sit-ups for abdominal strength, a nine-minute run for cardiovascular endurance, and the skinfold measure for body composition. Physical fitness tests given annually to children can, over a number of years, provide a profile of the child's fitness. Test results can then be used to plan a program of remedial exercises and suggested activities to improve areas of weakness. Physical fitness is developed through the principle of overload. Exercises must be of sufficient intensity, duration, and frequency to produce increases in fitness. Target heart rate must be maintained for fifteen minutes for an increase in cardiovascular efficiency to be produced.

Physical fitness can be incorporated into the theme of study, added to the lesson as a group activity, and increased through afterschool jogging/jump rope clubs and fitness trails/parcourses. The focus of physical fitness for the elementary school child is the development of a positive attitude toward an active lifestyle, a knowledge of the concepts of fitness, and an understanding of how to attain and maintain personal fitness.

READING COMPREHENSION QUESTIONS

1. Define physical fitness. Why can we no longer define the level of fitness as the capacity to carry out the day's activities without undue fatigue?
2. What is the difference between health-related and skill-related fitness?
3. Define cardiovascular efficiency. How is it developed? Name several activities that contribute to cardiovascular efficiency.
4. Within our physical education curriculum, what activities contribute to the development of muscular strength?
5. What does the phrase "specificity of flexibility" mean? What are the implications for physical education?
6. Explain the fitness component of body composition. What factors determine an individual's body fat?

7. Name the three principles of training. Give an example of each relative to cardio-vascular efficiency. (You can give your examples for muscular strength or for flexibility instead, but all three examples must be for the same component.)
8. Name two fitness concepts relating to each of the health-related components and tell why they're important for teachers of elementary physical education.

REFERENCES

Corbin, C. B., & Lindsey, R. (1983). *Fitness for life.* Glenview, IL: Scott, Foresman.

Gilliam, T. (1979). Coronary heart disease prevention begins with children. Research Report. Ann Arbor: University of Michigan.

Humphrey, P. (1979). Height/weight disproportions in elementary school children. *The Journal of School Health, 49,* 25–29.

Kennedy, J. F. (1960). The soft American. *Sports Illustrated, 13,* 15.

Personal fitness. (1984, June). Department of Education, State of Florida.

Weathers, W. (1983). *Physical fitness activity program for the health-related physical fitness test.* Special Projects Report. Middle Tennessee State University.

Winick, M. (1981). Which diet would work best for you? *U.S. News and World Report, 91,* 47–49.

C H A P T E R **30**

Mainstreaming Children with Handicapping Conditions in Physical Education

Movement is learning; movement is life. No matter how disabled a child, movement can make a difference in his/her life. Movement can help a child become oneself. If a child can move, he/she can become more a master of the environment rather than being controlled by it.

Jane R. Evans

Public Law 94-142 guarantees all handicapped children from four to twenty-one an education in the least restrictive environment. That education includes physical education. Thus the inclusion of children with special needs into regular physical education class populations is no longer by choice; it's mandatory. With an understanding of basic concepts, an awareness of the handicapped children's needs, and knowing how to adapt the environment and/or the curriculum, the teacher can create the enabling environment for these children with special needs. Children with handicapping conditions can function in an elementary physical education environment that allows individual response, fosters performance at the individual's skill level, and is taught by teachers who observe, reflect, and make changes in light of children's needs. This chapter addresses the concepts of special education, the major handicapping conditions that may require adaptations in physical education, special needs in physical education relative to the conditions, and ways to facilitate the integration of children with handicapping conditions.

MAINSTREAMING

Mainstreaming is the integration of exceptional children into the regular curriculum, as well as into art, music, and physical education classes. Public Law 94-142 itself doesn't include the word "mainstreaming," but it does mandate an educational program appropriate to the needs of each child. This program, to the extent appropriate, is to be provided in a learning environment that includes nonhandicapped students.

The appropriate education—both placement and curriculum—for each handicapped student is determined by a multidisciplinary team called the M-Team, composed of all persons involved in providing an appropriate education for the child: classroom teacher, special education teacher, child's parents, and professionals from related services. Following the educational assessment by the school psychologist and other professionals as needed, the M-Team designs the educational program for the child, including best placement, amount of time the child is to be mainstreamed, services of outside agencies to be secured, and the educational goals to be attained within the given school year. Placement options are the regular classroom, regular classroom with supplemental aids, regular classroom plus resource room, special self-contained class, or nonschool setting. The physical education specialist may be asked to serve on the M-Team or to be a consultant to the team for children whose handicapping conditions reflect strong needs in the motor skills area.

In individualized physical education classes, it is often difficult to identify the mainstreamed child.

INDIVIDUALIZED EDUCATION PROGRAM

Individualization of education for a diagnosed handicapped child is formulated through the individualized education program (IEP). Generally, the IEP is limited to curricular areas of special education and related services—instruction designed to meet the unique needs of the handicapped child and the related services necessary to help the child benefit from special education. The IEP includes

- Statement of the present level of the child's functioning
- Annual goals
- Short-term instructional objectives with time lines

- Extent to which the child will participate in the regular educational program
- Special services to be provided, including their duration and extent
- Plan for evaluation of annual goals

For some handicapped students, the IEP will address only a very limited part of their education, for example, speech; for others, the IEP may cover their total education. The IEP is a projection of what professionals and the parents think the child can accomplish. If the annual goals are inappropriate, reassessment of the child's curriculum by the M-Team can lead to new goals better suited to the child's needs. In many states, goals are also set for the parents in working at home with the child. The IEP may specify time for motor skills development in addition to physical education or remedial assistance in perceptual, sensory-motor, balance, or body image areas. If special services are to be provided under the direction of the physical education teacher, the M-Team will inform the teacher of such a decision, or the teacher will be asked to help develop the yearly plan.

Least Restrictive Environment

The least restrictive environment is the educational setting that is most appropriate, most enabling, for the handicapped child. To the maximum extent possible, children with handicaps are to be educated with children who don't have handicapping conditions. Legal reasons aside, there are sound educational reasons for educating handicapped children in the least restrictive environment. Research has shown that placing handicapped youngsters with nonhandicapped children yields positive benefits in behavior and life skills. Educators have long agreed on the effectiveness of peer modeling in academics and skill acquisition among children. Furthermore, the mainstreamed classroom and gymnasium more closely mirror the real world than do the classroom or physical education setting comprised of

all handicapped students. Most of the students with handicapping conditions we see in our public schools will reside and work within our communities and participate in community activities. The least restrictive, the more enabling educational environment should give handicapped students the same opportunities to learn, to develop personal potential, to interact and mature socially as all other students receive.

Implementation

After the M-Team has determined the least restrictive environment and the IEP has been written, it's the responsibility of all teachers working with the handicapped child to implement the educational program. For those children with an unrestricted classification, no adaptation of the environment or curriculum is necessary. For children with a modified classification, their handicapping conditions warrant an adaptation of the existing curriculum. Other children require an individualized remedial program. The mainstreaming of some handicapped children into physical education classes requires considerable modification of existing environmental and curricular tasks. Whether the IEP specifies an unrestricted, modified/adapted, or remedial program, we can no longer be content with letting the handicapped child be the scorekeeper in class. The program must be designed to mainstream the child into gymnastics, games, and dance. Adaptations in tasks, as is true for all children, will permit the child with handicaps to participate, to achieve, to develop the skills commensurate with personal ability.

Visual and hearing impairments, physical handicaps, and health impairments often necessitate a modification of the program. Following is a brief description of each of these handicapping conditions, with implications for physical education and suggestions for program modifications. Other handicapping conditions include mental retardation, severe emotional disturbance, and learning disabilities. Any adaptations for these conditions are noted in the child's IEP.

VISUAL IMPAIRMENTS

The two categories of visual impairment are blindness and partially sighted. Approximately 0.1 percent of school age children are seriously visually impaired, with impairments ranging from blindness to blurred/distorted vision, tunnel vision, and seeing out of the corners of the eyes only. Children with serious visual impairments may exhibit the following characteristics:

- Self-stimulating mannerisms, for example, stamping feet, rocking, clicking fingers, and turning the head from side to side. These mannerisms often result from boredom and lack of external stimulus.
- Awkward, clumsy, total body movements and poor motor skills from lack of experience and limited sensory information.
- Poor posture due to lack of visual modeling.
- Developmental lag of at least one year, often due to lack of stimulus and/or overprotective parents.
- Lack of fitness and tendency toward being overweight because of sedentary lifestyle.
- Difficulty dealing with abstractions and a limited conception of the "whole."
- Difficulty in conceptualizing boundaries.

The child with severe visual impairments needs auditory and tactile stimulation. As teachers, we need to encourage this child to venture beyond the known environment, to explore in the gymnasium and on the playground. We need to promote social interaction with peers as well as adults and to maximize learning through all the senses. IEPs for children with serious visual impairments focus on attention to sensory abilities, spatial awareness, and mobility. Visually impaired children need the maximum use of their proprioceptive, auditory, haptic, and spatial perceptions.

For visually impaired children, proprioceptive perception is important for maintaining balance. Body awareness and proprioceptive perception can be increased through activities that focus on the identification of body parts, awareness of the relationship of body parts to each other, and the body part's position in space. Children can be asked to move individual body parts when the body part is named and to perform certain movements with the isolated body part, for example, swing or tap. Proprioceptive awareness can be increased by adding small weights to body parts and then instructing children to move the parts. The gymnastics skills of balancing on different body parts and in different positions also helps this development.

The senses are also used to establish spatial awareness. Children who are blind have difficulty perceiving the relationship of objects in space and the spatial relationship of themselves to objects. Lateral and directional activities, such as identification of left and right sides; movement away from self—left, right, up, down, front, back; and posi-

Ron, a child blind since birth, was mainstreamed into a physical education class. The class was studying balance—balance on different bases of support and balance in inverted positions (Chapter 19). Ron was working independently in the space defined by the boundaries of his gymnastics mat. Suddenly Ron cried aloud; the entire class stopped and turned in his direction. Nothing was wrong; Ron was experiencing for the first time the change in body position and perception that accompanies being balanced in an inverted position on the hands only. Ron apologized for disturbing the class and activity continued. During sharing time at the end of the class, Ron shared his feelings of the experience and his excitement for more gymnastics.

tioning of self in relation to equipment, for example, a table or a chair, help develop this perception in children without the visual sense. Auditory cues determine distance in space for children with visual impairments. Auditory sounds can be placed on stationary equipment and the equipment used with a partner to help measure distance, location in space, and pathways of travel. Young children can face sounds made at different locations and thus determine near and far. Older children can follow a bike rider by the sound of cardboard on the spokes or copy the pathway of a partner by changes in intensity of the sound.

One of the greatest handicaps of visually impaired children is lack of mobility. A mobility training program in the gymnasium as well as the outdoor play area increases the child's independence and thus the ability and desire to participate fully. Three-dimensional models of both the indoor and outdoor physical education environments, including permanent equipment, give visually impaired children the concrete, hands-on experience to develop a conception of the whole and the ability to move within the physical education space. The mobility training should also include a peer-guided tour of the environment and time for personal exploration of the environment, including full use of tactile and auditory senses. The blind child should be free to walk, crawl, and touch the gymnasium without the embarrassment of a class of onlookers; the teacher, parent, or a trusted adult should be present to answer questions and ensure safety. Specific activities for orientation and mobility are presented in Bryant Cratty's book, *Movement and Spatial Awareness in Blind Children and Youth*, Springfield, IL: Thomas, 1971.

Most children with serious visual impairments lack the motor skills and patterns essential for successful participation in physical education activities. Many aren't able to perform the basic skills of running, skipping, jumping, throwing, and so on. The IEP for such children may include one-to-one instruction in these basic skills and movement patterns. Traditional teaching of locomotor skills and movement patterns relies heavily on the visual mode. The teacher of children with serious visual impairments will have to sharpen personal skills of movement analysis, clearly present the instruction, and provide effective feedback. An excellent resource for teaching basic movement skills to handicapped children is Jane R. Evans' book, *They Have to Be Carefully Taught: A Handbook for Parents and Teachers*, Reston, VA: AAHPERD, 1980.

Mainstreaming visually impaired children into physical education classes has implications for the teacher, the environment, and physical education equipment. Specific implications for the teacher include:

- Teaching with manual guidance accompanied by verbal directions.
- Remembering that the visually impaired child relies heavily on tactile perception. Manually guiding the visually impaired child can serve as the demonstration of the skill for other children, thus benefiting the group as well as the individual.
- Providing specific and immediate feedback. For profitable feedback, the teacher must thoroughly analyze movement skills and provide the verbal clues for correcting deviations.
- Using peer teaching to assist with the manual guidance and verbal feedback.
- Involving visually impaired children in small group and partner activities rather than large group situations.
- Avoiding activities that involve throwing and catching with fast speed and travel.
- Progressing from simple tasks in gymnastics and games to sequentially more difficult tasks to develop motor skill and cognitive complexity.
- Involving all children in the world of creative movement experiences and dance. Creative dance comes from the inner self; it is born of the senses. Vision is necessary only for the observer.

Adaptations in the environment include:

- Having the gymnasium well lighted, to help the handicapped child with residual vision.
- Varying the texture of the boundaries for game areas—dirt/grass for the play area, sand for the surrounding area.
- Making pathways for travel between targets or bases three to four feet wide and of a different texture.
- Keeping the outdoor teaching area and the gymnasium well organized and consistent. Introduce new equipment to visually impaired children, by means of three-dimensional models.
- Providing tactile markings on the floor as reference for teaching stations, the center for teacher directions, water fountains, and so on.

- Placing guide ropes across the gymnasium or playground, to permit the practice of locomotor skills and freedom of travel. Tie a series of knots in the ropes to signal the approach of the boundary.

The mainstreaming of visually impaired children into physical education may necessitate some special equipment needs, such as:

- Brightly colored balls and objects for children with limited vision
- Sponge and foam balls for projectile activities
- Protection for the eyes; eyeglasses
- Audible beep balls for tracking and location
- Battery-powered electronic sound devices within large marker cones to serve as bases
- A large gymnastic mat to serve as "personal space" for balancing and transferring of weight activities.

Write to the American Foundation for the Blind, New York, NY 10011, for catalogs of special equipment.

We expect children with visual handicaps to participate to their fullest potential in physical education, trying not to let the child use the handicap as an excuse to withdraw from activity and social interaction. Games situations that involve constant contact with the participants, for example, wheelbarrow travel, parachute activity, require the least adaptation. When new activities are introduced, having visually handicapped children play in slow motion will help their orientation to the play environment and the rules. The use of the buddy system also helps visually handicapped children participate in traveling activities. Note, however, that although young children naturally hold hands with partners, they do need to know the correct way to assist a visually impaired person. That is, the visually impaired person should grasp the guide's upper arm above the elbow, thus permitting the nonsighted person to maintain a sense of control rather than being led as if helpless.

Falls, scratches, and bruises are a part of physical education for children with serious visual impairments. Visually impaired children need to be permitted to recover on their own, to maintain dignity, and to attain maximum independence. The teacher must discuss with the nonhandicapped members of the class the danger of being overprotective. With the exception of ball-handling/striking activities, the visually impaired child can function quite independently in mainstreamed physical education classes. Following orientation and mobility training, the teacher's task is simply helping the child to develop a belief in self and potential skill development.

HEARING IMPAIRMENTS

Hearing impairment refers to hearing loss that can range from mild to profound. The handicap includes those who have trouble hearing normal speech and those who can't understand even amplified speech. Approximately 5 percent of school age children have a hearing loss that could affect learning, but only one in each twenty-five requires intensive special education. The term *deaf* is rarely used to classify a hearing impairment; most persons labeled deaf have some level of hearing, being able to understand speech with the help of amplification or by hearing combined with watching the speaker's lips, facial expressions, and gestures. The danger of labeling a child deaf is that the label may cause peers to stop interacting with the child and may actually make the child functionally deaf as an adult.

The social domain is the greatest problem for children with serious hearing loss. The hearing-impaired young child doesn't engage in play experiences with other children; speech, if present, is garbled, and communication quite limited. The hearing-impaired child doesn't understand his role in the play experience and often withdraws, thus denying himself the social interaction and development of motor skills that accompany play for young children. As children's games become more complex, the hearing-impaired child is likely to be left out of the activities. Rules are developed as the

game is played; instructions are shouted in the midst of play. Without special assistance, the hearing-impaired child is unable to comprehend all the intricacies of the game. Thus, the child with serious hearing loss fails to develop the social skills learned through group interaction in play. His withdrawal from activity causes a developmental lag in motor skills.

The frustration of being unable to communicate and not being understood by others plus the lack of experiences to learn how to express emotions in socially accepted ways often leads children with serious hearing impairments to express their emotions through physical means. Aggressive behavior is often the means of expressing negative emotions. Additional characteristics of a child with a serious hearing impairment may include:

- Slow development of inner and expressive language, often leading others to mistake the child as mentally retarded
- Poor pronunciation, garbled speech
- Absence of laughter
- Difficulty in dealing with abstractions due to slowness in developing inner language
- Hyperactive appearance because of constant movement to maintain visual contact
- Lack of good balance for some hearing-impaired children caused by inner ear damage
- Shuffling gait resulting from not hearing the sound of movement

Most children with hearing impairments don't need an adapted set of activities in physical education; they can be mainstreamed into the regular program of skill themes and movement concepts. As a rule, adaptations in equipment or environment won't be necessary. However, the physical education teacher needs to modify certain aspects of teaching:

- Position yourself so the child with a serious hearing impairment can read your lips; be conscious of not turning your back when speaking, and be close enough for lip reading.

We strongly recommend a course in sign language for teachers with hearing-impaired children in their classroom or gymnasium. Think of how much better the hearing-impaired child will feel if she or he is greeted the first day of physical education by a teacher she or he can communicate with!

- Face the sun when outdoors rather than positioning yourself so that the hearing-impaired child has to face the sun.
- Let the hearing-impaired child move freely in the teaching environment, to always be in the best position for hearing.
- Visually and manually demonstrate skills; don't rely on verbal directions alone.
- Remember, the hearing-impaired child can't read lips or hear a whistle across the playing field or gymnasium; accompany the auditory sound with large hand signals.
- Learn the basic sign language needed for communication. Figure 30-1 provides specific signs for physical education and basic communication.

For hearing-impaired children with a developmental lag in motor skills, an individualized physical education program to develop the motor skills and movement patterns needed for successful participation in mainstreamed physical education is necessary. Children with balance difficulties will benefit from a program of balance activities (precontrol tasks, Chapter 19). Children with poor motor skills or who have difficulty with balance are very conscious of their abilities as compared to those of their peers; a private place to practice can help overcome self-consciousness in attempting skills.

Like many children with a handicapping condition, the child with a serious hearing impairment may be handicapped due to a lack of experiences. As teachers, we try to maximize strengths rather than focusing on the weakness, the inability to hear. The child will have to experience success in activities to build the self-esteem for eager participation and social interaction. The understanding of directions and simple activities that the class takes for granted may have to be carefully explained to the child with a serious hearing impairment. Encourage nonhandicapped children to initiate conversation with the hearing-impaired child, to help the child understand class activities, yet not patronize the youngster. We need to educate all children in our classes to interact with the hearing impaired, to accept their less-than-perfect speech, and to involve them in both physical education and play activities.

PHYSICAL HANDICAPS

Physical handicaps include conditions resulting in orthopedic handicaps such as cerebral palsy and spina bifida, the crippling diseases of arthritis and muscular dystrophy, permanent loss of limbs, and the temporary disabilities caused by fractures. Other related health factors that can mean limited or restricted physical education for children include hemophilia, severe burns, congenital heart defects, and respiratory disorders.

Each child with a physical handicapping condition has different physical and motor capabilities, so the IEP must be designed to meet individual needs. The child's physical education program will include two aspects: the IEP of exercises and activities to meet specific needs and develop motor skills, and mainstreamed physical education. Auxier and Pyfer (1985) recommend the following procedure when planning this two-part program for children with physical handicaps:

1. Identify the child's clinical condition.
2. Determine what activities would be contraindicated based on medical recommendation.
3. Determine functional motor skills needed.
4. Select activities that will develop desired motor skills.

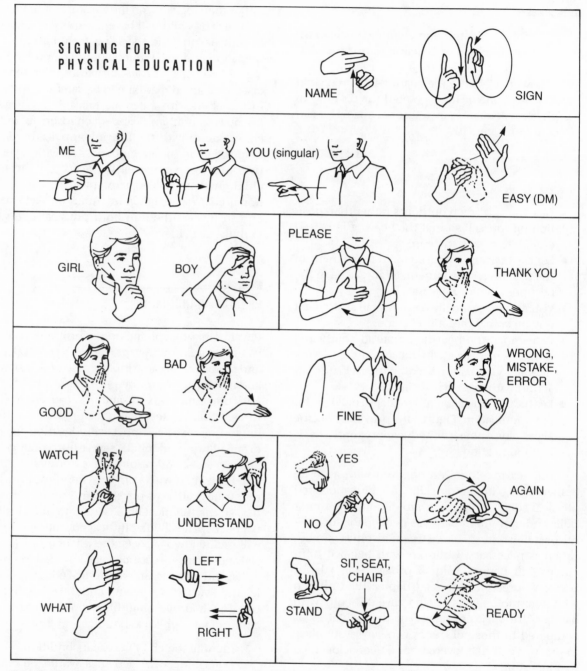

Figure 30-1 Signing for physical education. *Source:* "Signing for Physical Education," May 1978, *Journal of Physical Education and Recreation,* 49(5), 20–21.

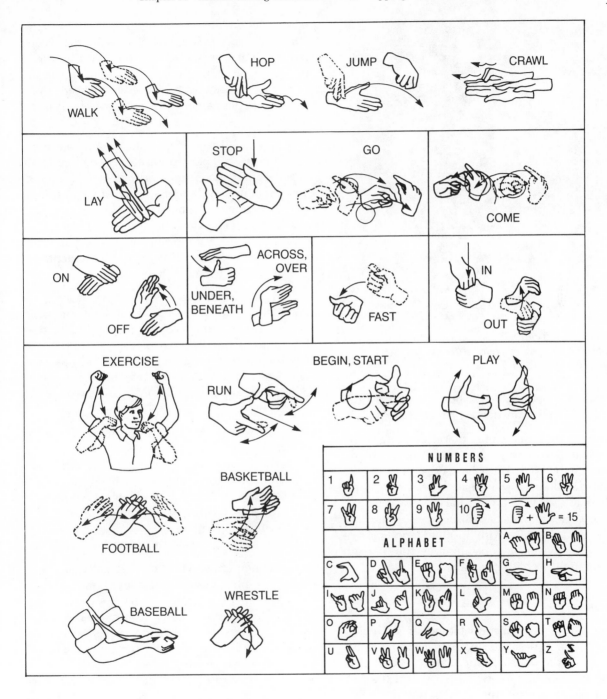

Locomotor activities are just as exciting to the physically handicapped child as they are to the nonhandicapped child.

5. Adapt the physical education environment and equipment as needed to provide the program.

It's important to remember that the program will be designed in consultation with a physician and a physical therapist. As teachers, we aren't expected to make a clinical diagnosis or to prescribe a program of individualized remedial exercises without the assistance of trained medical professionals. The professionals familiar with the child's medical history will be valuable consultants to the M-Team developing the child's program.

Cerebral Palsy

Perhaps the most misunderstood of all handicapped children is the one with cerebral palsy. Because of the language and auditory handicaps often accompanying cerebral palsy, and the lack of muscular control, the child is often labeled mentally retarded. Cerebral palsy is a neurological impairment; that is, the impairment is caused by a lack of complete development of or injury to the central nervous system. Cerebral palsy may occur as a result of prenatal factors, injuries during birth, or postnatal conditions, for example, serious childhood diseases with high fever or a head injury. Characteristics associated with cerebral palsy include:

- Associated handicaps in visual, auditory, speech, and perceptual areas of development
- Lack of concentration, distractability, overexcitability, and hyperactivity causing underachievement and poor behavior
- Poor coordination and lack of balance, resulting in awkward movements and frequent falls
- Difficulty in coordinating eye movements
- Tendency toward seizures

The individualized physical education program for a child with cerebral palsy will include a concentration on perceptual motor activities: locomotor patterns, balance, response to rhythm, development of ocular control, and form perception. The physical therapist may also recommend exercises that focus on the following factors:

- Muscle stretching to relieve contractures, prevent deformities, and permit fuller range of motion
- Muscle awareness exercises to control specific muscles
- Relaxation techniques to help control contractures, rigidity, and spasms
- Posture alignments
- Gait training for walking patterns

When a child with cerebral palsy is mainstreamed into physical education, it may be necessary to adapt facilities, equipment, or activities. Each type of cerebral palsy has unique characteristics and specific implications for physical education. The physical education teacher will benefit from extensive reading concerning the type of cerebral palsy and from discussion with the physical therapist concerning the remedial program and the adaptation of equipment and activities for maximum participation.

Spina Bifida

Spina bifida is a congenital condition in which the bony elements of the spine don't properly close during development in the womb. The condition may result in a cystlike formation on the spinal column that contains part of the spinal cord; a protruding sac containing covering tissue; or a malformation with no protrusion of spinal cord. In mild cases of spina bifida, the only effects may be weak muscles and deviations in posture. Since spina bifida causes paralysis in the legs and a loss of sensation in the lower limbs, children with mild spina bifida benefit from exercises to strengthen muscles and improve posture. Only slight modifications of physical education curriculum are necessary. Children with severe spina bifida can be mainstreamed with activities adapted for wheelchairs. These youngsters will need remedial programs emphasizing relaxation and passive range of motion exercises.

Like many children with handicaps, children with spina bifida benefit from the socialization inherent in mainstreaming, in addition to other learnings. Guiding this growth is perhaps the greatest contribution we as physical educators can make in the educating of children with handicaps.

Muscular Dystrophy

Childhood muscular dystrophy begins between the ages of two and six. It's an inherited disease; the exact nature of the inheritance isn't yet known. Muscular dystrophy is a progressive disease that affects the voluntary muscles, for example, legs and arms; involuntary muscles such as the diaphragm aren't affected. First affected are the muscles involved in walking and standing; the child with muscular dystrophy will begin to have difficulty maintaining posture, getting up from a chair, or walking up stairs. The degenerative nature of the disease causes the general deterioration of the muscle tissue and a replacement of muscle with fat. Thus the young child with muscular dystrophy

initially appears quite healthy as the legs and arms maintain or increase in "size."

The child with muscular dystrophy has a tendency to tire easily. Fine manual dexterity is gradually lost, and the progressive weakening of the muscles causes adverse postural changes. The IEP for the child with muscular dystrophy should concentrate on exercises to strengthen the muscles involved in the basic tasks of daily living, walking patterns, posture control, and stretching of contractures. However, these exercises must be selected in consultation with the child's physician. The child with muscular dystrophy should be kept actively involved in physical education to the extent the condition permits; inactivity only increases the atrophy of the muscles. Adaptations will be necessary as the child becomes dependent on crutches, braces, or a wheelchair.

HEALTH-RELATED IMPAIRMENTS

Although not normally thought of as physical handicaps, several other health-related impairments can affect a child's full participation in physical education. The following disorders may require temporary adaptations in the child's environment or limitations in physical activity: juvenile arthritis, diabetes, heart defects, sickle cell anemia, severe burns, and respiratory disorders.

LEARNING DISABILITIES

A specific learning disability is a disorder in one or more of the basic processes involving understanding or using language. According to the U.S. Department of Health, Education and Welfare, the disability may manifest itself as an imperfect ability to listen, think, speak, write, spell, or do mathematical calculations. Children with learning disabilities have normal intelligence but unlike other children, they're unable to perform academically within the normal IQ range. Children with learning disabilities are typically characterized by hyperactive behavior, short attention spans, impulsiveness, poor self-concepts, and often a delay in play development.

The motor skills of children with learning disabilities are difficult to categorize. Some children with learning disabilities experience no motor delays; others demonstrate a number of delays. The most common difficulties include visual-motor coordination, fine motor coordination, bilateral coordination, and balance. IEPs for children with learning disabilities have focused on perceptual-motor development (Cratty, 1980; Frostig & Maslow, 1970; Kephart, 1971) and more recently on sensory integration. Selection of the activities for the IEP must be based on an assessment of the child's deficiencies. Not all learning disabled children have motor/perceptual delays; not all have the same deficiencies.

With very few exceptions, children with learning disabilities are mainstreamed into regular physical education programs. They can be expected to participate fully in all activities. Slight teaching modifications may be needed for individual students:

- Prepare the lesson with several short activities in mind rather than one lengthy concentration, to reduce hyperactive tendencies.
- Give clear, brief instructions; ask the child to repeat the direction before beginning activity.
- Use small learning steps and praise the child's efforts and accomplishments. Remember, the attitude of the learning disabled child is, "I can't."
- Use a positive behavior modification program if needed (Chapter 7).
- End the lesson with a brief relaxation period.

Including children with handicapping conditions in physical education classes can be a most rewarding experience. Teachers can help the youngsters develop socialization skills, motor skills many didn't know existed, and self-confidence. We believe that children with handicaps can benefit from physical education and from integration with others.

One of the keys to successfully mainstreaming children with handicaps is the acceptance of those children by their peers. Many non-handicapped children have never been around children with handicaps and are hesitant about beginning conversations with them or engaging in activity. The physical education teacher should coordinate efforts with the classroom teacher to orient children to the nature of the handicap, its correct name, any limitations imposed by the handicap, and the potential for activity. Sensitivity training of the non-handicapped children can include physical activities such as:

- Forming a circle, standing with legs shoulder-width apart, and rolling a playground ball across the circle while the *eyes are closed.*
- Playing a simple game with no verbal sound—no verbal clues for directions, rules, and stopping the action.
- Executing simple ball-handling, racket skills with the nondominant hand.

TEACHER

I will know you.
I will touch you and hold you
And smell and taste and listen
To the noises that you make—and the
    words, if any.

I will know you.
Each atom of your small, lonely
Aching, raging, hurting being
Will be known to me
Before I try to teach you.
Before I try to teach
I must first reach you.

And then, when I have come to know you,
    intimately,
I will insist, gently, gradually, but insist
That you know me.
And later, that you trust me
And then yourself.

Now, knowing each other, we will begin to
    know the world—
The seasons, the trees, animals, food, the
    other children,

The printed word, books,
The knowledge of what has gone before and
    been recorded.

Then as surely as I moved toward you
I will move away.
As I once insisted on being close to you,
Demanding entrance to your half wild world
Of fear and fantasy, refusing you aloneness.

So now, I move away.
As your words come and your walk quickens,
As you laugh out loud
Or read clearly and with understanding,
I stand behind you—no longer close—
Available, but no longer vital to you.

And you—you grow!
You are! You will become!

And I, the teacher,
I turn, with pride in you,
Toward my next child.

                Mary MacCracken

SUMMARY

Integrating children with handicaps into regular educational settings is no longer a choice for teachers and administrators. Public Law 94-142 guarantees each child with a handicap a free and appropriate education in the least restrictive environment. The multidisciplinary team, commonly called the M-Team, determines the placement that constitutes the least restrictive environment.

The child's educational program, including annual goals, extent of mainstreaming, and any special services, is written into the individualized education program (IEP). The IEP includes any individualized program in physical education—motor skills, perceptual-motor, and sensory development. Individualized programs are designed in consultation with medical specialists and other professionals with the expertise to help fashion the program that will best meet the child's needs.

With very few exceptions, children with handicaps can be mainstreamed into physical education. Mainstreaming doesn't mean sitting on the sidelines keeping score or turning on the record player; mainstreaming means participating fully to the extent possible.

Most children with handicapping conditions have had a limited amount of childhood play experiences, so they're often deficient in social interaction and basic motor skills. Individualized programs of physical education can help close the developmental lags in motor skills; purposeful mainstreaming can assist in the development of social skills.

Each handicapping condition is different. Each child with a handicap has needs specific to him or her. When a child with a handicap is mainstreamed into physical education, we need to increase our knowledge of the condition through extensive reading about the handicap and its implications for physical education. We should consult with the child's medical doctor and physical therapist to determine activities for the individualized program and adaptations to facilitate full participation. We need to educate nonhandicapped children concerning the handicapping condition and orient them to the world of the handicapped child. By promoting the acceptance of all individuals and presenting a curriculum that focuses on the development of skills commensurate with ability, we can move forward in the acceptance of children with handicaps as contributing members of physical education.

READING COMPREHENSION QUESTIONS

1. What is Public Law 94-142? What is its impact on physical education?
2. What is a multidisciplinary team? What is its function? Who serves on the M-Team?
3. What is an individualized education program? What does it include?
4. Name three characteristics of children with visual impairments. Discuss the implications of each characteristic in relation to physical education.
5. Physical education can serve as a laboratory for socialization of the hearing-impaired child. What adaptations, if any, are necessary for this objective to be accomplished?
6. Choose one physical handicapping condition and explain the implications of that handicap for physical education. Discuss the adaptations involved in mainstreaming this child—adaptations for the child, adaptations for the total class, and adaptations for the teacher.

REFERENCES

Auxier, D., & Pyfer, J. (1985). *Principles and methods of adapted physical education and recreation.* St. Louis: Times Mirror/Mosby.

Cratty, B. J. (1980). *Adapted physical education for handicapped children and youth.* Denver: Love Publishing Co.

Dewey, M. A. (1980). *Assisting special students: Making mainstreaming work for you.* Portland, ME: J. Weston Walch.

Evans, J. R. (1980). *They have to be carefully taught: A handbook for parents and teachers of young children with handicapping conditions.* Reston, VA: AAHPERD.

Frostig, M., & Maslow, P. (1970). *Movement education: Theory and practice.* Chicago: Follett.

Kephart, N. C. (1971). *The slow learner in the classroom.* Columbus, OH: Merrill.

Kirk, S. A. (1972). *Education of exceptional children.* Boston: Houghton Mifflin.

MacCracken, M. (1978, July). Teacher. *In Touch, 1*(6).

Safford, P. L. (1978). *Teaching young children with special needs.* St. Louis: Mosby.

Schifani, J. W., Anderson, R. M., & Odle, S. J. (Eds.). (1980). *Implementing learning in the least restrictive environment.* Baltimore: University Park Press.

Sherrill, C. (1977). *Adapted physical education and recreation: A multidisciplinary approach.* Dubuque, IA: Brown.

Winnick, J. (1979). *Early movement experiences and development.* Philadelphia: Saunders.

PART seven

The Future

Our last two chapters emphasize future directions in physical education. Chapter 31, "Building Support for Your Program," describes how teachers can work with six different populations to gain support for their physical education programs. We offer practical ideas for working with other teachers in the school, the principal, parents, the school board, the children themselves, and the community at large.

Chapter 32, "Physical Education for Tomorrow's Children," is in many ways our favorite. We end the book by focusing on the future, presenting some of our thoughts. We hope our ideas will encourage you to dream too.

Building Support for Your Program

Many parents, students, teachers, and administrators do not know how physical education contributes to an individual's growth. The lack of a public relations plan can result in an absence of communication between the physical educator and the public, thereby hampering the growth of the physical education program.

Michael Tenoschok and Steve Sanders

One of the undisputed facts about teaching in schools is that teachers need support from a variety of sources if they're to develop the type of programs they want for their children. This is especially true in physical education, for two reasons. First, many people regard physical education as less important than other subjects, such as reading and math, for example. Second, physical education is a relatively expensive program to conduct because of the necessary equipment involved. Thus it's necessary to cultivate support from the various segments of a school community who have the potential to be allies in our quest for improved programs. We've identified six related populations who need to be aware of and supportive of our program: the school administration, especially the principal; other teachers

in the school; parents; the school board; the community at large; and the children.

This chapter discusses ideas for building support within each of these six populations. However, note that it's important that first a teacher build as good a physical education program as possible with the support available. Even with limited resources it's possible to begin a good program, and this should be done because much of the work that will go toward building more support involves opening the program to administrators, parents, and the community in general. Obviously, if the program doesn't get off to a good start, you don't want visitors.

Once the program is off to a reasonable start, however, the teacher can invite observers to visit the classes. It may take months before the teacher

Thorough planning by the physical education teacher helps ensure that programs receive support.

Open communication with the principal is one avenue leading to program support.

is ready, but the learning environment has to be established and the children and teacher working together comfortably before visitors are welcome. Once the teacher is ready, the principal and other teachers in the school will probably be the first visitors.

THE PRINCIPAL

Many principals, through no fault of their own, know very little about physical education—especially the approach we're advocating in this text. Thus it's important to not take for granted that the principal knows and understands the program you're trying to develop. We believe part of our job is to educate our principal and administrators about our physical education programs. This is probably our most important task for gaining support for our programs. Principals are extremely important. In fact, if a principal is "not on our side," the opportunity to develop our desired program is reduced considerably (Faucette, 1984). We suggest the following ideas for working with your principal. The ideas aren't arranged in order of implementation, and we don't suggest that they all need

to be done. They're simply a list of ideas, some of which you may find helpful in your particular situation.

- Invite the principal of your school to observe a program at a nearby school with you. Sit with your principal and be certain that he focuses on the aspects of the program that are critical to the growth of your own program. Be certain to schedule a visit with the principal at the school you're observing so that the two administrators can discuss their programs and your principal can ask questions.

- Invite your principal to your classes that are beginning to work the way you intend. Be certain to follow up her visit so that you can answer any questions that may have arisen. Some administrators, for example, are unaccustomed to seeing every child with a ball and may be concerned about the "chaotic" appearance of a class that differs from their experiences in which there was only one ball for an entire class.

- If you're able to obtain videotapes of other teachers, invite your principal to view one of the tapes with you. Be sure to comment on the critical aspects of the program as related to your needs. Remember that the principal is busy, so you may want him to watch only certain key features, not the entire videotape.

- Occasionally give your principal a copy of an article or book you think is particularly well done and relevant to your program. Be certain to discuss the document with your principal after she has had a chance to read it. This is especially important if, for example, you're teaching twelve classes a day and you're able to locate a publication that recommends nine classes a day as a complete load for a physical education specialist. We recommend the publication by the American Alliance for Health, Physical Education, Recreation and Dance (AAHPERD), "Essentials of a Quality Elementary School Physical Education Program" (1981) because it makes a number of such recommendations.

Try to avoid falling into the trap of thinking that your principal really doesn't like your program, or physical education in general, if she isn't initially overly enthusiastic about your program. It takes some principals several years to become active supporters of your program. In fact, we've worked with principals who took several months to find time to come view our programs. Eventually, however, they did support our program and came to view it as an asset to the school.

TEACHERS IN THE SCHOOL

As you build your program, it's important that other teachers in the school understand and support your efforts. For certain you'll want to invite these teachers to observe your classes. Some of the ideas you use with your principal can also be used with your colleagues. Physical education specialists also find the following ideas helpful:

- Suggest that you work in conjunction with the classroom teacher on certain projects. Child-designed games, for example, provide marvelous opportunities for writing, math, and art projects. Expressive dance is an excellent catalyst for creative writing.

- If you require your students to keep student logs (Chapter 10), some classroom teachers will provide class time for students to do the writing immediately after physical education class.

- Arrange for several of the primary grades to view the last ten minutes of an intermediate grade's lesson, to show the younger children the progress that the older children have made. This motivates the younger children, encourages the older children, and also has the impact of "in-servicing" the teachers who attend the "minishow."

- When a teacher's physical education class has done a particularly good job on a project, it's a treat for the children and the teacher to share in their efforts. Invite the teacher to observe the last ten minutes of a class while the children demonstrate their progress, for example, in child-designed games, gymnastics sequences. This also has the added incentive of encouraging the classroom teacher to observe your physical education program.

The classroom teacher's support of the physical education specialist is very important. Classroom teachers who understand that physical education is educational, not simply recess, won't keep children "in" to complete math or reading assignments. They also respect the fact that the physical education program has certain time limits and so make sure that their children arrive on time and are ready to return to the classroom on schedule. This may seem to be a minor point, but in fact it can be a source of considerable friction when all the teachers in a school aren't working together to provide the best program possible for children. When teachers understand the value and quality of a physical education program, their support is easier to obtain.

PARENTS

There are many ideas for generating support among parents. Parent support is important, but it's not enough without the assistance of the principal and the other teachers. The physical education teacher must be sure that there's administrator and colleague support before beginning a major program to cultivate enthusiasm among the parents. If such support doesn't exist, a principal might feel that you're going "over her head," which can be disastrous for a new program. Once the administration understands your program and its needs, in many instances, the principal will encourage you to generate parent support. And parents' support can be especially helpful in obtaining funds that aren't available in the school's budget. Following are ideas for gaining parents' support. Try a few of the ideas one year, a few the next year. Be sure to change the ideas to match the needs and interests of the parents in your community.

- Attend PTA (PTO) meetings regularly, even if you aren't required to. Try not to sit in the back corner with the other teachers; take the time to meet some of the parents—introduce yourself, tell them what you teach, and invite them to observe your classes. This isn't necessarily the most enjoyable part of building a program, but it certainly can be a major factor in creating support.
- If you're invited to do a presentation for the parents' group, try to involve as many children as possible, to ensure a large turnout for your program. Be certain to include all skill levels of children, not only the utilization- and proficiency-level youngsters.
- Send a letter home at the beginning of the year. Tell the parents about your program and the general rules the children will be expected to follow, for example, shoes for physical education class, clothing. Invite parents to visit. Include a phone number where you can be reached in the evening (this will depend on your personal judgment and school policy) so that parents can call if they have questions about the program or your policies.
- A monthly or quarterly newsletter one page long is very helpful for informing parents and creating enthusiasm. Include items such as community programs of interest, books and articles to read, special accomplishments of the children, upcoming television programs of interest, and future programs that you've scheduled. Also include a brief sketch of what you've been working on in physical education and suggest ideas for the parents and the children to do together; for example, include the directions from this text for making a nylon hose racket or golf club, and suggest several activities for the parents to do with their children. Be sure to have the newsletter proofread so there aren't any spelling or grammatical errors.
- Bulletin boards are a great way to let parents know about your program. If you don't have the skills to make attractive bulletin boards, try trading with another teacher, for example, one week of bus duty for one bulletin board. In many communities there are retail stores for teachers that have very attractive bulletin board letters, pictures, backgrounds, and so on that even the least skilled person can use to make an appealing bulletin board.
- Send home with the children a "good news" note, which informs the parents of their children's accomplishments in physical education class. Design and print a supply of notes at the beginning of the year, so it won't take long to send several every week (see Figure 31-1). These notes are particularly effective for the children who work very hard but rarely get noticed.
- Some teachers use positive phone calls to communicate with parents about the program. A positive phone call is just a brief phone call to tell a parent how pleased the teacher is about the child's progress (attitude, effort) in physical education. It doesn't take long, but

Physical education bulletin boards provide information to students, faculty, and parents.

the fact that the teacher takes the time to make the call means very much to the parent. In many instances it's also unexpected because most phone calls from the school tend to be negative.

- Several nights a year hold an open house for parents and the children. The children must have adults with them to gain admittance. At the open house, equipment is available, and the children show the adults what they've been practicing in physical education. Other ideas include mother-daughter, father-son, mother-son, etc., open houses. Some teachers hold these open houses on Saturday mornings because many of the parents work nights. If you schedule the open houses informally, parents are free to spend a few minutes or an hour, depending upon their schedule.

- Once a year schedule a parent work night, which is an evening in which parents can help build, repair, paint, etc., equipment for the physical education program. The advantage of such an evening is that it gives parents an understanding of the need for physical education equipment. Make sure the evening is well organized; two hours is adequate.

- Jogging is so popular today that parents may enjoy a family fun run once the children have built up their ability to run a limited distance. It's important to explain that it isn't a race but just a chance to get together and run. A local celebrity runner makes an appropriate guest for such an event.

- Schedule a speaker for parents only. For example, you might invite a child psychologist, a medical doctor, a former athlete. Be certain that you've heard the speaker personally—don't trust someone else's opinion because the speaker has to be worthwhile if the parents are going to enjoy and benefit from the speaker. The entire program should run a maximum of sixty minutes.

- Invite parents with special skills to visit your physical education classes and discuss their expertise, for example, rugby player, karate expert, triathlete.

THE SCHOOL BOARD

Another obviously important factor in building support for your program is the school board. Although the board may seem far removed, the members play an extremely important role in physical education. In fact, they're the ones who

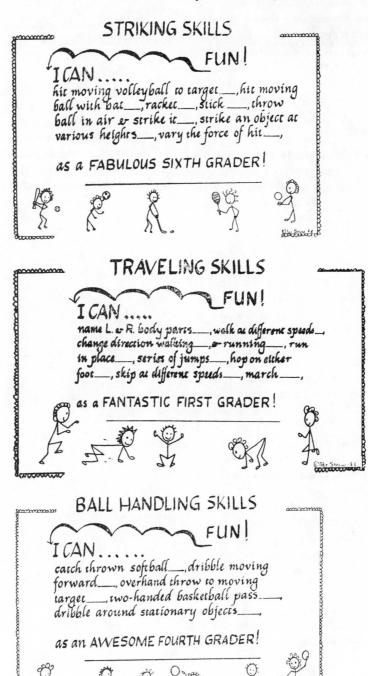

Figure 31-1 Examples of "good news" notes.

ultimately determine whether a school district will employ physical education specialists for their elementary schools. The time to gain the board's support is *not* when it's considering eliminating the physical education program at the elementary schools—that's often too late. Get to know the members, and let them get to know you and your program long before then.

- Attend several school board meetings each year. They won't be your most entertaining evenings, but you'll learn much about how decisions are made in school districts. If there's an opportunity, try to speak to one or more of the board members so that you get to know them. Don't ask for anything; just introduce yourself and talk about the current business before the board. If you ever have an occasion to speak to the board, the fact that you understand how the meetings are conducted and know a few members of the board will make things substantially easier for you.

- Whenever you're offering a special program at your school, send the board a written invitation. Be sure you've attended enough board meetings so you can recognize the members and call them by name if they come to your program. If you know in advance that the members will attend, try to have someone, such as the principal or another teacher, available to serve as a host.

- If you come across an article you think the school board members should read, send them a copy with a brief note. The article should be short, well written, and important to the board members.

Your relationship with the school board will be somewhat distant. It's important, however, to cultivate a relationship if your program of physical education is going to thrive within a school district.

THE COMMUNITY AT LARGE

Realistically, the community at large is less important than the populations discussed so far. You can potentially enhance your program, however, by conducting a program with community appeal. Typically, however, these are major undertakings that require substantial time and effort. The workload can be lightened by conducting programs with other schools in the community.

- If your community has a shopping mall, check with the managers; the managers of malls are often looking for demonstrations. Such a presentation will give your program a great deal of public visibility. It's a good idea to have handouts available so that people who stop by for a few minutes to watch the program know exactly what they're watching. These leaflets can be distributed by the children who aren't currently in action.

- The halftime of basketball games is a good opportunity for displaying some of the highlights of your program. For the program to be effective, the script for an announcer needs to be well done and rehearsed. Many children from different grades will make the program more appealing for the spectators. Contemporary, loud music is also stimulating. Be sure to include the younger children because they have enormous crowd appeal and can be very effective for getting across your message. Also, the children really enjoy performing, and their parents, grandparents, friends, and neighbors enjoy watching them.

CHILDREN AS ADVOCATES

We've saved the most important component until the end: the children. Obviously, if you hope to build support from the five populations just

described, the children will have to benefit from and enjoy the program. If the children aren't avid supporters of your program, you'll have difficulty gaining support from others in the immediate community.

Children become advocates and talk positively about teachers who help them learn and improve in any subject, not only physical education. In any school, the best teachers, not necessarily the easiest, are both known and respected by the children, other teachers, and the principal.

The word gets out when a teacher and a program are good.

Unfortunately, building a quality program of physical education requires more than being a successful teacher. To cultivate all the other populations that contribute to the success of a program, a teacher also needs to be part politician, part public relations director, and part fund-raiser. Some teachers find that part of the job distasteful, but it is necessary, especially when one's beginning a program of physical education.

SUMMARY

One of the roles that teachers of successful physical education programs play is that of generating support. Six different populations need to be aware and supportive of physical education if the programs are to be successful: school administration, other teachers in the school, parents, the school board, the community at large, and the children. Children are the most important advocates of a program, so a program must be of high quality if support from the other five populations is to be developed.

READING COMPREHENSION QUESTIONS

1. Why are six different populations identified for building support for a program? Can't the same ideas be used for all six groups?
2. What's the first step a teacher must take to develop a program with widespread support?
3. What does the phrase "principal education" mean?
4. Which of the suggestions for parents do you think you would use most frequently? Why?
5. Why is the school board so important to the success of a physical education program?
6. Why are the children the most important factor in developing support for a program?

REFERENCES

Buturusis, D. (1984). Gaining and keeping support for physical education. *Journal of Physical Education, Recreation and Dance, 55,* 44–45.

Carlson, G. (1982). A cooperative approach to public relations. *Journal of Physical Education, Recreation and Dance, 52,* 52–53.

Clay, W. (1981). First class and getting better. *Journal of Health, Physical Education, Recreation and Dance, 52,* 19–21.

Faucette, N. (1984). Implementing innovations: A qualitative analysis of the impact of an inservice program on the curricula and teaching behaviors of two elementary physical education teachers. *DAI, 45,* 1683a. (University Microfilms No. 80-21107)

Jenkins, D. (1981). A return to basics. *Journal of Health, Physical Education, Recreation and Dance, 52,* 25.

McLaughlin, R. (1979). The physical education demonstration: A different approach. *Physical Educator, 36,* 49–50.

Orr, B. (1983). Promoting local programs. *Journal of Physical Education, Recreation and Dance, 54,* 49–51.

Smith, J. L. (1981). Parents practice movement skills. *Journal of Health, Physical Education, Recreation and Dance, 52,* 24–25.

Tenoschok, M., & Sanders, S. (1984). Planning an effective public relations program. *Journal of Physical Education, Recreation and Dance, 55,* 48–49.

CHAPTER 32

Physical Education for Tomorrow's Children

Some men see things as they are and say why. I dream things that never were and say why not.

Robert F. Kennedy

All teachers have ideas about "the way things might be," and so do we. Some of our dreams are already reality in some schools for some teachers and some children. Some of our dreams may never become reality. We believe that it is as important to continue to dream as it is to see our dreams realized. Perhaps our hopes for the future will stimulate you to think and dream about the way things could be. The following discussion describes the world of the physical education teacher as it would be if we had our way.

Every child would have quality instruction in physical education every day.

Physical education, in both elementary and secondary schools, would receive as much emphasis as high school athletics. Communities would understand that an appropriate program of physical education for every child is at least as important as athletic programs for the gifted. And so all schools would have appropriate equipment, facilities, and budgets for physical education programs.

All school districts would recognize the importance of providing children with quality physical education programs. None would overlook the most important years of learning and wait until junior or senior high school to provide adequate instruction, equipment, and facilities.

All school districts would understand the differences between teaching children and teaching adolescents and would refuse to hire individuals whose primary interest and expertise is in coaching or teaching at a high school. Instead, school districts would hire, as elementary instructors, only teachers who are professionally qualified and dedicated to a career of teaching physical education to children.

Teacher education institutions would offer professional preparation programs for elementary school physical education specialists; these programs would be different from those for secondary school physical education teachers.

A national association designed specifically for teachers of children's physical education would be started. The meetings, journal, research, and other functions would be designed to specifically address and answer the questions teachers in the schools are asking.

Administrators and others who schedule classes would understand that physical education is intended to be an instructional experience, not a loosely organized recess. This understanding would be reflected by scheduling only one class rather than two or three classes with sixty or even ninety children at a time.

Teachers would have adequate time between lessons to jot down a few notes about the progress the last class made, rearrange equipment, review lesson plans, and shift their thoughts to the next class.

There would be time during the day to sit down with individual children and cooperatively plan a personalized curriculum for each child. This would help children to learn to make significant decisions about what they want to learn and how they want to learn it.

Assistance would be readily available for those children who require special remedial attention. This program would include instruction for parents so they could help their children at home.

Parents would become involved in their children's education. The concepts and skills introduced at school would be enhanced and embellished at home, through parent-child activity nights, afterschool programs for parents, and parent volunteer programs.

There would be times during each school day, beyond scheduled physical education classes, when children could choose to come to the gymnasium to practice something in which they were interested.

Classes would be scheduled to facilitate tutorial teaching—fifth graders working with first graders, or proficiency-level children working with precontrol children, for example.

Classes would be scheduled so that beginnings and endings were determined by the children's interest and involvement in a lesson rather than by an impersonal and insensitive time schedule.

Children could be grouped—by interest in a specific activity, by ability, by experience—to accomplish the specific goals of a series of lessons, then regrouped when the teacher decides to move to a new movement theme. For example, some upper grade children might be interested in putting on a dance performance for lower grade children. Those upper grade children could be grouped to meet together for two weeks, to prepare their dance and perform it. When they accomplish that goal, they could be regrouped as appropriate for another activity.

Children with handicapping conditions would benefit from programs designed specifically for them, to help them lead fuller lives. This implies that programs that attempt to force children to play (and enjoy) sports they'll never be able to play (or choose to play) on their own be eliminated from the physical education programs.

As a result of our programs, children would develop the healthy attitudes and habits that would lead to satisfying lifestyles as adults. Regular physical activity would become a part of their life as adults.

Teachers would have access to audiovisual equipment that would facilitate valuable projects. They would be able to make continuous videotapes of classes without having to reuse tapes. Teachers could do graph-check sequence filming of complex skills to help children develop the ability to analyze their own movements. Children would be able to make their own super-8 film strips, loop films, and videotapes.

Microcomputers would be readily available in

gyms for children to keep track of their own progress and for teachers to better design programs and report the children's progress to the parents.

Portable environments would be made available to schools throughout the year. Children would have opportunities to use portable swimming pools for swimming lessons, portable ski slopes for skiing lessons, and portable antigravity chambers to experience moving in a weightless atmosphere.

It would be common practice for individuals from the community to share their expertise and experiences with children. Children would learn about mountain climbing, hang gliding, hiking, human spatial ecology, and weightless gymnastics.

Teachers would be able to make arrangements to switch teaching assignments with other teachers for a day or a week. Then all teachers would have more experiences working in different environments and with children from various backgrounds.

Teachers would cooperate and organize curriculum into organic, natural contexts (consistent with the way children view the world), rather than artificially separating learning into compartmentalized subjects like reading, mathematics, art, and physical education. For example, building a house involves reading, mathematics, climbing, balancing, and working with others.

All classroom teachers would understand that a quality program of physical education can significantly contribute to children's total development. No one would prevent children from going to physical education class because they hadn't finished their work or because they had misbehaved.

All colleagues, parents, and administrators would be vitally interested in our teaching and physical education programs. They would demonstrate this interest by visiting our classes regularly, not only at the first PTA meeting of the year or during school lunch week.

All colleagues, parents, and administrators would understand the important contribution that a well-designed and effectively taught program of physical education can make in the quality of each individual's entire life.

Schools would become community centers that could involve parents and children in educational projects of mutual interest and benefit. These would include child/parent-designed and -constructed playscapes, child/parent-designed and -implemented field days for preschool children or underprivileged children, and child-parent programs designed for senior citizens.

Adequate funds would be made available for resource centers operated by teachers for teachers. Such centers would offer assistance in making materials or equipment, opportunities to hear visiting lecturers, in-service courses, discussion and sharing sessions, and up-to-date professional libraries.

All physical education programs, recreation programs, and youth serving agencies would cooperate to enhance the lives of children. No longer would they exist as independent agencies who serve the same children but rarely communicate or coordinate their efforts.

Teachers would be able to easily arrange frequent visits to other schools and teachers.

Elementary school teachers and college teachers would work together to discover better ways to enhance the learning experiences of children.

Elementary school teachers and college teachers would work together to discover better ways to enhance the learning experiences of preservice and in-service teachers.

Preservice teachers would work in elementary schools for several years before going to college so that they could learn the right questions to ask about children and teaching. Then as students they would ask the kinds of questions that real-world teachers ask.

College teachers would regularly trade teaching assignments with public school teachers, thus allowing the public school teachers to study current theories and practices at a college and giving the college teachers realistic opportunities to translate their theories into practice.

Nonthreatening, nonevaluative professional assistance would be available to teachers who want to improve their teaching effectiveness.

There would be ways to continually inform teachers about current educational thinking, to keep them from feeling isolated and out of touch.

Teachers would be involved in conceptualizing and conducting research. The resulting studies would have the potential for finding answers to the questions that teachers want answered.

Research results would be disseminated in forms that teachers of children would find useful, practical, and interesting, e.g., in weekly pamphlets or newsletters or monthly television programs that would use the language of the layperson, not professional jargon or advanced concepts related to experimental design or statistics.

We continue to dream about and search for better ways of teaching children. And we'd like to hear your dreams and ideas about children, teaching, and physical education. If you'd like to communicate with us, please write to us in care of the publisher.

One other dream emerged as we were writing this book. Wouldn't it be great if the ideas from our book help you become a more effective teacher of children! We've done our part—now it's up to you.

Sample School-Year Overviews

In this appendix we present four sample yearly overviews based on the material in *Children Moving*. The overviews are: (1) a two-day-a-week program for an inexperienced class, (2) a five-day-a-week program for an inexperienced class, (3) a two-day-a-week program for an experienced class, and (4) a five-day-a-week program for an experienced class. As you study the programs, keep these important points in mind:

1. The content outlines show how we organize a year using the material in *Children Moving*. They are intended not to be strictly followed, but rather to be used as starting points for developing your own yearly plans.
2. In this context, *inexperienced* generally refers to K–2 classes, *experienced* to grades 3–6. In your specific situation, *inexperienced* may refer to K–3 and *experienced* to grades 4–6. That's why the outlines should be used only as guides or examples and should not be taken literally.
3. The content listed for each day is intended to be the major focus of that day's lesson, but in many instances other content will be taught as well— e.g., a review of a skill theme or concept from the previous day, a skill that needs to be worked on frequently but for short periods of time, such as jumping rope and transferring weight from feet to hands.

4. In the five-day-a-week programs, the first few days are devoted to establishing a learning environment (see Chapter 7). Several other days are devoted to "reviewing" the learning environment. After Christmas or spring break, for instance, is often a good time to review the learning environment. Review days give you a chance to check the environment to determine if some areas, such as immediately stopping at the stop signal and paying careful attention when the teacher is talking, need additional work.

5. The sequencing of the skill themes and movement concepts takes typical weather patterns into account. Outdoor activities are grouped at the beginning and end of the school year, indoor activities toward the middle of the year. For the most part, the movement concepts are introduced early in the year and are revisited throughout the year when time permits.

6. Fitness concepts (see Chapter 29) are taught throughout the year on Wednesdays in these schedules. Obviously they could be grouped differently, but this placement allows you to teach a concept or two and set aside time for the children to incorporate the concept into their lifestyle before you introduce another fitness concept. It also allows you to review and reinforce concepts throughout the year, instead of lumping them into a block of lessons.

7. In our program, time is allowed throughout the year for special events that typically occur and take away time from teaching. (In most of the elementary schools we have taught in, there are days when physical education must be missed because of field trips, holiday shows or assemblies, voting, or picture days.)

8. Notice that skill themes tend to be massed at the beginning (several days combined) and then distributed throughout the remainder of the year. Notice too that in the programs for the experienced classes, several days in a row are sometimes spent on a single skill theme. The reason for this is that as children improve in skill proficiency they tend to want to spend more days on the same skill because their success rate is much higher. When success rates are low, children seem to concentrate better when the skill themes are changed frequently and reviewed regularly.

TWO-DAY-A-WEEK PROGRAM FOR AN INEXPERIENCED CLASS

Content Outline for an Inexperienced Class That Meets Two Days a Week

Topic of lesson/Activity	Percentage of school year[a]	Number of days
Establishing a Learning Environment	4	3
Space Awareness	9	6
Effort	5	4
Relationships	5	4

Topic of lesson/Activity	Percentage of school year[a]	Number of days
Traveling	7	5
Chasing/Fleeing/Dodging	4	3
Jumping and Landing	5	4
Rolling	7	5
Balancing	5	4
Weight Transfer	5	4
Kicking and Punting	7	5
Throwing and Catching	7	5
Volleying	3	2
Dribbling	3	2
Striking with Rackets	4	3
Striking with Hockey Sticks	2	1
Striking with Golf Clubs	2	1
Striking with Bats	3	2
Fitness Concepts	8	6
Field Day and Other Events	5	3
	100	72

[a]Percentages are approximate.

Two-Day-a-Week-Program for an Inexperienced Class (72 Days a Year)

Week	Chapter	Day	
1	7	1	Establishing a Learning Environment (p. 87)
	7	2	Establishing a Learning Environment (cont.) (p. 675)
2	12	1	Exploring Self-Space (p. 160)
	12	2	Exploring General Space (p. 164)
3	12	1	Exploring Directions (p. 168)
	12	2	Traveling and Freezing at Different Levels (p. 171)
4	15	1	Sliding; Galloping; Hopping; Skipping (p. 259)
	15	2	Performing Locomotor Sequences (p. 260)
5	16	1	Traveling to Flee; Fleeing from a Partner (pp. 284; 285)
	16	2	Traveling to Dodge; Dodging Moving Obstacles (pp. 285; 286)
6	29	1	Fitness Concepts (p. 675)
	21	2	Kicking a Stationary Ball from a Stationary Position (p. 426)
7	21	1	Approaching a Stationary Ball and Kicking; Kicking a Rolling Ball from a Stationary Position (pp. 427; 429)
	21	2	Dropping, Punting (p. 450)
8	22	1	Throwing at a Large Target (p. 470)
	22	2	Catching a Rolling Ball; Catching from a Skilled Thrower (p. 470)

Week	Chapter	Day	
9	23	1	Striking Balloons in the Air (p. 503)
	23	2	Striking a Ball Upward Continuously (p. 508)
10	23	1	Striking Down (Dribbling) Continuously with Both Hands (p. 527)
	23	2	Dribbling with One Hand (p. 527)
11	17	1	Jumping and Landing: Basic Patterns (p. 310)
	29	2	Fitness Concepts (p. 675)
12	13	1	Exploring Time (p. 188)
	13	2	Exploring Force (p. 195)
13	13	1	Traveling and Changing Force Qualities (p. 196)
	7	2	Establishing a Learning Environment
14	12	1	Exploring Pathways (p. 173)
	12	2	Exploring Extensions (p. 179)
15	15	1	Moving to Rhythmical Movements (p. 260)
	29	2	Fitness Concepts (p. 675)
16	14	1	Identifying Body Parts; Balancing on Matching and Non-matching Parts (pp. 211; 213)
	14	2	Traveling and Freezing in Different Body Shapes (p. 216)
17	17	1	Jumping over Low Obstacles: Hoops; Jumping over Low Obstacles: Hurdles (pp. 312; 313)
	17	2	Jumping over a Swinging Rope; Jumping a Self-Turned Rope (pp. 312; 318)
18	24	1	Striking Downward Continuously; Striking Upward Continuously (pp. 552; 553)
	24	2	Striking a Ball Rebounding from a Wall (p. 557)
19	29	1	Fitness Concepts (p. 675)
	15	2	Leaping (p. 263)
20	14	1	Studying Over, Under, Around, In Front Of, and Behind Concepts (p. 226)
	15	2	Playing Follow Me (p. 264)
21	18	1	Rocking; Matching Rocks (pp. 339; 340)
	18	2	Rolling like a Log; Rolling Forward (p. 340)
22		1	Special Event
	14	2	Matching and Mirroring (p. 236)
23	19	1	Balancing on Different Bases of Support; Balancing on Different Body Parts (p. 369)
	19	2	Balancing in Different Body Shapes (p. 372)
24	18	1	Rolling Sideways (p. 341)
	18	2	Rolling Backward (p. 341)
25	20	1	Transferring Weight from Feet to Other Body Parts Without Traveling (p. 398)
	20	2	Transferring Weight from Feet to Hands (p. 399)
26	19	1	Traveling on Low Gymnastics Equipment; Performing Stationary Balances on Equipment (pp. 373; 375)
	19	2	Balancing Sequence (p. 380)

Week	Chapter	Day	
27	13	1	Combining Time, Force, and Flow (p. 203)
	18	2	Jumping off Equipment, Landing, and Rolling (p. 345)
28	20	1	Transferring Weight Across Mats (p. 399)
	20	2	Traveling over Low Apparatus (p. 404)
29	21	1	Kicking to a Partner (p. 432)
	21	2	Punting Different Types of Balls (p. 451)
30	22	1	Throwing Overhand, Underhand, and Sidearm (p. 474)
	22	2	Throwing a Ball Against a Wall and Catching the Rebound (p. 481)
31	29	1	Fitness Concepts (p. 675)
	16	2	Overtaking a Fleeing Person (Catch-Up Chase) (p. 287)
32	22	1	Throwing and Catching with a Partner (p. 483)
	24	2	Striking a Ball Rebounding from a Wall (p. 557)
33	17	1	Jumping for Distance; Jumping for Height (p. 311)
	25	2	Striking a Stationary Ball on the Floor—Golf, Hockey (p. 582)
34	25	1	Striking for Distance—Golf (p. 584)
	25	2	Striking Off a Batting Tee (p. 585)
35	29	1	Fitness Concepts (p. 675)
	25	2	Striking a Pitched Ball—Bats (p. 597)
36		1	Field Day
		2	Field Day

FIVE-DAY-A-WEEK PROGRAM FOR AN INEXPERIENCED CLASS

Content Outline for an Inexperienced Class That Meets Five Days a Week

Topic of lesson/Activity	Percentage of school year[a]	Number of days
Establishing a Learning Environment	4	7
Space Awareness	9	16
Effort	5	9
Relationships	5	9
Traveling	7	12
Chasing/Fleeing/Dodging	4	7
Jumping and Landing	5	9
Rolling	7	12
Balancing	5	9
Weight Transfer	5	9
Kicking and Punting	7	12
Throwing and Catching	7	12
Volleying	3	6

Topic of lesson/Activity	Percentage of school year[a]	Number of days
Dribbling	3	6
Striking with Rackets	4	7
Striking with Hockey Sticks	2	4
Striking with Golf Clubs	2	4
Striking with Bats	3	6
Fitness Concepts	8	15
Field Day and Other Events	5	9
	100	180

[a]Percentages are approximate.

Five-Day-a-Week-Program for an Inexperienced Class (180 Days a Year)

Week	Chapter	Day	
1	7	1	Establishing a Learning Environment
	7	2	Establishing a Learning Environment
	7	3	Establishing a Learning Environment
	7	4	Establishing a Learning Environment
	12, 14	5	Exploring Self-Space; Identifying Body Parts (pp. 160; 211)
2	12	1	Curling, Stretching and Twisting in Self Space (p. 162)
	12	2	Moving the Whole Body in Self-Space (p. 162)
	12, 15	3	Exploring General Space; Traveling in General Space (pp. 164; 259)
	12	4	Dodging in General Space (p. 165)
	12	5	Traveling Over, Under, and Around Obstacles in General Space (p. 165)
3	12, 15	1	Traveling in Different Directions; Hopping; Skipping; Galloping; Sliding (pp. 167, 259)
	12	2	Turning While Moving in Different Directions (p. 169)
	12	3	Traveling and Freezing at Different Levels (p. 171)
	12	4	Rising and Sinking to Create Different Levels (p. 171)
	12	5	Exploring Pathways (p. 173)
4	12	1	Exploring Extensions (p. 179)
	13	2	Exploring Time (p. 188)
	13, 15	3	Moving at Different Speeds; Traveling at Different Speeds (p. 188; 265)
	13	4	Exploring Force (p. 195)
	13	5	Traveling and Changing Force Qualities (p. 196)
5	13	1	Traveling and Flow (p. 199)
	13	2	Eliciting Flow Qualities (p. 200)
	29	3	Fitness Concepts (p. 675)
	14	4	Balancing on Matching and Nonmatching Parts (p. 213)
	14	5	Teaching Body Shapes; Traveling and Freezing in Different Body Shapes (pp. 214; 216)

Week	Chapter	Day	
6	14	1	Traveling Over, Close To, Far Away, Inside (p. 222)
	14	2	Studying Over, Under, Around, In Front Of, and Behind Concepts (p. 226)
	14	3	Matching and Mirroring (p. 236)
	14	4	Traveling Alongside/Following (p. 237)
	15	5	Running (p. 260)
7	15	1	Performing Locomotor Sequences (p. 260)
	15	2	Moving to Rhythmical Movements (p. 260)
	29	3	Fitness Concepts (p. 675)
	15	4	Moving to Rhythmical Movements (cont.) (p. 260)
	22	5	Throwing a Yarn Ball Against the Wall (p. 469)
8	16	1	Traveling to Flee; Fleeing from a Partner (pp. 284; 285)
	16	2	Traveling to Dodge; Dodging in Response to a Signal (p. 285)
	16	3	Dodging with Quick Changes of Direction (p. 287)
	17	4	Jumping and Landing: Basic Patterns (p. 310)
	17	5	Jumping for Distance; Jumping for Height (p. 311)
9	21	1	Kicking a Stationary Ball from a Stationary Position (p. 426)
	21	2	Dropping, Bouncing, Kicking Lightweight Balls (p. 450)
	29	3	Fitness Concepts (p. 675)
	18	4	Rocking; Matching Rocks (pp. 339; 340)
	18	5	Rolling like a Log; Rolling Forward (p. 340)
10	16	1	Dodging Moving Obstacles (p. 286)
	17	2	Landing on One Foot (p. 312)
	17	3	Jumping Over a Swinging Rope (p. 312)
	21	4	Approaching a Stationary Ball and Kicking (p. 427)
	21	5	Dropping, Punting (p. 450)
11	7	1	Review of Learning Environment (p. 87)
	15	2	Traveling in Confined Spaces (p. 261)
	29	3	Fitness Concepts (p. 675)
	18	4	Rolling Sideways (p. 341)
	18	5	Rolling Backward (p. 341)
12	12	1	Creating Follow the Leader Pathways (p. 176)
	12	2	Using Extensions and Imagery (p. 180)
	16	3	Overtaking a Fleeing Person (Catch-Up Chase) (p. 287)
	17	4	Jumping over Low Obstacles: Hoops; Jumping over Low Obstacles: Hurdles (pp. 312; 313)
	17	5	Jumping Rhythmically (p. 315)
13	13	1	Combining Imagery and Time (p. 190)
	21	2	Kicking a Rolling Ball from a Stationary Position (p. 429)
	29	3	Fitness Concepts (p. 675)
	21	4	Tapping the Ball Along the Ground and Moving with It (p. 430)
	15	5	Traveling Through Rope Pathways (p. 261)
14	13	1	Using Imagery and Force (p. 196)
	22	2	Throwing at a Large Target (p. 470)

Week	Chapter	Day	
	18	3	Rolling in Different Directions (p. 343)
	18	4	Rolling from Different Positions (p. 343)
	19	5	Balancing on Different Bases of Support; Balancing on Different Body Parts (p. 369)
15	13	1	Practicing Flow Sequences (p. 201)
	22	2	Catching a Rolling Ball; Catching from a Skilled Thrower (p. 470)
	29	3	Fitness Concepts (p. 675)
	19	4	Traveling and Stopping in Balanced Positions; Balancing on a Wide Base of Support (p. 371)
	19	5	Moving off Balance (p. 372)
16	7	1	Review of Learning Environment
	14	2	Making Symmetrical and Nonsymmetrical Shapes (p. 216)
	16	3	Dodging a Thrown Object (Call Ball) (p. 288)
	18	4	Rolling from Different Directions and Positions (p. 344)
	18	5	Rolling at Different Speeds (p. 344)
17	14	1	Going Over and Under the Obstacle Course (p. 228)
		2	Special Event
	29	3	Fitness Concepts (p. 675)
	19	4	Balancing in Different Body Shapes (p. 372)
	19	5	Traveling on Low Gymnastics Equipment; Performing Balances on Equipment (pp. 373; 375)
18	20	1	Traveling on Body Parts; Traveling on Body Parts Other Than Feet (p. 398)
	15	2	Leaping (p. 263)
	14	3	Meeting/Parting (p. 238)
	17	4	Jumping a Turned Rope (p. 316)
	17	5	Jumping a Self-Turned Rope (p. 318)
19	19	1	Balancing on Boards (p. 377)
	19	2	Balancing with a Partner (p. 377)
	29	3	Fitness Concepts (p. 675)
	18	4	Rolling at Different Speeds (p. 344)
	18	5	Rolling Using Different Directions and Speeds (p. 344)
20	20	1	Transferring Weight from Feet to Other Body Parts Without Traveling; Transferring Weight from Feet to Hands (pp. 398; 399)
	20	2	Transferring Weight from Feet to Combinations of Body Parts (p. 399)
	20	3	Transferring Weight Across Mats (p. 399)
		4	Special Event
		5	Special Event
21	16	1	Maneuvering from a Thrown Object (Minidodgeball) (p. 289)
	17	2	Jumping Using Buoyant and Yielding Landings (p. 318)
	29	3	Fitness Concepts (p. 675)
	18	4	Jumping off Equipment, Landing, and Rolling (p. 345)

Week	Chapter	Day	
	22	5	Tossing to Self and Catching (p. 472)
22	7	1	Review of Learning Environment (p. 87)
	21	2	Kicking to a Distance Zone (p. 430)
	21	3	Kicking to Targets (p. 431)
	18	4	Jumping for Height, Landing, and Rolling (p. 346)
	18	5	Jumping from Different Heights and Rolling (p. 346)
23	19	1	Traveling on Large Apparatus (p. 379)
	19	2	Balance Sequence (p. 380)
	29	3	Fitness Concepts (p. 675)
	20	4	Transferring Weight from Feet to Back (p. 401)
	20	5	Stretching, Curling, Twisting into Transfers (p. 401)
24	23	1	Striking Balloons in the Air; Striking with Different Body Parts (pp. 503; 505)
	23	2	Striking the Ball to the Wall (p. 505)
	24	3	Balancing Objects on Paddles; Striking a Balloon with a Lightweight Paddle (p. 546)
	24	4	Striking a Self-Tossed Object or Dropped Ball (p. 550)
	24	5	Striking Downward Continuously; Striking Upward Continuously (pp. 552; 553)
25	21	1	Kicking to a Partner (p. 432)
	21	2	Tapping the Ball Along the Ground (Soccer Dribble) (p. 433)
	29	3	Fitness Concepts (p. 675)
	15	4	Traveling an Obstacle Course (p. 263)
	25	5	Striking for Distance—Golf (p. 584)
26	12	1	Traveling Pathways and Obstacles (p. 176)
	12	2	Combining Pathways, Levels, and Directions (p. 177)
	15	3	Playing Follow Me (p. 264)
	20	4	Performing Step/Spring Takeoffs; Performing Spring/Step Takeoffs onto Crates (pp. 402; 403)
	20	5	Traveling over Low Apparatus; Traveling onto Low Apparatus; Traveling off of Low Apparatus (pp. 404; 405; 406)
27	22	1	Throwing Overhand, Underhand, and Sidearm (p. 474)
	22	2	Bouncing a Ball to Self and Catching It (p. 474)
	29	3	Fitness Concepts (p. 675)
	23	4	Striking a Ball Down and Catching It; Striking Down (Dribbling) Continuously with Both Hands (p. 527)
	23	5	Dribbling with One Hand (p. 527)
28	15	1	Changing Speeds to Music (p. 265)
	21	2	Starting and Stopping; Traveling in Pathways (p. 434)
	21	3	Punting Different Types of Balls (p. 451)
	22	4	Throwing an Object to Different Levels and Catching It (p. 474)
	22	5	Catching in Different Places Around the Body (p. 475)
29	12	1	Review of Space Awareness Key Ideas
	20	2	Transferring Weight from Feet to Hands (p. 399)

Week	Chapter	Day	
	29	3	Fitness Concepts (p. 675)
	24	4	Striking a Ball Upward or Downward for More Than One Contact (p. 553)
		5	Special Event
30	23	1	Striking a Variety of Balls (p. 505)
	23	2	Striking a Ball Upward Continuously (p. 508)
	24	3	Sending an Object in the Desired Direction (p. 555)
	24	4	Varying the Force of the Hit (p. 555)
	24	5	Striking Through a Target (p. 556)
31	23	1	Dribbling at Different Heights (p. 528)
	23	2	Dribbling Continuously While Switching Hands (p. 528)
	29	3	Fitness Concepts (p. 675)
	25	4	Striking off a Batting Tee—Bats (p. 585)
	25	5	Striking Suspended Objects—Bats (p. 587)
32	25	1	Striking a Stationary Ball on the Floor—Golf or Hockey (p. 582)
	25	2	Striking to Targets—Hockey (p. 585)
	25	3	Striking a Pitched Ball—Bats (p. 597)
	25	4	Striking for Distance—Golf (p. 584)
	25	5	Striking for Distance—Golf (cont.) (p. 584)
33	23	1	Playing Keep It Up (p. 508)
	23	2	Volleying Game: Child-Designed (p. 510)
	29	3	Fitness Concepts (p. 675)
	25	4	Striking a Pitched Ball—Bats (p. 597)
	25	5	Striking a Pitched Ball—Bats (cont.) (p. 597)
34	22	1	Throwing at a Stationary Target; Throwing at Can Targets (p. 476)
	22	2	Catching with a Scoop (p. 479)
	25	3	Striking to Targets—Hockey (p. 585)
	25	4	Traveling, Stopping, and Controlling the Ball—Hockey (p. 591)
	25	5	Throwing a Ball in the Air and Striking It—Bats (p. 598)
35	22	1	Throwing a Ball Against a Wall and Catching the Rebound (p. 481)
	22	2	Throwing for Distance (p. 482)
	22	3	Throwing and Catching with a Partner (p. 483)
	23	4	Dribbling with the Body in Different Positions (p. 529)
	23	5	Dribbling and Traveling (p. 530)
36		1	Field Days and Special Events
		2	Field Days and Special Events
		3	Field Days and Special Events
		4	Field Days and Special Events
		5	Field Days and Special Events

TWO-DAY-A-WEEK PROGRAM FOR AN EXPERIENCED CLASS

Content Outline for an Experienced Class That Meets Two Days a Week

Topic of lesson/Activity	Percentage of school year[a]	Number of days
Establishing a Learning Environment	3	2
Space Awareness	3	2
Effort	5	4
Relationships	4	3
Traveling	4	3
Chasing/Fleeing/Dodging	4	3
Jumping and Landing	5	4
Rolling	7	5
Balancing	4	3
Weight Transfer	7	5
Kicking and Punting	7	5
Throwing and Catching	8	6
Volleying	5	4
Dribbling	4	3
Striking with Rackets	7	5
Striking with Hockey Sticks	3	2
Striking with Golf Clubs	3	2
Striking with Bats	3	2
Fitness Concepts	8	6
Field Day and Other Events	4	3
	98	72

[a]Percentages are approximate.

Two-Day-a-Week-Program for an Experienced Class (72 Days a Year)

Week	Chapter	Day	
1	7	1	Establishing a Learning Environment (p. 87)
	7	2	Establishing a Learning Environment (p. 87)
2	12	1	Dodging in General Space (p. 165)
	12	2	Combining Pathways, Levels, and Directions (p. 177)
3	20	1	Transferring Weight from Feet to Hands (p. 406)
	20	2	Transferring Weight to Hands: Walking (p. 407)
4	21	1	Kicking to a Partner (p. 432)
	21	2	Keeping It Perfect: Zero, Zero (p. 436)
5	22	1	Throwing Underhand, Overhand, and Sidearm (p. 474)
	22	2	Throwing for Distance (p. 482)
6	16	1	Dodging Stationary Obstacles (People Dodge) (p. 289)
	16	2	Dodging a Thrown Object Without Traveling (Glue Dodgeball) (p. 289)

Week	Chapter	Day	
7	21	1	Punting for Distance (p. 452)
	29	2	Fitness Concepts (p. 675)
8	13	1	Combining sport Skills and Time (p. 193)
	13	2	Using Imagery and Force (p. 196)
9	14	1	Creating Postcard Sculptures (p. 218)
	14	2	Building Body Shapes in the Air (p. 219)
10	15	1	Performing Locomotor Sequences (p. 260)
	15	2	Performing Slow Motion Replay (p. 266)
11	17	1	Jumping a Self-Turned Rope (p. 318)
	17	2	Jumping and Landing Task Sheet (p. 319)
12	18	1	Jumping off Equipment, Landing, and Rolling (p. 345)
	18	2	Playing Busy Mat (p. 350)
13	19	1	Performing Inverted Balances (p. 380)
	19	2	Balancing Symmetrically and nonsymmetrically (p. 381)
14	14	1	Meeting and Parting in a Cooperative Group (p. 239)
	29	2	Fitness Concepts (p. 675)
15	13	1	Using Flow Conversations (p. 202)
	13	2	Combining Time, Force, and Flow (p. 203)
16	23	1	Striking a Ball Upward Continuously (p. 508)
	23	2	Volleying to a Partner (p. 508)
17	18	1	Rolling over Equipment; Rolling on Equipment (pp. 350; 351)
	18	2	Rolling, Balancing, and Rolling (p. 353)
18	23	1	Dribbling and Traveling (p. 530)
	23	2	Dribbling Against an Opponent: One on One (p. 535)
19	24	1	Striking Downward Continuously; Striking Upward Continuously (pp. 552; 553)
	24	2	Striking a Ball Rebounding from a Wall (p. 557)
20	15	1	Shadowing (p. 269)
	29	2	Fitness Concepts (p. 675)
21	17	1	Jumping to an Accented Beat (p. 323)
	20	2	Transferring Weight to Hands, Followed by Rolling (p. 407)
22	19	1	Traveling into and out of Balances (p. 386)
	18	2	Rolling to Express an Idea (p. 382)
23	20	1	Transferring Weight over Apparatus (p. 411)
	20	2	Combining Weight Transfer and Balances in Sequences (p. 413)
24	23	1	Volleying Game: Child-Designed (p. 510)
	23	2	Playing One Bounce Volleyball (p. 513)
25		1	Special Event
	29	2	Fitness Concepts (p. 675)
26	23	1	Playing Dribble Tag (p. 536)
	24	2	Hitting Cooperatively and Continuously with a Partner (p. 559)

Week	Chapter	Day	
27	24	1	Playing Racket Call Ball (p. 562)
	24	2	Playing Minitennis (p. 566)
28	22	1	Throwing and Catching with a Partner (p. 483)
	22	2	Throwing and Catching While Traveling (p. 486)
29	25	1	Striking to Distant Targets of Various Sizes—Golf (p. 602)
	25	2	Playing Hoop Golf (p. 602)
30	16	1	Dodging and Chasing as Part of a Team (Octopus) (p. 291)
29	2		Fitness Concepts (p. 675)
31	21	1	Playing One on One Soccer; Playing Two on One Soccer (pp. 440; 441)
	21	2	Punting to a Partner (p. 454)
32	25	1	Traveling, Striking, and Changing Pathways with Partner—Hockey (p. 593)
	25	2	Striking to a Stationary Partner—Hockey (p. 596)
33	22	1	Throwing for Distance and Accuracy (p. 489)
	29	2	Fitness Concepts (p. 675)
34	22	1	Playing Keep Away (p. 494)
	17	2	Jumping to Throw; Jumping to Catch (p. 321)
35	25	1	Striking a Pitched Ball—Bats (p. 597)
	25	2	Playing One-Base Baseball (p. 611)
36		1	Field Day
		2	Field Day

FIVE-DAY-A-WEEK PROGRAM FOR AN EXPERIENCED CLASS

Content Outline for an Experienced Class That Meets Five Days a Week

Topic of lesson/Activity	Percentage of school year[a]	Number of days
Establishing a Learning Environment	3	6
Space Awareness	3	6
Effort	5	9
Relationships	4	7
Traveling	4	7
Chasing/Fleeing/Dodging	4	7
Jumping and Landing	5	9
Rolling	7	12
Balancing	5	9
Weight Transfer	7	12
Kicking and Punting	7	12
Throwing and Catching	8	15

Topic of lesson/Activity	Percentage of school year[a]	Number of days
Volleying	5	9
Dribbling	4	7
Striking with Rackets	7	12
Striking with Hockey Sticks	3	6
Striking with Golf Clubs	3	6
Striking with Bats	4	7
Fitness Concepts	8	15
Field Day and Other Events	4	7
	100	180

[a]Percentages are approximate.

Five-Day-a-Week-Program for an Experienced Class (180 Days a Year)

Week	Chapter	Day	
1	7	1	Establishing a Learning Environment (p. 87)
	7	2	Establishing a Learning Environment (p. 87)
	7	3	Establishing a Learning Environment (p. 87)
	12	4	Traveling Over, Under, and Around Obstacles in General Space (p. 165)
	12	5	Turning While Moving in Different Directions (p. 169)
2	12	1	Traveling While Rising and Sinking (p. 172)
	12	2	Traveling Pathways and Obstacles (p. 176)
	13	3	Combining Imagery and Time (p. 190)
	13	4	Differentiating Among Time Words (p. 191)
	13	5	Combining Sport Skills and Time (p. 193)
3	16	1	Dodging Stationary Obstacles (People Dodge) (p. 289)
	16	2	Dodging a Thrown Object Without Traveling (Glue Dodgeball) (p. 289)
	19	3	Performing Inverted Balances (p. 380)
	19	4	Performing Inverted Balances (cont.) (p. 380)
	17	5	Jumping a Self-Turned Rope (p. 318)
4	21	1	Kicking to a Partner (p. 432)
	21	2	Traveling in Pathways (p. 434)
	21	3	Dribbling Around Stationary Obstacles (p. 434)
	20	4	Transferring Weight from Feet to Hands (p. 406)
	20	5	Transferring Weight to Hands: Walking (p. 407)
5	22	1	Throwing Overhand, Underhand, and Sidearm (p. 474)
	22	2	Throwing a Ball Against a Wall and Catching the Rebound (p. 481)
	22	3	Throwing for Distance (p. 482)
	21	4	Punting with an Approach; Punting for Distance (pp. 451; 452)
	21	5	Punting for Accuracy; Punting for Height (p. 453)

Week	Chapter	Day	
6	16	1	Dodging and Faking Moves to Avoid a Chaser (Line Dodge) (p. 290)
	16	2	Dodging and Faking Moves to Avoid a Chaser (Freeze and Count Tag) (p. 291)
	22	3	Throwing and Catching over a Net with a Partner (p. 484)
	22	4	Throwing and Catching While Traveling (p. 486)
	22	5	Throwing to Make a Partner Move to Catch (p. 488)
7	12	1	Combining Pathways, Levels, and Directions (p. 177)
	12	2	Using Extensions and Imagery (p. 180)
	29	3	Fitness Concepts (p. 675)
	21	4	Keeping It Perfect: Zero, Zero (p. 436)
	21	5	Traveling, Kicking for a Goal (p. 437)
8	24	1	Striking Downward Continuously; Striking Upward Continuously (pp. 522; 553)
	24	2	Striking an Object in the Desired Direction (p. 554)
	24	3	Striking an Object to Send It over a Net (p. 556)
	24	4	Striking a Ball Rebounding from a Wall (p. 557)
	24	5	Hitting Cooperatively and Continuously with a Partner (p. 559)
9	25	1	Striking a Pitched Ball—Bats (p. 597)
	25	2	Striking a Pitched Ball—Bats (cont.) (p. 597)
	29	3	Fitness Concepts (p. 675)
	23	4	Dribbling Continuously While Switching Hands (p. 528)
	23	5	Dribbling and Traveling (p. 530)
10	23	1	Volleying to a Partner; Playing Keep It Up (p. 508)
	23	2	Volleying Game: Child-Designed (p. 510)
	23	3	Playing Two Square, Four Square (p. 510)
	23	4	Playing One Bounce Volleyball (p. 513)
	23	5	Striking a Ball Continuously with Different Body Parts (p. 514)
11	19	1	Balancing Symmetrically and Nonsymmetrically (p. 381)
	19	2	Balancing on Boxes (p. 384)
	29	3	Fitness Concepts (p. 675)
	19	4	Traveling into and out of Balances (p. 386)
	17	5	Jumping a Self-Turned Rope (p. 318)
12	7	1	Establishing a Learning Environment (p. 87)
	25	2	Striking for Distance—Golf (p. 584)
	25	3	Striking for Distance—Golf (p. 584)
	13	4	Showing Contrasts of Force; Using Imagery and Force (pp. 197; 196)
	15	5	Changing Speeds to Music (p. 265)
13	15	1	Traveling as Water, Steam, Ice (p. 266)
	15	2	Performing Slow Motion Replay (p. 266)
	29	3	Fitness Concepts (p. 675)
	17	4	Jumping Using Buoyant and Yielding Landings; Jumping on and off Equipment Using Buoyant and Yielding Landings (pp. 318; 319)
	17	5	Jumping and Landing Task sheet (p. 319)

Week	Chapter	Day	
14	17	1	Jumping and Landing Task Sheet (p. 319)
	19	2	Performing Inverted Balances on Equipment (p. 387)
	19	3	Performing Sequences That Combine Stationary Balances and Traveling on Mats (p. 388)
	19	4	Balancing While Supporting the Weight of a Partner (p. 390)
	19	5	Balancing on Hanging Ropes (p. 391)
15	20	1	Transferring Weight to Hands, Followed by Rolling (p. 407)
	20	2	Transferring Weight to Hands and Twisting (p. 407)
	29	3	Fitness Concepts (p. 675)
	25	4	Traveling While Changing Speeds, Pathways, and/or Directions—Hockey (p. 592)
		5	Special Event
16	18	1	Jumping over Equipment, Landing, and Rolling (p. 347)
	18	2	Rolling, Levels, Directions, and Jumping (p. 348)
	18	3	Traveling, Jumping, Landing, and Rolling (p. 349)
	18	4	Jumping, Landing, and Rolling: Follow the Leader (p. 349)
	18	5	Playing Busy Mat (p. 350)
17	7	1	Establishing a Learning Environment (p. 87)
	15	2	Traveling with a Partner: Matching Pathways (p. 266)
	29	3	Fitness Concepts (p. 675)
	20	4	Transferring Weight to Hands and Forming a Bridge (p. 409)
	25	5	Striking in Different Places Around the Body—Hockey (p. 595)
18	13	1	Following Flow Sequences; Practicing Flow Sequences (p. 201)
	13	2	Using Flow Conversations (p. 202)
	13	3	Combining Time, Force, and Flow (p. 203)
	23	4	Dribbling While Changing Directions (p. 531)
	23	5	Dribbling Around Stationary Obstacles (p. 534)
19	18	1	Practicing Touch and Go Rolls (p. 350)
	18	2	Rolling over Equipment; Rolling on Equipment (pp. 350; 351)
	29	3	Fitness Concepts (p. 675)
	15	4	Shadowing (p. 269)
	15	5	Performing Rhythmical Patterns (p. 269)
20	14	1	Creating Postcard Sculptures (p. 218)
	14	2	Building Body Shapes in the Air (p. 219)
	18	5	Traveling and Rolling Between Pieces of Equipment (p. 352)
	18	4	Diving over Low Obstacles to Roll (p. 354)
	14	5	Creating Postcard Sculptures (cont.) (p. 218)
21	18	1	Rolling to Express an Idea (p. 352)
	18	2	Rolling to Express an Idea (cont.) (p. 352)

Week	Chapter	Day	
	29	3	Fitness Concepts (p. 675)
	23	4	Dribbling Against an Opponent: One on One (p. 535)
	23	5	Playing Now You've Got It, Now You Don't (p. 536)
22	15	1	Traveling to Express Age: The Fountain of Youth (p. 270)
	20	2	Transferring Weight onto Large Apparatus (p. 409)
	20	3	Transferring Weight to Head and Hands on Apparatus (p. 410)
	20	4	Transferring Weight over Apparatus; Transferring Weight Along Apparatus (p. 411)
	20	5	Special Event
23	23	1	Playing Dribble Tag (p. 536)
	25	2	Striking to a Stationary Partner—Hockey (p. 596)
	29	3	Fitness Concepts (p. 675)
	17	4	Jumping to an Accented Beat (p. 323)
	17	5	Jumping with a Partner to Mirror Actions; Jumping with a Partner to Match Actions (p. 325)
24	25	1	Striking to a Partner, Varying Distance, and Force—Hockey (p. 597)
	14	2	Traveling Along Equipment (p. 227)
	14	3	Forming Cooperative and Collaborative Relationships (p. 238)
	14	4	Forming Cooperative and Collaborative Relationships (cont.) (p. 238)
	14	5	Meeting and Parting in a Cooperative Group (p. 239)
25	7	1	Establishing a Learning Environment (p. 87)
	18	2	Rolling onto and off Equipment (p. 357)
	29	3	Fitness Concepts (p. 675)
	22	4	Throwing to a Moving Target (p. 488)
	22	5	Throwing for Distance and Accuracy (p. 489)
26		1	Special Event
	20	2	Transferring Weight on Bars (p. 412)
	20	3	Combining Skills on Mats (p. 412)
	20	4	Combining Weight Transfer and Balances in Sequences (p. 413)
	20	5	Combining Weight Transfer and Balances in Sequences (cont.) (p. 413)
27	17	1	Jumping to Throw; Jumping to Catch (p. 321)
	17	2	Throwing and Catching While Jumping (p. 322)
	29	3	Fitness Concepts (p. 675)
	21	4	Playing Soccer Golf (p. 438)
	16	5	Octopus (p. 291)
28	23	1	Volleying with a Volleybird (p. 515)
	23	2	Playing Handball with a Partner; Playing Corner Handball (p. 516)
	23	3	Volleying Continuously to a Partner (p. 517)
	23	4	Volleying Three on Three; Playing Competitive Three on Three (p. 517)
	21	5	Playing One on One Soccer (p. 440)

Week	Chapter	Day	
29	25	1	Striking and Dodging Stationary Objects—Hockey (p. 601)
	25	2	Playing Hockey Bowl (p. 603)
	29	3	Fitness Concepts (p. 675)
	25	4	Striking for Distance—Golf (p. 584)
	16	5	Dodging and Chasing One Person in a Mass (Partner Dodge) (p. 292)
30	22	1	Catching to Throw Quickly to a Partner (p. 491)
	22	2	Tagging a Base Runner: Run Down (p. 493)
	22	3	Throwing to Avoid a Defender (p. 494)
	22	4	Playing Keep Away (p. 494)
	22	5	Playing Hitting the Pin (p. 494)
31	24	1	Striking to Different Places Around a Partner (p. 560)
	24	2	Playing Racket Call Ball (p. 562)
		3	Fitness Concepts (p. 675)
	24	4	Playing Wall Ball (p. 563)
	16	5	Dodging in a Dynamic Situation (Body Part Tag) (p. 293)
32	24	1	Playing Corner Ball (p. 565)
	24	2	Playing Minitennis (p. 566)
	24	3	Playing Minitennis (cont.) (p. 566)
	24	4	Playing Self-Designed Racket Games (p. 569)
	24	5	Playing Self-Designed Racket Games (cont.) (p. 569)
33	21	1	Punting Within a Limited Time (p. 456)
	21	2	Playing Rush the Circle (p. 456)
		3	Fitness Concepts (p. 675)
	21	4	Playing Two on One Soccer (p. 441)
	25	5	Directing the Air Pathway of the Object Struck—Golf (p. 604)
34	25	1	Directing the Air Pathway of the Object Struck—Golf (cont.) (p. 604)
	25	2	Playing Hoop Golf (p. 602)
	25	3	Hitting to Open Places—Bats (p. 600)
	25	4	Striking a Pitched Object, Varying the Distance—Bats (p. 600)
	25	5	Directing the Air Pathway of the Object Struck—Bats (p. 604)
35	22	1	Playing Frisbee Golf (p. 490)
	22	2	Playing Frisbee Stretch (p. 492)
		3	Fitness Concepts (p. 675)
	25	4	Playing Six-Player Teeball (p. 610)
	25	5	Playing One-Base Baseball (p. 611)
36		1	Special Event
		2	Special Event
		3	Special Event
		4	Field Day
		5	Field Day

Index

Hopping
  Assessment Guide, 258
  control level of, 262
  in general space, 165
  as locomotor skill, 30
  pattern of, 252
  practice needed in, 246–47
  precontrol level of, 259
  in self-space, 162
  skill development activities, 259, 262
  See also Traveling
Hot Potato, 361–62
Hurdles. *See* Obstacles
Hurdling, 313, 327

Imagery
  in dance, 632–33; *see also* Dance
  with effort concepts, 185, 190–91, 196–98
  with extensions concept, 180
  with jumping and landing, 326–27
  with rolling, 352
  with traveling skill theme, 266, 270
  vocabulary hints with, 191
Individualized educational plan (IEP), for
    fitness, 691
Individualized education program (IEP), for
    handicapped children, 697–98
Inner-city children, 7
Inquiry instructional approach, 75–76, 79,
    83, 84
Instructional approaches, 72
  child-designed, 73, 76, 79–82, 83, 84
  convergent inquiry, 75–76
  direct, 73–74, 79, 80, 83, 84
  divergent inquiry, 76, 77, 79
  inquiry, 75, 79, 83, 84
  in learning centers, 79
  and lesson formats, 83–84
  selecting, 76–77
Instructional time, 149, 150, 151
Intratask variation, 42, 43
  for accommodating skill levels, 172
  whole-class focus vs., 120, 121
  with whole-class lesson format, 77
Invariant teaching, reflective teaching vs.,
    6, 7
Inverted balances, 380–81, 382, 387, 388
Invitation, teaching by, 42–43
I See, 693

Jenkins, Ken, 630
Jogging, 165, 686–87, 688, 718
Joyce, Mary, 191
Jumping
  described, 298
  for distance, 306–9
  dynamic balance in, 364
  fundamental patterns of, 298–300, 302
  for height, 303–6
  in self-space, 162
  with traveling skill theme, 255
  See also Jumping and landing; Jumping
    rope
Jumping and landing, 17, 298–330
  Assessment Guide, 309
  body shapes and, 219–20, 314–15
  buoyant and yielding landings with,
    318–19

catching with, 321
control level of, 301, 302, 312–19
in dance, 298, 300, 324, 326–27
developmental stages of, 298–300
direct instructional approach for, 74
formative vs. summative evaluation of, 127
fundamental patterns of, 298–300, 302
in games, 298, 300, 324
in gymnastics, 298, 300, 324–26, 327–30,
    663
Key Observation Points, 302, 303–9
in learning center lesson format, 79
as nonmanipulative skill, 30
over equipment, 318–19, 326, 327–28
planning sample using, 54–55
precontrol level of, 300, 301, 310–12
proficiency level of, 301, 303, 324–30
relationships concepts in, 324
with rolling, 345–50
safety in, 329
sequences, 315, 325
skill development activities, 310–30
skill proficiency levels, 301, 302–3
Skill Theme Development Sequence, 301
task sheet, 319, 320
throwing with, 321, 322
utilization level of, 301, 302–3, 319,
    321–24
vaulting, 327–30
Jumping rope, 312, 316–18
  for cardiovascular efficiency, 686
  as dance activity, 651–52, 656
  inquiry approaches to, 75–76, 77
  music for, 651–52

Keep Away, 418, 419, 494
  Dribble/Pass, 524, 538
  Soccer, 418, 419, 442–43
Keeping It Moving, 573, 608
Keep It Up, 502, 508
Key Observation Points
  for catching, 463–64
  for jumping for distance, 306–9
  for jumping for height and landing,
    303–6
  for kicking along the ground, 421–22
  for kicking in the air, 422–24
  for punting, 446–48
  for rolling, 335–37
  for running, 249–51
  for sidearm striking with a bat, 574–76
  for striking with rackets and paddles,
    542–45
  for throwing, 460–61
  See also Observation cues; Observation
    techniques
Kickball, 618
Kicking, 417–44
  in the air, 422–24
  Assessment Guide, 425
  control level of, 418–19, 430–36
  developmental sequence, 424
  dribble/kick for distance, 421–22
  games, 418, 419, 436, 438, 439, 441, 442–44
  along the ground, 421–22
  Key Observation Points, 420, 421–24
  as manipulative skill, 30
  mature stage of, 424

observation cues for, 119, 120
outdoor facilities needed for, 50
precontrol level of, 418, 419, 425–30
proficiency level of, 418, 420, 441–44
skill development activities, 425–44
skill proficiency levels, 418–20
Skill Theme Development Sequence,
    418–19
Soccer dribble, 421
utilization level of, 418, 419, 436–41
See also Punting
Kickups, 381
Killer (game), 288
Kohl, Herbert, 51, 55, 73, 84
Kounin, J., 95–97, 105

Lambdin, Dolly, 72, 73
Landing. *See* Jumping and landing
Language arts analogy, 23
Layson, J., 115
Leading and following
  with jumping, landing, and rolling,
    349–50
  relationships in, 232, 233, 237–38
  traveling while, 237
Leaping
  control level of, 256, 263
  in general space, 165
  pattern of, 252–53
  practice needed in, 246–47
  skill development activities, 263
  utilization level of, 255
  See also Traveling
Learning center lesson format, 77–79, 83, 84
  for evaluations, 136
  fitness circuit and, 692–93
  for gymnastics, 669
  for jumping activities, 346–47
  for rolling activities, 335
Learning disabilities, 707–8
Learning environment, 6–12, 87–97
Legal considerations
  with handicapped children, 696, 697
  safety and, 117
Lesson formats, 72, 77–84
  contracts and, 79–82, 83, 84
  instructional approaches and, 83–84
  learning centers or stations and, 77–79,
    83, 84
  selecting, 82–83
  task sheets and, 79, 80, 83, 84
  whole-class, 77, 78, 83, 84, 90
Lesson planning form, 57–65. *See also*
    Planning
Levels (in space), concept of, 158, 169
  activities for understanding, 171–72
  Assessment Guide, 65, 66, 169–71
  combining with directions and pathways,
    177–78
  developing, 169
  teaching, 51
  time concept with, 205
Levels of skill. *See* Skill proficiency levels
Linear thinking, 6
Linear vs. reflective teaching, 6
Line Dodge, 290
Listening skills, 90, 91, 93–95, 110–11

Credits

Front endpaper   "Rhymes and Reasons" by John Denver. © Copyright 1969, 1970, Cherry Lane Music Publishing Co., Inc. International copyright secured. All rights reserved. Used by permission.

Page 5, 9, 102   From *Ribbin', Jivin' and Playin' the Dozens* by Herbert L. Foster. Copyright 1974 by Ballinger Publishing Company.

Pages 51, 55, 73, 84   Reprinted by permission of Schocken Books Inc. from *On Teaching* by Herbert Kohl. Copyright © 1976 by Herbert Kohl.

Page 101, 104   From *The Naked Children* by Daniel Fader. Copyright © 1971 by Daniel Fader.

Page 642   From "The Awful Beginning" by James A. Smith, *Today's Education*, April 1972.

Page 660   From "The Little Gymnast" by Dan Zadra. Published in *Young Athlete Magazine*, June 1976, p. 8.

Page 709   From "Teacher" by Mary McCracken, *In Touch*, 1(6), July 1978.